The Paper
George Catlett

Published under the auspices of
The George C. Marshall Foundation

Army Chief of Staff General George C. Marshall leads the inaugural parade, Washington, D.C., January 20, 1941.

The Papers of
George Catlett Marshall

Volume 2

"WE CANNOT DELAY"

JULY 1, 1939–DECEMBER 6, 1941

Larry I. Bland, Editor

Sharon R. Ritenour, Assistant Editor

Clarence E. Wunderlin, Jr., Assistant Editor

THE JOHNS HOPKINS UNIVERSITY PRESS

Baltimore and London

1986

The Johns Hopkins University Press
701 West 40th Street
Baltimore, Maryland 21211
The Johns Hopkins Press Ltd., London

∞™

Library of Congress Cataloging in Publication Data

(Revised for volume 2)

Marshall, George C. (George Catlett), 1880–1959.
The papers of George Catlett Marshall.

Includes indexes.
Contents: v. 1. "The soldierly spirit," December 1880–June 1939.
v. 2. "We cannot delay," July 1, 1939–December 6, 1941.
1. Marshall, George C. (George Catlett), 1880–1959.
2. United States—History, Military—20th century—Sources.
3. Generals—United States—Correspondence.
4. United States. Army—Biography.
I. Bland, Larry I.   II. Ritenour, Sharon R.   III. Title.
E745.M37 1981   973.918′092′4   81-47593
ISBN 0-8018-2552-0 (v. 1)
ISBN 0-8018-2553-9 (v. 2)

*The preparation and publication of this volume was made possible in
part by grants from the National Historical Publications and Records
Commission and from the Program for Editions of the National Endowment for the Humanities, both independent federal agencies.*

Contents

Preface

THE MARSHALL PAPERS

The George C. Marshall Research Library is the repository for General Marshall's personal papers. Since 1956 this collection has been supplemented by contributions of documents by the general's friends, associates, and admirers and by the Marshall Foundation's program of copying relevant documents in other repositories, primarily the National Archives. The core of this volume was drawn from nearly fifty linear feet of material in the Pentagon Office subgroup in the Marshall papers.

This volume presents a selection from the Marshall material available to the editors. With few exceptions, these documents were produced or dictated by General Marshall himself; occasionally he so substantially modified a staff-produced original that the editors have considered it Marshall's. The text of most documents published herein was taken from carbon copies in Marshall's files. On these the drafter's initials usually appear in the top right corner of the carbon copy and the typist's initials in the bottom left corner.

As the head of a large bureaucracy, Marshall signed numerous documents which he had little hand in drafting. Scholars are often less concerned about who actually drafted a document than with who authorized or signed it. Thus there are numerous citations in the secondary literature to important documents emanating from Marshall's office and bearing his signature that have not been included here. This volume does not seek to publish the papers of the Office of the Chief of Staff but only those of the chief of staff himself. Regardless of their importance, staff-written documents are not usually included.

In this volume, the editors have reproduced 564 documents. Of these 5 were not written by Marshall but were included because the editors believed that they were of unusual relevance to the published edition. Most Marshall documents were dictated by him; he produced only 4 himself—3 handwritten and 1 typed. In the annotation the editors have cited an additional 140 documents by Marshall, 245 to him, and 215 other unpublished documents. Fifty-nine illustrations have been reproduced.

ACKNOWLEDGMENTS

The editors which to acknowledge the assistance of those persons who helped them to produce this volume. The members of the Marshall Papers Advisory Committee offered valuable advice on the entire volume, and they deserve special thanks for their work. The committee consisted of Fred L. Hadsel (George C. Marshall Foundation director, 1974–85), Gordon R. Beyer (foundation president since June 1985), Edward M. Coffman (professor of military history, University of Wisconsin-Madison), Richardson Dougall (former deputy director, Historical Office, Department of State), William M. Franklin (former director, Historical Office, Department of State), Maurice Matloff (former chief historian, Center of Military History, Department of the Army), Forrest C. Pogue (General Marshall's authorized biographer), and Edwin A. Thompson (acting deputy director, National Archives and Records Administration).

The editors had the good fortune to inherit from Forrest C. Pogue and his staff—through the Marshall Library—a large body of research material of inestimable value to the Marshall papers project. Wilbur J. Nigh and Juanita D. Pitts worked in the biography project's offices to acquire, declassify, and index documents from which the editors have derived great benefit.

Joellen K. Bland keyed the volume into the editing terminal-typesetter, produced the galleys, and performed other essential technical duties.

Several other members of the Marshall Foundation staff contributed significantly to the volume. Jeanne E. Pedersen pasted-up chapter 1 and Tina Bowyer Harrison pasted-up the rest of the volume. The foundation's archival staff—John N. Jacob, Anita M. Weber, and Alice J. Lee—and librarians Marianne C. Bloxom and Teresa D. Linton provided essential reference services. William Valentine's assistance with the computer was invaluable.

The Marshall papers project has enjoyed close and beneficial relations with The Johns Hopkins University Press, and for that the editors would like to thank Henry Y. K. Tom, senior social sciences editor, Barbara Lamb, managing editor, and George F. Thompson, assistant acquisitions editor and paperbacks editor.

Since the Marshall papers project was initiated in 1976, the National Historical Publications and Records Commission and its staff have given the editors vital moral and financial support. The editors particularly wish to thank Publications Director Roger A. Bruns, Assistant Publications Director Richard N. Sheldon, and Assistant Director Mary A. Giunta. The National Endowment for the Humanities has also been generous in its support of the project; for her help the editors would like to thank Kathy Fuller, program specialist, Editions Section, Research Materials Division.

Anne Katherine Pond, formerly chief of the Documentary Editing Section of the Department of State, proofread this volume and made numerous valuable suggestions. The editors wish to thank her for her help.

Assistance in illustrating this volume was given by James E. Dedrick of the Lexington (Virginia) *News-Gazette;* Bill Kelley of Kelley Advertising Art; Thomas C. Bradshaw Professional Photography; André Studio; the Martin Luther King Library, Washington, D.C.; Mark Renovitch and Paul McLauchlin of the Franklin D. Roosevelt Library; Georgie Bradshaw and

Jodie Davis of the United States Army Center of Military History; Pam Michel and Virginia Horrell of the Defense Audiovisual Agency; and John E. Costello.

Without the assistance of historians and archivists from many repositories, no work such as this would be possible. The editors would like to express their appreciation for the assistance rendered by the following persons: Elaine C. Everly, Richard Gould, Wilbert B. Mahoney, Henry Mayer, Timothy K. Nenninger, Frederick W. Pernell, Charles A. Shaughnessy, and John E. Taylor of the National Archives and Records Administration; Gary Kohn and the staff of the Library of Congress Manuscript Reading Room; Raymond Teichman, John Ferris, and Robert Parks of the Franklin D. Roosevelt Library; Douglas Kinnard, Grady A. Smith, and Brooks E. Kleber of the United States Army Center of Military History; Kathryn Allamong Jacob of the Senate Historical Office; E. Raymond Lewis of the House of Representatives Library; Philip N. Cronenwett of the Dartmouth College Library; Judith Johnson of the Salvation Army Archives and Research Center; Alfred M. Thomas of the *Arkansas Gazette* News Library; William Glenn Robertson of the Combat Studies Institute, Command and General Staff College; Charles R. Ware of the National Security Agency; the Baker Library and the Public Information Office at Valley Forge Military Academy and Junior College; the Donovan Technical Library at the Infantry School, Fort Benning, Georgia; Mona K. Nason; and Robert L. Clifford.

The editors also wish to thank the staffs of the Virginia Military Institute's Preston Library and of the Washington and Lee University Library. In addition, Christine B. Clark, supervisor of the mail room and copying facilities at V.M.I. has helped the project.

The editors gratefully acknowledge the permission of the following individuals, publishers, and institutions to reproduce materials: Yale University Library, for the numerous quotations from the diary of Henry L. Stimson; Princeton University Library, for the quotations from various Bernard M. Baruch letters; Mrs. Edith Ward and Russell A. Gugeler for a copy of the 1939–41 portions of Orlando Ward's diary; Robert L. Sherrod for his November 15, 1941, press conference memorandum. The following have granted permission to reproduce photographs: Associated Press/Wide World Photos; Bettmann Archive; Condé Nast Publications Inc.; Historical Pictures Service, Inc. of Chicago; *Honolulu Star-Bulletin;* Life Picture Service of Time Inc.; New Orleans *Times-Picayune; New York Times;* and United Press International/Bettmann Newsphotos.

Guide to Editorial Policies

STYLE
Document texts and quotations in the annotation follow the writer's style, except as noted below. The editors' style generally conforms to that prescribed by *The Chicago Manual of Style,* 13th ed. (Chicago: University of Chicago Press, 1982).

TEXTUAL CHANGES AND INSERTIONS
Document Heading. The organization, sequence, and sometimes the content of the document heading have been supplied by the editors. This heading consists of between three and seven elements: addressee, date, originator, place of origin, message designation, security classification, and title.

The addressee for letters, telegrams, and radio messages is always in the form TO HARRY S. TRUMAN. Civil titles (i.e., Senator, Dr., The Honorable, Judge, etc.) are not included in the document heading. If the recipient was a married woman, Marshall usually used "Mrs." with her husband's name, if he knew it (e.g., Mrs. James J. Winn rather than Molly B. Winn). The editors have used the form Marshall indicated. For military personnel, including retired professionals, the rank used is that correct as of the date of the document. No distinction is made between permanent and temporary ranks in the annotation.

The addressee for memorandums is in the form MEMORANDUM FOR ____. The form of address Marshall used is followed, but abbreviations (e.g., A.C.S., Col., etc.) have been spelled out. If the memorandum is to an addressee's title only, that officer's last name is usually supplied in brackets or explained in a footnote (excepting the president and the secretary of war). A list of high-ranking War Department officials is printed in Appendix 1.

Some documents were addressed to an agency or person for transmission to a designated addressee. In these cases the ultimate recipient is listed on the top heading line and the transmitter is listed below. For example see Marshall to Lieutenant General Stanley D. Embick, May 7, 1940, p. 208. When the document is a telegram or radio message, this is indicated; the sender's message number is included, if known.

Salutation and Complimentary Close. When present, these elements have been printed with the first and last lines respectively of the document text rather than on separate lines as they appear in the original. The capitalization and punctuation of the original have been retained.

Signature.　Most documents in this volume have been reproduced from file (carbon) copies in the Marshall papers or in various War Department records. A name or initials at the end of a document published herein indicates that the editors have used the signed original as the copy text.

Silent Corrections.　In making silent corrections, the editors distinguished between documents physically produced by the author and those produced by a clerk or secretary. No silent changes have been introduced into author-produced documents. Although the original capitalization and punctuation have been retained, spelling errors have been silently corrected in staff-typed documents. Marshall sometimes made minor technical corrections to documents prior to having them sent. These changes are accepted as the final version of the copy text.

Brackets.　All information within brackets in this volume has been supplied by the editors. If the bracketed material is in italic type, it is to be read in place of the preceding word or letter (e.g., "fixed up for these four [*three*] divisions"). If the bracketed material is in roman type, it indicates additional rather than substitute information (e.g., "Wednesday afternoon [August 1] General Pershing").

Italics for Emphasis.　Except where used in brackets, italic type appears in the text of a document or in a quotation only if the emphasis was in the original—indicated on the copy text by underlining.

Ellipses.　In a few instances these are used to eliminate text from a lengthy document; the nature of the omission is explained in the annotation.

Cross-references.　Citations to volume 1 of this series are in the form *Papers of GCM,* 1: 000. References to documents within this volume are in the form: (a) letters: Marshall to Embick, date, p. 000; (b) memorandums: Memorandum for the President, date, p. 000.

Congressional Hearings References.　Wherever possible, the editors have cited Marshall's congressional testimony to the published version rather than to the transcripts in the Marshall papers. A somewhat shortened form of the citation is used in the annotation; the complete citation is given in Appendix 2.

DOCUMENT SOURCE CITATIONS

Source Line.　At the end of each document and before the footnotes, the source of the document is listed in the following format: Repository/Collection (Main entry, Subentry). Several copies of certain documents may exist, and these may be found in different repositories or collections. The version used by the editors as the copy text is the one cited.

Repository Abbreviations.　The following abbreviations are used in the source line for the repositories cited in this volume:

Dartmouth	=	Dartmouth College Library, Hanover, N.H.
FDRL	=	Franklin D. Roosevelt Library, Hyde Park, N.Y.
LC	=	Library of Congress, Washington, D.C.
MML	=	MacArthur Memorial Library, Norfolk, Va.
NA	=	National Archives and Records Administration, Washington, D.C.
Northwestern	=	Northwestern University Library, Evanston, Ill.
Oklahoma State	=	Oklahoma State University Library, Stillwater, Okla.
Princeton	=	Princeton University Library, Princeton, N.J.
USAMHI	=	United States Army Military History Institute, Carlisle Barracks, Pa.
Virginia	=	University of Virginia Library, Charlottesville, Va.
VMI	=	Virginia Military Institute, Lexington, Va.
Yale	=	Yale University Library, New Haven, Conn.

ANNOTATION

In the annotation the editors have attempted, insofar as possible, to explain all potentially obscure references, to provide cross-references to important related material, and to summarize the key parts of in-coming or out-going documents of relevance. The Marshall papers project is intended to provide a cohesive, intelligible story of Marshall in his own words, not to provide a detailed discussion of every facet of the general's life or to examine numerous questions not mentioned in Marshall documents.

In the annotation, the editors have avoided using secondary sources, which would date the edition. An exception to this policy has been made for certain official military histories, particularly the indispensable series *United States Army in World War II* (Washington: GPO, 1947–). Whenever appropriate and feasible, quotations from Marshall documents not selected for publication or from other primary sources have been used to annotate the published documents.

The editors have used but not cited certain reference works: *Official National Guard Register; Army Directory: Reserve and National Guard Officers on Active Duty, July 31, 1941; Official Army Register; Army Directory; Cullum's Biographical Register of the Officers and Graduates of the U.S. Military Academy; The 1984 VMI Register of Former Cadets;* and *Who's Who in America.*

Graduates of military colleges have been identified by school and year of graduation (e.g., V.M.I., 1901) the first time that person is cited. Initial personal identifications include only the status, rank, or role at the time of the citation. Subsequent citations usually give only the changes since the previous citation. The index should enable the reader to follow a particular individual's development or relationship to Marshall.

ABBREVIATIONS

If an abbreviation is used only once in the volume, it will be explained in brackets in the text. Repeatedly used abbreviations are listed below. Certain of these are used in this volume only in the document source lines; these are designated by †.

A.B.C.	=	American Broadcasting Company
A.C.S.	=	Assistant Chief of Staff
A.E.F.	=	American Expeditionary Forces
A.R.	=	Army Regulation
C.A.A.	=	Civil Aeronautics Administration
C.B.S.	=	Columbia Broadcasting System
C.C.C.	=	Civilian Conservation Corps
C.M.T.C.	=	Citizens' Military Training Camp
C.S.	=	Chief of Staff of the Army
D.C.S.	=	Deputy Chief of Staff
D.S.C.	=	Distinguished Service Cross
Exec.†	=	Executive Group File, OPD
F.S.R.	=	Field Service Regulation
F.Y.	=	fiscal year
G-1	=	Personnel Division, General Staff
G-2	=	Intelligence Division, General Staff
G-3	=	Operations and Training Division, General Staff
G-4	=	Supply Division, General Staff
G.H.Q.	=	General Headquarters
GPO	=	United States Government Printing Office
H†	=	document handwritten by author
H. J. Res.	=	House Joint Resolution
H.M.S.	=	His/Her Majesty's Ship
HMSO	=	His/Her Majesty's Stationery Office
H.R.	=	House of Representatives
I.P.F.	=	Initial Protective Force
M.T.C.A.	=	Military Training Camps Association
N.B.C.	=	National Broadcasting Company
N.C.O.	=	noncommissioned officer
N.D.A.C.	=	National Defense Advisory Commission
N.Y.A.	=	National Youth Administration
O.C.S.	=	Officer Candidate School
OCS†	=	Office of the Chief of Staff
OF†	=	Official File

OPD†	=	Operations Division, General Staff
O.P.M.	=	Office of Production Management
O.R.C.	=	Officers' Reserve Corps
P.M.P.	=	Protective Mobilization Plan
P.M.S.&T.	=	Professor of Military Science and Tactics
PSF†	=	President's Secretary's File
R.F.C.	=	Reconstruction Finance Corporation
RG†	=	Record Group
R.O.T.C.	=	Reserve Officers' Training Corps
S.	=	Senate
S.G.S.	=	Secretary, General Staff
SW	=	Secretary of War
T†	=	document typed by author
T.A.G.	=	The Adjutant General of the Army
T.R.	=	Training Regulation
U.S.M.A.	=	United States Military Academy (West Point)
U.S.N.A.	=	United States Naval Academy (Annapolis)
U.S.S.	=	United States Ship
USAFFE†	=	United States Army Forces in the Far East
V.M.I.	=	Virginia Military Institute
WDCSA†	=	War Department, Chief of Staff of the Army
W.D.G.S.	=	War Department General Staff
W.P.A.	=	Works Projects Administration
W.P.D.	=	War Plans Division, General Staff
Y.M.C.A.	=	Young Men's Christian Association

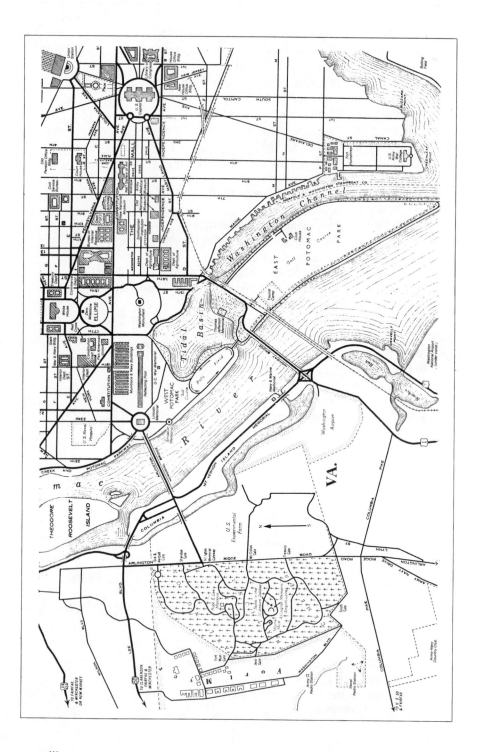

Illustrations

The following are the sources for the illustrations used in this volume. The abbreviations and the format of the source line are described in the "Guide to Editorial Policies."

frontispiece

Marshall leads the inaugural parade, January 20, 1941. Alfred Eisenstaedt, *Life* Magazine © Time Inc.; GCMRL/Photographs (7080)

page xviii

Map, downtown Washington, D.C., and Fort Myer, Virginia, 1940. GCMRL/Maps

page 250

Document, Marshall to Major General Daniel Van Voorhis, June 20, 1940. NA/RG 165 (WPD, 4326)

following page 260

1. War Resources Board, August 1939. U.S. Army Signal Corps Photo 108448; GCMRL/Photographs (7075)

2. Munitions Building, Washington, D.C. U.S. Army Signal Corps Photo 108102; GCMRL/Photographs (7081)

3. Marshall enjoys surf casting at Fire Island, New York. Thomas McAvoy, *Life* Magazine © 1939 Time Inc.; GCMRL/Photographs (1527)

4. Marshall picnics on the beach at Fire Island, New York, with his stepchildren. Thomas McAvoy, *Life* Magazine © 1939 Time Inc.; GCMRL/Photographs (1528)

5. Marshall fishing at Fire Island, New York. Thomas McAvoy, *Life* Magazine © 1939 Time Inc.; GCMRL/Photographs (6842)

6. Marshall relaxes at Fire Island, New York. Thomas McAvoy, *Life* Magazine © 1939 Time Inc.; GCMRL/Photographs (6837)

7. Katherine Tupper Marshall, 1939. GCMRL/Photographs (1235)

8. General George C. Marshall, September 1939. Bettmann Archive; GCMRL/Photographs (1048)

9. Quarters One, Fort Myer, Virginia. U.S. Army Photo; GCMRL/Photographs (6848)

10. Marshall is sworn in as chief of staff of the U.S. Army, September 1, 1939. U.S. Army Signal Corps Photo 114106; GCMRL/Photographs (970)

11. Marshall and Edward T. Taylor, chairman of the House Appropriations Committee, at the November 27, 1939, hearing. *New York Times* Photo; GCMRL/Photographs (7082)

Chronology
April 23, 1939–December 6, 1941

The following is a brief list of the more important events of Marshall's life (in roman type) and of influence on his job (in italic type) during the period covered by this volume. All events involving General Marshall took place in Washington, D.C., unless otherwise noted.

April 1939

23 Meeting at White House; president tells GCM that he is to become army chief of staff

27 CS appointment announced effective September 1; acting CS effective July 1; West Coast inspection trip begins (returns May 3)

May 1939

10 Departs New York City for Brazil aboard U.S.S. *Nashville*

17 Nomination confirmed by the Senate

25 Arrives in Rio de Janeiro, Brazil

June 1939

7 Departs Brazil aboard U.S.S. *Nashville* with General Góes Monteiro

20 Arrives Annapolis, Md., and Washington

July 1939

1 Becomes acting CS; arrives at Fire Island, N.Y. (returns 5th)

5 *Executive Order provides for direct contact between the White House and the CS*

6 Testimony, House Military Affairs Committee (age-in-grade retirement bill)

9 Hosts dinner for General Trujillo

11 Testimony, House Military Affairs Committee (lieutenant generals' bill); at White House for tea for General Trujillo

15 Travels to Fire Island, N.Y. (returns July 17)

18 Meeting with State and Navy departments and House Foreign Affairs Committee leaders to discuss the bill to permit the sale of U.S. materiel to Latin American nations

21 Travel to Chanute Field, Ill., and Chicago (returns 23d)

22 Speech, Illinois National Guard meeting in Chicago

26 *U.S. denounces 1911 Japan commercial treaty*

28 Marshall moves to Fort Myer (lives in Col. Patton's house pending completion of Quarters No. 1)

August 1939

2 *Albert Einstein's letter to the president on the possibility of creating an atomic bomb*

9 Reports on Manassas, Va., maneuvers

16 Attends V.M.I. alumni banquet, Leesburg, Va.

18 Meets with War Department General Council re measures to be taken upon the outbreak of war in Europe

23 *German-Russian nonaggression pact signed*

26 Meets with War Deparment General Council re reinforcements for the Panama Canal Zone

28 Meets with War Department General Council re measures to be taken if war begins in Europe

29 Speech, Virginia American Legion State Convention, Richmond; attends V.M.I. Club of Richmond testimonial dinner

September 1939

1 *Germany invades Poland; total mobilization ordered in Britain and France.* GCM takes oath as permanent major general, then is sworn in as CS (temporary general); meeting at White House re defense

3 *Britain and France declare war on Germany*

5 *President announces U.S. neutrality; arms embargo to belligerents; Canal Zone placed under military control;* meeting with DCS, ACS's, and TAG re reinforcement of Panama and Puerto Rico

7 Meets with War Department General Council re manpower increases to be requested; meeting at White House with president

8 Meets with War Department General Council re manpower increases; *president declares a state of "limited national emergency;" president issues executive orders authorizing increases in enlisted personnel for all U.S. military forces*

9 Speech at opening of Army Industrial College school year; travels to Connellsville, Pa., for speeches at airport dedication and Uniontown

15 Meets with War Department General Council re manpower and budget requests

16 Travels to Norfolk, Va., for V.M.I. Alumni Association meeting and dinner
17 *Soviet Union invades Poland*
21 *President calls special session of Congress to repeal arms embargo*
23 Meeting with chiefs of arms

October 1939

2 Meets with ACS's and Budget Branch re funding and manpower; *Congress of American Republics declares "Zone of Safety" around the Western Hemisphere*
10 Staff meeting re training and manpower
11 Joint Board meeting; speech at Army Ordnance Association meeting
13 Speech at annual banquet of the National Guard Association of Pennsylvania in Washington, Pa.
14 Receives honorary Doctor of Science degree and makes speech at Washington and Jefferson College, Washington, Pa.
20 Travels to Hollins College to meet Mrs. Marshall (returns 22d)
21 Attends V.M.I. homecoming
23 Meeting with ACS's re use of manpower increases; departs for New York City to attend civil aviation meeting (returns 25th)
27 Speech to National Guard convention, Baltimore, Md.
28 Travels to Indianapolis, Ind.; speaks to Indiana Reserve Officers' Association meeting (returns 29th)

November 1939

3 Travels to U.S.M.A. and returns
4 *President signs revised neutrality law allowing "cash-and-carry" arms sales to belligerents*
6 Attends Standing Liaison Committee meeting
9 Testimony, Bureau of the Budget hearing
10 Travels to Langley Field, Va., for radio broadcast on the departure of the flight of B-17s to Rio de Janeiro, Brazil
14 Speech, National Association of State Universities meeting; travels to Aberdeen, Md. (returns 15th)
16 Speech, Committee on Community Chest
20 Meets with War Department General Council re army expansion and training; attends Standing Liaison Committee meeting; at White House for budget meeting
25 Attends annual dinner, Aztec Club of 1847
27 Testimony, House Appropriations Committee; hosts luncheon for Brazilian Army aviators who returned with U.S. B-17 goodwill flight
29 Travels to Red Bank, N.J., and returns
30 *Soviet Union invades Finland;* testimony, House Appropriations Committee; meets with Corps Area commanders

December 1939

1 Reception for Army, Corp Area Commanders
6 Inspection trip to the southeast (returns 14th)
14 Diplomatic reception at the White House
15 Conference with Admiral Stark and Ambassador Joseph P. Kennedy
16 Dinner with Admiral Stark
17 *German battleship* Graf Spee *scuttled in the Plate River after battle with Royal Navy*
21 Meets with WPD and G-3 re fiscal year 1942 field exercises
28 Speech, joint meeting of the American Historical Association and the American Military Institute

January 1940

3 *77th Congress opens; president requests $1,800,000,000 for defense*
13 Attends budget conference
16 Testimony, House Military Affairs Committee re general defense needs; departs for California and cross-country inspection trip (returns 22d)
26 Dinner in honor of the president's mother
30 Dinner, Admiral & Mrs. Stark; attends president's ball
31 Dinner, Argentine Embassy

February 1940

1 *Army service schools' courses suspended;* speech to the Women's Patriotic Conference
2 Attends National Rifle Association Dinner
4 Caribbean inspection trip (returns 13th)
9 S*Dumner Welles mission to Europe*
14 *Britain begins arming North Sea merchant ships*
16 Reception for Reserve Officers Association (ROA), Fort Myer; NBC radio broadcast to ROA; attends ROA banquet
19 *U.S. extends moral embargo to Soviet Union*
20 Travels to Edgewood Arsenal, N.J.
23 Testimony, House Appropriations Committee re FY 1941 budget
26 Testimony, continued from 23d; speech, Salvation Army Diamond Jubilee Dinner, New York City (returns 27th)
29 Departs for Hawaiian inspection trip (returns March 15)

March 1940

12 *Russo-Finnish War ends*
18 *Hitler and Mussolini confer at Brenner Pass;* attends National Guard Dinner
19 National Guard division commanders conference; dinner, Association of Military Schools and Colleges
27 Testimony, House Military Affairs Committee re arms sales to foreign governments

28 Testimony, Senate Military Affairs Committee, re arms sales

30 Brief statement to the Society of the Cincinnati, Fredericksburg, Va.

April 1940

2 Attends Air Corps dinner, Bolling Field

3 *House cuts army appropriation bill 10 percent;* attends War College reception

5 Attends dinner honoring British ambassador

8 Testimony, Senate Military Affairs Committee re promotion list

9 *Germany invades Denmark and Norway;* testimony, House Military Affairs Committee, re promotion list

10 Meets selected group of congressional leaders re army appropriations

23 Off-the-record address at dinner of American Newspaper Publishers Assn., New York City

24 Departs New York City for Fort Benning, Ga.

26 Speech, Azalea Festival luncheon, Charleston, S.C. (returns to Washington, 28th)

30 Testimony, Senate Appropriations Committee re FY 1941 appropriation bill

May 1940

1 Testimony, Senate Appropriations Committee, continued from April 30

7 *President orders U.S. fleet to remain in Hawaiian waters indefinately*

9 Travels to Fort Belvoir, Va., and returns

10 *Germany invades Belgium, Luxembourg, and the Netherlands; Churchill becomes prime minister of U.K.; British troops occupy Iceland;* meeting at the White House

13 Meeting at the White House

14 *Netherlands surrenders;* meeting at the White House

16 *President addresses joint session of Congress; asks $1,200,000,000 for defense*

17 Testimony, Senate Appropriations Committee, continued from May 1

20 Testimony, House Military Affairs Committee (continued on 21st)

22 Meeting at the White House

25 *Office of Emergency Management established to assist the president and to coordinate defense activities*

26 *Evacuations begin at Dunkirk (end June 4)*

27 Speech, National Aeronautic Association Forum and Conference

28 *Belgium surrenders;* testimony, Senate Military Affairs Committee

29 *National Defense Advisory Committee established;* testimony, Senate Appropriations Committee re FY 1941 budget; meeting at White House

30 Meeting at White House

31 *President asks Congress for additional $1,300,000,000 for military;* testimony, Senate Appropriations Committee re emergency relief appropriation act

June 1940

1 Attends graduation ceremonies, Fishburne Military School, Waynesboro, Va.

4 Testimony, House Military Affairs Committee re H.J. Res. 555; testimony, House Appropriations Committee re supplemental appropriation bill for 1941

12 Speech at V.M.I. graduation, Lexington, Va.

13 *Age-in-grade promotion bill (H.R. 9243) approved by president; War Department budget for FY 1941 becomes law; military appropriation is $1,433,323,322*

14 *German troops march into Paris; president establishes National Defense Research Committee under direction of Vannevar Bush*

15 *Churchill requests U.S. destroyers;* testimony, Senate Appropriations Committee re supplemental appropriation bill for FY 1941

17 *Senate passes resolution precluding recognition of transfers of Western Hemisphere territories from one non-American power to another*

19 Speech, Veterans of Foreign Wars Encampment Banquet, Akron, Ohio

20 *President nominates Stimson and Knox to head War and Navy departments*

21 *France surrenders to Germany; Burke-Wadsworth selective service bill introduced*

22 *France signs armistice terms;* attends Allen T. Brown's wedding, New York

24 Meeting at the White House

25 *Fighting ceases in France*

26 *First Supplemental National Defense Appropriation Act becomes law; appropriation is $821,073,137*

27 Visits Henry L. Stimson at Long Island, N.Y., home

29 *Japan declares sphere of influence in southwest Pacific*

July 1940

1 Meeting at the White House

2 *Congress authorizes embargo on exports of munitions and critical materials*

3 *British attack French fleet at Oran, Algeria*

5 *President announces limited embargo of strategic material sales to Japan*

8 At Stimson's home discussing draft bill

9 Radio address from Washington to meeting of the Aviation Congress in Denver, Colorado; at Stimson's home discussing draft bill

10 *Armored Force established; president asks Congress for $4,800,000,000 in additional defense funds*

12 Testimony, Senate Military Affairs Committee re draft bill

21 *Havana Conference begins*

22 Meeting at the White House

24 Testimony, Senate Appropriations Committee re 2d supplemental appropriation bill for 1941; testimony, House Military Affairs Committee re draft bill

25 *Robert P. Patterson named assistant secretary of war.*

26 *Army General Headquarters activated;* testimony continued from 24th

30 Testimony, Senate Military Affairs Committee re call-up of reserve officers

August 1940

1 Meeting at the White House

2 Leaves for Fire Island, N.Y. (returns 5th)

5 Testimony, Senate Appropriations Committee re supplemental appropriation bill for 1941; radio broadcast on army field maneuvers

6 Testimony, continued from 5th

10 Inspection trip to maneuvers sites (returns 14th)

15 Testimony, continued from 6th

16 Meeting at the White House with E. M. Watson

20 Testimony, Senate Military Affairs Committee re temporary promotions bill

24 Inspection trip to Second Army maneuvers, Camp McCoy, Wis. (returns 26th)

27 *Congress authorizes federalization of the National Guard for 12 months*

September 1940

3 Testimony, Senate Military Affairs Committee; travels to Boston, Mass.; *U.S.-U.K. destroyers-bases agreement announced*

4 Attends First Corps Area staff conference; returns to Washington

7 *Germany begins massive air raids on London*

16 *President signs Selective Service Act;* radio broadcase on selective service

19 Testimony, House Appropriations Committee re 3d supplemental appropriation bill for 1941

25 *U.S. cryptanalysts able to decode complete Japanese message in top secret "purple" diplomatic code*

26 Testimony, House Military Affairs Committee re promotions, reserves, and National Guard; *U.S. stops sales of scrap iron and steel to Japan*

27 *Tripartite Pact (Germany-Italy-Japan) signed;* meeting at the White House

30 Testimony, Senate Appropriations Committee re supplemental appropriations for 1941

October 1940

1 Testimony, continued from September 30; speech welcoming visiting Latin American officers

11 Travels to Charlotte, N.C.

16 *Selective service registration begins*

22 Speech, National Guard Association Banquet

24 Meeting at the White House; gives dinner honoring visiting Latin American chiefs of staff

28 *Italy invades Greece*

29 *Stimson selects first draft number*

November 1940

4 Hunting trip with Arnold and Glenn L. Martin; inspection of Martin's aircraft factory near Baltimore, Md. (returns 5th)

5 *General Election Day*

10 Address at Armistice Day service, Valley Forge Military Academy, Wayne, Pa.

11 Radio broadcast on 101st anniversary of the founding of the V.M.I.

19 Meeting at the White House

20 Announces that U.S. gives U.K. 26 B-17s; travels to Roanoke, Va.

21 V.M.I. football game, Roanoke, Va.; returns

25 *First draftees report for induction*

29 Radio broadcast: "The Morale and Integrity of Our Army"

December 1940

3 Dinner, National Inventors Council

5 Plane trip with H. H. Arnold (returns 6th)

7 Speech, 100th anniversary dinner of the 108th Field Artillery of Pennsylvania, Philadelphia

13 Trip with Omar Bradley (returns 14th)

16 Gives dinner for Gen. Bittencourt of Brazil, Fort Myer

17 Speech, National Aeronautic Association dinner

25 Wedding of stepdaughter Molly P. Brown at Fort Myer

26 Vacation trip to White Sulphur Springs resort, W. Va. (returns January 2)

29 *President's "Arsenal of Democracy" speech*

January 1941

6 *President's speech on lend-lease and the "Four Freedoms"*

7 Radio broadcast on expansion of military; *Office of Production Management created*

8 *President's budget message asks $10,800,000,000 for defense*

10 *Lend-lease bill introduced in the House*

15 Meets with Ford Frick re exhibition baseball games for soldiers; meets with E. R. Stettinius, Jr. (O.P.M.) re aircraft production

16 Meeting at the White House re mobilization in case of war

19 Attends pre-inaugural dinner for state governors

21 *U.S. lifts "moral embargo" on shipments to U.S.S.R.*

27 Testimony, House Foreign Affairs Committee executive session re lend-lease
28 Testimony, continued from 27th
29 *First plenary session of U.S.-U.K. talks (ABC)*

February 1941

4 Conference with the president on global strategy
6 Conversation with Nelson Rockefeller re Axis airlines in Latin America; staff conference re defense of Pearl Harbor; meeting with Admiral Stark re defense of Pearl Harbor
8 Staff conference re officer training schools
10 Meeting at the White House re Far Eastern strategy
12 Testimony, House Appropriations Committee re 4th supplemental appropriation bill
17 Luncheon with Foreign Minister of Paraguay
19 Meeting at the White House
20 Testimony, executive session of the Senate Foreign Relations Committee re lend-lease bill
25 Speech, conference of corps area morale officers
26 Meeting at the White House
28 Staff conference re officer training

March 1941

3 Staff conference re British situation
4 Staff conference re lend-lease; conference in Secretary of State's office re lend-lease
5 Testimony, House Appropriations Committee re 5th supplemental appropriation bill
10 White House meeting with Harry Hopkins re lend-lease
11 *President signs lend-lease act;* speech, conference of public relations officers
13 Staff conference re barrage balloons; testimony, House Appropriations Committee re supplemental appropriation bill
14 Staff conference re CS's testimony and lend-lease; departs for inspection trip to southeast (returns 18th)
15 Radio broadcast from Montgomery, Ala., re anniversary of U.S.M.A. founding
17 Speech, U.S. Chamber of Commerce, Tampa, Fla.
19 Staff conference re health conditions in cantonments
20 Testimony, Senate Appropriations Committee re supplemental appropriation bill
23 Radio broadcast for the Red Cross
24 Standing Liaison Committee meeting
25 Staff conference re Air Crops needs; testimony, Senate Appropriations Committee re supplemental appropriations bill
26 Staff conference re GS jurisdiction over Air Corps matters
27 Staff conference re Air Corps materiel; testimony, House Military Affairs Committee re arms sales to foreign governments
31 *Gen. Rommel attacks British in Libya*

April 1941

2 Welcoming remarks to chaplain's conference; meeting at the White House
5 Army Day radio broadcast to 33d Division
6 *German Army attacks Yugoslavia and Greece*
8 Departs on inspection trip to southwest (returns 12th)
13 *Soviet-Japanese neutrality pact signed*
15 Meeting at the White House
16 Meeting at the White House with the president and Gen. Embick re strategy
17 *Yugoslavia surrenders*
22 Testimony, Truman Committee
23 *"America First" holds its first mass meeting*
24 *Greece surrenders*
26 Travels to Annapolis, Md.
28 Testimony, House and Senate appropriations committees re 1942 appropriation bill
29 Testimony, House Appropriations Committee, continued from 28th; speech to U.S. Chamber of Commerce

May 1941

2 Meeting at the White House; radio address re the role of the citizen in the national emergency
6 Meeting at the White House
10 Travels to Fire Island, New York (returns 12th)
14 Joint Board approves war plan Rainbow 5 and ABC-1
15 *Vichy collaborative agreements with Germany*
20 *German army invades Crete*
22 Meeting at the White House
27 *British sink German battleship* Bismarck; *president declares state of unlimited national emergency;* threatens to resign if Plattsburgstyle officers training camps are instituted
29 *Caribbean Defense Command inaugurated*
30 Meeting at the White House
31 *British forces complete evacuation of Crete*

June 1941

9 Delivers commencement address, College of William and Mary, Williamsburg, Va.
11 Testimony, House Appropriations Committee re 2d defficiency appropriation bill; statement on construction of a new War Department building
15 Delivers commencement address, Trinity College, Hartford, Conn.
18 Testimony, Senate Appropriations Committee re military appropriation bill for FY 1942; departs for New York City
20 *Army Air Forces created (end of GHQ Air Force and Army Air Corps)*
22 *Germany attacks the U.S.S.R.*
25 Meeting at the White House

July 1941

1 *Operation Indigo-3 begins (occupation of Iceland by U.S. troops)*
5 Meeting at the White House
7 *U.S. Marines land in Iceland, Trinidad, and British Guiana*
9 Testimony, Senate Military Affairs Committee re extension of service time for draftees, National Guard
14 Meeting at the White House
15 Testimony, House Military Affairs Committee re service-time extension, enlistment of former felons, and temporary appointment of officers
17 Testimony, Senate Military Affaris Committee re service-time extension
19 *U.S. Navy begins escorting ships to Iceland;-* departs for weekend with E. R. Stettinius family at Rapidan, Va.
21 *Japan occupies military bases in Indochina*
22 Testimony, House Military Affairs Committee re personnel matters
26 *U.S. freezes Japanese assets;* meets with Soviet military mission
28 Travels to Hartford, Conn. (returns 29th)
30 *Harry Hopkins arrives in Moscow on supply mission;* meeting at the White House

August 1941

3 Departs for Atlantic Conference, Placentia Bay, Newfoundland (returns 14th)
9 Meetings with British military leaders (end 12th)
12 *House passes service-time extension act 203–202*
19 Approves war plan Rainbow 5
20 Departs on inspection trip to the northwest with the secretary of war (returns 28th)

September 1941

1 *U.S. Navy extends convoy protection for all ships between Newfoundland and Iceland*
6 *At Japanese Imperial conference militants give Konoye government six weeks to reach diplomatic settlement with U.S. on Far East*
8 Attends First Army Headquarters conference, New York City
11 *U.S. Navy given orders to shoot-on-sight if ships threatened*
15 Departs for inspection trip to Fourth Army area (returns 18th); speech at American Legion Convention, Milwaukee, Wis.
22 Meeting at the White House; testimony, Senate Military Affairs Committee re army construction activities
25 Departs for Louisiana maneuvers (returns 28th)
28 *Harriman-Beaverbrook aid mission meetings begin in Moscow (end October 3)*

29 Testimony, House Appropriations Committee re 2d supplemental appropriation bill and lend-lease; departs from New York City (returns 30th)
30 Testimony, House Military Affairs Committee re transfer of construction activities to the Engineer Corps

October 1941

1 *U.S.-U.K.-U.S.S.R. aid agreement signed in Moscow*
9 *President asks Congress for authority to arm U.S. merchant ships*
13 Speech to Women's Advisory Council
14 Testimony, Senate Appropriations Committee re 2d supplemental appropriation bill, FY 1942
16 *General Tojo forms new Japanese government;* meeting at the White House
17 *U.S.S. Kearney torpedoed near Iceland, first casualties for U.S. (11 dead)*
18 Fishing trip to Virginia Beach, Va.
27 Speech at Navy Day dinner
31 *U.S.S. Reuben James sunk—first U.S. Navy vessel lost in hostile action*

November 1941

3 *U.S. evacuates military dependents from Guam, Wake, and Midway islands*
8 Travels to Baltimore, Md., for Navy–Notre Dame football game
11 Radio address on Citizens Defense Corps
15 Secret press briefing re reinforcement of the Philippines; meeting at the White House
16 Departs for inspection trip of Carolina maneuvers (returns 18th)
17 *Congress revises neutrality law to permit arming of U.S. merchant ships*
18 Testimony, House Appropriations Committee re supplemental appropriation bill, FY 1942
19 Departs for inspection trip of Carolina maneuvers (returns 22d)
25 Meeting at the White House
26 Departs on inspection trip of Carolina maneuvers (returns 27th); *Japanese task force sails for attack on Pearl Harbor*
27 *All U.S. forces in Pacific put on "final" or "war" alert*
28 Meeting at the White House

December 1941

3 *Joint Intelligence Committee established*
5 *Navy orders its offices in Tokyo, Bangkok, Peking, Tientsin, Shanghai, Guam, and Wake Island to destroy all but essential communication codes and secret documents*

Acting Chief of Staff

July 1–August 31, 1939

Brigadier General George C. Marshall, *General Staff Corps, is detailed as Acting Chief of Staff, effective 1 July 1939, and will report for duty accordingly.*

—War Department, Special Orders, No. 149
June 27, 1939

D EPUTY Chief of Staff George C. Marshall assumed the chief's duties on July 1, 1939. According to army regulations: "The Chief of Staff is the immediate adviser of the Secretary of War on all matters relating to the Military Establishment and is charged by the Secretary of War with the planning, development, and execution of the military program. He will cause the War Department General Staff to prepare the necessary plans for recruiting, mobilizing, organizing, supplying, equipping, and training the Army of the United States for use in the national defense and for demobilization. As the agent, and in the name of the Secretary of War, he issues such orders as will insure that the plans of the War Department are harmoniously executed by all agencies of the Military Establishment, and that the military program is carried out speedily and efficiently. . . . The Chief of Staff, in addition to his duties as such, is, in peace, by direction of the President, the Commanding General of the Field Forces and in that capacity directs the field operations and the general training of the several armies, of the oversea forces, and of GHQ units. He continues to exercise command of the field forces after the outbreak of war until such time as the President shall have specifically designated a commanding general thereof." (Army Regulation No. 10-15, August 18, 1936 [Washington: GPO, 1936], p. 1.)

With his July 5, 1939, Executive Order, President Roosevelt strengthened the commander in chief's relationship with the chief of staff. Roosevelt directed that the Joint Board and other service officers should report directly to him on certain issues instead of through their departmental heads. (Mark S. Watson, *Chief of Staff: Prewar Plans and Preparations,* a volume in the *United States Army in World War II* [Washington: GPO, 1950], p. 2.)

Marshall insisted on keeping his distance from Roosevelt while maintaining his loyalty to the president. He never visited the president in Hyde Park or Warm Springs, despite Harry Hopkins's urgings. "I was not on that basis of intimate relationship with the president that a number of others were," Marshall recalled. "I had to be proved. He had appointed me without any large war experience (except for being with General Pershing in the First World War and for a time chief of operations of an army of almost a million men), and I was pretty young. It was quite a long time before he built up confidence in me to anything like the extent that he apparently had in the last year of the war." (George C. Marshall, interviewed by Forrest C. Pogue, February 11, 1957, GCMRL.)

Beginning immediately after the April 27, 1939, announcement of Marshall's appointment, a wave of congratulatory letters and telegrams flooded his desk—so many that the general recruited his stepdaughter Molly Brown to assist the office staff in answering them. Thirty-six friends and colleagues wrote Marshall that they had earlier—in some cases decades earlier—predicted his appointment. Dozens more wrote that they had felt certain that he would someday become chief of staff. To one friend writing belatedly, Marshall replied: "I am very glad that you waited until about fifteen hundred or more letters went through at railroad speed, because I have the leisure this morning to enjoy and thoroughly appreciate that you were good enough to write." (Marshall to Captain O. D. Wells, July 19, 1939, GCMRL/ G. C. Marshall Papers [Pentagon Office, General]. Nine hundred eighty-seven congratulatory messages are preserved in Marshall's files.) ★

FROM MAJOR GENERAL MASAFUMI YAMAUTI[1]   July 1, 1939
                                                          Washington, D.C.

Dear General Marshall: Representing the Imperial Japanese Army, I wish to take this opportunity to extend my hearty congratulation upon your new appointment as Chief of Staff of the United States Army.

It will be my great pleasure to have our association during my official tour of duty in this country. Please be good enough to extend to us your courtesies officially as well as privately.[2]

Again on this opportunity I wish to extend my highest respects to your honour.   Yours sincerely,

                                                          M. Yamauti

GCMRL/G. C. Marshall Papers (Pentagon Office, Congratulations)

1. Yamauti was the military attaché at the Japanese Embassy.
2. Marshall replied that he was "sure that the cordial relations which have existed between the Imperial Japanese Army and the Army of the United States will continue, and I shall look forward to pleasant contacts with you during your tour of duty in Washington." (Marshall to Yamauti, July 5, 1939, GCMRL/G. C. Marshall Papers [Pentagon Office, Congratulations].)

TO LIEUTENANT COLONEL HAROLD R. BULL   July 1, 1939
                                                        [Washington, D.C.]

My dear Bull: While you have been the Secretary of the General Staff under General Craig since my transfer to the office of the Chief of Staff last October, yet a major portion of my business has been done with you and through you. Therefore, on your departure today I wish you to know that I have been most appreciative of the services you have rendered me.[1]

Officially, and as Chief of Staff, I wish to say now for the record that in judgment, loyalty, general understanding of the Army, and its administration and policies, and especially in contacts with officials and civilians generally, you rate superior. I wish you to know that in the event of any major crisis I will immediately want your services in an important capacity, if I am charged with heavy responsibilities.   Faithfully yours,

GCMRL/G. C. Marshall Papers (Pentagon Office, Selected)

1. Bull was taking a leave prior to the August 20 start of his assignment as professor of military science and tactics at Culver Military Academy in Culver, Indiana. (See Marshall's letter of recommendation for Bull in *Papers of GCM*, 1: 673.)

To GENERAL MALIN CRAIG   July 5, 1939
[Washington, D.C.]

Dear Craig: Your final note of appreciation and thanks was delivered to me Saturday morning.[1]

It is impossible for me to put on paper the depth of my appreciation of what you wrote regarding our relations here in the office, and your generous statements regarding my abilities. But however great the exaggeration, I will value your letter, not only as a high compliment, but more particularly as the generous expression of a grand soldier and a very human person—if that is good English.

I hear and read nothing but compliments of you since your departure. Certainly you should now feel that what I indicated earlier in the spring was correct, that is, you leave the War Department appreciated by everybody, beloved of the Army, and leaving behind you a record of progressive accomplishment which reached a peak in the bill which has just passed the Congress. But of course there is more to this than the mere passage of the bill; the fact that you succeeded in controlling the character of the bill is the greatest tribute of your service to the Army.[2]

I spent the week-end with Mrs. Marshall and flew back last night greatly rested and prepared for the battle.[3] I do hope that you and Mrs. Craig are finding utter relaxation, and that you are now willing to bask in the general public approval of your forty-five years as a soldier and your last four years as Chief of Staff.   Affectionately,

GCMRL/G. C. Marshall Papers (Pentagon Office, Selected)

1. Craig expressed his deep admiration for Marshall in a letter dated June 30. He lauded his deputy's "splendid character and able mind," and added that he had derived "great pleasure and mental stimulus" from their daily conversations. (*Papers of GCM*, 1: 721.)

2. On July 2, President Roosevelt announced that he had signed the $223,398,047 supplemental military appropriation bill which included funds for an increase in the Air Corps, for educational orders, and for five new air bases. The bill completed the $552,000,000 emergency defense program that the president outlined in his January 12, 1939, speech to Congress. (*New York Times*, July 3, 1939, p. 4.)

3. Mrs. Marshall usually spent a portion of her summers on Fire Island, New York.

To Juan T. Trippe[1]   July 6, 1939
                                                                 [Washington, D.C.]

My dear Mr. Trippe: I have you to thank, I think, for the very generous
and gracious treatment accorded me and the officers with me in Brazil, and
also for your message of service which was received by me and passed on to
General Monteiro on our way to Langley Field.

One reason I am particularly glad I was chosen to go to Brazil was the
opportunity to see something of the splendid plant that was being operated
by your Company. I want to tell you very frankly that I consider this of
great importance to the general program of national defense for this country and for the western hemisphere as a whole.[2]

I hope you will let me know when you are in Washington because I will
enjoy another opportunity to talk things over with you.   Faithfully yours,

GCMRL/G. C. Marshall Papers (Pentagon Office, General)

1. Juan T. Trippe, a veteran of the naval aviation service during the World War, had been
president of Pan American Airways since 1927.

2. Pan American, the world's largest international airline at this time, had acquired
numerous landing fields and other facilities (i.e., "plant") in Brazil since the early 1930s. The
company's airfields were not satisfactory for military use, however. The War Department was
anxious over the extent of influence of German and Italian interests in the South American
aviation industry, and had, as early as May 1938, advocated "the backing of American-owned
commercial aviation interests in Latin America." Other objectives included the development
of airfields with military capabilities and the preparation of these for air operations once
hostilities broke out. (Stetson Conn and Byron Fairchild, *The Framework of Hemisphere
Defense*, a volume in the *United States Army in World War II* [Washington: GPO, 1960], pp.
174, 238.)

To Major General Charles D. Herron[1]   July 7, 1939
Confidential   [Washington, D.C.]

Dear Herron: I have just this moment read your letter of July 5th, and I
hasten to tell you how sorry I am that I did not have the opportunity of
seeing you and Mrs. Herron here in the States.[2]

In glancing over my hasty correspondence during the few days I was in
Washington prior to sailing for Brazil, I note that my letter of appreciation
of your congratulations was decidedly pro forma. You know, and I feel
Mrs. Herron knows, that there are no people whose good will and good
wishes I value more highly than yours, and, incidentally, whom I admire
more.

Confidentially, I hope to get out to Hawaii, maybe this fall, possibly in
September. This is a mere dream at the present time, but Arnold and I are

trying to cook up a quick flight to the Coast, and then take the China clipper to Hawaii. Naturally I am not talking about it, but I hope it will be possible to find a way to do it both from the financial and administrative obligation standpoints.

My Brazilian venture was the hardest work I have ever done, but it was a wonderful trip and they put the big pot into the little one. However, I am no diplomat.

With my affectionate regards to you both,   Faithfully,

P.S.   Confidentially, Craig suggested Peyton as Deputy Chief of Staff, saying that he did not know whether I knew Peyton or not, and that I probably would not pay any attention to his suggestion.[3] I laughed and told him that he was my room-mate and that if I brought in a V.M.I. man as Deputy Chief of Staff, I would probably start up a new war between the States.

GCMRL/G. C. Marshall Papers (Pentagon Office, Selected)

1. Herron (U.S.M.A., 1899) and Marshall had been student officers at Fort Leavenworth between 1906 and 1908. During the World War, Herron had been chief of staff of the Seventy-eighth Division. He had been on duty with the General Staff in Washington, D.C., from June 1920 until August 1923. Between September 1935 and December 1936, he commanded the Sixth Field Artillery Brigade in Chicago, Illinois, and from January to September 1937, he commanded the Sixth Corps Area. Transferred to Hawaii, he commanded the Hawaiian Division from October 1937 to March 1938; since that time he had been commanding the Hawaiian Department.

2. From a train "somewhere in Kansas," Herron wrote: "I was in Washington, you were in South America and I did not go back again after your return because I knew that you would be swamped for the first month—but not like some of the rest of them, for four years!" (Herron to Marshall, July 5, 1939, GCMRL/G. C. Marshall Papers [Pentagon Office, Selected].)

3. In his letter, Herron observed: "The general officers in and coming to the islands are a splendid lot, who work well and without friction. Perhaps I think the most of your friend [Brigadier General Philip B.] Peyton—he would make a magnificent G-1 for you—he is a real human being which is not true of all Army officers!" (Ibid.)

To Major General Henry H. Arnold[1]   July 7, 1939
[Washington, D.C.]

My dear Arnold: Yesterday I met General Monteiro, of the Brazilian Army, and his officers on their arrival at Bolling Field, completing their circular tour of the United States by air.[2] This long flight was carried out on schedule without a single untoward incident. To my mind it is evidence of the high efficiency with which the Air Corps now operates, and I would appreciate your thanking the officers concerned for the splendid manner in which they performed their duties.

I also wish to comment on the program of Air demonstrations, honors, and entertainments provided for the Brazilian Mission at the Air Corps stations visited. In every respect these programs were most impressive, were beautifully carried out, and made a profound impression on General Monteiro and his officers. I have written direct to the various commanders concerned, but I would appreciate your conveying to them and their officers the formal appreciation of the War Department, and my personal thanks.   Faithfully yours,

GCMRL/G. C. Marshall Papers (Pentagon Office, General)

1. Arnold had been chief of the Air Corps since September 1938.
2. The defense of Brazil, particularly of its northeastern bulge, had assumed a high priority in the War Department's planning. The official history of United States Army–Latin American military relations is Conn and Fairchild, *Framework of Hemisphere Defense.* Documents on Marshall's tour of Brazil are in *Papers of GCM,* 1: 715–20. To repay Brazilian Army Chief of Staff General Pedro Aurélio de Góes Monteiro for this tour, Marshall arranged an airborne inspection trip for him to visit all major military establishments in the United States. (See Marshall to Pershing, July 17, 1939, p. 15.)

To COLONEL CHARLES C. HAFFNER[1]   July 12, 1939
Confidential   [Washington, D.C.]

Dear Haffner: I have just received your long-hand letter of July 10th, and while I have not had an opportunity to give it a very careful reading, I think it best for me to answer immediately, and possibly write more later.[2]

In the first place—and this is most confidential, I did not anticipate that Keehn would introduce my name into the matter. We were discussing the qualities desirable in a Chief of the Bureau, and I mentioned you as a type. He said there was no possibility of your considering the matter, that you would not have it. I replied that I was not so sure about that, and let it go at that.

Now the facts in the matter, so far as I am concerned, are these: I will be delighted to have you because I feel that you would not only courageously represent the best interests of the Guard with high intelligence, but that also you would be able to establish a desirable intimate and understanding contact with the General Staff. What I had in mind in tipping Keehn off was that you might be brought into the thing as an unexpected candidate after the numerous inevitable contestants had about neutralized each other. I assume that vigorous efforts will be made by the generals of the National Guard to secure the appointment, and I rather anticipate that they will make it very difficult for each other. I do know that it is going to be exceedingly difficult for the War Department to exercise the proper freedom of selection based on efficiency and other aspects of suitability. One can never tell what influences will work in these matters, and it is not beyond the bounds of possibility that your political affiliations might prove a difficulty beyond our control here. I do not imagine so, but from what I can learn the pursuit of this particular office is ruthlessly aggressive. It is for that reason in particular that I had in mind that your name should not be mentioned in the early stages, and then should be solidly backed by Illinois at the psychological[2] moment.

Now, as to you personally: I do not want you to feel a patriotic obligation, as it were, to make a great personal sacrifice. You know the measure of what that would be, and I think it only right that you should consider your own situation as of primary importance, unless conditions grow more critical.

I am rather strongly of the belief that the early mention of your name would be harmful, and that it would be much better to keep it out of the picture for the time being. These organized campaigns do not seem to lead very far. Witness General Leach's collection of resolutions and endorsements and association from practically every Governor and high National Guard official.[3] A little later, if you seriously consider the matter, then a few of the more powerful people, quietly tipped off, might be the best maneuver; to be followed, of course, at the proper moment by heavy Illinois pressure.

I am writing you most confidentially—for your eye alone.   Hastily,

GCMRL/G. C. Marshall Papers (Pentagon Office, Selected)

1. Haffner commanded the 124th Field Artillery Regiment, a Chicago unit of the Illinois National Guard.

2. Haffner wrote that Major General Roy D. Keehn, commanding general of the Illinois National Guard, had suggested that Marshall "might want to talk to me some time about the National Guard Bureau." The incumbent head of that office, Major General Albert H. Blanding, would complete his four-year tour in January 1940; consequently a group of Guard officers had recently asked Haffner to permit them to mount a campaign to secure that office for him. He had never sought to be any group's candidate, Haffner said, and he did not desire the position; but "no one who can afford it has the right to refuse governmental service if drafted and I could afford it." He asked for Marshall's advice before replying to the officers. (Haffner to Marshall, July 10, 1939, GCMRL/G. C. Marshall Papers [Pentagon Office, Selected].)

3. Brigadier General George E. Leach, commander of the Minnesota National Guard's Fifty-ninth Field Artillery Brigade, was the mayor of Minneapolis. He had been chief of the National Guard Bureau from 1931 to 1935.

To JOSEPH P. KENNEDY[1]   July 13, 1939
[Washington, D.C.]

Dear Joe: Replying to your letter of July 3d, I have had orders issued for Colonel Scanlon to remain available to you in his present status until January 1st, 1940.[2]

I am exceedingly sorry that you did not find Colonel Chynoweth personally acceptable. His relations with the British authorities seem to be cordial, and his reports to the War Department have been valuable. Naturally the War Department wishes to avoid injuring or humiliating an officer of Chynoweth's fine reputation and record in the Army by summarily relieving him from his present assignment. Furthermore, he has been put to considerable personal expense in preparing himself and his family for the detail.[3]

On the other hand, it is essential that you have an attaché with whom you can work in complete harmony. Therefore, I have given directions that another officer with the necessary military intelligence and general staff qualifications be selected who would be acceptable to you personally. In the meantime, I would appreciate your treating this phase of the matter as confidential, while allowing us a few months in which to rearrange matters.[4]

With warm personal regards,   Faithfully yours,

GCMRL/G. C. Marshall Papers (Pentagon Office, General)

1. Marshall drafted this letter for Secretary Woodring's signature. Kennedy, an investment banker and shipping industry executive, held positions on the Securities Exchange Commission and the Maritime Commission until his appointment as ambassador to the United Kingdom in 1937.

2. No copy of Kennedy's July 3 letter to Woodring is in the Marshall papers. Colonel Martin F. Scanlon, an Air Corps pilot who had been assistant military attaché, had been designated as Ambassador Kennedy's personal aide.

3. Lieutenant Colonel Bradford G. Chynoweth (U.S.M.A., 1912) was military attaché in London between March and October 1939. Chynoweth's account of his experiences is in *Bellamy Park* (Hicksville, N.Y.: Exposition Press, 1975), pp. 150–67.

4. Brigadier General Sherman Miles (U.S.M.A., 1905) was designated as military attaché and arrived in London in October. He was described to Ambassador Kennedy as "a dignified, well poised, quiet and agreeable man, who should be highly satisfactory in such a spot. Also he has a broad comprehension of military affairs. He has an attractive wife and they are accustomed to the ways of foreign capitals." (Woodring to Kennedy, July 21, 1939, GCMRL/G. C. Marshall Papers [Pentagon Office, General].)

To General Malin Craig   July 13, 1939
                                                        [Washington, D.C.]

Dear Craig: Your postal from Weatogue has been received, translated, and deeply appreciated.[1] I like the look of that set of quarters, which shows unmistakable evidence that no quartermaster ever got within a block of it.

I have been coming to the office at 7:30, trying to catch up with business, which necessarily is pretty heavy these days. It goes on about as you will recall it and up to the present moment I have been able to retain my sense of humor. Gasser, poor devil, is bowed under a mass of work.[2] I have rather walked out and left him flat in the role of master negotiator. I have given one dinner and gone to about seven of the Latin-American type, but I am almost through that business. I had tea on the south portico of the White House with the Dominicans the other day, Admiral Leahy and myself were the outsiders, about twelve people in all—very pleasant; the President poured.[3]

I went out to the house once for thirty minutes to give them Mrs. Marshall's selection of papers from the samples I had taken to Fire Island. Tell Mrs. Craig I am having them look into one purchase for her beautifully arranged kitchen, to see if it is not too expensive. That is a dish-washer, which I think is a very practical thought on the part of the Acting Chief of Staff. (Miss Young evidently doesn't think so judging from her expression).[4]

You are missed by everyone, as evidenced by daily comments. Up on the Hill, where I have been battling the Lieutenant General bill, your name is in every other sentence.[5] I told you in the spring during one of your most depressed and irritated moments that what was worrying you was kitchen stuff; that so far as the Army, the public, and Congress were concerned you occupied a unique position in their appreciation and confidence. I think that statement is completely borne out by the situation today.

I received a note from Hagood yesterday morning, sent a nickel across the street, and have been apologizing to myself ever since. He writes me up in the Saturday Evening Post. While I was at the White House Tea, one of the Aides gave the President a new buffalo nickel and said General Hagood had sent it to him to buy this copy of the Saturday Evening Post. At the time I did not know that I was involved.[6]

The Secretary called me in the other day to be photographed with him and McNutt. I think I was a sort of anti-political prophylactic.[7]

Tell Genevieve I received her sweet note and appreciate her taking the time to write. I quote below one paragraph from the letter of the Manager of the Pocono Manor Inn, to whom I had written for rates. You may be interested, but the rates paralyzed me. I have destroyed the catalogue but preserved the letter.

"We are indeed honored to learn that General Malin Craig enjoyed his brief visit to Pocono Manor to the extent that he would favorably comment regarding same upon his return to Washington. My great regret is that the General must have been intentionally very quiet and in the background, because until your letter arrived, I had no knowledge of his presence here. Otherwise I assure you that my personal attention would have been devoted to his comfort and pleasure."

My affectionate regards to you both.   Faithfully,

GCMRL/G. C. Marshall Papers (Pentagon Office, Selected)

1. General Craig's postcard from Weatogue, Connecticut, is not in the Marshall papers. Craig's handwriting was such that his staff frequently "translated" it word-by-word below his writing.

2. Brigadier General Lorenzo D. Gasser had been acting deputy chief of staff since July 1.

3. General Rafael Leonidas Trujillo Molina, army chief of staff of the Dominican Republic and that country's former president, was visiting the United States in order to discuss arms and security arrangements and to spur negotiations regarding customs revenues. (Department of State, *Foreign Relations of the United States: Diplomatic Papers, 1939,* 5 vols. [Washington: GPO, 1955–57], 5: 579–81; *Army and Navy Journal,* July 15, 1939, p. 1081.) Marshall gave a dinner for Trujillo on July 9. The White House tea took place on July 11.

4. Marshall was having the chief of staff's Quarters No. 1 at Fort Myer, Virginia, remodeled. (See the editorial note on pp. 20–21.) Maude A. Young, Marshall's personal secretary, had been secretary to the chiefs of staff since 1918.

5. Except for the chief of staff, the highest rank in the army at this time was that of major general. Officers of this rank commanded most service branches, the nine corps areas, and the three overseas departments. The four continental army headquarters were each headed by the senior corps area commander under that headquarters.

On July 11, Marshall testified before the House Committee on Military Affairs in support of H.R. 7093 which would promote the four army commanders to lieutenant general. This new rank would allow Marshall to select the most efficient officer, regardless of seniority, to command an army. In addition, as a lieutenant general was equal in rank to a vice admiral, of which there were several on duty, the army would gain a greater degree of rank and status parity with the navy. (GCMRL/G. C. Marshall Papers [Pentagon Office, Testimonies].) The lieutenant generals bill was signed by the president on August 5.

6. Retired Major General Johnson Hagood had written a laudatory essay entitled "Soldier" for the *Saturday Evening Post,* July 15, 1939, pp. 25, 62–64.

7. Paul V. McNutt took office on July 13 as the first Federal Security Agency administrator. A lawyer, he was formerly a national commander of the American Legion (1928–29) and governor of Indiana (1933–37). At this time there was some talk of him as a Democratic candidate for president in 1940. (For example see *New York Times,* July 8, 1939, p. 2.)

To Brigadier General Jay L. Benedict   July 13, 1939
                                                    [Washington, D.C.]

Dear Benedict: I have just this moment read your letter of July 12th regarding Monteiro's visit.[1] I can see that you put the big pot into the little one and gave him a perfect exhibition. I am especially appreciative of Mrs. Benedict's contribution to the affair. You two certainly have a hard time there. The honor of that post is considerably qualified by the laborious and expensive obligations that go along with it, but on every hand I hear compliments on the manner in which you carry it out.

I have been immersed in Brazilian and Dominican affairs. Like you, I found Monteiro a very agreeable person and unusually well informed. Please accept my personal thanks for your efficient response to this obligation, and my thanks to Mrs. Benedict. Faithfully yours,

GCMRL/G. C. Marshall Papers (Pentagon Office, General)

1. Benedict (U.S.M.A., 1904) had been superintendent of the United States Military Academy since February 1938. In his letter to Marshall, he described the visit by General Góes Monteiro and Second Corps Area Commander Major General Hugh A. Drum. Benedict presided over ceremonies in which Góes Monteiro presented the corps of cadets a replica of the sword of the Duke of Caxias (Luis Alves de Lima e Silva, 1803–1880), Brazilian

national hero, which was a gift from the cadets of the Brazilian Military Academy. "He was so touched by the ceremony," Benedict wrote, "that his emotions almost got the better of him. I feel certain the General was highly pleased with his visit here. After breaking through his reserve, I found him a delightful and well-informed soldier." (Benedict to Marshall, July 12, 1939, GCMRL/G.C. Marshall Papers [Pentagon Office, General].)

TO LIEUTENANT COLONEL HAROLD R. BULL   July 15, 1939
                                              [Washington, D.C.]

Dear Bull: I have just this moment read, or rather scanned for the time being, your fine letter of the 10th. I am so glad that you and Mrs. Bull are having a real rest, and a complete relief from the devastating pressure of Washington and the War Department. I think it was most important for you to get this before you took up business at Culver, because enough is a feast and you have long since passed your limit of the diet.

Things are moving along I hope smoothly, certainly all of the force are working hard to spare me. Gasser has taken over the entire burden of the office and I have left him pretty much alone. He deals direct with the Secretary in most matters, also the Assistant Secretary in many, and I have had Ward and Mickelsen dealing direct with the Secretary, and Parks with Mr. Johnson. This relieves me of a tremendous amount of interruption and I seldom hear Mr. Woodring's buzzer.[1] I have been deep in straightening out the construction program as to priorities, methods, control, etc., and Gasser has done an excellent job of coordination and harmonizing. I have been before Congress several times, particularly on the Lieutenant General's bill, which is through the House and should pass the Senate in a few days.

This week has been one of luncheons and dinners every day with someone, practically all semi-official. Monteiro returns to town Wednesday to see the President with me, and I will probably give him a luncheon. The Trujillo dinner was very successful, too so possibly. Monteiro gave me a lovely dinner. His trip has been a tremendous success apparently, and Drum has done a fine job in New York and Benedict at West Point. Monteiro was reduced to tears at West Point.

I flew up over the 4th of July to see Mrs. Marshall. It takes me two hours and ten minutes by air, using an amphibian to go over the water; and I am planning to fly up this morning to see her, I move out to Myer on August 1st.   Faithfully yours,

GCMRL/G. C. Marshall Papers (Pentagon Office, Selected)

1. Lieutenant Colonel Orlando Ward (U.S.M.A., 1914) replaced Bull as secretary of the General Staff on July 1, 1939. Major Stanley R. Mickelsen and Major Floyd L. Parks were assigned to the Office of the Chief of Staff. The chief's office was adjacent to that of the secretary of war, who could summon Marshall with a buzzer.

To General John J. Pershing   July 17, 1939
                                               Washington, D.C.

Dear General: I have been following your recent movements and condition through your letters to Adamson, which he has shown me. Also I have picked up a little data on you from the newspapers—your appearance at Marseilles for example.[1]

I am sorry you had such a gloomy, damp time in Paris, but apparently now you are enjoying fine weather and the surroundings are more stimulating.

I have been intensely busy of late, with accumulated business that occurred during my absence in Brazil, with the taking over of the new job, with the official duties and entertainments in connection with the visits of two Latin-Americans, General Monteiro of Brazil, and General Trujillo, of the Dominican Republic, and most pressing of all, the formal initiation of the Air Corps augumentation program and other matters pertaining to the Army included in that bill. We have been involved in settlements regarding contracts for almost $150,000,000 of construction and $120,000,000 for airplanes, including the matter of types, which is General Staff business, and the commencement of the actual business of recruiting, training, resorting or re-grouping personnel to meet the 32,000 men we are adding to the Air Corps and the Coast Artillery.[2] Then, I have had to be before Congress several times of late, and am very much pleased as apparently we have gotten the Lieutenant General bill through Congress, which I think essential for the development of the four field armies along business lines, particularly as pertains to planning and genuine organizing and set-up of the National Guard phases of munition and defense measures. I got by the Senate Committee in a three minute hearing, they acting for adoption while I was present. The House kept me thirty minutes, but passed the bill the next day. It is No. 2 on the Senate Calendar now and no fight is anticipated. We are having quite a battle with the revitalization measure.

I have only had a chance to see Mrs. Marshall for a few days since my return from Brazil. She is at Fire Island. I flew up there Saturday noon and back this morning. Incidentally, ten miles off shore from Long Island I was with her at seven a.m. today, took an amphibian plane near the dock, and was here at my desk at 8:10 a.m., of course having gained an hour in difference of time. Also, on my flight down I saw R.O.T.C. training at Sandy Hook, three columns of R.O.T.C. and C.M.T.C. units moving across the Parade ground apparently for a march, at Dix, practically the same situation at Meade; I saw drilling on the parade ground of R.O.T.C. and C.M.T.C. at Hoyle, took a look at the Ordnance Depot near Philadelphia, got a glance at Holabird—all before I reached my desk at 8:10 this morning. I have flown up several times.

I move out to Myer August 1st, but Mrs. Marshall will not return to town until September. Molly spent part of last week with me but has gone back to the seashore. My sister arrived this afternoon from Greensburg, Pennsylvania, to spend a week with me. I leave for Chanute Field, Illinois, Friday morning, inspect there that afternoon, and take the National Guard dinner for me in Chicago that night (Dawes, Robert Wood and some others you know will be there), lunch at the Arlington race course Saturday morning, and present a cup at the Arlington Classic that afternoon; I will have dinner with the Corps Area Commander at Sheridan Saturday night, and lunch with Dawes Sunday, leaving the air field near Evanston at two o'clock for Washington.[3]

The Brazilian trip was terrifically strenuous—I covered six states and generally was on the steady go from eight in the morning until one or two the next morning—flew something over 2,000 miles while there. They gave me a marvelous reception which built up after a few days to sometimes 50,000 to 75,000 people. I gave Monteiro a wonderful air trip entirely around the United States. He saw Langley Field, bombing; Fort Monroe, anti-aircraft; Barksdale Field with GHQ air group maneuvers; Randolph Field with students from there and Kelly; Fort Sam Houston and a review of our stream-lined division, Fort Bliss and the Cavalry Division, Grand Canyon, March Field and air group maneuvers, San Pedro and the Fleet, where he was received by the Admiral, Hollywood and Louis Mayer, where Norma Shearer was his dinner partner,[4] Hamilton Field and more air maneuvers, a review of the troops at the Presidio and Exposition, a view from the air of the entire fleet as it came through the Golden Gate, a luncheon in Kansas City, the Mechanized Force at Knox, the Ford factory in Detroit, cadets at West Point, troops near Governors Island, the Exposition in New York. Here he had luncheon with the President, and returns from New York Wednesday to have an interview with the President, Sumner Welles and myself. He sails for home on the 21st.[5]

I have had to give dinners and attend dinners around here until I am sick of the business.

Mrs. Marshall has gained seven pounds since her violent attack of poison oak serum, and she only has two more to pick up before she is back to normal.[6] Craig is automobiling about New England. I had a note from him this morning.

I am getting entirely too much publicity for my own good. It will start up resentment in the Army, I think. Hagood gave me an elaborate write-up in the Saturday Evening Post last week.

With my most affectionate regards, and the hope that you are not overdoing, Faithfully yours,

G. C. Marshall

P.S. We got Adamson on active duty July 1st.

LC/J. J. Pershing Papers (General Correspondence)

1. Marshall had been instrumental in having George E. Adamson, Pershing's personal secretary since before World War I, legally designated by Congress in March as "Military Secretary to the General of the Armies" with the rank of colonel and placed on the army active list. At this time Pershing was in France, where he normally spent his summers.

2. These issues are discussed in: (1) House Military Affairs Committee, *Facilitating Procurement of Aircraft,* report to accompany H.R. 7267, 76th Cong., 1st sess. (Washington: GPO, 1939); (2) House Appropriations Committee, *Third Deficiency Appropriation Bill, Fiscal Year 1939,* report to accompany H.R. 7462, 76th Cong., 1st sess. (Washington: GPO, 1939).

3. Molly P. Brown was Marshall's stepdaughter, and Marie Singer was his sister. The Illinois National Guard dinner at the University Club of Chicago on July 21 had a guest list of one hundred men, including Sixth Corps Area Commander Major General Stanley H. Ford; former Vice President Charles G. Dawes; Sears, Roebuck and Company President Robert E. Wood; and *Chicago Daily Tribune* publisher Robert R. McCormick. Julius Klein published a flattering story about Marshall's visit in the August issue of the *Illinois Guardsman* (pp. 4–5).

4. The United States Fleet was commanded by Admiral Claude C. Bloch. Louis B. Mayer was in charge of production at Metro-Goldwyn-Mayer studios where Norma Shearer had been a popular star since 1926.

5. Under Secretary of State Sumner Welles coordinated most United States relations with Latin America. On July 20, Marshall dictated a farewell message to Góes Monteiro which said, in part: "You are leaving behind in our army a host of new friends who have learned to admire you and who have faith in you as a great soldier. You leave me personally with a feeling of affectionate regard and understanding and the memory of a most delightful association as your guest and your host." (Marshall to Góes Monteiro, July 20, 1939, NA/ RG 407 [General, 210.482 Brazil (4–29–39)].)

6. In May Mrs. Marshall had spent three weeks in Walter Reed Army Medical Center, Washington, D.C. (Katherine Tupper Marshall, *Together: Annals of an Army Wife* [New York and Atlanta: Tupper and Love, 1946], p. 43.)

To Bernard M. Baruch[1]

July 20, 1939
[Washington, D.C.]

My dear Mr. Baruch: I have just this moment read your letter of July 19th,[2] and learned for the first time of your misfortune in having to undergo a mastoid operation. My full sympathy goes to you, and I am delighted to judge from your letter that you have fully recovered.

I have been concerned about General Pershing's health in France, as he had—most confidentially—several attacks. He has endeavored to minimize this, and emphatically denies them. I suppose they are inevitable under the circumstances, but it worries me to have him off in France even though he seems to be particularly happy there the pleasanter period of the year.

I am well aware of your important part in the stirring up of the national conscience to our serious situation last year, and the tremendous effect it had on public opinion. I also recall the views you expressed on South America in previous years, and your brief comment to me in my office here in the War Department not so long ago. I do hope I may have an opportunity to talk things over with you personally, and if I am in New York I will try to make an appointment with you in advance, and if you are in Washington I hope you will lunch with me.

I have an invitation to shoot ducks at the mouth of the Mississippi. It should be "to shoot at ducks", but it recalls a very amusing expedition with you.

With warm regards, and thanks for your letter   Faithfully yours,

GCMRL/G. C. Marshall Papers (Pentagon Office, Selected)

1. As General Pershing's aide, Marshall had become acquainted with Baruch, a politically influential financier and the former chairman (March–December 1918) of the War Industries Board. (See *Papers of GCM,* 1: 385.)

2. Baruch's letter mentioned his operation and that General Pershing had visited him in the hospital prior to his departure for France. "As you are aware, or can find out upon inquiry," Baruch wrote, "I did as much as anybody to stir up the action which resulted in the expenditures which are giving the Army a part of what they need. I know we have not yet a well balanced program and as soon as I get on my feet, I am going to go after it again. I was in hopes we would have a neutrality legislation that would permit the manufacture of airplanes and the export thereof during war, because I wanted to see a development in this country that our orders alone would not permit. Also, I wanted the United States to take first place again in quality and quantity. I do not know whether you have seen expressions of my views on the South American situation, and what I considered adequate preparedness. These were expressed back in 1936 and 1937. Always remember that the Army, and you particularly, have a friend in me if I can be of any use." (Baruch to Marshall, July 19, 1939, GCMRL/G. C. Marshall Papers [Pentagon Office, Selected].)

TO BRIGADIER GENERAL EDMUND L. DALEY[1]   July 20, 1939
[Washington, D.C.]

My dear Daley: I am sorry I did not have an opportunity to see you before you left for Puerto Rico, or during my recent visit to the Island. There was, and is, a great deal I would have liked to talk over with you, matters that do not lend themselves well to a written discussion.

I am intensely interested in the development of the Puerto Rican garrison. The Air Base is first priority, but that problem can be handled in the usual manner. I am particularly concerned now with the problem of furnishing an adequate garrison to secure the defense of the Air and Naval bases. War Plans has outlined the garrison they think suitable for this purpose, and you have been called upon for your views. There is not much question as to the suitability or adequacy of the garrison recommended, but there is considerable question as to the availability of the necessary regular troops for the purpose.[2]

It is conceivable that we might be able to secure the necessary increase in next year's legislation, or it is possible that a portion of the troops for this purpose might be secured when the units now existing in the United States are reorganized into the new smaller divisional organization. However, to build up a fairly large garrison of regular troops in Puerto Rico means that the military budget will have to be increased. I anticipate that sooner or later we will be faced with a cut in military appropriations and be called upon to undergo a strenuous process of economizing. Pay and rations are the simplest and most effective cuts that can be applied by Congress, so that we will therefore probably be subjected to serious reductions in regular personnel. We would then be concerned with the necessity of emasculating the ground forces of the Army within the United States in order to maintain our foreign garrisons.

I would, therefore, like to avoid building up a heavy regular personnel in our foreign garrisons, if this can be done without serious prejudice to their security.

I have in mind a scheme of making more effective use of the National Guard. For political and economic reasons, the National Guard can resist reductions better than can the Regular Army. At the same time, the use of National Guard units avoids the large cost of barracks, quarters and maintenance necessary for each additional regular unit.

For some time I have had the idea that the standard of Mobilization Day efficiency of certain categories of National Guard units could be materially raised and their availability for actual operations correspondingly speeded up, by a more intimate integration with Regular Army organizations.

I believe this can be accomplished by a close association between a regular unit and a corresponding National Guard unit in peace time training. This will be particularly true if the command and headquarters unit can, in effect, be that of the subordinate National Guard unit. For example, take antiaircraft troops. A skeleton regimental headquarters and possibly a full battalion would be regular troops, or maybe merely a battalion headquarters and one battery each of 3-inch and of 37 mm. guns. With this higher headquarters and regular unit, there could be affiliated two or more National Guard battalions. These later would have the identical status and standing of National Guard troops elsewhere as to control, training, etc. Instead of having merely an inspector-instructor from the Regular Army, they would have available the invaluable assistance and cooperation of the personnel of the Regular troops with whom they are associated. Their training should be particularly improved by supervision by the higher headquarters and by the use of selected non-commissioned officers. Upon being mobilized, these units would step off under regular regimental control. Additional separate battalions of antiaircraft might be added, all under the guidance of the higher regimental headquarters referred to above.

In like manner, instead of having a battalion of regular engineers, as proposed by the War Plans Division, it might be desirable to have a single engineer company of the Regular Army, with a skeleton battalion or regimental headquarters, paralleled by a battalion of National Guard engineers.

I look upon Puerto Rico as a natural laboratory in which to try this experiment. It would have to be accomplished with new units which would be in addition to the existing National Guard organizations on the Island. Governor Winship[3] and The Adjutant General of Puerto Rico assured me that they had the talent along the desired lines. The Chief of the National Guard Bureau is in favor of this procedure and it is my belief that politically it would be much easier to initiate this scheme in Puerto Rico than in the United States. It would not be suitable in Panama because of lack of personnel. In Hawaii, race mixtures complicate the problem.

I believe the type of organization outlined above is particularly adaptable to those organizations which do not have the compelling necessity for that iron battle-field discipline essential to infantry. National Guard Field Artillery seems to develop more efficiently than Infantry. The reason for this, apparently, is the greater simplicity of procedure. In addition, the heavy artillery materiel serves as an anchor for the personnel. There is not the great dispersion incident to infantry developments.

I have found that very satisfactory engineer units can be maintained in the National Guard, especially if the units are located near large cities where careful selection of technically trained personnel is possible. Highly satisfactory Medical and Signal Corps units can also be developed in the National Guard.

It is believed, therefore, that a large portion of your field artillery might be National Guard, likewise a major portion of your signal, medical and quartermaster troops.

The people there in Puerto Rico want a National Guard observation squadron to take care of the local missions around the island. From personal experience, I know that such an organization can be maintained at a high state of efficiency, more easily in some respects than in the Regular Army where the pilots are all anxious to get into the GHQ Air Force. In addition there are frequent changes in personnel and the air units do not serve intimately with ground troops. However, I believe that the proper organization for this mission in Puerto Rico would be a reserve squadron. Such a squadron could be maintained there with practically no expense other than the routine training of Reserve Pilots. It would not be necessary to have a full time engineer officer, mechanics, parachute service, etc., as are required in a National Guard squadron, because all of this service could be conveniently provided by the regular army base personnel in Puerto Rico. In other words, repairs, maintenance and other service, and storage could be handled without difficulty by the regular army. The pilots would come from those Reserve Officers, several of whom, I understand from Winship, are already flying their own planes. Some of them own private flying fields.

I wish you would think this over and then write to me, personally and confidentially, giving your impressions. My concern is to provide a reasonable means of defense, to conserve budget funds for much needed materiel, particularly in corps and army artillery, and at the same time to avoid the emasculation of our continental IPF in the near future.[4] I would like you to treat this whole matter, as far as my initiating and suggesting it are concerned, as personally confidential until we arrive at an acceptable base of departure.[5]   Faithfully yours,

GCMRL/G. C. Marshall Papers (Pentagon Office, Selected)

1. Daley (U.S.M.A., 1906), former commander of the First Coast Artillery District in Boston, Massachusetts, had been assigned to command the Puerto Rican Department which was activated on July 1. Initially the command's strength was less than one thousand. (Conn and Fairchild, *Framework of Hemisphere Defense,* pp. 15–16.)

2. The War Plans Division proposed an ultimate commitment of "Air Corps organizations and ground installations, a highly mobile force of infantry and field artillery, a considerable component of antiaircraft troops and installations, and, in all probability, a moderate project for harbor defense armament." Air strength expansion was to be accompanied by a comprehensive defense project. The division also envisaged an expansion of the local National Guard. (George V. Strong Memorandum for the Chief of Staff, February 7, 1939, NA/RG 407 [Classified, 323.231 (4–14–36)].)

3. Major General Blanton Winship had been governor of Puerto Rico since January 1934.

4. The I.P.F.—Initial Protective Force—was the emergency defensive force of currently existing Regular Army and National Guard units (on paper some 400,000 enlisted men at this time). The I.P.F. was the ready component of the P.M.P. (Protective Mobilization Plan) which, when a national emergency was declared, provided for the mobilization of 280,000 regulars, 450,000 guardsmen, and 270,000 new recruits for a total force of 1,000,000. General Staff planning between 1933 and 1939 aimed at providing weapons and equipment for the P.M.P. force, but Congress consistently refused to appropriate sufficient funds. (Watson, *Chief of Staff,* pp. 29–30, 128.)

5. Daley replied that he agreed fully with Marshall's ideas. "The National Guard is a splendid force for developing national spirit in the Island. Increased opportunities to serve in the National Guard, Organized Reserves, and R.O.T.C. will have definite values in bringing insular Puerto Rico closer to the continental United States.

"I am confident that an adequate defense of our Air and Naval bases will be planned which will make minimum demands on troops from the continental United States. As the National Guard components are progressively trained, the regular components in Puerto Rico may be somewhat reduced." (Daley to Marshall, July 28, 1939, GCMRL/G. C. Marshall Papers [Pentagon Office, Selected].)

TWO miles across the Arlington Memorial Bridge from Marshall's new office in the Munitions Building sat the official residence of the army chief of staff at Fort Myer, Virginia. Mrs. Marshall, recovering from her spring illness at her Fire Island cottage, had assigned to her husband the task of overseeing the preparation of their new quarters. "I have been dickering with the decorators, etc. regarding our new home at Fort Myer," Marshall told an Oregon friend. (Marshall to Hamilton Corbett, July 6,

1939, GCMRL/G. C. Marshall Papers [Pentagon Office, Selected].)

Since his arrival at the War Department in mid-1938, Marshall had been renting Major General Stanley D. Embick's house on Wyoming Avenue in northwest Washington. On July 28, Marshall wrote to Malin Craig that he was being moved that day, "the furniture being stored in the dining room pending the completion of papering and painting." He described in enthusiastic detail the changes he had ordered, including the installation of a dishwasher "which will do 1,000 dishes an hour. . . . The rooms look very lovely. . . . The bath rooms are mostly wet cement, so I cannot tell about them yet." (Marshall to Craig, July 28, 1939, ibid.)

Fort Myer and its Third Cavalry Regiment were commanded by Colonel George S. Patton, Jr., whom Marshall had known since their service with the American Expeditionary Forces in France in 1917. Patton wrote to Marshall on July 20 that he understood that the chief's furniture was being moved before the house was ready. "That being the case, it occurs to me that you will have no place to stay. All my family are away, but my house is open and running, and I am there. I can give you a room and bath and meals, and should be truly delighted to do so. I shall not treat you as a guest and shall not cramp your style in any way." (Patton to Marshall, July 20, 1939, ibid.) ★

To Colonel George S. Patton, Jr.   July 24, 1939
[Washington, D.C.]

Dear Patton: I have just found your letter of July 20th, with its hospitable invitation for me to "batch" with you while I am getting my house established at Myer. I will be glad to accept and will talk to you later over the 'phone. You are very kind to invite me.[1]   Faithfully yours,

GCMRL/G. C. Marshall Papers (Pentagon Office, Selected)

1. After receiving Marshall's acceptance, Patton wrote to his wife, who was at their permanent residence in Massachusetts: "I have just consumated a pretty snappy move. Gen George C Marshall is going to live at our house!!! he and I are batching it. I think that once I can get my natural charm working I won't need any letters from John J. P[ershing] or any one else. Of course it may cramp my style a little about going out but there are compensations." (Patton to Beatrice A. Patton, July 27, 1939, LC/G. S. Patton, Jr., Papers.)

Marshall fit perfectly into the Patton household and scheme of things, if not the Patton lifestyle. "Gen Marshall is just like an old shoe   last night he was dining out and instead of having a chauffeur he drove himself   He is going out in the boat with me to day. He does not seem to have many friends." (Patton to Beatrice A. Patton, July 29, 1939, ibid.)

To Jefferson Caffery[1]   July 24, 1939
                                                          [Washington, D.C.]

My dear Mr. Ambassador: General Monteiro sailed from New York on
Saturday, having completed his long tour and many engagements apparently in a better state of health than when he arrived. Of course the State
Department has, or will, inform you of their view as to the results of the
visit, but I thought you would be interested to get my personal reactions as I
gathered them from General Monteiro himself, from Colonel Miller who
seemed to be on a more intimate basis with him than his own staff officers,
and from other officials throughout the country.

On his arrival he got a rather nasty write-up in Time directed against his
appearance.[2] I seized upon a rather amusing incident at Gettysburg—for he
appealed to me to find out if the officer lecturing was not wrong about the
designation of a certain army corps—to give the press a basis for writing
him up as being a man of great intellectual abilities and having a remarkable familiarity with American history. This got about the country generally, and he was received as such practically everywhere he went.

General Monteiro carried himself very well, considering the limitations
on language and the lack of a dashing appearance. He really made a
splendid impression, however, better than I anticipated; and while we did
not get the public reaction of the people in the street and the children, such
as developed in Brazil, yet he was given a really remarkable reception. I do
not think any other individual has ever had quite the view of America in a
short time that this man did. No officer in our Army has ever had the same
opportunity to see our country as did Monteiro; and I think you will find
that he was profoundly impressed and carried away with him the feeling
that the potential power of this country is so great that, as he roughly
phrased it to me, in the end we could lick the world.[3] He was not only
impressed tremendously with the appearance of our men, as to physique
and intelligence, but especially with their great technical skill and high state
of discipline. I think he had in mind that we were rather careless people in a
military way, and he found in these concentrated garrisons that quite the
opposite was the case. The initial demonstration, which was the bombing
from high altitudes, and some machine gunnery, rather took his breath
away; as a matter of fact, the accuracy was a marvelous display of efficiency. From an airplane he saw the Fleet with its 100 or more vessels
steaming into the Golden Gate. I doubt if there could be a similar display of
power in the world, considering the setting.

I suppose you will hear all this at first hand, but I am going to have
Colonel Miller write a confidential report on his estimate of General Monteiro's reactions, and I will see that you receive a copy. Miller, incidentally,
while self-effacing and modest to a remarkable degree, played the leading

role in this affair. He made a profound impression everywhere he went—with the newspaper people, the public, and with our Army officials, who are rather hard-boiled in such matters. As a matter of fact, in some places he was written up almost as much as Monteiro, but he never pushed himself forward in the least. I mention this because he is a man of great value to us in connection with Brazil. I have changed his setting here and am sending him to the War College in September with a view—most confidentially—to his possible appointment as the next head of our Mission in Brazil. He seems to have Monteiro's confidence to a remarkable degree.[4]

On my departure from Rio I wrote you rather formally to express my very genuine appreciation of your courtesy to me, your hospitality, and wise guidance. I want to tell you again how very much I did appreciate all that you and Mrs. Caffery did for me, for I fully realize the vast importance you played in making it possible for me to carry through our mission to Brazil. Will you please present my compliments to Mrs. Caffery and give her my warm regards.   Faithfully yours,

GCMRL/G. C. Marshall Papers (Pentagon Office, General)

1. Caffery, career diplomat and Latin American specialist, had been appointed ambassador to Brazil in July 1937.

2. *Time* magazine called "beady-eyed, flap-chinned General Góes Monteiro . . . a hard-drinking ex-cowboy who worships Napoleon, has false teeth, and in part owes his rise to Oswaldo Aranha. He talks so much about imbuing Brazilians with military spirit that he has had to deny any personal ambition to be a military dictator. To all appearances he is a good & loyal servant of Dictator-President Getulio Vargas." In addition, the article stated that "that capable soldier-diplomat" Marshall had been sent to Brazil because Monteiro "began toasting the discipline, glory and honor of the German army and had accepted an invitation to review Nazi troops." (*Time* 33[June 26, 1939]: 20.)

3. Caffery replied that Góes Monteiro "talks constantly of the three factors he noted everywhere: liberty, order and discipline. He has come back here as sort of a hero and the general effect on our relations is an excellent one." (Caffery to Marshall, August 10, 1939, GCMRL/G. C. Marshall Papers [Pentagon Office, General (Brazil-American Military Mission)].)

4. Lieutenant Colonel Lehman W. Miller had been a member of the United States Military Mission to Brazil between 1934 and 1938; as a result he had been selected to accompany Marshall on his recent visit to Brazil. Marshall commended Miller "for the splendid contribution you made to the success of these missions. Your work with me in Brazil was of the highest importance to the success of the mission, and the efficiency with which you advised and guided General Monteiro on his tour of the United States was directly responsible for a large measure of the success of the visit." (Marshall to Miller, July 26, 1939, GCMRL/G. C. Marshall Papers [Pentagon Office, General].)

THE United States Army framed relations with Latin America within the limits of the president's Good Neighbor Policy. That policy of restrained interference in the region discouraged private munitions sales and military missions. By 1938, the army had assigned only six military attachés to the twenty nations. Lieutenant Colonel Joseph B. Pate, residing in Panama, also represented the United States Army in Venezuela, Colombia, and the five Central American republics. Two missions, four men in Brazil and one in Guatemala, rounded out the army presence in Latin America.

When Axis activity in the hemisphere seemed to mount in 1938, the State Department proposed closer cooperation with Latin American governments through admission of officers to United States service schools, visits by Latin American military leaders, and expansion in the number of attachés and missions assigned to the region. The War Department approved recommendations in 1938 for enlarged missions, military publications for Latin American libraries, and pilot training in the United States.

The army was particularly concerned with the degree of German influence in Colombia's SCADTA airline, which had flying fields within easy reach of the Panama Canal. In January 1939, Pan American Airways acknowledged that it had owned the company since 1931; for political and financial reasons it had permitted the Germans to continue operating the system. To exclude the Germans, it would be necessary to train Colombian replacements at all levels in the company. (Conn and Fairchild, *Framework of Hemisphere Defense,* pp. 172–75, 240–41.) ★

MEMORANDUM FOR THE CHIEF OF THE   July 26, 1939
AIR CORPS [ARNOLD]   [Washington, D.C.]

The Ambassador to Colombia[1] has represented to the State Department the importance of enlarging our mission to Colombia, and especially the importance of arranging for the training of mechanics. He points out that to send their men to this country involves very serious difficulties, since the type of mechanic would certainly not understand English, and probably would not have enough education to acquire sufficient knowledge within a reasonable time to facilitate his instruction. The language difficulty, of course, is also complicated from the viewpoint of our sending men to Colombia. He states that at the present time a large percentage of their airplanes are out of commission through necessity for repairs and lack of people to do the repairing.

A little later I will send you a more accurate quotation from the report, but in the meantime I would like you to consider what might be done to assist in this situation, which the State Department regards as very important to us diplomatically.

The thought occurs to me that we might gather together a small group of civilian mechanics, with one non-commissioned officer, or officer in charge, have the Colombian Government make a contract with them, and send them down there, first to start on repairing these planes, and then use Colombians as apprentices, and with their knowledge of the situation develop the beginnings of a school.

I suppose you have already heard directly from your people in Colombia what the situation is. In any event, we probably will have to do something about it, so I will appreciate your giving it careful consideration.

GCMRL/G. C. Marshall Papers (Pentagon Office, Selected)

1. Spruille Braden, financier and mining engineer, had extensive business experience in Latin America. After acting as adviser to various governments conducting loan negotiations with United States financial institutions from 1925 to 1928, Braden served in several diplomatic positions before President Roosevelt appointed him ambassador to Colombia in January 1939.

To Joseph K. Carson[1]
Confidential

August 1, 1939
[Washington, D.C.]

Dear Joe: I just this moment received your wire of congratulations, which is highly appreciated. However, I am inclined to think you are confused as to dates. While I have been Acting Chief of Staff since July 1st, I will continue to be a lowly brigadier general until September 1st, when I become a permanent major general and a temporary full general. Please don't pun on the "full." These dates are very important matters, because among other things, they mean a better understanding with the paymaster.[2] My present job on my present pay produces quite a depression. All this, of course, is casual comment for your eye alone.

I want to get out to the Northwest again this fall, with a day or two in Portland, but I can not tell now whether this is going to be possible of arrangement. Most confidentially, I have a reservation on a China clipper September 27th, and another reservation on another clipper leaving Hawaii October 3d for the States. I am hoping that possibly I may be able to inspect Portland on my way east, but my present engagements in October will make this difficult.

With warmest regards to Mrs. Carson and the family,   Faithfully yours,

GCMRL/G. C. Marshall Papers (Pentagon Office, Selected)

1. Carson was the mayor of Portland, Oregon. On December 5, 1938, Marshall had written to Brigadier General George Grunert, who had succeeded him as commanding officer at Vancouver Barracks, across the Columbia River from Portland, that Carson was "a fine fellow" who could be "of great help." (*Papers of GCM,* 1: 661.)

2. Marshall's pay and allowances as a brigadier general totaled $625 per month. As a major general this would increase to $808.33. The chief of staff received the pay and allowances of a major general plus $2,200 per year in additional allowances. Thus Marshall would receive an added $4,400 per year beginning September 1.

To Theodore Roosevelt, Jr.[1]
August 3, 1939
[Washington, D.C.]

Dear Roosevelt: I have just this moment read your letter regarding Colonel Cary Crockett, and am writing you immediately to tell you that I will look into the matter very carefully. I know him and am familiar with his fighting record, his special knowledge of Central and South America and the Philippines, and of his vigorous bearing as an officer, but I am glad to have your personal estimate to verify my own.[2]

This physical examination business has been pretty strenuous this summer, was specially ordered, and of course, we are having some tragic examples of the wrong man being tagged.[3] And, as you write, old man "precedent" steps in and prepares to prop open the door if we do any picking and choosing. Precedent is the rock on which our legal procedure is based, but here in Washington it seems to be our particular curse—to the extent that when we try to utilize or save the good men, we are confronted with the almost certain devastating results from the hordes of mediocrity who crowd through the door. This is old stuff to you, but I will give my personal attention to Crockett's case.

With warm regards,   Faithfully yours,

I find that he is being ordered to the Hot Springs Hospital for observation.[4]

GCMRL/G. C. Marshall Papers (Pentagon Office, Selected)

1. Roosevelt had known Marshall since 1917 when both sailed for France with the First Division. He had been governor of Puerto Rico (1929–32) and the Philippine Islands (1932–33); since 1935 he had been an editor at Doubleday, Doran and Company.

2. Crockett, a graduate of and currently an instructor at the Command and General Staff School, was scheduled to be retired because of physical disability. But according to Roosevelt, he could "take on most of the majors and a large percentage of the captains and outlast them." (Roosevelt to Marshall, August 1, 1939, GCMRL/G. C. Marshall Papers [Pentagon Office, Selected].) Crockett retired at the end of January 1940.

3. On April 27, the War Department announced a two-part program aimed at achieving a "rigorous vitalization" of the officer corps. First, Congress was sent a draft of a bill which sought to amend the 1935 promotion act so as to institute forced retirements of over-age field-grade officers. This bill, usually called the age-in-grade promotion bill, was one of the chief topics of discussion and comment in the spring and summer issues of the *Army and Navy Journal*. Second, special medical boards were convened to conduct "a rigid physical examination for all officers of the grade of captain and above" by June 30. (*Army and Navy Journal,* April 29, 1939, pp. 801, 818–19.)

4. This postscript, typed at the bottom of the file copy, was probably a handwritten addition by Marshall.

To Morris Sheppard[1]
Personal
August 3, 1939
[Washington, D.C.]

My dear Senator: I have delayed replying to your letter of July 18th, recommending the appointment of Major Watt as Assistant Adjutant General, until the Secretary of War had written you regarding the same matter.[2]

Watt is an old friend of mine, whose unusual efficiency I have long admired—as a matter of fact since my first contact with him as Chief Clerk of the Eastern Department at Governors Island in 1911. He worked with me on the Shanks' Board investigating the matter of rank among the War veterans commissioned in the Regular service in 1920. More recently, I have watched his highly efficient performance of duty as Liaison Officer with your Committee.

Personally, there is no one in The Adjutant General's Department whom I would take more satisfaction in backing for promotion, but I am forced to the conclusion that to do so would immediately involve us in a precedent which would seriously affect efficiency in other directions. Also, to advance him over the heads of all of the colonels and lieutenant colonels in The Adjutant General's Department, would probably develop enmity against him, and would adversely affect morale.

I am truly sorry, because of my fondness for him and my high opinion of his efficiency, that I do not feel free to urge his appointment.   Faithfully yours,

GCMRL/G. C. Marshall Papers (Pentagon Office, General)

1. Sheppard, a Democrat from Texas, was chairman of the Senate Military Affairs Committee.

2. The senator's letter was not retained in the Marshall papers. Major David A. Watt had entered the army as a private in the Spanish-American War.

MEMORANDUM FOR GENERAL GASSER   August 4, 1939
                                                [Washington, D.C.]

With reference to my uncompleted statement of this afternoon, regarding certain changes, I wish to have considered:

Gradually, without any publicity and undue stirring up of people, I wish to eliminate such features in the War Department as are a continuation of old days when the Army was a very small affair. I am referring to matters which are of a character applicable to post command rather than to a department of the Government charged with the national defense and spending of one billion dollars a year.

I hope to make a beginning in this business by transferring to the Headquarters of the District Commander of Washington certain present War Department activities. For example, the custom of officers arriving in

Washington and registering outside the office of The Adjutant General, should be transferred to the other headquarters; the actual list of registrations to be furnished The Adjutant General whenever he wants it or needs it, but the officers coming into town should report to General Murray's headquarters rather than to the War Department proper.[1]

General Murray's headquarters should take care of automobiles, of course, under such policy as the Chief of Staff establishes. I have found this being handled by the Secretary of the General Staff, the Chief of Staff's Aides, etc.

I have considered the possibility of authorizing General Murray's headquarters to issue all leave orders O.K'd and made by the Chief of arm or branch or section of the General Staff. Those that appear to require disapproval under the governing policy could be referred to The Adjutant General by General Murray.

Take the recent job of Colonel Crane in connection with General Monteiro's visit;[2] he was practically using G-2 as an administrative headquarters to coordinate things, except for the few arrangements made by General Murray. G-2 should lay down the policy but Gen. Murray should designate the officer to follow it through.

I would be opposed to enlarging General Murray's office to any material extent, if at all, because I think he should be merely authorized to call in officers from the surrounding garrisons for specific jobs of brief duration, just as White House Aides are brought over from Fort Myer, etc. This would be excellent training for a lot of young officers.

I wish you would look into this whole matter and see what you can develop. I have talked to General Murray about it without getting any distance, and I recently had a conversation with General Adams, in which he only conceded the automobile matter.

GCMRL/G. C. Marshall Papers (Pentagon Office, Selected)

1. Brigadier General Maxwell Murray (U.S.M.A., 1907) commanded the Washington Provisional Brigade; his offices were in the Munitions Building. Major General Emory S. Adams had been the adjutant general of the army since May 1, 1938.

2. Colonel John A. Crane, of the G-2 division, was chief of the Military Attaché Branch.

MEMORANDUM FOR GENERAL DE WITT[1] August 4, 1939
Washington, D.C.

I apologize for sending you this heavy bundle of papers, but I would appreciate very much your scanning them and letting me have a very informal opinion—as early as practicable.

The thought occurred to me, when reading previous proposals for a National Defense College, General Pershing's comments, etc. that a very practical solution might possibly be found by having a series of special lectures and conferences conducted at the War College, as part of the regular course, but so scheduled and arranged that specific personnel from other Departments of the Government would attend—and participate. This, off hand, would seem to have the advantage of not involving undue overhead, and of providing a course under conditions which would permit important officials to attend without undue loss of time, and would bring into the atmosphere of the War College under officials of the Government—to the advantage of the Army and planning of national defense.[2]

To expand on my idea a little bit: Suppose we assume that ten lectures of an hour each, followed by half of hour conference-discussion, were spaced one a week throughout a certain period of the course; suppose that conference groups were formed following this for special local discussion and report—this not requiring more than half a day's presence by the non-military personnel attending—the Military and Naval members contributing more of the spade work than the other parties. Suppose the reports of these conference groups were made on the basis of an hour's lecture and a thirty minutes' discussion. Such an arrangement would permit a highly informative course for civil officials, with a minimum of time obligated. The War College student would enter this somewhat in the role of a veteran, which would have an impressive effect on the civilian. I am supposing that the Naval phases of this are introduced, in Washington, for greater convenience than at Newport,[3] and at the War College for the same reason.

Now I know you will be shocked at the very thought of such an injection into your present course. And maybe you are entirely right. However, we should be prepared, with the proper logic and background, for a choice between a new time, personnel, and money consuming set-up, or of something integrated into our existing machinery—which means a certain amount of compromise.

It seems to me at the moment, that such an idea as I have hurriedly sketched, might be tremendously beneficial from the point of view of bringing into intimate contact with the War College prominent officials of the State and other Departments, and certainly engendering in them a feeling of more respect for that institution.[4]

[P.S.] This is a first dictation of an idea, without time for much thinking. Please accept it as such.—G. C. M.

USAMHI/Army War College Papers

1. Major General John L. De Witt had been commandant of the Army War College since July 1937.

2. In 1934 the War Plans Division disapproved a proposal for a defense college on several grounds: they opposed greater civilian participation, with the exception of the State Department, in defense planning; they found the plan inoperable because only the State Department had a permanent, professional bureaucracy; and they feared that such a college would become

a "super-joint-planning committee." Chief of Staff General Douglas MacArthur took no action at that time. (Captain Carter B. Magruder, "Digest—National Defense College," undated memo, USAMHI/Army War College Papers.)

In March 1939 Assistant Secretary of War Louis Johnson wrote President Roosevelt to urge the creation of a national defense college to study national strategy and the political, economic, and social problems of mobilization and war. Johnson wanted experts from each of the major executive departments to form a student body of twenty-five to thirty, unifying the planning and research functions of the executive branch. France, Germany, and Great Britain already had such colleges. (Johnson Memorandum for the President, March 8, 1939, ibid.)

On June 15 Brigadier General Edwin M. Watson, one of the president's secretaries, sent Johnson's proposal to Marshall and asked him to "give the President your views." In response, the War Plans Division reiterated its 1934 conclusions against such a college, adding that the college provided no curriculum advantages over the existing army and navy war colleges. (Watson Memorandum for General George C. Marshall, July 15, 1939; Magruder, "Digest—National Defense College," ibid.)

3. Newport, Rhode Island, is the site of the Naval War College.

4. De Witt replied that he favored Marshall's idea, but he thought experience had demonstrated that participation by other executive departments would be "casual and superficial." Assigning a few State Department and Commerce Department men as full-time students at the War College would be more beneficial than, as in the past, merely having them attend a few lectures and conferences. However, if certain lectures were to be added, "it would not be necessary to revise our program." He also agreed with War Plans Division that the planning function should be centralized in the Joint Board. (De Witt Memorandum for General Marshall, August 8, 1939, ibid.)

Marshall wrote to General Watson that he agreed with De Witt and proposed the expansion of the existing Army War College, without duplication of effort. Because of the European situation, which necessitated the expansion of the army and the closing of the service schools to provide more officers, it was impossible to take immediate action on a national defense college. (Memorandum for General Watson, October 19, 1939, FDRL/F. D. Roosevelt Papers [OF 335, National Defense].)

To Brigadier General Lesley J. McNair[1]   August 7, 1939
[Washington, D.C.]

My dear McNair: I have just read your letter of August 3d, regarding the Field Service Regulations. They came up for consideration on Saturday morning from G-3, and I think the matter will be settled almost immediately. I talked over the whole business with Gruber, and like you, I feel that he has done splendid work.[2]

Now, as to your job: I hear on every hand the most flattering comments regarding your effect on Leavenworth. You apparently—to use a hackneyed word—have vitalized the place and yet in a most harmonious manner. I told you in our last conversation that you had the authority to proceed as seemed best to you to bring about the general ends we have in mind, and that you could do this without feeling the necessity for securing approval for the various steps. I spoke then as Deputy, with the concurrence of General Craig. I am writing now as Chief of Staff, to confirm in a more positive manner what I told you then. Anything I can do to assist, you command me; but I want you to feel perfectly free to act, and we all have complete confidence in your judgment, your leadership, and your integrity.

I hope I can get out to Leavenworth this fall and talk things over with you. Faithfully yours,

GCMRL/G. C. Marshall Papers (Pentagon Office, Selected)
1. McNair was commandant of the Command and General Staff School, Fort Leavenworth, Kansas.
2. Colonel Edmund L. Gruber, chief of the Training Branch of the G-3 division of the General Staff, drafted the new Field Service Regulations. The Command and General Staff School reviewed that draft, made comments, but "did not challenge its fundamentals." McNair praised the new regulations: "If such a publication is to be abreast of the times, it necessarily must deal boldly with the newer and more controversial aspects borne of modern developments. If it ducks them, it loses much of its value, and the service drifts—as it has done in the past. This draft faces the issues." McNair wanted the new regulations to help fight the "inertia and intellectual resistance" to modernization in the army. (McNair to Marshall, August 3, 1939, GCMRL/G. C. Marshall Papers [Pentagon Office, Selected].)

To Brigadier General Bruce Magruder   August 7, 1939
Confidential   [Washington, D.C.]

Dear Magruder: I have just this moment read your little note of appreciation of August 4th, which I in turn appreciate. However, out of my deep regard for you and your future, I want to make a few very confidential, personal comments on this new business of yours of being a brigadier general.[1]

You have always worked too hard; you have done too many other people's work. This all but cost you your promotion—you see I am being very frank, but this for your eye only.

Now I counsel you to make a studied business of relaxing and taking things easy, getting to the office late, taking trips, and making everybody else work like hell. It is pretty hard for a leopard to change his spots, but you must cloak your new rank with a deliberate effort to be quite casual. I know that try as you will, it will be almost utterly impossible for you to take things too easy, and I fear it will be next to impossible for you to relax to anywhere near the degree that I think is important.

I woke up at about thirty-three to the fact that I was working myself to death, to my superior's advantage, and that I was acquiring the reputation of being merely a pick and shovel man. From that time on I made it a business to avoid, so far as possible, detail work, and to relax as completely as I could manage in a pleasurable fashion. Unfortunately, it was about six years before I could get away from details because they were in my lap. In China I made a good beginning, and at Benning I refused to read a great deal of the material worked up, and made a practice of pleasant diversions.

I have finally gotten to the point where I sometimes think I am too casual about things; but I think I have reaped a greater advantage than this other possible disadvantage.

Please take me very seriously. You have wonderful qualities, but you are too conscientious. I will be delighted to find that you have decided to take leave and do a little travelling before you report for duty, and I would be even more pleased if I had to write you later on and tell you that you were absenting yourself too frequently from your duties.

With my most sincere regard for your future,   Faithfully yours,

GCMRL/G. C. Marshall Papers (Pentagon Office, General)

1. Magruder, since 1937 the executive officer of the Infantry School at Fort Benning, had recently been notified of his promotion to brigadier general effective November 1.

MEMORANDUM FOR THE ASSISTANT   August 9, 1939
CHIEF OF STAFF, G-3 [ANDREWS]   [Washington, D.C.]

With reference to the attached letters,[1] and previous discussion of the matter, I wish you would seriously consider the establishment of an R.O.T.C. unit at the University of Alaska. I am not concerned about the matter of precedent, as the motive in this is national defense direct as pertains to a particular locality.[2]

The R.O.T.C. unit would be abnormal in many respects, as to numbers, as to character of courses, etc. We want to build up on as economical a basis as we can a military foothold in Alaska. An R.O.T.C. development would be very helpful, and the people would be available for instant use in an emergency.

I have included the letters pertaining to the Link Trainer, though this pertains directly to the office of the Chief of the Air Corps. But I agree with General Bowley that the development of a Reserve Air Corps in Alaska is important to us, and if the Trainer matter is not prohibitive, it might well be done.[3]

GCMRL/G. C. Marshall Papers (Pentagon Office, Selected)

1. The attachments are not in the Marshall papers. Documents on the army's interest in Alaska are in NA/RG 165 (WPD, 3512).

2. The War Department was being pressed by numerous secondary schools and universities which wished to inaugurate Reserve Officers' Training Corps units, each of which required at least one army officer as professor of military science and tactics. Other institutions wished to expand existing R.O.T.C. units. In late July, Marshall refused even to send a public message praising Culver Military Academy, fearing that his interest in that school might get him into "hotter water." "We are in the middle of a very difficult fight here with the Southern military schools, who have produced extremely heavy political pressure for the purpose of securing more officers with their R.O.T.C. units, based on the fact that Culver received two men this year." (Marshall to Leigh R. Gignilliat, July 26, 1939, GCMRL/G. C. Marshall Papers

[Pentagon Office, Selected].) On the R.O.T.C. issue, see the editorial note on pp. 104–6.

3. A "Link Trainer" is a machine—resembling a small, hooded airplane mounted on a pedestal—used in basic training to teach instrument flying. Lieutenant General Albert J. Bowley commanded the Fourth Army, whose district included Alaska. The first step toward implementing the army's long-range defense program for Alaska took place in August 1939 when construction began on an air base at Fairbanks. On the defense of Alaska, see Stetson Conn, Rose C. Engelman, and Byron Fairchild, *Guarding the United States and Its Outposts,* a volume in the *United States Army in World War II* (Washington: GPO, 1964), pp. 223–30.

TO JEFFERSON CAFFERY

August 11, 1939
[Washington, D.C.]

My dear Mr. Caffery: I am enclosing a clipping from last evening's Star, on the question of the joint resolution for the sale of munitions to South American Republics. I thought it would interest you, and encourage you— even though it will irritate you in spots.[1] Confidentially, I am under the impression that we will get very prompt action on the resolution on the re-convening of Congress. It is already through the House, is on the Senate calendar but has never been voted on. I understand it was not brought to a vote because a filibuster was threatened at the time, but it could have been passed with a large majority had the end of the session not been in sight.

I hope the failure of the passage of this legislation has not been a tragic disappointment in Brazil, and I feel reasonably certain that they can count on our getting matters straightened out at a fairly early date.[2]

With warm regards,   Faithfully yours,

GCMRL/G. C. Marshall Papers (Pentagon Office, General)

1. Preston Grover's "Washington Daybook" column in the Washington, D.C., *Evening Star* of August 10 (p. A–11) noted that "the last-minute legislative jam in the Senate stopped the War and Navy Departments from extending our hemispherical defense network down along the coasts of South America." After discussing the Roosevelt administration's support for the bill and the measure's opponents' views, he concluded that "the thing will come up again next session and probably will skid through like a wet duck."

2. The Latin American nations' interest in securing arms became a major problem in United States relations with that region in the late 1930s. German and Italian influence among high-ranking military officers in several nations in the area was aided by arms shipments, and this was an important factor in President Roosevelt's decision in mid-1938 to change United States arms sales policies and to seek new legislation to support that change. In March 1939 the Pittman Resolution (a joint resolution which would have ended the arms embargo provisions of the Neutrality Act of 1937 and permitted limited sales of military equipment to Latin American nations) was introduced in Congress. In the face of considerable opposition, a modified version of the proposal passed the House of Representatives on June 30, 1939. The Senate Foreign Relations Committee voted on July 11 to postpone until 1940 any consideration of neutrality legislation. However, even if the Pittman Resolution had been adopted, it would have limited the army's disposal of surplus materiel to Latin America to coast artillery and antiaircraft guns. (This subject is examined in Conn and Fairchild, *Framework of Hemisphere Defense,* pp. 207–10. See also *Foreign Relations, 1939,* 5: 1–14, and the minutes of the Standing Liaison Committee meetings in NA/RG 319 [WDCSA, SGS].)

To THEODORE ROOSEVELT, JR.   August 11, 1939
                                                          [Washington, D.C.]

Dear Roosevelt: I enjoyed your newsy letter, and appreciate the kind invitation to pull your latch-string.

In view of the problem that faces Ibn Saud it appears that the most suitable weapon for him would be either the Thompson sub-machine gun, caliber .45, Model 1928, A-1, or the Colt Monitor machine rifle.[1]

Since the Arabs would use the gun less as a weapon of precision than as a lead squirt, the Thompson sub-machine gun offers many advantages. It is light and relatively simple because it is a recoil-operated gun and has less mechanism than the gas-operated Colt Monitor. I enclose an Ordnance catalogue which shows the price is something under $200 for the gun without any spare parts. It is for sale by Auto Ordnance Corporation, 31 Nassau Street, New York.

The Colt machine rifle is similar to the type used by the cavalry. The experience of the cavalry has been that this heavier weapon requires a led horse. The greater weight of its ammuniton raises problems that would probably be difficult for the Arabs to solve. Furthermore, it is really a team weapon; its effective operation would probably require a higher degree of organization than Ibn Saud's troops are likely to have. The Colt machine rifle costs around $300.[2]

Our new M-1 rifle is in a "restricted" status. However, even if it could be released, it would not serve the purpose you outline for Ibn Saud as well as the Thompson sub-machine gun.[3]

I hope your holiday will be successful, and that we will not have to call on you again to carry a cane, a stiff leg and a full pack.[4]   Faithfully yours,

GCMRL/G. C. Marshall Papers (Pentagon Office, Selected)

1. Roosevelt had been approached by the munitions purchasing agent for the Arabian King Abdul-Aziz ibn Al Sa'ud regarding light machine guns "for keeping order in his kingdom." The Saudi king wanted "a weapon that can be carried easily by a man on horseback and that said man can use immediately on dismounting." (Roosevelt to Marshall, August 4, 1939, GCMRL/G. C. Marshall Papers [Pentagon Office, Selected].)

2. The Colt Monitor machine rifle was the commercial version of the Browning Automatic Rifle, the standard .30 caliber light machine gun in the Infantry rifle battalion.

3. The United States Rifle Caliber .30 M-1 had been designed by John C. Garand, an employee of the Springfield Armory. Tested during the 1920s, the rifle was adopted as the official Infantry arm in 1936. Roosevelt had immediately thought of the Garand rifle for the Saudis but was unaware of its status. (Ibid.)

4. Marshall was referring to the sight of Roosevelt, wounded at the battles of Cantigny and Soissons, leading his troops of the Twenty-sixth Infantry, First Division, in the last half of 1918. Roosevelt had written Marshall that he was "keeping in top hole condition for the next war. I'm sure I could still carry a full pack!" (Ibid. For Marshall's views on Roosevelt in World War I, see *Papers of GCM*, 1: 198–99.)

To Major General Walter S. Grant   August 12, 1939
Confidential   [Washington, D.C.]

Dear Walter: I have delayed in answering your last letter until the Lieutenant General business had clarified, and as you know now, this rank is only authorized for the four field armies. This undoubtedly will be a great disappointment to you, Dave Stone, and Herron, and I think you are entitled to know the facts of the case.[1]

It was thought imperative to secure real leadership of the four field armies. The present situation of equal rank with other corps area commanders, and attention largely centered on corps area affairs was getting us practically nowhere. And during this great augmentation period there were many things that required not only opinion and planning, but actual leadership. On the west coast the development of the color plans[2] and the defensive set-up in Alaska, was giving us a great deal of concern, and there were too many hundreds of millions [of dollars] involved to go ahead on the old basis.

It was apparent in the Congress that there was opposition to increased rank and additional headquarters. I found that a large number of influential Senators and members of the House felt we had too much administrative over-head. There was no possibility of passing a bill of this nature on the old grounds of approaching parity with the Navy, or as a reward or distinction for special service. It was apparent that the only way we could manage this was on a purely business basis—the necessity for increased rank on the part of the Army Commander, so that the right man could be put in the place and maintained there over a considerable period of time, and not have the office moved about for varying periods—usually short, as various men reached seniority. It was felt, after a careful examination of the situation, that our only chance of getting favorable action was to boil this thing down to its bare essentials. It was stated to the Committees that it would be most appropriate to have Lieutenant Generals in the foreign possessions, but that it was vital to have them at the head of the field armies. As a matter of fact, we expected that a motion would be made to amend the bill and include the foreign commands, and the War Department was going to favorably report on that. But even this had an element of risk connected with it, because we had difficulty in getting the approval on the original proposition out of the [Bureau of the] Budget—which means the President's O.K. The Budget incidentally does not act on these matters purely on the financial end, but on everything pertaining to legislation, whether money is involved or not.

In these circumstances the course was followed which brought about the final enactment of the bill, and I tell you confidentially, it was not easy even then. I had to seek out the objectors in the committee of the House and particularly the Senators who objected on the floor of the Senate, and convince each one of them that this thing was essential. I was very much gratified to secure the approval of Senator King, of Utah,[3] who had made a flat objection to the passage of the bill, and he made me feel that he would actually support the bill on its next presentation—though this did not prove to be necessary.

I am giving you all of the foregoing so you can understand why your position was left out in the cold in the matter of increased rank. That phase of the question will have to be taken up at a later date.

I will not confuse this letter with other matters, and please treat it as confidential.   Faithfully yours,

P.S.   There will arrive in the Philippines on October 13th or 14th on the S.S. Tjitjalengka a Mr. Lazarus (as you can see an intimate friend of Hitler's), who is one of the most powerful men of the Movie colony. I have been appealed to to get him some courtesies in Manila. He will only be there over-night, and as I understand it, all he wants is some person to tell him how best to go about seeing Manila, so if you have any young officer out there who would like to have a pass to the inner life of Hollywood, will you have him look this fellow up on the dock and tell him what to do next. If the idea bores you, forget it.[4]

GCMRL/G. C. Marshall Papers (Pentagon Office, Selected)

1. Grant, a cavalryman who had been Marshall's assistant in First Army G-3 in the autumn of 1918, had been promoted to brigadier general in 1936 and to major general on October 1, 1938. He took command of the Philippine Department in July 1939. The other overseas departments were commanded at this time by Major Generals David L. Stone (Panama Canal) and Charles D. Herron (Hawaii).

2. The army and navy routinely maintained contingency plans to cope with potential enemies. Each possible enemy was designated by a color (e.g., Joint War Plan Orange dealt with Japan). Work on newer plans envisaging coalition warfare had begun by the time Marshall arrived in Washington in mid-1938. The first of these—"Joint Army-Navy Plan I" (i.e., "Rainbow 1")—had been submitted to the Joint Board on July 27, 1939, and a revised version was approved by the president on October 14. Four other Rainbow plans were also being prepared at this time. (Watson, *Chief of Staff,* pp. 87, 103.) See the editorial note on pp. 100–101.

3. William H. King, a Democrat, was the second-ranking majority member of the Senate Finance Committee.

4. Marshall may have been referring to Hollywood press agent Paul N. Lazarus, Sr., but he was not among the ship's passengers listed in the *Manila Daily Bulletin* on October 13, 1939, sec. Pink, p. 4.

To Brigadier General Lesley J. McNair   August 16, 1939
Confidential   [Washington, D.C.]

Dear McNair: In looking over your recommendations for replacements of instructors I notice the names of former instructors included in the list. I have no intention of reneging on my assurance that you would be given a free hand in the solution of your problems, but I do want to call your attention to the fact that to recall an officer as an instructor, and not to a conspicuous key position, does serve to penalize the individual, and what seems to me of more importance, does further the continuation of old non-realistic methods to which there seems to be so much current objection. I suggest that it would be a good idea, and fairer to the officers, to ascertain informally whether they desire the re-detail.

Your recommendations will be approved, if at all possible to do so, and I am prepared to violate existing policies in order to give you the men you want. But I am moved again to suggest the advantages of new blood as against the previous overdose of repeaters.[1]

There is also another matter I want to suggest to you. That is the great advantage which would result from a shortening of the courses at Leavenworth for National Guard and Reserve officers. It is always very difficult to get the type of man we want when he has to give up his business for three months. *Confidentially*, under the present system at Leavenworth, at Benning, and at other schools, a three months' course is too apt to produce what might be termed "bread-ticket" people.[2]

I know that your instructors will say that three months is the minimum time in which a satisfactory course of study can be given. Confidentially, for your eye alone, I'll bet I could do everything they do and only take two months to do it in, if you wipe out certain unimportant details, and if the preparatory material sent in advance is carefully arranged toward the desired end.

Please do not treat this as something urgent, but merely as a casual comment from me.   Faithfully yours,

GCMRL/G. C. Marshall Papers (Pentagon Office, Selected)

1. "There will be no more calls for repeaters as instructors," McNair replied. "You are right in your stand." (McNair to Marshall, August 31, 1939, GCMRL/G. C. Marshall Papers [Pentagon Office, Selected].)

2. McNair agreed with Marshall that a "worth-while course of two months, or of one month for that matter" could be offered. However, he pointed out that the last class had been exceptional and that the army received "more for our money with the longer course." McNair left it up to Marshall to make changes for the 1941 school year, replying that he would plan accordingly. (Ibid.)

To General Malin Craig   August 21, 1939
                                                        [Washington, D.C.]

Dear Craig: I have just this moment read your letter of August 18th, and yesterday I read your telegram regarding my code message. I enjoyed your letter, appreciated your writing, and failed to understand your telegram.[1]

I moved into the house at Fort Myer this morning, or rather my things did—I report there tonight. Everything is pretty well straightened out though, of course, no pictures have been hung and we have not unpacked the silver, but the other portions of the furniture and fixings have been approximately put in place.

I find the new plumbing costs like the devil, but I suppose it is these short hours and high wages. Tell Mrs. Craig the large window in the up-stairs library completely metamorphoses that room. The only change I made in the set-up agreed to by Mrs. Marshall, Mrs. Craig, and the quartermaster, was to have a dishwasher installed, and I think this will probably be of the greatest help in taking care of large Teas, etc.

The house with its new paper looks very attractive, and the new mantel and fire-place in the library have transformed that room. They found the chimney was almost completely stopped up, and that was causing the trouble. I heard from someone that the house had been painted colonial yellow, but if it has I am color blind because it still looks like red brick to me.

The Munitions Building offices, that is, the Secretary of War's, Mr. Johnson's and mine, are delightful in temperature and attractive in appearance. Doing business in this building has increased the efficiency of operations very materially, for now it is a very simple thing to bring in the people you want and talk things over. The Secretaries of the General Staff are infinitely better off and are in spacious quarters. We have an air-cooled lounging room for the press people, which has produced a concentration of press men here instead of over on the Navy side. Whether this is for the better or worse, I do not know.

It has been infernally hot here with terrific humidity. I have not been able to get up to see Mrs. Marshall for about a month, but I had hoped to go up there over Labor Day. Whether the present tension will permit or not, I do not know. I am about to leave for Plattsburg with the Secretary of War.

With my affectionate regards to Genevieve and you.   Faithfully yours,

GCMRL/G. C. Marshall Papers (Pentagon Office, Selected)

1. Neither Craig's August 18 letter nor his telegram are in the Marshall papers. The restricted-code telegram Marshall sent to Craig at Fort Sill, Oklahoma, read: "Your daily training program for Margie and Helen [Craig's granddaughters] is approved. Deviations from program for purposes of golf are disapproved." (Marshall to Craig, August 19, 1939, GCMRL/G. C. Marshall Papers [Pentagon Office, Selected].)

B Y the time the first session of the Seventy-sixth Congress adjourned on August 5, the War Department's Budget and Legislative Planning Branch had assisted with the passage of the regular War Department Appropriation Act for 1940 ($508,723,344), a Supplemental Military Appropriation Act ($223,398,047), the War Department Civil Appropriation

Act ($305,188,514), and three deficiency appropriation bills (totaling $82,682,776) which together with some minor bills amounted to $1,100,-000,000 or 8.4 percent of the total federal budget. (Treasury Department, *Digest of Appropriations, 1940* [Washington: GPO, 1939], pp. 706, 781.)

Other legislation of importance to the army included bills to authorize the acquisition of "strategic and crucial" raw materials, to procure confidential aircraft instruments and parts, to authorize the sale of aviation supplies to foreign nations, to improve medical care for servicemen, to establish the rank of lieutenant general, and to enlarge the General Staff Corps. (A summary of service legislation is in the *Army and Navy Journal,* August 12, 1939, p. 1194.) ★

To Colonel Howard K. Loughry[1] August 22, 1939
[Washington, D.C.]

Subject: Appreciation.

My dear Colonel Loughry: Now that Congress has adjourned, I wish to express to you and your officers my deep appreciation of the highly efficient manner in which you conducted budget matters, supervised the War Department's presentations before the various committees of Congress, and, in general, influenced the handling of military legislation. Your office carried a greater burden of work than has ever been developed in the peace-time history of the Army, and this task was handled efficiently and with resultant success. It is a matter of great satisfaction to the War Department and merits high commendation for you and your staff.

I wish you would express to Colonel Brennan my thanks for his sound advice regarding the legal aspects of the presentations, and for the effective manner in which he advised and cooperated with the officials of Congress.[2] Faithfully yours,

GCMRL/G. C. Marshall Papers (Pentagon Office, General)
1. Loughry had served with the General Staff's Congressional Budget Section of the Budget and Legislative Planning Branch since May 1936.
2. Lieutenant Colonel Russell H. Brennan was assigned to handle legal affairs in the Office of the Deputy Chief of Staff.

To Mrs. Claude M. Adams August 24, 1939
[Washington, D.C.]

Dear Ruth: I enjoyed your letter and sent it on to Katherine at Fire Island,[1] though I must admit that your extreme generosity of expressions regarding me make it necessary for me to have a little salt at hand in order to keep my balance. I am afraid that all the publicity I have gotten recently is very harmful to me in the Army. Had I had any idea of the Hagood article, I would not have allowed the Press Section of the War Department to persuade me into cooperating with "Life" regarding their article.[2] However, I will have to live it down, but it is going to cause me a lot of trouble.

Flap's fish arrived at Fort Myer and were much enjoyed; but I had to write to the Express agent down in Mississippi to find out who sent them. It never occurred to me that he was down there.

I know you will enjoy Leavenworth. As for Flap, that will depend on his stepping out of his nerves and sitting in his skin, and refusing to be irritated or to cherish any contemptuous or violent internal disagreement with the attitude of the faculty. You charge yourself to keep him with both his feet on the ground, and remind him that many hundreds have gone through that school, who have tried to reform it on the basis of a few months' experience, and all the graduates have a very high opinion of the final result.[3]

The life there socially for you should be delightful, and Flap should enter into it sufficiently to get his mind off "shop."

Katherine will not return from Fire Island until about the second week in September. I hope to go up there over Labor Day, but it is merely a hope. Affectionately,

GCMRL/G. C. Marshall Papers (Pentagon Office, Selected)

1. Ruth Adams was the wife of Major Claude M. "Flap" Adams, the executive officer at Vancouver Barracks, Washington, when Marshall was there. The letter mentioned was not found in the Marshall papers. On the long association of the Adamses and the Marshalls, see *Papers of GCM,* 1: 377–78, 424, 551, 612–13.

2. Hugh S. Johnson, "The General Staff and Its New Chief," *Life* 7(August 21, 1939): 60–62, 64–68.

3. Adams attended the 1939–40 course of the Command and General Staff School, which began that fall.

To Colonel Charles W. Weeks[1]   August 26, 1939
[Washington, D.C.]

Dear Charlie: There came across my desk a reference to your retirement on September 30th, I think it was for my signature to the order for your retirement, and I was really shocked to find that you were about to leave the active list.

I have many memories in connection with you that have left a definite impression throughout the years. To begin with, when I first saw you at Calapan, you were to me the quintessence of Army experience and knowledge—the Adjutant who knew all the regulations and understood all the forms and methods of administration. Also, you had a laugh like Taft and I can still hear you chuckling over old Bill Pitcher's comments or strictures on this and that.[2]

Then, later came the period when you brought your bride to Santa Mesa.[3] I never will forget the many evenings that you haled me to your quarters, from that turbulent bachelor mess, to enjoy a delicious dessert and the peace and quiet of a real home, along with a little delightful music. At that time I was much in need of exactly that wholesome influence, and I have never forgotten the impression it made on me.

Odd to relate, I have a very definite recollection of your amusing description of running the Maytag washer and the ironing machinery in your cellar at the War College during the days of extremely high prices and more extremely low pay.

Please write and tell me what your plans are, and give my affectionate regards to Mrs. Weeks.   Faithfully yours,

GCMRL/G. C. Marshall Papers (Pentagon Office, General)

1. Weeks had been commissioned in July 1899 and was a first lieutenant in the Thirtieth Infantry in the Philippine Islands when Marshall first met him in May 1902. During the World War he had served with the Thirty-first Infantry in the Philippines and Siberia. He had been a student at the War College during the 1919–20 school year. He succeeded Marshall as assistant commandant at the Infantry School in 1933. In 1936 he became the professor of military science and tactics at Clemson Agricultural College in South Carolina, a post he held until his retirement. Following Weeks's retirement, Marshall wrote: "Personally, I am especially sorry to see you leave the active list. You were the officer to whom I reported for duty when I joined my first regiment, at Calapan on the Island of Mindoro, in the Philippines, and it was your advice and kindly offices that guided me through my earliest army service." (October 26, 1939, GCMRL/G. C. Marshall Papers [Pentagon Office, General].)

2. Major William L. Pitcher had been given command of the Thirtieth Infantry in August 1901 and removed one week before Marshall arrived in the Philippines on May 11, 1902. According to the regiment's official history, Pitcher, "being a man of great mental activity and extremely impulsive in his action, was quick to administer stern discipline, and after such disciplinary storms the skies often quickly cleared and all again was serene. So it happened that officers were placed in arrest or relieved from command some, a few days later, to [be] restored to their duties." ("History of the Thirtieth United States Infantry," typescript, NA/RG 391 [Thirtieth Infantry].)

3. Weeks and Marshall served together at the Santa Mesa Garrison, three miles east of the center of Manila, between March and September 1903. (Regarding Marshall's early service in the Philippines, see *Papers of GCM,* 1: 23–28.)

To Major General Milton A. Reckord[1]   August 30, 1939
Confidential   [Washington, D.C.]

Dear Reckord: Your letter of August 26th, with enclosures, regarding A.R.130–10, has been received, but due to absence from the city and the press of business, I have not had time to examine the mimeograph of comments and suggestions. I did have a few moments of discussion with General Blanding. But before going further into the matter, I wish to say, frankly and confidentially, that I much regret that you thought it desirable to make the critical comments in your memorandum of August 23d for the Adjutants General of the National Guard.[2]

Whatever the facts may be as to the practicability or advisability of the proposed changes, I feel that the form of your criticisms will do definite harm by promoting dissatisfaction and distrust as to the War Department. This is more harmful to the military efficiency of our Army, in my opinion, than lack of funds, materiel, or personnel. In fact, it is probable that past discord or distrust has prevented the securement from Congress of adequate funds.

My deepest concern in entering on the duties of Chief of Staff is to further in an unmistakable manner the development of a military team, otherwise the efficiency of the Army—especially for immediate employment in campaign—is jeopardized. For that reason, I am sorry that you saw fit to express yourself in the manner you did, whatever may have been your personal feelings.[3]   Faithfully yours,

GCMRL/G. C. Marshall Papers (Pentagon Office, Selected)

1. Reckord was the adjutant general of Maryland, the commanding general of the Maryland National Guard and of the Twenty-ninth Division, a key figure in the National Guard Association and one of its most important Washington lobbyists, and the president of the National Rifle Association.

2. Army Regulation 130-10 ("National Guard: Call and Draft into National Service"), originally issued in April 1923, was being revised. Reckord wrote that he "found the regulation to be very poorly drafted, in fact in some instances not even in step with the provisions of the National Defense Act. Whoever is responsible for the draft, in my opinion, lacks the proper conception of the position the National Guard now occupies as a part of the Army of the United States." Reckord, as chairman of the Legislative Committee of the National Guard Association, had sent a letter containing his objections to the new regulation for circulation to the adjutants general of the several states. (Reckord to Marshall, August 26, 1939, GCMRL/G. C. Marshall Papers [Pentagon Office, Selected].)

3. Reckord replied: "I share with you the desire to develop an efficient military team ready for any emergency and will work with you toward that end. You will agree with me, however, I am sure, that the foundation for such a team must be justice and equity, under the law. This is lacking in 130-10 and it was for that reason alone that I offered my criticism." (Reckord to Marshall, September 5, 1939, ibid.) Marshall sent Reckord's comments to the Personnel Division on August 31. The regulation was redrafted by the National Guard Bureau and issued in March 1940. At that time the new revision was hailed as a vast improvement by the Adjutant Generals Association. (See *Army and Navy Journal,* March 23, 1940, p. 672.)

TO WILLIAM R. MATHEWS[1]

August 31, 1939
[Washington, D.C.]

My dear Mr. Mathews: Due to my absence from Washington I have just received your note of August 23d regarding the apparent deficiency of Ordnance officers covering the European situation, and your comment as to the campaign hat instead of steel helmets. I am glad to have your suggestions and will give them careful consideration.[2]

However, I might make a comment on the steel helmet to the effect that it was developed and worn in the climate of Europe, and you can fry eggs in it in Arizona and could have broiled a steak on it in August at Manassas. Our National Guard troops are unseasoned when they turn out for training, and there is no suitable period for gradually hardening them, therefore compromise must be made to meet the actualities of the occasion. I must be frank and admit I am not aware of the immediate reasons for the point I am discussing, but I have worn a steel helmet in Texas. I do not mean by these remarks to indicate that one would not wear a steel helmet in a hot region, but relief would certainly be sought at every opportunity.

General Pershing seems to be building up strength very nicely. I saw him at the hospital Sunday.   Faithfully yours,

GCMRL/G. C. Marshall Papers (Pentagon Office, General)

1. The editor and publisher of the Tucson *Arizona Daily Star* since 1930, Mathews had been an officer in the Marine Corps in France in the World War.

2. Mathews wrote that he had talked with American military attachés all around the world and that he had great respect for their ability. However, he observed, "we have only one ordnance officer covering the four principal military powers of Europe. At this time this deficiency is a serious one." Secondly, he wrote, he had seen photographs of the recent army maneuvers which showed men under simulated battle conditions wearing campaign hats instead of steel helmets. "As a former infantryman who saw a lot of action this deficiency appears astounding and not in keeping with the high standards and realism which the army maintains in so many of its other activities." (Mathews to Marshall, August 23, 1939, GCMRL/G. C. Marshall Papers [Pentagon Office, General].)

STATEMENT ON THE RETIREMENT   August 31, 1939
OF GENERAL MALIN CRAIG   [Washington, D.C.]

General Craig leaves the Army in a state of efficiency as to morale, equipment, and training never before approximated in time of peace. He carries with him into retirement the loyal devotion of the officers of the Army and of the men in the ranks who had an opportunity to know him. And I do not believe anyone can dispute the statement that he is largely responsible for the unprecedented feeling of confidence which the public now has in the War Department.

Throughout his service he has been conspicuous for the positions of great responsibility which he has filled with uniform efficiency, and even more conspicuous for the self-effacing modesty with which he has always carried himself. It is a difficult task to follow in his footsteps, and I am keenly aware of the problems which will confront me and the obligations of the position I am about to assume.

GCMRL/G. C. Marshall Papers (Pentagon Office, Speeches)

The Time Factor

September 1 – December 31, 1939

You know, I know, all of us know that the time factor is the vital consideration—and vital in the correct meaning of the term—of our national defense program; that we must never be caught in the same situation we found ourselves in 1917.

—Speech to the Army Ordnance Association
October 11, 1939

IN the early hours of September 1, 1939, Marshall telephoned Lieutenant Colonel Orlando Ward, secretary of the War Department General Staff. Ward noted in his diary: "Gen Marshall got me out of bed at 3:50 AM more than usual his calm self– Directed I notify Overseas Dept and CA's [Corps Areas' headquarters]– of hostilities in Poland– Including statement reference bombing of Warsaw." (Orlando Ward Diary, September 1, 1939, photocopy in GCMRL/Research File.) Later that same morning George C. Marshall was promoted to the permanent rank of major general, filling the slot left by Malin Craig, and then sworn in as chief of staff (with the rank and title of general while holding that office) by Major General Emory S. Adams, the adjutant general. Shortly after taking the oath as chief of staff, Marshall attended a conference at the White House at 11:00 A.M.; President Roosevelt met with General Marshall, Secretary of War Harry H. Woodring, Assistant Secretary of War Louis A. Johnson, Acting Secretary of the Navy Charles Edison, and Chief of Naval Operations Admiral Harold R. Stark. (FDRL/White House Usher's Diary.)

That fateful day Marshall replied to one of many well-wishers who had sent congratulatory greetings to the new chief of staff: "I wish above everything else that I could feel that my time was to be occupied in sound development work, rather than in meeting the emergencies of a great catastrophe." (Marshall to Harold R. Bull, September 1, 1939, GCMRL/G. C. Marshall Papers [Pentagon Office, Selected].) A few days later the chief of staff wrote: "My day of induction into office was momentous, with the starting of what appears to be a World War." (Marshall to G. Edward MacGirvin, September 6, 1939, GCMRL/G. C. Marshall Papers [Pentagon Office, General].) ★

TO MRS. GEORGE S. PATTON, JR.
September 1, 1939
[Washington, D.C.]

My dear Mrs. Patton: I have been intending for some time to write you a note and tell you of the fine hospitality I received at the hands of your husband and how much I enjoyed my stay with him while my quarters were being put in order. I know I have you to thank for the comfort and pleasure of a well-ordered household, and I can only regret that I did not also have the pleasure of your presence.

Things look very disturbing in the world this morning, tragic for the Poles and the Germans, and there seems to be very little hope of a peaceful solution, in fact, England and France appear to be on the verge of declaring war within the next few hours.

Looking forward to the pleasure of seeing you on your return to Fort Myer,   Faithfully yours,

GCMRL/G. C. Marshall Papers (Pentagon Office, Selected)

To MAJOR GENERAL AND MRS.   September 2, 1939
FRANK R. McCOY[1]   Washington, D.C.

Dear Frank and Frances: I have just received your telegram of congratulations, and I want you to know that your good wishes mean more to me than almost any others I might receive. I chose an unfortunate day for my induction into office, and just as I took the oath a call came to go to the White House on national defense business.

You may remember that last fall, the day after I became Deputy Chief of Staff, the storm broke; and again the day of the announcement of my appointment, I had to dash off on a hasty tour of new Air Corps construction throughout the United States, and then to Brazil.[2] So, in the light of the present tragic catastrophe, I do not anticipate peaceful years ahead. All the more, your message is appreciated.   Affectionately,

G. C. Marshall

LC/F. R. McCoy Papers

1. McCoy was stationed at Governors Island, New York, commanding the Second Corps Area from May 1936—when he was transferred from Chicago—until his retirement on October 31, 1938. He assumed the duties of president of the Foreign Policy Association on September 1, 1939.

2. Marshall's first day in office as deputy chief of staff was October 15, 1938. Regarding the "storm" that broke at this time, Marshall may have been thinking of the troop movements into Czechoslovakia by Germany (October 1) and Poland (October 2) as a result of the Munich Agreement signed on September 29. Stanley D. Embick's last day as deputy chief of staff was September 30; this left Marshall—head of the War Plans Division, the senior General Staff division—as the chief of staff's principal deputy. (For information concerning Marshall's tour of West Coast installations and his trip to Brazil in the spring of 1939, see *Papers of GCM,* 1: 713–20.)

To MAJOR GENERAL DANIEL VAN VOORHIS   September 2, 1939
Personal and Confidential   [Washington, D.C.]

My dear Van Voorhis: I have a very confidential matter to take up with you, and I must ask you not to comment to any other person regarding what follows:

The Secretary of War is disturbed over the situation in Panama. He has just returned from an inspection there and is of the opinion that conditions are not what they should be. Frankly, he feels that the Governor of the Canal Zone has made little effort to cooperate with the Military Commander, but has centered his efforts to too great an extent on the economic or money-making phase of the Canal operation, to at least some neglect of essential military precautions. He feels that General Stone has made every effort to cooperate, but he is also strongly of the opinion that General Stone has not the force to command the situation, and does not visualize the more important aspects of the requirements.[1]

During the next few months, at least, the Canal Zone will probably be the point at which most of the critical international incidents will develop, concerning this country. For some time past six British cruisers have been lying off the Canal; we have the question of German submarines to consider; air fields in nearby Colombia have German reserve pilots operating planes, who have already excited the suspicions of our Embassy to the Colombian Government. So you can see the critical state of affairs in the Canal Zone.

Now I come to your connection with the matter. The Secretary of War refuses to consider General Lear as a possible Commander of the Zone. I have never met General Lear, but I do find a number of people who reflect the same opinion as the Secretary.[2] However that may be, Mr. Woodring is positive on this phase of the matter. So it becomes necessary to find an officer senior to Lear to relieve General Stone, and your name has been proposed as the man with the force, leadership, and good judgment to meet the situation.

To be perfectly clear in the matter, I will explain further—and again, most confidentially, that General De Witt is scheduled to relieve General Bowley in command of the Fourth Army, and General Brees, who might possibly be considered for Panama, not only has a short time left to serve, but some very important problems in the Air Corps augmentation program are occurring in his corps area, as well as in the planning for possible mobilization—which would center very heavily in his area.[3]

I see that on the Foreign Service roster you are credited with the longest service of any individual—over twelve years. Also you have been less than a year in command of the Fifth Corps Area—and I think it is most unfortunate to make frequent changes in corps area commanders. However, the facts are as I have outlined them above, and I wish you would write me immediately, confidentially, by air mail and give me your reaction.[4] I know you will loyally carry out any orders, but I would like to be aware of your feelings in the matter.   Faithfully yours,

P.S.   One phase of the matter I did not mention. I think it is not only important, but only fair that the shortening of General Stone's tour in Panama and the superseding of General Lear be carried out with as little loss of face to these two officers as is possible of arrangement. I hope we can stage the affair so that General Stone feels moved to reverse himself on the further extension of his foreign service tour. As to General Lear, there is no "out" that I can see at the moment. Naturally I presume he will be resentful of being denied the opportunity to command the Zone. But the situation is too critical to this country to settle on any personal basis.

GCMRL/G. C. Marshall Papers (Pentagon Office, Selected)

1. Secretary of War Woodring had been in the Canal Zone August 9 to 13; he returned to the United States on August 19. Brigadier General Clarence S. Ridley (U.S.M.A., 1905) had been governor of the Panama Canal Zone since August 1936. Major General David L. Stone had commanded the Panama Canal Department since April 1937 and was due to retire in August 1940.

2. Major General Ben Lear commanded the Pacific Sector of the Panama Canal Department. He was, as an officer who served under him briefly later recalled, "a big, gruff cavalryman, about whom I knew little. But there was something about him that I instinctively felt boded future trouble." (J. Lawton Collins, *Lightning Joe: An Autobiography* [Baton Rouge and London: Louisiana State University Press, 1979], p. 101.) Van Voorhis, whose commission as major general was three months prior to Lear's, outranked him by two files.

3. Lieutenant General Albert J. Bowley had commanded the Fourth Army and Ninth Corps Area since March 1938 and was due to retire November 30, 1939. Major General Herbert J. Brees commanded the Eighth Corps Area.

4. Van Voorhis replied: "I thoroughly appreciate the responsibility devolving upon the commander under the present circumstances. If, however, you feel that I am qualified to meet the situation, both present and future, I want to assure you of my willingness to meet your wishes and my availability at any time you command." (Van Voorhis to Marshall, September 4, 1939, GCMRL/G. C. Marshall Papers [Pentagon Office, Selected].) See Marshall to Stone, October 9, 1939, pp. 76–77.

To General Malin Craig   September 5, 1939
[Washington, D.C.]

Dear Craig: I received your fine telegram and letter of congratulations, and appreciate them more than you realize. It is a grand thing to start in the execution of a job of this character—and at this time, feeling the warm support and approval of your predecessor. Therefore, I appreciate deeply your generous expressions regarding me.[1]

As you will realize, things are very busy here, but I am immensely gratified with the efficient, quiet manner in which the Staff has gone about its business. We were well prepared to extend ourselves immediately, so there is no necessity for our rushing here and there and deciding things on the spur of the moment. As a matter of fact, I have a clear desk this morning. But I have a pretty important Staff conference in about thirty minutes.[2] Gasser has been splendid; I could not have done a wiser thing than bring him in. He has relieved me of a tremendous load, and as a matter of fact I have walked out of about 75% of the normal business and left it completely to him, without even knowing what was going on in that connection.

To turn to less serious matters, I am sending you a calling card handed me by a Cabinet officer in the Executive Office the other day. He claimed it was his card, but I think maybe it was yours. If you cannot figure it out, radio me for translation.[3]   Affectionately,

GCMRL/G. C. Marshall Papers (Pentagon Office, Selected)

1. Craig had written: "I owe you more than I can ever repay for the generous, loyal work you did for me in Vancouver, in War Plans and as Deputy. So old man, I salute you and promise you never to embarrass you. I shall volunteer nothing, but if you wish or need anything, I will give you my best efforts. All I ask of you is for you to take reasonable care of yourself." (Craig to Marshall, August 31, 1939, GCMRL/G. C. Marshall Papers [Pentagon Office, Selected].)

2. The most important actions taken at the meeting were to continue with the planned reinforcement of Puerto Rico and to send the Fifth Infantry and the Thirteenth Infantry regiments to Panama as soon as practicable. "All present were notified that the President had authorized the expansion of the Regular Army to National Defense [Act of 1920] strength, i.e., 280,000. G-1 was directed to prepare a letter from the President to the Secretary of War directing this expansion of the Regular Army, and also to prepare a similar letter to the Secretary of War directing this expansion of the Regular Army and the raising of the National Guard to peace strength [i.e., 450,000]." (Orlando Ward notes on a conference in the chief of staff's office, September 5, 1939, NA/RG 407 [334.8, General Council Report (8–21–41) Bulky].)

3. The editors have been unable to locate or to identify this card.

To Lieutenant General Hugh A. Drum   September 6, 1939
Confidential   [Washington, D.C.]

Dear Drum: Your personal radio of September 4th, received yesterday, has not been acknowledged earlier because it was my wish to write you at some length and time yesterday was not available.

I was pleased to receive your message, and at this particular time, the more so because it has seemed to me that you apparently felt a personal resentment towards me.[1] The results of such a reaction are unfortunate under any circumstances, and doubly so at the present time and in our respective positions. So, I repeat, I was pleased to receive your message, and I take you at your word.

There probably will be a conference of Army Commanders regarding matters of organization, and working details towards carrying out a program which, confidentially, we hope the President will authorize our announcing today. You will hear more about this later.

Meanwhile, with my sincere thanks for your message, believe me   Faithfully yours,

GCMRL/G. C. Marshall Papers (Pentagon Office, Selected)

1. Many observers had believed that General Drum was the leading candidate for the chief of staff's position until Marshall was nominated. (See *Papers of GCM,* 1: 713.) The editors have not located Drum's September 4 radiogram to Marshall.

MEMORANDUM FOR THE SECRETARY OF WAR   September 7, 1939
Washington, D.C.

Reference the question of immediate increase of the Regular Army and the National Guard—

Utilizing present authorized increases:

The last Appropriation Act authorizes increase of the Regular establishment from 165,000 to 202,000, in a series of increments, more than doubling the Air Corps and providing 6,000-odd anti-aircraft and coast defense troops for Panama.

Our urgent necessity of the moment is to complete the missing links of the ground forces of the IPF.[1] To utilize the foregoing increase, appropriated for by the last Congress, will create a deficiency in the same manner our proposed increase of the Regular Army to 280,000 would create a deficiency.

Furthermore, successful recruiting demands publicity, and publicity will probably mean an unfavorable reaction as Members of Congress learn that we are diverting the men away from the Air Service to the ground forces. Incidentally, we have already accelerated the Air Corps increments, but definitely do not wish to press it faster—otherwise indigestion.

Necessity for immediate increases:

It is highly desirable from a military standpoint, and I believe from the public reaction standpoint, to start immediately on the increase of the Regular Army and the National Guard to remedy the serious deficiencies in our Initial Protective Force. This is within the law (National Defense Act, which authorized 280,000 for the Regular Army and approximately 450,000 for the National Guard.) Also, it is believed of much importance that an announcement of an increase in the Regular Army should be coupled with a similar announcement regarding the National Guard.

Specific requests for authority:

Authority to increase the Regular Army to 250,000, *30,000 men below the peace strength of 280,000 now authorized by the National Defense Act,* is urgently recommended. Similar authority to recruit the National Guard to peace strength (an increase of 126,000 men—or about 130,000 below the strength authorized under the National Defense Act.)[2]

Procedure:

Both these increases to be made in *three increments*, the last on February 1st. It is possible, some think rather probable, that voluntary recruiting to the numbers indicated may be a slower process than planned. Publicity is essential in order to make reasonable progress.

Authority and manner for Recruiting National Guard:

Recruitment of the National Guard, under peace conditions is a matter for the respective Governors. The War Department merely *authorizes* the States to increase the strength of units by certain numbers—meaning that clothing, equipment, weekly drill night pay, and summer two weeks' training pay and rations, will be provided by the Federal Government. The Governor will increase his military forces above the War Department authorizations, but it would be entirely at the expense of the state, and no government equipment would be provided.

NA/RG 407 (Classified, 320.2 [9–7–39])

1. For information about the I.P.F. (Initial Protective Force), see note 4, Marshall to Daley, July 20, 1939, p. 20.

2. Memorandums were written for Secretary Woodring and he signed letters to the president recommending these increases, but they are in the files marked "Not Used."

MEMORANDUM FOR GENERAL GASSER   September 8, 1939
Secret   Washington, D.C.

Subject: Increases in the Army.

1. The President decided yesterday to announce—or authorize—increases of the Army and Navy by Executive Order, instead of by a more informal method, as he previously intended.

2. He stated that he cannot consider at this time more than the first increment, as he thought that was all the public would be ready to accept without undue excitement. He indicated that he would give us further increases up to the figures we proposed, but this prospect would have to be treated as highly confidential.

3. The draft of an Executive Order being sent to the Department of Justice this morning provides for an increase of the Regular establishment to 227,000, and of the National Guard to 235,000 enlisted men. It permits such increase of officers for the Regular Army as may be necessary, from

those already authorized—but not appropriated for—under the Thomason Act.[1] It also authorizes such additional officers for the National Guard as may be necessary for "command duty."

4. If this draft proves to be acceptable to the Department of Justice and to the President, it will be announced at a press conference of his today, at which time he will issue the Executive Order or Proclamation announcing a state of national emergency, of a restricted nature, as pertains to the maintenance of neutrality and to national defense requirements of the military forces. The increases of the Army and Navy, by Executive Order, are based on this national emergency and proclamation.[2]

5. Our people can proceed in their planning on the basis of an increase to 250,000 for the Regular establishment, and an increase of 126,000 (?) for the National Guard—provided that no publicity is given in connection with the arrangements for orders of execution and the fact that further increments are anticipated.

G. C. M.

NA/RG 407 (Classified, 320.2 [9–7–39])

1. The April 3, 1939, revision of the 1935 Thomason Act (Public Law 408, 74th Cong., 1st sess.) permitted the army to recruit 4,300 Reserve officers each year for one year's training with the Regular Army. At least 50 ground officers and up to 300 airmen could be selected from this group to receive commissions as second lieutenants in the Regular Army. The April 3 act also established the army's maximum commissioned strength at 16,719 beginning on July 1, 1939. (Public Law 18, 76th Cong., 1st sess.)

2. On September 8, 1939, President Roosevelt issued Proclamation 2352 stating that "a national emergency exists in connection with and to the extent necessary for the proper observance, safeguarding, and enforcing of the neutrality of the United States and the strengthening of our national defense within the limits of peace-time authorizations."

The same day, executive orders were issued authorizing increases in military strength. The Regular Army (authorized peacetime enlisted strength of 280,000) was instructed to increase its enlistments by 17,000 to a total of 227,000 men; while the National Guard (authorized peacetime enlisted strength of 424,800) was increased by 43,000 to 235,000 men. (Executive Order 8244.) The Regular Navy was ordered to increase its enlistments to 145,000 men; the Marine Corps was increased to 25,000. (Executive Order 8245.)

SPEECH[1]

September 9, 1939
Uniontown, Pennsylvania

. . . I suppose I must make some reference to my present occupation in relation to the existing crisis in world affairs. I have necessarily been concerned during the past year with the successive steps toward the building up of a respectable posture of national defense. It is a highly involved subject, a problem of great expenditures, and of vital importance to us as a people. It happens, fortunately, that your distinguished Representative in Congress, Mr. Snyder, is the head of the Military Appropriations Committee of the House of Representatives, which leads in the determination of just what expenditures will be made for the Army and his patriotic interest, good will and cooperation have been of inestimable value to the War Department.[2]

We citizens of this country have been fortunate in the bountiful state of our natural resources, in the freedom for expansion, and in the strong individuality of our people. Today we should be fully conscious of our good fortune in having broad oceans to the east and west, peaceful cousins to the north of us, and a friendly nation along our southern frontier. We are a highly favored people, and yet the march of time, of invention, and of mechanical perfection have brought us for the first time into very close relationship with all the world.

I will not trouble you with the perplexities, the problems, and requirements for the defense of this country, except to say that the importance of this matter is so great and the cost, unfortunately, is bound to be so high, that all that we do should be planned and executed in a business-like manner, without emotional hysteria, demagogic speeches, or other unfortunate methods which will befog the issue and might mislead our efforts. Finally, it seems to me that we should daily thank the good Lord that we live where we do, think as we do, and enjoy blessings that are becoming rare privileges on this earth. . . .

GCMRL/G. C. Marshall Papers (Pentagon Office, Speeches)

1. Marshall flew to Uniontown, his childhood home, the afternoon of September 9, 1939, and was welcomed at the nearby Connellsville Airport by three thousand people. (Marshall to Brigadier General Carlos E. Black, September 11, 1939, GCMRL/G. C. Marshall Papers [Pentagon Office, General].) That evening he delivered this speech during a banquet given in his honor. Marshall recalled, "I told a great many stories of my youth in order to avoid anything in relation to the war situation." (George C. Marshall, interviewed by Forrest C. Pogue, February 28, 1957, GCMRL.) Approximately 20 percent of this speech is printed here; another portion is printed in *Papers of GCM*, 1: 8–9.

2. J. Buell Snyder, a Democrat who had represented the Twenty-fourth District in southwestern Pennsylvania since 1933, spoke to the gathering just prior to Marshall's address.

To Brigadier General Ralph M. Immell   September 14, 1939
Confidential   [Washington, D.C.]

Dear General Immell: I have just this moment read your letter of September 11th, with suggestions regarding the increase of the Guard and its possible mobilization.[1] I am much impressed by your ideas and will have them carefully considered by G-1 and G-3 in consultation with the National Guard Bureau.[2]

Confidentially, I might tell you that I have had on the cards, from the start, the proposal to increase the number of drill nights, and to add a ration or two per month, to facilitate field training on week-ends and target practice. In this connection your suggestion regarding additional drills for certain units appears to be a sound one.

We have no intention of changing the minimum maintenance strength requirements, knowing that some companies are so located that they cannot draw sufficient people from their districts, but I rather like your idea of permitting over-strength in other units.

Also confidentially, I think I am free to tell you that our desire, and it probably will be approved, is to go ahead with the series of increments as soon as the first increment is recruited. I think in this way we can stride along without biting off more than we can chew, with consequent indigestion. Of course, in a great emergency the Guard would have to be concentrated for field training, but it appeals to me as being very much better if we can make steady rapid progress in normal surroundings rather than to indulge in the customary American-emergency violent lunge toward the ultimate goal.

You speak of the "probable mobilization of Army, Corps, Division, and Staffs of the lower echelons, together with their auxiliary services for their necessary training." The matter of Army Corps direction and leadership, and of corps staffs is one of great concern to me at the moment. Under the conditions of open warfare, and especially with the proposed smaller division, which assumes a greatly increased service by the corps, expert leadership, and skilled staff work with a high degree of team work, are essential. At present we have not the skeleton of such a set-up.

I made some progress in this direction after my return from Brazil, by getting Army command dignified above that of a decidedly secondary and casual business. The details of Army staff and direction have yet to be crystallized, but we are on our way. Now my concern, as stated above, is directed toward the Corps. Of course, should we mobilize, we could go ahead and create Army Corps, but that means preliminary confusion, with delays, mis-direction, and possibly ill-feeling. Therefore, it is to be avoided.

At present I have no Staff solution, but only a few private ideas of my own. A Staff solution is a tricky business, because the peacetime set-up (that is, pre-mobilization conditions) is abnormal. The Guard is a State institution and the Regular forces are badly scattered, as well as almost completely lacking Corps troops. I consider it essential that in the peacetime development of division staffs and command (which includes their direct influence on brigade and lower echelon training), there should be guidance, occasional direction and instruction, and semiannual inspections by a Corps commander with a skeleton staff, all well known to the division staffs and Corps troop commanders. This same outfit would exercise direct control over the Regular troops allotted to that Corps, and would exert a guiding influence over the Reserve developments concerned with that Corps. In other words, team work would be stimulated and intimate contacts within the Corps would be developed.

I wanted to experiment with this idea when I was in Chicago by having

General Herron, (then largely without a job there) act as Corps Commander and with his skeleton staff, try out the idea. My thought at the time was that Division Commanders might place one drill night a month, for their staff meeting or training, at the disposal of General Herron; also, instead of my making the mid-winter inspection of the Division Headquarters as senior instructor, General Herron should do it with his staff, and so on. Unfortunately, General McCoy left about this time and General Kilbourne was there too short a period during my brief remaining service in Chicago, to permit me to go ahead with the idea.[3]

If my thought is sound, the limiting factors seem to be these: The general acceptance by the Guard of the principle; the selection of the necessary Corps Commanders. The second factor presents more complications than the first, I believe Corps Commanders should be outstanding vigorous men. They should have temporary rank suitable to the position. Authority for this would be difficult to secure from Congress. What I would like to have is authority, similar to that recently secured for Army Commanders, which would give temporary rank of Major General to young Brigadier Generals designated for Corps commands. This would make duty with the National Guard the most sought-for detail in the Army. There would be the same relationship with the Reserve echelons, and for the same reason, an amalgamation of the Regular, National Guard, and Reserve units within the Corps, a highly desirable state of affairs.

I am really thinking out loud at the moment, and most confidentially, but I would like to get your reaction.[4]   Hastily yours,

GCMRL/G. C. Marshall Papers (Pentagon Office, General)

1. Immell, the adjutant general of Wisconsin and a friend from Marshall's days with the Illinois National Guard, had discussed Guard issues with Marshall during the latter's July 21–23 visit to Chicago. He wrote to offer some further "grass roots" observations in light of the possibility that the Guard might be mobilized to its full enlisted peace strength of 424,800. Immell's suggestions were: First, greater flexibility in recruiting than the traditional geographically based unit permitted. In order to broaden and improve training of new men, some units might be recruited to greater than authorized strength while some remained below; the leveling would occur upon mobilization. Second, "the number of armory drills might well be increased, and particularly for those units that comprise the group that might well be called the 'nervous system' of an army; specialists, staffs, communications, coordinating groups, and in short, the type of unit that requires long and tedious hours to bring efficiency." Third, units might be staggered for drill purposes so that all men might train with serviceable equipment. Fourth, over-age or uncommitted officers should be removed; "I think the present time offers a good opportunity to quietly clear the decks." Finally, the Guard's Infantry brigades should be reorganized completely in a single stroke; "under the present arrangement we are to do it peacemeal—a most vexatious arrangement." (Immell to Marshall, September 11, 1939, NA/ RG 407 [Classified, 320.2 (9–11–39)].)

2. The assistant chiefs of staff for G-1 (Brigadier General William E. Shedd) and G-3 (Brigadier General Frank M. Andrews) recommended no immediate action on Immell's suggestions since "the ideas suggested by General Immell are either already being applied in the National Guard or have been considered in the War Department and are still under study." (Shedd to Marshall, October 25, 1939; Andrews to Shedd, October 31, 1939; and

Shedd to Marshall, November 13, 1939, ibid.)

3. The Sixth Corps Area commanders Marshall mentioned were Major Generals Frank R. McCoy (February 1935 to May 1936) and Charles E. Kilbourne (June to December 1936). Brigadier General Charles D. Herron commanded the Sixth Field Artillery Brigade in Chicago from September 1935 to December 1936. Marshall was relieved from duty as senior instructor with the Illinois National Guard on October 5, 1936.

4. The editors have found no reply from Immell.

To Captain Charles T. Lanham   September 15, 1939
                                                          [Washington, D.C.]

Dear Lanham: I enjoyed your letter of September 9th, and appreciate the pleasant things you had to say about me.[1] I look back on my year at Screven as one of the finest in my Army career, and in many ways it was very instructive. The most gratifying phase of the period was contact with an unusual group of noncommissioned officers. I think we had the finest collection of first sergeants there I have ever seen together. I had them doing Officer of the Day duty and all close order drilling. Then, too, we found charming people in Savannah and out at Tybee.

I have passed your name on to the G-2 Section to include in their list for possible Military Observers.[2]   Faithfully yours,

GCMRL/G. C. Marshall Papers (Pentagon Office, General)

1. Having recently completed the 1938–39 academic year as a student officer at the Command and General Staff School, Lanham had been a company commander of the Eighth Infantry at Fort Screven, Georgia, since June 24, 1939. He wrote to Marshall: "Your old friends—the first sergeants down here—never tire of talking of you. . . . You certainly left an enduring impression on this little post." (Lanham to Marshall, September 9, 1939, GCMRL/ G. C. Marshall Papers [Pentagon Office, General].)

2. In his letter, Lanham recalled Marshall's October 1934 advice that he not allow low rank and infrequent promotion to ruin his morale. "Keep your wits about you and your eyes open; keep on working hard; sooner or later the opportunity will present itself, and then you must be prepared both tactically and temperamentally to profit by it." (See *Papers of GCM*, 1: 439.) Lanham wrote that he had "followed that advice up to the hilt," and that he had asked the Adjutant General's Department to consider him for a detail as military observer abroad. "My temerity in writing to you about my small affairs is great but I do it for two reasons: first, because you have always been the friend of the junior officer, and second, because the detail I desire is so potentially rich in professional values that I am willing to make any personal sacrifice involved and even, sir, to run the grave risk of your displeasure by troubling you at this serious time by a personal letter." (Lanham to Marshall, September 9, 1939, GCMRL/ G. C. Marshall Papers [Pentagon Office, General].) At the top of Lanham's letter in Marshall's hand is: "G-2: To note and return. A very aggressive and highly educated man.   GCM" Lanham remained with the Eighth Infantry for a two-year tour of duty.

To General Malin Craig   September 19, 1939
[Washington, D.C.]

Dear Craig: Since Parks left for the War College,[1] I do not follow your trail so well, but he did give me your San Francisco address.

Pa Watson was very anxious to locate you some time back—I gave all the details to Parks to handle—for the purpose of having you broadcast daily, I believe, for the Cincinnati Radio people. At about that time word came from you, I think from near the Grand Canyon, that you were being pursued by radio people and were saying nothing.

You know, I think you timed your affairs very beautifully, because you certainly left me on a hot spot. We are getting along fine, but the engine is never on idle speed. I find several great advantages in the offices being here in the Munitions Building. In the first place, you do business with the Staff with great convenience and celerity. I have the Assistant Chiefs of Staff in here frequently and it only costs them a minute or two to get here and we settle things in a hurry, and then they are back at work. Anyone else we happen to need can be brought in in a few minutes, and not notified until the need actually arises.

Then, there is the matter of lunch and relaxation. I go out to Myer for lunch; they telephone from here when I start and I walk right to the lunch table—on the glassed-in porch—from the car and then I have half an hour or more to relax in a more restful atmosphere than here at the office or at the Army and Navy Club. It only takes six minutes to go from here to the house, which is about three minutes less than required to go to the Army and Navy Club. Then, too, I find the change a very restful one, and return to work in much better spirits. Another thing, as it works out now, fifteen minutes after I leave the office I am in riding clothes and on a horse, and I have been getting in an hour's riding practically every day. Of course, some days I do not get started until 5:30, but I try to leave here about 4:10. This riding has done me a world of good and I am able to keep things in focus and shed almost all worries.[2]

I reach the office about 7:30 and by 8:30 I have pretty well cleaned up on things. Miss Young is losing sleep by coming in early too. For a time Parks drove her down on his way to the office. I find that if I do not get in here before 8:30 I never catch up, and there is so much of original planning, as it were, to do.

We have made many more motions than have appeared in the press and I think we are really on our way to a sound development. The new organization for Infantry divisions was adopted three days ago, and with this first increase we are going up to five of these divisions, along with corps troops.[3] We are headed to full peace strength of 280,000, and a total increase of 126,000 for the National Guard, with about double the number of pay drills and two rations a month—one for week-end shooting and one for week-end field training. Unfortunately, there is little that can be done regarding munitions which we lack which can be remedied quickly. Of course, we are after the money to place large orders.[4]

What do you think of General Pershing's statement and of its reception by the public and the press? Before you condemn it, I had better tell you—and most confidentially—that I wrote it.[5]

With affectionate regards to both of you,   Faithfully yours,

GCMRL/G. C. Marshall Papers (Pentagon Office, Selected)

1. Major Floyd L. Parks had left his position in the Office of the Chief of Staff on August 16, 1939.

2. Lieutenant Colonel Terry de la M. Allen had selected two horses from Fort Riley, Kansas, for Marshall's use. Marshall wrote to Allen: "I am delighted with the two animals. . . . It is very hard to get in any exercise here and I have to do it on the jump, riding after I leave the office in the evening, and at a most uncertain hour." (Marshall to Allen, September 7, 1939, GCMRL/G. C. Marshall Papers [Pentagon Office, Selected].)

3. The War Department announced on September 16 that the Regular Army would be organized into the new "triangular" divisions which had been under consideration since 1935. The existing First, Second, and Third divisions would be reorganized as soon as possible, and two new divisions—the Fifth and Sixth—were to be created. The United States was the last major military power to adopt this kind of organization.

The World War "square" division typically contained over 20,000 troops in two brigades of two regiments each. The objective of the new organization was to create a less cumbersome command and to obtain a more controllable and maneuverable unit. Several echelons of command were eliminated and better relations between combat branches were made possible. The new division would have a peace strength of approximately 8,953 (officer and enlisted) and a war strength of 11,903. Animal transportation was to be eliminated, thereby speeding the division's movements, although the infantry still walked. Divisional firepower was increased, despite a reduction in the number of artillery pieces. (Lieutenant Colonel Harry C. Ingles, "The New Division," *Infantry Journal* 46[November–December 1939]: 521–29; "The New Division" [editorial], ibid., 584–85.)

4. The previous day, Marshall wrote to Lieutenant General Albert J. Bowley that "things are in a very uncertain state now and will continue so until Congress is assembled, public opinion has crystallized a bit, and the President makes some basic decisions. Confidentially, we are pressing to grow up to peace strength for the Regular Army and to a total increase of 126,000 enlisted men for the National Guard, and to secure large appropriations for deficiencies in munitions and certain non-critical items. It is impossible to tell from day to day just what action will be authorized." (Marshall to Bowley, September 18, 1939, GCMRL/G. C. Marshall Papers [Pentagon Office, Selected].)

5. On September 13, 1939, his seventy-ninth birthday, General John J. Pershing issued a public statement praising President Roosevelt's efforts to strengthen the nation's armed preparedness. "I feel that this is especially necessary in the case of the Army, which had been reduced since 1921, so far as ground forces were concerned, to a mere skeleton of the peace establishment authorized by Congress in the National Defense Act of 1920." The statement also urged Congress to provide funds for increasing the army to full peace strength. Pershing had made numerous stylistic changes in Marshall's September 11 draft and added a concluding paragraph recalling the "deplorable situation" when the country entered the World War. "Then not a single move had been made, from a military point of view, to prepare for it. That experience, with its costly lesson, I am happy to say, appears certain to be avoided in the event that we should again become involved in war." ("Views on World Crisis," September 13,

1939, LC/J. J. Pershing Papers [General Correspondence, Statements].) The Washington, D.C., *Evening Star* and the New York *Sun* praised Pershing's statement. (Clippings from various newspapers are preserved in LC/J. J. Pershing Papers [Scrapbooks].)

To Major General James K. Parsons September 21, 1939
[Washington, D.C.]

Dear Kelly: I received your letter yesterday as I was leaving the office for lunch, and while I have only had time to read it in the car, I want you to know that I appreciate your writing and giving me the benefit of your views. I agree with you in general regarding most of them, and I will undertake to see that we get action immediately on some of them. Also, please accept my condolences over your illness, and particularly over the childish nature of the disease, considering that you are a Major General.[1]

I am being very sincere in what I state regarding your comments and I am very glad to have them. As soon as I became Acting Chief of Staff I forced ahead action on the Infantry division by about four months, and finally precipitated a decision in a couple of hours, and it is now an accomplished fact as far as the War Department is concerned. There were things about the proposed organization that I did not like and there were some changes from the previous test which did not particularly appeal to me; but I felt that time was the essence of the plot, and most of the matters were too minor to permit of further delay, and that I should accept the proposals of the officers who had been working with the troops.

I am glad you agree with me about the National Guard; I was interested in your comments regarding modernization of the big division. I feel, like you evidently do, that a change in the Guard at this time would be devastating; I also feel that an approximation of the new division could be quickly secured in the field, if it was found desirable, by the mere elimination of an infantry regiment, a regiment of artillery, and a battalion of engineers. It does seem better to me, aside from the confusion incident to change, to let things come to a tryout in the field before we commit ourselves to one type of division radically different from what we have ever had before.

The confusion of organization argument does not apply to the Regular Army, because we do not have any complete divisions, and something had to be done in any event; so it seemed better to go the whole hog. Hastily yours,

GCMRL/G. C. Marshall Papers (Pentagon Office, Selected)

1. Parsons, commanding general of the Third Corps Area, had been ill in quarters for several weeks with the mumps ("a disease I thought only juveniles had") and had used this

time to think and to write. "The results of my meditation concerning our Army I am submitting to you for what you may think they are worth." His letter commented on the new triangular division; complained about the new field uniform being tested, the inscrutable Tables of Basic Allowances, the War Department's mobilization plans, and its delays in acting upon recommendations from outside the department; and suggested the need for a permanent General Staff Corps and that civilians replace soldiers in certain duties. (Parsons to Marshall, September 20, 1939, NA/RG 165 [OCS, 21097].) Marshall sent the letter to Acting Deputy Chief of Staff Gasser with the stipulation that the various General Staff divisions study and respond to it. (Marshall Memorandum for General Gasser, September 21, 1939, ibid.)

MEMORANDUM FOR THE SECRETARY OF WAR   September 22, 1939
[Washington, D.C.]

With reference to the recruiting situation: On September 14th, recruiting for the Regular Army, under the Air Corps augmentation program, and that of the Panama garrison, to include the speeding up by 6,000 men for the Air Corps, was over 50% complete with one corps area still to be heard from.

At the moment we have no data on the National Guard recruiting, as the formal instructions were only initiated in the past forty-eight hours.

Recruiting of CCC discharged enrollees, who under the regulations are not permitted to re-enroll, are to be issued today. There has been a delay in this in order to explain to Mr. Fechner what we are proposing to do.[1]

There should be on your desk now a request from The Adjutant General for authority to advertise in newspapers, as this requires your approval.

The outdoor advertising companies have offered for recruiting 15,000 bill-boards scattered throughout the country, for which the posters are now being made. The car card advertising companies have offered space in the busses, street-cars, and similar vehicles for recruiting. This has been accepted.

Transcribed radio programs are now in use. This is the first time this has been tried. The number of side-walk stations has been trebled, and new posters prepared for this purpose.

I think it might be a good thing for you to make some reference to the recruiting problem in your American Legion speech in Chicago next week. There is attached suggestions for this which I hope can be worked up in a form satisfactory to you.[2]

GCMRL/G. C. Marshall Papers (Pentagon Office, Selected)

1. Robert Fechner had been director of the Civilian Conservation Corps since 1933.
2. The American Legion's national convention in Chicago opened on September 25. Brigadier General Frank M. Andrews, assistant chief of staff for Operations, spoke in place of Secretary Woodring. The two-paragraph enclosure (no author indicated) explained the ground army's recruiting problems and successes, and it concluded that the expansion "with

the additional grades and ratings involved, and with the many opportunities for technical training concerned with the demands of mechanization, motorization, and the Air activities, offers splendid opportunities for young men."

To General John J. Pershing   September 23, 1939
                                                    Washington, D.C.

Dear General: I am attaching some ideas, in the rough, for a possible radio broadcast by you. I rather imagine that my attempt at a discussion of the neutrality phase will be of little use to you. However, I have included it in order to develop a possible continuity leading up to purely military comments.

As to the timing of your broadcast, if you decide to make it, it seems to me that it should be scheduled for the middle of the coming week, presumably after the debates have started on the Hill. Will you have Adamson give me your reactions in the matter; and if you decide to do this and he advises me accordingly, we will make the necessary contacts with the Radio people, to arrange for the broadcasting from your room at the Hospital[1]—I am assuming that this can be managed.

I am very sorry to impose on you this burden of responsibility, but I know you personally are intensely interested in the outcome, and I also know that you can exert a greater influence than any other American, except the President, and on military matters I do not except him.[2]   Faithfully,

G. C. Marshall

LC/J. J. Pershing Papers (General Correspondence)

1. Pershing had been living at Walter Reed General Hospital since mid-August.

2. During the summer of 1939, President Roosevelt sought congressional repeal of the requirement of the Neutrality Act of 1937 that he embargo the sale and shipment by Americans of war materiel to *all* belligerents. This effort failed in mid-July when action was deferred until the January 1940 session. On September 13, the president called a special session of Congress to reconsider the embargo repeal, and on September 21 he delivered a message to a joint session urging that action. (See *The Public Papers and Addresses of Franklin D. Roosevelt,* 1939 volume, ed. Samuel I. Rosenman [New York: Macmillan Company, 1941], pp. 512–25.) The revised Neutrality Act was passed by substantial majorities in both houses and was signed by the president on November 4.

The attached draft of ideas (author not indicated) urged support for the president's position: "If we deny access to our shores and industry to the ships of belligerents, what will be our position should we become engaged in the defense of everything that we hold dear in American civilization?" The statement also asserted that "not less than a billion dollars is immediately required for our Army to make good the tragic neglects of the past years and to place ourselves in a secure position to guarantee our ability to lead in the maintenance of the democracy of the Western Hemisphere." It took years to "convert money into munitions," and the United States could not afford to wait. Pershing was also asked to urge increasing the Regular Army and National Guard to full peace strength and appropriating more funds for maneuvers. At the top of Marshall's letter, General Pershing wrote "not approved," and on the first page of the proposed statement, he wrote "not delivered."

September 26, 1939
[Washington, D.C.]

I have been reading the attached memorandum from the Chief of Infantry regarding the Infantry situation as of September 1st. The following comments occur to me, regarding which I would like to have an informal statement, orally if desired, from someone in the G-3 office:[1]

What are the prospects for weapons–ammunition carriers, within a reasonable time?

What is to be said in regard to the rifle or carbine for the members of special crews?

The low infantry strength in riflemen is a serious consideration. To my own mind, there are two points of view. Our large companies in the World War incurred a great many unnecessary casualties by reason of their size, as well as clumsy handling of the men. In other words, I do not think we derived a fighting effect in direct proportion to the strength of the company. From this point of view the new company would seem to have advantages over the old, of course assuming a fairly high degree of skill on the part of the riflemen with the new weapon.

My other thought on this matter suggests the necessity of more than routine arrangements to replace casualties. Just where would the replacements be just prior to a battle, under what control, and when fed to the unit? We have always discussed and debated at great length the exact position of the squad, a section, a platoon, and then these organizations have practically never had the exact strength finally decided upon due to a wide variety of reasons, camp ailments, especially at the outset being one of the heaviest contributing factors. I would assume that in an army of our character, at the opening of a campaign into which we have had to move without a delay of a year for preparation, that our temporary sick casualties would be very heavy, and our low rifle strength, therefore, correspondingly depleted. Therefore, replacements assume a great importance to my mind.

As to tactics, I wish a careful watch to be kept on this to see that if possible the fundamental principles are expressed in language that would impress the ordinary fellow, rather than in the usual colorless pedantic form. It required about three battles in France to demonstrate what was meant by tactical principle, and the reason to a large extent lay in the form of expression of the principle. To go back a bit, General Morrison at Leavenworth taught tactics and he was the only instructor I ever had on this subject who made any impression on my mind. And the reason was, he would not bother with small matters of technique or minor phases of tactics, but he slashed in units instead of tenths—as did the other instructors, when a fundamental principle was violated.[2] Practically all the tactical instruction I have seen in the Army has been 90% technique, and 10%

tactics. So the form of the Infantry Field Manual on Tactics is of great importance, and it should be written primarily to impress the mind of the National Guardsman or the Reserve officer, rather than for consumption by Regular Army personnel, who have years to employ on their training.

Under Training, I do not quite agree with the Chief of Infantry as to the effect of the CCC on regimental commanders. My observation has been that there is a tendency to too much control by the regimental commander, usually accentuated by the desire to use every moment of his brief two years to demonstrate capacity for promotion. It has appeared to me that the battalion commanders were exceptionally well qualified to train their battalions, and that the particular function of the regimental commander might well be to provide opportunities for training, personnel free from routine employment, terrain privileges acquired one way or another, problems arranged, etc. The CCC, it seemed to me, provided exceptional opportunities for developing leadership, in influencing young men, and in matters of administration and supply on a large scale. I know this was my own personal experience.

I thoroughly agree with the Chief of Infantry as to the too strong tendency of regimental commanders to rely on the service schools for the education of their officers. This is particularly the case with regard to new lieutenants in small posts. When there have been schools, I have been inclined to the opinion that too much of the school was on paper, with too much importance to fixed hours, etc. There was not an adjustment of instruction to the routine activities of the post, of training, etc., and the arrangements for school training were too formal, ignoring splendid opportunities.

Above I have been referring to the Regular Army in its peace-time garrisons, but there is much the same thing to be said in regard to armory training of the National Guard. I wish to emphasize the importance of the G-3 Section influencing all War Department doctrine, texts, training instructions, and inspections, towards their application to the citizen-soldier, who will compose the major portion of the Army. Many of our regulations, notably on rifle marksmanship, have been written to a large extent without regard to the time limitations of the National Guard. To leave the necessary modifications to the man on the ground, usually a partially trained officer, is bad practice and shows to my mind a lack of appreciation of what our war army is really to be. We have the National Guard and we must make it more efficient, and this can only be done by a very real understanding of the training opportunities, and possibilities. The same factor is dominant, and there are a world of things that can be done to carry out training more expeditiously and effectively than we now manage.

The Chief of Infantry's comments on lack of regimental duty are pertinent. I think this should be discussed with G-1 in an effort to reach some solution of a very serious situation. I fear that the knowledge of command and leadership is diminishing to a serious degree in the Regular establishment.

With regard to the necessity for closer supervision and observation of the training of units, I think this should be corrected through divisional command and the creation of army corps command and control.

Under Personnel, I think there is a fine opportunity here to meet the depletion of Regular officers in the summer season by building up a more effective use of Reserve officers. Our methods in this respect I think have been faulty, in that they consisted largely of having Reserve officers tag along and learn largely by observation. Americans do not respond quickly to such a method, they have to be thrown in to sink or swim. I know from my own experience that very satisfactory, really valuable results can be secured, and Regular officers greatly assisted—as well as freed from too close retention on duty for the summer period, by the proper use of Reserve personnel. I would like to talk this over with the G-3 Section.

The foregoing notes have been hastily dictated, and are not to be treated as a final word in any respect, but merely as a basis for discussion.

GCMRL/G. C. Marshall Papers (Pentagon Office, Selected)

1. No copy of the memorandum by Chief of Infantry Major General George A. Lynch was found in the Marshall papers. Some of Lynch's ideas at this time are expressed in his essay "Fire Power . . . Man Power . . . Maneuver," *Infantry Journal* 46[November–December 1939]: 498–505, 606. The editors have not found a written response to this memorandum from G-3.

2. In 1935 Marshall recalled his impressions of John F. Morrison: "He spoke a tactical language I have never heard from any other officer. He was self-educated, reading constantly and creating and solving problems for himself. He taught me all I will ever know of tactics." (Marshall to Colonel Bernard Lentz, October 2, 1935; the text of this letter is printed in *Papers of GCM,* 1: 45–47.) By "units" and "tenths," Marshall is referring to the minutely detailed grading scale in use when he attended the Infantry and Cavalry School. (Ibid., p. 37.)

To Brigadier General Charles H. Cole   September 26, 1939
Confidential   [Washington, D.C.]

Dear Cole: I have just received your letter of September 22d, and appreciate your regrets that I am unable to arrange to be in Boston at the time of the Convention.[1]

As to your questions: There is an embarrassment regarding the answers at the present time, pending the decision of the Administration as to just what is to be asked of Congress. However, there are some points that I am free to cover, and I pass on the information to you for your use.

While the Regular Army divisions are being reorganized on the new basis, largely because they are incomplete and ineffective in their present condition, we do not contemplate making any changes in the National Guard divisions for the present. The feeling is that to make such a change at this time would merely produce confusion and delay, whereas we wish to expedite training and build up efficiency.

We hope to get a further increase to bring the Guard up to 320,000 in enlisted personnel, but we are not free to make public mention of this at this time. This increase would permit the organization of special units, in which we are so deficient at the present time, anti-aircraft, heavy artillery, and organizations for the army corps. The increase would also carry the strength of division units well up to the full peace standard. What we are particularly desirous of getting is an authorization for 60 drills and for two rations a month; also, and this again is confidential, we are asking for money for two weeks of additional camp. Not that we contemplate calling out the Guard for such a camp, but using the two-week period merely as a basis of calculation for funds.

What we want to secure is the authorization and the money to permit staging at favorable moments for them, full battalion assemblies for two or three days, regimental assemblies for two or three days, and possibly brigade assemblies for two or three days on a pay basis, with the provision of necessary gasoline, etc. to permit such concentrations, and with money for leases where use of property devoid of crops in the winter might afford close-by opportunities for assembly. In other words, we want to have all the means for stimulating and expediting National Guard activity without the necessity of mobilizing the Guard prior to a considerable development in efficiency, if at all; and I wish at all cost to avoid taking men away from their personal pursuits until an emergency develops of such a nature that drastic action becomes necessary.

As an illustration of the general idea, we are not calling on the recently authorized Regular Army enlisted Reserve, which has reached a total of 25,000 at the present time. To call that force in would be a mandatory act and would take older men away from their occupations. However, they have had full training in the Regular Army, some for a number of enlistments, and they are available to be called on forty-eight hours' notice to raise the ranks of regular divisions to war strength.

I am dictating this hastily, but I am giving you a general idea, and I trust you will use it, so far as the confidential portions are concerned, so as not to embarrass the War Department, because, as I have explained above, we have no Presidential authorization as to a program at present, and with the Neutrality legislation up, this is a very delicate issue. Faithfully yours,

GCMRL/G. C. Marshall Papers (Pentagon Office, Selected)

1. A longtime friend of Marshall (see *Papers of GCM,* 1: 629) and former adjutant general of Massachusetts, Cole wrote to Marshall on September 5 to ask if Marshall could speak to the meeting of the National Guard Association of Massachusetts on October 14. Marshall replied on September 9 that he was committed on that date to attend a meeting of the Pennsylvania National Guard Association. Marshall arranged for Brigadier General Charles F. Thompson, executive for Reserve Affairs in the War Department since September 1938, to speak to the convention. Cole wrote on September 22, "It would be much appreciated if he could tell our officers what is in the offing as far as the new Division organization is concerned, and what, if any, further developments are contemplated for the National Guard in view of present world conditions." (Cole to Marshall, September 5 and 22, 1939; Marshall to Cole, September 9, 1939, GCMRL/G. C. Marshall Papers [Pentagon Office, Selected].)

To Brigadier General Lesley J. McNair[1] September 29, 1939
[Washington, D.C.]

My dear McNair: I am going into the matter of having a complete infantry battalion assigned to Leavenworth and believe it a very good idea as it will let the students see the basic combat unit of the Army. I am very glad that you can accommodate it.

Under our present augmentation of 17,000 no provision is made to activate or move any element of the 17th Infantry. However, in the event of raising the Army to 280,000, present plans contemplate assembling all of the 3d Battalion, 17th Infantry, at Leavenworth. You will appreciate the difficulties that would be encountered at this time were we to attempt the transfer of the 3d Battalion elements now at Crook to Leavenworth.

In going over the Field Service Regulation the other day prior to giving it tentative approval, a few points came to mind which I think might well be included in the next edition.

There should be a paragraph on continuity of effort. The initial impetus is seldom conclusive in effect, and final success will only be secured by maintaining the momentum once gained. Many factors enter into this, even the stabilizing effect of too early establishment of a complete command post. Reorganization for further activity after the disorganization incident to the first effort, should be practiced in time of peace. Incidentally, in the general tactical instructions for the conduct of troops at St. Mihiel, I provided for farther advances beyond final division objectives of battalions of regiments of infantry reenforced by some artillery. But few if any divisions did this. Training to overcome the disorder of unexpected casualties and unexpected events in battle will avoid to an important extent the demoralization which often follows such moments.

The procurement of maps and photographs should be emphasized as a function of command and the text should be written under the assumption that good maps will seldom be on hand without special command effort. A statement should be included in the text, if it is not already there, that when the number of radio channels indicate restriction as necessary, first priority for continued use of radio must be given to the combat troops who have no other means of communication. Greater emphasis should be put on the use of air photographs in reporting results of reconnaissance.

Greater emphasis should be placed on the use of cover in approaching to the assault position. Instruction on this subject usually is applied to the individual, and not, as it should be, to the platoon, company, and battalion unit. I gather that modern combat utilizes the individual weapon more within the hostile position than prior to reaching it.

I am glad you are pushing instruction in the new division. This division plus our new field service regulation constitutes a progressive step, one that should assist materially all our schools. Corps Areas are now effecting the reorganization of divisions; recruiting and activation of units has actually begun.   Faithfully yours,

GCMRL/G. C. Marshall Papers (Pentagon Office, Selected)

1. In a September 18 letter to McNair, Marshall enumerated the decisions that had been made on the new triangular division. "You will be interested to know that Field Service Regulation, as prepared by G-3 (Gruber), has been given tentative approval and general distribution will be made." He also wrote: "I will bear in mind your desire to have a complete rifle battalion at Leavenworth when a re-shuffle comes. Can you accommodate it?" (Marshall to McNair, September 18, 1939, GCMRL/G. C. Marshall Papers [Pentagon Office, Selected].)

McNair replied that he would have no trouble accommodating the new troops. He added: "The new division gives new zest to life; at last we know where we're going. Everything will be given new impetus, and even the new class here will get a good bit of it." (McNair to Marshall, September 22, 1939, NA/RG 407 [Classified, 320.2 (9–22–39)].)

To Major General David L. Stone   October 3, 1939
Confidential   [Washington, D.C.]

Dear Stone: I have had several notes and letters from you lately, but this is to acknowledge specifically your letter of September 19th, which was read by the Secretary of War.[1] I am very glad to learn how smoothly the transfer of authority in the Zone has been carried out,[2] and of the progress you are making in developing the construction program.

With reference to the latter: I talked to Colonel Danielson[3] just prior to his departure for Panama and suggested to him the great desirability of getting you to designate some engineer officer to maintain close liaison between the two of you. He was to do this apparently on his own initiative, but I am telling you confidentially that it is my suggestion. I told him that I think it highly desirable not only to make some such arrangement to facilitate and expedite business, but with a view to the possible re-enforcement of his office with two or three expert engineer officers to assist him in handling matters in such a way that the present centralization of control in the Quartermaster General's office would be rendered largely unnecessary.

I am telling you this most confidentially, because my motive is not quite that implied in my conversation with Colonel Danielson. I am greatly concerned by the lack of highly trained officers in the Construction Division of the Quartermaster's Department, and that Division is supersensitive on the subject and very fearful of engineer interference. They need assistance from the Engineer Corps terribly, and I was hopeful that by the method I chose on the spur of the moment in talking to Danielson we might realize that advantage in Panama. The Secretary of War has made the decision to have the work in Panama done upon a cost-plus-a-fixed-fee basis. Even under this plan careful supervision by the Government is essential. Colonel Danielson will need expert officers for this purpose.[4]

I should be leaving Hawaii this morning on the China clipper for San Francisco. I had a reservation on the plane and was supposed to have left San Francisco on September 27th with General Arnold. However, affairs here made me cancel the arrangement. My further plan had been to go to Panama in December; whether or not this can be carried out, I do not know, but I feel it is important that I should make the trip. I would probably fly down.

With warm regards,   Faithfully yours,

GCMRL/G. C. Marshall Papers (Pentagon Office, Selected)

1. Stone had written that operations were running smoothly in the Panama Canal Zone, that construction was under way for temporary quarters, and that he was encouraged at the prospects of building an army hospital in the Pacific Sector. "In accordance with the War Department's instructions, I have assumed command of the Panama Canal with all of its appurtenances, et cetera. In doing this I am taking full advantage of all the organizations that now exist, and have informed Governor Ridley that the planning and administrative affairs of the Canal will, so far as practicable, continue as heretofore under his direction. All matters of importance affecting neutrality and the safety and operation of the Canal will be submitted to me for decision. I keep in close touch with the operations of the Canal, especially those concerned with safeguarding of the locks, such as inspection of ships with cargoes of high explosives desiring to transit the Canal, and other matters of this nature.

"The Navy is with us 100% and I have a meeting each Friday morning, and oftener when necessary, with Governor Ridley and the two Admirals and their staffs, and talk over all questions and problems that we all may have in mind. . . . The construction of temporary quarters for the 18th Infantry Brigade and for increase in antiaircraft and Air Corps personnel is going along rapidly." (Stone to Marshall, September 19, 1939, GCMRL/G. C. Marshall Papers [Pentagon Office, Selected].)

2. President Roosevelt's September 5, 1939, Executive Order 8232 specified that "the Officer of the Army commanding the United States Troops stationed in the Canal Zone shall, until otherwise ordered, assume and have exclusive authority and jurisdiction over the opera-

tion of the Panama Canal and all its adjuncts, appendants, and appurtenances, including the entire control and government of the Canal Zone; and, while this order is in force, the Governor of the Panama Canal shall, in all respects and particulars as to the operation of the Panama Canal and all duties, matters and transactions affecting the Canal Zone, be subject to the order and direction of the Officer of the Army herein designated."

3. Colonel Wilmot A. Danielson was stationed with the Quartermaster Corps at the Panama Canal Department Headquarters.

4. Stone replied: "I am afraid the Construction Division of the Quartermaster General's Office will never change. The old civil service engineers and architects have been there a long time and have their way of doing things. They believe in strong centralization of everything in that office and are not very susceptible to changes and progress in the construction world." He concluded: "I believe that the best solution of all is to give the Department Commander control of all construction work here, under the supervision of the War Department. This seems to me a logical and businesslike way to handle the matter and the Department Commander would then be in a position to take such measures as might be necessary and helpful." (Stone to Marshall, October 11, 1939, GCMRL/G. C. Marshall Papers [Pentagon Office, Selected].)

To Brigadier General James L. Collins[1]   October 4, 1939
                                                          [Washington, D.C.]

Dear Collins: I received your letter of September 30th, with its comments regarding the new division.[2] I am very glad to have this frank expression of your opinion and I have had copies of your letter made and furnished WPD and G-3 that they might mull over your suggestions.

I took action in this matter very quickly because the essence of the problem now is the time factor, and I could not possibly enter into details myself. The business has been studied for a year and a half, and War Plans and G-3 here were almost in complete agreement with the report of the officers conducting the tests, and we had to do business without further delay.

I am like you, in that the organization does not please me; but I think it has the advantage of being a carefully considered product of some of the best minds in the Army. What is more to the point, it would be very easy to alter matters at a later date on a war establishment, if this appears necessary; just as it will be easy to modify the existing National Guard square division if it appears desirable after they take the field. The subtraction of a regiment of infantry, a regiment of artillery and a battalion of engineers would make it in effect a stream-lined division. Their infantry regiments are already being reorganized.

This reorganization of regular divisions is practically the only change I have given favorable consideration to at the present time. In the past we always held off and changed everything at the moment of the emergency, which I think is very bad practice.

Thank you for writing.   Faithfully yours,

GCMRL/G. C. Marshall Papers (Pentagon Office, Selected)

1. Collins commanded the Second Field Artillery Brigade, Second Division, at Fort Sam Houston, Texas, from May 8 to October 7, 1939, when the brigade was disbanded. He then became chief of the artillery section of the Second Division.

2. Collins had written: "The organization appears to be sound. What worries me, however, is how much punch the division will have left after a couple of days of fighting. As a nation, we are inclined to go from one extreme to the other. During the World War we had the largest division, now we are about to adopt the smallest. It is a step in the right direction but I wonder if we have not gone a bit too far. The peace strength of units barely cover minimum requirements so I would like to see a larger factor of safety in our war units. Also, I would like our medium artillery battalions to have three instead of two batteries—as our light battalions have. This could be done without adding a man to either regimental or battalion headquarters and incidentally this change would appreciably reduce the number of artillerymen per piece." (Collins to Marshall, September 30, 1939, GCMRL/G. C. Marshall Papers [Pentagon Office, Selected].)

To General Pedro Góes Monteiro   October 5, 1939
Secret   Washington, D.C.

My dear General Monteiro: Please accept my sincere thanks for your gracious letter of September 8th.[1] My reply has been delayed longer than I had intended, but I had hoped to hear the result of the inquiry made by your Embassy here regarding certain ordnance I had informed them we could furnish Brazil. For convenience and better understanding, I have had Colonel Miller handling these matters, and I also requested him to "write direct to you."[2]

It is unfortunate that the war in Europe has interfered with your contemplated visit abroad, because it would have given me the pleasure of greeting you here in the United States and renewing our pleasant association.

With regard to the question of the furnishing of armament and materiel by the United States Government to Brazil, Colonel Miller has given you detailed information. In order to clarify the matter, I shall explain the present status of the possibilities.

Under existing law, we have the authority to sell to a friendly government any materiel which is surplus and no longer needed for military purposes. I am sorry that this surplus materiel is limited in quantity and quality, because of our deficiencies in war materiel. However, there is armament on the list, mailed to you by Colonel Miller, which should be of considerable value to the Brazilian Army. The 6-inch mobile guns would be of special value in coast defense, and many of the guns of larger caliber could be modernized by the manufacture of suitable carriages in commercial factories. The principal deficiency in harbor defense armament is the lack of ammunition, of which we have a shortage. If this cannot be manufactured in Brazil, it could be procured from private manufacturers in the United States. The Secretary of War has approved the sale of surplus materiel to Brazil at nominal prices, and I am awaiting your decision in this matter, before asking the approval of the President. But it appears reasonably certain that he will give this authorization.

The present law does not permit us to sell new equipment manufactured in our government arsenals. The bill to authorize this failed to pass the Senate during the last session of Congress. It will be re-introduced and probably will be favorably acted upon at the regular session of Congress convening in January. However, we cannot place much dependence upon this source of procurement, even if the bill becomes law, because our government arsenals have insufficient capacity to meet our requirements in the present emergency.

Our program of ordnance procurement, just recently authorized, is designed to remedy the existing deficiencies in manufacturing facilities by giving priority to the purchase of such equipment from commercial firms in the United States. I think the same procedure should be developed in Brazil. As our procurement program progresses, we shall be able to declare surplus more materiel, such as 75 mm field and anti-aircraft guns. Such pieces, though not quite as efficient as more recent models, nevertheless would serve a very important immediate need in Brazil.

This, my dear General, is the situation in brief with regard to procurement. As Colonel Miller has suggested, it would be advantageous for you to send to the United States, a qualified officer who is authorized to represent you in matters of procurement. He could select, on the ground as it were, the surplus equipment desired by Brazil, as this materiel becomes available, and could place orders with commercial firms after obtaining plans from our War Department. It seems to me that this procedure would facilitate matters.

The general plan of the organization of your military forces, as outlined in your letter of August [*September*] 8th, appears sound, and I am glad to see that you contemplate the establishment of air bases in northeastern Brazil. Our General Staff is re-studying this question of the air bases, and I shall be glad to transmit to you information on the technical requirements.

It is very gratifying to learn that your government has tentatively approved certain measures for the increased effectiveness of our military cooperation, such as the strengthening of the United States Military Mission, the sending of Brazilian officers to this country, and the employment of technicians to orient your war industries. You may be assured that we will make available to you our most efficient personnel. This matter can be decided upon in later correspondence.

With reference to your question on the attitude of the American Congress on neutrality legislation, I might state that whatever action is taken regarding the present law it should not create obstacles to your procurements in the United States, as the neutrality legislation is directed toward belligerent nations.

With reference to the acquisition of Brazilian manganese by the United States and the methods of exchange, I shall make this the subject of later correspondence, after our requirements and funds available have been definitely determined.

Our present plans provide for the sending of the "flying fortresses" to Brazil, so that they may participate in the 50th anniversary of the proclamation of the Republic.[3] I am not yet able to state whether or not any of our government officials will accompany this flight, but will notify you later regarding this point. It will be convenient for the planes to transport to the United States a few officers of the Brazilian Army, the number being determined by the limited seating capacity of these bombers. I will give you more exact data on this point later. Incidentally, we carried your Ambassador from Cuba to Panama in a flying fortress last week.

In conclusion, I wish to assure you, my good friend, of my desire to cooperate to the full extent of my authority in all measures which will better prepare your country for its own defense, and that of the American continent. At this time of serious possibilities, we both have difficult problems to solve, but if I can be of any assistance to you, please do not hesitate to write to me direct, or to Colonel Miller, if you so desire, who will keep me informed.

With my compliments and respects to Senhora Monteiro, and with affectionate regards to you and best wishes for your health, I am   Faithfully yours,

NA/RG 165 (WPD, 4224)

1. General Góes Monteiro had written: "Brazil had purchased from Germany some material for the Army: field artillery, motorization and anti-aircraft equipments. It is natural that these orders are virtually cancelled and arrested. For that reason I should like to ask my friend to inquire the possibility for the United States to supply us with identical material with extreme urgency." (Monteiro to Marshall, August [*September*] 8, 1939, NA/RG 165 [WPD, 4224].)

2. Lieutenant Colonel Lehman W. Miller had been a student at the Army War College since September 1, 1939. (See note 4, Marshall to Caffery, July 24, 1939, p. 23.)

3. A flight of seven B-17s, with fifty-seven crewmen under the command of Major General Delos C. Emmons (U.S.M.A., 1909), left Langley Field, Virginia, on November 10. Marshall delivered a brief radio address at the field before take-off. The trip, he said, was not only "an aerial goodwill mission to our great sister republic of Brazil," but also another demonstration

of "the high state of development of our air vessels, the performance and reliability of American aircraft, and the excellence of the training of our airmen." (GCMRL/G. C. Marshall Papers [Pentagon Office, Speeches].) The flight's operations officer, First Lieutenant Curtis E. LeMay, comments on the trip in *Mission with LeMay* (Garden City, N.Y.: Doubleday and Company, 1965), pp. 175–82.

MEMORANDUM FOR ASSISTANT CHIEF   October 6, 1939
OF STAFF, G-3 [ANDREWS]   [Washington, D.C.]
Confidential

Training of Reserve Officers at Training Schools. (G-3/41500)

I have signed the letter proposed in your memorandum of September 26th for Senator Elbert D. Thomas,[1] but in this connection I wish several points to be considered, and reference to be made to the ideas in future letters of this kind.

We are going about the concentration of divisions in the South for a period of special training with large units this winter. After these reorganized divisions have gotten well under way with their divisional training, these concentrations will present wonderful opportunities for the schooling of senior National Guard commanders and key staff officers, as well as the younger fry of Reserve officers. I suppose we would have to include Reserve officers of other ranks for short periods.

I would like these possibilities carefully considered, having in mind two or three considerations:

(1) The procedure to be carried out on such a basis that the proper type of citizen soldier can manage to take the training—that is, a successful business man, and he is the one we want, cannot absent himself from his business for long periods. Division commanders and key staff officers, for example, should fly in, say on Friday afternoon, follow through the procedure Saturday and Sunday before taking over actual jobs on Monday, and fly home Tuesday morning. During such periods we would have to arrange our Regular Army training for Saturdays and Sundays and leave the holiday period to Tuesdays and Wednesdays, or some such arrangement.

(2) Young second lieutenants can stay for longer periods without the probability that we are merely supporting men so lacking in efficiency that they cannot secure jobs in civil life. Young lieutenants brought in on this basis could be made good use of, and I want this suggestion to be taken seriously. I know it is a fact because I have done it time and

again, yet in most cases in the Army we either demand a repeater on the basis of his previous experience, or we only permit the officer to follow along, with a great lack of interest and instruction for him, and interference and irritation to everybody else. I think in this coming situation we should make actual use to our own advantage of the 2d lieutenant Reserve material.[2]

GCMRL/G. C. Marshall Papers (Pentagon Office, Selected)

1. Thomas, Democrat from Utah, was a member of the Military Affairs Committee. Andrews's September 26 memorandum and the letter for Senator Thomas are not in the Marshall papers.

2. Attached to this memorandum was a typewritten note to Brigadier General Frank M. Andrews signed by Marshall: "For evident reasons I do not wish this informal memorandum of mine given general circulation in the section."

To MAJOR GENERAL DAVID L. STONE   October 9, 1939
Personal and Confidential   [Washington, D.C.]

Dear Stone: I have passed on your several letters to the Secretary of War in order that he might see what was being done by you under the changed conditions of control in the Canal Zone, and he is very much gratified. This morning I gave him your letter of October 4th, with the carbon copy of your communication to Mr. Sumner Welles.[1]

The Secretary is deeply interested in every aspect concerned with the Panama Canal, in view of the present world crisis. He is particularly concerned over the construction program—just as you are. Now, most confidentially, and for your eye alone, he is unwilling for the command to pass from you to General Lear, and I do not wish to see General Lear suffer a humiliation by his relief from duty in Panama prior to the expiration of his tour. This means that your successor must be senior to General Lear.[2] There is another phase of the matter; both the Secretary and I feel that your successor should arrive in the Canal Zone in time to have an important part in the development of that command, in tactical organization as well as in construction. We, therefore, think that your tour should be terminated before next summer, and we have settled on the first of the year as a desirable time.

General Van Voorhis is to succeed you. We would like, if practicable, to have him there about a week before your departure.

Will you please consider this matter from the standpoint of determining how best it can be done. Would you prefer to initiate the action from your end of the line, by requesting that your extension of foreign service be reconsidered on the basis of January 1st next? Please write me very frankly on the subject by *air mail*.[3]

Unless you have some other desire, you would be ordered to the Fifth Corps Area Headquarters until your retirement.   Faithfully yours,

GCMRL/G. C. Marshall Papers (Pentagon Office, Selected)

1. Stone's letter to Under Secretary of State Sumner Welles described in detail a conversation Stone had with Ecuador's minister of foreign affairs regarding that country's potential assistance and cooperation in the defense of the approaches to the Panama Canal. (Stone to Welles, October 4, 1939, GCMRL/G. C. Marshall Papers [Pentagon Office, Selected]. See Marshall to Stone, October 3, 1939, pp. 69–71.)

2. Concerning Major General Ben Lear, see Marshall to Van Voorhis, September 2, 1939, pp. 49–50.

3. Stone replied that he was requesting that his tour in the Panama Canal terminate on January 1, 1940. He concluded: "My high hopes regarding our defenses for the Canal and for which I have worked are now about to be realized and the foundation has been laid for the development of our defenses along the lines we have all had in mind. It, therefore, seems very wise that a man with a longer time to serve take hold and carry on and carry out the actual development of all our defense installations. Such an appointment will also guarantee continuity of command under whatever conditions we may face during the next few years." (Stone to Marshall, October 14, 1939, GCMRL/G. C. Marshall Papers [Pentagon Office, Selected]. See Marshall to Van Voorhis, September 2, 1939, pp. 48–50.) In a letter to Major General Van Voorhis, Marshall observed that Stone had "acceded to the proposal in a fine spirit." (October 16, 1939, GCMRL/G. C. Marshall Papers [Pentagon Office, Selected].) Marshall also wrote a letter of commendation for the secretary of war's signature praising Stone for "the splendid job you have done." (Harry H. Woodring to Stone, October 20, 1939, ibid.)

To Lieutenant General Stanley D. Embick   October 9, 1939
                                                 [Washington, D.C.]

My dear General Embick: I had with me in Chicago a staff sergeant, now a technical sergeant, named Frank S. Singer, on duty with the National Guard. He was my Adjutant for a year and a half, taking the place of a major at that time. He is not only a fine soldier technically—he is very high up on all infantry weapons—but in a staff capacity I used him for calculations, estimates, correspondence, and a wide variety of matters not customarily placed in the hands of an enlisted man. Furthermore, he was associated with me in the field in Army Maneuvers, where I was a commander, and understands this part of the Army.

Sergeant Singer is now at Benning taking special courses. He would like to remain there if possible. He was there once as a sergeant instructor in the school, but left to go to Clemson on the persuasion of the P.M.S.&T. at that place. Later he transferred to Chicago on account of his mother's health, and was caught in the doldrums of promotion with the National Guard. Singer has about 20-odd years of service.

I am writing to you because I understand that they are organizing the Fourth Corps Headquarters Detachment at Fort Benning, which means several vacancies for chief clerks. I commend Singer to the officer in charge of his organization, and hope he will give him a hearing.[1]   Faithfully yours,

GCMRL/G. C. Marshall Papers (Pentagon Office, Selected)

1. Embick, commanding general of the Fourth Corps Area and the Third Army, replied that Singer's assignment would be arranged. (Embick to Marshall, October 11, 1939, GCMRL/G. C. Marshall Papers [Pentagon Office, Selected].) The chief of staff sent a copy of Embick's letter to Singer with the comment: "Now it is up to you to be the best man in your particular job in the United States Army, regardless of mishaps, irritations, and other little things which sometimes wreck the ship. This is your opportunity and I know you will seize it." (Marshall to Singer, October 16, 1939, ibid.) Singer completed his course at the Infantry School and reported to Fourth Corps Headquarters at Fort Benning as a master sergeant on January 1, 1940. (Singer to Marshall, January 6, 1940, ibid.) On August 1, 1940, Marshall wrote to Colonel Iverson B. Summers at the Infantry School: "Thank you for sending me the copy of the commendation of Sergeant Singer. I am glad to know that he has made such a favorable impression, though I felt pretty certain of it. However, it is a relief when you put a man up to have him make good in such a generous measure." (GCMRL/G. C. Marshall Papers [Pentagon Office, General].)

To Louise Mills[1]   October 9, 1939
[Washington, D.C.]

My dear Miss Mills: I have just this moment read your note of inquiry as to how I achieved whatever success has been mine.

I am so busy these days that I have not time for sober reflection on the question of just how things were managed in my career, but—not to be quoted and more or less for your eye only—I rather think that giving the best I had to each job and not permitting myself to grow pessimistic over the slow progress or inevitable discouragements, were the most important factors. When one is young, there is great impatience with the slow development of a career, but it is a long race and the more firm the foundation of the "20's", the more the certainty of success after 50.   Faithfully yours,

GCMRL/G. C. Marshall Papers (Pentagon Office, General)

1. Louise Mills, a high school student from Seattle, Washington, wrote to Marshall as part of an assignment for a personal achievement class. The assignment was to ask a person of renown how he had achieved success. (Mills to Marshall, n.d., GCMRL/G. C. Marshall Papers [Pentagon Office, General].)

To Austin V. McClain[1]   October 10, 1939
[Washington, D.C.]

My dear Mr. McClain: Replying to your letter of October 9th, I must be very frank and tell you that up to the present moment I have nothing prepared for my talk on October 14th at Washington and Jefferson College. I am in the same predicament regarding remarks for the National Guard meeting on Friday evening, and before the 600 industrialists in Washington on Thursday [*Wednesday*] evening, and at the moment I see no hope of preparing anything. So I am afraid you will have to take me just as I am without benefit of preparation.

The fault is somewhat my own because of unwillingness to farm out such productions. I have been so extremely busy here in the War Department that I have not been able to attend to anything but the duties of the moment. I will simply have to do my best on Saturday.[2]   Faithfully yours,

GCMRL/G. C. Marshall Papers (Pentagon Office, Selected)

1. McClain was assistant to the president at Washington and Jefferson College in Washington, Pennsylvania. On Saturday, October 14, the college was bestowing the honorary degree of Doctor of Science upon Marshall, and he was to give a ten-minute address at dinner. McClain had written to ask Marshall to send a copy of his intended remarks. (McClain to Marshall, October 9, 1939, GCMRL/G. C. Marshall Papers [Pentagon Office, Selected].)

2. In the draft of his brief acceptance remarks, Marshall included the following observation: "I hope it will not be thought inappropriate to the occasion for me to express this thought, that what we have most to fear, at the moment, is the possible effect of superficial thinking and bellicose emotionalism, rather than the fear of militarism in this country. It seems to me that we might be compared at this hour to a very young giant in a position of tremendous power, possessing all those generous youthful qualities of virility, idealism and directness of purpose, untempered by the wisdom of the years." (Draft address [marked "revamped orally"], October 14, 1939, GCMRL/G. C. Marshall Papers [Pentagon Office, Speeches].)

To Lieutenant General Hugh A. Drum   October 10, 1939
Personal and Confidential   [Washington, D.C.]

Dear Drum: Thank you for your note of October 9th.[1] I think everybody in the mobile Army will be pleased with the fact that the "fleet is actually going to sea" in time of peace. We have been having a hard time of it finding ways and means to create legal deficits to get the funds to carry this through, but I think most of the impossibilities have been eliminated. Of course, we would be in a bad hole if Congress did not come to our rescue later on.

The most interesting point at the moment is the time factor, as illustrated by the motor transport problem. Confidentially, we succeeded in getting the President to give us his O.K. on the $12,000,000 deficit for motor vehicles, which is a tricky legal problem, and raise the normal $3,000,000 of f.y. 1940 to $15,000,000 in the advertisement for bids. We got this authority about ten days ago and got out the proposals, I think, the next day, but even so the first deliveries are the middle of January, with the major portion of the trucks being delivered in March. Of course we will try to push this faster, but with what success I cannot now say.

The foregoing means, of course, that the corps phase of the concentration will be delayed accordingly. However, and this is confidential as it is ahead of the completed plans, we hope to have a two division corps with some corps troops in action at Benning by the end of January. Later on in the spring, a corps of three divisions with corps troops will be completed, and if we are permitted to go ahead at that time, we will have another corps headquarters complete and a few of the corps troops, together with the Second Division, the Cavalry people, and the Mechanized force to operate against the first corps above referred to. Of course, if we are authorized to recruit up to full peace strength, which I think we will be, then the second corps will have a complete organization.

As to a landing operation, again confidentially, I am going to the Joint Board tomorrow to see if the Navy will modify their winter plans sufficiently to put on a landing operation of the entire Third Division on the California Coast between Santa Barbara and Half Moon Bay. We would use the West Coast Wing of the G.H.Q. Air Force on the defensive side, as well as the scattered troops that are not in the Third Division. Aside from the training value of such a joint staff operation, we would have the added advantage of leaving the Third Division at Camp Ord for the Northwest rainy season. With the 30th Infantry from San Francisco and other scattered troops, along with the corps troops to be organized at Ord, excellent maneuvers should be arranged.

The Neutrality debate, of course, has delayed all of our moves, and we were vastly relieved to get the authority to go ahead with the public announcements of Saturday and Sunday.

We have been planning to bring in all the Army Commanders and the Corps Area Commanders for a general conference. Just when we will do this is still undecided, as we want to have the rough outlines pretty well cast before starting discussions. One factor in the delay is the possibility, and this is most confidential, that we may succeed in getting a Joint Resolution considered at this special session of Congress for $165,000,000 for the Navy and $150,000,000 for the Army to carry us up to the end of January. With this money, many things that we are now improvising in a skeleton fashion, could be carried out to great advantage, and very important contracts placed for deliveries of much needed essential items. This money would also include a large sum made available for concentrations, maneuvers, etc., I think about $35,000,000.   Faithfully yours,

GCMRL/G. C. Marshall Papers (Pentagon Office, Selected)

1. Drum had handwritten: "May I extend congratulations on your decision to concentrate our regular army divisions in the South for Winter training. This will accomplish a long felt want, and will be well worth the financial cost. I hope that you can eventually group them into corps and a field army organization in order to produce the complete team so essential to teach & create the understanding of 'Mechanism of battle.'" (Drum to Marshall, October 9, 1939, GCMRL/G. C. Marshall Papers [Pentagon Office, Selected].)

SPEECH TO THE ARMY ORDNANCE ASSOCIATION[1] October 11, 1939
Washington, D.C.

General Crowell, Admiral Stark, General Wesson, Gentlemen: I am a little embarrassed tonight. First, in following the distinguished gentlemen who have already talked to you, but more particularly because of the recent decision of the War Department to discourage officers from engaging in public discussions of military matters, which to be interesting would immediately involve questions that still must be regarded as somewhat confidential. I will, however, do my best to talk frankly as to what our thought is today in regard to the Army generally; in regard to what is taking place in a military war and, especially, in relation to industrial preparedness.

As a beginning, I think it might be well to submit a few comments regarding the present discussions as to the great changes that have taken place in the manner of making war, judging, for example, from what has happened recently in Poland. I will preface that thought with a personal experience, if I may be permitted, which was to me a lesson in the matter of getting down to fundamentals, believing, as I do, that they are usually unchanging.

As the Toastmaster remarked, I sailed for France with the First Division in June, 1917. Filled with recruits and newly organized, the division went into the line that fall, and as a complete division, entered the sector north of Toul on the St. Mihiel front in January, 1918. We occupied a locality in which there had been no active fighting for almost three years. It had been maintained on the same basis until, in some respects, it was almost like a hotel—with divisions coming and going as the guests of the permanent sector organization. The troops were largely disposed in the forward zone of the sector, and I recall that the principal dugouts were under the parapets of the front trench.

We had been there but two or three weeks when there was received from the Intelligence Bureau of the French Army a description of an expected assault to be made by German forces, which had been heavily reinforced with divisions drawn from the collapsed Russian front. The reported nature of this new attack, termed a "maneuver of rupture," was such that it caused the French High Command to direct a complete reorganization of the defenses—from that of a shallow nature to one of considerable depth. This meant the complete change of a system which had existed for nearly three years. It meant, in brief, that a regiment which had occupied a deployed depth of about five or six hundred yards, would be disposed over a depth of a mile or more, and that the regiments, the companies, the individuals, could be much more widely dispersed; that a great many machine gun emplacements which had previously been located along the lines of trenches, would have to be re-located in staggered formation of great depth.

To the First Division it meant a tremendous planning problem, and for the troops hard manual labor and much exposure to the weather of that bitter winter of 1917–18. Snow was deep on the ground. Every move we made could be readily traced by the tracks of vehicles and of men on foot, as well as by the signs of extensive excavations. Construction was started and the men worked very, very hard. They suffered extreme hardships because of the inadequacy of the arrangements we could make for their shelter in the newly deployed positions in depth, but they did their work uncomplainingly. Then, when we were about half through with this program, the great German offensive of March 21, 1918, broke against the right of the British Army.

The First Division was hurriedly withdrawn from that sector and sent to Picardy. As its trains were arriving northwest of Paris, I personally reported to the headquarters of the group of French armies in which we were to serve. There I was informed that the system of organization in depth which we had just been carrying out on the St. Mihiel front, had since been greatly modified as a result of the experience of the recent heavy fighting. I was given the new method for taking up dispositions in depth which we were to follow as we went into the new sector, on ground but recently occupied and without trenches. We started work on the defenses under this new arrangement. Again the men worked in the cold and mud of early spring in Northern France, but just as they had gotten well into it, another German offensive broke, this time down the Valley of the Lys. Two weeks later new instructions were received for a further modifying of the method of deployment in depth. Once more we were forced to abandon the results of work that had been laboriously accomplished.

The troops were very tired. They had had no relief since early January. They had endured the cold, the mud, and the snow or rain of that bitter winter. It is true that they had not been engaged in an active operation, but they had been under such heavy fire that about three or four thousand men were casualties. Nevertheless, every man set about this newest task of reorganization in a fine, soldierly spirit. And then we entered into the Cantigny operation, where we suffered heavy losses due to a series of desperate German counter-attacks and violent artillery reactions. Simultaneously with that fight came the German attack on the Chemin des Dames, which thundered down to Chateau Thierry—to make of it historic ground for our Army. And then once more, two weeks later, we received a new set of instructions completely modifying the organization in depth that we were then in the process of completing.

I recall that in our reply to these new instructions we notified the French Headquarters that we could do one of two things; we could fight or we could dig, but it was no longer possible for us to do both.

We now come to the point of this series of events. That last modification (which was a modification of previous modifications—the first being a change in a system that had stood for almost three years), though written in French, was expressed literally in the language of the Field Service Regulations of the United States Army in 1914. In other words, there had been no change in fundamentals, but during three years of trench warfare those fundamentals had been lost sight of, and now in that critical summer of 1918, we were back again to first essentials of warfare.

To me that was an impressive lesson, and since then whenever changes are proposed, modern theories advanced, or surprising developments are brought to my attention, I automatically search for the fundamental principle involved in the particular matter at hand.

Many of the discussions at the present time, in relation to what we have learnt of the occurrences in Poland, seemingly propose new fundamentals as a basis for warfare. I might comment here on the fact that the American public is remarkably well informed on events in Europe as indicated by our confidential reports. But our knowledge at the present time, official and public, is superficial. However, it does appear that much of the procedure in Poland was merely a modification or a speeding up of the time-honored methods of making war, especially adapted to the terrain, the season of the year, the character of the people and the geographical set-up.

You have undoubtedly read in the papers of the concentrations we are inaugurating for the mobile troops of the Regular Army. Some four infantry divisions and one cavalry division, together with the necessary corps troops, a few of which now exist and others which are being organized, are being collected for special training. As soon as those divisional concentrations have permitted officers and men to gain familiarity with the new organizations, corps formations of three or four divisions, with the special troops concerned, will be carried out in large maneuvers to give the higher command experience with operations of large formations under modern conditions. This will be the most extensive maneuver ever attempted by our Army in time of peace. It will be, in effect, a great college of leadership for the higher officers, not only of the Regular Army, but of the National Guard and the Reserve Corps. It will provide a wonderful practical schooling for the young products of the ROTC in the Reserve Corps, and I hope it will lead to a policy for an annual concentration of a force of this general character of regular troops, so that we may keep abreast of the technique necessary for the handling of large bodies of troops, and keep before the public the evident necessity for maintaining a balanced force sufficiently complete for immediate employment.

In this connection I would like to make some comments which I think are rather pertinent. It has seemed to me, from a study of the hearings before Congress, that the Army has suffered continuously from lack of understanding by the public, and to a certain extent, by the Congress. The responsibility for this, in my opinion, rests largely with the Army because of the manner of our presentations and our use of military-technical terminology. At present, an army involves so many complex and varied activities and technical requirements that it is difficult even for a professional soldier to keep in close touch with the entire problem. I must confess that, in going into these matters in the War Department, I frequently have difficulty in understanding just what a particular staff officer is discussing, so far as all the related factors are concerned. If that is so in my case, it is probably much more the case with members of Congress, and must involve still more of misunderstanding by the general public.

We suffer from another disadvantage. The Army, I might say, is not photogenic. The more efficient, the better its organization, technique, and deployment, the more nearly it is invisible, except for the Air Force and the Mechanized Force. For that reason, these last two forces have less difficulty in convincing Congress of the necessity for appropriations; and for exactly the same reason, if we could offer for the mobile army something approximating the beautiful photographs of columns of battleships or destroyers bucking a heavy sea, I think we would have less trouble in developing our military program for the National Defense.

We recently had an excellent example of the force of such publicity. Several years ago publications were filled with photographs of the horrors of bombing women and children in China and in Spain. Promptly public pressure developed and Congress responded, and we finally received long overdue appropriations for antiaircraft materiel and airplanes. But until the war photographs had reached the public, there had been indifference or great reluctance to respond to our urgings for such equipment.

There is another factor—a most important factor, which pertains to our geographic location. The American people are naturally loath to see large appropriations made for war purposes, believing extensive defensive measures to be unnecessary due to our geographical location between two great oceans. The Atlantic and Pacific oceans are of tremendous value to our defensive situation, but they are not impassable.

In reviewing various hearings before committees of Congress, and the published articles stressing this, that, and the other military development, I have come to the conclusion that if we can find simpler terms for expressing our problem, if, for example, we can settle on a single unit, the Army Corps, for example, of two or three or four divisions, with the necessary corps troops—heavy artillery and antiaircraft, observation, engineers, squadrons, truck-trains, medical troops, signal corps battalions, and all the supporting elements that are essential in battle—if we can focus on an Army Corps as our unit of measurement, as our basis of calculation, then I believe we will have much less difficulty in making our problem understandable.[2] Such a policy, so far as concerns the materiel consideration that is foremost in the minds of you gentlemen, should offer a simple basis of calculation, and the fundamental consideration of your great problem is the basis for calculating actual requirements. So, if we take the Army Corps, insofar as the ground army is concerned, together with the proper percentages for other related forces, as a medium of measure—a yardstick, as it were—we will have a simple problem of arithmetic for the determination of the requirements in personnel, in materiel, and of reserves for any multiple of that force.

Incidental to the concentration we are now bringing about in the south, we have made a step forward in the reorganization of our infantry divisions. At present we will only reorganize divisions of the regular establishment, leaving the question of reorganizing the National Guard divisions to a later date. When it comes to corps troops, however, we will have to create a number of new units. This can be done only if we are permitted to expand to the authorized peace strength of both the Regular Army and the National Guard. When and if we reach such strength, we can provide four more divisions in the Regular Army, another group of corps troops, and some important special troops for the General Headquarters Reserve, as well as reinforcements for foreign garrisons; and in addition, create the necessary corps troops that logically should exist in the National Guard.

I believe that our military personnel problem in this country is often misunderstood by reason of the fact that we have such a large portion of the regular Army on foreign service. We might characterize these last posts of duty as naval garrisons, since they guard vital naval installations, such as the Panama Canal, or Pearl Harbor in Hawaii, and naval defenses we are developing in Puerto Rico as a rear-guard of the Panama Canal. There is thus left within the continental United States only a small combatant force of the Regular Army, for which we have found it difficult to arrange adequate training—training for our own education in the regular establishment, as well as for the education of the senior officers of the National Guard and of the Reserve Corps, who constitute the major portion of our war army. As a matter of fact, the National Guard must be considered as the first line of the Army, since it will form about 75% of our first army.

I have been talking about rather small forces, compared to the tremendous program with which you gentlemen are concerned in industrial preparedness. But the problem today is one of immediacy with regard to the existing troops that must be brought to a full state of efficiency as quickly as possible. I might remark, that we are most fortunate in the character and degree of military planning which has been accomplished. We are also exceedingly fortunate, and it is gratifying and reassuring to report, that we have at the present time a War Department staff composed of a highly educated group of officers who cooperate as a team in a remarkably efficient manner. This is one of the most reassuring and helpful features of the present situation. And along with that comment, it is appropriate for me, I think, to mention, in relation to questions of materiel or munitions, the large proportion of which are critical items of ordnance, that we have in the Ordnance Corps one of the most efficient, one of the finest group of officers in the Army. That is the common opinion of the Army, of everyone who has come in contact with the Ordnance Corps, and I am certain that it is the opinion of you gentlemen assembled here tonight.

I will not attempt to discuss the problem of industrial preparedness. General Wesson has already commented in some detail on the various factors involved. You have had your meetings since you came here, and you have known, most of you, for years what the great problem has been. You are familiar with the time factor, so it is unnecessary for me to go into that phase of the problem, except to say that you know, I know, all of us know that the time factor is the vital consideration—and vital in the correct meaning of the term—of our national defense program; that we must never be caught in the same situation we found ourselves in 1917.

General Harbord went to France as Chief of Staff of the American Expeditionary Force—a force devoid of materiel. I sailed with the First Division, on the first boat of the first convoy, and I cannot recall a better picture of the vast and terrible problem that General Pershing and his staff had to undertake, than a description of the conditions under which that expedition embarked for France. We embarked with a part of an entirely new division, of which I had never even seen a photostat of the organization until we were aboard ship. I then discovered—and I was a member of the General Staff of that Division—that we had units in the division of which I had never heard. They were on other boats, and because the use of the wireless was forbidden, we could not communicate with them to find out what they were and what they knew about themselves. We studied all the available charts. We sought to familiarize ourselves with the new organization, but there was very little literature on the war as it was then being conducted. We had one small English pamphlet, a single copy, which we studied conscientiously. But our thoughts would always go back to these new units and how they should be employed.

Landing at St. Nazaire, I was immediately sent on a circuit of the Division as the troops came ashore, to find out what they had, what manner of men they were, and what they knew about this new organization. I discovered that of 200 men to a company, approximately 180 were recruits. I found that some of these new units—Howitzer companies, the people with the Stokes mortars and with the 37 millimeter cannon—not only did not have the weapons, but the men themselves had never even heard of them. And we were landing on a foreign shore 3,000 miles from home, to enter the greatest war in history!

I recall the first time the American troops were put into line. They went in by battalions, and it fell to me to make the arrangements. We literally borrowed everything that was loose in France. Some items we didn't even borrow. We had no rolling kitchens; we didn't have this, and we didn't have that. I remember that some of the staff from the great GHQ, to which we looked in reverence rather as the rising sun and all the powers inherent in it, came down to inspect our departure, and were horrified because some of the soldiers had cut the brims off their campaign hats and were wearing the remaining crowns; others wore headgear made from bath towels, for with the steel helmet they had to have something that could be folded. Some of them had the Belgian kepi, probably because it had a gold tassel dangling in front. But we went into line in that shape for our first experience— everything begged, borrowed, or stolen—certainly not manufactured in America. That was a trying experience, a complicated affair to manage. Later I became involved in movements of troops up into the hundreds of thousands, but the problem didn't approximate the difficulties of managing that small first group of the First Division, of which nothing was normal except the fact that the men were Americans and they were willing to fight.

It has been an inspiration tonight to see a group of gentlemen of your quality of intellect and leadership assembled voluntarily to interest themselves in the very serious, the difficult, and really stupendous problem of the industrial program for the support of whatever military and naval effort we may have to make. I feel that it is a reassuring indication of the temper of the business men of America. Speaking for the Army I wish to express our appreciation of your patriotism, especially of the continued service you have rendered through the past twenty years.

I must apologize for this disconnected talk, and thank you for your generous reception and courteous attention.

GCMRL/G. C. Marshall Papers (Pentagon Office, Speeches)

1. Marshall delivered this address to a crowd of 770 at the twentieth anniversary dinner of the Army Ordnance Association at the Willard Hotel in Washington, D.C. This speech was published, in a slightly revised form, in "Changeless War: Modern Methods Have Not Altered the Fundamentals," *Army Ordnance* 20(January–February 1940): 213–15.

Army Ordnance published the addresses of other speakers at the dinner meeting (*Army Ordnance* 20[November–December 1939]): "America's Munitions Now," by Brigadier General Benedict Crowell, president of the Army Ordnance Association (p. 152); "Our Ordnance Heritage," by Major General Charles M. Wesson, chief of Ordnance (pp. 153–54); "Prepare and Stay Prepared," by Admiral Harold R. Stark (U.S.N.A., 1903), chief of naval operations (p. 156).

2. In describing the army's manpower and training needs to President Roosevelt on October 4, Marshall had emphasized the corps as the basic fighting unit, inviting the nautical-minded chief executive to consider the similarities between two organizational charts, one depicting a battleship and one an army corps. The chief of staff then described the impossibility of training in the use of the battleship by using only the captain's gig. The president agreed on the corps as the unit in future conversations. (Orlando Ward Report of meeting in the Chief of Staff's office, October 5, 1939, NA/RG 407 [334.8, General Council Reports (8-21-41) Bulky].)

SPEECH TO THE NATIONAL GUARD   October 13, 1939
ASSOCIATION OF PENNSYLVANIA[1]   Washington, Pennsylvania

. . . I spent three years with the Illinois National Guard, so I have a pretty general understanding of the various traditions, conditions, methods of the National Guard in various portions of the United States, and it has been of great assistance to me in this last year in Washington, particularly in the last three months.

You all know from the papers that we are starting on October 25th on the concentration in the South, as well as in the Northwest, of the newly reorganized divisions of the Regular Army under the President's Executive Order giving us 17,000 more men. We have succeeded in creating five divisions on the basis of strength where previously we had three large incomplete divisions. We are proceeding now with the organization of missing units of corps troops to provide one Army Corps—about 10,000 men. And we are also trying to get a portion of essential troops for another corps. These divisions are going into the South first to find themselves, and then to learn how to operate in an Army Corps in the field at their correct peace strength with necessary equipment, having available sufficient terrain to carry out the procedure on as nearly a war-time basis as can be managed in this country in time of peace. Before we get through, we hope to have sixty to seventy thousand troops in one general maneuver. Just where I do not know, but in the South toward the center of the concentration which is now being started in that direction. This is for the development of field efficiency of command and staff among the regular organizations for large units from the division and higher units. Through all the peace-time history of the United States, there has been very little opportunity to know anything of such training. I will revert to that in connection with its relation to the National Guard in a few minutes.

At this time, as General Reckord[2] has expressed very clearly, it is of great moment—it is vital, that the National Guard training be stimulated this winter to produce a greater degree of efficiency, and particularly to bring in these new men on a basis of quick development in order to make them familiar with the duties they will be called upon to perform. It is quite a problem, as you know even better than I, to accomplish this in time of peace. We have endeavored by every method which we can conceive, to see if ways can be found to manage this without the necessity of in any way separating a man from his job, which of course, is the most difficult phase of the entire matter.

. . . It is planned when these divisions in the South have sufficient transportation, of which they are at present very short, to arrange brief periods of duty for National Guard officers with the divisions. To what extent we can do that will have to be determined later. Certainly division commanders, the key men of their staffs, brigade commanders, at least their executive officers, possibly other regimental commanders, and key staff officers, will, so far as we can arrange, be given the opportunity to see what is going on, for a period of two or three days, and then have at least 24 hours of command and staff operations with officers seasoned and trained for maneuvers. As one adjustment, probably we will have to arrange to have their training concentrated on Saturdays and Sundays, and maybe Monday in a command or staff status with the troops, and then fly home on Monday evening or Tuesday morning. In other words, we will try to arrange for them to be away only a short time from business.

We will endeavor to arrange still further opportunities of that nature, and have cars. We have to go ahead now and pick up training of a large number of officers of the Reserve Corps whose only opportunity for that sort of experience would be with a regular organization.

I would like you to hear, personally and confidentially, what some of the difficulties are, so that you may have a general understanding of what is going on. We have reason to hope that shortly we will be authorized to go ahead with a further increase of the National Guard up to 320,000. That would make a total increase towards peace strength, which is a minimum of 420-odd thousand, of about 126,000 men, including this 45,000. Also a further increase of the Regular Army up to its authorized strength of 180,000. Of course, with that 280,000, some 7,000 are Philippine Scouts. When that increase comes, it will permit provision for an Army Corps—or you might say, the initial protective force: the 18 divisions of the National Guard, and the 8 divisions of the Regular Army into nine corps for peacetime development—of one regular division, two National Guard divisions, and 10,000 Corps troops. That then will give us a complete machine so far as the Corps is concerned to learn to operate and with which to quickly develop for use in time of real emergency. It will give us two corps of regular troops to use in any sudden emergency if we have to do anything in this hemisphere on very short notice; but it will also give us our ordinary peacetime development of nine Corps of three divisions, each with corps troops, which I might explain to you ladies are heavy artillery regiments, antiaircraft, trucks, trains, signal troops, engineers, bridge building attachment, and other special engineer functions in order to permit these divisions to operate in campaign.

Our shortage of officers in the Regular Army is a very serious one. I ask you to consider this confidentially as very serious. We do not want to touch the ROTC in its development at the colleges and the junior units; we do not want to disband our service schools and our special service schools, that is, the Artillery, Cavalry, Infantry, Signal Corps, Coast Artillery, and the larger service and staff schools at Fort Leavenworth. We do not want to disband them at the moment and lose all of them after we have gotten them together, so—this is most confidential—the courses are all being arranged on the basis of operating between November 1st and February 1st, so that you will have a balanced result instead of the thing being chopped off in the middle.

When those schools are closed, it will give us a large number of officers for the regular organizations, but we will still be short some 1200, I believe, on the present increase of 17,000. It is expected, and planned, and hoped that we will receive the authority to bring in the young Reserve Officers as platoon commanders for six months thus making it unnecessary to increase the Regular Army personnel. In other words, the Army in its upper grades, can stay practically as it is, as the broad basis of the entire development with reserve officers would have no relation to the promotion of the Regular Army.

It would reduce the expense; we would not have to increase the colonels, lieutenant colonels and captains to provide promotion for the large number of lieutenants we would have to have. That, however, is still in the planning and requires legal authority, but it is very essential to the operation of regular troops, and it would develop an entirely new basis for the training of Reserve officers who are activated on completion of their ROTC education from college and who at the time are not heavily involved in getting started in the business world or professional world.

Another limitation, and this again is confidential, but factual. I will revert to our limitation in transportation. I would like to use it as a measuring rod, as it were, for your comprehension of some of the problems that face this country at the present time. I told you that we are making the contracts and have gone ahead with the advertising and that sort of thing. I think the contracts are already made, or nearly so, for the vehicles required for five divisions of the Regular Army and the corps troops of one corps, and only the essential troops of that corps are now in the process of getting together. This is a very small number when we read of the divisions and other troops abroad, and yet with that procurement, we started several weeks ago to obtain material of the type that American industry is famous for turning out on a quantity production basis. The first delivery will be the middle of January, and the bulk of the deliveries will come the latter part of March and the first two weeks in April. That is for only five divisions of the Regular Army, to say nothing of the necessary transportation for 18 divisions of the National Guard, and corps troops for six of the seven corps troop units, for which there are no National Guard special troops at the present time. So you can see what a lengthy business it is, and what a serious situation we are in when it comes to the necessary materiel with which to go about our business.

There are other factors that are very interesting. One might think, with all this mass of motor transport in this country, we would seize and commandeer what we want. During the last ten years, or thereabouts, we have developed two types, first—I will exaggerate a bit—the leviathan truck, which we couldn't use in the field; if we had tried to use one of these trucks in the recent red clay dilemma down in Virginia, it would only have stalled, blocked everybody and I think it would have defied camouflage. From that huge type we jumped somewhat to the florist truck or grocery delivery wagon, which would last for three or four weeks. And there are very few of the dump carts; the engineer regiments take most of them. So a difficult problem is presented in a matter which it would appear that we should be better prepared to handle than any other country in the world.

. . . Now we are very, very fortunate that the last Congress, in addition to its augmentation of the Air Corps gave us $110,000,000 over and above the normal, which was rather large for the routine fiscal year appropriation. I do not remember, off-hand, what the total was, but they gave us a hundred and ten extra millions for materiel, plus about six millions for coast defense materiel. * *[3] I do not know what we would have done in this present situation if this money had not been appropriated last April. But the interesting point is this, talking most confidentially,—and I hope I shall not be betrayed—those orders will not be completed until the summer or fall of 1941, by the best calculation that can be made at the present time.

Now, we are a great country. Industrially we have great plants; we have the greatest go-ahead men in the manufacturing world, I think in the world, and yet we are confronted with that situation in the procurement of materiel. When you consider the models we have, I do not think anyone in the world has any better in general than we have in the semi-automatic rifle, in the machine guns, the 37 mm antiaircraft guns, the tanks, and 3-inch antiaircraft guns, but the time element is the problem, and making the public understand this is the greatest problem.

We have World War materiel for the troops, but you senior officers at least, undoubtedly have the same thought that I have. You don't want your son and I don't want my son fighting somebody else's son who is equipped with the most modern thing produced in the world, while our boys have something which is to a certain degree archaic. I am still talking confidentially.

I am not speaking as an alarmist * * but we have gotten started. These plants are going into production, and that is a tremendous step forward, but it does mean the more rapid turning out of all the things that are absolutely essential in war. You know, it is one of the most wasteful things in the world, and as you also must recognize, we are one of the most wasteful people in the world.

Now, to go back on the record: I apologize for talking so long, but I thought you would be interested. I think you are entitled to know, and where I have gone ahead of the plans, it is just for your general information and discussion among yourselves.

I want to congratulate you men of the 28th Division on the splendid work you did this summer, and General Reckord for his Division, the 29th, on their fine performance. I have heard high compliments of General Parsons,[4] and more particularly because that impresses me, with all due respect to him, from your enemies of the Black Forest, whom I know personally. They came back with very sincere expressions of what you men had been able to do, comparing your short period of preparation with the length of time and the entirely different circumstances under which they can get ready for such a maneuver.

I think those maneuvers were very popular; I think the public interest was a great advantage. Of course the condition of the world at the time produced that interest. And now our hope is that it will declare its position on a business-like basis of what is the correct thing to be done instead of recrimination and discussion about the past or too fanatical pursuit of this and that and the other fad or fancy. What we have to do is to approach this from our particular point of view, from the viewpoint of the way our Army is organized under the National Defense, and particularly from the standpoint of a balanced, coordinated result rather than an over-development of this or that. . . .

GCMRL/G. C. Marshall Papers (Pentagon Office, Speeches)

1. This version of Marshall's speech at the annual banquet of the National Guard Association of Pennsylvania was edited by a member of Marshall's staff from a reporter's notes. About 40 percent of the address is published here, and another excerpt is printed in *Papers of GCM,* 1: 42–45. The omitted portions include Marshall's review of his National Guard experiences, particularly in Pennsylvania, a discussion of certain changes in the National Guard program, a story about Adolf von Schell's reorganization of the German motor industry, and a brief closing paragraph.

2. Major General Milton A. Reckord was commanding general of the Maryland National Guard.

3. The asterisks here and below presumably indicated ellipses in the reporter's notes.

4. Major General James K. Parsons commanded the Third Corps Area, of which Pennsylvania was a part.

To MAJOR GENERAL FRANK R. McCOY   October 20, 1939
Confidential   Washington, D.C.

My dear McCoy: For some reason I did not see the citation of the Roosevelt Medal award to you,[1] and was first advised of what happened by reading an editorial commending your splendid service. As a matter of fact I have not yet seen the citation, and had the Press Section looking it up for me yesterday. But without further delay I must write you and tell you that while I understand you were paid high compliments and tributes, nevertheless from my point of view, you should have a much more impressive reward for your services in the broad field of international affairs. I know that you are delightfully situated at present, but I want to see you render a much greater service to the country.

This may be bad news for you, but I was talking to the Secretary of War day before yesterday about the propriety of speaking to the President with a view to having a trip for you to England and France financed, though you ostensibly went over purely as a civilian. I would value very highly your report on things military, rather than political, as they appear to you during the next six weeks. You have the contacts in both England and France and you have the military knowledge along with broad vision and sound judgment, to make you the most valuable agent the American Army could send over at the present time, for the purpose of securing helpful information. Of course you will treat this as confidential.[2]

With my congratulations and affectionate regards,   Faithfully yours,

G. C. Marshall

LC/ F. R. McCoy Papers

1. McCoy was to be awarded a Roosevelt Memorial Association medal on October 27, 1939, the eighty-first anniversary of Theodore Roosevelt's birth. The citation characterized McCoy as a "soldier and diplomat, working for his country without fanfare of trumpets or consideration of reward." The Roosevelt medals for 1939 were also awarded to agricultural chemist George Washington Carver and to poet and author Carl Sandburg. (*New York Times,* October 9, 1939, p. 21.)

2. McCoy replied that the proposed trip "gives me a fine feeling of anticipation." (McCoy to Marshall, October 23, 1939, GCMRL/ G. C. Marshall Papers [Pentagon Office, Selected].) Approval was apparently not forthcoming, as McCoy did not make the trip.

To Major General Walter C. Sweeney   October 23, 1939
[Washington, D.C.]

Dear Sweeney: Just read your note of October 19 and I am writing to tell you most confidentially—for your eye only—what our plans are for the Third Division.[1]

I have directed that the time of the concentration of the Division be delayed, and for the same reason you present in your letter—the winter rains. On the other hand, we must get busy, and at the moment the Navy is working on the proposition—which I have put to them—for a landing operation. The idea is, the entire Third Division to be embarked in Puget Sound, partially on transports and partially on chartered shipping—and landing somewhere on the California coast between Santa Barbara and San Francisco. The exact point to be a secret. We are asking the Navy to turn out a cruiser division, a destroyer division and a couple of airplane carriers, and to cooperate with our GHQ Air Force Wing with some long distance reconnaissance seaplanes. The timing is the question of the moment. We are proposing to them the first part of January, but it may be they will be forced to give us early December. But the further point to the matter—and this must be regarded as most confidential until the very last moment—the Division will remain in the South until the rains break in the Northwest.

I have used the expression confidential and for your eye only because the problem in these matters is not the maneuvers so much as it is a question of meeting the political pressures. I spend my time now personally fighting a rear guard action to protect the concentrations we are about to carry out in the Southeast, against home station influences, and also against pressures to move the concentrations to the other areas. You will understand this situation.   Faithfully yours,

GCMRL/G. C. Marshall Papers (Pentagon Office, Selected)

1. Sweeney commanded the Third Division at Fort Lewis, Washington. He had written that it would be advantageous for the Third Division field training to be located in the South rather than at Fort Lewis. The weather at Fort Lewis was mostly rainy and chilly from November through February, and if concentrated there half of the personnel would be living in permanent quarters and half in tents. (Sweeney to Marshall, October 19, 1939, GCMRL/G. C. Marshall Papers [Pentagon Office, Selected].)

SPEECH TO THE NATIONAL GUARD ASSOCIATION   October 27, 1939
OF THE UNITED STATES[1]   Baltimore, Maryland

I trust that what may be said will be considered as off the record. To be perfectly honest, there has actually been no time to prepare for this talk today. We have been busy up to the last moment before coming here, and all the hours counted on for preparation proved not to be available when they actually arrived. I was unwilling, however, to farm out to somebody else the preparation of these remarks, so I am talking without notes with due apology if the remarks are disjointed.

. . . In the first place, the situation today, insofar as concerns the development of the Army, and particularly the National Guard, resolves itself into a matter of timing. We have the consideration of plans leading on into the future which must be developed with a view toward continuity of policy. We have the affairs of the moment, where, as we all know, in this present world situation the element of time is the great and dominant factor which influences everything we do. This fact has particular application, not only to the recently authorized increase in strength—and further contemplated increases which we hope will be authorized—but to the actual training of the new men that we are bringing in at this time.

To illustrate—under the old scheme of training, which we have followed for years, new men taken into service at this time might go until next summer, and certainly as long as next May, without ever having fired a rifle. Think of it, 45,000 new men and possibly 126,000 new men, in uniform and being trained, but having to wait at least six months before having the experience of firing a weapon.

Now, however, in the opinion of the War Department, the time and the temper of the world does not permit a continuation of the old training policy. We have to move more rapidly. Just how we can carry out more rapid and effective training is, of course, another problem. It might be said in that connection that we recognize the fact that training conditions vary throughout the United States. There is a vast difference in the training problem of a National Guard regiment concentrated in a city like New York and a regiment scattered by units over a great part of a state like Texas.

The way units are trained and the way training plans can be carried out are bound to vary in different localities, especially in reference to the seven days now authorized for field training. For some units it might be convenient to have the concentration for a continuous week. For others such a concentration may be utterly impossible, and such units may have to utilize the additional training time on a day by day or week-end basis, or by some other means that are adaptable to local conditions.

Consequently, the War Department intends to leave decisions in the management of training affairs to the judgment of the several states so that training can be conducted in the way best suited to any particular locality, in the manner best adapted to the employment conditions which obtain, and with due regard to the climatic factor, the latter being a most serious consideration in the northern states, especially so for troops located in large cities, like New York City and Chicago.

So the major factor, as far as the National Guard particularly is concerned, is the time element which involves two distinct problems. The first is that of rapidly raising companies above their past small maintenance strength in order that they may be more workable and complete; and have an immediate availability greater than has been the case in the past; and finally to have a strength reserve to protect against personnel losses which will always be very heavy among troops that are not well seasoned. The second problem is that of training these new men—and the old ones too—above and beyond that which is possible on an armory floor.

Let me digress for a moment to talk about training in general. I have served and helped with the training of the National Guard in a great many parts of the United States—in the old days in Pennsylvania, later in New York and in Massachusetts, down in Florida, in Virginia, out in the West and in the Far West, in the Northwest, and more recently in Illinois, which also brought me in contact with the troops from Michigan and Wisconsin.

The methods, the procedure and the ingenuity displayed vary in each locality. Those who have travelled throughout the country during the training year, like General Leach here, and the present Chief of the National Guard Bureau, General Blanding, are thoroughly familiar with that condition.[2] I am, however, too often impressed with the fact that the officers of a particular locality know very little about what is done in other places, except as they may pick up details by hearsay at a convention like this. I am also impressed at each new experience with the different methods of training that are employed and with the variations in efficiency that result from the methods.

It is possible that in our training plans we haven't displayed nearly enough ingenuity either from the viewpoint of providing interest to the man, or from that of taking full advantage of training opportunities.

I am coming to the question of equipment a little later, but I would like to make one reference to it in connection with training. We are hopeful to receive funds that will permit us to procure for the National Guard a certain percentage of their peace strength requirement for transportation. We have just placed an order which will provide most of the peace-time authorization of four-wheel drive vehicles for the divisions of the Regular Army that are now concentrating and for the corps troops that are to be a part of that concentration.

It takes a long time to obtain motor transportation. Until we have it in hand we naturally can't proceed with full maneuvers. When you consider the 18 National Guard divisions of Infantry alone, disregarding for a moment the special troops and also the antiaircraft units that are absolutely dependent on motors for transportation of their equipment, you can see it is very important that a percentage of transportation considerably above the present allotment be available in case of mobilization. Otherwise, judging from our experience in dealing with even the fast-moving industrial process in America, a long period of months would elapse before, to use one of the typical Washingtonian expressions, we could implement these divisions so that they could do business.

The public may think that as long as a soldier can walk, he can still get through to his objective, but it overlooks the fact that he can't carry a cannon, a field range, ammunition, or all of the rest of the impedimenta that goes with the division. We feel that there should be an adequate percentage of transportation provided in peace so as to be immediately available in event of mobilization.

That same transportation, I believe, plays quite an important part in facilitating training during the period of the year other than during summer field training concentrations. In those places where I have served with the Guard, I have noticed the desire of the organization commanders—the efforts they make without funds, without equipment—to get off on weekends for various forms of training. Apparently, where the terrain is available for the smaller units to work, given the transportation, given a decent allowance of gasoline for the vehicles, given some small additional pay arrangement, tremendous progress can be made toward the development of a high state of field efficiency in time of peace.

It appears that in the armories there is much to be done. Recently, in talking to a convention of the Illinois National Guard, where it was possible to speak very frankly because I was one of them, I said something which I believe now just as strongly or even more so than I did then—that if we might develop in the Guard, in the armories, a custom, a tradition, a habit that when the drill hour comes, everything from the attic to the cellar should be conducted on a military basis comparable almost to that of West Point.

I always remember an incident, in connection with my experiences in Illinois, where we developed a system of division inspections of regiments, an hour and fifty-five minutes being the outside allowance for doing everything that was humanly possible to be done in the armory at that time— from the stores, the supplies, to the exhibition of the troops on the floor. Colonel Nelson,[3] who was G-3 of the division staff, met a janitor who had been in his battery in France. The man complained very bitterly over the fact that he had cleaned up the whole furnace and then the division commander and staff had failed to inspect his work. I think the general idea of the janitor was right. The same thought also carries through to produce more effective methods of training and develop ingenuity in the doing of it.

In the Regular Army at times we do not make sufficient use of our opportunities. As a matter of fact, we very often struggle too much with comparatively minor difficulties and forget the main objectives. The training of the civilian components is of such vast importance that we must develop our plans for training in a more efficient manner. We must accomplish more within the time available because it is too short to permit us to worry about minor difficulties. We need all the cleverness at our disposal to concentrate properly on the major objective.

Leaving the matter of the training for a moment and going into the general proposition of the recent concentrations that have already been announced in the papers, we believe that here again the time factor was dominant. The knowledge that has been common in the Army for generations, that the only way to learn how to do things properly is to get out on the ground and actually do them—an opportunity that we had been denied in the past through lack of appropriations which would permit tactical concentrations or maneuvers. In view of present world conditions, it was mandatory that something be done at once to increase the effectiveness of the Army. We proceeded first to reorganize the divisions, not because we wanted particularly to reorganize anything at the present moment, but because the then existing divisions were in such a state of incompleteness and the period of development of the new triangular division organization had already been stretched over such a period of time that it seemed the only wise course was to decide immediately to go ahead and accept an organization which would enable us at once to put complete divisions in the field.

After that decision, it still remained for us to find the means of carrying out the desired concentrations with the funds which were legally available. That was quite a problem. And it still remains quite a problem. But we have had wonderful cooperation from all sides which has made the problem easier of solution. I might at this time pay tribute to the President of your Association, who has cooperated with us in the most satisfactory manner.[4]

. . . Now, to go ahead a little bit further in what has been planned. As I have said, we will probably have corps concentrations with the necessary corps troops as soon as enough transportation has been delivered to make such concentrations possible. From that, we lead on to a general concentration involving somewhere in the neighborhood of 70,000 or 75,000 troops. Just where that will be held has not been determined as there is the big question of availability of terrain. We will also have in concentration the mechanized force and the cavalry division with some of the extra unattached cavalry regiments. We will eventually have in concentration the major portion of the mobile troops of the Regular establishment in the continental United States. In Army areas these various troops will be under the command of the Army Commander, although they may be divided so as to have opposing forces to fight each other. We see no great difficulty of allowing one Army commander to command two opposing forces as long as he doesn't get his G-3 information complicated, as it will probably facilitate keeping the two sides within reason as to terrain availability without having to adopt abnormal statements in the assumed situations.

There will not be one maneuver this winter but a series of maneuvers with varying strengths and arrangements of troops. Once we have reached the point where these divisions have enough transportation and have progressed sufficiently with their divisional training, we hope to have attached to them for a short period, key officers of the National Guard—division commanders with selected division staff officers and brigade commanders with at least one of their staff. It is planned to call these officers toward weekends to save time and to avoid causing them undue absence from their business. The plan is for them to follow the Regular officers through a few days of the maneuver to see how the machine runs and then to step in and function in their proper command or staff position so they can see exactly how it works when you have a trained animal with all his equipment and the necessary terrain.

This plan will be carried on in sequence in order to accommodate the various people involved. At the same time we will have to bring in officers of various grades of the Reserve Corps to give them training opportunities in the same manner.

In other words, as far as we can arrange it, that will be really our War College, certainly our Combat College for troop leading. It will be the first time, to use a naval term, that the Army fleet has been able to go to sea, and we are going to make the most of it in every way that we can.

There is a considerable discussion in the War Department as to the future organizational arrangements, and that, of course, becomes involved in what we have to do at the moment. As mentioned earlier, we have two factors to consider. One is the immediacy of things in the present world situation; and the other is fitting what we have, so far as we can, into an evenly-devised development towards the future of the Army in the United States.

As soon as military affairs are considered by Congress, I suppose there will be a great many discussions; there will be a great many views quite natural to any meeting of a legislative nature and equally common, I find, to any meeting of Army officers and very common to any group in the War Department staff.

The great problem we have in going before Congress is one of being able to present simply and understandably the general requirements and respective priorities. We know that there will be those who are intensely enthusiastic about mechanized troops because of what has been read as occurring in Poland. (Incidentally, we know quite a bit about the Poland campaign now, although our information still seems very superficial.) We also know there will be proponents of air power and its various methods.

. . . The Air program has not been discussed because fortunately for us it is in a well-rounded state of development—the mechanics, the young pilots and the planes; the whole thing is balancing up in a very satisfactory manner. So we haven't had that burden at the present time.

The most important question at the present moment is the types of planes that should be ordered in the future. We are naturally very deeply interested in knowing what has actually happened abroad and what may happen in the next few months before we commit ourselves to any fundamental changes or to any large orders. In the same way, we are deeply interested in regard to the mechanized forces, in regard to the corps troops, in regard to all the basic factors in the Army. . . .

GCMRL/G. C. Marshall Papers (Pentagon Office, Speeches)

1. Approximately 80 percent of the speech transcript is printed here. Omitted portions include some introductory comments, a discussion of the concentration at Camp Jackson, transportation problems, and Marshall's experiences at the 1936 and 1937 maneuvers, and a brief closing remark. The transcript noted at two places that portions of the speech had been off the record at General Marshall's request.

2. Brigadier General George E. Leach had been chief of the National Guard Bureau from December 1931 to November 1935. Major General Albert H. Blanding had been chief of the National Guard Bureau since January 1936.

3. Lieutenant Colonel Leroy E. Nelson had been G-3 at Thirty-third Division headquarters in Chicago when Marshall was senior instructor with the Illinois National Guard.

4. Brigadier General James C. Dozier, the adjutant general of South Carolina, was president of the National Guard Association of the United States. The next day Brigadier General Walter A. DeLamater, commander of the Eighty-seventh Brigade in New York City, was elected president of the association.

CONTINGENT plans for operations against Japan had been made by the summer of 1924, when the Joint Board issued Joint War Plan Orange. The plan emphasized an offensive naval war in the Pacific with the Philippines as the main base. From Manila Bay the United States would establish itself in the western Pacific "in strength superior to that of Japan." But by the mid-1930s, Japan's growing power had forced the planners to conclude that that nation could be defeated only by a long and costly war. The Philippines would probably be lost early in such a conflict, and the United States would have to reduce Japan's bases one at a time, beginning with those in the Marshall and Caroline islands. (Louis Morton, *Strategy and Command: The First Two Years*, a volume in the *United States Army in World War II* [Washington: GPO, 1962], pp. 28–30; Maurice Matloff and Edwin M. Snell, *Strategic Planning for Coalition Warfare, 1941–1942*, a volume in the *United States Army in World War II* [Washington: GPO, 1953], p. 2.)

Revisions of Plan Orange, however, continued to emphasize Manila Bay as the main outlying base of operations. In the late 1930s, changing world political conditions forced United States planners to reevaluate their strategic assumptions and to plan for coalition warfare. After enumerating possible contingencies, the Joint Board in April 1939 called for a series of war plans, each applicable to a different situation. As the various nations were designated by colors in the army-navy plans, coalitions naturally suggested a rainbow. Rainbow 1 was basic and preliminary to the execution of the other four plans; it provided for the defense of the Western Hemisphere north of 10° south latitude, including protection of the United States, its possessions, and its sea-borne trade. While Rainbow 1 assumed the United States to be without major allies, Rainbow 2 assumed that the United States, Great Britain, and France would act in concert, wherein the United States would have limited participation in continental Europe but would undertake offensive operations in the Pacific. Rainbow 3, while similar to 2, assumed no assistance from Great Britain and France. Rainbow 4 extended Rainbow 1 to include the entire Western Hemisphere. The most extensive of the plans, Rainbow 5 was like 2 in that it assumed the collaboration of Great Britain and France, but unlike 2 the United States would engage in major offensive operations in Africa and Europe in order to defeat Germany and Italy as soon as possible. Following the defeat of the European Axis, a major offensive would be launched in the Pacific. (Morton, *Strategy and Command*, pp. 67–72.)

War in Europe in September 1939 spurred United States strategists to develop Rainbow 2 further. The plan fit the situation since Great Britain and France would probably fight Germany in Europe, leaving the United States to defend the western Pacific. "Throughout the winter of 1939–1940, the period of the 'phony war,' the joint planners sought to develop plans to meet the Rainbow 2 contingency." (Ibid., p. 73.)

In a memorandum to Admiral Harold R. Stark drafted by the G-3 division, Marshall proposed a joint landing exercise "on the West Coast in early January, 1940, an operation closely simulating the possibilities of portions of the Rainbow Plan now being developed." Marshall suggested that the Third Division should embark from Puget Sound, rendezvous with the naval contingent off the California coast, and then conduct a joint landing operation somewhere between Santa Barbara and San Francisco. Air Corps units, naval reconnaissance planes, and mobile ground forces should defend the coast. Marshall was "especially interested in the functioning of the Joint Army and Navy staff in the planning and in the actual landing and supporting operations. For the Army air forces and the land-based Naval Aviation the exercise should be productive of important lessons. Finally, the exercise should be a genuinely practical test of the principles and procedures set forth in 'Joint Action of the Army and Navy.'" (Marshall Memorandum to Chief of Naval Operations, November 7, 1939, NA/RG 165 [OCS, 19715–94].) ★

To Lieutenant General Albert J. Bowley   November 9, 1939
[Washington, D.C.]

Dear Bowley: There has been mailed to you as Army Commander a copy of a memorandum I sent to the Chief of Naval Operations, regarding the proposed landing operation by the Third Division in January. A copy has also been furnished General DeWitt.[1] I think the memorandum is self-explanatory so far as the rough outline of the joint operation is concerned; but nothing in it referred to future plans for the Third Division.

We have in mind that on the completion of the landing operation the Division should go into camp either at Ord or San Luis Obispo for combined maneuvers to include such other troops as are available in the Corps Area. Then, after the rains have ceased in the Northwest, the Division would be returned to Fort Lewis,—whether by boat, road, or rail I do not know.

As for the Joint Army and Navy operation, we were hopeful of arranging a date in early January. This is very important from the viewpoint of the Wing of the GHQ Air Force on the West Coast, as they will be on the verge of what will almost amount to an emasculation in the expansion and special training involved in carrying out the tremendous augmentation for the Air Corps. The Navy people told me yesterday that Admiral Bloch[2] had found a spot in his previously arranged schedule, I think in the first week in February. I expressed deep concern over this delay because of the embarrassment it would cause our Air Corps, but refrained from mentioning the fact that the delay in the departure of the Third Division from Fort Lewis merely prolonged their period of waiting in the inclement weather of the Northwest winter. I was then informed that by considerable rearrangement Admiral Bloch might be able to have his people participate about January 22d, which would be a better date for our Air Corps than the one in February.

I am giving you this information as a background for your discussions with Admiral Bloch or his representatives. Please have in mind that this affair is our proposal, and involves a considerable disarrangement of the carefully blocked out plans for the United States Fleet. It would not have been possible to arrange, as a matter of fact we could not have had it even given consideration, except for the fact that Admiral Stark is very anxious to cooperate with the Army in every way possible, and he, therefore, directed that this be managed in some way or other.

I would appreciate your having someone on your staff keep General DeWitt advised as to the progress of the discussions or plans, as he naturally will be deeply interested.   Faithfully yours,

GCMRL/G. C. Marshall Papers (Pentagon Office, Selected)

1. Bowley was due to retire November 30, and Major General John L. De Witt was scheduled to succeed him as commander of the Fourth Army and the Ninth Corps Area.
2. Admiral Claude C. Bloch (U.S.N.A., 1899) was commander in chief of the United States Fleet.

To Charles Johnston[1]

November 10, 1939
[Washington, D.C.]

Dear Johnston: I have just received your note of November 9th, with its pleasant invitation for me to address the Philadelphia Chapter of the VMI Alumni, the date to be set by me.

I would be very glad to meet the Alumni around Philadelphia, but the truth of the matter is I have stretched myself to the limit here for three months, not having an afternoon off or even a Saturday or Sunday until I feel I must conserve my energies and time for the mass of business, now heavily budgetary, that is developing, as well as for the inspections of the field training just opening.

I have talked to the Alumni at Leesburg, near Richmond, at Norfolk, and spent a day and a night at the VMI the October 21st week-end,[2] and I do not believe I can undertake any other engagements for some time to come.

As soon as the weather clears, or I happen to find myself in the vicinity of Philadelphia, I will let you know.   Faithfully yours,

GCMRL/G. C. Marshall Papers (Pentagon Office, General)

1. Johnston, a 1902 graduate of Virginia Military Institute, was an insurance underwriter in Philadelphia.

2. Marshall attended Homecoming activities at Virginia Military Institute on Saturday, October 21. He reviewed the garrison and watched his alma mater's football team defeat the University of Virginia (16–13). He and Mrs. Marshall left Lexington by car the next morning. (Marshall to Major General Charles E. Kilbourne, October 18, 1939, GCMRL/G. C. Marshall Papers [Pentagon Office, General]; *The V.M.I. Cadet,* October 24, 1939, p. 1.)

SPEECH TO THE COMMITTEE ON   November 16, 1939
COMMUNITY CHEST   Washington, D.C.

The obligation to make a formal talk on an occasion of this kind, even on a military subject with which I am familiar is a very embarrassing one to me, but I find myself this morning in a different frame of mind, for a very excellent reason. Normally my discussions in public have relation to the national defense, as that is my occupation, and very active responsibility in the present world situation. I feel that it is my duty to discuss the various aspects of national defense in public, so far as practicable, for the general information of the citizens of the United States. But though that is my business and I am a soldier by profession, I am frank to confess to a decided reluctance to be forced invariably to a discussion of matters pertaining to the tragedies of war, not to mention the appalling expenditures necessarily involved.

But I have found comfort in the belief that what we are doing in the War Department and in the Army generally, will serve to make impossible the ghastly situation in which we found ourselves in 1917–18, with the attendant unnecessary wastage of young men to overcome the almost criminal lack of proper preparation. And there is the further very comforting belief that what we are doing now contributes in direct proportion to the soundness and extent of our preparation, towards rendering improbable the necessity for involving this country in war.

I seem to be involving myself in a discussion of matters pertaining to the national defense, but that is far from my purpose; I merely wish to emphasize the fact, or rather feeling on my part, that it is a gratifying experience to find my duty this morning pointing towards the humane and benevolent purposes of the local Community Chest.

With an assemblage of this particular character, it hardly seems necessary for me to dilate on the importance of the project now under way. I would suppose that no other group in Washington is as well aware of the necessities of the case,—the importance of this campaign, as the members of this gathering this morning.

It seems to me, however, that there is a phase to this matter which it might be well to mention. In this particular day and year, the success of the effort to raise the allotted sum of the Community Chest is of the utmost public importance. It is, in a large measure, a test of the attitude of the more fortunate of our people in meeting the problems of the less fortunate. It is in a measure a test of whether all the helpful measures are to be on a purely legislative basis rather than the personal and human obligation of the citizen in his community life.

There is another phase somewhat related to what I have just said which everyone I think recognizes as very important, and that is the matter of public morale. As a professional soldier, I know that high morale is the strongest and most powerful factor in the Army, just as lack of morale will bring about the defeat of almost any army however well armed. The morale of the people of this country, particularly at the present critical period in the world's history, is of tremendous importance, I think, and certainly the purposes of the Community Chest operate directly to build up morale, at least to prevent its destruction.

I think the average citizen is in thorough sympathy with everything concerned in the Community Chest enterprise, but he merely requires personal attention to overcome the procrastination that dogs most of us in affairs not specifically pertaining to our daily business. Therefore, those who are working so hard to carry out a successful campaign with the Community Chest in the District of Columbia this fall are not only entitled to a great deal of credit, but are even more entitled to our strong, active support, and for that reason I was glad to accept the invitation to talk at this particular luncheon.

GCMRL/G. C. Marshall Papers (Pentagon Office, Speeches)

E VEN while expanding enlisted manpower, Congress was reluctant to increase significantly the number of Regular Army officers; this meant that Marshall would have to call into active service an increasing number of men from the Officers' Reserve Corps for temporary duty. Since August 1935, the Thomason Act (see note, p. 54) had permitted the army to select and train several thousand Reserve Corps second lieutenants and to offer permanent commissions to a few each year. The chief source of such men was the college Reserve Officers' Training Corps program, which had granted just over 100,000 Reserve commissions since 1920.

In the late 1930s, interest in the R.O.T.C. was growing, and the number of students enrolled, at both the college-university and the high-school levels, had increased by approximately 11,000 (or 6 percent) from the autumn of 1938 to the autumn of 1939.

While of great potential value, this growth presented Marshall with immediate problems. The army's own expansion required more officers; it was difficult to spare more for the R.O.T.C. program. During the 1939–40 academic year, 5 percent of the entire Regular Army officer corps (824 men) were on R.O.T.C. duty. The army had permitted no increase in the number of units (365) in the program since 1938, despite applications for new units from 48 colleges and universities and 108 high schools. In addition, the facilities and equipment available to many existing units were of dubious quality. The army spent only $4.7 million on various R.O.T.C. projects during fiscal year 1939; $5 million was being requested for fiscal year 1941. (Statistics on the R.O.T.C. were presented to the House Appropriations Committee. See *Military Establishment Appropriation Bill for 1941, Hearings* [Washington: GPO, 1940], pp. 752–74. For further information see Marshall's testimony regarding the R.O.T.C. on pp. 167–68.)

On October 28, 1939, Marshall traveled to Indianapolis to speak to the Indiana Reserve Officers' Association. (There is no draft or transcript of this address in the Marshall papers.) At the gathering, he met a friend from the Infantry School, Colonel John F. Landis (U.S.M.A., 1910), who had been professor of military science and tactics at Indiana University since May 1938. A year previously, Landis had written to Marshall to explain the "strange situation" that the university's R.O.T.C. program faced. "Though the basic course here is compulsory and the authorities are friendly towards the unit, our training facilities are pitiful." Landis strongly advised that the War Department find a way of helping the institution to build an armory of a quality comparable to those at the University of Illinois and Purdue University, with which Marshall was familiar. "With such an armory it is no exaggeration to say that the value of our unit could be doubled." (Landis to Marshall, October 19, 1938, GCMRL/G. C. Marshall Papers [Pentagon Office, General].)

Following the Indianapolis meeting, Landis wrote that he hoped Marshall would find the time in the near future to examine the country's R.O.T.C. situation in detail. "After having spent a year on ROTC duty I have reached the conclusion that as regards their potentialities our ROTC units are, conservatively speaking, perhaps 25 or 30% efficient." Marshall replied, "Write me a little thesis on the subject. . . . I am much interested at the present time in the effective development of the R.O.T.C. and its closer amalgamation with the Reserve Corps." (Landis to Marshall, October 30, 1939; Marshall to Landis, November 1, 1939, ibid.) Landis sent his paper within the week, saying: "I fear that my conclusions about the ROTC situation may be different from any you have heretofore received. . . . During the recent government building program we should have obtained suitable armories for all our principal ROTC units. We missed a big bet." (Landis to Marshall, November 6, 1939, ibid. The editors have been unable to locate a copy of Landis's paper.)

On November 14, Marshall spoke on the R.O.T.C. problem at the meeting in Washington, D.C., of the National Association of State Universities. He told the assembled delegates: "I have felt that for the R.O.T.C. the last period of twenty-odd years since the World War was a period of evolution, as it were, in an attempt to find the best method to integrate that sort of training into the ordinary life of the country. I believe that the progress has been excellent, but there remains room for further improvement, and I always feel embarrassed as to War Department limitations in this respect."

He emphasized the difficulties the army faced not only in finding an adequate number of officers for R.O.T.C. duty, but also in finding those who had "the personality, the attraction, and the ability to accomplish his result without aid of the authority to give direct commands." Moreover, these officers had to be capable of adapting themselves to a college life which was "quite different from anything that he has had up to that time." Marshall invited the delegates to give the War Department their opinions on how to meet the pressing problems of "where to get the officers, how to provide the acceptable ones and also what should be the attitude of the War Department in relation to the colleges and universities in case we were called in some more serious crises to mobilize." (The transcript of Marshall's address contains only about 800 words, but he spoke off the record for some time. The speech was published in *Transactions and Proceedings of the National Association of State Universities* 37[1939]: 211-13.) ★

To Colonel John F. Landis   November 20, 1939
                                                          [Washington, D.C.]

Dear Landis: Thanks for preparing and for sending me your thesis on the ROTC. I have had it gone over by the particular staff officers concerned with the ROTC here in the War Department, and have given it a careful reading myself. There is not a complete agreement with you in all your points, but there is in regard to many of them.

I am inclined to think that a great difficulty with the ROTC lies in the fact that certain units were authorized too quickly, that is before they had the necessary facilities, so that we have them on our hands and they have not the means for the proper functioning of the unit. That seems to be the case somewhat at the University of Indiana, and it is a very difficult one for the

War Department to meet. The complication about all building problems lies in the fact that the precedent carries over into the National Guard, and a similar pressure is developed in connection with the Reserve Corps. You can see that if we become involved in a building problem that includes ROTC or National Guard, and maybe in the future certain facilities for the Reserve Corps, there will be practically no money left for the actual Army. Your own experience will indicate to you something of what is possible—witness the poverty stricken condition under which we operated at Benning for years and years.

I had a very pleasant conversation, entirely unexpected with Dr. Wells the other day, and also a gracious note from him following my visit to Indianapolis.[1]

With warm regards,   Faithfully yours,

GCMRL/G. C. Marshall Papers (Pentagon Office, General)

1. Herman B Wells, the president of Indiana University, had written to express his appreciation at hearing Marshall's address to the Reserve Officers' Association of Indiana on October 28. "I mingled with the crowd for some time following the dinner and found approbation of your remarks quite general. It was amazing what a feeling of confidence you instilled in the audience. On all sides, there was general agreement that our national defense is in safe hands." (Wells to Marshall, November 13, 1939, GCMRL/G. C. Marshall Papers [Pentagon Office, General].)

Wells had invited Marshall to speak to the student body at Indiana University while he was in the Indianapolis area for the Indiana Reserve Officers' Association meeting. "I am very intent on obtaining adequate R.O.T.C. armory facilities for our unit. At present we have none. Frankly, recent state appropriations to us have been so generous that I fear that it is going to be difficult to obtain additional amounts for construction. I can think of nothing that would stimulate interest in our R.O.T.C. more than your coming here and making a short convocation address, broadcast over a state-wide hook-up." (Wells to Marshall, October 2, 1939, ibid.) Marshall declined the invitation due to previously scheduled engagements. (Marshall to Wells, October 4, 1939, ibid.)

To Brigadier General Asa L. Singleton[1]   November 22, 1939
Confidential   [Washington, D.C.]

Dear Singleton: With reference to the President's visit to Warm Springs, I was talking over the 'phone to Watson just before they left.[2] I suggested that he go over and take a look at Benning, and he immediately said: "I will take the President over there."

Now, my point is this: I have seen the President there once or twice as a private citizen and as a Governor, and each time it was for some review effect. I do not believe he gets much out of that. So I suggest that if you can get Watson over to see some interesting field stuff—and without personal labor on his part, then you might pave the way for the President to see something of that nature which would awaken his interest in the practical training of the Army, just as the Navy has stimulated his interest over their big annual maneuvers.

I make this suggestion—that whatever arrangement is made, no one press him to see this or that or understand this or that; that whatever is furnished him in the way of data be on one sheet of paper, with all high-sounding language eliminated, and with very pertinent paragraphed under-lined headings; that a little sketch of ordinary page size is probably the most effective method, as he is quickly bored by papers, by lengthy discussions, and by anything short of a few pungent sentences of description. You have to intrigue his interest, and then it knows no limit. If you have a good sergeant with the gift of restrained gab, fine looking and impressive, you might work him in the plot and the proper moment beside the car. I have found that the ordinary Army method of presenting things to the President gets us nowhere and rather irritates him. I leave the solution to you.[3]

I am hoping that I can get down to Benning around the 7th or 8th of December, but this will depend entirely on an appointment with the President and a date for a Military Committee hearing. I want to stop first at Bragg, then at Columbia, and then if I can possibly arrange it, spend three days entirely with you—if this is convenient. I will write you later when I know more about my plans.   Faithfully yours,

GCMRL/G. C. Marshall Papers (Pentagon Office, Selected)

1. Singleton was the commandant of the Infantry School at Fort Benning, Georgia.
2. Brigadier General Edwin M. Watson was the president's military aide.
3. Writing later of his disappointment that President Roosevelt did not visit Fort Benning during his trip to Warm Springs, Singleton surmised that "the Presidential party left Georgia earlier than was planned. This is just a guess on my part premised on Watson's telephonic promise that he would phone me later, which he failed to do for reasons unknown to me. We indicated to Watson the many interesting new training features under way here. We learned of their departure through the press." (Singleton to Marshall, December 3, 1939, GCMRL/G. C. Marshall Papers [Pentagon Office, Selected].)

MEMORANDUM FOR GENERAL SHEDD[1]   November 22, 1939
                                                   [Washington, D.C.]

Subject: Military Police.

I have glanced over your study of November 10th on the subject of Military Police, and it is not sufficiently along the line I had in mind.[2] For example, the requirement, "Should have prior military service with a record of excellent character" practically eliminates the type of men I visualized. It seems to me, that for the control of younger men in the Army, particularly for the type of control we found essential in the rear zones of the army in the Meuse-Argonne, and all over the SOS [Service of Supply], we want men over thirty and up to forty and forty-five, men of some education, men who are keenly desirous of doing something for the country and yet are too old for active troop service and do not have a particular special knowledge so they could be commissioned at their age; men who would be tolerant with the wisdom of years in dealing with the younger soldiers and could advise and guide them, rather than merely tell them "No" and then use a club or a gun to carry out this or that prohibition.

I would have no objection to an older man who had had previous military service, particularly if he were a fine non-com.; but ordinarily I would prefer a man of the other type. We are now being pressed from every direction to find some job for men of some position, in connection with the Army. We do not want to give them Reserve commissions, certainly not at the present time, and we always have to be careful how we open up that gate at any time. It seems to me that the Military Police has fine possibilities. I proposed such a scheme in Paris in July, 1917, and I still think it would have saved General Pershing a thousand headaches that he later suffered from; and it would have been a profound satisfaction to the tremendous number of fine men in this country who found little to do other than make one-minute talks, or worked with the Red Cross or the Y.M.C.A.[3]

Have this looked over again, please. I do not mean merely to confirm my idea; but I would like it considered and analyzed.

GCMRL/G. C. Marshall Papers (Pentagon Office, General)

1. Brigadier General William E. Shedd (U.S.M.A., 1907) had been assistant chief of staff, G-1, since October 1939.

2. The editors have not found the study on military police to which Marshall refers.

3. In a September letter to *Chicago Daily Tribune* publisher Robert R. McCormick, Marshall mentioned his recommendation to General Pershing of July 14, 1917: "I suggested that they cable the United States to raise a group of about 10,000 men over thirty and under forty-five for the Military Police Corps. I think that men of years and consequent judgment in a Military Police force would be much more effective for our type of Army than such an organization composed of young fellows with the natural intolerance of youth, quick resentment to gibes, and too quick resource to violent execution of authority."

He further observed that when he was senior instructor with the Illinois National Guard (1933–36), he "had the men of the Military Police Company of the 33d Division imbued with the idea that their primary job was to assist and guide individuals and units into their proper slots in the deployments of movements. I had in mind that the officers of the Military Police Company should be of very high grade and be kept informed by G-3 of the tactical movements under way, and charged with the partial responsibility for assisting in carrying out such movements, and also to act as a dispatching service, as it were, to report the progress of movements from critical point to critical point." (Marshall to McCormick, September 2, 1939, GCMRL/G. C. Marshall Papers [Pentagon Office, General].)

To Colonel Morris E. Locke[1]   November 27, 1939
                                                                [Washington, D.C.]

Dear Locke: I found your note of the 24th when I reached home Saturday. I will be delighted to have lunch with you, but there seems to be no
prospect this week, as I am involved in lunching Brazilians, National Guard
Executives, Army and Corps Commanders, etc., etc.[2] I will call you up and
make a date at the first opportunity.

   Katherine and I have been scouting for an opportunity to return your call
of last spring, and the failure has been mine because I am rather adamant
about getting in a horse-back ride in the evening. I find that I have to keep
in real training to meet the pressure of this business and I have not let
anything get in the way of a daily ride, though it is usually done in the dusk.
The same thing occurs on Saturday afternoon and by Sunday I am frankly
so much in need of complete relaxation that I have failed completely in my
social duties. Though, incidentally, I have been out of town on official
engagements every Saturday and Sunday except for the last one, for almost
three months, so I am not so lazy as would appear.

   I want very much to see you and I want Katherine and Grace to meet. I
will telephone you.   Faithfully yours,

GCMRL/G. C. Marshall Papers (Pentagon Office, Selected)

   1. Locke, a graduate of Virginia Military Institute in 1899, had retired in November 1930
and was living in Washington, D.C. He had recently invited Marshall to lunch. (Locke to
Marshall, November 24, 1939, GCMRL/G. C. Marshall Papers [Pentagon Office, Selected].)
   2. On Monday, November 27, Marshall hosted a luncheon for the ten Brazilian Army
officers who had arrived at Bolling Field the previous day with the United States Army officers and men returning from their goodwill trip to Brazil. Six of the Brazilian Army officers
remained in the United States to study and examine American military aircraft equipment
and bases. (Washington *Evening Star,* November 27, 1939, p. A-5; *New York Times,* November 27, 1939, pp. 1, 9.)
   On Friday, December 1, General and Mrs. Marshall entertained at home the army and
corps area commanders who were in Washington November 30–December 1 for a conference.
The corps area commanders met with Marshall and other War Department officials to discuss
plans for the winter training program and reorganization of combat forces. (Washington
Times-Herald, November 25, p. 2-A, and December 1, 1939, p. 3-C.)

O N November 27 and 30 the chief of staff testified before a special
session of the House Appropriations Committee regarding the necessity of Congress providing a supplemental appropriation of $120,000,000
for fiscal year 1940. The funds were essential, Marshall told the congressmen, to pay for increasing the strength of the Regular Army and the
National Guard under the president's executive order of September 8, for
equipping the reactivated units, for reinforcing the Panama Canal and
Puerto Rican garrisons, for improving the army's training program, and for

providing motor transportation for certain units.

In concluding his prepared remarks on November 27, Marshall reemphasized "the deficiencies which have existed for years in the training of our larger units. Of the total annual War Department appropriations we have usually been able to devote less than the proverbial one-tenth of 1 percent to this phase of our problem, and the annual average of all direct charges against training of every kind has for some years been less than 5 percent. The unsoundness of such a procedure, particularly in view of the present critical world situation, is evident, I believe, to all of us, and it is hoped that the Congress will decide that the Army should never again be permitted to return to the condition of ineffectiveness which results from such a policy." (House Appropriations Committee, *Emergency Supplemental Appropriation Bill for 1940, Hearings* [Washington: GPO, 1939], p. 4.)

Marshall was careful to explain in detail the request for $16,000,000 for motor vehicles already ordered. "That sum will furnish motor vehicles for the five new triangular divisions, for the corps troops for one Army corps and for certain G.H.Q. and Army troops. . . . There has been a great deal in the press about the Army having a streamlined division. The discussions have indicated that the division is one which is completely motorized and which, as a unit, can travel at a high rate of speed. However, these are not motorized divisions in that sense. The motors take the place of animals. In the old divisions the mule or the horse carried ammunition and drew machine guns and cannon and supply trains; the men rode on the caissons of the artillery or on the artillery horses. In the new divisions, if the gun goes by motor the men also go by motor; but the infantryman, the rifleman still walks, except when it becomes necessary to move him rapidly, then motor trains, if available, would be employed." (Ibid., p. 6.)

Although trucks were faster and less expensive to maintain than animals, the horse and mule were not wholly outmoded, and there were no plans to eliminate them completely. Marshall observed that the German Army had opened its assault on Poland with animal-drawn divisions. "We have to be careful that we do not cut down on our horse-drawn elements to the point where we will lose the knowledge, the technique of handling animals. In France, for example, lack of this knowledge cost us a large part of over 50,000 animal casualties. In contrast, almost every boy in this country knows how to handle a motor vehicle and many of them understand a great deal about the repair of motor equipment. But we only have a few who know how to handle animals, and blacksmiths or farriers are hard to find. So, we have to be careful that we do not go below the point where the knowledge of horse-drawn equipment and the care of animals would be seriously lacking. We might find ourselves in a serious predicament if we had to operate in a country where we would be forced to employ that type of transportation." (Ibid., p. 7.)

In his testimony on November 30, Marshall discussed in considerable detail the need for funding the large-scale maneuvers that the army had planned for the next eight months. The additional money was needed primarily to cover transportation costs—pay and rations being largely fixed whether the army was in garrison or on maneuvers. The United States Army's lack of experience in large-scale maneuvers during the two previous decades and its lack of specialized corps troops meant that "we have been forced to build up our technique of command and control and even our development of leadership, largely on a theoretical basis. We have, I believe, the best military school system for the training of officers in the world, but of necessity the instruction has had to be based largely on theoretical conceptions in relation to units larger than a brigade. This is a source of weakness, just as it would be a source of weakness for a football team never even to have had team practice until the day of the game. What appears satisfactory on paper too frequently we find quite impracticable in actual operations. Organization and planning, based too largely on theoretical grounds, result in cumbersome organizations, too large staffs and too lengthy and complicated orders.

"Training the ground forces of an army for actual campaign in battle is a difficult business at best, as there is little that can be done in time of peace to simulate closely the conditions under which troops operate in war. Therefore, it is all the more important that we make every effort to learn the practical business of troop leadership and teamwork, utilizing field maneuvers for this purpose, and especially to wash out the over-theoretical or academic conceptions. We must have more simplicity of procedure, and that requires teamwork, and teamwork is possible only if we have an opportunity to practice as a team." (Ibid., pp. 134–35.)

The American Expeditionary Forces of 1917–18, he reminded the committee, was fortunate in having had "allies to protect it for more than a year, while it found itself. The future problems of our Army visualize no such protected period for overcoming peacetime military deficiencies. We must be prepared to stand on our own feet." (Ibid., p. 138. The bill—appropriating $109,416,689—became law on February 12, 1940.) ★

MEMORANDUM FOR GENERAL GASSER   November 28, 1939
Secret   [Washington, D.C.]

Subject: Increase of Regular Establishment to 280,000.

In my appearance before the Bureau of the Budget, I gathered the idea from Mr. Smith that he was hopeful we would not press for further increase to 280,000.[1] Just what the attitude of the President is I do not know, but probably we will learn a little later.

In a conversation this morning with Mr. Woodring, I learned that he is hopeful, if the European situation does not develop into a fierce land struggle, that we will not have to press for a full increase to 280,000. He has in mind as a compromise figure about 20,000 more men, giving the Regular Establishment a strength of 245,000 or 250,000. However, he does not intend to give any indication of this until we are forced to come to a decision.

Of course the whole thing is going to depend on the state of the war in Europe at the time of the Committee hearings and the actual voting in Congress. My idea at the moment is that if things remain virtually as they are now we should fight hard to get at least as many more men (1) as may be necessary to cover the two antiaircraft regiments we have borrowed for from the Air Corps; (2) to fill out two more divisions, which will form the basis of the corps to be maintained in the South for winter training, (3) to provide the necessary corps troops for a second corps, (4) to provide for the necessary Regular Army component, if it is to be a split unit for a corps cavalry reconnaissance outfit for each of the remaining seven army corps.

This is my thought at the moment, and it seems best for me to give it to you in writing. However, I do not think we should allow to creep into a general understanding of the staff any idea that we are giving up on the proposal to get 280,000 men.

GCMRL/G. C. Marshall Papers (Pentagon Office, Selected)

1. Harold D. Smith was the director of the Bureau of the Budget. Marshall had appeared before the bureau on November 9, and on November 20 he and Smith had met with President Roosevelt at the White House.

TO BRIGADIER GENERAL CLARENCE S. RIDLEY December 1, 1939
[Washington, D.C.]

Dear Governor Ridley: Your suggestion that the Executive Order of September 5, 1939, as it relates to the Panama Canal Zone, be rescinded or modified, has been carefully considered, and I am of the opinion that no change should be made at this time. The present system appears to be working satisfactorily and I am sure that there need be no fear of complications under the administration of General Van Voorhis, who sails for the Canal Zone on December the 20th.[1]

In the present world situation, with war activities in both the western Pacific and on the eastern side of the Atlantic, together with the various methods of attack against shipping being used in the latter struggle, I am of the opinion that we should take no chance of misunderstanding or other complication that might possibly result in jeopardy to the Canal. Furthermore, a change such as proposed by you might have the effect of creating the impression that the necessity for safeguarding the Canal had become less important.

Also, there is this final consideration; everyone in the Zone is there in direct connection with the safeguarding of the operation of the Canal. It is not as if we were suddenly imposing arbitrary military control on a peaceful civil population, in possession of their homes and pursuing civil occupations. Those in the Zone must conform to the necessities of the Zone.   Faithfully yours,

GCMRL/G. C. Marshall Papers (Pentagon Office, General)

1. Control of the Canal Zone had been transferred to the commander of the Panama Canal Department by executive order in September. See Marshall to Stone, October 3, 1939, pp. 69–71. No incoming correspondence from Ridley was found in the Marshall papers.

To JAMES W. WADSWORTH   December 6, 1939
                                                  [Washington, D.C.]

My dear Senator:[1]   I have just received in the mail a reprint of your remarks of November 2d on the Neutrality Bill, for which I thank you.[2] As a matter of fact, I had in my mind a number of times the intention to write you a letter regarding what you said, how you said it, and the remarkable impression you made at the time; but I have been traveling so rapidly and away so much that I am becoming quite unreliable as to remembering what I want to do personally—officially the office keeps me straight, but personally I am failing myself at every turn.

As you know, I have long been a very honest and frank admirer of yours; I believe I have told you that I thought you understood more about the Army than most of the officers in the Army. Now, to see you reap at least a small morsel of the reward that should come to you for wisdom or judgment, or whatever you term good common sense in public affairs, and particularly for the unique reputation you enjoy among all public men and well informed citizens as to your standard of integrity, is very satisfying to me.

I am off this morning by air for an inspection trip of the Southeast, and hope to include two days' shooting with Dwight Davis at his plantation near Tallahassee, Florida.[3]

With warm regards,   Faithfully yours,

GCMRL/G. C. Marshall Papers (Pentagon Office, Selected)

1. Marshall had first met Wadsworth during the 1919 hearings on army reorganization. Wadsworth served as a Republican senator from New York between 1915 and 1927; since

1933 he had represented New York's Thirty-ninth District in the House of Representatives.

2. In a well-received speech on the floor of the House, Wadsworth spoke in favor of the proposed revisions to the Neutrality Act, saying in part: "I believe the Senate in its cash-and-carry provision at least approaches this difficult problem realistically and that if legislation can keep us out of war, this particular provision will do more in this direction than any other provision that can be drafted." (*Congressional Record,* 76th Cong., 2d sess., 85, pt. 2: 1310–12.)

3. Dwight F. Davis had been secretary of war from 1925 to 1929 and governor-general of the Philippines from 1929 to 1932. On Marshall's association with him, see *Papers of GCM,* 1: 343–44.

B EGINNING in November 1939, the army concentrated three divisions in the southern states for spring corps and army maneuvers: the First at Fort Benning, Georgia, the Fifth at Fort McClellan, Alabama, and the Sixth at Camp Jackson, South Carolina. Marshall left Washington, D.C., at noon on December 6, 1939, for a brief inspection of these troop concentrations. Stopping that night at Fort Bragg, North Carolina, he left the next day to inspect the Sixth Division at Camp Jackson. Covering the remainder of the 930 miles of his airplane trip, Marshall viewed troops at Fort Benning on December 8 and at Fort McClellan on December 9. Returning to Georgia for some leisure time, he was joined by Mrs. Marshall, who had been vacationing in the South.

Ever conscious of his and Mrs. Marshall's privacy, the chief of staff wrote to the commanders of these posts requesting that they schedule a minimum of social obligations. To the commandant of the Infantry School, he noted: "We want to be polite and we must be considerate of our old friends in Columbus, but if there is any possible way in which Katherine and I can have a little peaceful time without entertaining, it will be greatly appreciated." (Marshall to Brigadier General Asa L. Singleton, December 4, 1939, GCMRL/G. C. Marshall Papers [Pentagon Office, Selected].)

Canceling possible side trips to Texas and Florida, the Marshalls returned to Washington, D.C., by automobile on December 14. ★

To Major General William N. Haskell[1]   December 14, 1939
Personal and Confidential   [Washington, D.C.]

Dear Haskell: I found your letter of December 11th on my return to the office this afternoon from an inspection trip to the Southeast.

I recall Colonel Tobin, and am very glad to have your suggestion as to his possible appointment for the National Guard. So far we have done nothing in the matter and, strange to say, there has been very little pressure. I think this has been due largely to the fine attitude of avoidance of embarrassing the War Department in the present crisis. Of course there is push and pull, but I gather that it is remarkably little in comparison to previous years.[2]

I wish you would write me a personal note of your own reactions to this extra training we had to hand out to the National Guard. It was very difficult of management in the northern latitudes, and I am anxious to learn just what the reaction has been, as to efficiency gained, as to loss of time from absence of job, and as to employers. I would appreciate your writing.[3] Faithfully yours,

GCMRL/G. C. Marshall Papers (Pentagon Office, Selected)

1. Haskell (U.S.M.A., 1901) had been appointed a major general and commanding general of the New York National Guard in 1926 after his resignation from the Regular Army.

2. Haskell recommended Colonel Ralph C. Tobin of New York's 107th Infantry for the position of chief of the National Guard Bureau. "I am sure that he is experienced in National Guard matters; is non-political, and will cooperate with the Regular Army." On the selection process for a new chief, Haskell commented, "I understand there are a bunch of political hacks that are after the job in Washington, but I am sure that Colonel Tobin would not enter into any such competition." (Haskell to Marshall, December 11, 1939, GCMRL/G. C. Marshall Papers [Pentagon Office, Selected].) Within a week, Marshall appointed John F. Williams, one of the three National Guard colonels in the bureau's office since 1936, to be the new chief effective January 31, 1940.

3. National Guard training had been increased to two drills a week and the troops spent seven days in the field in one- to three-day stretches starting in early November. Haskell replied that the training succeeded in improving efficiency: morale was high and the improvised schedule provided local commanders with experience in planning and supply. Employers registered little opposition to the winter training; small businesses suffered the most, but corporations with large labor forces had few difficulties. He recommended that cold weather clothing and equipment be issued to the National Guard if Marshall contemplated another winter training period; the New York troops had borrowed equipment from the Civilian Conservation Corps. Haskell wanted to increase the number of annual drills from forty-eight to sixty, but cautioned that few men could attend drills two days per week. (*New York Times,* October 23, 1939, p. 3; Haskell to Marshall, December 21, 1939, NA/RG 407 [Classified, 353 (12-21-39)].)

To Mrs. John J. Singer   December 18, 1939
[Washington, D.C.]

My dear Marie: Katherine and I want you to come down and spend Christmas and New Years with us. Allene is coming from New York, also Clifton and Allen. Then Molly's boy friend is coming in the middle of the week to stay over New Year's day, and I think Allen's girl from Staunton, Virginia, is coming for a few days, so we will be a sort of Grand Hotel.[1]

I suggest that you come down the day before Christmas, Sunday, and stay until the day after New Years. I am being specific as to dates, very frankly because if I left Katherine to her own over-generous devices, she would wreck herself, and she has a very hard time ahead of her in January and February. So I want her to have as much complete freedom from any responsibility as possible. However much she will enjoy the Holidays, it is going to be a heavy strain on her and I do not want to over-crowd her. I know you will understand.

I got back here late Thursday from an inspection of the Southeast, which was pretty strenuous for me, followed by the diplomatic reception at the White House that night and a later supper at Mrs. Truxtun Beale's;[2] then a dinner with Admiral Stark the next night, and one with the Deputy Chief of Staff last night. Meanwhile, Katherine is violently engaged in trying to catch up with her Christmas obligations. Affectionately,

GCMRL/G. C. Marshall Papers (Pentagon Office, Selected)

1. Marie Marshall (Mrs. John J.) Singer was the chief of staff's sister. Mrs. Allene Tupper Wilkes was Mrs. Marshall's sister. Clifton S., Allen T., and Molly P. Brown were Marshall's stepchildren.

2. Mrs. Beale was the widow of a former United States minister to Greece, Rumania, Serbia, and Persia. Her Washington home, the Stephen Decatur mansion, had long been one of the city's social and intellectual centers.

TO KAUFMAN T. KELLER[1]   December 18, 1939
Confidential   [Washington, D.C.]

My dear Mr. Keller: General Gibbins, The Quartermaster General,[2] mentioned on Saturday that he had had a very satisfactory talk with you regarding the delivery of the motor vehicles recently ordered for the Army from the Chrysler Company. I am very glad to learn that you were most generous in your attitude in the matter and that we may have some hope that the dates of delivery can be expedited. In view of the importance of the matter to the Army, I am taking the opportunity of outlining the situation.

For the first time in the peace-time history of the Army we have been permitted to concentrate and complete the organization of divisions and corps troops of the Regular establishment, and to look forward to a practical experience in the technique of leadership of these large groups. Heretofore we have had to proceed on a basis which was largely theoretical, so the present concentration is of extreme importance to the Army and will have a tremendous effect on its efficiency and standards of training, as well as the teaching in all the Army schools and development of policy generally.

Unfortunately, though the divisions are now concentrated and the corps troops are being organized, we can make no headway until the motor transportation is received; and more unfortunately, we are under heavy pressure to return the troops to their home stations at as early a date as possible. Also, there is the necessity for their employment in the training of the civilian components, which is a heavy yearly task. We are, therefore, anxious to get under way with the corps maneuvers at as early a date as possible, and we are even forced to the conclusion that we must start these maneuvers before we have received the full complement of motor vehicles.

Under the circumstances, I hope that your people can work one of those industrial miracles for which American industry has become famous, and give us deliveries at a much earlier date than we now anticipate.

I am writing very frankly and somewhat confidentially, but the matter is so important and your attitude with General Gibbins was so encouraging that I am moved to communicate with you personally and directly.[3]   Faithfully yours,

GCMRL/G. C. Marshall Papers (Pentagon Office, General)

1. Keller had been president and general manager of the Chrysler Corporation since 1935.
2. Major General Henry Gibbins had been the quartermaster general since April 1, 1936.
3. Keller replied that if the samples the army was testing were approved, production of all contract items would be completed "at least by the 13th of May . . . and we hope to beat these figures. . . . We have been so conscious of your desire to get these jobs at the earliest possible moment that we are doing everything physically possible to get them to you at the earliest possible date." He declared that Chrysler's interest in production for the army made them work even more efficiently. In spite of the 1939 strike, he believed his company could deliver their trucks almost a month ahead of schedule. In fact, Keller noted, the strike had freed management to concentrate on the army's orders. (Keller to Marshall, December 22, 1939, GCMRL/G. C. Marshall Papers [Pentagon Office, General].)

Marshall wrote similar letters to Robert F. Black, president of the White Motor Company, and to Irving B. Babcock, president of the Yellow Truck and Coach Manufacturing Company, urging them to speed truck production. (Marshall to Black, January 16, 1940; Marshall to Babcock, January 23, 1940, ibid.) Both companies replied that they would try to do so. Transportation shortages delayed the completion of maneuvers in the southeastern United States. Marshall, under fire from Congress because of the expense of these exercises, sought to secure trucks as early in the spring of 1940 as possible. (See Marshall to James F. Byrnes, January 25, 1940, pp. 147–48.)

To Lieutenant General Stanley D. Embick   December 18, 1939
Confidential   [Washington, D.C.]

Dear Embick: In my note to you the other day I forgot to mention something that seems important to me.

I found your three division commanders had many of the same problems, but different approaches to the solution.[1] I found different reactions on the ration and to what extent it was satisfactory. I also found that it took me less than forty minutes to fly up to McClellan from Benning, which moves me to suggest that those fellows visit each other, using a plane, and see how they are working out their problems.

Right after the New Year I am going to have a group of staff officers make a flying tour in your region in order to see how these divisions are getting along and what they need. I found several matters concerned with developing more comfortable situations for the work were circulating through the War Department in the laborious time-consuming peace-time fashion. There may be other things following the same slow trail, and I think a staff visit may prove helpful.

In addition to the data given you regarding motor vehicles, I am led to believe, after a conversation between General Gibbins and Mr. Keller, President of the Chrysler Corporation, that we may expect much earlier deliveries. I have just written him a note thanking him for his attitude and explaining in detail the situation, with the request that he exert his influence to further accelerate deliveries. I should hear from him in a few days, and may have some data to give you. In any event I think it is important not to allow the maneuvers to run over late into the spring.[2]

I now want to give you a little confidential tip, if I have not already spoken to you about it, as to what we have in mind for the Army Corps. I am assuming that Walter Short will be the next Major General, and that being the case, that he will be designated as the Corps Commander, and I think you can make your own private plans on that basis.[3] Another thing, while the Corps Commander and his staff for the moment will be somewhat on a temporary basis, I have in mind that we may settle this permanently by making the Corps Commander the Commandant of the Infantry School, and the key members of his staff additional members of the faculty of the School. That would enable us to continue the Corps set-up without having to use new installations and a complete expensive set-up; also guarantee the practical training to the Infantry School, which I hope to develop into the real leadership agency of the Army, facilitate obtaining the use of troops in a large way for the student officers, along with facility in utilizing the student officers to assist with the troops. Of course this change would not be made a definite thing until the retirement of General Singleton. It has not been passed on by the General Staff, but I think that is what the decision will be.

I am giving you this hurriedly and most confidentially, and for your eye alone, at the present time.   Faithfully yours,

*Poor English, but I have not time to correct.[4]

GCMRL/G. C. Marshall Papers (Pentagon Office, Selected)
1. Marshall was referring to Brigadier General Walter C. Short, commander of the First

Division; Brigadier General Clement A. Trott (U.S.M.A., 1899), commander of the Sixth Division; and Brigadier General Campbell B. Hodges, commander of the Fifth Division.

2. Three days earlier, Marshall had instructed Embick to plan his Third Army maneuvers "on the basis of 50 or 75% of deliveries of motor transportation. I do not think we can afford to wait until May, and I think a pretty satisfactory maneuver can be conducted without the complete transportation. The pressure is going to be so heavy for the return of these troops, and the heat and other climatic conditions will be much less favorable in May, so if at all possible, I would like to see the main maneuver at least started not later than the 15th of April." (Marshall to Embick, December 15, 1939, GCMRL/G. C. Marshall Papers [Pentagon Office, Selected].)

3. For the purpose of large-scale maneuvers, the army created the Fourth Army Corps with the divisions and support troops concentrated in the Southeast. Short was promoted to major general effective March 1, 1940.

4. Marshall added this handwritten note after the letter had been typed.

To Brigadier General Adna R. Chaffee   December 20, 1939
[Washington, D.C.]

Dear Chaffee: I had thought of sending Major Black[1] on a brief tour to several stations, Knox among others, to discuss with regular officers the impressions he gathered during the first months of the war; but I find that it is not advisable to initiate these discussions at the present moment. The information which Black obtained will be made available to you in convenient form as quickly as possible.   Faithfully yours,

Confidentially, Black made statements to the press that have produced a violent Jewish reaction; so, for the present, we are not advertising him.[2]

GCMRL/G. C. Marshall Papers (Pentagon Office, Selected)

1. Major Percy G. Black (U.S.M.A., April 1917), assistant military attaché in Germany from February 1937 to November 1939, had witnessed the capture of Warsaw in late September 1939. "He had been allowed to accompany the German army in Poland, where he had had an exceptional opportunity to view the usage of the German mobile mechanization," Chaffee had written to the chief of staff. The Fort Knox commander had requested Black for an overnight visit so that his staff could hear firsthand about German operations in Poland. (Chaffee to Marshall, December 11, 1939, GCMRL/G. C. Marshall Papers [Pentagon Office, Selected].)

2. "I do not believe any of the atrocity stories," declared Black when he landed in the United States in November 1939. He claimed that German soldiers had fed the demoralized women and children of Poland's capital at soup kitchens. He believed that German morale was high despite acute food shortages in some areas. "I think reports of internal dissension in Germany are largely exaggerated. Remember, any people who go to war feel their cause is just and that they are being attacked. The German people from the top to the bottom are more afraid of another Treaty of Versailles than of anything else." (*New York Times,* November 30, 1939, p. 11.) Marshall changed his mind about Black in 1940 and sent him to visit various commands. (See Marshall to James G. Harbord, February 17, 1940, pp. 161–62.)

MEMORANDUM FOR GENERAL BLANDING December 20, 1939
[Washington, D.C.]

I have been much impressed with the splendid response of the Guard to the special training program, now about completed. But I am also impressed by the fact that the initial excitement of September has somewhat cooled, and as a result the question of employers and employees in the maintenance of jobs is becoming a matter of serious concern. This, I assume, will continue to develop until a fresh excitement generates a new impulse.

In view of the foregoing it seems to me that for the time being we should rather turn off the heat, as it were, at the same time not giving public indication of any intention to abandon these additional drills—particularly in view of the fact that we are now involved in appropriation requests for the purpose of maintaining them. I, therefore, suggest sending out direct to The Adjutants General and by air mail some such statement as the following:

The splendid work that has been carried out in the special training of the National Guard during the past two months is very commendable. The serious sacrifices made by employees and by employers in relation to their jobs is also greatly appreciated. In view of the splendid progress that has been made to date, and in order to not cause too much interference with the civilian employment of members of the Guard, the War Department wishes to inform you that it sees no objection to relaxing in the matter of additional drills. It is therefore directed that the period for holding the special Army drills already authorized, be extended to March 1, 1940.

GCMRL/G. C. Marshall Papers (Pentagon Office, Selected)

TO MAJOR CLAUDE M. ADAMS December 28, 1939
Confidential [Washington, D.C.]

Dear Flap: I have just this moment read your letter of December 26th, and will endeavor to satisfy your curiosity. I would have written earlier, but the fact is my days are about eighteen hours long and I have been so busy I have almost no time to give to personal things, not even to shop for a present for Mrs. Marshall.

Originally I had intended for you to be assigned as a General Staff officer to a division in the South so that you could get the benefit of these coming maneuvers before joining me, but on the spur of the moment following your telegram, and in view of your situation at the time, I arranged to have you ordered here directly.[1]

I have an Aide—he is more of a Military Secretary than an Aide, in Colonel Buchanan, of the National Guard.[2] Buchanan had been here about three years when I brought him in, and so far as the office work here is concerned, he is able to handle the business.

My intention is to bring you into my office for whatever work comes up, and to be in a position to replace Buchanan in his particular job. It would be necessary for you to be intimately familiar with the workings of the General Staff and the War Department as a whole, in order to be able to serve me at the express speed that is usually necessary, so when you arrive, I propose having you attached successively to the branches of the General Staff for about two weeks each until you acquire a fair familiarity with the machinery of administration.

Now as to quarters. The Lieutenant's double set, similar to those on Augur Avenue at Leavenworth, have been vacant since I took office. The plans have been made and we are waiting for the appropriation in January having utilized all available funds for this concentration, to permit the complete remodeling of the house. It is to be thrown into one set of quarters, to be assigned to the Deputy Chief of Staff when completed, probably not before June, as WPA labor is involved. This particular item is to be treated as confidential, as it will not be announced until the new Deputy reports for duty the first of May. I suggest that you make no effort to locate quarters here until after your arrival, and that then you go about it very deliberately.

There is another possibility, which bears on the preceding paragraph. I want you to take things easy, and under no circumstances to overdo; but if you feel so disposed, I would like to have you see the divisions in the field, at some length, before settling down here. This, however, should be a matter for Ruth to decide and not for you. If she thinks it all right, understanding that it is not absolutely necessary, I would want you to spend several weeks at Benning, and at least a few days at Columbia, South Carolina, Camp McClellan, at Knox and at Bragg; and also a visit to Randolph and Kelly Fields, to Barksdale Field and to Langley Field. But I repeat, the decision in this should be Ruth's and not yours.

I am writing very hurriedly, but I think I have given you the information you wish.   Faithfully yours,

P.S.   We were delighted with the presents. Katherine is charmed with her picnic sack, and tell Ruth that her donkey has charmed up the library and the visitors.

GCMRL/G. C. Marshall Papers (Pentagon Office, Selected)

1. At this time, Adams was a student at the Command and General Staff School. (See Marshall to Mrs. Claude M. Adams, August 24, 1939, p. 40.) On November 14, he had suffered a heart attack, although he was able to return to his course work after a brief hospitalization. Marshall had previously ordered him to report to the War Department for

General Staff duty when the school closed at the end of January 1940. Adams had written to Marshall concerning his future assignment, since he had to inform the quartermaster at Fort Leavenworth about shipping and had to find housing in Washington, D.C. (Adams to Marshall, December 26, 1939, GCMRL/G. C. Marshall Papers [Pentagon Office, Selected].) See Marshall to Mrs. Claude M. Adams, January 2, 1940, pp. 133–34.

2. Lieutenant Colonel Kenneth Buchanan was on detached duty from the Illinois National Guard.

SPEECH TO THE AMERICAN HISTORICAL ASSOCIATION[1]

December 28, 1939
Washington, D.C.

National Organization for War

The character of the organization of nations for war appears to be determined largely by their state of civilization, their geography, and their politics. From a military point of view, the state of civilization of the dominant nations approximates the same level; all use similar weapons, organize their forces in corresponding units, and man and equip their armies in much the same manner. Their military set-up differs principally in the extent of organization and in the degree of readiness of the major forces, and these differences appear to be dictated principally by geographical and political considerations.

The influences of geography are numerous and usually obvious. Invading forces, for example, prefer open frontiers and avoid ocean barriers. The possibility of conflicting interests between nations diminishes as the distance between them increases. This country is fortunate in its geographical position, and if the Atlantic Ocean has not guaranteed complete immunity from wars with European powers, it has made such wars so difficult of management as to be approached with caution and reluctance, and it does make sudden attack on us seem unlikely. The influence of distance has been modified by the airplane, along with increased speeds on land and water, but these changes have not as yet materially affected our unusually favorable situation.

If these views regarding the effect of civilization and geography on the organization of this country for war are accepted, then we must turn to political considerations to find the dominating influence in this vital matter. In our democracy where the government is truly an agent of the popular will, military policy is dependent on public opinion, and our organization for war will be good or bad as the public is well informed or poorly informed regarding the factors that bear on the subject.

Public appreciation of international affairs is of course important to a sound view regarding military policy, and the radio and press are doing a remarkable job of keeping the public informed. School children today are probably more fully informed on current international developments than were many high government officials of thirty years ago. But even more important are the lessons of history. Therefore, it is to the historian, to you gentlemen, that we must turn for the most essential service in determining the public policy relating to national defense.

Popular knowledge of history, I believe, is largely based on information derived from school text-books, and unfortunately these sources often tell only a portion of the truth with regard to our war experiences. Historians have been inclined to record the victories and gloss over the mistakes and wasteful sacrifices. Cause and effect have been, to an important extent, ignored. Few Americans learn that we enrolled nearly 400,000 men in the Revolutionary War to defeat an enemy that numbered less than 45,000, or that we employed half a million in 1812 against an opponent whose strength never exceeded 16,000 at any one place, and fewer still have learned why these overwhelming numbers were so ineffective. The War between the States pointed numerous lessons for our future protection, yet seldom has a nation entered a war so completely unprepared, and yet so boastfully, as did the United States in 1898. Veterans of the World War often seem to overlook the fact that almost a year and a half elapsed after the declaration of war before we could bring a field army into being and even then its weapons, ammunition and other materiel were provided by our Allies. And many of them seem unaware of the fact that the partially trained state of our troops proved a costly and tragic business despite the eventual success.

What the casual student does learn is that we have won all our wars and he is, therefore, justified in assuming that since we have defeated the enemies of the past we shall continue to defeat the enemies of the future. This comfortable belief in our invincibility has been reflected legislatively in the inadequate military organization of past years, resulting in stupendous expenditures in each emergency, invariably followed by a parsimonious attitude, if not the complete neglect of ordinary military necessities. In addition to the perils of war there is the issue of huge war debts with their aftermath of bitter years of heavy taxes. I think it apparent that much of this misfortune in the life of our democracy could have been avoided by the influence of a better informed public on the decisions of the Congress.

Personally I am convinced that the colossal wastefulness of our war organization in the past, and the near tragedies to which it has led us, have been due primarily to the character of our school text-books and the ineffective manner in which history has been taught in the public schools of this country. In other words, I am saying that if we are to have a sound organization for war we must first have better school histories and a better technique for teaching history.

I have had no opportunity for research in preparation for this discussion but I have found in a brief survey of some of the present school text-books on American history that there has been a great improvement since the days of my early schooling, and a material improvement since the period, a few years after the close of the World War, when I became officially interested in this question. I should confess that I was particularly impressed with Dr. Albert Bushnell Hart's volume, but I have no data as to the extent to which it is used in the schools of this country.[2]

I might attempt a philosophical discussion this morning regarding the proper organization of this country for war, or, to put it more tactfully, for the national defense; but however convincing this might be, the effect would be negligible—or at least but momentary. The members of a Congress, wise on heels of a war, will legislate with serious purpose to avoid a repetition of the crises, the plights and frights of their recent experience; but what is done is usually undone, the military arrangements emasculated, the old story of unpreparedness continued on into the next chapter of repetitions, because of the pressure of public opinion.

To maintain a sound organization the public must understand the general requirements for the defense of this particular country—the requirements for the maintenance of peace as we soldiers believe, before Congress can be expected, year in and year out, to provide the necessary legislation with due regard both for the economics of the situation and for the essential requirements for an adequate Army and Navy, with the necessary industrial organization behind them. When the high-school student knows exactly what happened, and most important of all, why it happened, then our most serious military problem will be solved. Potentially the strongest nation on earth, we will become the strongest and at a much smaller cost than has been paid for our mistaken course in the past. The historian, the school history and its teacher are the important factors in the solution of the problem I am discussing so superficially this morning.

History as a science has many specialties. The military historian is a specialist. Normally he is not concerned in the preparation of school text-books. Furthermore, military history, since it deals with wars, is unpopular, and probably more so today than at any other time. Yet I believe it is very important that the true facts, the causes and consequences that make our military history, should be matters of common knowledge. War is a deadly disease, which today afflicts hundreds of millions of people. It exists; therefore, there must be a reason for its existence. We should do everything in our power to isolate the disease, protect ourselves against it, and to discover the specific which will destroy it. A complete knowledge of the disease is essential before we can hope to find a cure. Daily we see attacks on war and tabulations regarding its cost, but rarely do we find a careful effort being made to analyze the various factors in order to determine the nature of war; to audit the accounts as it were, and to see to whom or to what each item of the staggering total is really chargeable.

As to the character of the organization for war suitable and acceptable to this country, I might say that certain definite policies have been developed through the years, and given a degree of permanence in the general amendments to the National Defense Act, of June 1920:

1st A small Regular Army as the keystone of our land defense program. It should provide the small force that might be immediately required for the security of the interests of this country, and supply the training standards and the training staff for the development of a citizen army.

2nd A territorial force, the National Guard, voluntarily maintained by the State governments in cooperation with the Federal Government, to supplement the small standing Army for the first phase of the defense of the country in the event of war.

3rd A democratic system for developing a Reserve of trained officer material—the ROTC and the CMTC, and a practical plan for the prompt procurement of man-power to fill up the ranks of the Regular Establishment and the National Guard, and later to provide the necessary replacements and the men for the new units which will be required.

4th A reserve of non-commercial munitions.

5th A practical set-up for the prompt mobilization of the industrial resources of the nation, to provide, with the least practicable delay, the munitions that are required.

And lastly, an adequate reserve of the raw materials essential for war purposes, which are not available in this country.

The foregoing policies have been generally accepted by the public and are a part of the organic law. Properly administered and developed, they provide a democratic basis for the national defense suitable to our form of government and to our particular international situation.

In the development of these policies two factors dominate the thought of the War Department. The first pertains to economic considerations. Everything in this country is expensive, in keeping with the high standards of living demanded by our people. Therefore, the military establishment is very expensive, and its maintenance on a sound basis is always endangered by the natural demand of the people for economy in government. This demand concentrates first on the Army and Navy immediately following a period of war, gradually grows more insistent in time of peace, and finally becomes politically compulsory with a depression in business. The War Department, therefore, concentrates earnestly on the problem of how best to maintain an adequate standard of national defense for a minimum of expenditure.

The time factor is the other dominant consideration which influences the planning of the Department. It is related to all our preparations—the production of materiel, the training of troops, of pilots and of mechanics, the organization of new units, and the mobilization of a war Army. The Navy in peace is 75% fully prepared. The Army machine is probably less than 25% ready for immediate action. Our problem, therefore, involves the development of a war force after the emergency has arrived. The time factor dominates the situation to a degree not approximated in any other great country. For this reason in particular the problem of a suitable war organization for the United States is one of many complications, and the influence of a well-informed public is of profound importance.[3]

GCMRL/G. C. Marshall Papers (Pentagon Office, Speeches)

1. Marshall addressed a joint meeting of the American Military Institute and the American Historical Association at the Mayflower Hotel in Washington, D.C. The content of this speech on preparedness is similar to his February 10, 1923, address to the members of the Headmasters Association in Boston, Massachusetts. (See *Papers of GCM,* 1: 219–22.)

2. Marshall had instructed his orderly, Sergeant James W. Powder, to select a sample of United States history textbooks from the Washington, D.C., Public Library on December 26, 1939. (Kenneth Buchanan Memorandum for the Public Library, Washington, D.C., December 26, 1939, GCMRL/G. C. Marshall Papers [Pentagon Office, Categorical].)

3. After the speech, Senator Elbert D. Thomas, Democrat from Utah, challenged Marshall. Thomas believed it would be "dangerous" for individuals in public life, including teachers, to criticize soldiers and inefficient military methods. (New York *Daily News,* December 29, 1939, p. 5.) Commenting later on the chief of staff's remarks, Charles A. Beard, past president of the American Historical Association, asserted that "if Gen. Marshall will get the American Legion to tell the real truth about the War of 1812 and will get the pure history law of Wisconsin repealed and convince parents that the true history of the War of 1812 ought to be taught their children, it is probable that historians might be willing to tell it." (*Washington Post,* December 30, 1939, p. 4.)

To Major General Ewing E. Booth[1]   December 29, 1939
[Washington, D.C.]

Dear Booth: I have received your letter, check for $5, the box of manuscript, and all have been turned over to The Adjutant General for the customary War Department check.

I endeavored during the Christmas week-end to find a chance to go over what you have written, and while I was not able to read through the manuscript, I did read the major portions of it and glanced through the remainder.

I hesitate seriously to make any comments on the manuscript of an Army officer for proposed publication. In the first place I am an amateur and in the second place he is an amateur in the writing business. In the third, and most important place, I generally find that I have hurt feelings or offended.

To be perfectly frank with regard to your manuscript: I was amazed at the complete outline of events it records, at the delightful sense of humor you display in places, and at the clever technique you showed in hitching together in such a smooth fashion so much detail of events along with discussions of the rights and wrongs of things.

That portion of the manuscript that refers to your boyhood is a little classic, charming to read, and very impressive as to the conclusions drawn from the character of your early experiences. I was much struck with the fact that the reaction to your call of thanks as a young man in Pueblo had an almost exact counterpart in the life of General Charles G. Dawes, particularly as to the result. This portion of the proposed book is a "best seller."

Now, as to the purely military portion: I was tremendously interested in what you had to say, naturally because of my knowledge of many of the events, and particularly because of my relationship with General Bell and with you. I believe in every criticism you made, and was most strenuously involved in trying to correct some of them when I joined the GHQ staff in May 1919. If you recall, I had a telephone war with you over the handling of units and individuals at LeMans and Brest, and you brought about a cure of the unfortunate situation I was reporting by having the LeMans officials meet with the Brest officials in a sort of Runnymede island half way between the two points. Whether all of this will be interesting to the ordinary reader, I cannot form an opinion. My guess is, and it is purely a guess, that it will not intrigue the attention sufficiently to bring about a reasonable sale of the book. What you have written will be read by the senior survivors in the Regular Army, of the AEF, and with the greatest interest; but I doubt whether it will make a general appeal to the military reader. I may be all wrong about this, and it is quite probable that I am, but I am giving you the benefit of my honest reaction.

The only point of your account that I was a little dubious about, that is as to its propriety, was the discussion of the method of command by Generals, which occurred at Langres. I gathered that you were referring to General McAndrew, and it is hard for me to believe that he was proposing such an unfortunate technique for troop leadership of Americans.[2] I know that we suffered too much from that sort of business.

I have had to handle this very hurriedly, and I submit the foregoing with many apologies and with most sincere congratulations on the remarkably fine job you have done. I knew you were conscientious, and tenacious in carrying out your duty as you saw it, to a degree that few men approximate, but I did not realize that you had concealed within you so much of literary ability.³   Faithfully yours,

GCMRL/G. C. Marshall Papers (Pentagon Office, General)

1. Booth had known Marshall since 1906 when the former was an instructor at Fort Leavenworth. Booth also served as aide-de-camp to Major General J. Franklin Bell from 1912 to 1915; Marshall assumed that position in July 1916. As commander of the Fourth Division's Eighth Brigade in the offensives of 1918, Booth continued his association with his former student.

2. Major General James W. McAndrew had established and was the first commandant of the A.E.F. General Staff School at Langres, France. (See *Papers of GCM*, 1: 195–97, 360–61.) Booth replied: "As soon as the manuscript is returned to me I shall eliminate at once this particular feature. Not for anything would I have anyone think I was referring to General McAndrew." (Booth to Marshall, January 2, 1940, GCMRL/G. C. Marshall Papers [Pentagon Office, General].)

3. "I would like to publish at least enough copies to present one with my compliments to each of my friends and associates in the Army," Booth wrote to Marshall. (Ibid.) The Adjutant General's Office returned the manuscript in early February 1940. Booth had his autobiography privately printed as *My Observations and Experiences in the United States Army* (Los Angeles: n.p., 1944).

To COLONEL MORRISON C. STAYER¹   December 29, 1939
                                                   Washington, D.C.

Dear Stayer: Your letter of December 16th arrived before Christmas, and I was very glad to hear from you. I intended to answer it by air mail at the time, but it got away from me, clipped accidentally to the back of another paper.

I was much interested in what you had to say about your work. Your name was mentioned in a cable a few days ago regarding a former Panamanian, a German, removed sick from a British prize passing through the Canal.

You refer to the contrast between your work with purely civilian groups and that of the life in Army circles. I am experiencing something similar because there is no comparison between the War Department's hurly burly and an Army post.²

I was in Benning the other day for 48 hours, but moving at such a terrific pace that I did not have much time to look about. After inspecting the First Division cantonment on the Cussetta Road south of Harmony church, I did ride horseback through the post over the Marne Road. The following morning I got up at five for a dove shoot and got my limit by eight o'clock; looked for quail until nine, killed a pheasant, changed into uniform, and arrived by plane at Camp McClellan at 10:15 to inspect the division there. I completed that at three o'clock and was in a turkey blind at Benning at 4:30, but no turkey. Stayed with Singleton. Katherine motored down in advance of my departure from Washington, and joined me at Benning. I dismissed the plane there and returned by way of Savannah, with one day there for hunting. I was to have gone to Tampa and to San Antonio, and to have had a day or two hunting near Tallahassee, but a White House engagement brought me back.

My plans are very uncertain now, complicated by uncertainty as to hearings before committee of Congress and other similar matters of great importance. There is to be a big maneuver on the West Coast the third week in January, which I want to see, but may not reach. But I am planning to insert a trip to Panama at the first opportunity.

With affectionate regards to Mrs. Stayer,   Faithfully yours,

G. C. Marshall

P.S.   I may add I am in splendid shape, though I tap wood. I am riding every day after the office, usually into the dusk; walked home yesterday on account of the snow and ice, 2½ miles. I feel so well and have such a good appetite that it is very difficult to keep down my weight, but I am getting good and hard again. I am not working at night and am keeping clear of most of the social-official obligations. So far all goes well.

GCMRL/ M. C. Stayer Collection

1. Stayer, the chief health officer of the Panama Canal Zone, had been Marshall's physician at the Infantry School. (On their association and Stayer's knowledge of Marshall's health, see *Papers of GCM*, 1: 539–40, 682–84, 696–97.)

2. After noting the intensity of work in the Canal Zone and the Health Department's accomplishments, Stayer observed: "I can not help but wish for the days that I spent at Benning when I could ride as I did many times with you. At present I am unable to take any exercise. We work every day until 4 or 5 o'clock, including Saturdays and sometimes on Sundays. The work is very interesting, very strenuous and needs a great deal of planning, but I am homesick for the Army with which I associated for many years. It is my first experience with civil people in my 32 years of Army life. I can not help but go back and recall how fine my tour of service was with you at Benning." (Stayer to Marshall, December 16, 1939, GCMRL/ G. C. Marshall Papers [Pentagon Office, General].)

Watchful Waiting

January 1 – April 11, 1940

If I may be permitted, I will go back to the late fall when the War Department submitted estimates to the Budget Bureau for $240,000,000 for critical items of equipment which take a long time to manufacture, to complete the first or initial equipment for the protective mobilization plan force of 750,000 men in units plus replacements. Estimates were submitted also for $205,000,000 to provide for that force its essential items of equipment. . . . These particular estimates that I have just mentioned were not included in the Budget submitted to Congress last January. For some time thereafter we went through a period of what might be called "watchful waiting."

—Testimony Before the Senate Committee on Appropriations
June 15, 1940

MARSHALL considered the spring 1940 maneuvers of paramount importance to the modernization of the army, and he devoted a large portion of his time to the defense of appropriations for these exercises. "With a view to providing for the training of large units we have concentrated in southern camps and on the Pacific coast five Infantry divisions, corps troops, two Cavalry divisions, and the Mechanized Cavalry Brigade. Before the end of this fiscal year divisional training will be completed and the divisions will be assembled with corps units into two corps, for what we believe will be the most instructive and the most productive maneuvers in our history." The army scheduled the joint army-navy Pacific coast operations for January 15 through 20; the Caribbean joint exercise for mid-January through February, the Panama Canal Zone mobile forces exercises for the week of March 10, the Fourth Corps maneuvers at Fort Benning between April 15 and 27, and the massive Third Army maneuvers along the Sabine River in Texas and Louisiana for May 9 through 25. (Marshall testimony of February 23, 1940, House Appropriations Committee, *Military Establishment Appropriation Bill for 1941, Hearings* [Washington: GPO, 1940], p. 13.)

In the three months preceding the April 9 invasion of Denmark and Norway, Marshall testified at five crucial congressional hearings. On January 16, he appeared before the House Military Affairs Committee to outline defense needs and the president's emergency supplemental appropriation bill. On February 23 and 26, the chief of staff submitted a lengthy statement and answered questions regarding budget appropriations for fiscal year 1941. He returned for the House Military Affairs Committee's hearings on arms sales to the Allied nations on March 27, and appeared before the Senate Military Affairs Committee the following day. The age-in-grade promotions legislation brought Marshall back to the Senate committee on April 8, and to the House committee on the next day. ★

To Mrs. Claude M. Adams   January 2, 1940
Confidential   [Washington, D.C.]

Dear Ruth: Your birthday telegram arrived in the midst of a riding party breakfast with which we were celebrating the event, though why celebrate my increasing yearage is really a question. But it was good of you to remember me, and I wish you and Flap could have been with us.

I dictated a hurried note to him the other day and answered some of his questions.[1] I wish you would reply with your views on the various phases of the situation. It seemed to me, at long range, that it might be an excellent thing to have him get a camouflage rest, as it were, before coming into

Washington. I could have him ordered down for an inspection and then fix it up on a detached service basis or some other way to permit him to enjoy some of the beautiful late winter weather of the South and get thoroughly on his feet before coming in here.

I do not want you to show him this letter, because it would merely trouble him; but I should think it would be very important for him to get thoroughly strengthened up after the strain of the course at Leavenworth and following the attack he had. That is too serious to trifle with. What he probably would not understand is the terrific strain of things here in the War Department. We are doing so much, practically working on a war-time basis with all the difficulty and irritating limitations of peace-time procedure. You cannot imagine what happens here in a single day, and I would be deeply concerned over his taking on such a load before he had had a full opportunity to build up his resistance. Once in the machine here, it is very difficult to spare anybody because I have to work fast and rather ruthlessly, and we are under continuous pressure from the outside, which will increase tremendously with the convening of Congress. Forbearance and self-restraint are very wearing on the individual, and probably do more harm than violent physical exercise; and there will be a tremendous amount of that required this late winter and early spring.

Flap spoke about wanting to send his stuff here by van which, of course, involves the necessity of having an immediate place to set up a household. Would it not be a good thing to delay that, hold your quarters there, which you can do, and carry out that portion of the move later on.

Write to me direct, sending your letter to the office, and under no circumstances show this to Flap.[2] I am injecting this dictation in the midst of the early morning business after the New Year's week-end, so I must apologize for the form of the letter.   Affectionately yours,

GCMRL/G. C. Marshall Papers (Pentagon Office, Selected)

1. See Marshall to Major Claude M. Adams, December 28, 1939, pp. 121–23.

2. Ruth Adams responded that "Flap is so eager to rejoin you" that he would not want leave. "I cannot imagine and I'm sure he does not fully realize the tremendous strain under which you and your staff work. He thinks he is physically fit to take over anything you would want him to do." (Mrs. Claude M. Adams to Marshall, January 6, 1940, GCMRL/G. C. Marshall Papers [Pentagon Office, Selected].)

To Colonel Charles C. Haffner   January 4, 1940
[Washington, D.C.]

Dear Haffner: I received the Christmas copy of "Vanished Arizona", and was delighted to have it.

Thanks for your letter with reference to some of my suggestions as to materiel. As a matter of fact, I read "Vanished Arizona" in 1906; a copy was given me by the Commanding General of the Pennsylvania National Guard, as a wonderful Army story.[1]

Mrs. Summerhayes I saw at David's Island, Fort Slocum, New York, when I reported there enroute to the Philippines in 1902.

I had your copy of "The Cannoneer" with reference to the fall training, and also your letter on the subject of extra training. This last question is one for which the answer varies with the international situation. Public opinion in early September was quite different from public opinion today, and that of today will probably be completely altered in March if heavy land fighting develops in Europe.[2]

It is essential for us to have the new men, both the increase and the replacements following the summer camps, whipped into a fairly practical shape as quickly as possible. Then if mobilization should become necessary, the next step could be made with reasonable smoothness and not be the stumbling performance that has occurred in the past.

Then, there is another point which I mention very confidentially. There is no question but that if the Guard had been ignored in the special military program in early September, there would have been a heavy reaction against the attitude of the War Department.

I have been exceedingly busy but have managed to ride in the late afternoon, usually in the dusk, every day—and Sunday mornings; also I did get away for a flying trip of inspection in the Southeast, and probably will be off again in a few days for the West Coast to see the big joint Army-Navy maneuver and divisional landing affair out there, as well as inspecting some troops in Texas.   Faithfully yours,

GCMRL/G. C. Marshall Papers (Pentagon Office, Selected)

1. Martha Summerhayes wrote *Vanished Arizona: Recollections of My Army Life* (Philadelphia: J. B. Lippincott Company, 1908). Marshall was an instructor with the Pennsylvania National Guard during the summers of 1907, 1908, and 1909. Haffner's Chicago publishing firm, R. R. Donnelley and Sons, annually reprinted an out-of-print book of historical interest. For several years, Haffner had been sending Marshall a copy of these volumes.

2. Marshall presented his views on the extension of National Guard training to the House Appropriations Committee on February 23, 1940. (See the editorial note on pp. 163–64.)

MEMORANDUM FOR G-2 [MCCABE]   January 5, 1940
                                              [Washington, D.C.]

There is developing on the Hill the basis for an attack on the Army for extravagance in the setting up of the Corps Maneuvers in the Southeast.

This, I think, is largely the result of a misleading Associated Press dispatch which left the implication that $26,000,000 would be spent on these specific maneuvers.[1]

The 1940 supplemental appropriations proposal will come up for debate almost immediately, and passage is expected within about two weeks. It is therefore important that we have prepared and available suggested presentations for the use of Mr. Woodrum, Chairman of the Deficiency Appropriation Committee, Mr. Snyder, of the Sub-Committee for Military Appropriations, and for any other of the Democratic leaders who have to defend the War Department estimates. These were accepted practically without reduction or amendment by the Budget.[2]

Please have a draft for the defense of these estimates, so far as pertains to Maneuvers, prepared in language that the layman can understand. In this treatment the following are suggested as points that might be made:

> These maneuvers present the first training opportunity for the Army in warfare movement above the division, and on a fairly realistic basis above the brigade, in the peace-time history of the Army.
>
> We have been forced to base almost all of our conclusions, regarding the tactical organization, supply and leadership of bodies of troops larger than a brigade in warfare movement, on theory or hearsay—we have lacked the troops, or rather the organization; we have never had the terrain available, we have lacked the transportation, and all the higher organizations had to be improvised. The Navy has such training; certainly at some time in its history, especially in this time of world crisis, the Army is entitled to at least one opportunity to learn to play the game the way it has to be played in actual campaign. Only thus can wastage of money and human life be avoided, and the national defense made secure.
>
> The cost of these particular maneuvers in the Southeast involves the transportation of units from their home stations to the concentration areas, and the return movement to home stations. This is the heaviest charge and could only be avoided by a complete revamping of the Army station set-up, abandoning numerous small posts, concentrating troops, expending large amounts for permanent construction, etc. If this cost of transportation, in the opinion of the people or of Congress, is considered too heavy to accept, then the answer is that the manner in which the Army is stationed prohibits its training. Along with this should be emphasized the fact that we are confronted by the condition of things as they are in the set-up of the Army, along with an emergency in the affairs of the world. The issue at the moment is not what might in the past have been better done, or what might be done better in the future; the issue at this moment is, what can be done today better to prepare ourselves to defend the peaceful integrity of this country.

Another initial expense involved in these maneuvers is or was for the preparation of the winter cantonments in which the troops have to be sheltered. In every way possible we have utilized existing facilities, borrowing National Guard concurrent camps and summer training camps of the CMTC and ROTC; there has been nothing of extravagance in the arrangements for these maneuver operations. The Army has been raised on too parsimonious a basis to have acquired extravagant habits. Every device or means that we could utilize to accomplish this concentration economically has been employed.

There has been some confusion in the public mind, apparently due to press reports, as to the cost of these maneuvers. The fact that the amounts covered training in the Philippines, Hawaii, Panama, and Puerto Rico, and for troops in the corps areas which are not going to the larger maneuvers, has been ignored. With the cantonment sites in the South set up and with the motor transportation provided, future concentrations, especially on a smaller scale, may be carried out much more economically.

This concentration makes possible the training of the Infantry regiments and the Artillery regiments under the new regimental organization, with actual weapon and fire instruction that would otherwise have been impossible until next summer, the development of the new combat team of infantry and artillery, the first test of the divisions in the new organization, and the beginnings, as it were, of the training of the corps troops and corps staffs of command, which has never before been possible.[3]

GCMRL/G. C. Marshall Papers (Pentagon Office, Selected)

1. The editors have been unable to identify this story.

2. Clifton A. Woodrum, Democrat from Virginia, was a member of the House Appropriations Committee. J. Buell Snyder, Democrat from Pennsylvania, also served on the committee.

3. In reply to the damaging Associated Press story, the army issued a press release explaining the use of the $26,000,000 for a number of territorial exercises and joint operations with the navy. The army then publicly explained the need for the additional sums requested to cover the corps and army maneuvers in the spring. (Press release on the cost of maneuvers, n.d., GCMRL/G. C. Marshall Papers [Pentagon Office, General].)

To Brigadier General Duncan K. Major, Jr.[1]   January 8, 1940
Confidential   [Washington, D.C.]

Dear Major: I have just this moment read your highly informative letter of January 5th, and I am delighted to find that everything seems to be going so harmoniously and effectively on the West Coast.[2]

I would not attempt to evaluate the profit that will come from these maneuvers, because in one sense it is intangible, and in other ways it is very concrete. In every respect it is tremendously important, because I believe during these coming maneuvers, commencing with your maneuver, we are going to wash more theory, cumbersome practice and excessive mimeographing out of the Army than even the most optimistic could hope for.

I am in hopes that I can get away in time to see the landing, but at the present moment I am involved with very important hearings before Committees of Congress which are extremely critical in their possible effect. Confidentially, already an attack is building up against the cost of these maneuvers, largely due to an unfortunate statement in the Associated Press which caused the hoi-poloi and many people on the Hill to think that I am involving them in the expenditure of $26,000,000 for one concentration in the Southeast. This is going to be rough sledding for me before the Committees, but belief in the righteousness of the cause makes me rather indifferent to the attack. My only worry is to find the necessary diplomatic skill to secure what we need. All this is most confidential.

Thank you for writing in such detail.   Faithfully yours,

P.S.   I checked over your old quarters at Benning the other day. Now-a-days rank goes up on the hill near the golf course, and your quarters are in second priority.

GCMRL/G. C. Marshall Papers (Pentagon Office, General)

1. Major was commander of the San Francisco Port of Embarkation.

2. The navy's cooperation for the January 15 joint exercise had been secured, commercial shipping arranged, and labor problems resolved, Major reported. "The Navy was most cooperative and willing and I had a perfect understanding with them as to our respective jobs and the line of demarkation between them when I left." The navy also arranged to train the army's transport masters. "As this is the first time more than one Army transport has participated in such a joint exercise this training will be of great value to our transport masters." Commercial vessels for the exercise were hard to obtain because of the short period of use and the labor instability on the West Coast. "My own guess is that we will never have any difficulty with the unions. My impression is that they don't want to mix up with the Army." (Major to Marshall, January 5, 1940, GCMRL/ G. C. Marshall Papers [Pentagon Office, General]. The politics of the maritime industry's labor organizations received extensive coverage in the American press in 1939; for example, see the *New York Times,* November 4, 1939, p. 9, and November 6, 1939, p. 3.) On the problems associated with ports of embarkation, see Memorandum for General Gasser, March 26, 1940, pp. 178–80.

MEMORANDUM FOR COLONEL WARD   January 10, 1940
Confidential   [Washington, D.C.]

Accumulate concise data for me in preparation for hearings before Congress on the following subjects:

Why it was better to go ahead with the modernization of the 75 [mm] gun rather than to plunge on the 105 mm. I think something on this was worked up last year, and the data should include a line or two indicating that present program has already 105's.

Data on the expected time of the distribution of the semi-automatic rifles up to completion of the 165,000 now under orders. Along with this a very brief digest of Wesson's presentation or ideas regarding the reasons why the Garand rather than the Johnson gun.

The cost respectively of the division cantonments, and for the corps units recently created or enlarged.

The comparison of the motor transportation equipment now being assigned triangular divisions with the old horse and mule transportation, along with estimates of comparative cost both as to procurement and as to maintenance.

Estimate of time saved by the new Drill Regulations in the training of soldiers, of ROTC cadets, etc.

An estimate of the cost of concentrating the divisions, compared with the probable cost of returning them to their stations, particularly in view of the new motor equipment which will be available.

A paragraph on anti-tank defense as to organizations available and required.

A short outline (and the preparation of this must be highly confidential as to officers concerned) on what we consider as highly necessary additions to special troops or corps troops from the National Guard, and how they might be obtained by conversion prior to a reorganization of National Guard divisions.

A very brief statement of what Edgewood Arsenal has today (and the approximate amount that has been invested in it), along with additional pieces that we wish to add. This to reduce appropriations for Edgewood in order to promote a large brand new arsenal somewhere else.

I presume you can handle this thing without advertising these points to the world and without making it so secret that everybody becomes excited. But whatever you get, it has to be brief, and easily understandable.

GCMRL/G. C. Marshall Papers (Pentagon Office, Selected)

TO ROBERT R. MCCORMICK   January 11, 1940
                                          [Washington, D.C.]

My dear Colonel McCormick: A number of people have sent me clippings from the TRIBUNE regarding an impromptu talk I made before the National

Historical Societies here in Washington several weeks ago. I thought I was talking in a rare cultural calm that has little of newspaper publicity, but I find myself plastered all over the pages of the papers.

Unfortunately most of the quotations were not verbatim and some of the conclusions were drawn from the sentences extracted from a paragraph without regard to the context. For this reason I am sending you, as something of an historian yourself, a mimeographed copy of what I actually said, less a preamble and a few conclusions.[1] Faithfully yours,

GCMRL/G. C. Marshall Papers (Pentagon Office, General)

1. Marshall was probably referring to a story by Walter Trohan, a *Chicago Daily Tribune* Washington correspondent, which was widely reprinted. Trohan said that the chief of staff had "exploded an oratorical bomb in the laps of several hundred historians today by attributing colossal wastefulness in past wars to botchy histories and slipshod teaching lessons of the past." Trohan purported to quote Marshall's speech at some length. (*Chicago Daily Tribune,* December 29, 1939, p. 3.)

In his reply, McCormick, *Chicago Tribune* editor and publisher, and formerly a colonel in the American Expeditionary Forces in France, replied that he doubted Marshall's premise that in the past United States organization for war had been colossally wasteful. "I will add a last opinion . . . that I do not believe National Guard Troops can ever be made into first class troops, as they have become satisfied with a low standard. I feel it is necessary to keep them, not for national defense against an alien enemy, but to have them sufficiently numerous to overwhelm the regular army when, and if, the time comes when it will be used to overthrow the republic." (McCormick to Marshall, January 15, 1940, GCMRL/G. C. Marshall Papers [Pentagon Office, General]; ellipsis in the original.)

MEMORANDUM FOR MAJOR EWERT[1]   January 13, 1940
                                                 Washington, D.C.

I am attaching a letter from Judge May, of the Military Affairs Committee, which specifically refers to recruiting.[2] In view of the fact that we have jumped up to practically 220,000 today, that we have enlisted since July 1st 51,000 in additions to the Army and _____ (get this from the Adjutant General) to replace discharges, I think the recruiting program has been an amazing success.

It seems a release is needed to off-set this damned idea.

G. C. M.

GCMRL/G. C. Marshall Papers (Pentagon Office, General)

1. Major Earl C. Ewert worked in the Public Relations Branch of G-2.

2. Andrew J. May, Democrat from Kentucky's Seventh District, had forwarded an editorial cut from the weekly *Labor,* which criticized Marshall's American Historical Association speech and Army recruitment policy. *"Instead of permitting soldiers to rewrite our histories, it might be well for Congress or the Executive to order an impartial inquiry to determine what's wrong with our army.* Why is it less than 25 per cent ready? Why do young men refuse to enlist? . . . We can't very well expect the answers to come from the generals. They are responsible for whatever may be wrong with the army. . . . Our guess is that young men do

not enlist because the caste system, so rigidly enforced, is obnoxious to the average red-blooded American." ("What Is the Matter With Our Army?" *Labor,* January 9, 1940, p. 4.)

To MAJOR GENERAL CHARLES H. MARTIN   January 16, 1940
                                                      [Washington, D.C.]

Dear Governor: I have just received your note of January 11th, thanking me for my small contribution to the occasion of your confirmation as "First Citizen" of Oregon. I appreciate your writing, and am sorry that I could not have been present to have personally said what I felt.[1]

I am appearing before a Committee of Congress in about half an hour, and expect to leave there, if they will let me get away, direct for Bolling Field to fly to Sacramento in order to check up on the Joint Maneuvers just starting on the West Coast. Incidentally, I have managed a degree of cooperation on the water, in the air, and on the ground with the Navy in this matter that is without previous precedent, and I believe it paves the way to a much better understanding in the future. It has all come about very smoothly. Admiral Stark is a splendid fellow.

I will probably only be in California two days, one at Sacramento and the other at the landing point, wherever that is to be. Then I must hustle from there to review the Cavalry Division, which I have not seen and which is concentrated at El Paso and due to break up for the time being to be re-united for the big maneuvers in April, and also to see the Second Division which is in the field south of San Antonio, and the Mechanized force near Knox. Then I have to be back here just a week from today, so there is not much time left over.[2]

With affectionate regards to you both,   Faithfully yours,

GCMRL/G. C. Marshall Papers (Pentagon Office, Selected)
   1. Martin had been governor of Oregon from 1935 to 1939.
   2. That same morning, Marshall also wrote to Kenyon A. Joyce and Adna R. Chaffee. To Major General Joyce, commanding officer of the First Cavalry Division, Fort Bliss, Texas, Marshall wrote that his "stay there will have to be very short, possibly not more than three or four hours, so I ask you to omit honors, and just let me see what you are doing and give me an opportunity to talk to you and your principal people. . . . Please use your best tact to save me from time-killing functions which would keep me from finding out what I want to learn in the way of business." (Marshall to Joyce, January 16, 1940, GCMRL/G. C. Marshall Papers [Pentagon Office, Selected].)
   To Brigadier General Chaffee, commanding general of the Seventh Cavalry Brigade (Mechanized), Fort Knox, Kentucky, the chief of staff noted that after his inspection of the Second Division, "if I am not pulled from Washington, and the weather is favorable I may fly in to see your people." He also cautioned Chaffee to minimize formalities. (Marshall to Chaffee, January 16, 1940, ibid.) Marshall did not visit Fort Knox; see Marshall to Chaffee, January 25, 1940, p. 146.

M ARSHALL testified before the House Military Affairs Committee before his departure for California on the afternoon of January 16. (Regarding his testimony, see Memorandum for Colonel Ward, January 10, 1940, pp. 138–39.) Before his return to Bolling Field on January 22, the chief of staff inspected the joint army-navy operations, the First Cavalry Division, and the Second Division. He flew approximately 5,390 miles in seven days.

Shortly after his return, Marshall declared: "Due to continual hearings before Congress and the necessity of watching every move in order to protect our Army appropriations, my inspection trips, if I am going to get anywhere about the country, have to be so hurried that I cannot proceed with much deliberation and am seldom certain until the last moment of just where I will be able to stop. However, I find so much profit in seeing the man on the ground that fleeting as my visits may be, they are a great advantage to me here in the work of the War Department." (Marshall to Millard F. Harmon, January 26, 1940, GCMRL/G. C. Marshall Papers [Pentagon Office, Selected].) ★

To CAPTAIN WILLIAM T. SEXTON[1]   January 23, 1940
                                                     [Washington, D.C.]

My dear Captain Sexton: I have just returned this morning from an air trip to the Maneuvers on the West Coast, along with an inspection of the divisions in the South and Southwest.

At Randolph Field Colonel Brooks presented me with a copy of "Soldiers in the Sun", which I read during the air portion of my journey between San Antonio and Fort Benning.[2]

On my second trip to the Philippines, in 1913 I occupied a great deal of my spare time during the three years in going completely through War Department records covering the military events, in the field and in government, between the arrival of the first expeditionary force in 1898 and the campaign in Mindanao in 1904. Of course I also read General Funston's book and several other private publications. During this period I arranged to visit as many of the scenes of action as possible, and tried to take with me officers who had been actual participants in the events. I planned and participated in a Staff ride up the central valley of Luzon through Angelo, Bautista, Mangatarem and Lingayan Gulf, and returned in the reverse direction of General Lawton's expedition. In the vicinity of Manila, the Batangas region, San Pablo Valley, and other easily accessible points, it was relatively a simple matter to go over the ground of the interesting events which had transpired during the insurrection.[3]

With this as a background for my critical opinion of your book, I would like to congratulate you on a remarkable piece of research and writing. I can think of nothing of importance that you have omitted, and there seems to be nothing you have included which might well have been omitted. Your book is a remarkable record of what took place in the Philippines, of the aspects of cause and effect, and of the state of mind of the times.[4]

My congratulations on a splendid piece of work.   Faithfully yours,

P.S.   When I came to sign this letter, I realized that probably your publishers would like to use it in the customary campaign of marketing the book, but I must ask you to treat this as a personal letter.

GCMRL/G. C. Marshall Papers (Pentagon Office, General)

1. Sexton (U.S.M.A., 1924) had served in the Philippine Islands from 1930 to 1932, taught history at the United States Military Academy, and was a student at the Command and General Staff School, Fort Leavenworth, Kansas, during the 1939–40 school year.

2. Colonel John B. Brooks, Air Corps, was stationed at Randolph Field, fifteen miles northeast of San Antonio, Texas. Sexton's book, *Soldiers in the Sun: An Adventure in Imperialism* (Harrisburg, Pa.: Military Service Publishing Company, 1939), was a history of the United States occupation of the Philippine Islands from May 1, 1898, when Admiral Dewey's fleet destroyed the Spanish fleet, until June 20, 1901, when President Theodore Roosevelt's proclamation transferred executive authority over the islands from the military to a civilian commission.

3. Major General Frederick B. Funston, Sr., commandant of the Army Service Schools during Marshall's tour of duty as student and instructor, had written *Memories of Two Wars: Cuban and Philippine Experiences* in 1912. (On Marshall's experiences in the Philippines, see *Papers of GCM*, 1: 23–29, 75–95.)

4. Sexton replied that "the same interest which motivated you to travel so extensively throughout Luzon in 1913 impelled me to finish a long but interesting project which at the beginning seemed fairly simple. Also as I progressed with the work, I became determined that the exploits of a group of brave men who were struggling through sun and fever to carry out the will of the national government, should be made known to the American people. I tried to make the book interesting yet objective. If that desire has been attained I feel that the time was well spent." (Sexton to Marshall, January 28, 1940, GCMRL/G. C. Marshall Papers [Pentagon Office, General].)

In mid-April, Marshall had Sexton send a copy of the book to Major General Frank R. McCoy. Marshall suggested to McCoy that he try to have the *New York Times* review the volume. (Marshall to McCoy, April 13, 1940, GCMRL/G. C. Marshall Papers [Pentagon Office, Selected].) A review by Major General William C. Rivers appeared in the *New York Times Book Review* of May 5, 1940, p. 4.

To Mrs. Lowell F. Hobart   January 23, 1940
                                                              [Washington, D.C.]

My dear Mrs. Hobart: I returned from the West Coast this morning to find your letter of January 20th, inviting me to appear before the Women's

Patriotic Conference on National Defense at The Mayflower on February 1st, or to designate someone to represent me.[1]

My engagements at the present time make it impossible for me to accept on the basis of a formal talk. If you will permit me to talk informally for a few minutes, off the record as it were, I will undertake to enter into this engagement. My embarrassment is that I have no time at all in the rush of the moment, to make formal preparation for such a talk, and at this time practically anything I say is apt to be given wide publicity. Now, if it is possible without creating undue interest because of arrangement for my appearance without press report, I would be glad to make a few comments. I do not believe this can be managed except by the two of us having an agreement as to the approximate time that might be convenient, and my appearing without any previous notice or warning. I am afraid if you advertised the fact that I am to talk off the record, it will, as far as I am concerned, make matters worse. But, if you could allow me to appear at a moment when it would be a simple matter to give me ten minutes on the program, I would be very glad to do so.   Faithfully yours,

GCMRL/G. C. Marshall Papers (Pentagon Office, General)

1. Mrs. Hobart, president of the National Society of New England Women, served as chairman of the fifteenth annual Women's Patriotic Conference at the Mayflower Hotel in Washington, D.C. She told Marshall that "the members of these participating organizations are very much in earnest over the proper protection of our Country. We are anxious to receive the latest needs of the Armed Forces. Which bills we will want to approve or disapprove that are coming before this Congress." (Hobart to Marshall, January 20, 1940, GCMRL/G. C. Marshall Papers [Pentagon Office, General].) Marshall spoke to the conference on the morning of February 1; no record of his remarks was preserved in the Marshall papers.

TO BRIGADIER GENERAL LESLEY J. MCNAIR   January 24, 1940
[Washington, D.C.]

Dear McNair: I appreciated your coming down to the Air field in the cold and snow of last Tuesday evening, and while we did not have much opportunity to talk things over, yet I picked up at least one valuable bit of information.[1] We are looking into the matter of having some of your people in the faculty see the Maneuvers in late April or May.

When I talked things over with the faculty at the Air Corps Tactical School, just having seen the large classes of flying cadets, straight from colleges, who will form the great body of the augmented Air Corps, I was again impressed with the importance of developing every means to give the Air Corps an understanding of the ground army. I completed the tentative arrangements while en route to have the class of 300 flying cadets who finish at Kelly Field in the first of April attached for six weeks to the headquarters of companies, batteries, battalions and regiments of all the troops which are to participate in the Maneuvers.[2]

I am trying to make a similar arrangement for the class at the Air Corps Tactical School. Also we are trying to find a proper basis for delaying the assignment of graduates of West Point to the Air Corps until they have had at least a year with large units of the ground army. This last is very difficult of arrangement because it appears to mean that while such officers would be senior in rank to the flying cadets who were commissioned at the same time, the latter, would be two years their senior as experienced pilots, and therefore the assignment of the West Point graduate to the command of flights or squadrons could not be made on the basis of rank without serious consequences. Just how we will get around this, I do not know, but we are trying to find a solution.

I mention the foregoing to you because it has probably some relationship to your Air Corps ground Army force at Leavenworth, just as the presence of a representative number of your faculty at these Army maneuvers appears to be absolutely essential if Leavenworth is to retain its prestige as the teacher of division and corps tactics, logistics and technique. Otherwise, the student will be the veteran and the member of the faculty will be the novice. I am dictating this off-hand as the thoughts occur to me, so treat it as more or less of a casual conversation.

I wish you would have the doctor who examined Major Adams write me personally a statement of his condition, and with the probabilities, in terms understandable to me. The two doctors on his medical board told me Tuesday night of the result of their examination, but I paid very little attention to that as Major Adams was listening in on what they said. Specifically, I am wondering if it would not have been better to have put him on at least two months' sick leave instead of just one. In a sense I am trying to protect him against himself, because with these important Army activities coming to a head and the press of business here in Washington, he quite evidently feels deeply embarrassed at delaying his reporting for duty.[3]

I hope you conveyed my apologies to Mrs. McNair for allowing her to prepare a dinner for us, and then not reporting to enjoy it. Please tell her I am sorry to have been the cause of so much trouble.   Faithfully yours,

GCMRL/G. C. Marshall Papers (Pentagon Office, Selected)

1. Marshall was forced to leave Fort Leavenworth by the onslaught of a snow storm after a one hour visit on January 16, 1940.

2. Marshall stopped at the Air Corps Tactical School, Maxwell Field, Alabama, en route home from his inspection of the western maneuvers on January 22, 1940. Prior to that visit, he had inspected the Advanced Flying School at Kelly Field, Texas, on January 20.

3. Physicians at Fort Leavenworth recommended to McNair that Major Claude M. Adams receive one month of sick leave. (Memorandum to the Commandant, Command and General Staff School, January 27, 1940, GCMRL/G. C. Marshall Papers [Pentagon Office, Selected].)

MEMORANDUM FOR ALL STAFF DIVISIONS,   January 25, 1940
CHIEFS OF ARMS AND SERVICES   Washington, D.C.
[*Confidential*]

The concentration of troops in the field amounts to a partial mobilization of the regular establishment of the Army. The men are wintering in tent camps, the training schedule is arduous and has been carried out determinedly despite unusually cold weather. It is the War Department's most important project of this fiscal year. Therefore, action which affects the comfort, efficiency or unhampered operation of these units, whether originating in the field or in the War Department, will be followed through to its conclusion by the responsible officer of the Staff, or of the arm or service concerned, to avoid the inevitable delays incident to routine procedure, and to insure that the interests of the troops and the training objectives are given the desired priority.

G. C. Marshall

GCMRL/G. C. Marshall Papers (Pentagon Office, Selected)

TO BRIGADIER GENERAL ADNA R. CHAFFEE   January 25, 1940
[Washington, D.C.]

Dear Chaffee: I was very sorry not to be able to reach Knox, but when we reached San Antonio in a very fast trip of inspection along the Southern border, I found that not only was a storm closing in on us but that you were down to five degrees below zero. As I had to be in Washington on Tuesday morning, I could not afford to risk being delayed in your region, and I did not think it would be a very comfortable inspection either for the troops or for me personally. However, at the first opportunity I will fly out there from here direct.

As matters now stand, confidentially I expect to take off in a B-17 direct for Panama about February 4th in order to make that inspection and also of Puerto Rico before I appear before the Appropriations Committee on the 1941 budget. Just now I am in a heavy battle on the Senate side of the Hill to protect our maneuvers from serious cuts; spent almost all of yesterday visiting various Senators in order to build up some resistance to the cuts. I was successful on the House side in getting through without trouble.[1]   Hastily yours,

GCMRL/G. C. Marshall Papers (Pentagon Office, Selected)

1. In addition to various senators, Marshall spoke to Milton H. West, Democrat from Texas and member of the House Ways and Means Committee, on January 24, 1940.

To James F. Byrnes[1]   January 25, 1940
                                         [Washington, D.C.]

My dear Senator: In thinking over our conversation of yesterday afternoon, when you were good enough to give me an opportunity to discuss the 1940 Deficiency Appropriation bill, I am inclined to think there were several matters which I did not make sufficiently clear.[2]

In the first place, the length of the maneuvers has no bearing on the expense, but what is more important, the prolongation of the period is due entirely to the delay in receiving the necessary motor transportation. We had hoped, and I had given instructions, that the maneuvers in the Southeast would be completed by April 15, not as a matter of economy—because none would be effected, but in order to get these troops back to their home stations in time to undertake the heavy program of civilian military training for the summer. However, I found that we would be seriously defeating the purpose of the maneuvers if we did this, because the troops would be forced to operate with such a limited portion of their transportation that the lessons of the maneuvers would be lost to a serious extent. The undertaking involves too much money and is too important to the Army and national defense to be so seriously limited by premature termination of the exercises.

In order that you may have a clear picture of this, I am attaching a list of the scheduled deliveries from the various manufacturers who are involved in the motor transportation question. In this connection, aside from the heavy pressure being exerted by the Quartermaster General's Department, I have personally been in communication with the heads of the various firms, and while they are doing everything they can to expedite deliveries, and we are assuming that they will make some gains, yet you can see to what extent we are embarrassed, notwithstanding the fact that the advertisement for the bids was circulated last October.[3]

There is also this further consideration, that after the date of delivery, the vehicle must be received, broken in and integrated into trains and tactical organizations.

The second matter to a certain extent relates to the foregoing in that it has to do with transportation. I gathered from what you said that there had been a confusion of understanding with relation to the charges for transportation. I feel that the War Department is at fault in this matter because it used the same word "transportation" to refer to two different items, one was a ride in a common carrier or by Army transport, or for gasoline to propel a truck; while the other item under "transportation" referred to the purchase of vehicles which had heretofore been lacking, and which are needed to tow or carry the heavy weapons and the crews for the same, and to transport supplies, tasks formerly performed by horse and mule teams.

The third point relates to the acquisition of land in Puerto Rico. I radioed

General Daley, as you suggested, and hope to have an answer from him very shortly. I find that the settlement of this land is or was to be determined on the basis of condemnation proceedings, so if any excess should be appropriated, it would revert to the Government in any event. I also find that during my absence on the West Coast, General Daley had reported that in order to effect a reduction in the property cost of this land, he was planning to permit the owners to harvest their sugar cane so far as would be practicable without interfering with the urgently needed temporary construction. Faithfully yours,

GCMRL/G. C. Marshall Papers (Pentagon Office, Selected)

1. A Democrat from South Carolina, Byrnes served on the Senate Appropriations Committee.

2. Marshall was referring to the Emergency Supplemental Appropriation Bill for 1940, [H.R. 7805] which was enacted on February 12, 1940.

3. The transportation problem is discussed in Marshall to Kaufman T. Keller, December 18, 1939, pp. 117–18.

TO WILLIAM ALLEN WHITE[1]   January 25, 1940
[Washington, D.C.]

My dear Mr. White: The attached editorial was brought to my attention today on returning from an inspection trip on the West Coast. There have been a number of somewhat similar comments regarding the remarks I made before a meeting of the Historical Society here in Washington, but your reaction is of more importance to me than that of the ordinary commentator.[2]

I am enclosing you a copy of what actually was said, which I thought at the time was being confined to a rather academic calm rather than a highly publicized meeting. The 25% referred to was not a comment as to the strength of the Army but one, as you will see, regarding a comparison of the mobilization status of the Navy and the Army. I was talking about systems rather than strength, and specifically, I was not criticizing our present system but was endeavoring to explain the problem which is normal to all Army planning.[3]   Faithfully yours,

GCMRL/G. C. Marshall Papers (Pentagon Office, General)

1. White was the well known editor and owner of the *Emporia* [Kansas] *Gazette*.

2. The editorial "What's the Matter?" appeared on January 11, p. 4. White wrote that if Marshall's statement that the army was not 25 percent ready for action was true, then President Roosevelt must "answer to this gross and terrible charge of incompetence." As commander in chief of the army for the past seven years, Roosevelt had, White asserted, apparently let the army run down to 25 percent efficiency in preparedness; yet he has had "every request he has made for the army granted," and was now asking for much more.

3. Responding to Marshall's letter, White wrote: "I am sorry that I gave the wrong impression. I shall try soon to straighten it out." (White to Marshall, January 30, 1940, GCMRL/G. C. Marshall Papers [Pentagon Office, General].)

To LIEUTENANT GENERAL STANLEY D. EMBICK January 26, 1940
[Washington, D.C.]

Dear Embick: The visiting of other divisions by the various division commanders will, I believe, have some good results. I notice in the 5th Division News of January 14th that Trott has visited Hodges' Division.

Due to the fact that the 2d Division has its transportation, and has had long practice with the new organization, I would like the division commanders of the 1st, 5th and 6th Divisions to see the 2d Division functioning in field maneuvers. The 2d Division completes a period of maneuvers in the field on January 28th. It then returns to Fort Sam Houston and will engage in target practice during the month of February. Krueger has informed me that, after about two weeks of target practice, the 2d Division will probably have another maneuver. I would like you to find out from Brees and Krueger when this maneuver will be held and arrange for the attendance of the division commanders of the 1st, 5th and 6th Divisions. The division commanders may be accompanied, if desired, by one or two other officers of their respective divisions. Travel by military airplane is authorized. The costs of the trip may be defrayed from training funds now at allotted status to you.[1]

Please let me know of your arrangements concerning this matter, as I may want to send one or two of my staff officers from here to see what a triangular division with full transportation looks like and to see how it functions. Faithfully yours,

GCMRL/G. C. Marshall Papers (Pentagon Office, Selected)

1. Both the Fifth and Sixth divisions had been recently reorganized into the three-regiment organization which the Second Division had tested under the leadership of Major General Walter Krueger.

To COLONEL EDMUND L. GRUBER[1] January 27, 1940
[Washington, D.C.]

Dear Gruber: I learned with great regret during my few hours at Benning last Monday that you had had the hard luck to contract pneumonia, but I was relieved to find out that you are well on the way to recovery. Colonel

Ward and I had intended to go to the hospital to see you Monday night, but just as we sat down to dinner, we received word of the rapidly approaching storm of snow and sleet from the Gulf, and we left on twenty minutes' notice. Incidentally, we made the trip to Washington in a trifle under three hours due to a seventy mile an hour tail wind.

I hope very much that your convalescence proceeds rapidly, and also that you do not try to force the issue, but rather that you carefully follow out the instructions of the doctors.

We had a very interesting, though very rapid trip around the country. The maneuvers on the West Coast were the most impressive I have ever seen in time of peace and represented a milestone, I think, in cooperation between the Army and the Navy, as well as the civilian components. The Cavalry Division was marching in from a four-day maneuver with a temperature of 10 degrees above zero, and I reviewed them—a hard-bitten, efficient looking lot. The Second Division was in the field at 18 above zero, and they looked equally sturdy and seasoned. I was sorry I could not stay long enough to see the First Division take the field Monday night.   Faithfully yours,

GCMRL/G. C. Marshall Papers (Pentagon Office, Selected)

1. Gruber was acting chief of staff for the Fourth Army Corps from January 2 to February 10, 1940; from February to October he was deputy control officer for the Third Army maneuvers.

To General Pedro Góes Monteiro   January 29, 1940
[Washington, D.C.]

My dear General Góes: It distressed me greatly to learn of the loss of your brother, Durval. Although it was not my good fortune to know him personally, I know what a misfortune his passing has been to you. Yet, it is certain that you are facing this trouble with the same courage that you have displayed so many times in the past. Confirming my radiogram of January 26th, I send you my most sincere condolence.

Your letter of December 27, 1939, was most welcome and I thank you for the expressions of friendship contained therein. Since its receipt, I have been absent from Washington for about ten days, returning here about a week ago. General Arnold and I flew to California to witness the Joint Army and Navy Maneuvers there. We made the flight from Washington to Sacramento, California, in one day. On the return trip, we stopped to inspect training activities at various places. Saw several of your friends, including General Fickel at March Field, General Joyce at El Paso, Generals Brees, Krueger and Collins at San Antonio, General Martin at Barksdale Field, and General Short at Fort Benning. All spoke enthusiastically of your visit last summer. General Fickel is coming to Washington for duty as Assistant Chief of the Air Corps. General Short will Command the "Blue" Army Corps during the maneuvers in the South next spring, and General Krueger will command the "Red" opposing forces.[1]

On my return to Washington, I was pleased to learn that His Excellency, President Vargas, has approved the acquisition by the Brazilian Army of the 90 six-inch guns. This armament, although not of recent manufacture, has many good characteristics and is capable of filling an important role in the defense of your many harbors.

You will be interested to know that the Ordnance and Electrical Engineers, whom you sent to the United States, are now engaged on a schedule of visits to various arsenals and factories. The Electrical Engineers are including in this itinerary: General Electric factories at Schenectady, Harvard University and Massachusetts Institute of Technology at Boston, the Sperry Co. plant at Brooklyn, West Point, the Army Signal School, Bethlehem Steel Co. plant at Bethlehem, Pennsylvania, and the Westinghouse and Carnegie Steel factories in Pittsburgh. The Electrical [*Ordnance?*] Engineers, in addition to visiting Boston, are spending a week at each of the following places: Army arsenals at Philadelphia, Picatinny, Watertown, Springfield, Watervliet, and the Bethlehem and Carnegie Steel companies. These visits will terminate about the middle of March, after which we shall plan an additional program which I trust will be profitable to these officers.

It is a pleasure for me to inform you that the United States Senate has recently approved the Joint Resolution which will permit the acquisition of armament by South American countries from our government arsenals. The Senate inserted an amendment providing that such acquisition shall not be permitted to interfere with the execution of the armament program on which the United States is now engaged. The Resolution has been returned to the House of Representatives for their action on the amendment, and I feel sure that the measure will soon become law. Unfortunately, our army arsenals will not be able to render assistance to you for the next year or two, on account of the flood of government orders confronting them. However, the passage of the resolution will enable us to eventually give material cooperation to our good friend, the Brazilian Army.[2]

With reference to the United States mission to Rio, I am still planning to send Miller there as Chief of the Mission, after he completes his course at the War College in June. Confidentially, I plan to return the present members of the Mission to the United States at the expiration of their two years of service, with the possible exception of Major Elliott.[3] My earnest desire is to give you the best qualified officers that we can select, so that the Mission will be of maximum benefit to your army. If you have any suggestions or desires in this matter, please communicate them to me.

Believe me, my dear General Góes, your sincere friend and admirer. I take pleasure in sending my respectful compliments to Mrs. Monteiro and your daughter, and an "abraco" to you. With best wishes for your health, I remain Faithfully yours,

NA/RG 165 (WPD, 4224)

1. Brigadier General Jacob E. Fickel served as wing commander, March Field, Riverside, California. Brigadier General James L. Collins commanded the artillery section of the Second Division at Fort Sam Houston. Brigadier General Frederick L. Martin commanded the Air Corps wing at Barksdale Field, Shreveport, Louisiana. The maneuvers that Marshall referred to were the Third Army exercises in the Sabine River region of Louisiana and Texas.

2. House Joint Resolution 367 (adopted on June 15, 1940) authorized the manufacture, procurement, and sale of coastal defense and antiaircraft materiel to Latin American governments. The Judge Advocate General's Department had previously interpreted this language as excluding all other munitions. (For the 1939 efforts to permit certain arms sales to Latin America, see the editorial note on pp. 23–24.) The questions of the proper policy with regard to selling obsolete or surplus small arms and of the policy regarding new and modern arms continued to plague the Roosevelt administration and the War Department for months. Marshall was not prepared to part with any of his modern equipment for a long time to come. (Stetson Conn and Byron Fairchild, *The Framework of Hemisphere Defense,* a volume in the *United States Army in World War II* [Washington: GPO, 1960], pp. 209–11.)

3. Lowell A. Elliott, of the Chemical Warfare Service, continued with the military mission in Brazil through 1941.

TO WILLIAM DAVEY   January 29, 1940
                                                   [Washington, D.C.]

My dear Mr. Davey: Your letter was received this morning, calling my attention to the inconvenience, as well as the irritation, of having soldiers on maneuvers in such close proximity to your house. I much regret that you have been disturbed and also that apparently you have been somewhat prejudiced against the Army.[1]

I was present on the West Coast when the landing was made at Monterey, though I was not able to remain long enough to see the development of the operations on shore. Under the circumstances—availability of land, character of the beaches, time restrictions, expense, etc., Monterey was the only place where this landing could be carried out; and there were serious risks in the operation even at Monterey.

Such training is essential both to the Army and for the Navy, just as similar training is essential for a baseball, football, or any other team. So far as possible we try to avoid any interference with the ordinary civil pursuits and with the affairs of citizens. Sometimes, as in this case at Monterey, it is impossible to stage the maneuvers at a distance from the local community. The Army, however, is but doing its best to prepare to perform the function for which it is supported by the citizens of this country.[2] Faithfully yours,

GCMRL/G. C. Marshall Papers (Pentagon Office, General)

1. Davey, an "irritated civilian" from Carmel, California, asked Marshall why "in the present war games on the Monterey Peninsula, is it necessary to have the Blues or the Blacks or whatever they are camping three feet from my window and actually leaning against my house? . . . It may be doing the Army a service even of the smallest to report that, aside from whatever tactical discoveries are achieved, the strategy of surrounding small non-combatant houses with groups of soldiers . . . is, from the point of view of the one living within the house, undoubtedly of low psychological value." Davey hoped "that civilians still retain certain mythical 'rights', such as privacy." (Davey to Marshall, n.d., GCMRL/G. C. Marshall Papers [Pentagon Office, General].)

2. In a letter written in February 1940, Davey expressed his "admiration for the really American dignity of your reply. . . . Such a direct reply certainly makes me think much of the Army with a Chief of Staff whose qualities transcend even the very high ones required." (Davey to Marshall, n.d., GCMRL/G. C. Marshall Papers [Pentagon Office, General].)

To John C. O'Laughlin   January 29, 1940
                                                     [Washington, D.C.]

My dear Cal: This morning I read the editorial in the Army and Navy Journal of January 27th, referring to my recent inspection trips. I appreciate the generous treatment you have given me, and I think it will be very helpful with the Service at large.[1]

I had some radio communication with General Pershing the afternoon of the day of his arrival in Tucson. I was flying east from March Field trying to reach El Paso in time to review the Cavalry Division as it returned from the field; I made it by about fifteen minutes. Incidentally, we enjoyed perfect flying weather throughout, but we flew all the way from Leavenworth to the West Coast, east to Georgia and north to Washington followed by vicious weather, which got closer and closer on our heels. Arnold sent me a note this morning from General Martin at Barksdale Field, who said sleet and snow struck them thirty minutes after our departure. We were just sitting down to dinner at Benning when the weather report caused us to abandon the meal and the assembling guests, and take off for Washington. We had a perfect flight up here, as the visibility was good and we had a tail wind of from 50 to 70 miles an hour; made the trip in 2 hours and 50 minutes. Faithfully yours,

P.S.   Apropos of the editorial in the Army and Navy Journal, I am enclosing a confidential memorandum of a few days ago to the Staff.[2]

GCMRL/G. C. Marshall Papers (Pentagon Office, Selected)

1. O'Laughlin was the publisher of the *Army and Navy Journal.* The editorial observed that Marshall "is wisely building an en rapport between the high command in Washington and the forces in the field. A lack of understanding between the War Department General Staff and the field could hold dire possibilities for the success of the programs and policies laid

down by the Secretary of War. To avoid this and to assure complete coordination of purposes and methods, General Marshall has been taking every precaution to keep in closest touch with the Army units." It also noted Marshall's conference with the Corps Area commanders and his inspection trips to the maneuvers in the west and south. Emphasizing the importance of the chief of staff's personal presence in the field, the editorial said: "a thousand letters could not convey the picture he brought back in his mind."

2. The memorandum to which Marshall refers is that of January 25, printed on p. 146. O'Laughlin replied that he was "glad the editorial pleased you. It is only the beginning of the campaign I have in mind." (O'Laughlin to Marshall, January 30, 1940, GCMRL/G. C. Marshall Papers [Pentagon Office, Selected].)

To David W. Hazen   February 2, 1940
                                                  [Washington, D.C.]

Dear Hazen: I have just this moment read your note of January 31st, with its picture of spring weather and temptations to take the field in Oregon.[1]

I was out on the Coast but a portion of three days, after a straight flight from Washington to Sacramento. I went to the plane here directly from the Military Committee, and continued around the circuit of inspections along the Southern frontier in time to be back here for another hearing six days later. While I saw practically all the troops, it was at horse race speed.

The joint maneuver with the Navy in California was a remarkable exercise and productive of a tremendous amount of valuable training, especially for the Air Corps of the two services—almost 500 planes involved; for the transport service and the joint staffs of the Army and Navy. Of course the 3d Division got a great experience out of going to sea in business like fashion and making their landing; the anti-aircraft and National Guard in California, the Coast Defense people, also of the National Guard, and the Aircraft warning service, which included civilian agencies as well as military, made the whole affair productive of a great deal of valuable experience.[2]

I have been tremendously busy keeping abreast of the rapid changes in the War Department and appearing before Committees; spent six hours before the Military Committee last Wednesday. I am off to Panama in a Flying Fortress Sunday morning, to do that in a hurry and also Puerto Rico, and I only have six days for the trip.

With warm regards,   Faithfully yours,

GCMRL/G. C. Marshall Papers (Pentagon Office, General)

1. A correspondent for the Portland *Oregonian,* Hazen tempted Marshall with the image of a pleasant horseback ride along some woodland path. "Since last Saturday it has been like

spring; a few days before there was a touch of snow, but not enough to take the green out of the grass." (Hazen to Marshall, January 31, 1940, GCMRL/G. C. Marshall Papers [Pentagon Office, General].)

2. Hazen informed Marshall that the West Coast maneuvers had awakened Oregonians to the fact of war, and the international situation then became a constant point of discussion. (Ibid.)

To Lieutenant General John L. De Witt[1]   February 3, 1940
[Washington, D.C.]

Dear De Witt: I have been intending to write to you ever since my return from the West Coast to give you my reactions on the Maneuvers. However, the tremendous pressure of business, along with time-consuming hearings, have delayed me. Now this morning I have your letter of January 31st, which I have only been able to scan, as I am leaving almost immediately by a B-17 plane for Panama.

I am delighted with your report of the conference. I think the Maneuver was a grand performance and the most practical I have seen in the peacetime training of the Army. Most of all I was impressed with your leadership in making it one of complete cooperation with the Navy and the most practical, realistic training exercise we have yet had. I feel that you have justified in your first two months the policy of having Lieutenant Generals, and I want you to know that I deeply appreciate the fine job you have done.[2]

Your letter is very informative, and I will see that it is passed around in the Staff and that Admiral Stark sees it.   Hastily yours,

GCMRL/G. C. Marshall Papers (Pentagon Office, Selected)

1. De Witt had been given command of the Fourth Army and the Ninth Corps Area—with headquarters in San Francisco—and promoted to lieutenant general in December 1939.

2. Despite communications problems during the maneuvers, De Witt reported, both the army and navy cooperated fully in the operations. He had made certain that his general officers met and knew the senior naval officers prior to the maneuvers. "There was not a single case of friction . . . [and] the basis for it all, of course, exists in the relationship between yourself and Admiral Stark and it has permeated down through all echelons in both services."

Briefing the chief of staff on his critique, De Witt wrote: "the Army has much to learn and can only overcome the defects existing in its organization and its training by service in the field, and it can only be made ready to accomplish this mission both in peace and war by extended training in the field; to live and work under field conditions, for only by such means can those defects found to exist be corrected. I think one of the finest things that has ever happened to the Army was your action in getting these troops into the field and divisional training started. It is going to pay tremendous dividends in the end." (De Witt to Marshall, January 31, 1940, GCMRL/G. C. Marshall Papers [Pentagon Office, Selected].)

FLYING in a B-17, Marshall left Bolling Field in Washington, D.C., on the morning of February 4, 1940, for a whirlwind inspection trip of the army's installations in the Caribbean. He inspected the defenses of the Panama Canal Zone and the new Puerto Rican Department. Having logged 5,250 miles in the air, Marshall was back at his desk in the Munitions Building on the morning of February 14.

Part of the reason for his trip, he later told members of the House Appropriations Committee, was to study the possibilities of further army-navy cooperation. He also pressed the congressmen for larger appropriations for land acquisition and construction in the region. Could not money be saved, Democrat David D. Terry from Arkansas asked the chief of staff on February 26, by combining army and navy facilities? Despite his desire for interservice cooperation, Marshall was opposed to the "overconcentration" that would result when enormously large and complex bases were combined: "we do not want to put all our eggs in one basket." Moreover, Marshall observed, "each service is responsible to our Government for the efficiency and economy of its own particular operations. These responsibilities cannot be delegated, one to the other. More important, though, and I say this very specifically, we must not concentrate too much." (House Appropriations Committee, *Military Establishment Appropriation Bill for 1941, Hearings* [Washington: GPO, 1940], pp. 31–32.) ★

To Major General Edmund L. Daley   February 14, 1940
                                                     [Washington, D.C.]

Dear Daley: I reached Miami 4 hours and 30 minutes out from Borinquen, a record flight I believe.[1] After a night in Miami, we left the next morning to beat the bad weather into Washington. It was fortunate that we did because today there is a blizzard, and you can barely see across the street, with the snow blowing almost horizontally.

My visit to Puerto Rico was satisfying and gratifying, and I was tremendously impressed by the highly efficient manner in which you had both developed the Department and met the emergencies of the situation. I have no comment to make except by way of congratulation and appreciation.

I think the opportunity to see what was happening there will prove very beneficial to me and helpful to the War Department, and I hope will be of direct service to you and your command. Certainly we will make every effort to see that you get all possible assistance.

I inquired this morning immediately on coming to the office about the money for the piece of land near your headquarters, and I am glad to tell you that it has just gone through successfully for $250,000.00 I believe. I have told them to notify you of this, and also of the amount of construction money that will be available to you out of the deficiency appropriation, so you will not be delayed in your preliminary planning.[2]

Again let me thank you for your fine hospitality, the lovely dinner, and all of the courtesy and consideration shown me.[3]

With my congratulations on your job, and my personal thanks, believe me   Faithfully yours,

GCMRL/G. C. Marshall Papers (Pentagon Office, Selected)

1. Borinquen Field was in western Puerto Rico, approximately one thousand miles from Miami, Florida.

2. On February 12, Congress appropriated $200,000 for eight hundred acres for a general depot and cantonment area and the enlargement of Camp Buchanan. The Emergency Supplemental Appropriation Act for 1940, also allocated $319,000 for Air Corps shelter construction. On June 29, 1940, Congress also appropriated $616,700 for the construction, rehabilitation, and installation of necessary buildings and utilities.

3. Daley wrote: "To the officers and men in the field, your presence was of incalculable morale value. To myself and my staff, you outlined definitely the position of Puerto Rico in the national defense and our task to prepare the Puerto Rican Department for its mission." (Daley to Marshall, February 14, 1940, GCMRL/G. C. Marshall Papers [Pentagon Office, Selected].)

To MAJOR GENERAL CHARLES D. HERRON   February 14, 1940
Confidential   [Washington, D.C.]

Dear Herron: I returned last night from Panama and Puerto Rico, to find your letter of February 3d, and am passing it over to War Plans to mull over.[1] I will write you a little more with reference to the matter later on. Meanwhile I have told them to let you have the first data and outline that we get of the Joint Maneuver on the West Coast. It was tremendously impressive and highly instructive, easily the most realistic affair in the air and on the ground, in my military experience, short of war.

Admiral Stark and I are getting along very intimately and I hope we will have a genuine basis to complete cooperation shortly.

I had a fine, though greatly hurried trip through the Caribbean area. Incidentally, I flew from Puerto Rico to Miami in 4 hours and 30 minutes, a record I believe.

Now, most confidentially, I hope to fly to Hawaii the first part of March, between the House hearings on the Appropriation Bill and those of the Senate. I may go by China Clipper, though more probably by the new B-17B Flying Fortress. I will be unable to give you much advance notice, as it will be a matter of getting away the moment I find myself clear, and also of spotting the weather before leaving Washington.

If I do make the trip, please spare me so far as possible from official entertaining and repeated "honors." Formal honors on arrival will be sufficient. I would like the rest of the time for business, and maybe a moment to sit down and rest, something I have not had for about five months. I had hoped to have a day of relaxation at Miami Beach with Mrs. Marshall yesterday, but the weather drove me on to Washington.

This is a hasty note, as I have a huge pile of business on hand.

With affectionate greetings to you both,   Faithfully yours,

P.S.   I may have you a Lieutenant Generalcy if I have any luck in the House.[2]

GCMRL/G. C. Marshall Papers (Pentagon Office, Selected)

1. Herron, commanding general of the Hawaiian Department, had written that he was cultivating relations with the navy. He expressed his "considerable suspicion" that the navy desired to expand their facilities in Hawaii. Herron admired the thorough development of navy maneuvers. "They do not have to put on demonstrations instead of maneuvers, in order that there may be some profit to the command, as we often do. . . . There is no excitement among local orientals in regard to the world situation. This part of your kingdom seems to ride on an even keel." (Herron to Marshall, February 3, 1940, GCMRL/G. C. Marshall Papers [Pentagon Office, Selected].)

2. On February 1 the Senate passed S. 3200, which provided for the temporary rank of lieutenant general for the commanders of the Panama Canal and Hawaiian departments. The House passed the bill on July 25, and it was signed by the president on July 31, 1940.

To MAJOR GENERAL DANIEL VAN VOORHIS[1]   February 14, 1940
[Washington, D.C.]

Dear Van Voorhis: My trip to Puerto Rico was very informative, and I was greatly impressed with what had been done in the short period of that Department's existence. As in Panama, I picked up many things regarding which the War Department could take a more helpful attitude. En route from Puerto Rico to the Mainland, I sent you a radio to the effect that I had instructed Daley to fly over to Panama to talk things over with you. He will have his Air officer with him and possibly another staff officer. I think it is very important that the complementary relationship between Puerto Rico and Panama be developed through personal conversations.

I am not satisfied with the present Air set-up, at least so far as the Atlantic side is concerned. It seems to me that we might have less bombers in Panama and more in Puerto Rico, also more of pursuit in Puerto Rico, though no less of this type in Panama. However, this is very superficial thinking, and I am hopeful that you and Daley can establish a sound base of departure.[2]

So far as the Panama Canal Department is concerned, I want you to know that I was greatly impressed with how much you had done in the brief period of your leadership, you have given me a feeling of complete confidence regarding matters in the Canal Zone. It is very satisfying to my state of mind to feel that you are at the helm during this critical period.

I am grateful to you for the honors and courtesies paid me during my visit, and especially for the effective manner in which you arranged my program. Mrs. Van Voorhis was delightful in her hospitality, and I think she is a very valuable asset to that command.

This is my first morning at the office, and I am pretty well overwhelmed, but I wanted to write to you immediately.

With warm regards,   Faithfully yours,

P.S.   Please have your A.D.C. [aide-de-camp] let me know cost of those two neckties and the helmet ornament.

GCMRL/G. C. Marshall Papers (Pentagon Office, Selected)

1. Van Voorhis assumed command of the Panama Canal Department in January 1940.

2. Daley believed that the proper peacetime bomber strength for the Puerto Rican Department was one heavy bombardment group. This would be accompanied by a pursuit group and a reconnaissance squadron. (Daley Memorandum to The Adjutant General, January 31, 1940, NA/RG 407 [381].) Van Voorhis considered that the proposed long-range reconnaissance wing of eighty-four planes would carry out their assignment on both ocean fronts. He asserted, however, that medium-range reconnaissance and bomber groups be replaced by long-range bombers to stop an attack on the canal from sea or land. (Van Voorhis Memorandum to The Adjutant General, February 12, 1940, NA/RG 407 [660.2-2/1D].)

To Lieutenant Colonel Francis A. Byrne[1]   February 16, 1940
[Washington, D.C.]

My dear Colonel Byrne: I am enclosing a letter from Captain Storck regarding Sergeant Morossow, at Screven, which is largely self-explanatory.

Morossow was with me in China, and later was my provost sergeant at Screven, the job he has been continued in for a good many years. Of course I know nothing of his service since I left Screven in 1933, but at that time he was the most efficient provost sergeant I had ever seen in the Army, and I think it was merely a case of doing efficiently whatever he was charged with. The handling of almost all the fatigue work at Screven and even construction by the prisoners, was the outstanding example in my Army experience of how this business should be carried out in garrison. The troops were spared practically every distraction from their purely military business; the prisoners were worked harder than any I have ever seen, and yet Screven was a popular point for deserters to turn in. I recall that when we had 35 prisoners at Screven, there was only one at Moultrie; but I would not say that this should be taken as an indication of relative efficiency to the disadvantage of Screven, as I commanded Moultrie after leaving Screven.

I am completely unfamiliar with the present situation as to promotions in the 8th Infantry and as to Morrosow's work since I left the regiment, but I submit this commendation of his past services.[2]   Faithfully yours,

GCMRL/G. C. Marshall Papers (Pentagon Office, General)

1. Byrne had commanded the Eighth Infantry at Fort Moultrie, South Carolina, until November 27, 1939.

2. Captain Louis J. Storck (U.S.M.A., 1923), who had served at Fort Screven, Georgia, with Marshall in 1933, had written on February 12 seeking the chief of staff's help in promoting and finding a suitable post for First Sergeant Joseph Morossow, who was approaching retirement and therefore was prevented by regulations from being promoted to master sergeant. Marshall sent Storck a copy of his letter to Byrne with the admonition that he not tell Morossow of his intervention. Byrne replied on February 19 that "every effort will be made to take care of this deserving soldier." On April 9, 1941, Morossow wrote to Marshall that he was retiring on April 28 and asked if he could be placed in a civilian job at Fort Screven. Marshall arranged this. (All correspondence on this subject is in GCMRL/G. C. Marshall Papers [Pentagon Office, General].)

To Major Mark W. Clark   February 16, 1940
                                                        [Washington, D.C.]

My dear Clark: When I returned from the Pacific Coast I directed your detail as instructor at the War College. G-1 informed me however that you have had only three months of actual duty with troops since 1920 and in view of this fact I withdrew my instructions concerning your War College assignment, because I thought it would be harmful to your career.

If you still feel that you want to go ahead with it I will reopen the matter. However, I would like you to tell me where you would like troop duty, and I will try to arrange exactly that.[1]   Faithfully yours,

NA/RG 165 (OCS, 14625-193)

1. Clark had spent most of his time in the 1920s and 1930s in school—he was a graduate of the Infantry School (1925), the Command and General Staff School (1935), and the Army War College (1937)—or as an instructor or in staff positions. Since June 1937 he had been the Third Division plans and training officer (G-3) at Fort Lewis, Washington, and had planned and helped to direct the division's participation in the joint army-navy maneuvers in January 1940. He had requested assignment as an instructor at the Army War College. In March 1940, Marshall arranged this assignment for him. Clark reported to the War College in July 1940, but since it had closed, he joined the staff of the newly activated General Headquarters. (See Mark W. Clark, *Calculated Risk* [New York: Harper and Brothers, 1950], pp. 9–11.)

To Major General James G. Harbord[1]   February 17, 1940
                                                [Washington, D.C.]

Dear General: I have just read your note of February 16th regarding Truman Smith's talk, and I appreciate your generous expressions of appreciation. Smith has a pretty thorough understanding of things German, and his prognosis a year before Munich was one of the most remarkable reports of a Military Attaché.[2] Incidentally, should you have occasion for another talk—not to be publicized—I have a Major Black, of the Field Artillery, over recently from Germany, who I am sure would interest any formal gathering. He is being sent the rounds of the Divisions concentrated in the field.[3]

At the present time, we are trying every way to both inform the troops of what we learn abroad, and to inform the War Department staff of what is the actual condition of affairs with the troops. Every time I go on the road I am surprised anew at how utterly impossible it is to exercise any control over troops in the field from a desk and expect to do a good job of it. However, it doesn't give me much time to think or operate here, and especially to prepare for lengthy hearings before the Committees of Congress. They had me before the Military Committee from 10:30 to a quarter to five the other day, and this is the important battle I must fight for the Army.

Confidentially, I am planning to take off for Hawaii about March 2d so as to make that inspection between the House hearings and those of the Senate. After that I will only have several very pleasant and easily made inspections of the troops in the Southeast and, of course, during the maneuvers of some 65,000 troops. In the summer I must fly to Alaska, but that should be a very delightful trip. Then, if Hitler and Stalin will let up on me a little bit, I am going to take a vacation.

I wish I could hear you and General Pershing and General Dawes get together in Arizona; I would love to hear your discussions. I sent a radio to General Pershing from the plane as we were flying over the Candado-Vanderbilt Hotel beach, where the General and I played around for a week following a shipwreck in 1920. The message went direct from the plane to the Army operator of the Tucson air field, and within five minutes I got a report back that Miss May Pershing had received the message.[4]

Mrs. Marshall was at Miami Beach and is now at Key West. She plans to return the end of the month, but I want her to stay until after I get back from Hawaii.

With affectionate regards to you and Anne,   Faithfully yours,

GCMRL/G. C. Marshall Papers (Pentagon Office, Selected)

1. Harbord had been Pershing's chief of staff in France and later deputy chief of staff of the army.

2. Lieutenant Colonel Truman Smith had been military attaché in Berlin in the 1920s and again between August 1935 and April 1939. Since August 1939 he had been in the G-2 section of the General Staff. (For Smith's observations on Germany, see *Berlin Alert: The Memoirs and Reports of Truman Smith,* ed. Robert Hessen [Stanford, Calif.: Hoover Institution Press, 1984].) Smith was also a good friend of Charles A. Lindbergh, who noted in his diary of July 25, 1939: "I found that Marshall had a very high regard for Smith." (*The Wartime Journals of Charles A. Lindbergh* [New York: Harcourt Brace Jovanovich, 1970], p. 235. See also *Papers of GCM,* 1: 479, 482–84, 670.) In his February 6 letter, Harbord asked for Smith to speak at the Second Division dinner in New York City. Smith "delivered a most excellent talk on the Polish Campaign. He was kind enough to submit himself to questions afterward and the questions were about what you would expect from sixty former officers more than twenty years out of service, but he handled himself very well and a good many of the questions were not foolish." (Harbord to Marshall, February 16, 1940, GCMRL/G. C. Marshall Papers [Pentagon Office, Selected].)

3. Concerning Percy G. Black, see Marshall to Chaffee, December 20, 1939, p. 120.

4. General and Mrs. Harbord vacationed with General Pershing and Brigadier General and Mrs. Charles G. Dawes in Tucson, Arizona; Guaymas, Mexico; and Rancho Santa Fe, California. The "shipwreck" to which Marshall refers occurred on May 10, 1920, when the U.S.A.T. *Northern Pacific* ran aground while leaving San Juan, Puerto Rico. (See *Papers of GCM,* 1: 293.) May was General Pershing's sister.

To LIEUTENANT COLONEL JOHN C. MONTGOMERY[1]   February 21, 1940
[Washington, D.C.]

My dear Montgomery: Thanks for your cordial note of February 20th, with the pleasant exaggerations about my radio talk. I personally think it was rather a mess, having rushed it together during the lunch period that day and then mixing up the pages when I started to read it. However, if Virginia and you thought it was O.K., it is reassuring to me.[2]

I did not know Clifton knew you, but I appreciate your giving him a pleasant reception.

Give my love to Virginia.   Faithfully yours,

GCMRL/G. C. Marshall Papers (Pentagon Office, General)

1. Montgomery (U.S.M.A., 1903) was a vice president of the First Boston Corporation in New York City.

2. On February 16, Marshall spoke at 7:00 P.M. to a national radio audience from the Hotel Washington, where he was attending the Reserve Officers' Association's national convention banquet. In the broadcast—which was part of association-sponsored "National Defense Week"—Marshall spoke on many of the same issues that he had been addressing since becoming chief of staff (e.g., the army's deficiencies and the importance of R.O.T.C. and the Reserve Corps). The nation was traditionally committed to a small army, he concluded, "but we must have the best Army of its size in the world. . . . Until the world is a much more peaceful place, with men's minds directed towards homes and firesides, farms and factories, the military necessities for our security must be carefully weighed and then created in fact, and not in theory." (GCMRL/G. C. Marshall Papers [Pentagon Office, Speeches].)

MARSHALL asserted, "If Europe blazes in the late spring or summer, we must put our house in order before the sparks reach the Western Hemisphere." These words highlighted the first formal testimony by the chief of staff before the subcommittee on the War Department of the House Appropriations Committee on February 23, 1940. (*Military Establishment Appropriation Bill for 1941, Hearings* [Washington: GPO, 1940], p. 3.) Congress at this time vigorously debated the appropriations for fiscal year 1941 and the use of funds for large-scale maneuvers. Subcommittee chairman J. Buell Snyder stated the issue succinctly: "The Congress is in a position where it has got to reduce these annual appropriation bills, the defense measures not excepted." (Ibid., p. 587. See also Mark S. Watson, *Chief of Staff: Prewar Plans and Preparations,* a volume in the *United States Army in World War II* [Washington: GPO, 1950], pp. 164–65.) Marshall cautioned his staff that "the impact of economy will probably be terrific. It will react to our advantage if our bill is acted on at the latest possible date. It is probable that events in Europe will develop in such a way as to affect Congressional action." (Walter B. Smith Report of Conference held in the Chief of Staff's office, February 16, 1940, NA/RG 165 [OCS, Chief of Staff Conferences File].)

Marshall clearly stated the War Department's priorities: "Our great objective is the procurement of the critical items of equipment—ammunition, rifles, artillery, tanks, and so forth, for the Protective Mobilization Plan Force (the P.M.P.) of 750,000 men in units, and about 250,000 individuals as replacements. These munitions will be needed immediately in an emergency. They require from 1 to 2 years to procure. They would be like gold in the vault against a financial crisis." The immediate objective, he contended, was to outfit the Regular Army's 227,000 authorized men and the National Guard's 235,000. An additional $19,000,000 should be appropriated for the creation of a sixth division, special corps troops for a second army corps, and the expansion of the mechanized brigade. This expansion would carry the army to a total of 242,000 Regular enlisted men, a force that should be maintained "until world conditions have stabilized." Marshall reminded the subcommittee members, however, that "this increase should come after the materiel requirements for the Protective Mobilization Plan Force have been provided." (*Military Establishment Appropriation Bill for 1941,* p. 3.)

Embattled by the congressional opposition to increased expenditures on maneuvers, the chief of staff resolutely defended, on February 23 and 26, the on-going corps concentrations and explained the necessity for summer field army maneuvers in fiscal year 1941. Divisions from each field army in the current southern maneuvers, he explained, would return to their bases and form the nucleus for the coming summer exercises. Marshall asked for funds to extend National Guard field training from fifteen to twenty-seven days—twenty-one days of field maneuvers and six days for small-unit training. (Ibid., pp. 12–13, 18–19.) In pressing for an expanded role for the National Guard, Marshall had to maneuver carefully as he was pitting himself against many state adjutants general, who did not want control of training to get outside state borders, and against Major General Milton A. Reckord, a key figure in the National Guard Association, who opposed lengthening the Guard's field training. Marshall was determined to settle the issue without stirring up animosity in powerful Guard elements—unless he had to. (Smith, Report of Conference, February 16, 1940.) ★

MEMORANDUM FOR COLONEL BURNS[1] February 23, 1940
[Washington, D.C.]

Colonel Burns: These are some notes regarding Maneuvers which Mr. Johnson asked me for the other day.

[Enclosure]

In brief, the situation as to maneuvers is this:

The Regular establishment in continental United States is scattered in more than 100 posts. To concentrate regiments and brigades for maneuvers involves a heavy and unavoidable expense, possibly four-fifths of the cost of the maneuver. There are only two solutions, from the viewpoint of economy, to this situation. One is to abandon a number of small posts and concentrate the Army with more relation to training necessities. This would require years to accomplish, if politically possible. The other is to abandon the idea of maneuvers because of the unfortunate location of our troops.

The second choice though proposed as an economy measure, would actually be a great governmental extravagance. The expense of maintaining our Army is heavy, but to maintain the troops without properly training them would be inexcusably wasteful, as well as highly dangerous in the present world situation.

The Army has never been permitted to train in time of peace except on a basis so limited that the officers have been largely without practical knowledge of the management and leadership of brigades, divisions and army corps. Battalions and regiments have had little or no experience in the necessary adjustments and mutual contacts common to large deployments. The Army in continental United States has been largely a collection of battalions. The battle team is an army corps of two or three divisions, with some 10,000 (peace strength) corps troops of heavy and antiaircraft artillery, engineers, anti-tank battalions, observation planes, quartermaster truck trains, signal corps units, medical organizations, etc. This team in action covers a wide zone, and a sector of great depth. It involves very skillful handling, the more so with mechanized and motorized units and considering the increasing ranges of weapons.

We now have our division and corps troops in the field. Some of the divisions have not yet been able to engage in divisional work, as it has been necessary to recruit, organize and train entirely new units, and there is a serious lack of motor transportation for all units. We have not yet assembled an army corps.

The first corps maneuver, to be only a one-sided "try-out", cannot be initiated until the first week in April because of the lack of transportation, motors for weapons, equipment and supplies. The larger general maneuver should get under way the second week in May. In results, it should dominate the teaching at the Army Schools, particularly Leavenworth and the War College; it should cause the amendment to a more practical basis of many of our regulations and tactical directions; it should vitalize the Army from the standpoint of leadership in campaign and a general knowledge of how to go about the modern business of fighting.

The duration of the maneuver has no relation to the cost. The principal expense is for transportation. Pay, rations, and similar charges go on whether in the field or in the post.

An Associated Press dispatch conveyed the impression to the public that $26,000,000 was to be expended for the coming maneuvers in the Southeast. This $26,000,000 provided for training, including ammunition for combat practice, in the Philippines, Hawaii, Panama, and Puerto Rico; it provided the money for the Joint Army and Navy exercise of last January on the West Coast; it permitted small concentrations and field training for regular troops in the North who were not moved to southern latitudes; it provided the money for the concentrations of the divisions in the Southeast, and it must yet provide the money for their return to their home stations. In other words, the major portion of this money has already been expended or must be expended by the end of May to return these troops to their home stations, regardless of whether or not we have a corps maneuver.

Throughout its history the Regular Army has been the victim of scattered posts, high costs of transportation for concentrations, limited areas on which to maneuver when concentrated, and complicated appropriation items and restrictions covering costs for training. This year a great emergency, and the wise direction of the President, has given the army, for the first time in peace, an opportunity to learn how to fight as a team against the necessity of safe-guarding American interests. It has not meant a period of indulgence or pleasurable opportunity for the officers and men. It has meant hardships, great hardships at times, living in tents or actually in the field in zero weather, and it has meant separation of families and added expenses.

But all have been enthusiastic at this long last opportunity. Morale is high, we are actually building up a field Army.

GCMRL/G. C. Marshall Papers (Pentagon Office, General)

1. Colonel James H. Burns (U.S.M.A., 1908) was the executive officer in Assistant Secretary of War Louis A. Johnson's office.

MEMORANDUM FOR ADMIRAL STARK   February 24, 1940
Confidential   [Washington, D.C.]

Subject: Joint Air Advisory Committee.

Referring to our conversation of Wednesday morning following The Joint Board meeting:

I suggest that we proceed with the organization of this committee on whatever basis, formal or informal, that you think best. The committee to prepare to advise us on the general subject of the relation of Army and Navy Air interests, (1) as to employment, (2) as to joint operations, (3) as to types of planes, and (4) as to possible joint use or operation of facilities in such special cases as may be found practicable and more economical—research for example, or certain depots, etc. It seems to me that with some such instructions to the committee, we could allow them to reach an agreement for our approval as to various subjects and matters that might be well for them to study.

I have in mind that where there is unanimity of opinion, and we approve, such matters could be placed in normal channels for formal consideration. The principal benefit should flow from the fact that we are getting together, on a more intimate and workable basis than in the past.[1]

I propose for this committee as Army members,

Major General H. H. Arnold, Chief of the Air Corps.
Brigadier General George H. Brett, Chief of the Materiel
Division, Office of the Chief of the Air Corps.
Lieut. Colonel Thomas T. Handy, G.S., War Plans Division.[2]

NA/RG 165 (OCS, 20218-50)

1. On January 9, 1940, Marshall—in a conversation with Acting Deputy Chief of Staff Brigadier General Lorenzo D. Gasser and Assistant Chief of Staff, War Plans Division, Brigadier General George V. Strong—suggested "an unofficial Joint Army-Navy Air Board" to handle mutual aeronautical interests, and particularly to determine the numbers of planes that each service should procure. At that time three army-navy agencies dealt with aeronautical problems: the Aeronautical Board for materiel and operating facilities; the Army and Navy Munitions Board for armaments and their production; and the Joint Board for functions, missions, and questions of duplication. Strong reminded the chief of staff that annual

procurements had never been discussed in army-navy meetings. He preferred that the Joint Board estimate procurement figures rather than creating a new unofficial committee. Such action presented the danger of freezing air requirements for the army during a period of very fluid international conditions. Strong suggested that the Joint Board provide a mandate for any new system of future planning. He warned Marshall that joint planning might "reopen the violent controversies which for years impaired all the working relations between the Army and the Navy." The assistant chief of staff claimed that naval officers never wanted a joint discussion of naval air procurement. The vague 1935 revision of the "Joint Action of the Army and Navy," Chapter IV, failed to delineate the functions of each service's air component. Strong advised that a joint committee, however composed, should "avoid scrupulously any effort to transcend its provisions." (Strong Memorandum for the Chief of Staff, January 13, 1940, NA/RG 165 [WPD, 888–107].)

2. A Joint Air Advisory Committee was appointed on May 16, 1940, for the purposes Marshall outlined. In addition to the army officers nominated by the chief of staff, Admiral Stark appointed Rear Admirals Frederick J. Horne (U.S.N.A., 1899) and John H. Towers (U.S.N.A., 1906) and Commander Forrest Sherman (U.S.N.A., 1917). (Joint Memorandum, May 16, 1940, ibid.) On the problem of army-navy cooperation concerning aircraft, see Memorandum for Admiral Stark, July 7, 1941, pp. 562–64.

M ARSHALL answered questions from members of the House Sub-committee on War Department Appropriations on February 26, 1940. He explained that the Initial Protective Force (I.P.F.), a portion of the Protective Mobilization Plan (P.M.P.) force, consisted of the entire National Guard and a portion of the Regular Army. "Our present plan contemplates that in time of emergency our initial force will be expanded to the protective mobilization plan force within a period of approximately 4 months. It is therefore obvious that critical items required for the balance of the protective mobilization plan force must be on hand before an emergency arises." Marshall estimated that an appropriation of $76 million ($37 million in fiscal year 1941) was necessary to provide critical items for the I.P.F. For the remainder of the force, another $240 million had to be appropriated. (*Military Establishment Appropriation Bill for 1941,* p. 28.)

Asking for an additional 4,700 men to supplement existing units of the National Guard, Marshall met immediate opposition from subcommittee Chairman J. Buell Snyder. The chief of staff countered: "If National Guard units are to be effective in the early days of an emergency, it is imperative that they be maintained as nearly as practicable at full peace strength. Consequently, the diversion of any of the increase for the activation of new units is not considered to be in the best interests of preparedness." (Ibid., pp. 28–29.)

Marshall was asked to elaborate the War Department's policy on the expansion of the Reserve Officers' Training Corps. "Could you not establish more of these units over the country?" asked David D. Terry, Democrat from Arkansas. Marshall's reply is illustrative of his ideas on mobilization in general: "The policy has been and is that, until we are able to provide an adequate number of officers for the existing R.O.T.C. units, we should not establish any additional ones. We have a shortage of officers with the existing units, which becomes more marked as enrollment increases. In the last year the increase was approximately 10,000.

"The shortage of instructor personnel creates an unfortunate situation for the Army and also for the individual officer on R.O.T.C. duty. He is becoming badly overworked.

"We have felt it best to consider the needs of existing units rather than to establish additional ones." (Ibid., p. 33.)

Marshall seized this opportunity to educate Congress on the growing responsibilities of officers in the modern army. "I would like to present one other aspect at this time which has not yet been discussed. There has grown, up largely since 1919, many added responsibilities of the Regular Army which take an officer away from the important duty of commanding troops of his arm. On duty with the R.O.T.C. we have 826 officers; with the National Guard, a few under 500; 475 with the Organized Reserves. In addition, there are the faculties and students of the service schools, the General Staff, the overhead personnel of the various corps area and departments. All of these details take officers away from troops.

"Today we have a situation where the average line officer has little opportunity to handle men. He is losing the practical experience, and that is one of the things I am thinking very much about. There is a strong demand to have officers assigned to troops, but the best officers are in demand everywhere and if something weren't done to help them they would rarely serve with troops. We cannot continue to take officers away from troops in the Army without jeopardizing leadership, and I am inclined to think that we have about reached the limit at the present time." (Ibid., p. 34.)

The chief of staff met stiff opposition that day from D. Lane Powers, Republican from New Jersey, who responded to Marshall's comments on officer strength in the military establishment: "Year after year it is the same. This is the eighth year I have sat here, and I have heard Army officers come and say, 'If you will just do this this year, no matter what happens, we are absolutely set; we won't require any more. That will give us a nucleus of what we want.' And then the next year something different is advocated. I sat here in 1933 and heard General MacArthur say, 'If we had 165,000 enlisted men in this Army, we would not fear anything that might happen.' Can't we arrive at some jumping-off place where you gentlemen can come to this committee and say, 'Here is our program, and this is what we think it is going to cost over a period of years,' and then figure out whether we can do it?" General Marshall replied: "To a certain extent we can do it, but conditions change. The present world situation has changed conditions." (Ibid., p. 40.) ★

SPEECH TO THE SALVATION ARMY[1]   February 26, 1940
                                                                  New York, New York

Miracles of this world seem to be associated exclusively with the remote past, but tonight we have an opportunity to congratulate the Salvation Army upon the accomplishment of a modern miracle. Sixty years ago a single official of this great Army of peace and mercy landed in New York, armed with a beneficent purpose and firm determination to invade America, to spread the influence of the Salvation Army the length and breadth of this country. The proportions of this plan seemed beyond the realm of possibility. Nevertheless, they have been realized.

I believe there has always existed among professional soldiers a special regard for men and women of the Salvation Army. We understand and can fully appreciate their standards of loyalty and discipline, and their complete devotion to duty. They have a special claim upon the affections of the veterans of the American Expeditionary Forces of 1917 and 1918. On behalf of those veterans of the Army in general, I salute and congratulate the Salvation Army on its sixtieth American birthday.

My initial contact with that Army occurred on an evening in July of 1917 in my billet in Gondrecourt, France. Its first representative to join the American Expeditionary Forces spent the evening with me, talking over the possibilities of serving our troops.[2]

I recall that he described conditions in England and the work the Salvation Army was engaged in with the British Army;—the difficulties encountered, and what had been accomplished. He told me what his people hoped to do for the American troops. How well they succeeded is too generally known to require further reference by me.

The American soldier has a keen eye for both sham and sincerity. The soldier in France instantly recognized physical and mental courage when he saw it, and he reacted quickly to the calm, untheatrical acceptance of danger, of discomfort and fatigue which distinguished all ranks of the Salvation Army. The contribution of this devoted band of workers to the morale of our soldiers at the front will never be forgotten.

A few years after the war, I accompanied General Pershing to Pittsburgh, Pennsylvania, and there for the first time had the honor and the good fortune to meet your great leader Evangeline Booth. I heard her deliver a powerful and moving address.[3] Her charm of personality, her intensity of benevolent purpose, and her outstanding ability as a leader of people, marked her apart as one of the great figures of this country and of the world at large.

I have been reminded that Miss Booth's father was approached in Paris by a General of the French Army who said to him—"General Booth, you are not an Englishman—you belong to humanity," and I am rather proud that a member of the military profession is credited with such discernment. What was true of the father has been equally true of the daughter. The citation with which our Government awarded her The Distinguished Service Medal does only partial justice to her great contribution of those war years. Evangeline Booth today represents the pinnacle of womanhood, among those whose contribution to humanity is of supreme importance to this distracted world.

I have been referring to the Salvation Army in war, but there are crises in peace as well as in war. We have been passing through a crisis where lack of food, of clothing, and of shelter were the enemies. As the government mobilized to meet these formidable opponents it found the Salvation Army, as usual, in the front line struggling against the tragedies and disabilities of the poor and needy.

The blue and red uniform is no mere decoration. Its wearers ask for no individual reward for their labors. They accept the unselfish satisfaction of a life devoted to the service of others. They subject themselves to rigid military discipline. They receive orders and carry them out unquestioningly. Some years ago during an emergency in this city the Salvation Army was suddenly called upon to feed a large number of hungry men. Within four hours eight large stations had been established in widely separated localities and were dispensing food. That is efficiency which soldiers can understand and admire.

Every official of our armed forces recognizes the tremendous moral value represented by the thousands of trained and devoted Salvation Army officers and soldiers deployed in more than 1,800 centers throughout this country. This benevolent army is a loyal and invaluable part of our system of National Defense. As a factor for maintaining morale, it is a great and positive asset to the National Defense.

May the Salvationists of this country continue in their cultivation of the gentle arts of peace, but since they are practical men and women they doubtless agree with Dean Inge's forceful remark that it does little good for the sheep to pass resolutions in favor of vegetarianism unless the wolves are also voting that way. Today we are forced to think in terms of total war— the process of marshaling every mental, moral and material resource within a nation to meet a threat to national existence, in forms of government. We face a tragic world, but like a silver lining to the dark clouds is the concept of lasting peace, when men's minds will be directed to homes and firesides, to farms and industry; to the time when nations will be striving to improve the lot of their citizens within their own resources, and not at the expense of neighbors. Among those few groups qualified, by conviction and faith, to keep alive this cherished hope of total peace, the Salvation Army stands preeminent. To me, it is a genuine rallying point for democracy at home. For it commands the whole-hearted support of men and women who stand at opposite poles on almost every other question in life. It has proved its devotion to the needs and sufferings of men and women of all nations, of all colors and creeds, and on every occasion both in peace and in time of war.

There is a military etiquette which governs the formal salute of one army to another, and in my opinion the Salvation Army and its great commander rate the full twenty-one guns of international respect.

And now, by way of supplement to the formal remarks which I have just read, may I add a rather personal conclusion: for almost three hours this afternoon I was before the Appropriations Committee of the House of Representatives, answering questions regarding proposals for the expenditure of hundreds of millions for National Defense; I came directly from the Committee Room to the train and to New York and to this dinner, and I would like to make the comment, that although it was very much my business and my great responsibility to urge the expenditure of large sums of money to guarantee our national security in this chaotic world, yet for that very reason, it is now a profound relief and a great satisfaction to me to participate in this gathering to honor and assist this other army, which has for its sole purpose that which appeals to the heart and generous instincts of all mankind.

General Booth, I envy you your beneficent mission.[4]

GCMRL/G. C. Marshall Papers (Pentagon Office, Speeches)

1. Marshall delivered this address at a Hotel Pierre banquet marking the seventy-fifth anniversary of the founding of the Salvation Army in London by William Booth, the sixtieth anniversary of the arrival of the Army's first commissioned officer in the United States, and the opening of the Army's $375,000 Diamond Jubilee fund raising drive.

2. Marshall was in Gondrecourt as Operations officer of the First Division between July 14, 1917, and January 18, 1918. (See *Papers of GCM*, 1: 109–29.) He probably met Salvation Army Lieutenant Colonel William S. Barker, who had General John J. Pershing's permission to establish facilities in the First Division's military district. Barker's account of his mission is in *The War Cry*, October 26, 1918, pp. 8–9.

3. Evangeline Booth, Pershing, and Marshall were in Pittsburgh for a Salvation Army fund raising meeting on Sunday, October 31, 1920. General Booth's comments on the meeting and her synopsis of the remarks made are in *The War Cry*, November 6, 1920, pp. 9, 14.

4. Marshall may have written this sentence and the previous paragraph while on the train to New York City. The handwritten version is on the back of a letter from Salvation Army Colonel John J. Allan to Marshall, February 23, 1940, GCMRL/G. C. Marshall Papers [Pentagon Office, General].)

MEMORANDUM FOR THE CHIEF OF   February 27, 1940
INFANTRY [LYNCH]   [Washington, D.C.]

I am interested in Colonel Alexander Stark. He was in to see me the other day, and I assume had been to your office in regard to possible details.[1]

Stark was a wild buck at one time, but has since settled down. My interest comes from the fact that I regard him as one of the outstanding field soldiers in the Army. He demonstrated successfully in the War in the Meuse-Argonne, and gave me a peace-time demonstration with the CCC. He repeated the latter for General McCoy in another region, and I believe for other officers. He, Terry Allen,[2] and one or two others, there are very few of them, are of that unusual type who enthuse all of their subordinates and carry through almost impossible tasks.

I do not know what you have in mind for him, but let me know before the decision is taken.[3]

GCMRL/G. C. Marshall Papers (Pentagon Office, General)

1. Lieutenant Colonel Alexander N. Stark, Jr., an instructor of the California National Guard, had visited Marshall on February 3, 1940.

2. Lieutenant Colonel Terry de la M. Allen was stationed at Fort Bliss, Texas, with the Cavalry.

3. The chief of Infantry assigned Stark to the Twenty-sixth Infantry at Plattsburg Barracks, New York.

TO GENERAL JOHN J. PERSHING   February 27, 1940
                                          Washington, D.C.

Dear General: I returned this morning from the Salvation Army dinner in New York, where I sat next to Evangeline Booth. She looked even more a soldier than when I last saw her in Washington in about 1923. She spoke of you a number of times during the evening, and with great admiration. I know you would be interested in her reaction; she tells me that she still rides ten or fifteen miles a day.

Katherine reached home at midnight last night, while I was in New York. She has been at Miami Beach and Key West for a month and has returned much rested and the gainer by four pounds. Unfortunately she arrived in the midst of a snow-storm and with three or four dinners that we cannot evade.

I have only been back a short time from my trip to Panama and Puerto Rico. Incidentally, I sent you a radio from the plane while flying over the Candado-Vanderbilt beach at San Juan, and about fifteen minutes later received an acknowledgment from the Army operator in Tucson to the effect that he had telephoned it to Miss May. I spent the night with Katherine at Miami Beach, and was driven away from there a day ahead of time by approaching bad weather; she showed me a gracious note from you, in which you referred to my not stopping at Tucson when I was flying East the other day. The reason was I was racing against time to catch the Cavalry Division before it got in from the field at El Paso—and got there just fifteen minutes ahead of its arrival in the post, and to keep ahead of an approaching wave of bad weather. The snow was three hours behind me at El Paso, two hours after me at San Antonio, where I inspected the Second Division in the field; only thirty minutes off my tail at Barksdale Field in Louisiana, and as I was sitting down to dinner at Benning the weather report indicated a new cold front from the Gulf was coming in. So we left the guests before dinner was served and reached Washington two hours and fifty minutes later. Three hours after our arrival here, snow and sleet and a real blizzard developed.

As things now stand, I will leave here Thursday afternoon or early Friday morning for San Francisco, to take a China Clipper Saturday for Hawaii. I will leave Hawaii on the return trip March 10th or 11th, but will have to rush straight to Washington to appear before the Senate Appropriations Committee. I was before the House Appropriations Committee yesterday afternoon, as well as a few days ago; this morning I was before the House Military Committee. In the intervals I answer the 'phone or receive Senators or Representatives, all with an iron in the fire and some of them raising hell over troop dispositions. It is pretty hard to manage what amounts to a minor mobilization on a peace-time basis, at the same time struggling against the cuts that public opinion is now forcing on Congress.

Please give my warm regards to Miss May.   Affectionately,

G. C. Marshall

LC/J. J. Pershing Papers (General Correspondence)

To Walter Hoving[1]

February 28, 1940
[Washington, D.C.]

My dear Mr. Hoving: I did not see you as I left the Salvation Army dinner the other night, and I want you to know I appreciated the courtesy of your reception and your kind references to me. It was a genuine pleasure for me to do whatever small things were within my power to assist Evangeline Booth and her Army. I feel that their position is unique in such matters and their procedure has been without blemish or the possibility of criticism.

I hope very much that you will be successful in your campaign for funds. Faithfully yours,

GCMRL/G. C. Marshall Papers (Pentagon Office, General)
1. Hoving was chairman of the Salvation Army's fund raising drive as well as president and chairman of the board of Lord and Taylor department store in New York City.

To Brigadier General Asa L. Singleton   February 28, 1940
[Washington, D.C.]

Dear Singleton: In my various trips I have been following up delays that have resulted in the War Department towards the supplying of troops in the field. There have been many that came about through the functioning of depots, and we are obtaining valuable information about the inevitable delays that would result in the event of mobilization, particularly as to supplying of the various items of a single equipment where they are not stored in the same place.

However, there are other delays that have been checked up as a result of my various trips, and one of them occurs at Benning. I do not want to move into official channels for this, but I do want to follow every one to its source. The question of this particular delay resulted from my pressure as to the supplying of equipment to newly organized units, and it pertains to engineer equipment for field artillery of the First Division. One delay was of eighteen days at Fort Benning, according to dates on requisition of November 10, 1939 from the Field Artillery Section, First Division. Whether this delay occurred in the Division or in the office of the post engineer officer at Fort Benning, or between the two of them, the records do not show, but there was an eighteen-day delay in clearing a paper which had for its purpose the prompt supplying of materiel to troops in the field.[1]

Incidentally, I find that Corps Area Headquarters, or the young Engineer officer, imposed apparently an arbitrary cut of 50%. Altogether you can see that this is not a very helpful procedure.[2]

I do not want to stir up any official investigation over this, but I wish you and Short[3] would talk to each other and your respective people and see just who caused this eighteen-day delay at Benning; because if this is multiplied out in general effect, it would result in an appalling delay in mobilization, and I am endeavoring to find the necessary permanent corrective measures against such procedure.   Faithfully yours,

GCMRL/G. C. Marshall Papers (Pentagon Office, Selected)
1. Singleton, commandant of the Infantry School, replied in detail to Marshall's inquiry. He submitted data to justify the eighteen-day delay necessary to process the requisitions for the First Division. Given the shortage of personnel and the increased workload, Singleton believed that the period was not excessive. (Singleton to Marshall, March 20, 1940, GCMRL/ G. C. Marshall Papers [Pentagon Office, Selected].)

2. Singleton's staff noted that this requisition cut was not made at Fort Benning. (Ibid.)
3. On March 1, Major General Walter C. Short would assume command of the Fourth Army Corps.

To MAJOR GENERAL CHARLES D. HERRON   February 28, 1940
Radio   [Washington, D.C.]

Planning to leave San Francisco Saturday March Second on China Clipper for Hawaii. Please hold in abeyance and tactfully discourage official-social engagements pending my arrival. I expect to spend Monday to Wednesday being educated on Hawaiian defense conditions. Then confidentially I hope to get an unobtrusive rest with Mrs. Herron and you the first I will have had since the Fourth of July weekend and I need it.

NA/RG 165 (OCS, Miscellaneous Correspondence)

HIS air journey to Hawaii was "most interesting," Marshall wrote to Brazilian Army Chief of Staff Góes Monteiro. He had departed from Bolling Field in Washington, D.C., on the morning of February 29. "On the way out I went by the Southern Route stopping off overnight with General Pershing at Tucson, Arizona. . . . I originally intended to fly from here [Washington, D.C.] non-stop to San Francisco in one of the 'Flying Fortresses' and then to take another one of these fine ships and fly from there to Hawaii. At the last moment circumstances compelled changes in this plan and I went from San Francisco to Hawaii and return by one of the Pan-American Airways clippers." (Marshall to Góes Monteiro, March 18, 1940, NA/RG 165 [WPD, 4224].) After spending two days in California, Marshall arrived in Honolulu on March 3 for a nine-day stay. He left Hawaii on March 13, arriving at Bolling Field two days later after traveling a total of 9,500 miles by air. ★

To JUAN T. TRIPPE   March 16, 1940
[Washington, D.C.]

My dear Trippe: I returned yesterday from my trip out to Hawaii, and I want to thank you very sincerely for the courtesies extended me by the Pan

American system on the flight from San Francisco to Honolulu and return. I was tremendously impressed by the efficiency of your service, and by the comfort and luxury of the trip, as well as the speed. I found the ocean traveling more restful than transcontinental air trips, and certainly from my observation of every procedure, one is much safer in the air in a China Clipper than in crossing the street here in Washington.

My sincere thanks for your courtesy.   Faithfully yours,

GCMRL/G. C. Marshall Papers (Pentagon Office, General)

MEMORANDUM FOR THE ASSISTANT   March 18, 1940
CHIEF OF STAFF, G-1 [SHEDD]   [Washington, D.C.]

I talked to a committee of the Bandsmen's Association and heard all their representations.[1] They brought up the business of commissioning the Band Leader last. Their first request was for some representation in the War Department on band matters.

Apparently the leader of the Army Band is not very popular with these fellows because they (General Burt being the spokesman)[2] were urgently of the opinion that he was much too busy and that he had been disassociated with the service bands and regiments for over twenty years.

They also urged larger bands, but I gave them the details of our personnel struggles for the Regular Army, which convinced them that that was out of the question.[3] However, I see no reason why we might not easily arrange to have a larger band personnel with the National Guard. Look into this, please.

Consider the possibility of having a semi-formal board composed of about three band leaders to make recommendations about band matters in general. This might be a way to offset the powerful pressure that is now pressing on us.[4] I am afraid with the present popularity of orchestra leaders and their prominence in public life, in night clubs and on the radio, that if we are not clever about this business our hand will be forced in a way that will be unfortunate.

I made no commitments on the question of rank. There is a possible "out" there for the head of the Division bands. But in any event I think we should press to have the higher grade warrant officers.

GCMRL/G. C. Marshall Papers (Pentagon Office, General)

1. Marshall met with a group representing the United States Army and Navy Bandsmen's Association on the morning of March 16.
2. Reynolds J. Burt was a retired brigadier general.

3. The head of all army bands was Thomas F. Darcy, Jr., a warrant officer with a temporary rank of captain; under his command were seventy-five warrant officer bandleaders.

In the February 10, 1940, *Army and Navy Journal* (p. 540), Warrant Officer (Bandleader) Arthur S. Haynes wrote an article ("What's the Matter With the Band?") criticizing the condition of the Regular Army's musical organizations. "The band has not kept pace with the rapid development in the modernization of other branches of the army. Lacking representation on the General Staff, there has been no one conversant with band problems to assay changes or make recommendations. Too many of our bands are steeped in the outmoded programs of generations past and have no acquaintance with music in the modern idiom."

Haynes blamed the poor conditions of the bands on the abolition of the Army Music School. Bandleaders had no formal training in martial music, as did the graduates of the music schools in the great European armies. He also observed: "Discipline is lax, alignment faulty, and march music poor and unsuitable in many of our organizations. As a result, they lack the swing, precision, and martial spirit of the European bands." Moreover, he believed that the twenty-eight-piece band was "unimpressive, both in volume and appearance, and deficient in tonal coloring." He thought a minimum of thirty-five pieces was necessary.

4. At this time, the House had already passed a bill (H.R. 3840) creating the commissioned rank of bandmaster, and Senate consideration of the measure had begun. The bill was sent to the president on June 18, but on June 24 he vetoed the measure as constituting "a novel departure in the organization of the Army for which there is no necessity from a military standpoint." (*Congressional Record,* 76th Cong., 3d sess., 86, pt. 8: 9109.)

To Lieutenant General Stanley D. Embick   March 23, 1940
[Washington, D.C.]

Dear Embick: This is just a hasty note in regard to the Air officers from Kelly Field attached to troops for maneuvers.[1] I have been a little fearful that G-3 would act on this on a routine basis with the inevitable unfortunate reactions, so I am writing to you direct.

What I want is to have these men "attached" to the Commanders of companies, batteries, troops, platoons, and regiments. If they are ordinarily assigned for platoon duties, the inevitable reaction will be that they do not know anything about commanding a platoon and the procedure was unfortunate. Some of them may be able to command platoons and, if so, all right, but I had in mind their injection into the plot more as an aide to the commander concerned, where they may be useful and maybe find a definite place for themselves. But, most of all, where they will get some idea of the ground army before they start on their intensive air training with the GHQ Air Force.   Faithfully yours,

GCMRL/G. C. Marshall Papers (Pentagon Office, Selected)

1. Kelly Field, Texas, was the headquarters for the Advanced Flying School.

To Brigadier General Asa L. Singleton   March 23, 1940
                                                         [Washington, D.C.]

Dear Singleton: I have just received your detailed reply to my note of February 28th, regarding the requisition for engineer equipment. I appreciate the careful check you made on this because, as I inferred in my letter, while the matter involved is very small, it does represent the trial of a system.[1]

I have been following up a number of similar matters to see what the prospect was of our being able to activate a number of units and really equip them within a reasonable time. At the present moment I have come to this conclusion,—that the present system, in general, is all right, but that we must effect a decided change in the state of mind of all staff officers, particularly in the War Department and at Corps Area Headquarters, to the end that anything that concerns troops in the field will be considered as of more importance than any other matter to be handled at the moment. Also, that the officer first concerned will feel a definite responsibility to speed the matter on its way in the most effective fashion.

In the incident of getting blankets for the First Division, I found delays all along the line, but most of all here in the War Department, with the final touch, after weeks of delay, when the officers concerned at Benning were informed in a routine manner to submit a requisition, notwithstanding the facts that weeks had elapsed, that the troops were in the field, and that the coldest winter of many years was creating a critical situation.

I am going into this detail so that you will not feel that I was being critical in any way of your administration, but rather that I was in the general business of stirring up all officers involved in supply to a feeling that any delays in supplying troops rebounds directly in the lap of the Chief of Staff. I do not know any other way to bring about a change.

Thank you for your letter, and incidentally, I knew the cut of 50% was made at Atlanta.

I hope to get down to see you again because I have not forgotten the loss of that turkey.   Faithfully yours,

GCMRL/G. C. Marshall Papers (Pentagon Office, Selected)
1. For Marshall's letter to Singleton, see p. 174.

Memorandum for General Gasser   March 26, 1940
                                                        [Washington, D.C.]

Subject: Ports of Embarkation.

Troop movements at sea last fall and during the maneuvers on the West Coast in January have brought to my attention what I fear is an impracticable aspect of our present regulations concerning ports of embarkation. As I recall, when the reinforcements were sent to Puerto Rico and Panama, there was a failure to send the proper notice at the proper time to the commander of the Port of Embarkation in New York; again, in connection with the movement of the Third Division by the fleet of transports during the joint maneuvers, there was a failure to notify the Commander of the Port of Embarkation in San Francisco at the proper time. In each instance, the corrective measure seemed to be one of placating the two Commanders of the ports of embarkation, but my concern is over a system which lends itself so easily to such oversights.

It seems to me the trouble is we are trying to operate from the War Department, which when large matters are at stake is bound to mean inevitable oversights; or it means we must change our system after the emergency arises. The latter is almost a more serious fault than the former. I talked to De Witt about the matter when I was in San Francisco, or rather he brought it up to me; and I found that he had discovered two things, the first was that General Major had received no instructions, and the second was that the Port of Embarkation there was not organized on a basis to function for such purpose. De Witt also mentioned that he was more or less responsible—being the Quartermaster General at the time—for the present regulations on this subject.[1]

I do not know what the cure should be, but I am convinced that the War Department should not have operative responsibilities of this nature, because it cannot work in the midst of the many obligations that must be met here, as well as the state of mind of the staff officers who do not have a close responsibility for the attendant failures. Offhand, I should think that the Corps Area Commanders should be given responsibility, while the War Department should determine the policy; that the Corps Area commanders should be decentralized to a certain extent from the detailed transport passenger schedules and freight consignments and that so far as possible the War Department be cut out from immediate directive connection. I believe this is the case in the Philippines and Hawaii; therefore I do not see why it should not be the case here.

Along with this same subject comes up the question of exempted stations. I was much impressed at Christmas time with the tremendous number of letters I had to sign to exempted stations, and I do not believe such scattered responsibility can ever be coordinated by the War Department.[2] I hesitate to involve the Staff in a prolonged study on this subject, but I do want the Ports of Embarkation considered immediately and put on a solid basis for operation in time of war.

I attach some comments that just came to me this morning, which may or may not have some bearing on the plot.[3]

GCMRL/G. C. Marshall Papers (Pentagon Office, Selected)

1. There were two army ports of embarkation at this time (New York and San Francisco) under the quartermaster general; they were defined and regulated by A.R. 30–1110. Brigadier General Duncan K. Major, Jr., commanded the San Francisco Port of Embarkation at Fort Mason, California, from October 1938 until his retirement on February 1, 1940. Lieutenant General John L. De Witt, commander of the Fourth Army and the Ninth Corps Area, had been quartermaster general between February 1930 and February 1934.

2. Exempted stations were those not under the jurisdiction of their respective corps area commanders. These included such stations as schools, medical facilities, arsenals, ordnance depots, most air bases, and the ports of embarkation. In April 1940, there were 112 active exempted stations listed in the *Army Directory;* the commanders of many of these could report directly to the chief of staff under certain conditions.

3. Copies of the enclosures to Gasser are not in the Marshall papers. The G-3 division of the General Staff prepared a study on embarkation port procedures and submitted it to the chief of staff in May 1940. Marshall was dissatisfied with the study, commenting: "I do not learn from your memorandum enough to reassure me that you have a working system now." (Marshall Memorandum for Assistant Chief of Staff, G-3, May 20, 1940, GCMRL/G. C. Marshall Papers [Pentagon Office, Selected].)

To BERNARD M. BARUCH   March 29, 1940
                                                     [Washington, D.C.]

Dear Mr. Baruch: I have just received your telegram of March 28th, stating that you would arrive by airplane at eleven o'clock today at Columbia and would visit Benning after April 8th.

I telephoned down to Camp Jackson at Columbia and told the Division Commander, General Trott, to detail a special officer as your Aide, Colonel Peabody.[1] I did this because Peabody has been in the War Department and is familiar with our materiel struggles, and has also been present during the formation of this new Division.

I do not know that you can pick up very much information at Columbia at the moment, but I am glad you are going there. What particularly pleases me is that you plan to go to Benning, and I want that visit arranged at the best time and under circumstances which would give you the maximum of information. I propose sending down from the War Department an officer to be your Aide, and also particularly to be your informant on a lot of details which the local men might not have available.

You should not go to Benning before the 15th as that is the period of the First [*Fourth*] Corps Exercises—incidentally the first one in the peacetime history of our Army, I believe. So please let me know your possible dates well in advance so that I can arrange everything in the best possible manner.

Later on in May you must see something of the big Army Maneuvers when everything will be going full blast, Infantry divisions, Corps organizations, Cavalry divisions, and mechanized divisions, three or four hundred tanks, and the planes in the air.[2]   Hastily yours,

GCMRL/G. C. Marshall Papers (Pentagon Office, Selected)

1. Brigadier General Clement A. Trott had been commander of the Sixth Division and Camp Jackson since October 27, 1939. Lieutenant Colonel Paul E. Peabody served with the Twentieth Infantry of the Sixth Division.

2. Following Baruch's visit, Trott wrote to Marshall that "we discussed with him the general subject of preparedness, covering all points mentioned in your telephone conversation, together with others which occurred to us." Although Baruch missed the divisional review, he "seemed to be most interested in everything we told him and I feel quite sure that he absorbed a few new ideas concerning Preparedness as well as having others confirmed which he probably had before." Trott thought it was "a most beneficial visit." Baruch had promised to visit the corps maneuvers at Fort Benning in April. (Trott to Marshall, March 30, 1940, GCMRL/G. C. Marshall Papers [Pentagon Office, Selected]. See Marshall to Baruch, April 3, 1940, pp. 188–89.)

MEMORANDUM FOR COLONEL BRADLEY   March 30, 1940
Confidential   [Washington, D.C.]

Try your hand at this Training draft.[1] It is far too long, it is pedantic, it doesn't put across an idea anywhere with a wallop, it scatters the shot, it might just as well be omitted rather than issued in its present form. These comments of course are confidential to you.

In general, what I think the National Guard needs is to get the idea that there must be a more effective use of the armory training periods, and the arrival in camp for the summer training with as little to interfere with straight field training as possible (the accomplishment of small arms firing of known distance practice before summer camps means a great saving in time for things that can be done around the armories.)

If every unit of the National Guard could be brought by tradition and custom to the habit of treating the weekly drill period of an hour and a half from the moment of fall-in until recall is sounded, after the order of West Point, by this mean that during that period every military formality would be observed, there would be nothing casual, no first names, no groups gossiping on the drill floor, no hit or miss drills, no group straggling from one appointment to another. Of course this could not be written into a training directive, but the rough idea might be conveyed in a couple of sentences—as to purpose and method.

A serious weakness of the National Guard is the lack of trained staffs from battalion up, meaning staff teams that know how to function expeditiously and to the advantage of the troops. Extension courses are merely primary for the training of the individual; team work can only be gained by operating on the basis of a team, whether it is in the armory or in the field, whether it is over some matter or a tactical operation. This staff weakness will be destructive of troop efficiency unless it is thoroughly understood as a weakness and everybody works to meet it.

Just what can be said about the use of our too expansive training regulations, by units which have a very limited time at their disposal, I do not know. For example, if the Guard were left to follow McNair's training preparations for target practice, it would have little time for anything else but that one thing—practically no time for anything else. Yet to leave them to make the choice of what is to be slighted and what is to be done, is bad business.

There is a great deal that can be done in the armories clear up to regimental training, that is actually thought out of the question. For example, An infantry communication and artillery communication system can be set up entirely in an armory just as a matter of drill and operated. Air officers when available can make fine contacts by inspecting the liaison service of ground and air; signal officers can check over all the signal equipment to see that it is effective, and properly understood; all this assuming that signal, engineer, and air officers are available and in the vicinity of the units.

Training in larger problems is rarely done because the Leavenworth system is too ponderous and as a rule it only deals with some distant affair, like a Gettysburg map. I found in Chicago that we could work out a splendid divisional tactical problem on 3-inch maps within three hours' motor trip of the Chicago Loop, where there was a world of open country accessible to everybody.[2] We did things as a practicable problem, over the telephone, or by telegraph, or by direct conversations, and it merged into a CPX [Command Post Exercise]—all indoors, but all based on the map of a nearby piece of ground where the men could, if they chose, look it over on Saturdays and Sundays; finally from the journal of operations, the people would go in the field on the actual ground, without damage to property and check up everything they did—observation posts, battery machine guns, one-pounder positions, locality of kitchens, arrangements of command posts, set-up of dumps—everything without spending a cent.

Of course no such description of this can be written into a training order, but maybe the idea can be expressed in a sentence or two. I found these things could be done away from the city, with a small unit under pretty good conditions if there was imagination, ingenuity and a determination to advance training.

GCMRL/G. C. Marshall Papers (Pentagon Office, Selected)

1. Lieutenant Colonel Omar N. Bradley was one of the assistant secretaries of the General Staff. Marshall was referring to training regulations for the National Guard (T.R. 130–10).

For Marshall's views on these National Guard problems, see his speech on armory training in *Papers of GCM,* 1: 448–50.

2. "The Leavenworth system" referred to the policies and procedures published by the Command and General Staff School, Fort Leavenworth, Kansas. The "Gettysburg Map" was a highly detailed map of the region between Antietam, Maryland, and Gettysburg, Pennsylvania, which was used to lay out school tactical problems. (On Marshall's concern with map problems, see *Papers of GCM,* 1: 320, 336, 410, 414–16, 478, 530, 533, 704, 707–8.)

To Major General Charles D. Herron   April 1, 1940
                [Washington, D.C.]

Dear Herron: I feel very remiss in not having written to you earlier to tell you how much I appreciated the perfectly delightful hospitality you and Mrs. Herron and Jimmie offered me during my visit to Hawaii. I felt that everything pertaining to my stay was exactly as I would like to have it, and I know of no two people that it would give me so much pleasure to visit as you and Louise. Jimmie was an unexpected pleasure.

I have been under terrific pressure since my return, not only with the business which piled up during my absence, but with presentations before the Appropriations Committee, but also, and particularly, with a battle over airplanes, and the preparations of a battle to protect our appropriations in the Senate against heavy economy slashes. This last is really hard work, because I have to see so many people, convince them, provide them with arguments, and then see that the whole scheme of defense dovetails together. I feel that if I can keep the Army training program going, then my most important business is to see that the money is forth-coming to provide adequate preparedness.

It has been cold here until yesterday, which developed into a real spring day with the redbuds out in the early morning and the forsythia blooming by late afternoon. Molly and I had a fine ride and then I walked for an hour with Katherine.

I have been taking up your various propositions one by one to see what can be done to help out. You will hear from me from time to time regarding them.[1]

With my affectionate regards to you all. Faithfully yours,

P.S. Your striker put Mrs. Herron's shoe-horn in my baggage. I am returning it under separate cover. I am also sending my photograph to Jimmie.

The fruit came as a great surprise and delighted us. It was in perfect condition. I am writing Louise to thank her.[2]

GCMRL/G. C. Marshall Papers (Pentagon Office, Selected)

1. Herron had written a memorandum to Marshall regarding aides to general officers. He contended that at the corps level one aide-de-camp was sufficient. "Aides above this number are either doing work belonging to staff departments, or covering up their idleness. If they are company officers, they are sorely needed with troops." Herron then noted that too many aides were relatives. Generals followed the "choice of their wives" and this usually reduced the morale of the command and reflected poorly on the commander. "An aide should be an outstanding officer—the best of his grade. When he is, the General's prestige is enhanced thereby." Herron recommended that a letter from the secretary of war opposing the detail of relatives to the staffs of general officers be circulated. (Herron to Marshall, March 26, 1940, GCMRL/G. C. Marshall Papers [Pentagon Office, Selected].)

Marshall referred the memorandum to G-1. General Shedd concurred with the limitation on numbers of aides, but thought that relatives should be permitted because of the close relationship necessary between general officers and their aides. (Shedd to Marshall, April 2, 1940, NA/RG 165 [G-1, 16083-1].)

2. Louise was Mrs. Herron. Their daughter, also named Louise, was called "Jimmie."

MEMORANDUM FOR GENERAL WATSON[1]   April 1, 1940
[Washington, D.C.]

Subject: Transfer of Construction from Q.M.G. to Engineers.

The question of transferring construction functions from the Quartermaster Corps to the Chief of Engineers, as suggested by Mr. Starnes, has been considered by the War Department for some time. We have been particularly interested in this project as a possible move in connection with the President's Reorganization Program.[2]

However, at present there are two complications, both opposed to such a transfer. One is that the Quartermaster General is now responsible for maintenance and operation of utilities as well as for construction. There is a decided advantage in having the same organization handle both maintenance and construction. The other is the fact that the Quartermaster Department is involved in a tremendous construction program, and a transfer of direction and responsibility at this particular time would be hazardous procedure.

The Assistant Chief of Staff (General Moore), who is responsible for supervision of these activities, happens to have been for many years an officer of the Corps of Engineers and has a very broad view of the entire subject. He has this to say:

"The Corps of Engineers is capable of performing efficiently all of the construction for which the Quartermaster General is now responsible. Construction is a specialized type of engineering and it could very appropriately be placed under a technical branch such as the Engineer Corps rather than under a Supply Branch and to do this would tend to bring to the construction activities of the Army a standard of efficiency not possible under the existing set-up. On the other hand to transfer away from the Quartermaster General the construction for which he is now responsible will result in separating construction from maintenance, repair and operation. The cost of maintenance is dependent on the quality of construction work and, conversely, the lessons learned from maintenance are useful in designing new construction. Much actual construction is necessary under the head of maintenance and it is almost impossible to draw a line of demarcation between these two functions; but while this is not an insurmountable difficulty, to do so would result in duplication, which would nullify to a large extent the advantages that might result from the proposed consolidation.

"The present time is highly inopportune for the proposed consolidation. There is an enormous amount of construction now in progress. The Quartermaster Corps is thoroughly committed to the program and any immediate transfer of responsibility would inevitably result in confusion and delay."

I concur in the belief that it would be most inopportune to effect a transfer of responsibility at this time, but I am of the opinion that the transfer should be made when the time is more opportune.

Acting Secretary of War.

(not signed)[3]

GCMRL/G. C. Marshall Papers (Pentagon Office, Selected)

1. Brigadier General Edwin M. Watson was President Roosevelt's military aide and secretary.

2. In October 1939 House Appropriations Committee members Albert J. Engel, Republican from Michigan, and Joe Starnes, Democrat from Alabama, decided to sponsor legislation transferring the construction function from the Quartermaster Corps to the Corps of Engineers. "The news was not particularly welcome. A premature attempt to bring about the change might ruin the Engineers' chances for years to come. Although the congressmen seemed in no hurry, General Marshall had to be ready to take a stand should a bill be introduced. Somewhat reluctantly, he reopened the question. The Staff reviewed earlier studies and kept an eye on Quartermaster progress." (Lenore Fine and Jesse A. Remington, *The Corps of Engineers: Construction in the United States,* a volume in the *United States Army in World War II* [Washington: GPO, 1972], p. 107.)

Chief of Engineers Major General Julian L. Schley (U.S.M.A., 1903) opposed the idea of any organizational change during this period of global emergency. This argument influenced his U.S.M.A. classmate and fellow engineer, the new Assistant Chief of Staff, G-4, Brigadier General Richard C. Moore. Moore wanted a postponement of at least a year on any transfer and persuaded Marshall and Woodring to wait. (Ibid., p. 108.)

3. Acting Secretary of War Louis Johnson prepared a personal memorandum to General Watson expressing a differing opinion: "The enclosed memorandum dated April 1, 1940, which was prepared for my signature, presents the Staff viewpoint on this question. I have not signed this memorandum because I am not wholly in accord with the viewpoint presented. After extensive study and long conferences with General Craig, then Chief of Staff, I reached the conclusion months ago that the best interests of the War Department would be served by placing all military or semi-military construction work under the Corps of Engineers." Johnson also informed Watson that he had not discussed this matter with Congressman Starnes, but was in accord with his ideas. (Memorandum for General Watson, April 4, 1940, GCMRL/ G. C. Marshall Papers [Pentagon Office, Selected].)

To Brigadier General Clement A. Trott   April 1, 1940
Confidential   [Washington, D.C.]

Dear Trott: I have just received your note of the 30th, about Mr. Baruch's delayed and uncertain visit. I am sorry you had so much trouble but very glad that you were able to give him the attention you describe. I had a telegram from him stating that he would arrive there at eleven o'clock, and that was all I knew.

The fact of the matter is, confidentially, Baruch and Hugh Johnson have turned to for the purpose of preventing a heavy Senate slash in our appropriation bill, and both of them are very powerful at that sort of thing, and for that reason I am all the more appreciative of your effort to look after Baruch.[1]   Faithfully yours,

GCMRL/G. C. Marshall Papers (Pentagon Office, Selected)

1. Brigadier General Hugh S. Johnson (U.S.M.A., 1903) had been administrator of the National Recovery Administration from June 1933 to October 1934. Johnson had long been associated with Baruch as a statistician and investigator of industrial stabilization problems.

To Major General Daniel Van Voorhis   April 2, 1940
                                 [Washington, D.C.]

Dear Van Voorhis: I have delayed acknowledging your letter of March 23rd until I had had some time to discuss the various matters you raised with people here on the Staff.

In the first place, the source of the data for the article that appeared in the Army and Navy Journal regarding the modifications in the Panama Canal setup, is unknown to us here. It was not released in the War Department. General Strong feels that the organization you have set up appears to be thoroughly justified. The only question in his mind is whether it may not be necessary ultimately to go still further than was indicated in your letter of February 12th. Your letter was referred to the Chiefs of Arms for remark and recommendation, and is still in process.[1]

The matter of the permanent allocation of four infantry regiments to Panama is still under study in War Plans Division and I have had several discussions with General Andrews and General Strong on the subject. It is probable that the factors of cost and maintenance in Panama, availability of transportation, and other considerations will play a part in the final decision. I hope we can give you a definite reply very shortly.[2]

The matter of the cost of quarters is, of course, of great concern, but General Moore tells me that the bids that have just been opened have reduced costs about 25 percent.

The Chief of Air Corps has recommended that there be no change at present in the allocation of aircraft to Panama. After construction and preparation in Puerto Rico is further advanced we may reopen the question and, as you say, the Pacific side is the major consideration.[3]

Your comments on the South American situation are in accordance with the thought here. The President has just made a decision regarding the payment of missions being held down to the actual necessities.[4]

I talked over with Gregory the question of the Engineer setup in the Canal towards the construction and I am very glad that Gregory saw you and looked over the conditions there. I think it was a highly profitable trip. I am also relieved that Daley has been over to see you and when you feel disposed I think it would be a good thing for you to go over there and see what he has done.[5]

My offhand impression is that we are creating a congestion in Panama, in view of the limited terrain available for new garrisons and installations, the climatic difficulties, etc.; also, costs are so much greater there for maintenance than here in the States, or even in Puerto Rico, that where we can make troops quickly available for Panama, we certainly ought to proceed on that basis. Just how we can do this is of course another question. Arnold is flying down on Saturday to talk things over with you and the Air people.

Very confidentially, I found Frank in Hawaii in much the same state of mind as General Dargue in Panama—that is, highly suspicious of the Navy.[6] These are two very able men, but they must leave Navy adjustments to me and to the War Department and direct all their energies to straight Army business. Herron is attending to Frank and I hope, in a tactful way when the opportunity casually arises, that you will get this thought over to Dargue. Incidentally, Admiral Stark is trying in every way to play ball with us and we could not ask for more cooperation and more of effort to understand our side of the various questions, so I want these other fellows to stay strictly within their own field and above all not to keep such talk alive.

I had a very interesting trip to Hawaii and now feel that I have a fairly clear point of view as to the relative priority of matters in the United States, Panama, Puerto Rico and Hawaii. I am going up to Alaska the last week in June.

With warm regards to Mrs. Van Voorhis and you,   Faithfully yours,

GCMRL/G. C. Marshall Papers (Pentagon Office, Selected)

1. An *Army and Navy Journal* article on the "Panama Canal Dept. Expansion" (March 16, 1940, p. 643) angered Van Voorhis. It presented details on new antiaircraft, coast artillery, and mobile forces arrangements. Van Voorhis declared that he had "an aversion to publicity" and had "a thorough realization that any action which I might take is subject to change by higher authority." (Van Voorhis to Marshall, March 23, 1940, GCMRL/G. C. Marshall Papers [Pentagon Office, Selected].)

2. Van Voorhis wanted a decision on the permanent garrisoning of four Infantry regiments

in the Canal Zone because it was a problem that "ties in with that of morale and housing. The lack of quarters to accommodate dependents is a serious one." Authorization for suitable housing could be made once their duty station became permanent. (Ibid.)

3. General Strong agreed with the Canal Zone commander that Puerto Rico was an outpost for Panama. In light of this strategic thinking, Van Voorhis's recommendation to maintain the existing disposition of air power in the Caribbean was followed. (Ibid.)

4. Following his March 10–16, 1940, bomber flight to South America, Van Voorhis observed that something "tangible" now had to be done for the Latin American republics. He noted that their poor financial condition taxed their ability to support American military missions which insisted on payment for officers detailed. "I do feel, however, from a defense standpoint that there could be some contribution made which would not place a great burden on our Government." (Ibid.)

5. Quartermaster General Edmund B. Gregory (U.S.M.A., 1904) had arrived in Panama on March 21, 1940, to discuss construction problems. Van Voorhis contended that the Canal Zone Engineers could not handle the enlarged construction load without increased overhead and the acquisition of new equipment. Also, estimates in Panama ran far ahead of those prepared by the quartermaster general. As a result of conferences with Canal Zone officials, the quartermaster general assumed the burden of Canal Zone Department construction. General Daley of the Puerto Rican Department reviewed the Canal Zone Department's operations and then staged a briefing for Van Voorhis and his staff on the development of the Puerto Rican command's defenses. (Ibid.)

6. Brigadier General Walter H. Frank (U.S.M.A., 1910) was commanding general of the Eighteenth Wing, Hickam Field, Hawaii. Brigadier General Herbert A. Dargue (U.S.M.A., 1911) commanded the Nineteenth Wing at Albrook Field in the Canal Zone.

To BERNARD M. BARUCH   April 3, 1940
Confidential   [Washington, D.C.]

Dear Mr. Baruch: I was sorry to learn from General Trott at Camp Jackson that you were delayed in your arrival there, did not have an opportunity to see the Division under arms, and as a matter of fact, only had a very brief opportunity to see how things were going. However, I am encouraged by the fact that you think you will be able to go over to Benning.

The First [*Fourth*] Army Corps exercise there, and incidentally, the first in our peace-time history, gets under way, I think, on April 15th, but a more interesting exercise will occur a few days later. I possibly will be down there on April 22d or 23d,—but when you go I wish to send an officer from the War Department to meet you there and to stay with you throughout your visit. I wish to do this because, while the people on the ground can give you excellent descriptions of the various phases of what they are doing, yet their knowledge is confined to the immediate unit rather than to the larger application to National Defense as a whole. If you are going down by rail, I would like to send my man to make the trip with you from Georgetown or Charleston, or from wherever you start.

We have just had the report this morning of the House Subcommittee on Appropriations, in which they slice approximately $67,000,000. in cash from our proposal as approved by the Budget Bureau. My particular concern at the moment is over the elimination of the $11,000,000. we asked for the establishment of an air base at Anchorage, Alaska. While I could go along with a cut, yet I think it is a highly dangerous business not to give us at least sufficient money to get started up there. For that reason I am sending you herewith a statement on the Anchorage situation, together with a map, both of which are copies of documents which I sent to the White House this morning. I must ask you to treat this information as confidential in so far as would indicate that I had given you an exact duplicate of what I had just sent to the President. However, if the opportunity presents itself I believe it would be very helpful if you could say a word to the President in support of this proposition. His active interest is of far more importance to us in getting results than that of men on the Hill.[1]

I am also sending you some other data, which may be of interest.

With warm regards,   Faithfully yours,

GCMRL/G. C. Marshall Papers (Pentagon Office, Selected)

1. Baruch went to General Watson with a recommendation that the president restore to the budget "at least $4,000,000 with which to start" the Alaskan base. (Baruch to Watson, April 5, 1940, Princeton/B. M. Baruch Papers [Selected Correspondence].) The War Department appropriation for 1941 (signed on June 13, 1940), included $12,104,060 for the construction of the air base.

To Bernard M. Baruch   April 9, 1940
                                                [Washington, D.C.]

My dear Mr. Baruch: When I returned from the House Committee this morning I found a note of your telephone message at 10:30, stating that "everything was set" and that you had seen the people concerned and that it was up to me to say what was wanted and I would get it. I called you at the Carlton but found that you had checked out, and I was very sorry not to have had at least a few moments to talk to you over what had occurred and particularly to thank you for what you had done.[1]

I am deeply grateful for the unselfish and patriotic effort you have made to help the Army out, and I am certain that your interest will have an important effect on the result because undoubtedly you have convinced leading men on the Hill of the gravity of the situation and of the importance of something being done immediately.[2]

From your message I gather that you will probably go to Benning about the 15th and that Miss Baruch will go with you. I will see that the necessary arrangements are made for you there, and I am very much pleased that you have decided to make that trip.

With warm regards and my very personal thanks,   Faithfully yours,

GCMRL/G. C. Marshall Papers (Pentagon Office, Selected)

1. Baruch informed the secretary of the General Staff that he had arranged a dinner to be given by Senator Byrnes for the Senate leadership on the evening of April 10, 1940. Marshall was invited to attend and to present his views on military preparedness and the budget. (Memorandum to Chief of Staff, April 9, 1940, GCMRL/G. C. Marshall Papers [Pentagon Office, Selected]; Bernard M. Baruch, *Baruch: The Public Years* [New York: Holt, Rinehart, and Winston, 1960], p. 278.)

2. Baruch was widely thought in Washington to have important influence in Congress. In mid-1937, Secretary of the Interior Harold Ickes had noted in his diary, "Bernie Baruch has very strong influence with quite a group of southern Senators and Representatives. He has moved in on occasions when they needed funds for campaign purposes or otherwise and has financed them generously, with the result that, other things being equal, they are likely to do what he wants in matters of legislation." *The Secret Diary of Harold L. Ickes,* 3 vols. (New York: Simon and Schuster, 1945), 2: 164.

TO BRIGADIER GENERAL LESLEY J. MCNAIR   April 9, 1940
[Washington, D.C.]

Dear McNair: I have just received the enclosed letter from John O. B. Wallace, and am asking you to have one of your people give me an idea of what the nature of my reply should be.[1]

I had hoped to get out to see you during this period of preparation for the new regime at Leavenworth, but the days have not enough hours and Congress is very pressing on a multitude of matters, not to mention the threat of heavy cuts, which I am organizing to offset.

The reaction to the new arrangement at Leavenworth seems to be generally good, though of course I do not hear much from those on the side of the former system. I would not have risked such a change had you not been at the helm, but I feel very comfortable in the thought that you are handling this business in a most effective fashion.

The old school all feel that there is not enough time to do a fair job on the education that Leavenworth is supposed to give. The two-year men are the most critical, of course, but most of the one-year men I think feel that the standards will be so greatly lowered that the school will not be looked up to as it has been in the past. These are very natural reactions, but they are based on the proposition that the way instruction has been managed in the past is the only manner in which it can be conducted efficiently. To this I take strong exception.

In the first place, I found during the five years I was at Benning—which gave me a lengthy opportunity to examine into such things—that our greatest loss of time lay in the unbalanced state of preparation of the members of the classes as they arrived. We tried to have organized through the Chief of Infantry preparatory measures for officers to take before they came to Benning, but so many difficulties were put in the way that I was unable to get through the bog. So, I believe that with a proper preparatory reading or self-preparation course—not merely a repetition of dry extension courses— a material gain in time can be made under the new system.

In the second place, I found the waste of time at Benning was, to my mind, inexcusable, and the economies I was able to manage in this respect enabled me to add a great deal to the course despite the fact that the office of the Chief of Infantry would not permit me to shorten any of the existing courses, however strong my recommendation. I found that part of the time-wasting system apparently resulted from an old condition at Leavenworth, one of my day before the World War. In those days we were required to write out in long-hand a lengthy estimate of the situation, which occupied about two hours; and then there followed a brief decision and the preparation of the order to carry it out. At Benning they were still allowing the two hours and not requiring the long-hand presentation with the estimate of the situation. Also, the requirements were timed to the slowest member of the class. I found from a personal test with a stop-watch that in illustrative problems that were scheduled for three hours, the work could be much better accomplished in an hour—better from the point of view of rapid, concise thinking, stimulation to alertness, and paced in time to the 75% of the class who were the more able.

I also found, for example, that when the advanced class at Benning was composed of a nondescript group, so far as wide variations in educational background and in age were concerned, and the company class was a homogeneous group in age, West Point training, etc.,—in presenting the same subject to the two groups it required twice as long for presentation and instruction of the advanced class as it did for the younger men of the company class. This was particularly evident in supply courses, the large portions of which were common to both classes.

I have talked to a number of recent Leavenworth students, and I find quite a few of them feel that two and three hour periods on some of the subjects in the afternoon could have been effectively handled in an hour.

Time is the dominant factor in all of our military preparations, the more so, I believe, with us than with any other power. The time factor is particularly important in dealing with the National Guard and the Reserves. Unfortunately our Regular Army methods of training take little account of the economy of time, and the officers going from regular troops to the citizen forces are not indoctrinated with either the idea of economy of time or with the technique of the most expeditious methods. I am hopeful that the pressure of the short courses at Leavenworth will make the time factor of more commonly recognized importance, with the general result of great advantage to the training systems for the Army.

I will probably see you during the maneuvers, but I want to have an opportunity for a lengthy talk with you either here or at Leavenworth. Meanwhile, keep in mind the fact that you are not tied down by policies or regulations which in your good judgment are detrimental to the most efficient arrangement.   Faithfully yours,

GCMRL/G. C. Marshall Papers (Pentagon Office, Selected)

1. Wallace, city editor of the *Leavenworth* [Kansas] *Times,* had written to Marshall on April 7 to enlist the chief of staff's aid in preparing an article for one of the summer issues of the *Infantry Journal* on the Command and General Staff School and its influence upon the American military establishment. Wallace mentioned that he was also enlisting General McNair in his project. On April 17, Marshall sent Wallace a brief statement praising the school's record and influence, noting that the school's curriculum had been reorganized "so as to permit a larger number of officers to profit by the training," and expressing confidence that "the shortening of the period of instruction will not lessen the professional standards credited to the graduate of 'Leavenworth.'" (GCMRL/G. C. Marshall Papers [Pentagon Office, General].) No article by Wallace on the Fort Leavenworth school appeared in the *Infantry Journal.*

FINANCES were hardly Marshall's sole congressional concern in early April. He also testified before the military affairs committees of the Senate (April 8) and House (April 9) on the long-festering age-in-grade promotion bill. This legislation sought to restructure the officers' promotion system in order to rectify the problems caused by the "hump" of World War commissionings. Intended to provide field grade officers who were fit for the physical and mental demands of wartime command, this revision of A.R. 605–40 specified years of active service and years in grade as guideposts for promotion. "Captains, majors, and lieutenant colonels shall be promoted to the respective grades of major, lieutenant colonel, and colonel immediately upon completing respectively 17 years', 23 years', and 28 years' continuous commissioned service in the Regular Army" and passing the required physical fitness examination. No field-grade officer could have less than six-years service as a major and five-years service as a lieutenant colonel before promotion. The colonels list could not exceed 705 and the mandatory retirement age was lowered from sixty-four to sixty. (War Department, Circular No. 94, August 29, 1940.)

Before both committees, Marshall supported the bill "from two points of view." The chief of staff first considered the rights of individuals. He found the new system afforded the best protection of individual rights within the profession that was legally possible. Second, Marshall believed that military efficiency and national defense was best served by a reorganization of the promotion list along these lines.

Officers commissioned during the World War, and fit for command in 1940, would be selected from a larger group including many unfit for command. "You have a man's experience, you have his judgment. And that increases in the average individual with the years. But, unfortunately, from the military point of view his muscles and his tendons do not go along with that development of judgment and of experience. And they are absolutely necessary to field leadership.

"In my experience in the war—and I saw about 27 of 29 divisions in battle—there were more failures, more crushed careers of officers of considerable rank that grew out of physical exhaustion than by reason of any other one cause."

Marshall also feared that officers commissioned after 1920, those following the "hump," would be unfit for field-grade service in the event of war. "They will be so old when the time comes that they might eventually reach promotion to lieutenant colonel and colonel and so limited in experience in handling men, except in small groups, that it would be a very unfortunate thing for the Army to have them suddenly jump to positions of high command and control." (Marshall testimony, Senate Military Affairs Committee, April 8, 1940, GCMRL/G. C. Marshall Papers [Pentagon Office, Testimonies].)

"You have to lead men in war by requiring more from the individual than he thinks he can do," Marshall told the members of the Senate Military Affairs Committee on April 8. "You have to lead men in war by bringing them along to endure and to display qualities of fortitude that are beyond the average man's thought of what he should be expected to do. You have to inspire them when they are hungry and exhausted and desperately uncomfortable and in great danger; and only a man of positive characteristics of leadership, with the physical stamina that goes with it, can function under those conditions." (Ibid.)

Concerned over the future of the officer corps, Marshall discussed the newest commissioned ranks in his House testimony on April 9, 1940. "Now, for the present, young men coming into the service, while the law gives them certainty of rank up to the grade of captain, thereafter they will advance too rapidly, due to the retirement of the World War officers. This bill, however, would control that situation. It would not allow undue rapidity of promotion as has occurred in the past; otherwise we would have a repetition of the vicious circle of rapid promotion for one group and too slow promotion for another." (Marshall testimony, House Military Affairs Committee, April 9, 1940, GCMRL/G. C. Marshall Papers [Pentagon Office, Testimonies].) The House and Senate finally reached agreement on the bill's provisions in early June, and President Roosevelt signed it into law on June 13, 1940. (See Marshall to Morris Sheppard, June 5, 1940, pp. 236–37.) ★

To Brigadier General Asa L. Singleton   April 11, 1940
Confidential   [Washington, D.C.]

Dear Singleton: Mr. Bernard M. Baruch and his daughter will probably fly in to Ft. Benning about the 15th—I will give you the exact data on this as early as possible. He will be there two days to get a look at the Corps Maneuver, as a matter of fact to gain a concrete idea of just what an Army corps is.

I propose having Major W. B. Smith, Assistant Secretary of the General Staff, report at Benning at the same time to act as Aide and to give him the necessary data both from the War Department side and that of the actual troops.

Very confidentially, Baruch has just been in Washington lobbying to prevent the cut of our appropriation bill before the Senate. He is thoroughly familiar with the problem of providing materiel, but not at all familiar with the troop set-up, that is to use the materiel. He and Hugh Johnson have been critical of our presentations and requirements on the basis of their being too modest, (Actually they were in accordance with the President's directions) and because they were in executive session, over which we had no control. I am giving you this data, most confidentially, so that you will know my reason for having him go to Benning, and particularly for sending Smith down there with him. Smith has already been in conference with him up here, and you need not bother at all in the matter other than to give him the cordial reception which, of course, I know you would do.

I would like you to reserve accommodations at the Club for Mr. Baruch and his daughter, and to have a man to look after him. Also I must ask you to provide him with motor transportation.

I am sending a copy of this letter to Short.   Hastily yours,

P.S.   Please do not give out any publicity on Mr. Baruch's presence. If the press happens to pick it up, all well and good, but I do not think it will help us to have this widely advertised, and it is especially important that we do not circulate the reasons for his presence.

GCMRL/G. C. Marshall Papers (Pentagon Office, Selected)

Step by Step

April 12–June 30, 1940

My own thought is that as the situation grows more critical abroad we ought, step by step—not in a single plunge to repeat those past mistakes in our history where we have gotten indigestion from trying to do everything at once at the last moment—but step by step, to do those things which will put us in a little stronger position; to do those things which are most important to be done, so that the military advisors of other governments will recognize our immediate strength and grow cautious accordingly.

—Testimony before the House Appropriations Committee
May 1, 1940

FOUR minutes after midnight on April 9, 1940, the State Department received a terse telegram from its minister in Oslo: "Norway is at war with Germany!" The news was shocking but not unexpected. The European war had now entered a new and more dangerous phase. On May 10 the German Army swept into the Low Countries, but the gravity of the military change in Europe was not evident until the French lines broke at Sedan on May 14.

"During May and June of 1940," Marshall wrote a year afterward, "the German avalanche completely upset the equilibrium of the European continent. France was eliminated as a world power and the British Army lost most of its heavy equipment. To many the invasion of Great Britain appeared imminent. The precariousness of the situation and its threat to the security of the United States became suddenly apparent to our people, and the pendulum of public opinion reversed itself, swinging violently to the other extreme, in an urgent demand for enormous and immediate increases in modern equipment and of the armed forces." ("Biennial Report of the Chief of Staff, July 1, 1941," in War Department, *Report of the Secretary of War to the President, 1941* [Washington: GPO, 1941], pp. 49–50.)

Marshall continued to remind Congress of the great expense and time required to produce a modern fighting force. Now he added warnings (public) and complaints (private) of the menace of *enthusiasm,* by which he meant curative schemes of great expectations which, when they failed, led to recriminations. He believed that excessive enthusiasm was the antithesis of rational planning. Moreover, election-year politics added to the burdens of his office. "These are serious times," he wrote to a friend in Oregon, "more serious possibly because this is a Presidential year, which is an embarrassment to everyone." (Marshall to David W. Hazen, May 3, 1940, GCMRL/ G. C. Marshall Papers [Pentagon Office, General].) ★

To GENERAL JOHN J. PERSHING April 12, 1940
Washington, D.C.

Dear General: I have tried to get off a letter to you for several days, but each time I start something happens—and a great deal has been happening in the last seventy-two hours.

I understand you made the trip in fine shape to Hot Springs,[1] and that you are coming to Washington the end of the month. We will be looking forward to seeing you with a great deal of pleasure.

Just now I am in a battle with the Appropriation bill, with the Army promotion or revitalization bill, and with one or two other very important pieces of legislation; on top of which there is the matter of the maneuvers in the Southeast, and what is to be done in view of the increased tenseness of the situation abroad. I fear that affairs are rapidly moving to a crash of ground forces and air activity.

With most affectionate regards from Katherine and me,   Faithfully yours,

G. C. Marshall

LC/J. J. Pershing Papers (General Correspondence)

1. Pershing was at the Army and Navy General Hospital, Hot Springs National Park, Arkansas.

MEMORANDUM FOR THE SECRETARY OF WAR   April 15, 1940
[Washington, D.C.]

The increasing gravity of the international situation makes it appear necessary for me to urge a further increase in our state of military preparation.

Should the present Congress vote the $37,000,000 for critical items of equipment set up in the President's budget for 1941, and also the additional amount of $14,250,000 which was added for this purpose by the House of Representatives, there would still be a deficiency of $25,000,000 for the modern equipment necessary to outfit the existing units of the Regular establishment and the National Guard and to provide the special equipment, the new detectors, for our aircraft warning service, which is a pressing requirement. In my opinion we cannot afford to delay longer in placing the orders for this materiel.

I therefore propose that an urgent recommendation be submitted to the President to secure immediate budgetary authorization for an additional $39,250,000 for critical items over and above the approved 1941 budget. This sum includes the $14,250,000 referred to above, which, for the moment, has been added to the approved budget by the House.[1]

NA/RG 165 (OCS, 20983-106)

1. This document was sent to the White House with a covering memorandum—also drafted by Marshall but signed by Secretary of War Harry H. Woodring—which concluded: "I concur fully in his recommendation and urgently recommend that it be approved. I feel that we cannot delay in this matter." President Roosevelt penciled "Seems necessary. F.D.R." on Marshall's memorandum printed here.

To MRS. JOHN J. SINGER   April 16, 1940
                                                     [Washington, D.C.]

Dear Marie: I have been trying to get a letter off to you since my return
from Hawaii, but there are not enough hours in the day and I am terribly
pressed with business every moment I am at the office.

Out at the house we have been suffering from a steady stream of luncheon
guests and visitors. Allen had his fiancée down;[1] my new Aide, Major
[Claude M.] Adams and his wife spent last week with us—they were out at
Vancouver Barracks my last year there, and people have been pouring into
town from all over the country in connection with legislation. Going home
from the Gridiron Dinner Saturday night,[2] Katherine and I were taking
stock of the week, and we found that someone had come out for lunch every
day since the previous Sunday, along with Allen and Adams and their
ladies, making six or eight for lunch on most days. Then the next morning,
last Sunday, we were about to have twenty for breakfast; in between times I
work.

I am hard at it now with some important personnel legislation that I am
trying to steer through Congress, and I am getting ready to appear before
the Senate on the Appropriation bill, which was badly cut in the House.
Incidentally, last night I had a very successful talk with Senator Tydings. We
were at a dinner at the Canadian Minister's, and he volunteered to take the
lead in defending my point of view in the Senate.[3]

I have to be in New York the night of the 23d, but expect to fly from
Mitchel Field to Fort Benning on the morning of the 24th and will be there
for two days of Corps Maneuvers, and then will fly in to Charleston, South
Carolina, on the morning of the 26th. I am due to make a talk there, at the
request of the Governor. Katherine plans to get out of town on the 22d and
motor down to K. & J. Metcalf's near Georgetown, north of Charleston and
she will meet me in Charleston; then, if I am not too pushed, we will motor
back together—otherwise, I must fly. It may be that I will have to return to
Benning for three or four days for Maneuvers, but that will depend considerably on the pressure up here in connection with the passage of the
Army Appropriation Bill.

As soon as we both get back the first week in May, before I leave again
for the Sabine River Valley in Louisiana for the big Army Maneuvers about
the 12th or 15th, we will have our last At Home. It will run up to about 1200
people, I am afraid, but we are doing it as a Garden party; if the weather
fails us it will be just too bad. Katherine wants you to come down and spend
a week with us at about that time. We will let you know as soon as our
return to town is certain and the dates are fixed.[4]

This is a very hasty note, but about three times as long as any you ever wrote to me.

With my love   Affectionately,

GCMRL/G. C. Marshall Papers (Pentagon Office, Selected)

1. Allen T. Brown, Marshall's younger stepson, was engaged to be married on June 22 to Margaret Goodman Shedden of Westchester County, New York.

2. The Gridiron Club, a journalists' organization, held its annual spring dinner on April 13. The affair featured satirical political skits pertaining to the approaching national political conventions and to possible presidential candidates. Club members performed for an audience which included President Roosevelt and numerous persons of importance in the government and in politics.

3. Marshall had written "confidential" in the left margin beside this paragraph. Millard E. Tydings, a United States senator from Maryland since 1927, was a member of the Appropriations Committee. He had written to Marshall in July 1939 to congratulate the new chief of staff and to offer his support in the Senate. Marshall replied, "Your congratulations are genuinely appreciated, the more so as they come from a citizen soldier with an unusual battle record. While I knew you as the Senator from Maryland, yet my interest and appreciation was largely based on the fact that in having a military text on tactics prepared at Benning, I found an incident of your participation in the Meuse-Argonne which was an outstanding example of the effect of successful leadership and technical efficiency on the battle-field, toward the success of an operation, particularly in conserving the lives of the soldiers involved. I am referring to the reference to you in 'Infantry in Battle,' a book which I understand has received more approval and consideration in England and Germany than among the home folks." (Marshall to Tydings, July 12, 1939, GCMRL/G. C. Marshall Papers [Pentagon Office, Selected].)

4. The Marshalls' garden party was held on May 10 and attracted nearly two thousand guests.

To Brigadier General Asa L. Singleton   April 22, 1940
                                                  [Washington, D.C.]

Dear Singleton: I was about to write you a note this morning when the mail brought yours of April 19th to me, so I am a little embarrassed in saying what I intended to tell you.[1]

The Secretary plans to be at Benning the 24th and 25th, and I may be there then, though my visit is on a more dubious basis due to congressional involvements regarding the Appropriation bill and the Promotion Bill. At the present time I am due to leave here Tuesday night for New York,[2] and I am planning to leave there—from Newark Field at seven o'clock for Fort Benning, where I should arrive about eleven o'clock on Wednesday morning. Now, I want you to devote yourself exclusively to the Secretary of War. It is of great importance that he see everything and receive every attention,—it is of equal importance that I get a chance to see the things I want to see, which I cannot very well do if otherwise involved.

So, I wish you would arrange for me to stay with the Walter Fultons, if convenient to them; otherwise with Courtney Hodges.[3] I mentioned Fulton first because I am fond of him and admire him and regret very much that he could not be promoted. For that reason it might help out a bit if I stayed with him, but I leave you to judge of this.

I will radio you the moment my plans crystallize, which is going to depend entirely on the vicissitudes of Army hearings and legislative battles in Congress.

Major [Walter B.] Smith has not had an opportunity yet to tell me of Baruch's visit, but I am glad to learn from you that it was apparently successful, and I received an appreciative telegram from him.[4]   Faithfully yours,

P.S.   The Secretary has just told me that he is still uncertain as to whether or not he will be at Benning on the 24th and 25th.[5]

Since dictating the above Major Smith has told me of the very perfect arrangements you made for Baruch and the highly successful manner in which everything worked out in connection with his visit. I am deeply grateful.

GCMRL/G. C. Marshall Papers (Pentagon Office, Selected)

1. Singleton had written, "I know that you know I expect you to stop with me when you come to Benning." (Singleton to Marshall, April 19, 1940, GCMRL/G. C. Marshall Papers [Pentagon Office, Selected].)

2. On April 23 Marshall delivered an off-the-record address to the American Newspaper Publishers Association convention in New York City's Waldorf-Astoria Hotel. There is no text for or transcript of this speech in the Marshall papers.

3. Colonel Walter S. Fulton (U.S.M.A., 1904) had been in the National Guard Bureau until March 1939 when he was detailed to the Infantry School. Courtney H. Hodges, who had enlisted in the army in 1906, had been promoted to brigadier general on April 1, and at this time was the assistant commandant at the Infantry School.

4. Baruch wrote: "Most instructive visit. Everyone has been exceedingly courteous and attentive. Many thanks." (Baruch to Marshall, Telegram, April 18, 1940, GCMRL/G. C. Marshall Papers [Pentagon Office, Selected].)

5. Secretary of War Woodring did not go to Fort Benning.

To Brigadier General James E. Chaney[1]   April 23, 1940
[Washington, D.C.]

Dear Chaney: I have just received your letter of April 22d, and while I have had to go over it very hurriedly as I am leaving town this afternoon, not to be back until Monday, I think I have gotten the general idea of your proposals, all of which appear excellent.[2] However, there is one point I had in mind which I do not believe you have quite visualized as yet. I am much concerned to see that in the beginning these civilian measures are started in a small way in a single locality, so that they will be a model which all the others will seek to copy. Also, that wherever we can, we reach into an organization that has a history, a tradition.

For example, suppose we take the veteran organization of the Seventh Regiment[3] and, sub rosa, get an outstanding figure there to get together a group of about twenty men both vigorous and of distinction in civil life, and get them to appeal to you or the War Department to assist them in organizing a volunteer anti-aircraft unit. The distinction of the individuals in it would be a great drawing card, just as the presence of former Ambassadors, Secretaries of State and Mayors of New York cause the Plattsburg Camps to go over with such a bang. We could offer to help them without involving the War Department in any expense by having selected officers talk at their get together dinners, and by having their group taken on for an afternoon or evening or week-end with the regular anti-aircraft unit at Fort Hamilton. The idea would be to make this volunteer unit representative of the type of men who could manage such a thing, of the type of men who would attract others, of the type of men who have the necessary educational or mechanical ability.

I visualize a company of men between thirty-five and fifty years of age, composed of leading citizens, wealthy men, elderly mechanics, radio experts, officials of trucking companies, etc. etc. If one such unit could be quietly started, and then publicized in just the right way, other cities would leap to the fore in their effort to produce more units. We could anticipate that by picking out the proper individuals and organizations to start such a movement, such as the Ancient and Honorable Artillery Company in Boston, the veterans of the City Troop in Philadelphia, etc.

Some units as you suggest in these shipyards and industrial areas, composed of officials of the plant and the leading mechanics, would be tremendously helpful. Wherever there is a regular or National Guard anti-aircraft unit, the problem is vastly simplified, because there is no materiel problem at the start.

I am looking to you to generate the business in this direction, and for that reason have been writing to you directly and informally. Please do not take any of my proposals as things that must be done; and do not feel at all embarrassed in differing with me. I can only give momentary thought to this business while you are concentrating on it, so I want to feel that I am not an embarrassment to you in developing the plot.   Faithfully yours,

GCMRL/G. C. Marshall Papers (Pentagon Office, Selected)

1. Chaney was promoted to brigadier general on January 1, 1940; on March 12 he was made commanding general of the Air Defense Command at Mitchel Field near Hempstead, Long Island. The command was an experimental organization primarily concerned with planning.
2. On April 16 Marshall sent Chaney a letter he had received from a New Jersey man who

had written: "The people are more willing to be ready and take training than is realized at Washington. . . . Can't you think of some plan on a voluntary basis for this great mass of men that would be an actual help to the U.S. when needed." Marshall told Chaney: "It occurred to me when I read this that one move we might generate would be to use men over thirty and up to fifty in organizing 'volunteer' antiaircraft units in the various states. I suppose there would be many difficulties, but I think it is worth considering." (Marshall to Chaney, April 16, 1940, GCMRL/G. C. Marshall Papers [Pentagon Office, Selected].)

In his lengthy reply Chaney agreed that volunteers would have to be organized, trained, and armed as they had been in Great Britain. He concluded that volunteer antiaircraft and air raid precaution units should be formed plus a national air defense observers corps and eight National Guard pursuit squadrons—four on each of the Atlantic and Pacific coasts. The War Plans and the Operations and Training (G-3) divisions generally concurred with Chaney's recommendations. (Chaney to Marshall, April 22, 1940, NA/RG 407 [Classified, 580 (4-16-40)].)

3. The old elite Seventh Infantry, based in New York City, had been redesignated the 107th Infantry of the Twenty-seventh Division, New York National Guard, in October 1917.

To Lieutenant General Stanley D. Embick   April 29, 1940
[Washington, D.C.]

Dear Embick: Ten members of Congress headed by Representative J. Buell Snyder will arrive at Natchitoches, Louisiana, by air sometime on Monday, May 13, to spend three days witnessing the Third Army maneuvers.[1] Their particular interest is to see some of the results of recent expenditures for military materiel.

As you will recall, Mr. Snyder is chairman of the Subcommittee on Military Appropriations of the House, and we want him and his associates to see such things as the new antiaircraft weapons, artillery, motor transportation and combat vehicles, with a view to the restoration of some of these items to the Fiscal Year 1941 Appropriation, recently slashed by the House Committee. We also wish them to get a definite idea of what an Army corps really is. The importance of the Army corps, the fact that its divisions are not fully effective without the special corps troops, is a special point for their comprehension.

Major E. H. Brooks of the Statistics Branch General Staff will accompany the Committee, to supervise their itinerary and to give them any data they require both from the War Department standpoint and that of the troops.

Please have a tentative schedule prepared, for three days commencing May 14, and so arranged as to allow the Committee to see materiel and organizations under the most favorable circumstances, and let me have it up here. Faithfully yours,

GCMRL/G. C. Marshall Papers (Pentagon Office, Selected)

1. Upon completion of the Fourth Corps maneuvers at Fort Benning, Major General Walter C. Short's troops began moving to the Kisatchie National Forest between Natchitoches and Alexandria in central Louisiana. There they were scheduled to maneuver against Major General Walter Krueger's Ninth Corps which was to concentrate in the Angelina and the Sabine national forests in east Texas. Embick, the Third Army commander, was to lead this operation involving approximately 65,000 men. (*Army and Navy Journal,* February 10, 1940, p. 521.)

To BERNARD M. BARUCH   April 29, 1940
Confidential   [Washington, D.C.]

My dear Mr. Baruch: Your letter of April 22d was forwarded to me at Fort Benning, where I was making a hasty visit during the maneuvers.

I am glad you think that the going will be good before the Senate towards an increase in our appropriations, and am well aware of the responsibility I carry in the matter. Confidentially, at the same time as I received your letter, a radio came from the War Department to the effect that the Budget (meaning the President) had just cut six and one-half million from the thirty-nine million materiel estimate that I had submitted as being urgently required at the present time over and above the materiel included in the 1941 budget.

I reached the office this morning and immediately took up matters with the Bureau of the Budget people at their office, but learned that the President had already signed the communication transmitting the deficiency estimates to the Congress, so I will have to maneuver this somehow in spite of legal restrictions in the matter.

The money I am referring to was that required for the materiel, and particularly the Aircraft warning detectors,[1] for the Initial Protective Force—the existing units of the Regular establishment and the National Guard, and it did not take into consideration at all the two hundred and forty million deficiency in materiel of modern type for the whole Protective Mobilization Plan force.

I will let you know what happens; I am appearing tomorrow morning before the Senate Appropriations Committee.

With my thanks again for your tremendous assistance in this matter, Faithfully yours,

GCMRL/G. C. Marshall Papers (Pentagon Office, Selected)

1. On November 29, 1939, Marshall, Secretary of War Harry H. Woodring, and Major General Henry H. Arnold had gone to the Signal Corps center at Fort Monmouth, New Jersey, to witness an important test of the army's "radio position finding" system. The army officially adopted the device, designated SCR–270, in May 1940, and it remained a standard unit for several years. (Dulany Terrett, *The Signal Corps: The Emergency,* a volume in the

United States Army in World War II [Washington: GPO, 1956], pp. 41, 128–29.) The United States Navy acronym RADAR (from "radio detection and ranging") had not yet come into general use for these electronic devices.

To LIEUTENANT GENERAL STANLEY D. EMBICK   May 1, 1940
Personal and Confidential   [Washington, D.C.]

Dear Embick: I have just received your note of April 30th, apologizing for your not getting down to Benning while I was there. Thank Goodness you did not make the trip; I felt vastly relieved when your Aide told me you had submitted to the doctor's directions that you go to bed. Now, my concern is that you do not leave for Beauregard too soon;[1] please don't take any such chance, you have a good staff and they will wrestle with the concentration.

I haven't had a cold for a year and a half, but I picked up one, apparently from the dust at Benning, and am just now shaking it off. I had to take to my bed, between drinks as it were, during the trip, both at Benning and at Charleston. At the latter place I was running a slight fever, about a degree, but had to make a talk at a luncheon and then review General Summerall's fine cadet corps.[2] By the time I got to Washington I was pretty well shot, but next morning—yesterday, I spent two hours before the Senate Appropriations Committee, return again this morning, and go before the House Military Committee Thursday morning.[3] There is not much rest and relaxation about this business, but I cannot complain because up to the present moment I have felt splendidly and I think I will be entirely free of my cold by tomorrow or the next day.

Very confidentially, for your eye alone, I found what you probably are already aware of, that relations between Short and Singleton at Benning are on a very delicate basis. Singleton has made every effort to cooperate—I doubt if there is any man in the Army who would try harder saving yourself; and Short is an aggressive type, with a large responsibility for a new development in training on his hands.

During the early period of the concentration I found on each visit, always staying with Singleton, that he was highly supersensitive about Short and the First Division. Short made no comments to me of any kind, and incidentally, I never had an opportunity to talk to him alone because Singleton never left my side on either trip. If any question as to supply or any matter relating to Benning as a whole came up Singleton would at once intervene in the discussion even though I might be talking to the Division Commander and his assembled staff. He was acutely supersensitive, at the same time he was trying with all the loyalty of his being to cooperate.

Of course, the situation of two independent commanders, with inter-related affairs, is an impossible one at best, and I am much relieved that the concentration in Louisiana terminates this situation. I found on this last trip that Singleton had gotten to the point where everything regarding the First Division was poison to him, and to exaggerate very slightly, everything else whatever it was, was better. Yet Short had nothing to say to me on the subject, though on this trip I did drive about with him alone a portion of the time. I know Short well; he is a very able, determined, and rather stubborn type. Incidentally, Krueger, with a different complexion, is much the same sort.[4] Both of them are aggressive, energetic, and to a certain extent, self-opinionated. Both of them, I believe, are leaders with a sufficient under-standing of mobile army problems to produce valuable results. You will probably find them "head on" regarding many considerations brought up by results of the maneuvers.

I hope to get down to Louisiana between the 12th and 15th and stay until the completion of the last exercise. The Secretary of War is going down for a couple of days and wishes me to be with him during that period. Otherwise, I am asking you not to make any special arrangements for me whatsoever, except to see that I have a car and a place at the camp or Beauregard to sleep.

On my return to Benning, I was tremendously impressed with the splen-did job that Gruber is doing and the confidence that everyone seems to have in him. I wish it had been possible to promote him; I tried to manage it but without success. (Incidentally, in any of these discussions, the question of Manus McCloskey always arises).[5] Now, I want to find the place he wishes to go and try to arrange it accordingly.

This is a longer note than I intended, but as I did not have an opportunity to talk to you personally, I will take it out in writing.

With further cautions against a too hasty convalescence, and my warm regards,   Faithfully yours,

GCMRL/G. C. Marshall Papers (Pentagon Office, Selected)

1. Camp Beauregard—eight miles north of Alexandria, Louisiana—was to be the location of the headquarters for the Third Army maneuvers.

2. On April 26 Marshall was the featured speaker at the politically important Azalea Festival luncheon in Charleston, South Carolina. If his address followed the notes his staff prepared for him, Marshall talked about the recent improvements in army funding, training, and equipment, and warned that adequate defense was going to be expensive. (Notes for the Chief of Staff, GCMRL/G. C. Marshall Papers [Pentagon Office, Speeches].) Marshall's friend and the former army chief of staff Major General Charles P. Summerall also attended the luncheon. He had been president of the Citadel, South Carolina's state military college, since 1931.

3. The chief of staff's April 15 memorandum to the secretary of war (p. 198) resulted in a request by the president on April 29 to add $18,000,000 (rather than the $25,000,000 Marshall had asserted was urgently required) to the 1941 army supply budget specifically for the pur-chase of certain critical items for the Signal and the Ordnance corps. On April 30 and May 1,

Marshall spent a total of four hours before the Senate Appropriations Subcommittee seeking to restore approximately 60 percent of the $112,000,000 cut by the House. Personnel problems were less pressing than weapons, ordnance, and supplies, Marshall told the subcommittee. Taking care not to appear to ask Congress for funding greater than the president's requests, he sought the restoration of the House's cuts in clothing allowance, flight pay for certain officers, 109 aircraft, the construction of an air base at Anchorage, Alaska, and critical-items purchases. (Senate Appropriations Committee, *Military Establishment Appropriation Bill for 1941, Hearings* [Washington: GPO, 1940], pp. 14–71.)

4. Walter Krueger joined the army in 1899, as a private, after serving with the volunteer forces in Cuba. In June 1901 he was commissioned as a second lieutenant in the Thirtieth Infantry in the Philippine Islands, the regiment Marshall joined in May 1902. Krueger was known as an expert on discipline and training and also as a historian and scholar of military affairs. In February 1939 he was promoted to major general and given command of the Second Division at Fort Sam Houston, Texas.

5. Colonel Edmund L. Gruber had prepared the plan of the corps maneuvers at Fort Benning and was working on the Third Army maneuvers plan. Brigadier General McCloskey retired at the end of April 1938, and since August 1938 he had been superintendent of Cook County Hospital in Chicago, Illinois. (Regarding McCloskey see *Papers of GCM*, 1: 528.)

To Major General Benjamin A. Poore   May 4, 1940
Confidential   [Washington, D.C.]

Dear General Poore: General Harbord brought to my attention your letter to him of April 30th, enclosing a statement of the services of Colonel Robinson, and I think it best to reply to you direct.[1]

The situation, and this must be confidential, is this: The President insists on a certain length of service availability for brigadier generals, and up to the present time he has declined to make any exception. Once an officer has passed the age of fifty-seven, we can do nothing to advance him, except in the case of a Chief of Arm on a four-year detail; he must have a full four years to serve. I have picked men up who have been passed over, but in each instance they had more than six years to serve. Normally, they will not reach the grade of brigadier general. The more critical the situation in the world, the more adamant the President has become.

I was familiar with Colonel Robinson's services, and am sorry that he is at an age which, short of an actual war situation, prevents anything being done in the matter. Faithfully yours,

GCMRL/G. C. Marshall Papers (Pentagon Office, Selected)

1. General Poore (U.S.M.A., 1886) was the father-in-law of Colonel Donald A. Robinson (U.S.M.A., 1906), who had been chief of staff of the First Cavalry Division at Fort Bliss, Texas, since July 1939. General Poore hoped that Robinson might be considered, despite his age (59), for one of the four new brigadier general positions that Congress was considering. In January 1941 Robinson was promoted to brigadier general.

To Lieutenant General Stanley D. Embick   May 7, 1940
Memorandum for The Adjutant General   Washington, D.C.
Telegram. *Confidential*

Please send the following telegram in CODE to the Headquarters, Third
Army, Camp Beauregard, Louisiana:

"Confidential: Associated Press dispatches notably of May fourth
from New Orleans refer to Army Maneuvers from May eleventh to
May twenty-fifth as costing twenty-eight million. This particular phase
of the maneuvers probably cost about two million. Such publicity is
very harmful to the processing of Army appropriations before Congress.
Please see that future releases avoid such unfortunate misstatements.
ADAMS."[1]

G. C. M.

NA/RG 165 (OCS, 14440-306)

1. Marshall wrote this memorandum for the signature of The Adjutant General Emory S.
Adams. Embick replied that the spurious figure had originated in a February 7 Associated
Press story quoting Senator John H. Overton of Louisiana. The only press release regarding
maneuver costs issued from Third Army Headquarters estimated the total to be $1,888,950.
(Embick to Adams, May 9, 1940, NA/RG 165 [OCS, 14440-306].) On this same issue see pp.
135-36.

To Major General Daniel Van Voorhis   May 10, 1940
[Washington, D.C.]

Dear Van Voorhis: I feel that I have neglected you sadly in the past few
weeks, particularly in view of the fact that you did such a splendid job in
connection with the fire disaster in Colon. I did draft a radiogram for the
Secretary to send you, which reflected the views of both of us. The Ambassador from Panama, our State Department and apparently, the President
were all very much gratified and pleased with the rapidity with which you
acted, and the completeness of your arrangements. Mr. Norman Davis, of
the Red Cross, was especially complimentary in his relation with you in the
matter of funds, etc.[1]

I have taken rather a busy day to write a letter because since midnight last
night when the word came in of the German move on Holland, we have
been very busy with special estimates and other proposals, which the
President will now approve. I have just returned from the White House an
hour ago and am having a number of detailed statements prepared which I
must take up with Mr. Morgenthau and the Budget people at 9:15 tomorrow.
Meanwhile, to make everything extremely simple, Mrs. Marshall is on the
verge of receiving about 2,000 people this afternoon at a reception and

garden party. I say she is doing it, because it looks a little bit dubious about my getting there at all.

I do not think I have written you since my trip to Hawaii. That journey was delightful and astonishingly quick. My time from Honolulu to Shreveport, Louisiana, was 27 hours, I could have come into Washington in 30 hours had there not been foul weather over the Rockies and a sleet storm in Washington. I learned a great deal in Hawaii about the general status of affairs and the personnel and an understanding of their problem and the general Army problem. As a matter of fact, I have found these hurried trips of mine of incalculable value in giving me a reasonably sound basis for determining the relative priority of requirements, as well as a splendid opportunity to acquaint myself with general conditions and the point of view of the local personnel.

Unless the European situation prevents, I expect to leave here the latter part of June for Alaska, and that should complete my foreign garrison inspections for some time to come. I do have to go to the Maneuvers in Texas and Louisiana next week, and I will have to go clear around the United States to drop in at each Army maneuver in August.

Some day I do want to sit down and enjoy a period of lazy contemplation, but with the world growing more desperate and chaotic, the outlook for a rest in the near future is not very inspiring.

Please give my warm regards to Mrs. Van Voorhis; incidentally I am still in a battle with the Customs people to give me a clearance to permit the entry of those grass rugs. They have been almost a month answering my last letter.   Faithfully yours,

GCMRL/G. C. Marshall Papers (Pentagon Office, Selected)

1. On the night of April 13–14 about one-third of Colon burned, leaving about 10,000 persons homeless in the tenement section. General Van Voorhis sent troops to patrol the city—at the Caribbean end of the Panama Canal—and to set up a large number of tents and field kitchens. The American Red Cross cabled $15,000 for relief on April 14. The next day, Marshall wrote the following radiogram for the secretary's signature: "Your prompt action to assist and succor the people of Colon is to be commended. The War Department feels confident in trusting to your good judgment as to the further requirements of this situation." (Woodring to Van Voorhis, Radio, April 15, 1940, GCMRL/G. C. Marshall Papers [Pentagon Office, Selected].)

O N the morning of May 10, scarcely twelve hours after word of the German attack on the Low Countries reached Washington, the president met with General Marshall, Secretary of the Treasury Henry Morgenthau, Jr., and several others. Marshall discussed the materiel situation and asked for an immediate manpower increase for the Regular Army to be followed by a further increase in the autumn to raise it to full peace strength of 280,000 enlisted men. Having been instructed by President Roosevelt to "get all of this together" by Monday, Secretary Morgenthau arranged to meet with Marshall on Saturday morning, May 11. (FDRL/H. Morgenthau, Jr., Papers [Presidential Diary, 2: 538–40]. For comments by Marshall and others on the May 10 meeting, see FDRL/H. Morgenthau, Jr., Papers [Diary, 150: 275–81].)

At the meeting Morgenthau told Marshall that the War Department's budgetary tactics were wrong; "the trouble is . . . the President is getting little pieces and what he ought to have is an over-all picture." Marshall at once produced "a rough outline of the over-all picture" summarizing additional requirements for the fiscal year 1941 budget amounting to $640,000,000 for 38,000 more men (to bring the total to 280,000), for critical and essential items of equipment, for aircraft, for seacoast defenses, and for expediting materiel production. The secretary declared that he was not frightened by the numbers, but Marshall said, "It makes me dizzy." "It makes me dizzy if we don't get it," Morgenthau responded. (Ibid., pp. 291–92. A revised version [May 12] of the memorandum Marshall presented—"Summary of Additional Requirements for National Defense . . ."—is in NA/RG 165 [OCS, Emergency File].)

A major problem the military faced in seeking to stimulate greater and more rapid production was, in Marshall's view, that the country was undergoing an unprecedented period of transition from peacetime industry but without the stimulus and efficiency of full mobilization. "We have never in the past made deliberate moves one after the other to build up to a preparation before we were in the business." If it became necessary for the country to pass beyond preparation, the costs would become tremendous. "When we step beyond this, we are really going into mobilization, that is what it amounts to." After a lengthy discussion of the proper strategy to adopt in approaching the president with these unprecedented requests, Secretary Morgenthau called the White House to arrange for a Monday morning (May 13) meeting. (FDRL/H. Morgenthau, Jr., Papers [Diary, 150: 300–302].)

At eleven o'clock Monday morning, Marshall, Morgenthau, Woodring, Johnson, and Budget Director Harold Smith "went to see the president who, it was quite evident, was not desirous of seeing us," Marshall recalled later. "The conversation through most of the meeting—in fact all of it for a long time—was between the president and Mr. Morgenthau, and he was getting very little chance to state his case. I rather assumed that the president was staging this rather drastic handling of Mr. Morgenthau for my benefit, because they were old friends and neighbors."

At first Morgenthau talked about the need for an advisory committee for the Council of National Defense, but the president did not favor this on the ground that existing agencies could handle the industrial preparedness effort. "Then Mr. Morgenthau got around to military aspects—military equipment—and the president was exceedingly short with him. Finally, Mr. Morgenthau said, 'Well, Mr. President, will you hear General Marshall?' The president replied (I remember this most distinctly), 'Well, I know exactly what he would say. There is no necessity for my hearing him at all.' It was a desperate situation. I felt that he might be president but I had certain knowledge which I was sure he didn't possess or which he didn't grasp. I thought the whole thing was catastrophic in its possibilities, and this last cut [i.e., the president's reduction of Marshall's April 15 request (see pp. 206–7)] just emphasized the point. Recalling that a man has a great advantage, psychologically, when he stands looking down on a fellow, I took advantage—in a sense—of the president's condition. When he terminated the meeting, I, not having had a chance to say anything, walked over and stood looking down at him and said, 'Mr. President, may I have three minutes?' Then in a complete change of mood and in a most gracious fashion he said, 'Of course, General Marshall.'

"I said, 'Now, first Mr. Morgenthau spoke to you about this civilian organization to represent all the civil side of these matters, and you said that Hopkins would handle one part and Morgenthau one part.' And he [the president] himself was handling one part of it. 'With all frankness, none of you are supermen, and Mr. Morgenthau has no more chance of managing this thing than of flying. We just had lunch and he gave orders he was not to be interrupted. He was interrupted three times by the matter of the closing of the Stock Exchange. He can't possibly grasp all these things. He was trying to get the straight of the enormity of our situation regarding military preparedness, and he wasn't even allowed to do that. If you don't do something like that [the advisory committee]—and do it right away—I don't know what is going to happen to this country.'

"'As to the military part, I just came here in the first place about a cut—of something which had previously been approved by the Budget Bureau and turned down in the Congress—which is actually a small sum of money. It seems to us large these days, but it will eventually be considered a small sum. I don't know quite how to express myself about this to the president of the United States, but I will say this, *you have got to do something and you've got to do it today.*'" (George C. Marshall, interviewed by Forrest C. Pogue, November 15, 1956, GCMRL. The emphasis is in the original. For Morgenthau's record of this meeting, see FDRL/ H. Morgenthau, Jr., Papers [Presidential Diary, 2: 531].)

Secretary Morgenthau—who observed in his diary that "the President has to take a great deal of the responsibility that the Army is in as bad shape as it is"—told Marshall that evening, "You did a swell job and I think you are going to get about 75% of what you want." The secretary was "tremendously impressed with General Marshall. He stood right up to the President." (Ibid., pp. 533–34.) ★

To Bernard M. Baruch   May 14, 1940
Confidential   [Washington, D.C.]

Dear Mr. Baruch: Major Smith has just shown me your note to him of May 11th.[1]

With reference to the second paragraph, in regard to the 280,000 men: Very confidentially, I think you will be interested in knowing that I battled twice yesterday to have the President include in his special defense message, which presumably goes to Congress tomorrow, the 280,000. At the moment he declined to go further than 15,000; but even more confidentially, and for your eye alone, he stated that he would give me the remaining 38,000 in July by Executive Order, creating a deficiency. Mr. Morgenthau, who meets me with the President this morning, is hopeful that he can get him to come out in the open in this. I merely mention these items that you may see the difficulties in getting even what you call "a pitiful number."

The President is deeply interested in increasing airplane production.[2] Our air production has been materially increased by Allied orders, and continues to increase. What General Arnold is interested in is again the personnel question—an increase in the number of pilots trained to operate planes, and of course the bombs and weapons for the planes. That is the bottle-neck at the moment in the Air program. It takes longer to develop the crew than it does to build the plane. Thank God we have fair production now, but we have nothing like enough pilots to maintain our *present* GHQ force on a going basis in campaign.

This is a very hasty note; I am due at the White House in about an hour.[3]   Faithfully yours,

GCMRL/G. C. Marshall Papers (Pentagon Office, Selected)

1. On May 10, Marshall had Major Walter B. Smith send Baruch a three-page memorandum exemplifying the chief of staff's desire for prompt increases in Regular Army manpower. Baruch replied the next day encouraging Marshall to "go after the money necessary to increase the arms to equip what seems like a pitiful number of men—280,000." Baruch requested information regarding appropriations during the previous decade. (Baruch to Smith, May 11, 1940, Princeton/B. M. Baruch Papers.) Smith's letter to Baruch of May 14 listed the War Department's military appropriations 1930–40, and noted that the total of $3,496,000,000 was $1,164,000,000 "less than the estimates of minimum requirements made by the Chiefs of Arms and Services." (Both of Smith's letters are in NA/RG 165 [OCS, Emergency File].)

2. Following the May 13 meeting with the president, Secretary Morgenthau noted in his diary: "The part that worries me most is the President's statement that he wants to have 50,000 planes and wants the Government to build a lot of factories. I just can't see it and I told him so. No one has thought the plan through." (FDRL/H. Morgenthau, Jr., Papers [Presidential Diary, 2: 533].)

3. Marshall had two meetings at the White House on May 14. At the first, beginning at 10:30 A.M., Marshall, Morgenthau, Woodring, Johnson, Arnold, and several others discussed Air Corps appropriations. (Notes on this are in Morgenthau Diary, 262: 174–76.) Following this meeting, General Marshall met with President Roosevelt, who eliminated the army's

request for an immediate 15,000 men and cut seacoast defense requests thereby reducing the army's supplemental requests by $24,000,000. But he added $80,000,000 for two hundred B-17's and $106,000,000 for pilot training. The president was thus prepared to request $732,000,000 in added funds for fiscal year 1941 for the army. (The documents concerning this discussion—several with handwritten notations by Marshall and one handwritten budget summary by Roosevelt—are in NA/RG 165 [OCS, Emergency File].)

MEMORANDUM FOR GENERAL MILES, G-2   May 14, 1940
[Washington, D.C.]

Please look into the question of submitting a periodic summary of the lessons being learned from abroad, tactical, technical, organizational, etc.[1] At the present time, this subject, it seems to me, is somewhat submerged under the general presentations of what is going on.

Also, please consider the matter of maintaining a current estimate of predicted activity, in the Caribbean area, Latin and South American area, Alaskan region, and the Far East.

Also, please consider the organization of your section from the viewpoint of present groupings. I am not intimately familiar with your set-up, but have the impression that you have British, French, German, Italian, Japanese, Chinese compartments. If this is so, do you think there would be an advantage in collecting these desks, or officers, into "power groupings", as it were. This might not be an efficient arrangement, but it occurred to me that for the purposes of current estimates, etc., it might be an effective one.

GCMRL/G. C. Marshall Papers (Pentagon Office, Selected)

1. The first issue of the *Tentative Lessons Bulletin* was dated May 22; it concerned German tanks, weapons, and tactics. In all, 170 bulletins had been issued by November 1941. They are in NA/RG 165 (OCS, G-2, Publications File); information concerning them is in NA/RG 319 (G-2, 461[5–22–40] and [10–11–40]).

MEMORANDUM FOR COLONEL WARD   May 15, 1940
[Washington, D.C.]

We must be prepared in the next few days—and immediately in conversations with the press, to off-set the clamor that will be raised by the opponents of the Administration and by the pacifists on the basis that tremendous amounts of money have been spent and now we claim we are not prepared and are asking for much more.

Of course, we know the answer, but it is necessary to get the data in such form that it is readily usable. Please have rough estimates of the following prepared for my use and that of the Secretary of War, and the Press Section:

Percentage of annual appropriations from 1934 to 1940, year by year, that went for fixed charges,—that is, pay, rations, clothing, transportation, maintenance, and matters of this sort, which are high according to American standards of living, and the cumbersome manner in which the Army must be administered under the peculiar laws which have been passed, and the dispersed state of the troops in many posts, and the necessity of handling each individual soldier in such a manner that we can report on his health, allowances, and location, at any time to Congress.

I think it will be best to make the break-down without the amounts, so that I may see the manner in which the data is to be gathered. I repeat again, these are to be rough requirements; I do not want minute calculations, we have not time for such.[1]

GCMRL/G. C. Marshall Papers (Pentagon Office, Selected)

1. During his May 17 testimony before the Senate Appropriations Subcommittee, Marshall discussed this issue and presented two charts: one giving regular and supplemental War Department military appropriations for 1920 through 1940, and the second giving a functional breakdown of army expenditures and obligations for 1937 through 1940. (See *Military Establishment Appropriation Bill for 1941*, pp. 429–31.)

To Franklin D. Roosevelt   May 15, 1940
From Henry Morgenthau, Jr.   Washington, D.C.

My dear Mr. President: In view of my experience with the Army during the last couple of days, I am taking the liberty of making a suggestion.

Let General Marshall, and only General Marshall, do all the testifying in connection with the Bill which you are about to send up for additional appropriations for the Army.[1]   Yours sincerely,

H. Morgenthau, Jr.

FDRL/F. D. Roosevelt Papers (PSF, Morgenthau)

1. In his diary Morgenthau noted that he had told Marshall on May 17 that he had "written to the President that he, General Marshall, handle the bill on the Hill; that if he had any trouble with Woodring or Johnson and wanted to let me know, that I would let the President know. He said 'Is the President worried?' and I said he is worried as to how the bill is going to be handled on the Hill, because he spoke to me about it last night." (FDRL/ H. Morgenthau, Jr., Papers [Diary, 263: 249].)

In 1956 Marshall told Forrest C. Pogue that he was allowed to handle the administration's War Department budget defense before Congress because: "In the first place, they [the congressmen] were certain I had no ulterior motive. In the next place, they had begun to trust my judgment. But most important of all, if Republicans could assure their constituents that they were doing it on my suggestion, and not on Mr. Roosevelt's suggestion, they could go ahead and back the thing. He had such enemies that otherwise members of Congress didn't dare, it seemed, to line up with him. And that was true of certain Democrats who were getting pretty bitter." (Marshall interview, November 15, 1956.)

TO WALTER G. ANDREWS[1]   May 16, 1940
Confidential   [Washington, D.C.]

Dear Andrews: I have just received your note of May 15, with the enclosure of copy of letter to Senator Wadsworth from General O'Ryan.[2]

In line with what General O'Ryan says I think in effect that today, meaning this Thursday, the Government is moving to advance the state of National Defense in response to the pressure of public opinion to which General O'Ryan refers. All is not included that should be at this time, and I refer specifically to the fact that there is no material increase of the Regular Army. But I think that will come closely on the heels of the move about to be made.

With reference to his thought "People now seem to be leagues ahead of the Government in the understanding of aggression menace", I think it only fair to the President to say that he had moved in each instance almost as rapidly as public opinion would permit. Naturally, I have not always agreed with the specific character of each move, but that is merely a matter of opinion as to the best means for accomplishing a general purpose. But I do think that in each measure, beginning with his special defense message of January, 1939, and on down to date, he has pressed about as rapidly as public opinion would permit. Possibly—and I mean also politically—the Army could have been given a larger budget sum for the fiscal year 1941. But there again, it is a question of what the public and the Party at that time would stand for.

The tag end of February I was before the Appropriation Committee of the House, and while they did give the Army an increase over budget funds of money for materiel, they also cut our plane program down to 57 planes and wiped out the Anchorage Base. And the point is, that apparently met public approval, not of course the approval of well informed men like General O'Ryan, and certainly not my approval. Since that date, there has occurred the affair in Norway, which brought about almost a reversal of public opinion; and the assault on the Western front has created a deluge of recommendations for the increase of our military forces. This is a typical American process, apparently with nothing abnormal about it.

I stated what I thought was a wise policy before the Military Appropriation Committee of the House last February, to advance step by step with the situation abroad. There were two considerations then; one related to materiel, and on that I urged the immediate provision of what we needed for the PMP. I did not go into the Assistant Secretary's portion of the plot as to the building of additional facilities, leaving that entirely to his presentation. I urged then that the Regular establishment be brought up by a small sum of 15,000 men, whose importance was out of all proportion to the small number involved, because it meant the rounding out of organizations now in existence. I had in mind when I spoke of step by step, the further increase of the Regular establishment to 280,000 and beyond, and, of course, the eventual mobilization of the National Guard.

I think at the present moment the War Department should be permitted to go ahead with enlistments in order that we may have available as early as possible seasoned soldiers, in highly trained units, to meet sudden responsibilities in the Western hemisphere. We can reach 280,000 on an ordinary volunteer basis by September, and from there we should go on towards 400,000.

As to the National Guard, and whether or not it should be mobilized at this moment is a question in my mind. I am rather inclined to think that it would be better to consider that a little later and in relation to the Army Maneuvers, which portions of the Guard have been so violently opposed to. And incidentally I might say that while it is a fine thing to train companies and battalions, unless we get these brigade and division staffs, we will have an impossible situation, and there is no other way to do it except by large maneuvers.

In relation to a possible mobilization of the National Guard, I have the feeling at the moment that we should avoid a complication of burdens in order that the development of highly trained, seasoned division and corps troops in the Regular Army can be brought to a pitch of instant preparedness to take action in this hemisphere. If you remember that chart I showed you, that gives the first objective which should be reached, certainly as to enlistments for the Regular establishment by September, and we should go on beyond that towards war strength rather than peace strength which, as I have said above, carries us towards 400,000.

The question in my mind again in relation to the mobilization of the National Guard, is whether in this crisis, with its menace of the moment along with the indefinite period which may be involved, it would not be better, particularly so far as jobs, families, etc. are concerned, to get a temporary increase to the Regular establishment, which will be brought about by those men who feel perfectly free to volunteer,—young reserve officers, young fellows of the type now being cared for by the Government in the CCC, etc., rather than to mobilize the Guard at this particular juncture. We will have no trouble in giving it the extra training in this crisis; everybody will cooperate towards that end.

This is very hastily written, but it gives you my ideas of the moment. Faithfully yours,

P.S. The foregoing idea of temporarily increasing the Regular Army rather than mobilizing the National Guard, might seem to be a return to the former unfortunate policy of initially trying to fight a war with Regular troops. However, today the situation is quite different, and I am not talking about the permanent advancement of Regular officers, but rather of the rounding out of forces already on the make, and the urgent necessity of having trained people ready to operate in the Western hemisphere. Our initial missions will inevitably be those of relatively small forces here and there, for which the troops must be instantly available.

GCMRL/G. C. Marshall Papers (Pentagon Office, General)

1. Andrews was the ranking Republican on the House Military Affairs Committee.
2. Major General John F. O'Ryan—a New York City lawyer, the World War commander of New York's Twenty-seventh Division, and a strong supporter of aid to the Allies—had sent a telegram on May 10 to Congressman James W. Wadsworth (Republican from New York) urging greater military preparedness. "People now seem leagues ahead of government in understanding of aggression menace. Wilson mobilized guard divisions on border as war measure without hostile public reaction though with presidential campaign pending. This of greatest value to later war efficiency. Our man power urgently requires mobilization and training as defense measure for eventualities." Andrews had received a copy and had forwarded it to Marshall for comment.

UNTIL the night of May 13, German successes in the land battle in Western Europe did not appear particularly alarming to the Allies, according to an official British history. But thereafter the tide ran strongly in Germany's favor. On May 14 the Germans crossed the Meuse River at Dinant and broke through French defenses around Sedan. In the air Allied losses were heavy. Overwhelmed, the Dutch Army ceased fighting on the fifteenth. By the following day the chief of the British Imperial General Staff reported that the situation was most critical. (J. R. M. Butler, *Grand Strategy, September 1938–June 1941,* a volume in the *History of the Second World War* [London: HMSO, 1957], pp. 182–83.)

Implementing the decisions arrived at with Marshall on May 13, President Roosevelt personally delivered a message to Congress on May 16 requesting a supplemental military appropriation of $1,184,000,000, including $732,000,000 for the army. This new money was to cover the cost of increasing the Regular Army from 227,000 to 255,000 enlisted men and of providing the critical and essential items necessary to field a Protective Mobilization Plan force of 750,000 plus replacements.

The morning following the president's address, Marshall appeared before the Senate Appropriations subcommittee to explain the implications of the new request. Repeatedly he told the committee members that added troops and funds were for the defense of the Western Hemisphere, that strengthening the army should be done in a series of carefully planned steps, and that further spending and manpower increases might be required, depending upon the changing international situation. He did not favor the immediate mobilization of the National Guard at this time, but he emphasized the need to begin at once to increase the Regular Army. Pressed by Subcommittee Chairman Elbert D. Thomas to tell the senators what he, as chief of staff, wanted in addition to the president's proposals, Marshall replied, "it is my personal opinion that we should immediately proceed with the further increase of the Army up to its authorized peacetime limit of 280,000 men, and, as we approach that limit, in the light of the situation at that time, we must then decide to what extent we should go beyond that strength. I anticipate the necessity of 400,000 men before we finish with this business of preparing for emergencies short of full mobilization." He would also need more money, and if further steps toward full mobilization were required, that sum would become quite large. (Senate Appropriations Committee, *Military Establishment Appropriation Bill for 1941,* pp. 403–33; the quotations are from pp. 422–23.) ★

MEMORANDUM[1]   May 22, 1940
Secret   [Washington, D.C.]

Subject: National Strategic Decisions.

1. Further imminently probable complications of to-day's situation are:
    a. Nazi-inspired revolution in Brazil.
    b. Widespread disorders with attacks on U.S. citizens in Mexico and raids along our southern border.
    c. Japanese hostilities against the United States in the Far East.
    d. Decisive Allied defeat, followed by German aggression in the Western Hemisphere.
    e. All combined.
2. We have vital interests in three general areas:
    a. The Far East.
    b. South America.
    c. Europe.
3. There should be an immediate decision as to what major military operations we must be prepared to conduct.

4. It is not practicable to send forces to the Far East, to Europe, and to South America all at once, nor can we do so to a combination of any two of these areas without dangerous dispersion of force.

5. We cannot conduct major operations either in the Far East or in Europe due both to lack of means at present and because of the resultant abandonment of the United States' interest in the area to which we do not send forces.

6. It would appear that conditions now developing limit us for at least a year, more or less, to the conduct of offensive-defensive operations in South America in defense of the Western Hemisphere and of our own vital interests; such limited offensive operations in Mexico as the situation may require; possible protective occupation of European possessions in the Western Hemisphere; and the defense of Continental United States and its overseas possessions East of the 180th Meridian.

This appears to be the maximum effort of which we are capable to-day.

7. Intelligent, practical planning, and later successful action, require an early decision regarding these matters:

1st—As to what we are *not* going to do,

2d—As to what we *must prepare* to do.

NA/RG 165 (WPD, 4175-7)

1. This document was not addressed to any specific person, but Marshall took copies to President Roosevelt, Admiral Stark, and Under Secretary of State Sumner Welles. In a note for the record dated May 23, 1940, and typed on the file copy, Major Matthew B. Ridgway, a Latin America specialist in the War Plans Division, commented, "Mr. Welles read this Memo in Gen. Marshall's presence, this date, and expressed his 'complete agreement with every word of it.'" Ridgway's initials appear on the file copy of this memorandum as the writer, but the final version was the result of Marshall's heavy editing, particularly in paragraphs 3 through 7.

MEMORANDUM FOR THE SECRETARY OF WAR   May 22, 1940
[Washington, D.C.]

I have read the letter you handed me from the lady in Owensboro, Kentucky, with reference to General Krueger.[1]

Krueger and I were second lieutenants in the same regiment in 1903. He is of typical German stock, thorough, hard-working, ambitious, and devoid of humor. At the time of the return of our regiment from the Philippines in 1902 [*1903*] and the stopping of the transport at Nagasaki to coal, I recall he was hoping to see his brother there, and that his brother was a General Staff officer of the German Army then on duty as a Military Attaché at Tokyo. He did not see his brother.

Krueger has made a commendable record in the Army as an intellectual; he was an instructor at the Army War College, and, I believe, also at the

Naval War College. During the World War I believe his return from France was requested by the French Government, and he was quietly returned to France the second time and utilized, I think, in the Training Section of the GHQ. I have no doubt whatever as to his loyalty. I know he is ambitious, and that he is a very stubborn character.

It is nothing remarkable to have high ranking officers in our Army of German stock. General Haan, in command of the Ninth Corps, on the march to the Rhine, called at the home of his father in Germany.[2] I believe there are other similar instances.

GCMRL/G. C. Marshall Papers (Pentagon Office, Selected)

1. This letter was not found. General Krueger's name had been in the news as commander of the Ninth Corps or "Red" side in the Louisiana-Texas maneuvers. The *Army and Navy Journal* (June 8, 1940, p. 989) observed: "General Krueger is the 'Daddy' of the 2nd Division, having organized and commanded it, in its present form, since its inception and naturally is proud of his command. In turn, the rank and file of the Division, now popularly known as 'Blitzkruegers,' are proud of their commander."

2. Major General William G. Haan (U.S.M.A., 1889) had commanded the Thirty-second Division in France during 1918. After the Armistice, he was assigned to command the Seventh Corps, which formed part of the American Army of Occupation in Germany.

MEMORANDUM FOR THE WAR PLANS DIVISION   May 23, 1940
Secret   Washington, D.C.

In a discussion with the President yesterday afternoon, and with Mr. Sumner Welles this morning, the memorandum prepared yesterday on the subject "National Strategic Decisions", I found the President in general agreement, also Admiral Stark, and specifically, Mr. Welles. They all felt that we must not become involved with Japan, that we must not concern ourselves beyond the 180 meridian, and that we must concentrate on the South American situation. All were in comparative agreement with the proposal which I made to have cruisers, with marines aboard, in certain South American ports on the East coast, to be available to support the existing governments in the event of an attempted Nazi overthrow.

I left the original of this memorandum with the President, and a copy with Mr. Welles, and with Admiral Stark. I think the matter is now well under way in their minds, and I believe that definite action will be taken.

I stated to Mr. Welles that some such idea as this should be one of the matters which our representatives about to be sent to South America should discuss on a definite basis with the authorities of certain of the governments there.

G. C. Marshall

NA/RG 165 (WPD, 4175-10)

MEMORANDUM FOR THE DEPUTY   May 23, 1940
CHIEF OF STAFF [GASSER]   [Washington, D.C.]
Confidential

Subject: Further objectives for Staff Planning.

I think we should get under way with definite studies or plans for further military development.[1] As a basis for initiating such procedure, it first becomes necessary, it seems to me, to make certain general decisions as to objectives. For example:

Existing Forces: – Approximately 500,000 at present, to be ready for continuous combat by July 1, 1941.

Protective Mobilization Plan: – Approximately double existing forces, to be in a similar state of preparation by January, 1942.

First Augmentation beyond PMP: – Either one and a half million or two million men, to be in a similar condition of preparation by July 1942.

With relation to the Air Forces, the successive stages of plane development, meaning completely manned, serviced, and supplied units, should be determined upon in general numbers of planes.

GCMRL/G. C. Marshall Papers (Pentagon Office, Selected)

1. On the morning of May 20, representatives of the General Staff's Personnel and Supply divisions and the Quartermaster Corps met with Marshall to discuss the implications of a sudden increase in manpower. Marshall inquired as to how long it would take, assuming that Congress passed a selective service act, to procure enough men to expand the army to its Protective Mobilization Plan quota of 750,000 plus 250,000 replacements. The Personnel representative said forty-five days. Marshall told Bernard Baruch that it would take about four months. Marshall requested that studies be made of the problems of providing shelter and clothing for the P.M.P. force. (Walter B. Smith Notes of Conference in Chief of Staff's Office, May 20, 1940, NA/RG 165 [OCS, Chief of Staff Conferences File].)

PRIOR to mid-May 1940, the Roosevelt administration and the War Department considered the stock of World War vintage surplus or obsolete munitions and ordnance to be largely earmarked for disposal to Latin American nations. British and French purchasing agents in the United States had expressed no interest in acquiring surplus army materiel; the legality of such sales to belligerents was in doubt, and Secretary of War Woodring was adamantly opposed to the sale of any surplus army property, particularly to belligerents. In mid-March the army, the navy, and the State Department finally agreed upon a procedure to handle arms sales to neutral governments. (See the documents in NA/RG 165 [OCS, 15270]. See also Secretary Woodring's handwritten comments on Brigadier General Richard

C. Moore's Memorandum for the Chief of Staff, March 9, 1940, NA/RG 165 [G-4, 31684].)

German military successes forced a rapid reassessment of arms sales policies. On May 21 the heads of the British and French purchasing commissions presented to Secretary of the Treasury Morgenthau a lengthy memorandum listing urgently needed supplies they wished to purchase from the United States's World War stocks. That same day General Marshall directed Major General Charles M. Wesson, the chief of Ordnance, to prepare a memorandum listing the supplies that could be sold.

Paralleling the developments in regard to surplus materiel was the issue of sales of aircraft to belligerents. In this area, British and French purchases had stimulated the United States aircraft industry far more than War or Navy department budget authorizations had permitted. The War Department sought to encourage foreign aircraft purchases. On March 25 Marshall had written a memorandum which endeavored to delineate government policy; President Roosevelt approved it with some modifications. ("Government Policy on Aircraft Foreign Sales," NA/RG 165 [OCS, 15270–938].) Within certain limits, manufacturers could negotiate deferred deliveries of aircraft for which the army had contracted if this allowed them to take advantage of foreign orders. The manufacturer would later fulfill the army's contract with newer models.

On March 28, in testimony before the Senate Military Affairs Committee, Marshall sketched his reasons for supporting a revised aircraft sales policy. "We will have the benefit of the tragic situation which produces a market for a plane that foreign governments want immediately and which we would prefer to release in favor of a more modern plane, and in order to get that plane as soon as possible other governments will pay a good price for it. Therefore, it is to the advantage of the manufacturer if he is allowed to sell the plane, particularly if it is nearly ready for delivery. If he is permitted to do that, he can sell to his own profit and give us the benefit of a better plane, we hope practically without cost and in many instances we know without any cost to us. So then we should be able to go along progressively changing our orders to get the maximum modernization of airplanes in the program, which will project further into the future the day of obsoletion of our types, and thereby delay the date when their replacement will be necessary." (Senate Military Affairs Committee, *Purchase of Implements of War by Foreign Governments, Hearings* [Washington: GPO, 1940], pp. 12–13.)

Before the German attack on the Netherlands and Belgium, Allied aircraft orders in the United States provided the British and French with an important but marginal source of supply. After that date both London and Paris pressed the Roosevelt administration ever more urgently for all possible planes. (H. Duncan Hall, *North American Supply,* a volume in the *History of the Second World War* [London: HMSO and Longmans, Green and Company, 1955], pp. 125, 128.) Marshall now found himself thrust into the position of struggling to prevent the Allies from absorbing the entire United States aircraft output and thereby upsetting the army's own preparedness plans. ★

MEMORANDUM FOR THE WAR PLANS DIVISION[1]   May 23, 1940
Secret   Washington, D.C.

Sale of Airplanes and Ammunition to Allied Purchasing Agents.

I discussed with Mr. Sumner Welles the list of munitions in the memorandum submitted by the Chief of Ordnance on May 22d (400,3295/4226) this morning. This list had been gone over by the President yesterday afternoon.[2] His directions were that I go further into the matter of determining what I might be able to state, under the terms of the law, was surplus, and what other legal methods I might be able to find to arrange for releasing various items of this equipment for the use of the Allies. He further directed me to confer with Mr. Welles this morning, in order to see what might be done towards meeting the Allies' request.

Mr. Welles is familiar with the items on the list, and with the complications regarding their being declared surplus. In effect, he stated that under the law the War Department could not sell this surplus materiel to the Allies; that he felt that international law would similarly forbid such transaction.

I told Mr. Welles that the matter was now in his hands; that I would continue to study it to see what means or methods we might find—such as turning in the 30 caliber ammunition for the purpose of securing better ammunition,—towards facilitating the release of these munitions to the Allies. Mr. Welles stated that he would consider the matter, that we quite evidently had done our best and it was really a matter of governmental policy and law, which he would look into.

I explained to Mr. Welles the situation regarding aircraft, that we could not jeopardize the completion of our augmentation of operating units, by releasing planes under process of manufacture for delivery to the Army; that the situation as to pilots would become an impossible one in a very few months if we did not receive deliveries of planes.[3] He agreed with this. I told him that in the smaller matters of accommodating them regarding engines and things of that sort, we would do practically all of this as desired by the Allies.

G. C. Marshall

NA/RG 165 (WPD, 4244-6)

1. This memorandum was also addressed to the assistant chief of staff, G-4 (Moore), and to General Wesson, the chief of Ordnance.

2. The original copy of General Wesson's memorandum for the chief of staff bears the president's check marks beside the materiel to be released. (NA/RG 165 [OCS, Emergency File]. Much of the documentation for the complex issue of releasing materiel to the Anglo-French Purchasing Board—changed to British Purchasing Commission after the fall of France—is in NA/RG 165 [OCS, Foreign Sale or Exchange of Munitions File].)

3. During his May 17 meeting with Secretary Morgenthau, Marshall had commented at length about the importance of keeping available a sufficient number of modern pursuit planes to train the new pilots the army was beginning to produce at the rate of 220 per month. "We are right at that moment of all these things being synchronized—we keep on receiving the pilots but we have lost the training ships." At the moment, Marshall said, the army had 150 P-36s. If the United States shipped the British 100 of these—which Marshall asserted was about a three-day supply under current battle conditions—the army's pilot training schedule would be set back nearly six months. (FDRL/H. Morgenthau, Jr., Papers [Diary, 263: 241-49].)

INCREASED support for military preparedness manifested itself in part in an outpouring of suggestions and plans by various private persons, government leaders, and organizations outside the War Department.

One portion of the president's May 16 message to Congress on the military budget attracted widespread interest and comment. Mr. Roosevelt said, "I should like to see this nation geared up to the ability to turn out at least 50,000 planes a year. Furthermore, I believe that this nation should plan at this time a program that would provide us with 50,000 military and naval planes." He mentioned this number again in his May 26 fireside chat. (*The Public Papers and Addresses of Franklin D. Roosevelt*, 1940 volume, ed. Samuel I. Rosenman [New York: Macmillan Company, 1941], pp. 202, 234.) Proposals to train large numbers of pilots in civilian schools were soon being discussed in Congress and in the press; the *Aero Digest* commented on a scheme to train fifty thousand civilian pilots during fiscal year 1941. These numbers were far in excess of army plans. (*Aero Digest* 36[June 1940]: 102. See the various studies in NA/RG 165 [WPD, 3807-55] and [OCS, Emergency File].)

Frank Knox, publisher of the *Chicago Daily News* and the Republican party nominee for vice-president in 1936, formed a committee in mid-May to cooperate with the government's pilot-training program. On May 14, he met with the president and received Roosevelt's endorsement of a plan to create volunteer camps—similar in scope and intent to the Plattsburg camps of 1915-17 and aimed primarily at college students—in each of the nine army corps areas. Preliminary flight training was to be extended to ten thousand men during the summer of 1940. Knox presumably discussed his ideas with Marshall and Arnold at their luncheon on May 15.

The Knox committee's "air Plattsburgs" complemented the ideas being pressed for the ground army by the Military Training Camps Association (M.T.C.A.) under the leadership of New York lawyer Grenville Clark. On May 25 representatives of the Knox and Clark groups, plus leaders from several civilian air organizations, met in Washington, D.C., with Civil Aeronautics Authority Chairman Robert H. Hickley and two army representatives. The Knox committee designated four men—Malin Craig, Frank R. McCoy, William J. Donovan, and Lewis W. Douglas—to cooperate with the military and the C.A.A. on plans for civilian pilot training. At the May 25 meeting, General McCoy stated that the army, navy, and C.A.A. already possessed the machinery for doing what the Knox group had in mind; he believed that the committee should concentrate on oiling this machinery. (Lieutenant Colonel Orlando Ward Memorandum for General Marshall, May 27, 1940, NA/RG 165 [OCS, Emergency File]. See Marshall to Craig, May 29, 1940, pp. 227–28.)

John McAuley Palmer, another of Marshall's longtime friends, performed what Marshall considered a moderating role in efforts by the M.T.C.A. to draft a universal compulsory military training act to be introduced in Congress. Palmer visited Marshall's office on May 23 to suggest that the association's drafting committee be given access to the model conscription bill that had been produced after years of study by the Joint Army and Navy Selective Service Committee. (John McAuley Palmer, *America in Arms* [New Haven: Yale University Press, 1941], pp. 198–99; Selective Service System, *Backgrounds of Selective Service* [Washington: GPO, 1947], 1: 77–78.)

General Staff officers Lieutenant Colonel Victor J. O'Kelliher, Major Lewis B. Hershey (executive officer of the joint committee), and Captain Walter L. Weible conferred with Palmer during the next two days. Hershey and Palmer met briefly with Marshall on the morning of May 25. The next day, Palmer sent Marshall a telegram from New York City requesting that the two officers be permitted to confer with the M.T.C.A. drafting committee. This was not an unusual procedure, as the joint committee had long made a practice of meeting with such citizens' groups. Marshall's approval was sent on May 27. ★

SPEECH TO THE NATIONAL AVIATION FORUM[1]   May 27, 1940
                                                                              Washington, D.C.

Mr. Beck,[2] Ladies and Gentlemen: I have no prepared address to deliver this morning. In the pressure of business of the past few weeks, I have been without opportunity to make careful preparation for such engagements as this. So I must ask you to accept my comments this morning as the informal best I can manage under the circumstances.

I did feel that it was important that the Chief of Staff should put in an appearance this morning before the National Aeronautic Association Forum, to express the appreciation of the Army for the fine cooperation received from all branches of civil aeronautics, and more especially to make acknowledgment of the tremendous importance of civil aeronautics to the Army Air Corps.

The President himself has stated that "civil aviation is recognized as the back-log of national defense in the Civil Aeronautics Act." We have established the principle that the country's welfare in time of peace and its safety in time of war depends to an important extent upon the existence of a highly organized aircraft industry for the production of the planes, and a well established system for their operation for commercial transportation. For almost twelve months we have had under way a tremendous expansion of our Army air, and I think it is very appropriate to mention the unexpected success which has met our first experiment in making direct use of civil aviation schools in training our Army pilots. Now we are about to enlarge tremendously on this logical procedure, which both stimulates civil aviation and facilitates the development of Army aviation.

During the past week we have all heard a great deal about the increases in plane production and training of thousands of pilots, and of the other activities which are believed necessary to further fortify the national defense. I cannot undertake a discussion of the various phases of these matters this morning, but I would like to make a few general comments.

The history of our difficulties of the last World War in developing air power provides several pointed lessons for our guidance today, and I believe the most important of these relates to the American tendency, under the emotional strain and importance of a great emergency, to talk and plan in large numbers and for vast projects.[3] In 1917 there was an immediate appropriation of $640,000,000 for the development of air power. So far so good. But there immediately followed a campaign of publicity, probably to reassure or to impress the public, that led the people and the Congress to expect stupendous results in short order. This procedure led inevitably to a tragic disillusionment when the planes and trained pilots failed to materialize in a few months, or even by the end of the first year.

Investigation followed, violent attacks were made on various individuals, some of whom were discredited. The impossible had been promised and the public had been left in ignorance of the difficulties to be overcome. The country did not realize then, as I do not think it realizes today, the long time required under the most efficient procedure, first to initiate a production program and then to arrive at the hour of mass production; the time necessary to train the personnel and to transport the equipment and personnel to the field of action.

As I recall, America at that time was asked to manufacture in one year more airplane engines than the entire British output in the fifty-one months of their participation in the World War. We were asked to build more aircraft than the Allies turned out during the entire War. To exaggerate a bit, when the smoke of the battle died away almost as much time was occupied in explaining why the planes were not forthcoming for our Army in France as was devoted to the manufacturing effort in this country.

We must approach this present situation in a state of calm determination not to be foiled by exaggerations or the emotions of the moment, or any of the multitude of difficulties which are certain to be involved in a tremendous and sudden expansion.

My thought is that we should promise less than we expect to achieve; that we should resist ideas or enthusiasms that will not stand the searching test of common sense.

The impulse of patriotic America is a wonderful thing, but its impatience to overcome the delays of past indifference, can be a destructive force. The public indifference of the past to our national defense requirements is a matter of fact which we are powerless to alter, and we must accept the resultant situation as our base of departure to remedy our deficiencies. Today all of us must cooperate, must think of ourselves as a team in a united effort to produce the most practical result in the shortest possible time.

GCMRL/G. C. Marshall Papers (Pentagon Office, Speeches)

1. This address was prepared for delivery in the Department of Commerce Building auditorium to the forum (May 26–29) sponsored by the National Aeronautic Association. The text here is slightly different from the version quoted in the *New York Times* (May 28, p. 17). Some of the talk's themes had been suggested by Colonel Edgar S. Gorrell (U.S.M.A., 1912), a Chicago industrial engineer who had been chief of staff of the A.E.F. Air Service in 1919; since 1936 he had been president of the Air Transport Association of America. Gorrell had also been prominently mentioned as a possible presidential assistant for national defense. (*Aero Digest* 36[June 1940]: 117.)

2. Thomas H. Beck, chairman of the forum, was the director of the National Aeronautical Association and the president of Crowell-Collier Publishing Corporation.

3. Marshall repeated this sentence and the last two paragraphs of this speech to the War Department Subcommittee of the House Appropriations Committee on May 29. As then delivered, the last phrase of this sentence read, "to assume vast projects can be completed on a basis of enthusiasm, without regard to the practical realities of the problem." (House Appropriations Committee, *Senate Amendments to the Military Establishment Appropriation Bill for 1941, Hearings* [Washington: GPO, 1940], p. 10.)

To General Malin Craig   May 29, 1940
                                           [Washington, D.C.]

Dear Craig: I am really sorry I missed you yesterday, but I was in about ten places at once throughout the day and in each of them handling pretty important matters. Today will be even worse, beginning with the Appropriation Committee, going on to see Mr. Morgenthau and then to the President regarding the 50,000 planes. As a rule I have to educate myself on each subject while riding back and forth. My difficulty now is that I have only about an hour and a half at my desk, and have to treat things with such rapidity that I have little chance to digest them. However, in a week or two I hope to have all these trickles, streams, and rivers of energy flowing into well organized channels with a definite basis of appropriation or law for us to handle things.

I was delighted to see that they had you on the Knox Board. I think if it had not been for you, McCoy and Palmer, one way or another, we would have been sunk by enthusiasms.

Bryden took over completely yesterday afternoon and has been buried ever since.[1]   Hastily yours,

GCMRL/G. C. Marshall Papers (Pentagon Office, Selected)

1. On June 1, 1940, Brigadier General William Bryden (U.S.M.A., 1904) was officially to replace Brigadier General Lorenzo D. Gasser, who was retiring at the end of May, as deputy chief of staff. During the first half of General Craig's term as army chief of staff, Bryden served in the Mobilization Branch of G-3 (August 1935 to September 1937). He then commanded the Sixteenth Infantry (September 1937 to May 1938) and the Thirteenth Field Artillery (May 1938 to May 1940).

ALTHOUGH the House of Representatives had not yet held hearings on the changes the Senate had made in the army's budget or on the president's additional requests of May 16, Marshall and his staff were at work on a request for still more money, primarily for ordnance, tanks, and aircraft. In 1946, while editing his wife's memoirs, General Marshall inserted a long handwritten addition regarding the army's budget requests of May 1940; a portion of this addition concerns the president's May 31 request for a supplement to the military budget.

"Meanwhile the German Army swept down over France, the world seemed to be rocking on its axis. Now manufacturers who previously would not bid on government contracts for fear of labor uncertainties, etc., and to conserve the interests of their stock holders, were in a purely patriotic frame of mind ready to take chances on literally any contract. Hence the second message to Congress about two weeks later which asked for 709 million for the army. At first the President was outraged at Mr. Morgenthau and George bringing up a proposal for a second message after so short a time, but he was quickly convinced that he really had no choice in the matter, it clearly must be done, and George worked on the draft of a second message." (The above is printed with minor editorial changes in Katherine Tupper

Marshall, *Together: Annals of an Army Wife* [New York and Atlanta: Tupper and Love, 1946], p. 70. This episode is also mentioned in Marshall interview, November 15, 1956: "Morgenthau called me up and told me that the manufacturing industry now would bid on these things which they had refused to do before. . . . The president was furious.") ★

Memorandum for the President[1]   May 29, 1940
                                                          [Washington, D.C.]

The following is submitted for possible inclusion in your Message to Congress:

The almost incredible events of the past two weeks in the European conflict, particularly as a result of the use of aviation and mechanized equipment, together with the possible consequences of further developments, necessitate another impulse for our military program. An investigation into manufacturing resources since my message of May 16th, to determine the practicability of placing additional orders with industry for special materiel, both to provide an early expansion of existing production facilities, and to obtain increased quantities of the special weapons concerned, has caused the War Department to submit to me an urgent recommendation that increased appropriations for the National Defense be secured before the adjournment of the present Congress.

Over and beyond these requests for materiel is the evident requirement for the immediate creation of additional production facilities to meet present deficiencies in facilities for the manufacturing of munitions, such as guns, ammunition and fire control equipment, since they require a long time to create and to reach quantity production. The increased gravity of the situation indicates that action should be taken without delay.

The following supplemental estimates are therefore submitted to the Congress: For tanks and mechanized equipment—$90,000,000; for additional bombs and other ammunition for planes—$26,900,000; for storage facilities for additional bombs and ammunition—$2,900,000; for 105 mm guns and ammunition—$8,640,000; for antiaircraft materiel to equip eight additional regiments—$30,400,000; for 2,850 combat airplanes completely equipped to speed up existing production facilities and to provide for the further increase of the GHQ Air Force—$300,000,000. For further research and development of all airplanes and all types of munitions—$23,700,000; for the erection of additional production facilities for guns, ammunition and fire control equipment—$200,000,000.[2]

NA/RG 165 (OCS, Emergency File)

1. Marshall wrote this for Secretary Woodring's signature.

2. In his message, the president refused to specify a figure beyond "over a billion dollars" for both the army and the navy. The agencies involved would present their specific programs to Congress. The memorandum Marshall discussed with the president on May 29 asked for $706,274,000. (Copies of the army documents pertaining to this request are in NA/RG 165 [OCS, Emergency File]. The president's message is printed in *Public Papers and Addresses of Franklin D. Roosevelt,* 1940, pp. 250–52.)

To Mrs. Reynolds Brown   May 29, 1940
                                                  [Washington, D.C.]

Dear Emily: Thank you so much for telling me about Fifille. I have written her a note, and I am distressed, greatly distressed, to have this sad news of her condition.[1]

Things move with such rapidity here, particularly in the pile-up of public opinion and extreme emotionalism that I have no time whatever for anything more than business before Congressional Committees, the Budget Bureau and the White House from daylight to dark. I hope we can survive the next two weeks and get things on a sound basis.

Thank you very much for writing me, and please pardon this hasty note. Affectionately,

GCMRL/G. C. Marshall Papers (Pentagon Office, Selected)

1. Marshall's longtime friend Emily Perry Russell Brown lived in Milton, Massachusetts, and Charleston, South Carolina. She had written to say that "our darling Fifi Ames is very sick. . . . She has not long to live." (Brown to Marshall, n.d., GCMRL/G. C. Marshall Papers [Pentagon Office, Selected].) Mrs. Ames was the wife of former Congressman Butler Ames of Massachusetts.

THE chief of staff's schedule between May 29 and June 5 was indeed hectic. In addition to the normal swarm of visitors, meetings, and conferences, Marshall made four trips to the White House and seven to the Capitol, testifying at hearings on five different days concerning four subjects before three committees. One of his constant refrains at these hearings was that the time the nation had for military preparedness was growing short. He also carefully reiterated that the army's efforts were directed toward defending the Western Hemisphere. For this he at once needed more money, materiel, and manpower—and given the fluid international situation, perhaps yet more in the near future.

On May 29 Marshall appeared before the War Department Subcommittee of the House Appropriations Committee for the first time since the German invasion of Norway. Proposed changes in the House-passed army budget of April 4 (i.e., additions by the Senate plus increases contained in the president's May 16 speech) had more than doubled the original appropriation. When the supplemental funds President Roosevelt requested in his May 31 message were included, the total Marshall was called upon to justify was $2,530,482,624—equal to the total army budget for the previous five years. Some committee members wished to know if this amount was sufficient and could be spent properly. Marshall replied that funding for materiel was adequate.

"Personnel happens to be our tragic shortage at the moment. There is no doubt in my mind of the extreme importance of getting this materiel of the more modern types and, I stated before this committee in February, that I put materiel ahead of anything else. I even put it ahead, in view of the conditions at the time, before we had seen Norway blow up, of the desire for the small number of 15,000 men.

"In the past, it has been a question of the costs involved. We have our American standard, which we have to live up to. If we are going to maintain a volunteer Army, we must provide pay, food, shelter, and medical attention on a basis that is far beyond the requirements of other countries, particularly of those with conscript or universal-service requirements.

"The materiel items we are dealing with always are, of course, for the protective mobilization plan force of 750,000 men, plus replacements; whereas the personnel items were for the existing troops of the Regular Army and National Guard. But, the Senate amendment, adding to the enlisted strength for the Regular Army, only carries the total up to 515,000, including all of the National Guard.

"Personnel at the present moment is our most serious deficiency, in the light of the requirements that are being brought to bear on the War Department particularly in the past week or more, and the necessity of having seasoned, trained men, who can use the new weapons effectively and immediately and with a state of discipline that makes them completely dependable.

"I have struggled in the past to hold the personnel requirements down because the materiel is a permanent asset, good for 20 or 25 years, with a low cost of maintenance and, whatever the economies that may be forced on us, we would still have the materiel on hand to capitalize our man power at a later day. But now the situation has changed and personnel is the only thing, in a large measure, that can produce immediate results, within a period, roughly, of 6 months." (House Appropriations Committee, *Senate*

Amendments to the Military Establishment Appropriation Bill for 1941, pp. 6–7.)

This added manpower would come mainly from volunteers for three-year enlistments in the Regular Army. These had been running at about 8,000 per month; Marshall expected the European crisis to increase that rate substantially. He was certain that the goal of 280,000 enlisted men in the Regular Army would be met by September. (House Appropriations Committee, *Supplemental National Defense Appropriation Bill for 1941, Hearings* [Washington: GPO, 1940], p. 66; House Appropriations Committee, *Senate Amendments,* p. 30.)

Second, Marshall attempted to persuade Congress to fund the Enlisted Reserve Corps, authorized by the 1920 army reorganization act but never implemented. Under this program 200,000 volunteers would be given three or four months of training and then returned to their civil pursuits. (Unsigned Memorandum for Harry Hopkins, May 25, 1940, NA/RG 165 [OCS, Emergency File]; House Appropriations Committee, *Senate Amendments,* pp. 22–23.)

Third, Marshall's staff drafted an amendment to a bill, which Senator James F. Byrnes introduced, aimed at using the Civilian Conservation Corps to recruit and to train service personnel (e.g., cooks, mechanics, and radio operators). Despite Marshall's favorable testimony, this bill was defeated in mid-June. (Senate Appropriations Committee, *Emergency Relief Appropriation Act, Fiscal Year 1941, Hearings* [Washington: GPO, 1940], pp. 191–97. Marshall testified on May 31.)

Marshall never mentioned the possibility of conscription at these hearings. Neither did he wish to mobilize the National Guard. It was less than half its authorized strength, and it would take a long time to close this gap by recruitment. Moreover, Guard units would require extensive training before they became militarily effective. "In order to delay or to avoid the possible necessity for mobilizing the National Guard, or a part of it," Marshall told the House Appropriations Committee, "there is a requirement for a further increase in the strength of the Regular Army of 55,000 men on a voluntary basis pure and simple." As a second priority, 40,000 more men were needed for the Air Corps. "We wish to enlist the additional 95,000, however, on the basis of a purely temporary force for the emergency." The cost of this was an additional $321,921,898. He did not, however, have the president's permission to request this increase, he told the committee.

"Beyond a Regular Army strength of about 400,000 we can arrive at additional trained and seasoned units more rapidly by utilizing the National Guard than by expanding further the Regular Army. The reason for the difference is that the odd companies and battalions in the Regular Army provide a leaven to a new unit that will enable it to be very quickly organized and trained. When a strength of about 400,000 is reached, that leaven will have been absorbed." (House Appropriations Committee, *Supplemental National Defense Appropriation Bill for 1941*, pp. 68–72.) ★

Public Relations Branch Press Release　　　　　June 1, 1940
[Washington, D.C.]

Statement by Chief of Staff on use of National Guard

The Chief of Staff, General George C. Marshall, when questioned as to the recommendation in the President's message of yesterday regarding the possibility of ordering the National Guard into Federal service,[1] made the following statement:

"In view of the limited number of seasoned Regular troops available in the continental United States—we have but 5 peace strength triangular divisions with a sixth now in process of organization—and it is necessary that more troops be made available, trained, and seasoned, to enable missions to be carried out without denuding this country of ground troops in a state of sufficient preparation to meet unexpected eventualities in some other direction. Time is the essential factor in such matters. In other words, this means that we should make the preliminary moves in time to be prepared against the unfortunate necessity of definite action.

"The War Department is opposed to ordering the National Guard out for active duty, and it is hopeful that by quickly building up, on the foundation of scattered organizations of the Regular Army still available, additional divisions and some special corps troops, we can avoid the necessity of utilizing the National Guard at this time. Even if it were found necessary to bring the National Guard into service it is believed that for the present only a portion of the Guard would be involved. However, it is essential in these days that the War Department, through the Commander-in-Chief, be in a position to act with rapidity and to plan with the definite assurance that such plans can be made effective without uncertain delays.

"The President now has the authority to 'call' the National Guard into service, but under that call it would be impossible to send any units of the National Guard to assist a Regular Division in any one of the possible situations which might arise in this hemisphere.[2] Time again is the essential factor in these matters, and the first requirement in any event, would be the opportunity for giving at least a portion of the Guard intensive training and possibly some degree of reorganization."

GCMRL/G. C. Marshall Papers (Pentagon Office, Speeches)

1. In his May 31 message to Congress, President Roosevelt said, "There is a specific recommendation I would make in concluding this message, that before adjournment this Congress grant me the authority to call into active service such portion of the National Guard as may be deemed necessary to maintain our position of neutrality and to safeguard the National Defense, this to include authority to call into active service the necessary Reserve personnel." (*Public Papers and Addresses of Franklin D. Roosevelt,* 1940, p. 252.)

2. The statutes providing for the federalization of the National Guard provided "that whenever the United States is invaded or in danger of invasion from any foreign nation, or of rebellion against the authority of the Government of the United States, or the President is unable with the regular forces at his command to execute the laws of the Union, it shall be lawful for the President to call forth such number of the militia of the State or of the States or Territories or of the District of Columbia as he may deem necessary." Moreover, that service could be "either within or without the Territory of the United States." (Office of the Judge Advocate General, *Military Laws of the United States,* 8th ed. [Washington: GPO, 1940], paragraph 1295.) Senate Joint Resolution 286, introduced on July 30, 1940, and signed by the president on August 27, stipulated "that the members and units of the reserve components of the Army of the United States ordered into active Federal service under this authority shall not be employed beyond the limits of the Western Hemisphere except in the territories and possessions of the United States, including the Philippine Islands." (Office of the Judge Advocate General, *Supplement III to the Military Laws of the United States, Eighth Edition, 1939* [Washington: GPO, 1945], paragraph 2220-1.)

To Major General William N. Haskell   June 3, 1940
Confidential   [Washington, D.C.]

Dear Haskell: I received your letter of May 28th and was very much interested in your point of view regarding the possible mobilization of the National Guard.[1]

As you have seen since writing your letter, the President made reference to this in his message. The purpose of that reference was not to proceed to the immediate mobilization of the National Guard—quite the contrary; what was wanted was the authority to move in the matter at such a time and to such a degree as the situation in Central and South America (this is confidential to you), might demand. We did not want this Congress to adjourn and leave us in the situation of having to ask that Congress be recalled for the purpose of granting authority to order into service the equivalent of two or three divisions, or to be compelled to call them in a much less effective status on the basis of a call.[2]

I am due to go before a Congressional Committee tomorrow on this subject, and I expect they will give me a hard time. All our plans are to get such quick increases of volunteers enlisted for duration, as we can manage in order to avoid the necessity of calling for elements of the National Guard. Of course in all of this much will depend on the further developments abroad, as each crisis there produces an important action of the sub rosa forces in this hemisphere.   Faithfully yours,

GCMRL/G. C. Marshall Papers (Pentagon Office, Selected)

1. Haskell, commanding general of the New York National Guard, had received a copy of Major General John F. O'Ryan's telegram of May 10 and Marshall's letter to Congressman Walter G. Andrews of May 16 (see pp. 215–17.) Haskell wrote to say that he agreed with Marshall's decision against mobilizing the National Guard at this time. "I just thought I would drop you this note to let you know that everyone up here doesn't agree with General O'Ryan's telegram. At least they don't agree with it unless and until you are able to foresee the continued use of the Guard in the Federal service and the imminence of the involvement of the United States in war." (Haskell to Marshall, May 28, 1940, GCMRL/G. C. Marshall Papers [Pentagon Office, Selected].)

2. Marshall's staff prepared a document introduced as House Joint Resolution 555, which provided that in the event that a national emergency arose between the adjournment of the Seventy-sixth Congress and the convening of the Seventy-seventh in January 1941, the president was authorized to call to duty the nation's army reserve "in such manner as he may deem necessary." At his hearing on the resolution on June 4, Marshall said that the War Department was not seeking to mobilize the National Guard but merely to permit the department's emergency planning for hemispheric defense to proceed on the assumption that the Guard was available to replace Regular units sent to various spots in the Western Hemisphere. (GCMRL/G. C. Marshall Papers [Pentagon Office, Testimonies].) A struggle developed in the House between those who wished to limit the president's authority to use the Guard outside United States possessions and those who wished him free to defend the entire hemisphere as he saw fit. The point soon became moot, as the session continued until the new Congress convened.

To Irving B. Babcock[1]   June 3, 1940
[Washington, D.C.]

My dear Mr. Babcock: The large maneuvers in the Southeast have just been completed, and have been of great value to the Army in preparation for its further training and possible expansion.

As explained in my letter to you of January 23d, the early delivery of the new motor transportation to the units to be engaged in these maneuvers was of great importance to the Army. Your organization assisted so whole-heartedly in the matter by expediting these deliveries, that I wish you to know that the maneuvers were a great success and that your direct contribution to this success is very much appreciated. I hope you will have your Secretary convey my thanks to the Executives and other officials who helped us equip our little force in the short time available before the maneuvers.   Faithfully yours,

GCMRL/G. C. Marshall Papers (Pentagon Office, General)

1. Babcock was president and general manager of the General Motors Truck and Coach Division of Yellow Truck and Coach Manufacturing Company. Similar letters were sent to Presidents Robert F. Black of the White Motor Company and Kaufman T. Keller of the Chrysler Corporation. (See pp. 117–18.)

To Morris Sheppard[1]   June 5, 1940
                                                    [Washington, D.C.]

My dear Senator: I have read some of the criticisms that have been made
of the Army Promotion Bill now before the Senate, and I find that a cable
of mine on this subject, sent from France to the Secretary of War, has been
referred to by the War Department as an argument towards favorable
consideration of the current bill. In view of the gravity of the times, and of
my personal experience in this matter, I am taking the liberty of submitting
a few comments.

Rank means command, and command involves leadership, and leadership in a military emergency is, in my opinion, the most important single
consideration. The difficulties of leadership which existed in 1917–18 have
been enormously multiplied today by the increased mobility and fire power
of modern armies, and the necessity for vigorous commanders is greater
now than it has ever been before. I am familiar with the Promotion bill now
before your Committee only in the most general terms; but I believe I am
sufficiently familiar with military requirements to submit that the passage of
this measure is of great importance. Elimination of such basic provisions of
the bill as retirement at sixty, and certain similar requirements, would
nullify its effectiveness to a large extent. It would be most unfortunate at this
critical moment in our history to tie the hands of the War Department with
restrictions or amendments calculated to favor a group of senior officers at
the expense of their juniors on whom we must largely depend for leadership
in every phase of training and possible mobilization, as well as for troop
command, and certain to embarrass the War Department in the heavy task
of administering our military system.

I apologize for intruding my views in this matter, particularly as I have
not studied the bill; but my belief in the importance of such a measure at this
time must be my excuse for taking this liberty. As a matter of fact my
criticism of the bill would be that in the present situation the retirement
feature should become effective immediately rather than two years hence.
Faithfully yours,

GCMRL/G. C. Marshall Papers (Pentagon Office, Selected)

1. Marshall wrote this letter for John J. Pershing's signature. On April 4 the War Department sent to Congress a new version of its long-sought officers' promotion bill (H.R. 9243).
The bill proposed that length of service-in-grade be considered as important for promotion
and that the limits on the maximum number of officers in a specific grade be removed, except
on colonels. The objectives were to place an upper limit on the time an officer could spend in a
grade without promotion, to eliminate the "hump" of officers in field grades which resulted
from the World War expansion, and to reduce the retirement age (effective July 1, 1942) to
sixty years for officers below brigadier general. The effect of this would be to retire numerous
older majors and colonels and to speed promotion for younger officers.

The House passed the bill with little dissent on April 23, but opposition, particularly to the age of mandatory retirement, developed in the Senate. A Senate-House conference committee removed the Senate's amendments, but the bill's opponents carried their fight to the Senate floor. To prevent further delay, perhaps for several months, Marshall signed a letter to Senator Sheppard strongly supporting the bill. One of the bill's floor managers, Senator Lister Hill (Democrat from Alabama) read the letter printed here during the final moments of debate on June 5. A few days later, Marshall wrote to Senator Millard E. Tydings of Maryland, "I disliked appealing to you at the time—it made me feel a little like a lobbyist, but the issue was so important as a basis for future action, that I felt I should use every effort to secure a favorable decision." (Marshall to Tydings, June 8, 1940, GCMRL/G. C. Marshall Papers [Pentagon Office, General].) The bill was passed 61 to 11 on June 5 and signed by the president on June 13.

MEMORANDUM FOR THE ASSISTANT CHIEF   June 6, 1940
OF STAFF, G-3 [ANDREWS]   Washington, D.C.
Secret

It is felt to be very important that the Air Corps appear in the Army Maneuvers this summer, despite the difficulties involved during the expansion procedure. However, it is believed that by having a flight represent a squadron[1] and arranging for participation on the basis of 24 to 36 hours during the critical periods—rather than blocking off a week or more for the purpose, a satisfactory method can be arranged for without disorganizing training procedure of the GHQ Air Force.

Please have the matter developed along this line.

G. C. M.

NA/RG 165 (OCS, 14440-311)

1. A *flight* consisted of three or four aircraft and was the equivalent of an Infantry company or a Field Artillery battery; three or four flights made a *squadron,* analogous to a ground forces battalion.

MEMORANDUM FOR THE FILE   June 7, 1940
                              [Washington, D.C.]

The attached is my suggestion for the President's statement to the Press this morning[1]—not used by him.

G. C. M.

[Attachment]

Since 1919 the Army and Navy have had on hand a tremendous supply of ordnance materiel which has gradually deteriorated and become obsolete.

In July of 1919 the Congress passed an Act which gave to the Secretary of War the authority to sell such of this materiel which had become surplus to our respective needs. From time to time such sales have been carried out under the authority of this Act. The same Statute permits an inter-change of supplies and equipment between the Army and Navy.

Congress in 1918 passed an Act which authorized airplanes to be turned in in the same manner old automobiles are accepted by dealers as partial payments on new equipment. There is also a law on the books since 1926 which authorizes the Secretary of War to trade in deteriorated ammunition against the procurement of new ammunition.

Of course in all such procedures there must be a buyer for this old equipment or materiel in order to enable the Government to secure any advantage from the provisions of the law. Today this old equipment and deteriorated ammunition is of immediate value to certain countries and therefore there is a market, a buyer, which will permit this Government to dispose of this materiel.

A number of items of Army ordnance have recently been sold to Brazil. Other South American countries are in the market for similar materiel. The Allied Purchasing Agent is desirous of obtaining as much of this old materiel as is surplus to our requirements.[2]

That is the situation in a nutshell.

NA/RG 165 (OCS, Foreign Sale or Exchange of Munitions File)

1. At his press conference, President Roosevelt announced the signing of agreements whereby the United States would sell obsolete or surplus military equipment to private firms which would immediately resell them to the Allies. (*New York Times*, June 8, 1940, p. 1.)

2. The question of the legality of transferring arms to the Allies was settled, in so far as surplus or obsolete materials were concerned, by Acting Attorney General Francis Biddle's June 3 letter to Secretary of War Woodring. Marshall summarizes that letter here. The letter is published in S. Shepard Jones and Denys P. Myers, eds., *Documents on American Foreign Relations: July 1939–June 1940* (Boston: World Peace Foundation, 1940), pp. 790–91.

On June 3 Marshall approved the Ordnance Department's list of surplus materiel, and Arthur B. Purvis, director general of the British Purchasing Commission, asked for nearly everything on the list: 400 (later increased to 900) 75-mm field guns and 1,075,000 shells; 500,000 Enfield rifles and 130,000,000 rounds; 308 3-inch Stokes trench mortars and 97,680 shells; 80,000 machine guns of various types; 25,000 Browning automatic rifles; 20,000 revolvers and 1,000,000 cartridges; plus a large number of accessories. Increases were later made in certain of these items. The movement of supplies to the army's docks at Raritan, New Jersey, began on June 4, although a formal contract was not signed until June 11—the day the first ship began loading. (See Hall, *North American Supply,* pp. 134–38, and NA/RG 165 [OCS, Foreign Sale or Exchange of Munitions File].)

MEMORANDUM FOR THE PRESIDENT[1]　　　　　　　　　　　June 8, 1940
Secret　　　　　　　　　　　　　　　　　　　　　　　[Washington, D.C.]

Subject: Release of aircraft.

Tentative arrangements have been made to exchange 93 A–17–A Army airplanes (attack bombers). Bombs to make the airplanes immediately effective must be of our type. Two to three months would be required to re-work these planes to accommodate foreign type bombs. In order to supply bombs, it will be necessary to consider the bombs as an accessory of the airplane. Whether or not this can be legally sustained is questionable.

To furnish approximately one-fifteenth of the number of bombs desired by the Allied Purchasing Agent it will be necessary to release approximately one-seventh of our entire bomb stock in the two sizes required,—30 and 100 pound bombs. Additional bombs are under order, but the first deliveries will not be made for another six months.

In view of our shortage of bombs, I request your decision in the matter.[2]

NA/RG 165 (OCS, Foreign Sale or Exchange of Munitions File)

1. Marshall wrote this document for Secretary of War Harry H. Woodring's signature.

2. This memorandum was delivered to the White House by Major Walter B. Smith on June 8. An agreement signed on June 12, between the War Department and the Douglas Aircraft Company, transferred the ninety-three Northrup light bombers to the Allies in return for a credit allowance of $2,928,592 to be applied to the purchase of twenty Douglas A-20 "Havoc" bombers. The first group of Northrups were flown to Halifax, Nova Scotia, on June 21 and loaded on a British aircraft carrier. Marshall received permission to withdraw the army's bomb commitment. The Navy supplied 5,908 bombs. (Arnold Memorandum for the Chief of Staff, June 12, 1940, NA/RG 165 [OCS, Foreign Sale or Exchange of Munitions File].)

To Edwin C. Johnson   June 8, 1940
                                              [Washington, D.C.]

Dear Senator Johnson: Relative to the recent debate in the Senate on the Army Promotion Bill, I want you to know that I read very carefully your comments, and particularly those regarding the elimination of so-called "dead wood". Although you and I were not in complete agreement as to the best method of approaching the promotion problem, we had the same general end in view and I was glad to read your concluding comments regarding the further improvement of officer personnel. I think when the smoke of this present discussion has cleared away, and Congress is again in session, the War Department can approach Congress with a more practical plan for bettering the efficiency of the Officer corps than is now on the books.[1]

Please accept my thanks for the courtesy with which you treated my presentation of this matter.   Faithfully yours,

GCMRL/G. C. Marshall Papers (Pentagon Office, General)

1. Johnson, a Democrat from Colorado, and Tom Connally, a Democrat from Texas, had led the efforts in the Senate to amend the promotion bill. Johnson was displeased with what

he considered a large amount of "dead wood" in the officer corps and with the army's difficulty in cutting this group. He also believed that the new bill permitted the army far too many lieutenant colonels, and he did not like the provision setting the mandatory retirement age as low as sixty. (*Congressional Record,* 76th Cong., 3d sess., vol. 86, pt. 7: 7591.)

To MAJOR GENERAL JOHN F. WILLIAMS[1] June 8, 1940
[Washington, D.C.]

Dear Williams: Recently General Key, of the 45th Division, made an inquiry relative to the assignment of a Regular Army officer as Chief of Staff for his Division. I am attaching a copy of my reply to Key, for your information.[2]

Personally, I have not been in favor of piecemeal business about the detail of Regular Army officers to the National Guard. I think a formal policy should be worked out and adopted uniformly for the entire National Guard, which must mean, of course, the acquiescence of each state—a very difficult thing to launch. My conception of the most effective manner of increasing the staff efficiency of the National Guard and promoting its training, would be to fill certain positions with Regular officers, young ones given increased rank; to have all these officers forbidden by regulations from having anything whatever to do with promotions, selection of personnel, and local relations. To have them specifically charged with problems of training and particularly with the development of team work in the staffs.

The present is no time to bring this up, therefore I am not giving you this for distribution; rather, merely to give you my idea on the subject. I think the following posts in the National Guard should be filled, as vacancies occur, by young Regular officers on a three-year detail—maybe four: Division Chief of Staff, brigade and regimental executive officers. With such an arrangement I do not think it would be necessary to detail instructors with the National Guard, because the posts I have mentioned are proper positions for officers engaged in instructional work. Incidentally, they could do their job as instructor with authority from such posts, whereas at present it is by indirection or circumlocution.   Faithfully yours,

GCMRL/G. C. Marshall Papers (Pentagon Office, Selected)

1. Williams was chief of the National Guard Bureau.
2. Major General William S. Key, an Oklahoma oil producer, commanded the National Guard division which included units from Oklahoma, Arizona, New Mexico, and Colorado. Marshall's letter to him of May 17 (NA/RG 165 [OCS, 18107–32]) was similar in content to this document.

MEMORANDUM FOR THE ASSISTANT   June 13, 1940
CHIEF OF STAFF, G-1 [SHEDD]   [Washington, D.C.]

Mr. Mastick and Mr. Cross came to me to see if I would help them to approach the President for the purpose of securing $5,000,000 of his $200,000,000 fund, to enable them to set up the necessary YMCA facilities to meet the augmentation of the Regular Army this summer and into the winter.[1]

I told them that there would be many considerations of probable priority for the use of the President's $200,000,000, and I did not think I could specifically recommend this.[2] However, I did say, and I do think that it is very important that the YMCA be prepared in advance to set up in the nearby towns clubs and assembly places for the enlisted men of these new organizations, and around the Air schools that we are getting under way. It is important that the arrangement be managed so that such assembly places will be installed immediately rather than two or three months late, as occurred to a certain extent with the First Division.

I am not interested in the entertainment feature; I think the ordinary movies and things provide for this. I am not interested in the distribution of free goods; the soldier gets pay to buy these. I am intensely interested in his having a warm, cheerful place to sit down, play cards or engage in similar simple activities; and keep him off the streets as much as possible. I am particularly interested that whatever is to be done be so arranged for that it is accomplished quickly and not after the usual two or three months of fighting to maintain morale and set up a bad situation in the nearby towns.

GCMRL/G. C. Marshall Papers (Pentagon Office, General)

1. General and Mrs. Marshall had been invited to, but were unable to attend, a June 3 luncheon meeting given by Mrs. Roosevelt at the White House for the purpose of discussing proposals for enlarging the Young Men's Christian Association's role in providing recreational facilities for servicemen near military installations. Seabury C. Mastick, a New York lawyer and the chairman of the Y.M.C.A.'s Army and Navy Department, had presented the luncheon program. Harry D. Cross was a member of Senator Mastick's department. Frank R. McCoy sent Marshall a report on the meeting. (See Marshall to McCoy, June 12, 1940, LC/F. R. McCoy Papers.) The War Department announced its policy regarding civilian welfare activities on July 15. (See *New York Times,* July 16, 1940, p. 14.)

2. In his message to Congress of May 16, President Roosevelt had requested—in addition to the $696,000,000 for the army and the navy—$200,000,000 in discretionary funds for the president. This became law on June 13. (*Public Papers and Addresses of Franklin D. Roosevelt,* 1940, p. 203.)

TO ALLEN T. BROWN   June 13, 1940
                                                    [Washington, D.C.]

Dear Allen: This, what must be a hurried note, carries to you my warmest congratulations for your birthday, along with my apologies for not having had more to say regarding the approaching wedding.[1] However, I think you understand the pace at which I am traveling, and like the doctor, have difficulty in finding time to attend to my own family.

This will be a pretty important birthday in your life, because you are headed into so many important changes, about the two most important in any man's life, his wife and his job. I feel pretty certain about you now that you have gotten good control over your emotions, and have demonstrated a continuity of purpose. I think Madge will be a splendid stabilizer and after you two have adjusted yourselves one to the other in this business of living together—and that will require a year or more with some pretty sharp differences, then I think you ought to make an ideal couple.

Your mother is so filled with the wedding that she can talk of little else. I am trying to arrange my plans so that I will certainly get there. As matters now stand, she will drive up the day before with Sergeant Powder,[2] and I assume, Molly will go with her. I will either fly up late that evening so as to be at the dinner and rehearsal, or I may be delayed until about noon the next day. I am having them look up the closest airport with at least 2500 foot runways. I believe they told your mother of one, but she has forgotten what they told her; it was about ten miles away.

With my love to Madge and all the good things of life to you beyond this birthday,   Affectionately,

GCMRL/Research File (Family)

1. Marshall's stepson, who would be twenty-four years old on June 15, was marrying Margaret Goodman Shedden on June 22 in Westchester County, New York.

2. Sergeant James Powder had been one of Marshall's chauffeurs and a personal orderly since October 1938.

MEMORANDUM FOR GENERAL SHEDD   June 14, 1940
[Washington, D.C.]

Increasingly each day there come to me requests from men of past experience, to be given some opportunity to do their part. Many of these, of course, are of the type we would not wish to accept; but others are men who would be a great asset to the Army. Yesterday, for example, Colonel Patton at Myer, had three or four of the men who were with him in the Tank corps in the Meuse-Argonne come to him to see if they could not in some way get into this. At least two of them were men of high position in civil life, who were willing to contribute their services in any way possible; had been wounded in France and given the DSC, and understood thoroughly what it meant actually to fight tanks.

Most of the applicants could only fit into staff jobs; however there are many others who might contribute a very valuable veterans touch in some of our new units. There is a large representation of men who have outstanding qualifications, though entirely without previous military experience.

If any use is to be made of these people, the matter of selection would be the most critical question. But I think we should arrive at a prospective solution at as early a date as possible, otherwise we will be either overwhelmed with pressure or bitterly attacked for our failure to utilize existing talent. Over all this remains, of course, the question of protecting the existing Reserve Corps.

GCMRL/G. C. Marshall Papers (Pentagon Office, Selected)

To LIEUTENANT GENERAL STANLEY D. EMBICK   June 15, 1940
[Washington, D.C.]

Dear Embick: I have been so buried under new business, as it were,—just got back from a hearing on one billion appropriation bill[1]—that I have utterly neglected you. It has been my intention morning after morning on coming to the War Department to start the day by dictating a letter of appreciation for the really splendid manner in which you organized and carried through the recent maneuvers.

As I told you when you were last in Washington, it was a source of great comfort and satisfaction to me to know that you were at the head of the Third Army, in charge of the development and conduct of these maneuvers—the largest and most pretentious we have ever attempted. From all I can learn and from what little I saw, I think that your leadership and direction led to the most stimulating and instructive Army demonstration of our time. I am certain the effects will be far-reaching on the Army, on its officer personnel, and its school system; but I feel also that the whole affair was managed with such smoothness and efficiency that it has educated the public, and certainly the Congress to an understanding of the necessity for such maneuvers at frequent intervals.

I want you to know that I am deeply appreciative of the loyalty and remarkable efficiency with which you organized and carried, to a successful completion the Third Army maneuvers.[2]   Faithfully yours,

GCMRL/G. C. Marshall Papers (Pentagon Office, Selected)

1. Marshall had testified that morning before the Senate Appropriations Committee in support of the first Supplemental Appropriation Bill (H.R. 10055). He emphasized the need for the contemplated appropriations of approximately $821,000,000 in cash and $254,000,000 in contract authorizations, in order to place new materiel orders as soon as possible to increase supplies quickly, to assure manufacturers that they could plan for continued full production when current contracts expired (particularly in the aircraft industry), to broaden the manufacturing base for future demands, and to expedite production by removing bottle-

necks and by building new facilities. The bill also increased the number of enlisted men permitted in the Regular Army by 95,000 to a total of 375,000. Senator Millard E. Tydings tried to get the chief of staff to say that he really needed a total of 500,000 men as soon as possible, but Marshall refused. (Senate Appropriations Committee, *First Supplemental National Defense Appropriation Bill for 1941, Hearings* [Washington: GPO, 1940], pp. 3–10.)

2. Approximately 70,000 Regular Army troops had participated in a series of blitzkrieg-style maneuvers in Louisiana between May 6 and May 24.

TO MAJOR GENERAL CHARLES E. KILBOURNE June 17, 1940
[Washington, D.C.]

Dear Kilbourne: Since my return to Washington on Wednesday, I have been so pressed with business and meetings here and in other departments, and with testimony on the Hill that I failed to acknowledge your fine hospitality and the honor you paid me last Wednesday morning.[1]

I was sorry to rush off in the manner I did, but as it was I only had ten minutes to fortify myself regarding new arrangements before appearing at a rather momentous meeting at the Treasury Department.[2] My appearance on the program occurred so quickly and I left so hastily that I hardly had time to form very definite impressions of the Corps and the graduation class. From what little I saw I was much impressed with the general tone and high morale of the Corps and I gathered the impression from many that you have done a splendid piece of work this past year, and have gotten everything on a solid foundation.

Immediately on my return I took up the question of the coordination of government efforts regarding the utilization of various facilities, such as yours at the VMI. I found that the first investigation, which had reached you, was a hasty affair launched in a minute by the services concerned. Now, I believe, all is being coordinated under Mr. Harry Hopkins' guidance.

With my warm regards to Mrs. Kilbourne and you and my most sincere thanks for your fine hospitality and all the trouble you took for my comfort,   Faithfully yours,

GCMRL/G. C. Marshall Papers (Pentagon Office, General)

1. Marshall had delivered the Virginia Military Institute's commencement address on Wednesday, June 12. After reminiscing about his own V.M.I. days and his early experiences in the army, he told the graduates: "It is your graduation day, but it may also be one of the most fateful in the history of the world. No man can predict the outcome of the tragic struggle in Europe. No American can foresee the eventual effect on the Americas. The world we have known may be revolutionized; the peaceful liberty we have accepted so casually may be a hazard in this ghastly game abroad.

"All of us hope with all our hearts that you young men may be free to go ahead with the civil pursuits for which you have been in training. All of us hope for a continuation of our blessings on this continent. But no one knows just what the outcome may be. Those of us specifically charged with the duty of safe-guarding our defenses are fully aware of the vast

responsibility implied. We are planning and preparing in every way possible under our law to put this country in such a state of preparation that we may be spared the agony of war. All of us, all of you, I am sure, realize that the day of drum and bugle armies is over. And we are determined that if it should become necessary for us to use a club to defend our democracy and our interests in the Western Hemisphere, that it shall be a club of hard wood, and not of rubber hose." (GCMRL/G. C. Marshall Papers [Pentagon Office, Speeches].)
  2. The meeting concerned the allied purchasing program. (FDRL/H. Morgenthau, Jr., Papers [Diary, 272: 13–45].)

To Major General Roy D. Keehn June 18, 1940
[Washington, D.C.]

Dear Keehn: I received your note of the other day and sent it to the proper section of the Staff for report; I have not yet gotten their reply. This morning came your further note of June 17th regarding the same matter, and also going into more pleasant details regarding Arlington and the Races.[1]

As you surmised, I am busy to an extent I did not even reach in the World War, with the added difficulty of meeting a wide variety of people who can contribute or complicate things for us to an important degree. Also I spend a great deal of time before committees of Congress and most of the time have the disadvantage of being caught off the base, for one cannot talk, sometimes five hours at a time, without exposing himself to a great deal of misquoting or unfortunate implications. Also the situation has advanced with such lightning rapidity, with one of a very critical nature for us, that my time and thoughts are very heavily absorbed in what the next move should be.

This is a very hasty note, but I did not want you to think that I was neglecting you. Faithfully yours,

GCMRL/G. C. Marshall Papers (Pentagon Office, Selected)
  1. On June 11 and 17 General Keehn had sent Marshall copies of correspondence with Sixth Corps Area Commander Major General Stanley H. Ford concerning Keehn's unsuccessful opposition to the promotion of Colonel Charles C. Haffner, whom Keehn considered avaricious and insubordinate. Keehn's letter of June 17 ended with an invitation to Marshall to visit Chicago on July 10 for the "Classic Stakes" at Arlington Park Race Track.

FRANCE'S collapse and the looming German threat to Great Britain forced Marshall to consider worst-case scenarios for the Western Hemisphere. At a June 17 morning meeting with George V. Strong (W.P.D.), Frank M. Andrews (G-3), and Richard C. Moore (G-4), the chief of staff said that, considering the various possibilities, the United States might suddenly find

Japan and Russia acting in concert to hold the American fleet in the Pacific Ocean while the Germans pressed ahead with whatever plans they had for South America. It seemed likely that the United States fleet would have to be concentrated in the Atlantic Ocean and the Caribbean Sea. General Strong observed that he anticipated a desperate need for United States troops to protect Brazil and Uruguay within the next sixty days. The international situation seemed to indicate, Marshall said, that the National Guard should be mobilized. The others agreed.

General Marshall also suggested that the Hawaiian garrison might be reinforced with five or ten Flying Fortress bombers; he noted that the Japanese could be four-fifths of the way to Hawaii before the United States knew that they had moved. But General Andrews thought that having a few more bombers in Hawaii would not be effective; the Air Corps should send many more or none and avoid dividing its forces.

President Roosevelt, replying on June 15 to French Premier Paul Reynaud's plea for materiel support, assured the French that so long as they fought for their liberty, "so long will they rest assured that materiel and supplies will be sent to them from the United States in ever-increasing quantities and kinds." Marshall observed to his staff, however, that the army had already "scraped the bottom" for supplies for the Allies. (Major Walter B. Smith Notes of conference in office of Chief of Staff, June 17, 1940, LC/RG 165 [OCS, Chief of Staff Conferences File]. President Roosevelt's message to Reynaud is in *Public Papers and Addresses of Franklin D. Roosevelt, 1940*, pp. 266–67.)

Meanwhile, Arthur B. Purvis, head of the British Purchasing Commission, submitted a list of pressing needs, including heavy bombers, to Treasury Secretary Morgenthau. The next day, June 17, the secretary and President Roosevelt informally agreed to give the British a few of the oldest model B-17s. (FDRL/H. Morgenthau, Jr., Papers [Diary, 273: 123].) When he was told of this plan early in the afternoon of June 18, Marshall immediately began to prepare a memorandum opposing this action. (Major Walter B. Smith Memorandum for Mr. Morgenthau, June 25, 1940, NA/RG 165 [OCS, Foreign Sale or Exchange of Munitions File].) ★

MEMORANDUM FOR THE SECRETARY OF WAR[1]   June 18, 1940
Secret   [Washington, D.C.]

Subject: Transfer to British of 12 Flying Fortress type planes (B-17)

On hand today   52
Due for delivery this summer   2

Time required to replace 12 planes — December 1940

Remarks

This is the only efficient bomber we now possess. Our B–18's have a speed under 200 miles, and are poorly armed.

Our secret bombsight is built into the plane. The next most efficient sight,—the Sperry, would require four months for installation. The Estoppey—an inferior sight—would require two months to install.

We have recognized the urgent necessity for locating a few of these planes in Hawaii, but have not done so because of the small number available. They must also be held available for the defense of the Canal Zone and the Caribbean areas.

Recommendation

It is the unanimous opinion of the War Department officers concerned, that it would be seriously prejudicial to our own defensive situation to release any of these ships.[2]

NA/RG 165 (OCS, Foreign Sale or Exchange of Munitions File)

1. Marshall originally drafted this on the afternoon of June 18 as a memorandum for the president from the secretary of war. The next morning, at the request of Secretary Woodring, Marshall redrafted the document in its present form, adding the final sentence in the third paragraph under "Remarks."

2. Major Walter B. Smith delivered copies of this memorandum to General Watson at the White House and to Secretary Morgenthau. While Smith was in Morgenthau's office, Marshall telephoned the secretary to request, as a favor, that he do nothing further about giving bombers to the British until he returned from his Akron, Ohio, speaking engagement. (FDRL/H. Morgenthau, Jr., Papers [Diary, 274: 22].) Shortly after Marshall returned, on the morning of June 20, President Roosevelt informed the War Department that the proposed transfer had been dropped. (Smith Memorandum for Mr. Morgenthau, June 25, 1940, NA/RG 165 [OCS, Foreign Sale or Exchange of Munitions File].) The idea was soon revived, however; see Conference Notes, August 20, 1940, p. 292.

SPEECH TO THE VETERANS OF FOREIGN WARS[1]   June 19, 1940
Akron, Ohio

In talking to veterans I feel free to go straight to the point in discussing the problems of national defense. You men understand the meaning, the requirements of war, and I feel that you will readily comprehend the point of view of the War Department.

Today, the United States faces probably the most critical period in its history. Within the year we have seen the map of the Old World radically altered in a succession of startling moves. We have seen political faiths and forms of government common to our age, placed in jeopardy or exterminated. Commonly accepted military technique and methods in the art of war have been consigned to the ash heap. And finally we here in distant America find ourselves facing the imminent possibility of being suddenly required to defend the independence of the Western Hemisphere.

Those of us who are charged with the responsibility for preparing our defenses are fully aware of the seriousness of the situation and the difficulties of the task. We realize that the soundness of our decisions have suddenly become of immense importance to the people in this country. In every way, in every possible manner, we are endeavoring to resolve our plans in the light of what has occurred, but most of all, on a basis of sound common sense.

In common with other democracies, the United States has always been lax in matters of national preparedness during periods of peace. Such a policy inevitably results in a convulsive, expensive expansion in an emergency. Following the World War, efforts to have the condition of our national defense abreast of possible developments in the international situation were invariably halted by the steady resistance of public opinion. The period of boom markets, of the great industrial expansion gave no help to the national defense. In fact those were parsimonious years for the Army. Last week in looking over some old papers I found this paragraph in a letter from General Pershing, addressed to me in China in December [*November*] 1924, "I find on my return here that the War Department seems to be up against the real thing. The Budget Officer insists on reducing our estimates so that we shall not be able to have over 110,000 men. Just what this means I cannot understand. I do not know what is going to be done about it, but to my mind it is very discouraging."[2]

The blame for this state of affairs can not be laid to any one individual or political party. It is the result of our form of government, of our sense of security behind what have seemed to be great ocean barriers.

Last February, I stated before a Congressional Committee that if Europe blazed in the late spring or summer we should put our house in order before the sparks reached this hemisphere. I also stated that we should proceed step by step abreast of each major development of the crisis abroad. Though this was but a few months ago, yet I was criticized in editorials for expressing such a view.[3] Later, the cut of the War Department appropriation down to 57 planes received considerable public approval. Less than three months later, when the situation abroad burst into a general conflagration, public opinion swung so rapidly in the other direction that I was being criticized for daring to mention so small a number as 10,000 planes. These, incidentally, were for immediate procurement, before Congress would again be in session. Today the American people want the nation to be prepared. They want a large army, fully equipped with the latest vehicles and weapons; and they want this transformation to be accomplished immediately.

Now, you veterans know, that an army—a large army—can not be recruited, equipped, and trained over-night. It is a long and tedious process, especially as to materiel. The present situation has two aspects, the problem of immediate measures for our security, and the long range planning for a year or two years hence. Most of the millions of recent Presidential messages and appropriations will bear no fruit for at least a year, and for the majority of items, a year and a half to two years.

Our people must realize that the flag-waving days of warfare are gone. The successful Army of today is composed of specialists, thoroughly trained in every detail of military science, and above all, organized into a perfect team. Today, it is imperative that cold factual analysis prevail over enthusiastic emotional outbursts. Sentiment must submit to common sense.

The War Department has long prepared for possible expansions of the army and has definite plans for a step-by-step coordinated increase. We have started on our way, and are endeavoring to proceed in an orderly manner. Let me strongly emphasize the fact that we must not become involved by impatience or ignorance in an ill-considered, over-night expansion, which would smother well-considered methods and leave us in a dilemma of confused results, half-baked and fatally unbalanced.

If I may leave a message with you, let it be this: The War Department knows what is needed, the American people know that they want preparedness; and the time for endless debate and other differences of opinion is past. We must get down to hard pan and carry out our preparations without vacillations or confusion.

My visit with you, however short, has been a very pleasant interlude in the heavy press of business in Washington. Your very able and genuinely patriotic representative at the National Capitol, Congressman Harter,[4] and I must fly back to Washington without delay. I admire your organization for what it stands, and express my sincere appreciation for the courtesies and kindnesses you have shown me this evening. If the quarter of a million members of the Veterans of Foreign Wars do nothing more than to promote unity of thought and action in our military preparations, they will have served their country well.

GCMRL/G. C. Marshall Papers (Pentagon Office, Speeches)

1. Marshall delivered this address to the Annual Encampment of the Veterans of Foreign Wars at the Mayflower Hotel in Akron, Ohio.
2. Pershing to Marshall, November 18, 1924, GCMRL/G. C. Marshall Papers (Pentagon Office, Selected).
3. For Marshall's comments to the House Appropriations Committee on February 23, see p. 163.
4. Dow W. Harter of Akron had represented Ohio's Fourteenth District since 1933. He was the third-ranking Democratic member of the House Military Affairs Committee.

To Major General Daniel Van Voorhis   June 20, 1940
Radio No. 1.   *Secret*   [Washington, D.C.]

Fleet may be ordered to Atlantic stop   Possibility of attempt at sabotage of
canal anticipated stop   Continue present precautions accordingly stop
acknowledge[1]

                                                                Marshall

NA/RG 165 (WPD, 4326); H

1. On June 17, the War Plans Division sent a radio message directing that Van Voorhis
"quietly but immediately take every possible precaution against surprise action, naval, air or
sabotage which may be intended to put the Canal out of commission. Your air component
and antiaircraft forces must be in state of preparedness for action at any hour." (Brigadier
General George V. Strong Memorandum for The Adjutant General, June 17, 1940, NA/RG
165 [WPD, 4326].) For a further explanation of this alert, see Marshall to Herron, August 28,
1940, pp. 296–97.

O N June 19, two days after the French Government had requested armistice terms from the Germans, President Roosevelt asked Henry L. Stimson to become secretary of war. Stimson noted in his diary that "the President said he was very anxious to have me accept because everybody was running around at loose ends in Washington and he thought I would be a stabilizing factor in whom both the army and the public would have confidence." After ascertaining that his strong public support for generous aid to the Allies, for the rapid building up of the nation's military strength, and for a general compulsory military service law was acceptable to the president, Stimson accepted, with the understanding that he could name Robert P. Patterson as assistant secretary of war. (Yale/H. L. Stimson Papers [Diary, 29: 56].) Another Republican, Frank Knox, was simultaneously to be named secretary of the navy.

The controversial announcements were made on June 20, the same day that Secretary of War Woodring resigned. Marshall had been acquainted with Stimson since 1918, although they had not been close friends. (See *Papers of GCM,* 1: 322.) John McAuley Palmer wrote to Marshall on June 21 "enclosing a copy of a telegram I have taken the liberty to send to an old friend of mine." Addressed to Henry L. Stimson, the message read: "Your appointment is a great public event. As you return to the War Department please let me say that I have known the Chief of Staff intimately since he was a first lieutenant and picked him years ago as the ablest officer in the Army. You will find his loyalty disinterestedness and integrity equal to his high ability and professional standing." (GCMRL/G. C. Marshall Papers [Pentagon Office, Selected].) ★

To Brigadier General John McA. Palmer June 24, 1940
                 Washington, D.C.

Dear John: I returned from New York yesterday to find your note of June 21st, together with a copy of the telegram you had sent Mr. Stimson. I want you to know that I appreciate very deeply not only just what you said of me to him, but particularly your thoughtfulness in doing this. I can always count on you for a fine unselfish act.

I am sorry I did not have a chance to see anything of you when you were in town.[1] It is getting so these days that I am having difficulty in seeing anything of Katherine, and when I am with her I have to spend so much time relaxing that I am not very much of a husband. Affectionately,

G. C. M.

LC/J. McA. Palmer Papers

1. Palmer had been in Washington in connection with the introduction in Congress of "A Bill to Protect the Integrity and Institutions of the United States Through a System of Selective Compulsory Military Training and Service" by Senator Edward R. Burke (Democrat from Nebraska) on June 20 (S. 4164) and by Congressman James W. Wadsworth (Republican from New York) on June 21 (H.R. 10132).

To Major General Frank R. McCoy   June 26, 1940
                                                   Washington, D.C.

Dear McCoy: Will you give me a tip on Mr. Stimson, what you may happen to know of his special ideas and what advice you would give me in my approach to him. Confidentially, I am flying up there late tomorrow evening—to Mitchel Field and on to his Long Island place, and returning early Friday morning.[1] If you think there is anything for me to know before going up, please telephone me tomorrow morning prior to ten o'clock eastern time on a reverse charge basis. Hastily,

                                                   G. C. Marshall

LC/F. R. McCoy Papers

1. Marshall wrote to his wife at Fire Island on June 28: "I left the office at three yesterday, flew up to Mitchel Field, and from there motored twenty minutes to the Stimson's country place. They are both delightful people and their farm is charming; he has owned it for forty years. We talked until almost midnight; then I had breakfast with him at 6:30 this morning and hustled back to town, arriving here at eight." (GCMRL/Research File [Family].)

To Bernard M. Baruch   June 29, 1940
                                                   [Washington, D.C.]

My dear Mr. Baruch: Thanks for your letter of June 25th, and the suggestions you were good enough to let me have. I have gone over them myself very carefully and have had them studied by a particularly able officer of the Staff.[1]

Up to the present moment I think there has been a reasonable synchronization of requirements in relation to the program. The estimates before Congress for planes that are carried in the approved appropriation bills, have included all the spare parts, the engines, and armament and ammunition that are needed for the planes. For some time I have been having one of my ablest people search out each of our programs like the foregoing, for bottlenecks, and of course, heavy powders and fuses still give me a headache.

The tank program has carried armament with it. The bomb and explosives program has been greatly increased, not only for the additional planes, but for far more bombing by these planes than had been visualized heretofore. Again, of course, the time factor is the difficulty, and we are pressing very hard for corrections and improvements.

The contract for the powder plant has not yet been placed. We have been searching through the field for particular men to accomplish special purposes, but at the moment most of these men seem to fit in between a civilian (Knudsen-Stettinius) set-up, but we are going after some from the staff direct. We have already had some special advice and suggestions.

Your suggestion that we get a conspectus of the program is excellent, and a start has been made; but there is still a lot of work that must be done along this line, which we will push as soon as the first rush of procurement by contract is over. This, as I see it, is primarily a General Staff function in coordination with the Assistant Secretary's office.

A good many of your points pertain more directly to the Assistant Secretary's office than they do to mine, but I am very glad to have your point of view.

I think the Research Committee recently appointed by the President is going to be an important receptacle for several of our problems, especially inventions, and I am having this investigated.[2]

As a matter of fact, my struggle at the moment has been to get appropriations and certain legislation through Congress without undue delay, to get Executive approval for certain actions, and get our General Staff data in up to date shape for outside agencies to work from,[3] and, hardest of all, to meet the flood of suggestions, urgings, enthusiasms, etc. that are aimed at the War Department these weeks, and each of these from very powerful channels. My problem has been to keep our heads above the flood of these critical weeks, more particularly to prevent the emasculation of most of the plans we have in favor of what—to be brutally frank—are a series of superficialities. I have felt it of vital importance to do everything in my power to keep public confidence in the War Department, but it really has been extremely hard to do this when we were involved in turning down 1,000 schemes a day.

I am going over with our Public Relations Section this morning the question of protecting the Ordnance Department. In brief, it runs something like this: We are getting about 1,000 letters a day with proposals for this and that, the largest number of them pertaining to inventions, new processes, or other matters of a general ordnance nature. Naturally not a tenth of one per cent that pertain to the ordnance have a sound working basis. The trouble then is that the Ordnance Department in a way makes about 600 enemies, or at least disappointed people a day, and this rapidly rapidly becomes cumulative. I am having their response system carefully checked—this has already been done a number of times by my inspector—but the situation is a tremendous number of people of importance in civil life have descended on the Ordnance by mail and by personal presentation, and each is sure in his own mind that his particular idea is the correct one.[4]

Of course, when we get to a general mobilization status—not merely that of materiel as at present, we can handle these things much more easily, but at the present moment, National Defense is everybody's business, and I find a great deal of my time involved in endeavoring to maintain public confidence in the War Department despite the fact that we cannot accede to the mass of public suggestions or demands.

Thanks very much for your helpful letter.   Faithfully yours,

GCMRL/G. C. Marshall Papers (Pentagon Office, Selected)

1. Baruch had written to suggest how Marshall might most efficiently turn his appropriated funds into materiel. He was concerned about a number of specific problems, particularly that Marshall recruit good executive talent. "I do not know what personnel you have in the various branches of the service, but I do know that it would be wise to get for yourself and the other procurement officers some first-class industrial men aside from those taken on by [industrial production adviser William S.] Knudsen and the others. . . . The best thing in the world is brains, and they are very hard to get. I would like to see you get the best, because you now have all the money you asked for." (Baruch to Marshall, June 25, 1940, GCMRL/G. C. Marshall Papers [Pentagon Office, Selected].) Marshall had requested that Brigadier General Richard C. Moore (assistant chief of staff, G-4) study Baruch's comments and write recommendations regarding them. (See Moore Memorandum for the Chief of Staff, June 27, 1940, ibid.)

2. On June 27 President Roosevelt established the National Defense Research Committee under the direction of Dr. Vannevar Bush, president of the Carnegie Institution.

3. At this time various War Department officers were drafting a massive new materiel procurement program. See the editorial note on pp. 285–87.

4. An example of the sort of political pressure that a determined inventor could bring to bear on the War Department was Lester Barlow's activities during the spring of 1940 on behalf of his "oxygen bomb." The idea of making an explosive out of liquid oxygen and carbon was not new and its use would create serious technical problems for the Ordnance Department, which did not wish to pursue the subject. Barlow, asserting that his weapon would "keep enemy warships 1,000 miles from American shores," persuaded Congress to press the War Department to test his device; it failed to perform satisfactorily. (*New York Times*, March 14, p. 12; March 27, p. 7; May 26, p. 9; May 28, p. 22.)

In mid-May Lawrence Langner, a New York City patent lawyer, wrote to President Roosevelt to suggest the creation of an "Inventors' Council for National Defense," similar to one formed during the World War, one of whose duties would be to examine inventors' ideas and to advise the military on promising subjects for further investigation. On July 11 Secretary of Commerce Harry L. Hopkins appointed Charles F. Kettering, the president of General Motors Research Corporation, to head the department's National Inventors' Council, with Langner as secretary. (Documents concerning this council are in NA/RG 165 [New Developments Division, National Inventors' Council].) In 1945, Langner sent a résumé of the council's work to Marshall; it asserted that the council had evaluated and classified over 220,000 inventions. The busiest period was in early 1942 when over 10,000 suggestions were submitted in one week. (Langner to Marshall, July 2, 1945, GCMRL/G. C. Marshall Papers [Pentagon Office, General].)

No Royal Road

July 1 – September 30, 1940

The importance of specialized training is apparent to all observers, but the tremendous importance of seasoned soldiers, welded into a perfect team is the outstanding impression. There is no royal road to such training. It cannot be obtained by reading books or sitting in barracks.

—C.B.S. Radio Address on Selective Service
September 16, 1940

ARMY Chief of Staff George C. Marshall and Chief of Naval Operations Harold R. Stark sought, despite the traditional rivalries and the differences in outlook between their respective services, to foster army-navy cooperation. Recalling his association with Marshall, Admiral Stark later said that they worked "very closely, almost intimately. I don't see how we could have worked more closely than we did or more happily as far as our pulling together and solving our own problems." (Harold R. Stark, interviewed by Forrest C. Pogue, March 13, 1959, GCMRL.)

The January 1940 landing exercise on the California coast had been an important manifestation of Marshall and Stark's efforts at cooperation. The service chiefs' ideas, however, were frequently slow to influence behavior at lower levels. In an April 2, 1940, letter to Major General Daniel Van Voorhis, commanding general of the Panama Canal Department, Marshall directed him to convey, "in a tactful way," to the local Air Corps commander the need for greater cooperation with the navy. (See p. 187.) But solutions to the problems of jurisdiction and of the advisability of unified command over the three critical areas in the nation's western defense perimeter (the Canal Zone, Hawaii, and Alaska) were difficult to achieve.

"We were having constant difficulties over the command question which I was endeavoring to settle," Marshall recalled in 1957. "I wanted the navy to have overall command in the Alaskan district. I proposed that, thinking that if we could get that settled we could move down to Hawaii and settle that in time and then go down to the Panama Canal and settle that. But the navy was very loathe to accept my proposals about the Alaskan Theater, and I suppose for the reason that they thought that would obligate them to accept my views as to Hawaii. My view as to Hawaii—although I had not expressed it, as I recall, at that time—was that the navy should have the overall command. But when it came down to Panama, I thought the army should have the command. But it never got around to my expression of that fact." (George C. Marshall, interviewed by Forrest C. Pogue, January 15, 1957, GCMRL.)

By executive order, Van Voorhis had "exclusive authority" over the Panama Canal (see pp. 70–71) and instructions to defend it. His relations with the two local naval commanders had been "most friendly," he told Marshall. "I have not assumed that the Navy elements were under my command and have dealt with them on the basis of request, my position being somewhat embarrassed as both Admirals rank me. This procedure operated very well until we began to tighten up on preventative measures." At this point, the navy commanders objected to the tone of certain memorandums they had received from Van Voorhis's headquarters and pointedly reminded him that they were not in his chain of command. Believing strongly that "the means available to the Navy and the very hazy situation as far as jurisdiction over those means are concerned are not conducive to well coordinated operations of the two services in the defense of the Canal," Van Voorhis appealed to the chief of staff. (Van Voorhis to Marshall, June 24, 1940, GCMRL/G. C. Marshall Papers [Pentagon Office, Selected].) ★

To Major General Daniel Van Voorhis   July 3, 1940
Washington, D.C.

Dear Van Voorhis: A cable was sent you yesterday, I believe, with information regarding Naval adjustments to meet some of the comments in your letter of June 24th to me.

As to the other points concerned, regarding inter-relationships, there is not at this time anything I can do from this end of the line. I realize how embarrassing it is to you to be the junior of the three,[1] and I hope within the next few days to see you a Lieutenant General. Stone's amendment has blocked us for this long period of time. I have been endeavoring recently, and particularly the last few days, to break the jam and get the legislation through. It is not easy to put these things over even when practically no money is involved.[2]

I think your staff let you in for complications by not leading up to the meetings with a personal touch. However, your ability to get along with people will surmount the difficulties, but it is too bad that such important matters have to be approached in this manner. I hope we can do better by the situation a little later. I am going into the entire matter with Admiral Stark.   Faithfully yours,

GCMRL/G. C. Marshall Papers (Pentagon Office, Selected)

1. Rear Admiral Frank H. Sadler (U.S.N.A., 1903), commandant of the Fifteenth Naval District, had his headquarters in Balboa, Canal Zone, and he reported to the chief of naval operations. The other naval officer involved was Rear Admiral John W. Wilcox, Jr. (U.S.N.A., 1905), commander of the Special Service Squadron, also based in the Canal Zone, who reported to the commander in chief of the United States Fleet.

2. The bill to raise to lieutenant general rank the commanders of the Hawaiian and Panama Canal departments was introduced into both houses of Congress on January 25, 1940. The Senate bill (S. 3200) passed on February 1, but the House bill (H.R. 7611) was delayed by an amendment which would have made a lieutenant general of any one who had commanded either department since August 5, 1939. This amendment applied only to Major General David L. Stone. Lieutenant generals and vice admirals received an additional $500 each in salary per year. The Senate bill was accepted by the House on July 25; it was signed by President Roosevelt on July 31.

MEMORANDUM FOR GENERAL STRONG   July 3, 1940
Confidential   Washington, D.C.

Please fix me a sheet, with the following properly arranged:

First: "Memorandum for Admiral Stark:

Please glance over the following and then talk to me about it. The Canal is a pretty important consideration in our National Defense structure, and any accident there might have calamitous results. We cannot defend it with a debating society.[1]

General Van Voorhis a short time back circulated the following: . . .[2]

The Commandant of the 15th Naval District is not under General Van Voorhis, but the whole tone of this procedure awakens my concern as to satisfactory arrangements for the defense of the Canal. We cannot be involved in quibbles over such matters at the present time, and I am deeply concerned over the reaction shown in these communications. Van Voorhis has a long record of getting along with people. He became conspicuous for that quality in the handling of the flood situation in the middle West. I am certain of his qualities.

I think it would be unfortunate to bring this up in an official manner, but I do think you and I will have to arrive at some more satisfactory basis for the defense of the Canal. Germany has given us too good an illustration of the contrast between unity of command and the reverse."

G. C. M.

NA/RG 165 (WPD, 4326)

1. This document was revised several times before it was sent. In the final version (July 8, 1940), the last sentence in this paragraph had been deleted.

2. Marshall listed five documents between the Panama Canal Department and the two local naval commanders that he wished to have quoted. This episode is discussed in Mark S. Watson, *Chief of Staff: Prewar Plans and Preparations*, a volume in the *United States Army in World War II* (Washington: GPO, 1950), pp. 458–61.

MEMORANDUM FOR THE UNDER SECRETARY   May [*July*] 5, 1940
OF STATE [WELLES]   [Washington, D.C.]
Secret

Subject: Consideration by Liaison Committee of critical situation at Martinique, and other French possessions in the Caribbean Area.

In the light of what has just occurred between the French and British

Naval forces at Oran, it seems to me that the Liaison Committee should meet to consider whether any action other than diplomatic is now indicated for the United States in connection with possible, even probable developments in the French possessions in the Caribbean area.[1]

I understand that there are at present three French Naval vessels in the harbor at Martinique, and that at least two British Naval vessels are present in the same harbor. A serious development is therefore possible. Furthermore, yesterday's change of attitude between the French and British Governments presents serious possibilities in connection with the disposal of the French possessions in this hemisphere.

Should the United States take any definite action at this time other than diplomatic; and if so, of what nature?[2]

I am sending a copy of this memorandum to Admiral Stark, and I am suggesting that we discuss this in an early meeting of the Liaison Committee.[3]

GCMRL/G. C. Marshall Papers (Pentagon Office, Selected)

1. On July 3 the British government had issued ultimatums to the French naval commanders at Alexandria, Egypt, and Oran, Algeria. When the commander at Oran refused to surrender his ships, the British attacked and destroyed or disabled the French vessels in a brief but intense battle. No ultimatum was delivered to the commander at Martinique, Admiral Georges Robert, who had aligned himself with the Vichy government, but on July 4 Britain instituted a blockade of the French ships—including an aircraft carrier, a fast cruiser, and several other vessels—in port there.

2. In early May 1940, President Roosevelt and Under Secretary of State Welles had agreed that some form of trusteeship under the aegis of the Pan American Union might be necessary to administer the European nations' Western Hemisphere possessions. Shortly thereafter, Germany's military successes in Western Europe caused the United States to press Pan American Union members to attend a meeting in Havana to consider the possessions issue. The conference could not be convened before July 21. (Stetson Conn and Byron Fairchild, *The Framework of Hemisphere Defense*, a volume in the *United States Army in World War II* [Washington: GPO, 1960], pp. 46–48.)

Martinique, Secretary of State Cordell Hull observed in his memoirs, "proved a magnet attracting much of our diplomacy in the summer of 1940." (*The Memoirs of Cordell Hull* [New York: Macmillan, 1948], p. 818.) On July 5 Marshall joined with Admiral Stark in directing the Joint Planning Committee to prepare a "Joint Plan for the Occupation of Martinique and Guadeloupe." The initial plan, completed on July 8, asserted that "any attempt by British or Canadian forces to land or take sovereignty of French possessions in the Western Hemisphere will be considered by the United States as an infraction of the Monroe Doctrine. . . . The use by the Axis of bases in the French West Indies would constitute a violation of the Monroe Doctrine. In order to prevent this, our occupation of Martinique and Guadeloupe may become necessary." The proposed expeditionary force was to include an initial naval force of fifteen fighting ships and 2,800 Marines to be supported by 6,800 men from the army's First Division. (NA/RG 319 [OPD, Joint Board, Serial 666].) The Martinique issue rose repeatedly as a diplomatic and potential military problem during the next eighteen months. Conn and Fairchild, *Framework of Hemisphere Defense*, pp. 49–51, 84–88, 161–63.

3. General Marshall attended one meeting of the Standing Liaison Committee at 11:30 A.M. on July 5 (from which this memorandum may have derived) and another at 11:00 A.M. on July 10.

(1) War Resources Board, August 17, 1939. Seated, left to right: Harold G. Moulton, Charles Edison, Edward R. Stettinius, Jr., and Louis A. Johnson. Standing: Commander Anton B. Anderson, Admiral Harold R. Stark, Karl T. Compton, John L. Pratt, Brigadier General George C. Marshall, and Colonel Harry K. Rutherford.

(2) Munitions Building, Nineteenth Street and Constitution Avenue, N.W., Washington, D.C., July 1938.

(3) Marshall enjoys surf casting at Fire Island, New York, summer 1939.

(4) Marshall picnics on the beach at Fire Island, New York, with his stepchildren Allen, Molly, and Clifton Brown, summer 1939. Allene Tupper Wilkes is in the right foreground.

(5) Marshall fishing at Fire Island, New York, summer 1939.

(6) Marshall relaxes at Fire Island, New York, summer 1939.

(7) Katherine Tupper Marshall, 1939.

(8) General George C. Marshall, September 1939.

(9) Quarters One, Fort Myer, Virginia. (This photograph was taken in 1954.)

(10) George C. Marshall is sworn in as chief of staff of the United States Army, September 1, 1939. Left to right: Secretary of War Harry H. Woodring, Marshall, and The Adjutant General Major General Emory S. Adams.

(11) General George C. Marshall (left) and Edward T. Taylor, chairman of the House Appropriations Committee, at the November 27, 1939, hearing.

(12) Conference of Army and Corps Area (C.A.) commanders held at the War Department
General Council Room, November 30, 1939. Left to right: Brig. Gen. Lorenzo D. Gasser,
D.C.S.; Maj. Gen. Daniel Van Voorhis, 5th C.A.; Maj. Gen. Percy P. Bishop, 7th C.A.; Maj.
Gen. Herbert J. Brees, 8th C.A.; Lt. Gen. Stanley D. Embick, 3d Army and 4th C.A.; Lt.
Gen. Hugh A. Drum, 1st Army and 2d C.A.; Gen. George C. Marshall, chief of staff;
Secretary of War Harry H. Woodring; Lt. Gen. Stanley H. Ford, 2d Army and 6th C.A.;
Maj. Gen. John L. De Witt, who became commanding general of the 4th Army and 9th C.A.
in December with rank of lieutenant general; Maj. Gen. James K. Parsons, 3d C.A.; Maj.
Gen. James A. Woodruff, 1st C.A.; Brig. Gen. George P. Tyner, A.C.S., G-4; standing by
window, Lt. Col. Orlando Ward, secretary of the General Staff; seated in front of Ward,
Mona K. Nason, Marshall's secretary, and an unidentified woman; seated behind Woodruff,
Brig. Gen. George V. Strong, A.C.S., W.P.D.

The New York Times
(13) Marshall, Commissioner Alexander M. Damon, and Evangeline
Booth at the Salvation Army's Diamond Jubilee dinner, New York
City, February 26, 1940.

(14) Marshall inspects the plans for Fort Miles, Puerto Rico, February 1940. Left to right: Major Feodor O. Schmidt, Lieutenant Colonel Charles W. Bundy, Marshall, Brigadier General Edmund L. Daley, and Major James F. C. Hyde.

(15) Marshall is welcomed to Hawaii with a lei and a glass of pineapple juice as Major General Charles D. Herron looks on, March 1940.

(16) Marshall and Major General Charles D. Herron during the chief of staff's trip to Hawaii, March 1940.

(17) General Marshall during his trip to Hawaii, March 1940.

(18) Major General Edmund B. Gregory, the new quartermaster general, and Major General Henry Gibbins, the outgoing quartermaster general, April 1, 1940.

(19) Major General Henry H. Arnold, November 1941.

(20) Colonel William T. Sexton, 1942.

(21) Brig. Gen. Walter B. Smith, 1942.

(22) Major General George Grunert, 1940.   *(23) Brig. Gen. Courtney H. Hodges, 1941.*

(24) Major Matthew B. Ridgway, 1940.

(25) Marshall talks with Air Corps men during his visit to Fort Benning, Georgia, April 1940.

(26) Marshall greets Brigadier General Asa L. Singleton and Major General Walter C. Short during his trip to Fort Benning, Georgia, April 1940.

(27) General Marshall confers with Major General Walter C. Short during maneuvers, Fort Benning, Georgia, April 1940.

(28) *General Marshall confers with Colonel Martin C. Shallenberger, Colonel George S. Patton, and Brigadier General William Bryden during maneuvers, Fort Benning, Georgia, April 1940.*

(29) *In the Control Room at Third Army Headquarters during the Third Army maneuvers in the Louisiana-Texas area, May 1940. Left to right: Major General Herbert J. Brees, Lieutenant General Stanley D. Embick, and Colonel Edmund L. Gruber.*

(30) Marshall meets with Lieutenant General Stanley H. Ford (right) and an unidentified National Guard officer during the Second Army maneuvers at Camp McCoy, Wisconsin, August 1940.

(31) General Marshall inspects the Cadet Corps of Fishburne Military School, Waynesboro, Virginia, June 1, 1940.

The New York Times

(32) *President Roosevelt signs the Burke-Wadsworth conscription bill in the presence of Secretary of War Henry L. Stimson; Congressman Andrew J. May, chairman of the House Military Affairs Committee; General George C. Marshall; and Senator Morris Sheppard, chairman of the Senate Military Affairs Committee, September 16, 1940.*

MEMORANDUM FOR GENERAL GREEN[1]   July 5, 1940
                                                          [Washington, D.C.]

I have noticed Major Phillips' comments on antiaircraft defense. Whatever the soundness of his ideas may be, he makes a good presentation of his point of view.

Whenever I find these fellows who seem to have ability and a certain amount of disagreement with what we are doing, I am always interested in seeing them, and getting first hand impressions. What do you think of bringing him here, either temporarily or permanently?[2]

GCMRL/G. C. Marshall Papers (Pentagon Office, General)

1. Major General Joseph A. Green (U.S.M.A., 1906) had been chief of the Coast Artillery Corps since April 1, 1940.

2. Thomas R. Phillips, Coast Artillery Corps, had been promoted to lieutenant colonel on July 1. He had recently completed an assignment as instructor at the Command and General Staff School and was scheduled to go to the headquarters of the Puerto Rican Department. Marshall's interest in him might have been stimulated by Phillips's "Defense Against Night Bombing," *Army Ordnance* 21(July–August 1940): 24–28. There he argued that daylight bombing of the enemy's interior was becoming too dangerous to be risked, but defense against night attacks was difficult. He suggested that spending great amounts of money and manpower on pursuit planes for night defense was probably ineffective and recommended that the United States undertake experiments to solve the problem of night interception, giving consideration to increased use of antiaircraft artillery and barrage balloon defenses. Phillips did not receive an assignment to the War Department.

CERTIFICATE OF COMPLIANCE[1]   July 12, 1940
Confidential   [Washington, D.C.]

Under provisions of the Act approved June 28, 1940 (Public 671, 76th Congress), I hereby certify that the following ordnance materiel is not essential to the defense of the United States:

a. Surplus or obsolete equipment transferred from Navy Department as not essential to the defense of the United States (see certificate of Chief of Naval Operations, dated July 9, 1940, attached) —

      3,000 Lewis Machine Guns (used) Aircraft
      3,000 Lewis Machine Guns (used) Ground Type
  18,000 ~~10,000~~ Spare Barrels for Both Types of Lewis Machine Guns
   30,000 Magazines for Lewis Machine Guns
     500 Caliber .38 Smith & Wesson Revolvers
1,281,000 ~~1,000,000~~ Rounds Ammunition for Caliber .38 Smith & Wesson Revolvers (more or less)

6,367,647 ~~6,600,000~~ Caliber .30 Ball, M1 Ammunition for Machine Guns (more or less) (deteriorated)

  b. Surplus Arms from War Department Stock —
  35,000 Enfield Rifles, caliber .30, Model 1917 (used).[2]

NA/RG 165 (OCS, Foreign Sale or Exchange of Munitions File)

  1. This document is typical of scores Marshall was required to sign between July 1, 1940, and the passage of the lend-lease act in March 1941. The certificates were required under the provisions of the naval appropriation bill (H.R. 9822) approved by the president on June 28, 1940. The provision—sometimes called the "Walsh amendment" because it was fostered by Senator David I. Walsh, Massachusetts Democrat and chairman of the Naval Affairs Committee—stipulated that no materiel belonging to the army or navy could be disposed of in any manner without a certificate signed by the chief of staff (if army equipment was involved) or the chief of naval operations asserting that the materiel was not essential to the nation's defense. Further, a copy of this certification had to be delivered to the chairmen of the relevant House and Senate Military or Naval Affairs committees within twenty-four hours of signature. (*United States Statutes at Large*, vol. 54, pt. 1 [Washington: GPO, 1941], p. 681 [Public Law 671, Title I, 14(b)].)

  Marshall considered the provision unconstitutional, as it gave him, a subordinate to the commander in chief, authority to override the president's decisions. (Claude M. Adams Notes on Conference in Office of Chief of Staff, November 13, 1940, NA/RG 165 [OCS, Chief of Staff Conferences File].) He later commented that he was careful to abide by the law. "I tried not to crowd the issue at all, and I thought it was imperative that Congress feel that they could trust me, and then I could get them to do things that otherwise they would oppose. . . . It was the only time that I recall that I did something that there was a certain amount of duplicity in it." (Marshall interview, December 7, 1956. See also the interviews of January 15 and 22, 1957. A lengthy discussion of the law's implications took place at a meeting Marshall attended in Secretary of the Treasury Morgenthau's office on July 3, 1940, FDRL/H. Morgenthau, Jr., Papers [Diary, 279: 140–48].)

  2. The changes indicated here in italics were made under the authority of the chief of staff on July 22.

IN a series of meetings of the Standing Liaison Committee in mid-June, General Marshall, Admiral Stark, Under Secretary of State Welles, and their assistants prepared a secret memorandum for President Roosevelt, dated June 22, and entitled "Basis for Immediate Decisions Concerning the National Defense." On June 24 Marshall, Stark, and Welles met with the president to discuss the document which requested decisions on the disposition of the United States Fleet, the military's opposition to further commitments of war materiel to Great Britain, and various aspects of Western Hemisphere defense. In the final point, Marshall and Stark stated: "The naval and military operations necessary to assure successful Hemisphere Defense call for a major effort which we are not now ready to accomplish. Time is of the essence in overcoming our unreadiness. To overcome our disadvantage in time, the concerted effort of our whole national life is required. The outstanding demands on this national effort are: – first, a radical speed-up of production, and second, the assembly and training of organized manpower." To accomplish this latter goal, they recommended that "immediate enactment be sought of a Selective Service Law along the lines of existing plans, to be followed at once by complete [Marshall inserted "progressive" here] military and naval mobilization." The president agreed that a draft bill was needed. (This memorandum and Marshall's report on the president's responses to it are in NA/RG 165 [WPD, 4250–3].)

During the next six weeks, manpower policy was the main focus of Marshall's attention. The Burke-Wadsworth selective compulsory military training and service bill had already been submitted to Congress at the instigation of an influential group of civilians associated with the Military Training Camps Association. Marshall remarked some years afterward: "I was much criticized because I didn't take the lead in the selective service legislation. I very pointedly did not take the lead. I wanted it to come from others. . . . Then I could take the floor and do all the urging that was required. But if I had led off with this urging, I would have defeated myself before I started." He had to be careful, he felt, "not to create the feeling" that he, "as the military leader . . . was trying to force the country into a lot of actions which it opposed." (Marshall interview, January 22, 1957.)

Prior to the fall of France, Marshall had thought that voluntary three-year enlistments would enable the Regular Army and the National Guard to reach their authorized "peacetime strengths" (375,000 and 400,000 enlisted men respectively) in sufficient time. Regular Army enlistments in June had been the largest in two decades, producing a net increase of 15,000 men, but at that rate it would take ten months to reach peace strength. In view of the international situation, Marshall told the Senate Military Affairs Committee on July 12, "we will be procuring them at much too slow a rate." Therefore a draft was needed. But there was another important consideration. "If such a measure is accepted by the Congress, the practical proposition of putting it into effect requires one of two things. Either we must mobilize the National Guard for the purpose of training these men in its ranks, and also in the ranks of the Regular Army units, where we must have more men as quickly as possible, or we will have to emasculate the Regular Army and emasculate the National Guard, at this time, in order to provide the necessary training cadres to handle the new men in the manner that it would be desirable. In other words, the training of young men in large training camps on the basis of compulsory training is something that we cannot manage at the present time. We do not have the trained officers and men—the instructors, to spare; also, we do not have the necessary materiel. We lack the special training set-up at the moment, and we cannot afford to create it. Therefore, we would have to make the first step within the ranks of the Regular Establishment, and within the ranks of the National Guard." Marshall wanted the National Guard called into federal service at once for a minimum of one year. (Senate Military Affairs Committee, *Compulsory Military Training and Service, Hearings* [Washington: GPO, 1940], pp. 328–31, 340.)

In testifying on the House version of the draft bill on July 24, Marshall repeated his desire for quick action. "We must get these men very quickly. Materiel we cannot rush to meet the immediate emergency, but men we can procure. There should be no delay. . . . My relief of mind would be tremendous if we just had too much of something besides patriotism and spirit." In order to reach the Protective Mobilization Plan goals of a "war strength" army of 900,000 enlisted men plus 300,000 replacements, Marshall proposed the induction of between 300,000 and 350,000 in October 1940, with another call-up the following April; the men were to be in the twenty-one to thirty age range without dependents. (House Military Affairs Committee, *Selective Compulsory Military Training and Service, Hearings* [Washington: GPO, 1940], pp. 101–3, 109.)

Six days later, before the Senate Military Affairs Committee, Marshall reiterated his plea that the National Guard be called to active duty: "I strongly urge that we be permitted to go ahead in a businesslike, orderly way and go ahead with these units to give the effective result as needed. We have been proceeding, I think, on a very conservative basis. It is a question as the time grows late whether we can continue on that basis. . . . The one difference here over our experience in the past is that we are trying to do in time of peace what we have always delayed until the actual moment of war. I say 'time of peace,' but if you will pardon me, I think it is a time of peril, and I think everybody admits that aside from the matter of the defense of this country it would be a high crime to send our men out unprepared." (Senate Military Affairs Committee, *Ordering Reserve Components and Retired Personnel into Active Military Service, Hearing* [Washington: GPO, 1940], p. 14.) ★

STATEMENT FOR *LIFE* MAGAZINE   July 13, 1940
[Washington, D.C.]

The War Department considers some form of compulsory selective service and training as essential to our system of national defense, and pressingly necessary in the present international situation. It is a scientific, a democratic, and an economical method for maintaining a defensive force.[1] It is my belief, out of the experience of the last World War and a recent intimate association with the Civilian Conservation Corps, that such a system would be tremendously effective in improving our citizenship.

The Burke-Wadsworth Bill, with minor modifications, proposes a satisfactory system for selective service. In the first step it would be necessary to mobilize the National Guard and Reserve officers to assist the Regular Army in the task of training the individuals to be selected.

The immediate adoption of some such method for increasing the strength of our armed forces is vital to our security.[2]

GCMRL/G. C. Marshall Papers (Pentagon Office, Selected)

1. Only these first two sentences were quoted in *Life* 9(July 22, 1940): 16.

2. Writing a few days later to Daniel Longwell, executive editor of *Life,* Marshall said, "I am acknowledging your acknowledgment because I want you to know that I was not only glad to do so [i.e., write the statement printed above], and fully realize the importance of educating the public to the necessities, but more particularly because I have felt under obligation to LIFE ever since you undertook the article on Materiel ["50,000 Airplanes: U.S. to Multiply Fleets & Factories," *Life* 9(May 27, 1940): 83–93] which, in my opinion, played an effective part in enabling us to get one hundred and ten millions for this purpose out of the special defense measure." (Marshall to Longwell, July 19, 1940, GCMRL/G. C. Marshall Papers [Pentagon Office, Selected].)

MEMORANDUM FOR GENERAL ANDREWS[1]   July 13, 1940
Confidential   [Washington, D.C.]

There is attached a letter which has just been received by the Secretary of War from Grenville Clark, also a letter from Colonel Adler to Mr. Johnson, and a draft of a reply to it, and a resolution from Howard Slade and Peter Jay, and a draft of reply for my signature. All pertain to the same problem, that of Business Men's Training Camps in September.[2]

Confidentially, it appears to be the earnest, the rather intense desire of the Secretary of War to have us undertake these camps. He referred to this in the first few minutes of our first interview at his home on Long Island. He referred to this in the last few minutes of a conversation before he left the office yesterday to go to New York.

I am well aware of the difficulties. The problem is, how do we meet this particular situation? Colonel Stimson feels that such camps are a necessary movement to build up strong public opinion throughout the country to make the country acutely conscious of a unity of purpose towards preparations for the National Defense. The fact that the situation as to the War Department and the Army's burden is vastly different now from what it was in 1916, at the time of the Leonard Wood Plattsburg Camps, is not realized other than by those of us who are deep in the problem here in the War Department.

Think this over during the week-end and talk to me about it Monday morning. What I want is your proposal as to how to put this matter up to the Secretary. I have already explained our difficulties, but the desire remains to conduct these camps. As a matter of fact, in our last conversation the Secretary suggested the possible desirability of calling off the National Guard Maneuvers. I mention this so you can understand the intensity of his views on the subject of the Business Men's Training Camps.[3]

NA/RG 319 (WDCSA, 326 [7-13-40])

1. Brigadier General Frank M. Andrews was assistant chief of staff for Operations and Training (G-3).

2. The Military Training Camps Association—of which Grenville Clark was a leader and Julius Ochs Adler of the *New York Times* and bankers Pierre Jay and Howard Slade of the Fiduciary Trust Company were vigorous supporters—sponsored annual month-long Citizens' Military Training Camps in the summer for young men between the ages of seventeen and twenty-five. Most of the public attention, however, focused on the "special" camps for older men, ranging in age from twenty-five to fifty. During July 1940, 3,000 business and professional men attended, at their own expense, eight training camps reminiscent of those held at Plattsburg, New York, in 1915 and 1916. A common assumption behind the special camps for older men was that "the blitzkrieg in the Low Countries and Northern France showed, among other things, that the physical requirements for a successful refugee may be more exacting than those for mechanized soldiering." (Samuel T. Williamson, "Plattsburg, 1915-1940," *New York Times Magazine*, July 28, 1940, p. 5.)

Secretary of War Stimson had attended the Plattsburg camp in 1916, and the man who was soon to become assistant secretary, Robert P. Patterson, was at the M.T.C.A. camp at this time. Marshall did not wish to offer commissions to camp graduates or to spare the Regular Army and Reserve Corps officers necessary to run them. The basis of planning for the September camps, according to Marshall's handwritten addendum to the memorandum printed here, was 18,000 trainees; this would require establishing some twenty-five camps utilizing 575 officers.

3. On Tuesday, July 16, Andrews and Brigadier General William E. Shedd—assistant chief of staff for Personnel (G-1)—held a lengthy conference with Secretary Stimson on the army's objections to holding the September camps. Afterwards, Stimson noted in his diary that cancelling the camps "would be a great blow to the courage and enthusiasm of the Military Training Camps Association." Moreover, the Plattsburg camps had demonstrated their value during the World War. "In the end I told them to hold up their report until later on and we could see better how the situation was turning out in regard to the passage of the Selective Service Act." The camps would be less necessary if the draft bill passed quickly—which he doubted would happen. (July 16, 1940, Yale/H. L. Stimson Papers [Diary, 30: 12-13].) See Marshall to Davis, July 20, 1940, pp. 273-74.

To Major General Roy D. Keehn   July 15, 1940
Confidential   [Washington, D.C.]

Dear Keehn: I have just this moment read your letter of July 12th, and I will first reply regarding Arlington.[1] I would love to get away, but I have not a Chinaman's chance under present conditions. Last July, a year ago, I had three days up at Fire Island with Mrs. Marshall. That has been my vacation, except as I read or slept on an airplane flying here and there. I have gotten down to Virginia Saturday evening for Sunday several times, but even that has been difficult of arrangement. Yesterday, Sunday, for example, Owen D. Young came out to the house, also General Dawes;[2] Mr. Stimson, the new Secretary of War, tried to get me, and half a dozen somewhat similar calls of importance came during the day. Fortunately I was not there, but it goes on like this interminably.

I ride at six o'clock in the morning with Molly; this is the only time I can be certain of exercise. Until Congress completes action on the basic proposals, and we get under way further with our readjustment and reorganization of troops, I am pretty well tied to this vicinity. More occurs here in a day now than used to occur in a month, and it seems to grow a little worse each day.

I am interested in what you had to say about the National Guard. Quite confidentially, I might say to you that your expression "the situation will have to be more imminent to justify an immediate call", suggests very positively the thought that you in your contacts are not aware at all of the possibilities of the immediate future. Time is the dominant factor in all this business. We cannot advertise every thought and item of knowledge we have; we are charged with the National Defense, meaning national safety. Once the dilemma has arisen, it is too late; we have to take our preliminary measures in time to reach some degree of preparation. I wish I could feel as sure of the situation as you and your people apparently do. The past three months have been catastrophic in the history of the world, the next six months may be more paralyzing. Understand this is confidential and not to be quoted.   Faithfully yours,

GCMRL/G. C. Marshall Papers (Pentagon Office, Selected)

1. Keehn repeated his invitation (see p. 245) to Marshall to come to Chicago and attend some horse races; "you can get a little relaxation and contact a few people." Keehn's letter was primarily concerned with the National Guard, however. "Everybody is calling up about the headlines in the newspapers, concerning what you say about calling out the National Guard *immediately*. . . . Just between you and me, don't you let anybody kid you that the National Guard officers here want to be called for training. Everybody is up in the air today. . . . Of course, everybody is excited about the war and wants to kill Hitler, but in my opinion the situation will have to be more imminent to justify an immediate call of the Guard with their scant equipment, etc. Besides, many of them are just getting jobs." (Keehn to Marshall, July 12, 1940, GCMRL/G. C. Marshall Papers [Pentagon Office, Selected].)

2. Young, former chairman of the board of the General Electric Company, was an adviser on industrial training,—or, as he himself said, "a sort of handy man"—for the Roosevelt administration on transportation and defense problems. (*New York Times*, July 25, 1940, p. 8.) Marshall habitually called former Vice-President Charles G. Dawes "general." Dawes had been a brigadier general in the World War when he was the general purchasing agent for the A.E.F.

MEMORANDUM FOR THE PRESIDENT   July 17, 1940
                                                         [Washington, D.C.]

I am taking the liberty of presenting a suggestion regarding certain arrangements for the Secretary of War, Colonel Stimson's comfort and
convenience.

Colonel Stimson's home on Long Island is about fifteen to twenty minutes' drive from Mitchel Field and, therefore, he can conveniently leave his
desk in the War Department for the week-end and be at his home in Long
Island in about an hour and forty-five minutes—even more quickly if the
wind is favorable. This, of course, assumes the use of an Army plane.

The trouble is Colonel Stimson, I am certain, would feel obligated to
make the trip with Mrs. Stimson by commercial plane—as he did in returning to the office last Monday morning.[1] Travel by this means confines him
to a commercial schedule and involves a lengthy drive from his home to
LaGuardia Field, Flushing, and would lack the restful convenience and
quiet of an Army plane.

Colonel Stimson's burden, particularly during the next two months, will
be tremendous. He is seventy-two years of age. I think it would be a direct
contribution to the efficiency with which he discharges his duties as Secretary
of War if the President thought it practicable, and desirable, to inform
Colonel Stimson that there is no objection to Mrs. Stimson's travelling with
him on his trips between Washington and Mitchel Field, Long Island, and
return.

This is being presented to the President direct because I feel certain that
Colonel Stimson himself would never raise the question.[2]

GCMRL/G. C. Marshall Papers (Pentagon Office, Selected)

1. In his diary on July 15, Stimson observed that the military plane to and from Mitchel
Field "would have been much more convenient but on thinking it over, I decided not to do it,
in view of the present regulation against taking women on an Army plane. I did not wish to
break that, even though it seems to have been quite the custom in the past to do so among
Congressmen and others, so I decided to, as long as the regulation stood, go by commercial
plane and I cancelled my own plane and got tickets at LaGuardia Field." (Yale/ H. L. Stimson
Papers [Diary, 30:10].)

2. Secretary Stimson began using his transport plane on July 19. (Ibid., p. 25.)

TO ARTHUR J. HAYES   July 17, 1940
                                                         [Washington, D.C.]

My dear Arthur: I am very busy these days but not too busy to answer a
letter as interesting as yours.[1]

The art of military strategy as we in the Army understand it can be mastered only after years of intensive study and through progressive training which must begin with the instruction you have been receiving in your ROTC unit. For you to start on a serious study of strategy at the present time would be somewhat like trying to understand algebra and geometry without a previous background of arithmetic; or like trying to win football games with players who did not know how to tackle and block.

I admire your desire to acquire knowledge, and I hope that the fact that you have not yet been able to obtain books on the subject will not discourage you. Any book on military history is full of examples of good and bad strategy. If you thoroughly understand the military history of the United States, you have already made a good start on the subject of strategy.

As you suggested in your letter, a great military leader of the future might be among your own group of friends in the ROTC. But remember that the eminent commanders usually rose to great heights only after they had mastered the fundamentals such as are now being taught to you. Faithfully yours,

GCMRL/G. C. Marshall Papers (Pentagon Office, General)

1. Hayes wrote to the army chief of staff on July 12 to say that when he had joined the Junior R.O.T.C. in Dubuque, Iowa, he had expected to be taught "strategy and its use in various campaigns." But he was surprised to find this subject absent from R.O.T.C. studies and books on it difficult to find. He suggested that R.O.T.C. cadets be given at least a "taste" of the subject. (Hayes to Chief of Staff, July 12, 1940, GCMRL/G. C. Marshall Papers [Pentagon Office, General].)

To ALLEN T. BROWN

July 17, 1940
[Washington, D.C.]

Dear Allen: This letter while addressed to you is intended for both Madge and you, to thank you for having me in mind on a honeymoon to the extent of thinking to get for me that fine leather belt. It is a beautiful piece of leather and I am very, very glad to have it. Thank you both very much.

Your mother has been much excited over the reports of your initial experiences at housekeeping, and I gather that so far there have been none of the preliminary battles over tooth paste in the bathroom, the shirt on the floor, and other casual gestures common to men, about the house. If you can prevent these superficial irritations from annoying you, the remainder of the adjustments should be very simple of management.

I hope that I will get a chance to drop in on you at Poughkeepsie, and if I fly up to West Point for any purpose, I am going to get you to put me up for the night. At present, as for the past twelve months, I am very busy, probably more so now than at any time, and the future doesn't hold much prospect of a respite.[1]

My love to you both and my thanks.   Affectionately,

GCMRL/Research File (Family)

1. For Marshall's previous advice to his stepson on marriage, see p. 242. Brown was working as a salesman for a radio station and living in Poughkeepsie, New York.

MEMORANDUM FOR THE PRESIDENT[1]   July 18, 1940
[Washington, D.C.]

Existing laws empower the President, either in peace or in war, to make temporary promotions of officers of the National Guard of the United States, and of the Officers' Reserve Corps *when ordered to active duty in the Federal service.* But, except in time of war, no such authority exists for the temporary promotion of officers of the Regular Army. Therefore, leadership in our present program of army expansion is jeopardized.

The authority now granted the President to promote officers of the Officers' Reserve Corps and of the National Guard of the United States should immediately be extended to include the Regular Army, during the present emergency. This becomes the more urgently necessary as we progress with the organization of five new divisions and various special organizations, involving 32 new regiments, 115 battalions, and 729 companies to be completed by September.

For example, the Regular Army now has insufficient captains and general officers, and by the time the foregoing new organizations are formed will be short some 2200 captains for duty with troop units, and will lack 57 general officers for divisions, brigades and important staff assignments, exclusive of the general officers required for the approaching increases of the GHQ Air Force, whose temporary promotion is already authorized by law. Most of our regular divisions are now commanded by brigadiers, and practically all of them lack the two general officers for the infantry and artillery brigades.

For the first time in our history we have been given the opportunity in time of peace to engage in serious preparation to insure the national security. We must have commanders who are outstanding leaders, who possess the requisite initiative and drive to secure the rapid development of the troops, and to insure their success in campaign. The selection of those commanders should not be confined to the oldest colonels, for example, merely on the basis of seniority, as at present, but unless the expedient of temporary rank is immediately adopted, that will be the situation. The temporary advancement of the experienced and specially schooled first lieutenants of the Regular Army is equally important, as it relates to the selection of commanders for these new companies, in view of the large number of Reserve officers now being called to active duty who naturally are less well equipped to organize, train and lead a company unit.

Attached is a draft of an amendment to the National Defense Act which empowers the President to make these temporary promotions. The cost involved is small. To secure the 2200 captains and 57 general officers which constitute our most pressing shortage at present will cost less than $60,000 for the present fiscal year.[2]

Formal request has been made in the usual manner to the Director of the Bureau of the Budget for information as to whether the proposed legislation would be in accord with your program.

I strongly urge its approval.[3]

NA/RG 165 (OCS, 21151-1)

1. Marshall had written this document for Secretary of War Stimson's signature.
2. Marshall alluded to this need to advance experienced Regular Army officers in his Senate testimony on the bill. "Time is of vast importance, is really the dominant factor. It is a well-known fact that some men, given a year or 2 years, will do a beautiful job but they are utterly unable to do it in short order and under many difficulties, with the lack of this and the lack of that. That situation was notorious, I suppose that is the right word, in the A.E.F. where time meant so much. It is quite evident right now that we cannot afford to place in a position of great responsibility one of these men who works very slowly and deliberately. We must have somebody that will take one of these units and bring about a result in the most expeditious manner possible. That means we must select the men to give the necessary direction and vigor to units in the field." (Senate Military Affairs Committee, *Uniformity in Temporary Promotions in the Army, Hearing* [Washington: GPO, 1941], p. 4.)
3. The bills were introduced in the Senate on July 25 (S. 4207) and in the House on August 1 (H.R. 10279), but only the Senate held hearings before Congress adjourned. The issue was resolved in substance by an amendment to the Second Supplemental National Defense Appropriation Bill for 1941, and was passed; it was signed by the president on September 9.

MEMORANDUM FOR GENERAL G. A. LYNCH[1]   July 19, 1940
Confidential   [Washington, D.C.]

I am endeavoring to have Congress authorize the President, in the present situation, to make temporary promotions. He has already the authority for the Reserves and the National Guard when called into active duty. In my opinion it is exceedingly important that as quickly as possible we give effect to the vital influence of leadership, by creating major generals for the command of divisions, and corps if the National Guard comes into the service, and brigadier generals for the important posts in the development of troops. It is also, I believe, of equal importance that we be able to give the temporary rank of captain to most of our first lieutenants.

What I would like you to do, on a purely personal basis without the knowledge of anyone in your office, is to give me a list of the colonels and lieutenant colonels who stand at the top of leadership efficiency, in your opinion, for selection for temporary brigadiers. I would like these all arranged on a basis of priority, and it would probably be best for you to make up your list in three groups, one of older officers whom you feel can give vigorous leadership in the organization and training of combat units, another group of younger men, who would come under the present policy for making permanent promotions, and a third group of still younger men in age, and lower in rank if not in age, whom you think are outstanding to the extent of justifying their advancement over the heads of large numbers of officers.

I would like to have such a list the latter part of next week.

GCMRL/G. C. Marshall Papers (Pentagon Office, Selected)

1. Major General George A. Lynch was the chief of Infantry. This memorandum was also addressed to Major Generals John K. Herr (chief of Cavalry), Robert M. Danford (chief of Field Artillery), and Joseph A. Green (chief of Coast Artillery).

To Colonel George S. Patton, Jr.   July 19, 1940
Washington, D.C.

Dear Patton: I have just received your note of July 16th, thanking me for your assignment to the brigade of an armored division. I am glad this arrangement is pleasing to you, for I thought it would be just the sort of thing you would like most to do at the moment. Also, I felt that no one could do that particular job better.[1]

I am looking forward to seeing you and having a talk with you before you leave for the South.   Hastily,

G. C. Marshall

LC/G. S. Patton, Jr., Papers

1. Patton had been given command of the Second Brigade of the Second Armored Division at Fort Benning, Georgia, effective July 10. He wrote to Marshall: "Nothing could please me more. I shall do my uttermost to justify your kindness." (Patton to Marshall, July 16, 1940, GCMRL/G. C. Marshall Papers [Pentagon Office, Selected].) When Patton was promoted to brigadier general, effective October 1, he wrote another thank-you note to Marshall, which elicited the following response from the chief of staff: "Dear George: . . . You should thank yourself rather than me for your nomination for promotion. The service you have rendered demanded such action on my part, and I think it was the consensus of opinion elsewhere." (Marshall to Patton, October 2, 1940, ibid.)

To COLONEL CHESTER R. DAVIS   July 20, 1940
                                                    [Washington, D.C.]

Dear Davis: I have just this moment read your letter of July 18th, regarding
your visit to the business men's training camp at Sheridan, and your
reactions, particularly the comment that "none of them seem to know
exactly why they are there or what the purpose may be of their training."[1]
    The Business Men's Training camps were instituted at the request and
under the heavy pressure of the New York branch of the Military Training
Camps Association. The original request was for a very large number,
twenty-five or fifty thousand I believe. We compromised finally at 3,000, but
the instructions were specific that these camps would not in any way involve
the Government to bestow commissions on the trainees. The Training
Camps Association thought that this would crystalize public opinion as to
the urgent necessity of all citizens doing a part toward building up National
Defense. They are now urging a minimum of 18,000 men for similar camps
in September.[2]
    Please treat the foregoing, in so far as an expression of the Chief of Staff
is concerned, as *confidential.*
    I note your renewed offer of service and I shall certainly keep you in
mind, but I was astonished to be reminded that two years had passed since
your resignation; it seemed a matter of a few months to me.
    With my warm regards to Mrs. Davis,   Faithfully yours,

GCMRL/G. C. Marshall Papers (Pentagon Office, Selected)
    1. Davis, a Chicago banker, had been a colonel in the Illinois National Guard until he
resigned in 1938. He wrote to Marshall that he had recently visited a company at the Citizens'
Military Training Camp at Fort Sheridan, Illinois. "For the most part I was very much
impressed with the caliber of the men and their sincerity, although none of them seemed to
know exactly why they are there or what the purpose may be of their training. . . . Most of
them seemed to feel that their training will lead to a Reserve Commission of some sort."
(Davis to Marshall, July 18, 1940, GCMRL/G. C. Marshall Papers [Pentagon Office,
Selected].)
    2. Grenville Clark of the Military Training Camps Association was particularly displeased
with Marshall's opposition to holding the camps. Clark's friend, John McAuley Palmer, wrote
a lengthy defense of the chief of staff's position, asserting that Clark was wrong. "If Marshall
opposes it [i.e. the September camps program], it is not from timidity or lack of imagination
but because he believes that the War Department's limited resources can be used to better
advantage." (Palmer to Clark, July 26, 1940, Dartmouth/Grenville Clark Papers. This document is published in I. B. Holley, Jr., *General John M. Palmer, Citizen Soldiers, and the
Army of a Democracy* [Westport, Conn.: Greenwood Press, 1982], pp. 597–99.) On July 18
Secretary Stimson received information that enthusiasm for the September camps was less
widespread than he had believed. On August 8 he had a long talk with Marshall about the
camps after which he noted in his diary that the conditions which the army insisted upon
imposing on the camps, the delay in passing the draft bill, and the other work the army had to
do made "it very questionable whether we ought to have them." Finally, on August 14,

Stimson told Clark that he was "inclined to think that whole project had better be abandoned for the present." (July 18, August 8 and 14, 1940, Yale/ H. L. Stimson Papers [Diary, 30: 19, 74, 87].)

MEMORANDUM FOR CAPTAIN SEXTON[1]   July 22, 1940
Washington, D.C.

Reduce this to a series of paragraphs of ideas or policies rather than a prepared speech.[2] For example, on the question of selective service,

In the present critical situation, the question of compulsory service is hardly debatable. We have to have more men immediately to fill up ranks of the Regular Army and National Guard, and we cannot obtain them by voluntary enlistments. Therefore, some form of compulsory service is immediately necessary and every week of delay presents a definite and increasing hazard. The exact form that such a law should take is, of course, a matter of public policy, but the situation in which the United States now finds itself this summer demands rapid congressional action.

Today time is the dominant factor in the problem of national defense. For almost twenty years we had all of the time and almost none of the money; today we have all of the money and no time. It is a long time between the appropriation of the money and the actual procurement of the article, especially when it is of a non-commercial nature. A contract for a small weapon let September '39 will produce the first delivery ten months later, November '40. A contract for an anti-aircraft gun let March '40 promises the first delivery in February '41. It requires longer to train the crew for a plane than it does to build the plane, and while it does require longer to build a tank than it does to train the crew for a tank, yet at least a year is necessary for the preparation of that crew. Long years of indifference on the part of the public towards national defense are now crowned by a tremendous impatience to get results immediately.

G. C. M.

GCMRL/G. C. Marshall Papers (Pentagon Office, Selected)

1. William T. Sexton had recently been designated an assistant secretary of the General Staff.

2. Marshall's friend Stephen O. Fuqua, formerly chief of Infantry and at this time military editor of *Newsweek* magazine, had written that he was preparing to deliver an address at Louisiana State University. "I wonder if you would like me to include any particular thought of yours on the subject of national defense. . . . Our magazine is of course watching your work, and as you know, our policy is strong in the support not only of national defense, but of your interpretation of it." (Fuqua to Marshall, July 18, 1940, GCMRL/G. C. Marshall Papers [Pentagon Office, Selected].)

To J. Edgar Hoover   July 22, 1940
                                                              [Washington, D.C.]

My dear Mr. Hoover: With reference to your memorandum of June 5, 1940, to the Attorney General,[1] to the effect that "the War Department does not desire to incur any expense of responsibility in connection with the apprehension of deserters", I would like to make it clear that it is not a question of a desire on the part of the War Department not to incur any expense or responsibility in the matter, but that the War Department lacks the necessary funds. Prior to 1932 funds in excess of $100,000 were appropriated annually for the purpose of rewards for the apprehension of deserters, etc., but since that date it has not been possible to pay a reward or to reimburse the apprehender for the actual expenses involved.

The War Department does desire to have deserters apprehended and will exercise such responsibility as it is financially able to manage.   Sincerely yours,

GCMRL/G. C. Marshall Papers (Pentagon Office, General)

1. Marshall had written this letter for the adjutant general's signature. As director of the Federal Bureau of Investigation, Hoover had asked the adjutant general whether the army was interested in the return of deserters whose whereabouts come to the attention of this Bureau during the course of its usual investigations." The adjutant general replied by indorsement that the army did desire to apprehend deserters, but that it had no funds to pay any costs incurred. (Hoover to Adams, April 8, 1940, NA/RG 407 [General, 251.21].) On June 5 Hoover sent Attorney General Robert H. Jackson the memorandum from which Marshall quotes.

To Mrs. John J. Singer   July 23, 1940
                                                              [Washington, D.C.]

Dear Marie: I have been so extremely busy—of course I cannot compete with you at Pike Run—that I have not managed a letter to you for some time.

There is little to tell you except that each day is a repetition of the previous one, only the pressure seems to increase and the necessities become more imperative. Am due before two Committees of Congress this morning and am now so full of facts and figures that I fear I may strip my gears.

During the heat I have managed my ride every morning with Molly at six o'clock, and we have generally gone in swimming after I get home from the office in the late afternoon, in the Fort Myer pool. Very frequently during the week we get in a canoe and paddle up to Chain Bridge, and then eat our picnic supper while drifting back. The river is lovely in its upper reaches and there is usually a cool breeze. The paddling is splendid exercise for me and the whole business most restful. We get home between nine and eleven at night.

My plans for the next month are very uncertain; I have the necessity of going entirely around the United States for an inspection of the maneuvers, but just how far I will be able to go through with this, I do not know at the present moment.

With my love,   Affectionately,

GCMRL/G. C. Marshall Papers (Pentagon Office, Selected)

To Brigadier General Adna R. Chaffee[1]   July 24, 1940
                                                       [Washington, D.C.]

Dear Chaffee: I recall that I mentioned to you the other day the desirability, in my opinion, of your picking up some educational institutions in the Middle West where a special course could readily be instituted for training men from the armored units. I had in mind engines and radio in particular.

Last week I received a number of letters from heads of universities and colleges pleading with me to give them something to do. They were being solicited by the NYA and other similar activities, but were hearing nothing from the War Department. Gignilliat, of Culver, gave me the best analysis of the situation, and he commented on the fact that the entire technical plants of most of these big establishments were lying idle this summer and yet everybody was talking about the need for such training.[2]

The situation came to a focus in my mind when I learned of your small disaster by fire out at Knox. I wish you would have someone immediately look over a number of these university plants to see if you cannot set up technical training arrangements for the armored corps on the basis of enlisted men taking the courses, with probably one officer and an assistant at the institution to help out in coordinating matters and to see to the financial arrangements for bed and board. I am convinced that the university people would be enthusiastic over such an opportunity, particularly in the role rather as sponsors of the armored corps. I am assuming that you would start rather in a small way and that you cannot visualize all of requirements or complications; but you can make a beginning and let it be an evolution to avoid building up complete establishments within the army, where existing facilities in civil life may be utilized for the same purpose.[3]

I am sending you a letter from Bruce Palmer, on which I would like your comments.[4]   Faithfully yours,

GCMRL/G. C. Marshall Papers (Pentagon Office, Selected)

1. Chaffee was the commanding general of the Seventh Cavalry Brigade (Mechanized) at

Fort Knox, Kentucky.
2. Brigadier General Leigh R. Gignilliat, superintendent of Culver Military Academy, had visited Marshall on June 24; Marshall asked him for suggestions for using some colleges for summer army specialized training programs. Gignilliat replied with a lengthy letter. (Gignilliat to Marshall, July 3, 1940, GCMRL/G. C. Marshall Papers [Pentagon Office, Selected].) An analysis by the G-3 staff stated that colleges and universities were ill suited for the type of specialized training the War Department contemplated and for the caliber of men the army was likely to send. "But these difficulties could have been overcome if there had been any necessity for using the institutions. No such necessity has been discovered or brought to the attention of this Division. The Trade and Vocational Schools are generally much more suited to our use than are the colleges." (Brigadier General Frank M. Andrews Memorandum for the Chief of Staff, July 20, 1940, ibid.)
3. Chaffee replied to Marshall on July 27. "Considerable spade work in preparation for full utilization of training facilities in civilian institutions for my enlisted specialists has already been completed. . . . I am in complete accord with the view that civilian institutions should be utilized to provide basic training for such army specialists as motor mechanics, radio operators and repair personnel, electricians, welders and like occupational specialists." (Chaffee to Marshall, July 27, 1940, ibid.)
4. Marshall's friend Colonel Bruce Palmer was serving with the Sixty-second Cavalry Division of the Organized Reserves. He wrote to Marshall to complain that he was "being completely ignored by the Army" and that "*the Army is in essential need of my services at this time.*" He believed that the direction of development and organization of the army's mechanized and armored forces had taken a wrong turn after he had left the Seventh Cavalry Brigade. "The organization of your new armored division, because of the inflexibility of its fighting part and the over-size of its non-fighting part, does not adapt itself to an employment similar to that of the Germans' in Belgium and France." (Palmer to Marshall, July 20, 1940, GCMRL/G. C. Marshall Papers [Pentagon Office, General].) Chaffee rejected Palmer's assertions. (Chaffee to Marshall, July 26, 1940, GCMRL/G. C. Marshall Papers [Pentagon Office, Selected].) Marshall replied to Palmer that "the organization is purely on an experimental basis until we are quite clear as to the actual experience of similar units in Europe." (Marshall to Palmer, July 31, 1940, GCMRL/G. C. Marshall Papers [Pentagon Office, General].) For additional comments on the Armored Force, see p. 462.

MEMORANDUM FOR THE CHIEF OF
ORDNANCE [WESSON]

July 26, 1940
[Washington, D.C.]

Along with the usual assaults on our Army system, particularly the progress of our present procedure in securing prompt production of materiel, there was reported to me the frank antagonism of Mr. Spear, President of the Electric Boat Company. This seems to be based on the fact that he had brought up a gun, the Davison Antiaircraft gun, about a year ago for consideration by the Army; that he felt he had received shabby treatment; that, as I understand it, the gun was tried out at least briefly at Fort Monroe, and the officers there were rather enthusiastic about it; and finally that he sold the gun to the British Government.[1]

Have someone give me a brief memorandum of what happened with Mr. Spear that I may offset such criticism from men of his important position.

The trouble with this is, he does submarine work for the Navy, and with others, compares the Navy efficiency to the disadvantage of the Army in such matters.

GCMRL/G. C. Marshall Papers (Pentagon Office, Selected)

1. John C. O'Laughlin, a friend of both Marshall and of Lawrence Y. Spear, had visited the chief of staff's office on the afternoon of July 26 and had raised Spear's complaints. (See Marshall to O'Laughlin, August 8, 1940, pp. 287–88.)

MEMORANDUM FOR THE SECRETARY OF WAR July 29, 1940
[Washington, D.C.]

The following is an extract from the President's Press Conference last Friday:

"The President was asked if he had any further program to submit to Congress that might hold them in session but he answered that as far as he knew now the Selective Service bill was holding their attention and that he had no other measure contemplated at this time that would be of sufficient importance to hold them in session."

This would seem to indicate that he either did not intend to go forward with the National Guard mobilization or that he had overlooked the legislative possibilities or difficulties connected with the Joint Resolution for that purpose. I called up Saturday morning on the status of the Joint Resolution authorizing the President to order out the National Guard, and while we were not able to obtain definite information, it appears that he has not sent that Resolution to Congress. These delays are daily growing more serious from several points of view: the lack of adequate numbers of trained troops, in the present international situation; and now the dilemma in which the War Department is rapidly being thrown by reason of our inability to start construction in the camps necessary for the National Guard, and for the compulsory trainees, in time to have them ready in the event that the necessary legislative authority is given us.

At the moment the situation is the more serious because we not only have the need for the immediate mobilization of a portion of the Guard, but the longer this matter is delayed the less time we have to make preparations against the cold weather of the early fall.

I am having prepared for your consideration a memorandum to the President on the subject, in the hope that he may be willing to give us a temporary allotment of a portion of his special fund in order to permit us to enter contracts and get the work started for sewage, roads, water, and hospital layout for a portion of these camps.[2]

GCMRL/G. C. Marshall Papers (Pentagon Office, Selected)

1. This same day President Roosevelt sent a letter transmitting the draft joint resolution to the president of the Senate; it was introduced in the Senate the next day by Morris Sheppard, chairman of the Military Affairs Committee. Within hours of its introduction, a hearing was arranged and Marshall was called to testify. The president's letter, the draft resolution, and Marshall's testimony are published in Senate Military Affairs Committee, *Ordering Reserve Components and Retired Personnel into Active Military Service, Hearing* (Washington: GPO, 1940). After a compromise was reached on the differences in the amendments between the Senate and House versions, Senate Joint Resolution 286 was sent to the president, who approved it on August 27.

2. In his testimony before the Senate Appropriations Committee on August 5, Marshall stressed the importance of starting cantonment construction. "Shelter is a serious problem at the present moment. We have known for some time where we wanted to put these people. We had decided on the type of shelter to be erected and had plans and specifications for it. We thought that Congress would settle the question of authority to order out the National Guard, and the matter of compulsory training by the 1st of August. On that basis, the Guard was to be brought into the Federal service during September and the first induction of men under the selective service act during October.

"What has happened is that the weeks have been passing and we have no authority to enter into contracts to provide the additional shelter required. We have been trying to find some manner, some means for getting started. We want to proceed in an orderly and businesslike manner. We know exactly what we want to do and exactly where we want to do it, but we have neither the authority nor the funds and time is fleeting. So far as construction is concerned the winter is upon us, because it requires from 3 to 4 months to provide proper shelter.

"We had hopes at first to gain time by providing a progressive mobilization of the National Guard during the summer. We planned to put troops in tent camps, while better shelter was being prepared in the climates that demand special protection against the winter. However, weeks have come and have gone and we have been unable to make a start. The present uncertainties make a businesslike procedure almost impossible. We must make a start toward getting water lines laid; a start on the sewage-disposal systems; a start on the temporary roads and certainly the walks to keep our people out of the mud; and we must get under way the start of construction of temporary hospital facilities. These are fundamental necessities and take time to develop." (Senate Appropriations Committee, *Second Supplemental National Defense Appropriation Bill for 1941, Hearings* [Washington: GPO, 1940], p. 4.) The construction problems are further discussed in the editorial note on pp. 482–83.

To EDWARD R. STETTINIUS, JR.[1]   August 2, 1940
[Washington, D.C.]

Dear Ed: I understand that the hearings on the four billion dollar appropriation bill are to be taken up by the Senate next week. I suggest that if you and Mr. Knudsen appear before the Committee and the same line of questioning is followed as that that took place before the House Committee, you make clear your reactions in regard to the sufficiency of the appropriations under discussion. I am referring to the matter of the wisdom of deferments from the original recommendation of six billion.[2]

There is attached a break-down, which shows the original totals, and the deferments I have just referred to.[3]

Confidentially, the situation is this: The War Department made a recommendation to the President, which was processed by the Budget. In that process a little short of two billions was subtracted from the totals recommended. Faithfully yours,

GCMRL/G. C. Marshall Papers (Pentagon Office, Selected)

1. Marshall had been acquainted with Stettinius for many years, having had business dealings with his father following the World War. (See *Papers of GCM*, 1: 275.) Stettinius had been chairman of the board of the U.S. Steel Corporation until June 4, 1940, when he resigned to devote his time to mobilization work. On August 9, 1939, he had been appointed chairman of the War Resources Board, and on May 29, 1940, he had been appointed head of the industrial materials section of the Advisory Commission to the Council of National Defense (popularly called the National Defense Advisory Commission or N.D.A.C.)

2. William S. Knudsen, the former president of General Motors Corporation, had been the commissioner for industrial production on the N.D.A.C. since May 1940. Concerning Marshall's testimony on the second supplemental defense appropriation bill, see the editorial note on pp. 286–87.

3. See "The Materiel Program of June 20, 1940, and Immediate Requirements," July 8, 1940, NA/RG 165 (OCS, Emergency File).

N.B.C. Radio Address on the Maneuvers   August 5, 1940
[Washington, D.C.]

Commencing today and continuing through August, our Army will be engaged in the most extensive and, we hope, the most productive field maneuvers we have ever attempted.

Since the American people foot the bill for all military expenditures, they are entitled to a detailed explanation of the purpose and importance of these maneuvers.

On September 8, 1939, nearly a year ago, and following the outbreak of hostilities in Europe, President Roosevelt issued the limited emergency proclamation and authorized the Army to recruit to an enlisted strength of 227,000 for the Regular Army and 235,000 for the National Guard. Immediately, five Regular Army Divisions were organized and ordered into the field for intensive training, which culminated in Army maneuvers for 70,000 Regular troops in the Sabine River Valley of Louisiana and Texas last May.

One purpose of the present maneuvers is to capitalize on the lessons of the past six months. About 85% of the mobile Regular Army and National Guard troops in Continental United States will participate, and in this way, the knowledge and experience recently gained by the Regular troops can be brought to the National Guard. During the maneuvers last May, National Guard Division and Brigade Commanders, with their staffs, served with the

Regular troops and during a 24-hour period of action were given actual command.

As a culmination to this year's training, the Regular Army and the National Guard will engage, during the next three weeks, in maneuvers in each of the four territorial Army Areas. In Northern New York, approximately 100,000 troops of the First Army will simulate combat conditions beween Plattsburg and Watertown.

In the Second Army, 65,000 men will operate in the vicinity of Sparta in Western Wisconsin.

The Sabine River Area in Louisiana will furnish the locale for the maneuvers of 65,000 troops of the Third Army; and the 80,000 troops of the Fourth Army will concentate at Fort Lewis, near Tacoma, Washington, and at Camp Ripley in Minnesota. This area is so large that it is not economical to assemble the Fourth Army troops in one region.

It is a matter of regret that our newly organized Armored Corps will not be free to participate in these maneuvers. The great distances of this country separating the maneuver areas and the necessity of permitting the two new armored divisions to complete their organization and training, as quickly as possible, have made this decision necessary.

It has also been necessary to hold to a minimum the squadrons of the Air Force which will participate in the maneuvers, because that component of the Army is in the midst of a tremendous expansion from a comparatively small force to the large organization recently authorized by Congress.

The present era of science and invention has exerted a dominating influence on the ways and means of conducting warfare. Teaching a man to shoot a rifle or to ride a horse, or to drive a motor vehicle, are only primary steps in the education of the modern soldier. He must not only be technically trained in many subjects and duties, but he must also be seasoned for rigorous field duty and taught the mechanics of operating as an intelligent cog in a highly complicated machine.

During the World War, it was my opportunity to see 27 of our divisions operating on the battlefields of France, and it seemed to me at the time that the great tragedy of our participation in that war was the wastage of the tremendous potential advantage we had in the quality of our personnel because of the limited opportunity the men were given to prepare themselves for action. No one has ever really told the full truth of what might have been and what actually was; and the fault was that of our nation at large in not giving those men a fair chance to prepare themselves for the ordeal of battle.

Another factor in the last World War is little understood in judging the necessities of today. Our experience in France was that of semi-siege warfare. Our divisions operated in sectors delimited by specified boundaries. Thus restricted, the errors in a large measure were confined to limited areas. Open warfare, that is, warfare of movement, such as recently took place in France and Belgium, knows no boundaries nor similar limitations, and is far more difficult of management.

In open warfare, the artillery, the signal communications, everything in fact is exceedingly hard to manage, even at best. This difficulty has been the more serious for us by reason of the lack of training of large units, such as divisions and Army Corps. We are hopeful that our theoretical ideas, as taught at our service schools, are correct; but hitherto we have been unable to prove them out by actual maneuvers on the ground. In other words, theory was forced upon us because we had no sizeable formations of troops to demonstrate the practical side. The Navy has a great Fleet. Paradoxical as it may sound, the Army has had no Army until the small field force of Regulars was concentrated last May.

Such maneuvers as we have been able to hold during the past five years have indicated the necessity for the more frequent assembling of the divisions and for the establishment of Army Corps—meaning a grouping of several divisions into a team. The general deficiency in Army Corps troops, that is, heavy artillery, antiaircraft units, Engineers, Medical regiments, Signal battalions, Quartermaster truck trains, and the complete lack of Corps Headquarters and experienced leadership, have made it extremely difficult for the mobile combat troops of the Regular Army to be trained as an immediately available, effective, first-line combat force, experienced in the conduct of large-scale field operations. Higher commanders and staffs must be given opportunities for training in the technique, tactics, and team work involved, and the troops must be accustomed to operating in large groups. These August maneuvers, among other things, are designed to give Brigade, Division, and Corps Commanders and their staffs, necessary experience which can be gained in no other way, and the lack of which would mean the wastage or sacrifice of men and means, if not the loss of great decisions.

Another purpose of these maneuvers is to improve the teamwork that is so necessary for the efficient operation of the modern Army. I wish to mention a few of the elements which enter into this. For instance, in an Army Corps of several divisions, there are the old faithfuls, the Infantry and the Artillery. Success in battle is closely attuned to the extent of their cooperation. We have the Cavalry, horse or mechanized, which must feel out and locate the enemy. We have the antiaircraft units, which must furnish protection against air attack; the Signal Corps troops, who install and operate the telephone lines and the radio sets; the Ordnance troops, who repair the broken vehicles and guns; the Engineers, who build the bridges, repair the roads, and clear blockades; the Quartermaster troops, who haul and distribute the supplies; the Observation Aviation, which has been called the eyes of the Army; the anti-tank units, which furnish protection against tank attack; the Medical troops, who care for the wounded. There are now, also, the distantly based squadrons of bombers, who must be hailed and brought to the focal point at a precise instant, to blast away hostile resistance. All of these elements must be taught to work with each other. We would not expect a football team, the members of which met for the first time on the playing field the day of the game, to furnish much opposition to a well-trained opponent. It is the same with an army, only more so.

There is no short cut to adequate combat training. The First Division of the AEF arrived in France in July, 1917, and entered into intensive training as a division within the sound of guns on the battlefront. Most of its officers were Regulars, and under the protection of the Allies, it was given 12 months in which to find itself, its first operation being launched a full year after the concentration at Hoboken. Yet in that first battle, following the most favorable practical situation for training conceivable, there were lessons without end, for both officers and men. There was courage a-plenty, but as we surveyed the operation, successful as it was, we felt a little like recruits at the business.

The situation today is utterly different from those days. There may be no such prolonged period for preparation, and there will be no friendly powers able to provide all our weapons and ammunition. Everything to be done will have to be done by ourselves alone. We must stand on our own feet.

I am hopeful that these August maneuvers will have a tremendous effect towards seasoning that important element of our defense forces, the National Guard, which is forced to conduct most of its training indoors. The Guard occupies an important place in our defensive system. It has suffered in equipment shortages as a result of the lean post-war years when appropriations were pared to the bone. The very recent billions for material can produce no effect for many months until quantity deliveries commence. The men of the National Guard are volunteers, enthusiastic, conscientious members of our Army; and great credit is due them for the time they have freely given from their civil pursuits to make a patriotic contribution to National Defense. These maneuvers will enable the National Guard Divisions to work with supporting units such as Cavalry, Anti-aircraft troops, and combat and observation aviation to an extent which has until this time been impossible.

Thousands of Reserve officers should benefit by the practical training in command and staff work which they will receive. These men are members of a Corps which is one of our great defense assets, and which has been built up progressively since 1919 to the present approximate strength of 120,000 commissioned officers.

One of the outstanding purposes of these maneuvers is to prepare in the present emergency the manpower which is our only resource for the immediate future. You have read of the billions which Congress is appropriating for National Defense. These appropriations constitute an important, a vital step toward adequate preparedness, but years must elapse before they declare their dividends in the way of finished material, that is, guns, ammunition, and heavy equipment. Time—and let me repeat—time is our pressing necessity today, and manpower is the only thing which can be provided on short notice. We must train men immediately against the possibilities of the next few months, which may be the most critical in the history of this country.

Ordering the National Guard to active duty and the passage of some form of selective service are the best, and the War Department is convinced, the only practical means by which we can prepare to meet the immediate situation. It was expected that in the process of obtaining authority for these various measures, there would be, of necessity, a period of discussion and debate, particularly with relation to a Selective Service Act; however, the passage of the weeks—this loss of time—is a constantly growing embarrassment to the War Department. Speaking from a purely professional viewpoint, I must say that further delays might seriously jeopardize the effectiveness of our preparations to provide the country with adequate military defense. We must not speculate with the security of this nation.

GCMRL/G. C. Marshall Papers (Pentagon Office, Speeches)

MEMORANDUM FOR THE CHIEF, NATIONAL   August 6, 1940
GUARD BUREAU [WILLIAMS]   [Washington, D.C.]

Subject: Exemptions and Relief Measures.

I wish you would have somebody in your office make a study and keep abreast of both the questions of exemptions, and especially of possible relief measures where the exemptions are not practicable of arrangement without too destructive an effect on National Guard units.

I want the War Department to be ready to make the necessary proposals to Congress, if proposals should be made, to meet these problems in the event of a mobilization of the National Guard. As I recall, a measure of this character was put into effect when the Guard was on the Border in 1916, but the trouble was months elapsed before action was taken. If it is necessary to take such action, we should be timely with the first move. It occurs to me that possibly we can arrange for some assistance through an existing fund outside the control of the War Department. In any event, have the field of requirements and possible solutions carefully covered.[1]

NA/RG 165 (OCS, 16810-134)

1. At the July 30 Senate Military Affairs Committee hearing, Marshall had discussed the necessity of exempting certain members of the National Guard from being called up with their

units. See *Ordering Reserve Components and Retired Personnel into Active Military Service*, pp. 6–8, 20.

TO MRS. REYNOLDS BROWN   August 6, 1940
                                              [Washington, D.C.]

Dear Emily: Thank you for your note about Fifille; I was so glad to hear something definite about her present condition.[1] I have just finished dictating a note to her, about the best I can do in these days of continued rush and pressure. It is very difficult to know what to write about and I fall back on a brief description of what I have actually been doing.

I flew up to Fire Island Friday night and flew back early Monday morning. Katherine and Molly have been there for about ten days. This is my first "lengthy" holiday since three days over the fourth of July in 1939. However, I reached my desk yesterday morning before nine and was so overwhelmed with various difficulties and problems, including two hours before the Senate Appropriations Committee, and a broadcast at 8:30 last night, that I lost most of the benefits of the week-end. Today holds no hope of better things; I am due again before the Senate Committee at 10:30 for a number of other difficult problems on important things that must be solved before night.

Wouldn't it be a delightful thing if we could have again the peaceful days of Naushon in 1919, without the menace of war and a world in apparent dissolution?

With my love to you both,   Affectionately,

GCMRL/G. C. Marshall Papers (Pentagon Office, Selected)
   1. Mrs. Butler Ames was in a Boston hospital. See Marshall to Mrs. Reynolds Brown, May 29, 1940, p. 230.

P RIOR to mid-June 1940, the various deficiency and supplemental appropriations for the army had been essentially short-term responses to European events whose future developments were unpredictable and whose full implications were obscure. Germany's victories, however, clearly demanded a bolder, longer-range program to stimulate United States military industrial production. By June 20 an itemized and detailed materiel procurement having a projected cost of $7,300,000,000 had been delineated by the War Department staff. The president's advisers suggested that the total appropriation should be held to around $4,000,000,000 by deferring certain costs for possible future supplemental appropriations. Accordingly, the revised Munitions Program of June 30 was adopted; according to one army historian, this marked "a major development in the preparedness policy." It called for the production of essential (i.e., commercially producible) items for a ground force of 1,000,000 men; the critical (i.e., specialty or noncommercial) items for a force of 2,000,000; the creation of production facilities to supply an army of 4,000,000; the procurement of 16,000 new aircraft; and the creation of the capacity to produce 18,000 aircraft per year. (R. Elberton Smith, *The Army and Economic Mobilization,* a volume in the *United States Army in World War II* [Washington: GPO, 1959], pp. 130–32.)

The new army munitions program was introduced into Congress as part of the second supplemental appropriation bill for fiscal year 1941. Marshall testified before the House Appropriations Subcommittee on June 24 and reappeared briefly on July 26; he appeared before the Senate Appropriations Subcommittee on August 5 and 6. Funds for materiel concerned the nation's representatives less than the implications of manpower increases.

Much of the discussion at Marshall's August 5 hearing concerned recruiting, the draft, the National Guard call-up, and the construction necessary to house the growing army. On August 6 Marshall began his testimony with some remarks on the great cost of mobilizing. "I think it is tragic that we find ourselves in a situation which requires the spending of these colossal amounts of money for purely a war-making purpose. I think it is indeed unfortunate that the so-called enlightened peoples of the world should be engaged in devoting such a large part of their resources to nonproductive, war-making purposes. The spending of huge sums for national defense is a most serious business. However, I want to be equally frank in saying that I do not see any other solution at the moment. Written history is full of the records of the destruction of peace-loving, unprepared nations by neighbors who were guided by the policy of force of arms. We must meet the situation that is facing us, and I see no way of doing that except by preparing. Huge sums of money must be spent, but that spending must be done in the most businesslike manner possible. There must be no undue waste. Hasty and ill-considered expenditures must be avoided."

Senator Gerald P. Nye of North Dakota inquired whether developments abroad would soon make it possible to abandon a considerable part of the expensive program. "Senator," Marshall responded, "I am sorry that I cannot entertain any such hope at present. My fear is not that I am recommending too much but rather that I may find at some time in the future that I recommended too little. In fact, if I could feel now that I might expect some day to face an investigation for having recommended too much, my mind would be more at rest than it is at present." (Senate Appropriations Committee, *Second Supplemental National Defense Appropriation Bill, 1941,*

Hearings [Washington: GPO, 1940], pp. 21–22.)

Marshall testified on the bill again on August 15, but it was primarily to reiterate what he had said on August 5 and 6. Senate amendments caused the total appropriation to increase slightly. After considerable debate and negotiation between the House and Senate, the bill passed and was signed by the president on September 9, 1940. ★

MEMORANDUM FOR GENERAL SHEDD
Confidential

August 7, 1940
[Washington, D.C.]

Dear Shedd: Mr. McReynolds, of the White House, Acting Executive of the Advisory Defense Commission, telephoned me yesterday in regard to Mr. Joe Harris, who is attached to their group. It seems that Harris had talked to Major Hershey, going over the draft blanks, etc., but that Hershey was going to send some Captain to talk further to Harris. McReynolds says no such officer has shown up.[1]

The point is, this Harris is an expert on election machinery and was the adviser on the procedure for the Social Security set-up. Further, McReynolds is one of the President's confidential advisers. Therefore, it is important that something more than routine notice be taken of this man Harris. Will you please have the proper officer make an appointment with him, see him, get his views, and then talk to me. If we do not follow some such procedure as this, we will be embarrassed by directives, so please protect me against these irritating interruptions.

GCMRL/G. C. Marshall Papers (Pentagon Office, General)

1. William H. McReynolds was secretary and acting executive for the Advisory Committee to the Council of National Defense. Major Lewis B. Hershey, a member of the G-1 staff, had been secretary and executive officer for the Joint Army and Navy Selective Service Committee since 1936.

TO JOHN C. O'LAUGHLIN
Confidential

August 8, 1940
[Washington, D.C.]

Dear Cal: I am sending you confidentially a detailed report on the matter of the Davison Antiaircraft gun and the treatment of Mr. Spear, which you brought to my attention the other day. I would like you to glance through this and then talk to me about it the next time you are down in the Munitions Building.[1]

This is the only specific case you mentioned; therefore it is the only one I could follow through. For the past six or eight months, I have had run down each instance that has come to my attention of a cold or routine front on the part of sub-divisions of the War Department in meeting outside contacts, whether for contracts, inventions, or any other idea or proposal. I have several times followed through on matters brought up in connection with invidious comparisons as to our method of doing business with that of the Navy's. In practically every instance I have found that the conditions are utterly different and the Army problem many times more complicated and difficult to crystallize or bring to a head.

As you probably know from your long experience, an appreciable percentage of disappointed customers resort to many unfair measures to embarrass the section of the War Department concerned. We had glaring examples of this in connection with construction in Panama, and I found it necessary to defend officers who were being destroyed in the mind of the Secretary of War by agents or representatives of firms who did not get the business they wanted. The War Department is by no means perfect in personnel, and there is always the necessity for guarding against the bureaucratic self-satisfied state of mind. However, I find very few traces of it in the present staff, and I have had the Inspector General, not once, but a number of times in the past four months personally search through the Department for evidences of just such conditions.   Faithfully yours,

GCMRL/G. C. Marshall Papers (Pentagon Office, Selected)

1. O'Laughlin, who was the publisher of the *Army and Navy Journal*, returned the report, but it is not in the Marshall papers. He wrote to Lawrence Y. Spear, president of the Electric Boat Company, to tell him some of the army's objections to the Davison gun, all of which, Spear replied, were "just a rehash of the old Ordnance alibis." (O'Laughlin to Spear, August 9, 1940, LC/J. C. O'Laughlin Papers; Spear to O'Laughlin, August 12, 1940, ibid.) See Memorandum for the Chief of Ordnance, July 26, 1940, pp. 277–78.

MEMORANDUM FOR GENERAL MOORE[1]   August 9, 1940
[Washington, D.C.]

Subject: Extension of Airports at Roanoke and Lynchburg, Virginia.

Mr. Woodrum, Chairman of the Deficiency Appropriation Committee of the House, called to see me this morning. He is interested in the development of the Roanoke Airport, and for Senator Glass in the development of the Lynchburg Airport.[2] He is familiar with our policy of restricting national defense arguments in such matters to the Northeast, the Northwest and Southeastern areas. However, Roanoke is on the edge of the Mountains and directly on the route between Nashville and Washington. It seems to me that the extension of the runways at least at Roanoke is of enough importance to give us reason for advocating action.

I wish this looked into as quickly as possible to see what we might do toward increasing the WPA or other allotments for improvement of this field. Specifically, Mr. Woodrum would like to visit both places on Tuesday, with a representative of the War Department, to meet the delegations there and satisfy them that the War Department is considering their interests. I have in mind Major Wilson as being the proper officer to make the trip.[3]

I have seen Wilson and sent him to you GCM[4]

GCMRL/G. C. Marshall Papers (Pentagon Office, Selected)

1. Brigadier General Richard C. Moore, formerly assistant chief of staff for Supply (G-4), had been additional deputy chief of staff since July 22. Moore's new job was to handle all matters pertaining to supply and construction and all Air Corps and Armored Force matters except training and personnel.

2. Clifton A. Woodrum of Virginia was the third-ranking Democrat on the House Appropriations Committee. Senator Carter Glass, also a Virginia Democrat, was the chairman of the Senate Appropriations Committee.

3. Major Arthur R. Wilson was the G-4 officer assigned as liaison to the Federal Works Agency. The War Department Aviation Board inspected the Roanoke airport and recommended against improving the runways or establishing an air unit there. In December Marshall told Wilson: "If you can think of anything else we might do around Roanoke of any character relating to national defense, will you let me know because I would like to accommodate Mr. Woodrum if it is possible to do so." (Marshall Memorandum for Colonel Arthur Wilson, December 9, 1940, GCMRL/G. C. Marshall Papers [Pentagon Office, General].)

4. Marshall probably added this postscript by hand on the original; it had been typed on the carbon copy.

TO MRS. BUTLER AMES
August 16, 1940
[Washington, D.C.]

Dear Fifille: I left Washington suddenly Saturday morning [August 10] by air on an inspection trip around the United States of the troops now in the field for maneuvers—some 300,000. I had not seen my way clear to leave until the last moment, and then only had the prospect of a few days, so I flew direct to Minnesota; reached there at noon, went through some 40,000 troops, and left in the early evening for the West Coast expecting to spend the night at Miles City, Montana. There I sent you a wire, but the weather being favorable for flying I continued on and landed at Fort Lewis, near Tacoma, Washington, at 10:45 the same night. Sunday I inspected some 40,000 troops in the field between Tacoma and Centralia, flying to Portland that night. I stayed with a friend there, who grilled an elaborate supper on the bluff in their grounds overlooking the River. They gave me breakfast at 5:30 and I left at 6 the next morning, and paused near San Francisco to inspect an air base, paused again in southern California at an air base there, and spent the night at El Paso; left there at 6 the next morning and reached the Sabine River region of western Louisiana at noon and went through some 50,000 troops there. I took the air again at 6 the next morning and stopped at Montgomery, Alabama to inspect an Air school, flew to Fort Benning, Georgia, where we have about 20,000 troops, and then made a final flight into Washington, arriving here at 9 P.M. Wednesday.

Yesterday I found a heavy accumulation of business awaiting me and had to spend three hours before a Committee of the Senate, so it was a bad day.[1] Then I had to go to a small dinner, stag, for Senator McNary the Republican Vice-Presidential candidate, but I managed to get away from there at 9:30 and "so to bed."[2] I think I am the one who needs the hospital and a nurse, certainly I would find it very restful to eat a meal in bed.

Katherine has been at Fire Island for several weeks and leaves today for Northwestern Maine with Molly and my Aide and his wife.[3] The plan is for me to fly up there in an amphibian and land on the lake, but I think there is small chance that I will get away. I have to fly up to the maneuvers in Northern New York next week and also to those in Wisconsin, some 100,000 troops in the first affair and 70,000 in the second, I believe.

All of this will probably bore you, but it at least [is] a record of what is happening to me, and notice that you are in my thoughts.[4]   Affectionately,

GCMRL/K. T. Marshall Collection

1. Lieutenant Colonel Orlando Ward, secretary of the General Staff, noted in his diary that Marshall had returned to the office on August 15 "full of ideas." The next day was "an unusually busy day at the office. Got about a dozen directives out in connection with the discoveries that GCM had made on his inspection." (Orlando Ward Diary, August 15 and 16, 1940, photocopy in GCMRL/Research File.)

2. As opposition in Congress to the selective service bill seemed to be growing, the measure's supporters believed that it was important to convince Wendell L. Willkie, the Republican presidential candidate, and his running mate, Senate Minority Leader Charles L. McNary of Oregon, to endorse the bill. After the August 15 dinner, Marshall telephoned Secretary of War Stimson to say that he had talked with the senator and that McNary would vote for the bill. (August 15, 1940, Yale/H. L. Stimson Papers [Diary, 30: 91–92].)

3. Lieutenant Colonel Claude M. Adams, who had recently been promoted, and his wife Ruth, were longtime friends of the Marshalls.

4. Mrs. Ames died September 1. Marshall served as an honorary pallbearer at her funeral in Boston, September 4. (Marshall to Mrs. Reynolds Brown, September 13, 1940, GCMRL/ G. C. Marshall Papers [Pentagon Office, Selected]; *Boston Daily Globe,* September 5, 1940, p. 15.)

To the Editor of the *Oregonian*   August 20, 1940
                                                                  [Washington, D.C.]

Dear Sir: I have just received the editorial published in The Oregonian of August 14, in which there is a short comment devoted to my recent inspection trip.[1] I appreciate the complimentary references to me, but in the interest of facts, I would like to say this:

For months I have been scheduled to inspect each of the Army maneuvers, commencing on the West Coast on August 13th, and then proceeding to Camp Ripley, Minnesota, for the 15th, Louisiana for the 17th, the First Army maneuvers in northern New York on the 19th, and the Second Army maneuvers on the 24th. It became evident that, due to my hearings before Congress and other matters of great moment here in Washington, I would not be able to be absent from the city for such a length of time or on the dates mentioned. As a matter of fact, my decision to take the recent trip was made on Friday afternoon, August 9th when I learned that there would be no hearings before Congress until the following Thursday, the 15th, and that no important decisions would be required in regard to other matters in the interim. The Secretary of War did not know of my proposed departure until four o'clock on that afternoon, and the President, I am quite certain, knew nothing of my departure or plans, and I would not be at all surprised if he still is unaware that I took the trip.

My purpose was solely to learn at first hand something of the conditions of the troops in the field, to talk to the particular officers, get their reactions, find out what their difficulties were, and see what could be done to improve matters.

The interview given to Mr. Hazen in Portland was purely accidental; I saw no other members of the press and he reached me, purely on a basis of past friendship and his acquaintance with Mr. Hamilton Corbett.[2]   Faithfully yours,

GCMRL/G. C. Marshall Papers (Pentagon Office, General)

1. The editorial, entitled "General Marshall's Journey," said: "This page yields to no one in admiration for General Marshall, chief of staff of the United States army. It believes he has the capabilities for being one of the greatest commanders in the history of the American army. But he is a soldier. He takes his orders. And we do not doubt that he was ordered to make his present whirlwind trip around the country, during the course of which he appears to be stopping just long enough at each place to give out interviews on the question of conscription. It is not a question of the general's insincerity. He obviously feels deeply on the subject. And the majority of the people are with him. But the White House and the war department are well aware that such a round-the-country journey by the chief of staff, when the Burke-Wadsworth bill is in its crucial stage, will cause an increase in the telegrams and letters pouring in upon congress. Generals do not make such trips at such critical times without approval and without being under orders."

2. David W. Hazen, a correspondent for the *Oregonian*, and Hamilton F. Corbett—who had given Marshall the supper and breakfast mentioned in Marshall to Mrs. Butler Ames, August 16—were friends from the days when Marshall commanded Vancouver Barracks, Washington. In response to another Portland friend's criticisms of the editorial, Marshall observed: "I was rather sorry that I wrote to The OREGONIAN, though maybe it was just as well I did. I have never before written to any one of the papers in relation to any attack on me, and I would not have written that letter except for the fact that it prefaced the statement by complimentary references, which made it impersonal rather than personal." (Marshall to

Ralph A. Fenton, August 31, 1940, GCMRL/G. C. Marshall Papers [Pentagon Office, Selected].) The *Oregonian* printed Marshall's letter and said, "we apologize for fearing that he had been subjected to such pressure."

CONFERENCE NOTES   August 20, 1940
Secret   [Washington, D.C.]

Conference held in Office Chief of Staff at 12:30 p.m. this date.[1]

"The transfer of the following materiel to the British is O.K.:[2]

 5 B-17 planes, without bomb-sights.
 250,000 Enfield rifles.
 5,000,000 rounds cal. 30 ammunition.

Colonel Stimson understood that the 5 million rounds of cal. .30 ammunition was from the fifty million rounds at ten million a month previously promised the British, which I now consider too essential to our defense to permit the transfer.[3]

                   G. C. M."

  900,000   cal. .30 Springfield
  1,200,000   Enfield
  Army 2,000,000 — need 1,000,000
  Home Guards   500,000

NA/RG 165 (OCS, Foreign Sale or Exchange of Munitions File)

1. Lieutenant Colonel Orlando Ward took these notes.

2. During the negotiations with the British over the exchange of United States destroyers for the right to create military bases in certain British possessions in the Western Hemisphere, the United States agreed to include several additional military items. Under Secretary of State Sumner Welles prepared drafts of an agreement on August 19. At noon the following day, Marshall held a staff discussion of the army's role in the proposed agreement. The memorandum printed here resulted from that meeting. The additional military items were not included in the September 2 destroyers-bases agreement, but they were ultimately furnished. (For further details see Conn and Fairchild, *Framework of Hemisphere Defense*, pp. 52–60.)

3. Marshall had previously urged Secretary of War Stimson to cancel the United States obligation, made in a June 6 agreement, to allocate to the British 50,000,000 rounds of .30 caliber ammuniton from current production. "The critical situation in the Philippines makes further releases to the British Purchasing Commission now impracticable, as the caliber .30 ammunition involved must be diverted to the Philippines to meet in part the urgent requirements of the Commanding General of that Department. I feel therefore that it is imperative that I notify the British Purchasing Commission that the War Department is unable to release any additional caliber .30 ammunition at this time." (Marshall Memorandum [drafted by Major Walter B. Smith] for the Secretary of War, August 7, 1940, NA/RG 165 [OCS, Foreign Sale or Exchange of Munitions File].)

To Lieutenant General Daniel Van Voorhis[1]   August 22, 1940
Secret   [Washington, D.C.]

Dear Van Voorhis: I was glad to receive your detailed letter of August 15.[2] I had been hoping you would write and tell me how things were going.

The reactions you got from the Navy are very interesting to me. Most confidentially, I am enclosing two papers, one a memorandum of mine to Admiral Stark and the other a letter of Admiral Stark to his people on the Canal Zone.[3] I am going to ask you not to show these to anybody. I am sending them merely to show you that your troubles of that incident in the long run would be profitable. But they have produced a decided result, and I hope shortly to have a definite decision on the question of command, establishing you clearly as the actual commander of all forces in that region.

In connection with this, we are now in the business of determining a further extension of your command influence, against the possibility of operations in the Caribbean area. I think it will be necessary to give you a definite leadership in the development of plans down there so that you may control reconnaissance recommendations and studies both of your people and those in Puerto Rico. As soon as our basic Caribbean plans are further developed, particularly from the viewpoint of logistics, I think such operations as are applicable to you will be sent to you in order that all the reconnaissance and detailed plans can be developed by officers who have visited the actual localities concerned. I am sending you this ahead of decisions and before I have seen the recommendations of the War Plans Division. So do not advertise it to your staff.

We are very busy here, a little busier every day; but the decentralization I have gradually been accomplishing, first the sub-division of matters between the two Deputies, and now the decentralization of all unit training to General McNair ensconced at the Headquarters of the GHQ at the Army War College should greatly simplify my problem. If I can do it, I am going to organize myself out of a job.[4]

With warm regards to Mrs. Van Voorhis and my congratulations to you, Faithfully yours,

P.S.   There is a further confidential comment regarding your recent difficulty with the Navy contingent. I might tell you that I used that situation in the abstract to force immediate action by the Military Committee of the House. Without that I probably still would be laboring to get action. Stone's amendment to the bill delayed it at least four months.[5]

GCMRL/G. C. Marshall Papers (Pentagon Office, Selected)

1. Van Voorhis had been promoted to lieutenant general on July 31.
2. The letter from the commander of the Panama Canal Department is not in the Marshall papers.

3. Marshall enclosed a copy of his July 8 Memorandum for Admiral Stark (the gist of which is printed as Memorandum for General Strong, July 3, 1940, p. 259) and a copy of Stark's letter to the commandant of the Fifteenth Naval District in Balboa, Canal Zone. Stark observed in his letter that the army wished the navy to have command in the Alaska area, including command over the army units there. "I mention this just to show how thoroughly Army is playing the game here with us and in fact I think it not an over-statement to say that here in the Department cooperation was never closer, if as close, as it is now. If we had any worry in this connection it would be that the Army some time this Fall will move to another building where we can not be at each other's elbow's for our constant work together on our problems.

"These recent studies led me to inquire into the situation at the Canal where I find command is vested in the Army for the responsibility of joint defense and this seems to me correct. I hope that there is complete pull-together down there so far as we are concerned. Of course in the last analysis we have to take orders from them whether we like it or not, just as we have to do in our own service at times from the top authority. I trust, however, that the spirit of cooperation and absolute loyalty as well as our knowledge of their primary responsibility will result in a happy and efficient team, so far as is possible with the tools at hand. I trust your gang all thoroughly understand this and if not, that you will give it your personal attention to insure it." (Stark to Rear Admiral Frank H. Sadler, July 29, 1940, GCMRL/G. C. Marshall Papers [Pentagon Office, Selected].)

4. A second deputy chief of staff position had been created effective July 22. (See note 1, Memorandum for General Moore, August 9, 1940, p. 289.) The nucleus of General Headquarters had been activated July 26 with Brigadier General Lesley J. McNair as its chief of staff. (For the background of this organization and a discussion of its role and duties, see Kent Roberts Greenfield, Robert R. Palmer, and Bell I. Wiley, *The Organization of Ground Combat Troops*, a volume in the *United States Army in World War II* [Washington: GPO, 1947], pp. 1–15.)

5. See note 2, Marshall to Van Voorhis, July 3, 1940, p. 258.

To Brigadier General Asa L. Singleton
August 27, 1940
[Washington, D.C.]

Dear Singleton: I have just received your letter of August 24th, and am glad to hear what you have to say about the matter of supply.

The searching investigations which I instigated after my return from Benning and other points on my recent inspection trip have developed quite a few valuable points which should be productive of better results in the future. Every time I go into the field I find something of the same nature and invariably the Staff can prove to me that I am wrong; but sooner or later they themselves find a repetition of the same condition. This happened just a few days ago to one of the men who was explaining why there was no shortage at Benning; he ran into a worse shortage at another post which could not be explained away—so I think we are gradually getting organized on a basis that will enable us to handle large numbers of men without the complications and delays of past experience of this nature.[1]   Hastily yours,

GCMRL/G. C. Marshall Papers (Pentagon Office, Selected)

1. Singleton, the commandant of the Infantry School, had written to Marshall that the reported shortages of supplies at Fort Benning were not serious, that remedial action was under way where problems did exist, and that "you have nothing to worry about insofar as relates to clothing and individual equipment of the soldiers at Fort Benning." (Singleton to Marshall, August 24, 1940, GCMRL/G. C. Marshall Papers [Pentagon Office, Selected].) The day after he returned from his inspection trip, Marshall reported to those officials concerned with supply the various problems that he wished investigated and solved. He instructed the quartermaster general to direct his officers at all levels to anticipate the needs of units in the field rather than waiting until they complained of shortages. (Orlando Ward Report of Conference held in the Chief of Staff's office, August 15, 1940, NA/RG 165 [OCS, Chief of Staff Conferences File].)

MEMORANDUM FOR THE PRESIDENT[1]   August 27, 1940
Secret   [Washington, D.C.]

I understand that you have authorized a board of Naval officers to survey the sites for prospective bases in the Newfoundland and Caribbean areas under the proposed arrangement with Great Britain.[2]

Since the close-in defense of these bases, as well as Army air fields in the same localities will be the responsibility of the Army, I think it desirable that there be representatives of the Army on this board. I do not know how large a group you have under consideration, but I suggest that Brigadier General Edmund L. Daley (now in command in Puerto Rico) and Lieutenant Colonel Harold F. Loomis, War Plans Division of the General Staff, be included in the membership of this board.

GCMRL/G. C. Marshall Papers (Pentagon Office, Selected)

1. Marshall wrote this memorandum for Secretary of War Stimson's signature.

2. The destroyers-bases agreement was contained in an exchange of notes between British Ambassador Lord Lothian and Secretary of State Cordell Hull on September 2, 1940. The ambassador's note stipulated that Great Britain would "make available to the United States for immediate establishment and use naval and air bases and facilities for entrance thereto and the operation and protection thereof" in Newfoundland, Bermuda, Jamaica, St. Lucia, Trinidad, Antigua, and British Guiana "free from all rent" for ninety-nine years. (Department of State, *Foreign Relations of the United States: Diplomatic Papers, 1940,* 5 vols. [Washington: GPO, 1955–61], 3: 73–74.) Secretary Hull's note declared that the United States would immediately transfer fifty destroyers. In addition, "the Government of the United States will immediately designate experts to meet with experts designated by His Majesty's Government to determine upon the exact location of the naval and air bases mentioned." (Ibid., 3: 74–75.)

MEMORANDUM FOR THE SECRETARY OF WAR August 28, 1940
[Washington, D.C.]

At the sudden request of the State Department Colonel Maguire was sent there at 3 P.M. yesterday to be present at a discussion reference Canadian use of Greenland.[1]

Colonel Maguire informed Mr. Berle of State Department that the War Department had no objections to the Canadians using Greenland as a ferrying station across the Atlantic, and that it was a matter for the State Department to decide. Mr. Berle gave the impression that he was surprised that the War Department did not object.[2]

However, the matter was discussed and as it now stands the Canadians are authorized to investigate the feasibility of using Greenland as a ferrying station. As we now understand it, ships could not land stocks of gas and oil on the east coast of Greenland before next spring.

GCMRL/G. C. Marshall Papers (Pentagon Office, Selected)

1. Lieutenant Colonel Hamilton E. Maguire (U.S.M.A., 1916) was a member of the Intelligence section (G-2) of the General Staff.

2. Adolf A. Berle, Jr., assistant secretary of state, observed in his diary that the problem with the British-Canadian plan was: "If planes can go East that way they can likewise come West; and I'm not enthusiastic about developing an air route which might be used by an enemy to make trouble for us. Also, we have pretty sincerely tried to keep Greenland out of this. And of course the moment it becomes an air ferry station, we should have to contemplate the possibility that the Germans might try to interrupt the place. This brings in the Monroe Doctrine with a vengeance and I regard it as possibly crucial." Moreover, he believed that "if anybody has a base in Greenland I prefer that we do." (*Navigating the Rapids, 1918-1971: From the Papers of Adolf A. Berle*, ed. Beatrice Bishop Berle and Travis Beal Jacobs [New York: Harcourt Brace Jovanovich, 1973], pp. 331-32.) See *Foreign Relations, 1940*, 2: 352-76; and Stetson Conn, Rose C. Engelman, and Byron Fairchild, *Guarding the United States and Its Outposts*, a volume in the *United States Army in World War II* (Washington: GPO, 1964), pp. 442-58.

TO LIEUTENANT GENERAL CHARLES D. HERRON[1] August 28, 1940
Confidential Washington, D.C.

Dear Herron: I have appreciated very much your letters and notes keeping me generally advised of the situation.[2]

As to "the alert", what is your frank reaction? Do you think it is imposing too heavy a tax to continue on the present basis? In Panama the condition is much more difficult. We have had to give them about $300,000 to construct temporary shelters for the numerous antiaircraft stations in the high hills. The rainy season makes life under these circumstances very difficult, but I do not feel that we can expose ourselves to the risks of a sudden lunge from some unexpected quarter. It is a very difficult business and I am deeply concerned that we do not exhaust the morale of the command by heavy requirements during what is supposed to be a period of peace, yet a failure would be catastrophic.

Let me have your frank opinion.[3]   Faithfully yours,

GCMRL/G. C. Marshall Papers (Pentagon Office, Selected)

1. As commanding general of the Hawaiian Department, Herron had been promoted to lieutenant general on July 31, 1940.

2. On June 10 the Japanese and Soviet governments announced that they had concluded an agreement settling the disputed border between Outer Mongolia and Manchuria that had recently caused serious fighting between them. (*Foreign Relations, 1940*, 1: 641–42.) The Hawaiian Department had been ordered to go on alert status on June 17 because the War Department deduced that the "recent Japanese-Russian agreement to compose their differences in the Far East was arrived at and so timed as to permit Japan to undertake a trans-Pacific raid against Oahu, following the departure of the U.S. Fleet from Hawaii." (War Plans Division draft—marked "not used"—of Marshall to Herron, June 27, 1940, NA/RG 165 [WPD, 4326].) A month later Herron had been authorized to relax the alert except for training air patrols and precautions against sabotage, which "will be continued on the basis of instant readiness." (Marshall to Herron, July 16, 1940, NA/RG 165 [WPD, 4322].)

3. Herron replied: "My absolutely frank and honest opinion is that 'the alert' as now carried on here does not dull the keen edge, or exhaust morale. . . . As things now are, I feel that you need not have this place on your mind at all." (Herron to Marshall, September 6, 1940, GCMRL/G. C. Marshall Papers [Pentagon Office, Selected].)

TO ROBERT R. MCCORMICK   August 28, 1940
                                                           [Washington, D.C.]

Dear Colonel McCormick: Thanks for your comments on the TRIBUNE editorial "Negroes in the Army."[1]

The negro strength of the Regular Army is being more than doubled and will include a new regiment of Field Artillery, one of Engineers, two anti-aircraft artillery battalions, and a number of smaller units. The older regiments are organized and functioning definitely on a combat basis. Even so, the problem is a delicate one and a constant, almost daily embarrassment to the War Department.[2] I appreciate, therefore, all the more your attitude. Faithfully yours,

GCMRL/G. C. Marshall Papers (Pentagon Office, General)

1. The August 16 *Chicago Daily Tribune* editorial (p. 12) castigated the army for discriminating against black soldiers. "The army's prejudice against colored troops is only one of its numerous stupidities that should be abandoned in the interest of sound national defense." McCormick, the newspaper's publisher, told Marshall that the editorial had been printed in his absence. (McCormick to Marshall, August 21, 1940, GCMRL/G. C. Marshall Papers [Pentagon Office, General].) No copy of McCormick's comments on the editorial was found in the Marshall papers.

2. A total number of 4,595 enlisted men were to be added with these units. "The War

Department is of the opinion that the above action will remove any criticism of prejudicial treatment of the Negro race by the Army." (Marshall Memorandum for [Acting Secretary of War] Mr. Johnson, July 6, 1940, GCMRL/G. C. Marshall Papers [Pentagon Office, Selected].)

TO GENERAL MALIN CRAIG September 3, 1940
[Washington, D.C.]

Dear Malin: I received your very fine and affecting note of August 31st Saturday evening, and wired you immediately my appreciation, but I wish you to be certain how much I really do appreciate your writing.[1]

This first year has been hectic. As a matter of fact, it is a little more than a year because the circus began July 1st with what I thought was a pretty full blast at that time. The Fall was busy and packed with new things, and the winter seemed more so; but the last two weeks have been without precedent.

You were good enough to predict that the coming twelve months will not be so hard, but I rather anticipate the next three months as being the hardest of all because it will be the first experience of a troop concentration of the National Guard, and probably compulsory service trainees in time of peace. With the full liberty of the press and with no repression as in 1917, we are going to have a hard time meeting the captious criticisms that are bound to develop. However, I will continue to follow your scheme of "doing my damndest and to hell with the result".

With my thanks again, and love and affection to you both   Faithfully yours,

GCMRL/G. C. Marshall Papers (Pentagon Office, Selected)

1. In his letter Craig observed that he had reviewed Marshall's first year as chief of staff: "I . . . am sure that you have made no mistakes and feel that you have handled yourself and your problems very wonderfully. You have the confidence of Congress and altogether, you can not have many regrets. I fully believe that this first year has been harder and more upsetting, than the next years will be." (Craig to Marshall, August 31, 1940, GCMRL/G. C. Marshall Papers [Pentagon Office, Selected].)

TO MAJOR GENERAL CAMPBELL KING September 5, 1940
[Washington, D.C.]

Dear King: I have just this moment read your letter of September 2d, with the query regarding your nephew Mitchell, and his desire to enter an Officer's Training Camp.[1] At the present time, there are no prospects of an Officer's Training Camp. We have more than enough Reserve Officers, products of the ROTC since 1920, to fill the requirements of an army of more than one million men—as a matter of fact, the first assignments for two million, but not the replacements.

The first step toward the commissioning of additional men other than out of the ROTC will, according to present plans of the War Department, be Candidate Schools—at Benning, Sill, Riley, etc., the men selected from the ranks. I do not know that there will be any more Officer's Training Camps of the old type. In the first place, it is impossible to put into three months what an ROTC graduate gets in four years, including a six months' camp; and in the next place, the whole Reserve Corps is aligned against such procedure. Tremendous pressure is brought on the War Department from both directions, and particularly from the sons of very prominent people who had hitherto taken no interest in national defense. It is a very difficult thing to handle.

A couple of weeks ago I went around the United States within a few days, and after returning to Washington for a few days, had to fly out to the maneuvers in Wisconsin; yesterday I flew to Boston.

Katherine got back from Maine for the Labor Day week-end and is with me now. Molly got back as far as New York. I will give them your message.

With my love to you both,   Faithfully yours,

GCMRL/G. C. Marshall Papers (Pentagon Office, Selected)

1. King had retired from the army in 1933 and was living in North Carolina. He had written to ask "if any provision now exists for accepting volunteer candidates for Officers Training Camps or what future plans the War Department has for this purpose." (King to Marshall, September 2, 1940, GCMRL/G. C. Marshall Papers [Pentagon Office, General].)

MEMORANDUM FOR GENERAL BRYDEN   September 6, 1940
[Washington, D.C.]

The "scrambler" for disguising telephone messages, which is being set up in each Corps Area Headquarters and is to be set up here in the War Department is now ready for installation here. It is a box 10 x 30 inches long and about 6 inches higher than the top of my desk. It should be near a wall plug. The question is where to have it installed.

With these "scramblers" we can conduct conversations with reasonable privacy with each of the Corps Area Commanders. Also, with the more complicated and difficult to decipher trans-Atlantic "scrambler" installed in Panama and Anchorage and in Seattle, we can superimpose our privacy scrambled effect on the more complicated scrambler and produce a still more difficult situation for anybody to decipher—this is not entirely the word for a telephone conversation, but it conveys my meaning.

Will you think over where this box might be placed. They supposed it would go in my office, but I do not know as that would be the most desirable place to have it.[1]

GCMRL/G. C. Marshall Papers (Pentagon Office, Selected)

1. The Bell Telephone Laboratory device was installed in Deputy Chief of Staff William Bryden's office, where it was tested on September 18. Other "scramblers" were soon installed in Orlando Ward's and Richard C. Moore's offices. ("Test of New Telephone Device," September 18, 1940, NA/RG 165 [OCS, Chronological, Miscellaneous].)

To Major General Claude V. Birkhead   September 9, 1940
[Washington, D.C.]

Dear Birkhead: I received your note of September 3d, enclosing a memorandum of comments to your brigade, regimental, and separate unit commanders following the Maneuvers. I had not seen General Williams' red ball letter, but I can guess what he had to say. I was much interested in reading your comments, and appreciate your very positive endeavor to quiet down the unfortunate effect of all these unnecessary and baseless rumors.[1]

I find that about three quarters of my time is occupied in meeting such things, not only as to the Guard but as to production of equipment, as to selective service, and as to every phase of national defense; it is a very difficult business.

My first objective is to see a genuine team developed, but it is a terrific job under the give and take procedure of a democracy. Just at present we are struggling with the uncertainties of selective service, when we will obtain the money for their training and shelter, and other matters of that kind. Fortunately I was able to squeeze in at the last moment in the munitions program appropriation of five billion, the money required for the construction of shelter for the National Guard. You can imagine how difficult it has been to make the necessary preparations under the conditions of uncertainty and lack of funds, and at the same time to guard against the inevitable assaults that would be or will be made if there should be any delay in conforming to a tentative schedule discussed before Congress a long time ago on the basis that definite action both as to authorizations and as to funds would be taken without the long delays that have since developed. However, I think we are getting the situation in hand, but the first requirement is that we have a team, and I thank you for your contribution to that idea.   Faithfully yours,

GCMRL/G. C. Marshall Papers (Pentagon Office, General)

1. Birkhead, commanding general of the Thirty-sixth Division, Texas National Guard, had sent his subordinates a memorandum congratulating them on the progress the division had made in its training. He also noted that Major General John F. Williams, chief of the National Guard Bureau, had recently sent Guard commanders a letter suggesting that he had heard numerous false rumors and unjust criticisms of the Regular Army were circulating. In his memorandum, Birkhead said that the rumors that the Regular Army intended to use rigorous physical examinations to eliminate the Guard's higher commanders and that it intended to destroy the Guard, after its mobilization, by highly critical inspection reports were without foundation. He directed his commanders to instruct their officers to "prevent the building up of unfounded apprehensions and resentments which, if they exist, will in themselves have a very adverse effect on our efforts for National Defense. I cannot conceive of gentlemen of the high standard of the officers of our Army doing so dishonorable a thing and one so subversive of real National Defense. On the contrary, I believe that the Army is going to do its best to shoot square over the table with the Guard and not repeat the mistakes of the World War which sent so many civilian officers out of the service with bitter resentment towards the Regular Army." (Birkhead Memorandum to Brigade, Regimental, and Separate Unit Commanders, August 31, 1940, GCMRL/G. C. Marshall Papers [Pentagon Office, General].)

MEMORANDUM FOR ADMIRAL HAROLD R. STARK September 10, 1940
[Washington, D.C.]

I have given considerable thought to your telephone call of the 6th, and in order that you may have a better understanding of the problem, I feel that I should give you in some detail the space situation within the War Department.

A year ago a careful study was made of the space requirements for the War Department in the event of an emergency. It showed a requirement for 805,000 additional square feet. These requirements were sent to the Public Buildings Administration in September 1939, in order that our needs might be anticipated.

In early June of this year, the Commissioner of the Public Buildings Administration informed us of the plan to allocate the Social Security and Railroad Retirement Buildings, about September 1st, to the War Department, but no mention was made of releasing space in the Munitions Building to the Navy. When the official notice of the above assignment was received, it carried the proviso that the Advisory Committee for National Defense would also be accommodated in these buildings. Since that time the office of the Administrator for Export Control has been created and we are also taking care of the requirements of that office. These two activities will reduce our allotment accordingly. To further curtail the War Department space by releasing some 250,000 square feet in the Munitions Building to the Navy would reduce to approximately half the amount of space essential for the present expansion.

When the question of penthouses for both the Munitions and Navy buildings was raised, our representative indicated that our requirements would still not be satisfied, while on the other hand the Navy representative stated the penthouses would meet the Navy requirements.

The plan to release a part of the Munitions Building to the Navy was made before the War Department representative had an opportunity to calculate the effect of such arrangement. Also, at that time the Selective Service legislation and the legislation for calling the National Guard into active service were in the formative stage, and we could not be at all certain that this legislation would be enacted. Now that this legislation has become law, the War Department is faced with a situation which demands the full 805,000 square feet beyond the entire space of the Munitions Building and its penthouses.[1]

Offices of the War Department are now housed in eleven separate and widely separated buildings. When we occupy the Social Security and Railroad Retirement Buildings, the number of separate buildings will be reduced to seven. The effect of this dispersion will be evident to you. As it is, we must now move the entire establishments of The Quartermaster General and the Chief of Ordnance out of this building, a very serious interference with the transaction of reorganization business at the present moment. If we should be directed finally to turn over the three wings to your Department, it would mean moving the offices of the Chiefs of Infantry, Cavalry and Field Artillery and Coast Artillery away from the General Staff, with whom they are in almost hourly conferences these days when the military establishment is being tremendously enlarged, put into the field and started on the new experiment of selective service. These departments would have to go to some other building, and I understand there is no space, even reasonably convenient, available.

Another factor in our difficulties is the delay encountered in the completion of the Social Security and Railroad Retirement Buildings. They were supposed to be completed by September 1st, but now since the Social Security Building may not be available until as late as December 1st, the Secretary of War has decided that his office must remain in this building. With our new building due for completion on July 1st, 1941, to move the Secretary of War and my office in December would mean a succession of interrupting moves.

Any plan to give the Navy space at this particular time in the Munitions Building places the entire burden on the War Department, which is already suffering seriously from an unfortunate dispersion. I am sorry I cannot find a solution which would permit an adjustment more favorable to you.

GCMRL/G. C. Marshall Papers (Pentagon Office, Selected)

1. The joint resolution permitting the federalization of the National Guard (S. J. Res. 286) had been approved on August 27. The Selective Compulsory Military Training and Service

Bill had passed the Senate (58–31) on August 28 and the House (263–149) on September 7. At the time Marshall wrote this memorandum, the bill was in a conference committee. On September 14 the committee's report was accepted by both houses and the compromise bill was sent to the president, who signed it at a September 16 ceremony.

MEMORANDUM FOR MR. LOWELL MELLETT[1]   September 10, 1940
[Washington, D.C.]

My dear Mr. Mellett: I am worried over the problem of the possibility of the Selective Service Act being made effective without an immediately available background of publicity, calculated to dignify the position of the prospective trainee—as was so successfully managed in 1917.

In the Selective Service Section of the War Department, they have prepared data for pamphlets, questionnaires, etc.; but what I am interested in is a much more extensive publicity service, geared ready to go into action as soon as the law becomes effective.

I would appreciate your looking over the attached notes.[2]

GCMRL/G. C. Marshall Papers (Pentagon Office, General)

1. Mellett was a special assistant to the president and director of the Office of Government Reports.
2. The editors have not found these attachments.

MEMORANDUM FOR ASSISTANT CHIEF   September 12, 1940
OF STAFF, G-3 [ANDREWS]   [Washington, D.C.]

Subject: Skiing.

Attached is a memorandum submitted to me personally by Mr. Dole, Chairman of the National Ski Patrol, who has been in contact with Colonel Huebner in your Section, and with the Chief of Infantry's Office. Mr. Dole came to me through the efforts of Mr. Palmer, Special Assistant to the Secretary of War, and is very highly spoken of. He is evidently quite a person, and the organization is not a fly-by-night affair.[1]

I do not see our way clear at the moment to entering into the ski business on a large scale, but I do think that we ought to approach this from two points of view. In the first place, for troops like the First Division at Devens, those at Ethan Allen, the Third Division in the Northwest, and possibly those in Alaska, and in other units in the northern latitude of central United States, the problem of morale during the winter is going to be a difficult one. Skiing with proper instructors and with available equipment would be very helpful to morale, and for that reason alone it merits serious attention. The matter of the proper type of equipment, its availability; the question of suitable instructors, etc. could easily be arranged through this organization.

In the second place, I should think that the First Division and the Third Division might well receive some ski training, in view of possible missions— particularly the First Division in regard to Canada. The same thing holds with the 44th Division to be concentrated at Dix, though the first problem there is purely one of hardening and seasoning the people. Later on as the winter develops, it might be well to start week-end skiing detachments for instruction at some camp selected in the Adirondacks or other available region. In due time, after the straight or disciplinary training has gotten under way, but this winter, a more extensive skiing program could be gotten under way. Confidentially, we also have the possibility of some duty in Greenland; we have right now the possibility of having to send a battalion of infantry to Newfoundland. This last unit will undoubtedly have a very hard time for quarters and anything that would pick up morale would be very important.

I do not want to embarrass you with my reaction, so please go ahead as seems wise to your section. My interest in the first place is with regard to morale, especially for the troops in the northern latitude.[2]

GCMRL/G. C. Marshall Papers (Pentagon Office, General)

1. The chief of the Training Branch was Lieutenant Colonel Clarence R. Huebner. Arthur E. Palmer, a young lawyer from Secretary of War Stimson's New York City law firm, was a special assistant to the secretary. C. Minot Dole, also from New York City, was chairman of the National Ski Patrol Committee, a branch of the National Ski Association of America; he had met with Marshall on September 12. Marshall did not retain a copy of Dole's memorandum volunteering the patrol's assistance in organizing winter training and recreation.

2. Marshall soon directed the Training and Operations, Supply, and War Plans divisions to begin planning, estimates, and instructions for winter training and equipment. (Lieutenant Colonel Orlando Ward Memorandum for the Assistant Chiefs of Staff, G-3, G-4, WPD, October 10, 1940, NA/RG 165 [OCS, 21112–13].) See Memorandum for G-3, May 16, 1941, pp. 510–11.

To Brigadier General Edmund L. Daley[1]　　　　September 13, 1940
[Washington, D.C.]

Dear Daley:　I have treated you to a long silence, though it has been in my mind to write to you quite frequently. The truth is, you must take it as a compliment that you hear so little from me, because I have a feeling of great confidence in your handling of the job in Puerto Rico.

The other day we were within a few minutes of dispatching a radio to you to come to Washington immediately on temporary duty. I was going to put you on this joint Army and Navy board for the survey of bases between Newfoundland and Trinidad. However, things moved too rapidly and I only had a few hours in which to get together the Army representation; so Devers was selected.[2] He has been to Bermuda and leaves for Newfoundland tonight.

I do not know when I will get to Puerto Rico but I am very anxious to see how you are progressing. It has just been barely possible for me to get around the United States by air in order to keep track of the expansion now under way—which is really very extensive particularly as to schools and as to new divisions and construction. The first increment of the National Guard goes out on Monday and that will mean another series of pressing events, particularly as to shelter and expedition of training.

Next week we will alter the organization—really just a deliberate step in the program we have had under way for some time—by removing from the corps areas any responsibility for the training of units. We are organizing tactical corps, removing army commanders from corps area affairs, and heading up the whole business under General McNair at the head of the GHQ, now at the War College. He is taking over a large part of the faculty and we have added to it selected officers; I think he will be able to exercise a profound influence on both training and leadership.

I wish you would write me a little informally and tell me how things are progressing, and also to assure me that you have not felt neglected by my long silence.   Faithfully yours,

GCMRL/G. C. Marshall Papers (Pentagon Office, Selected)

1. Daley had been commanding general of the Puerto Rican Department since its activation on July 1, 1939.

2. Brigadier General Jacob L. Devers (U.S.M.A., 1909) had been chief of staff of the Panama Canal Department until July 1940. He served on the presidential board for the selection of air and naval base sites in the Atlantic until October 9, 1940.

MEMORANDUM FOR GENERAL MOORE   September 14, 1940
[Washington, D.C.]

At the Cabinet meeting yesterday, there was a considerable discussion of housing. The Secretary of War wishes to have a full resumé of what we have done or are doing in this respect and how far we have gone.

The discussion in the Cabinet covered the possible methods of obtaining cheap housing. The only matter with which the President was concerned was that such construction should be as economical as possible and that the interest of our expenditures be protected as far as possible. He suggested the usefulness of discussions with Mr. John Carmody.[1]

Will you please get this under way. It may be that the Secretary will wish to talk to you about it when he returns Monday.

GCMRL/G. C. Marshall Papers (Pentagon Office, Selected)
1. John M. Carmody was the administrator of the Federal Works Agency.

MEMORANDUM FOR GENERAL SHEDD

September 14, 1940
[Washington, D.C.]

At the Cabinet meeting yesterday the President stated that he had been troubled by representations of the negroes that their race under the draft was limited to labor battalions. He has been informed by Army authorities that it is contemplated giving the negroes proportionate shares in all branches of the Army, in the proper ratio to their population—approximately 10%. He suggests that steps be taken by the War Department, in conjunction with the Navy Department, to publicize this fact.

The Secretary of War wishes an exact statement of the facts in the case, and as to how far we can go in the matter.[1]

GCMRL/G. C. Marshall Papers (Pentagon Office, Selected)
1. Black-army relations are further treated on pp. 336–39.

MEMORANDUM FOR MR. MARTYN[1]
Confidential

September 14, 1940
[Washington, D.C.]

At the cabinet meeting yesterday the question of importation of Jamaican negroes by the Canal Zone authorities was discussed. The President is unwilling to consent at present to the importation of further Jamaicans. He suggests that the authorities in the Canal Zone notify the President of Panama that unless the strikers go back to work we will have to import negroes from Jamaica by a fixed near date. He predicts that will settle the strike.[2]

This business is not in my department, so I am passing it on to you to be put into the proper channel. However, the result of it is a matter of deep concern to me, particularly any turbulence that might develop, which is a purely military question.

I will give a copy of this to Colonel Morrison Stayer, of Governor Edgerton's staff, who is now in town and who has been charged, I understand, with the presentation of this phase of the Canal problem in Washington.[3]

GCMRL/G. C. Marshall Papers (Pentagon Office, Selected)

1. John W. Martyn was the War Department's administrative assistant and chief clerk.
2. A strike began on September 5 among workers clearing land for a new set of locks for the Panama Canal at Gatun. Most of the men, who were Panamanians protesting over wages and food, were back at work by September 9. (*New York Times,* September 7, p. 6, and September 10, 1940, p. 3.)
3. Morrison C. Stayer was the chief health officer and Colonel Glen E. Edgerton (U.S.M.A., 1908) was the governor of the Panama Canal Zone. Both were Regular Army men scheduled to be promoted to brigadier general on October 1, 1940.

TO MAJOR GENERAL ROY D. KEEHN September 14, 1940
[Washington, D.C.]

Dear Keehn: I have held your letter of September 10th for a couple of days in a mental effort to see if I could meet your wishes. I am sorry that I cannot.[1]

My situation is so difficult at the present time, so exceedingly hard to handle, that I must not complicate it by engagements which would be a great embarrassment to those making the arrangements, as well as to me if something turned up to prevent my appearance. For example, I was due in Fort Knox today on an inspection, which I had to set for Saturday—with all its ill effects on morale—because the Chairman of the Military Committee of the House was most insistent that I appear with him this evening at Louisville. All of that I had to wash out this morning.

I am involved in a number of important changes in the figures of a program of about a billion and a half which I have to justify before the Appropriations Committee of the House Monday morning. I was to have appeared Friday, it was postponed until Saturday; now the estimates have had to be changed, for reasons which I cannot mention, and all of this calculation I have to get in my head in time to appear reasonably well informed on Monday morning. This business goes on continuously in relation to a wide number of matters, and I just am not able to make any plans in advance.[2]

I will do this—keep your date in mind, and see if at the time I can get there, can work it in with some inspection trip, and can put in an appearance, but I must not be featured. I am sorry. Faithfully yours,

GCMRL/G. C. Marshall Papers (Pentagon Office, Selected)

1. Keehn had written on September 4 inviting the chief of staff to the early October dedication of the Illinois National Guard's new airplane hangar. Marshall replied on September 6 that, given the "heavier and heavier demands" of daily business, he did "not dare accept." Keehn wrote on September 10 of his disappointment with this decision, as the dedication would be one of his last official acts before he was relieved as commanding general of the Thirty-third Division. (All documents are in GCMRL/G. C. Marshall Papers [Pen-

tagon Office, Selected].)

2. Marshall's House testimony in support of the $1,589,056,538 third supplemental appropriation bill for fiscal year 1941 was delayed until Thursday, September 19. The money was requested primarily to cover the costs of: (1) calling the National Guard into federal service; (2) inducting, training, and equipping the men to be drafted; (3) providing certain critical and essential items for expanding the army by an additional 200,000, to a total of 1,400,000 enlisted men, by the end of June 1941—including increasing the Air Corps from 95,000 to 160,000 men; and (4) speeding the production of aircraft for the Air Corps' new fifty-four-combat-group program. (House Appropriations Committee, *Third Supplemental National Defense Appropriation Bill for 1941, Hearings* [Washington: GPO, 1940], pp. 31–42.) With certain minor amendments, this bill was passed by Congress and approved by the president on October 8.

C.B.S. RADIO ADDRESS ON SELECTIVE SERVICE[1] September 16, 1940
Washington, D.C.

This afternoon President Roosevelt gave the final approval to the act of Congress creating a system of selective service for compulsory military training, a great fundamental stride toward the preparation of this country to defend itself, to protect its form of government and its compelling interests in the Western Hemisphere. *This morning* some 60,000 citizen-soldiers of the National Guard left comfortable homes, their families and their jobs to fulfill their patriotic mission as members of the Army of the United States.

Within the next ten days most of these troops will concentrate in *divisional* camps in New Jersey, South Carolina, Oklahoma, and the State of Washington, to start on a period of intensive military training. Along the East and West Coasts of the United States, Harbor Defense and other units of the Guard will move into camps and commence their training in the handling of heavy seacoast guns and smaller weapons. Antiaircraft regiments will assemble at special firing centers to commence practical training in this vital service. National Guard air squadrons of observation planes will move to air fields to perfect their coordinated training with other branches of the Army.

I wish to emphasize the *importance* of these preparations. We are at *peace* with every nation in the world. *Nevertheless* it is the feeling of the War Department that the next six months *include the possibility* of being the most critical period in the history of this nation. Ordinary common sense indicates that our preparations should be made accordingly.

The situation today is utterly different from that of 1917. *Then* we were at war—but we foresaw small possibility of military danger to this country. *Today* though at peace, such a possibility trembles on the verge of becoming a probability. *Then* we could proceed with deliberation. We could wait until we built cantonments, until we first trained officers later to train the men, until we were prepared to form a field Army. We did not need to worry about arms, equipment and ammunition—our Allies were prepared to supply those necessities.

Today time is at a premium and modern arms and equipment must be provided by our *own* industries—not by allies. We must be prepared to stand alone. We cannot depend on others for protection during a prolonged period of preparation.

Therefore, the mobilization this morning of the first increment of the National Guard is the *first long step* in the preparation of an adequate Army of citizen-soldiers to man our defenses.

Testifying before a Congressional Committee last February, I made the statement that our preparations for defense should be carried out in an orderly, businesslike manner, proceeding step by step, in accordance with the major developments abroad; that if Europe blazed in the late Spring or Summer, we must put our house in order before the sparks reached the Western Hemisphere. Even so, it must be admitted that I only partially visualized the full extent of the conflagration, and the rapidity with which it was to overwhelm the Continent of Europe. Yet, at the time, there was severe criticism of that statement as being unnecessarily alarming.

Today the public and the press are demanding action, immediate and all-inclusive, and there is a general appreciation of the hazards of our situation. But I fear that there is not so clear an understanding of just what is required in order to produce the desired results.

The time-consuming process in manufacturing materiel—planes, guns, tanks, and other munitions—is partially comprehended, though impatience and forebodings are productive of demands for miracles to overcome delays due to past public indifference.

Also, I fear that we expect *too much of machines.* We fail to realize two things: First, that the finest plane or tank or gun in the world is literally worthless without technicians trained as soldiers—*hardened, seasoned, and highly disciplined* to maintain and operate it; and second, that success in combat depends primarily upon the development of the trained combat team composed of all arms. This battle team is the most difficult, the most complicated of all teams to create, because it must operate on unknown ground, in darkness, as well as in daylight, amidst incredible confusion, danger, hardship, and discouragements. It is a team of many parts, the decisive element of which remains the same little-advertised, hard-bitten foot soldier with his artillery support.

From a foreign source, a distinguished veteran of the recent fighting, we get this comment: "Wars are still fought by men even though they use elaborate weapons. Troops of all kinds must therefore have physical fitness and toughness that will guarantee their vitality and endurance under prolonged strain."

A German general staff officer is credited with this summary of that army's recent campaign. He stated: "Our success is due to close team work between the air force, armored troops, motorized engineers and infantry. Of course the infantry must finally hold the ground, but all others help to bring it up. Our methods are simple in the extreme; they are understood by every soldier in the Army. Our foot infantry is the best in the world. Their principal job is marching, and *the job of every other arm* is to keep them marching forward into enemy land." "We move," he says, "on a broad front with armored divisions and air force. Where the initial resistance is too strong for the armored troops to penetrate, it is broken by dive bombers and additional artillery. The way must be cleared for the infantry with whom the final decision lies. This requires perfect communication and coordination between arms; further, it requires a singleness of command and purpose." He is describing a highly-organized team, a balanced team, in contrast to a few highly developed specialties each operating somewhat according to its own theory of combat.

The War Department has carefully followed the development of the War in Europe for the purpose of analyzing the reasons for the success of one army or the failure of another. The importance of specialized training is apparent to all observers, but the tremendous importance of seasoned soldiers, welded into a perfect team is the outstanding impression. There is no royal road to such training. It cannot be obtained by reading books or sitting in barracks. The only way we can prepare ourselves for the future is to get out in the open, in all kinds of weather, and take advantage of the lessons forced on nations who are less fortunately situated.

The original recommendation of the War Department that this *first* increment of the National Guard be ordered into active service last July, was based on the necessity for hurrying to develop a *special, seasoned* reenforcement for the small body of mobile troops of the Regular Army available in Continental United States. *Today,* the entry of this portion of the National Guard on active duty must also serve another purpose. These divisions, these regiments and squadrons that joined the active Army of the United States this morning, must prepare themselves as quickly as possible to receive and train their portion of the young men selected under the democratic terms of the new law just given force and effect by the signature of the President.

Both the troops of the Regular establishment and those of the National Guard must absorb in their ranks the men of the Selective Service Act and give them their military training. *Furthermore,* thousands of officers of the Reserve Corps, mainly products of the ROTC in our colleges and universities, are either on active duty or are being called to such duty to provide the necessary additional leaders. *In other words,* the National Defense Act of 1920, the lesson of our lack of preparation in 1917 and 1918, is being put into effect in a progressive, business-like manner. The Selective Service Act has added the final touch of authority to enable America to go to work effectively at the business of preparing herself against the uncertainties, the threatening dangers of the immediate future.

The consummation of the War Department plans must be governed by the speed with which adequate shelter can be provided. *Until* funds *were made available* the Department could only *plan* for such important details. Now the problem is the prompt completion of temporary hospitals, sewage and water systems, buildings and other necessities of healthful life. So long as the international situation permits, we will proceed *only* as rapidly as adequate shelter can be provided. In turn, the trainees under the Selective Service Act will be called out only as rapidly as units of the Regular Establishment and National Guard are prepared to receive them—both from the viewpoint of training and of shelter—the first increment probably about the middle of November.

October 15th it is planned to order a second increment of the National Guard to join the active Army—the 27th Division from New York, the 37th Division of Ohio, the 32d Division from Michigan and Wisconsin, and air squadrons of observation planes from New York, Michigan and Mississippi. Also included will be the entire National Guard of Puerto Rico and Hawaii.

For years the National Guard has been preparing for service in the event of a great national emergency. *Today* that emergency is recognized, and the first of these troops of citizen-soldiers *have reported* for duty. Their task is most difficult. They must establish themselves in camp and in the shortest possible time season and prepare their small nucleus of men—about thirty per cent of full strength—to receive and train treble their number.

This means long hours of arduous work. For the officers and non-commissioned officers it means not only hard physical work but also intensive daily study of the manuals covering the latest technique in warfare. It is only through discomfort and fatigue that progress can be made toward the triumph of mind and muscles over the softness of the life to which we have all become accustomed.

All this not only takes time, but requires wholehearted effort. It demands a standard of discipline which will prevail over fatigue, hunger, confusion, or disaster. Given the opportunity to prepare himself, the American makes the finest soldier in the world, and for the first time in our history we are beginning in time of peace to prepare against the possibility of war. We are starting to train an army of citizen-soldiers which may save us from the tragedy of war.

If we are strong enough, *peace, democracy,* and our American way of life should be the reward.

GCMRL/G. C. Marshall Papers (Pentagon Office, Speeches)

1. Marshall delivered this address over the Columbia Broadcasting System's Washington, D.C., affiliate WJSV at 10:15 P.M. This speech was printed in the *Army and Navy Journal* of September 21, 1940, pp. 78–82.

MEMORANDUM FOR THE SECRETARY OF WAR   September 17, 1940
[Washington D.C.]

Subject: Arlington Cantonment and Arlington Experimental Farm.

With the personal approval of the President the War Department recently increased the garrisons of regular troops at the Arlington Cantonment and Fort Myer, concentrating two regiments which had heretofore been widely separated—the 12th Infantry and the 3d Cavalry. This action was taken because of the importance of having a strong garrison of regular troops permanently located near the federal area of the national Capital.

The President also approved the transfer of Arlington Farm from the Department of Agriculture to the War Department in order to provide additional space required by this increase. The Budget Bureau approved $3,200,000 for the Department of Agriculture to purchase a site in lieu of Arlington Farm, and $4,000,000 for the War Department to construct the necessary buildings and installations on the Arlington Farm site.[1]

The Senate recently passed the necessary legislation to make this action effective. In the House, the bill (S. 4107) was referred to the Committee on Agriculture. It has been placed on the Union and Consent Calendars, but may die a natural death unless a determined effort is made to process it through the House.

Since the importance of this project is greater now than at the time the bill was introduced, and since the President has been personally interested in this matter, I recommend that action be taken through the White House urging the Chairman of the Committee on Agriculture to expedite passage of this legislation before Congress adjourns.[2]

GCMRL/G. C. Marshall Papers (Pentagon Office, Selected)

1. The United States Experimental Farm was at the southwestern end of the Arlington Memorial Bridge. See the map on p. xviii. Since early 1939, the army had sought to establish a

permanent Infantry garrison near the Virginia end of the bridge, "within quick reach by motor or marching of Capitol Hill." (Malin Craig Memorandum for the Secretary of War, March 16, 1939, NA/RG 165 [OCS, 21050]. In this file are also several memorandums on this subject written by then Deputy Chief of Staff Marshall.)

2. The Senate bill divided the farm between the Interior and War departments. On September 30, the House amended the bill to give the entire area to the army and to increase the construction funds to $5,000,000. With certain modifications, the Senate agreed to these amendments, and the revised bill was signed by the president on November 29.

MEMORANDUM FOR GENERAL WATSON[1]   September 17, 1940
                                                          [Washington, D.C.]

Daily the War Department is receiving numerous requests from individual members of Congress for detailed information on the procurement of arms and munitions, reports on the comparative status of military equipment, and on various specific dates. Each request requires research and careful checking and some of them have involved one or more officers and several clerks for two or three days, to the delay of War Department business.[2]

Much of the information requested is of a confidential or secret nature, and reports recently given in confidence have been made public to favorite individuals of the Press, with results that are confusing to the public and highly detrimental to the War Department in its relation to the Press generally.

The War Department is in an embarrassing situation in this matter for the reason that each refusal to give out such information creates an antagonism which may be of considerable importance in connection with the passage of necessary legislation. There is no question but what the time has come when we cannot continue to do business in this particular matter in the uncoordinated and uncontrolled fashion that it is now being done. The War Department would like to have all such requests for information cleared through the Chairmen of the military committees of the Senate and House, and the Department directed to furnish information on the status of arms and equipment only when requested by these Committee Chairmen.

GCMRL/G. C. Marshall Papers (Pentagon Office, Selected)

1. Brigadier General Edwin M. Watson was President Roosevelt's secretary and military aide. Marshall drafted this document, but it was signed by Major Walter B. Smith.

2. Orlando Ward, secretary of the General Staff, recorded one instance of such congressional requests in his diary: "Sen [Harry F.] Byrd wanted some detailed data on tanks and planes under order in order to throw dead cats. The[y] fiddle while Rome is getting ready to burn." (August 27, 1940, photocopy in GCMRL/Research File.)

MEMORANDUM FOR THE ASSISTANT   September 17, 1940
CHIEF OF STAFF, G-1   [Washington, D.C.]

Have we ever considered the award of a good conduct medal or other decoration that might be used to stimulate pride in such a force as we are about to enter into training? It seems to me that if the development of this citizen Army should take place entirely on a peace basis, it would be quite important to figure out some distinctions other than mere athletic medals, for which men would strive and point to later with pride.[1]

It may be that this has all been considered but I wish you could let me have an informal report.

GCMRL/G. C. Marshall Papers (Pentagon Office, Selected)

1. Medals or badges for good conduct previously had been authorized for the other services: Navy (1869); Marine Corps (1896); Coast Guard (1923). Executive Order 8809 of June 28, 1941, authorized the Army Good Conduct Medal for award to enlisted men who had honorably completed three continuous years of active service subsequent to August 26, 1940, among other qualifications. (Evans E. Kenigan, *American War Medals and Decorations* [New York: Viking Press, 1964], pp. 48–51.)

TO MAJOR GENERAL GEORGE GRUNERT   September 20, 1940
Confidential   [Washington, D.C.]

Dear Grunert: I have received your several letters including the one of September first, the last one, which is now being carefully gone over by the War Plans Division in the light of all other communications.[1] Meanwhile I think a radio has been sent to you with information as to additional ammunition that we are sending over. I am going into the matter of planes very carefully with General Arnold to see whether we might get you some modern pursuit at an earlier date than planned.

I am fully aware of your difficulties and they have been a matter of almost daily discussion between the Secretary of War and myself. The trouble is, as you may not fully appreciate at your distance from Washington: We are involved in a tremendous expansion, new obligations in Newfoundland, Nova Scotia and all the recently acquired bases in the Atlantic and Caribbean area—for all of which materiel is required. Meanwhile quantity production has not yet had time to develop and everywhere there are shortages or complete deficiencies.

As a single example, consider the problem of calibre .30 ammunition. We are now legally on our way to a million four hundred thousand men in ranks before the end of this fiscal year and thousands of planes. Training requires the expenditure of small arms ammunition, and the number of machine gunners for a modern airplane will require tremendously increased consumption. Meanwhile, though we have striven by every hook or crook to expedite powder production, we cannot achieve quantity output before next summer.

In this same connection, immediately after the disaster of the British Army in Belgium and Northern France where it lost all of its equipment, its accumulation of munitions in dumps, etc., we released to that Government the deteriorated calibre .30 ammunition that had been disapproved for use in shoulder rifles. Without this ammunition the British would not have been able to utilize the Enfield rifles, obsolete machine guns and the automatic rifles we were giving them, without disadvantage to ourselves, to form the bulk of the equipment of the reconstituted army in England. Even so the number of rounds per rifle was, and remains, pathetic. But it was a long ways better than nothing at all.

I am giving you some highly confidential information which is for your eye alone. Probably I should not trust this to ordinary air mail, but I think it is important that you know something of our situation, and that you feel that I am alert to your dilemma and will do my very best in every way to help you out.

As to press announcements creating unfavorable reactions on the morale of your people, that is a matter extremely difficult to control and we can but do our best.

This is a hastily written letter and I want to get it off to you by air mail today.   Faithfully yours,

P.S.   I hope to get clearance for a large number of temporary promotions Monday, largely to fill troop leadership vacancies. There must be more Staff promotions later. I don't think Wilson on Corregidor is on the list but you can assure him that he will be moved into a position for advancement later.[2] You yourself need not be concerned about a Lieutenant Generalcy. I expect to see you moved into that rank in due time.

GCMRL/G. C. Marshall Papers (Pentagon Office, Selected)

1. The commanding general of the Philippine Department had written to the War Department on July 5, 8, 10, 22, 25, and August 2 requesting small arms ammunition, antiaircraft materiel, permission to recruit the Philippine Scouts to full peace strength, Air Corps personnel and materiel, funds for storage installations, and a supply of mustard gas. He had also written to Marshall personally on certain of these matters on July 5 and 10. On September 1 he again wrote to the chief of staff recapitulating his previous communications and remarking upon the decisions made or the lack of replies. He also enclosed a copy of a United Press dispatch which he said was typical of reports which dwelt on the defenselessness of the Philippines. "My campaign to bolster morale and to eliminate fear and defeatism has met with some success but the lack of an announced policy, backed by visual evidence of defense means and measures, works against me. . . . I can imagine how busy and involved you are and dislike to add to your burden, but I must assure myself that you understand the problems and conditions in this department." (Grunert to Marshall, September 1, 1940, NA/RG 407 [Classified, 093.5 Philippine Islands (7-2-40)].)

2. Major Albert T. Wilson was a member of the Forty-fifth Infantry (Philippine Scouts).

To Bernard M. Baruch   September 24, 1940
                                                        [Washington, D.C.]

Dear Mr. Baruch: Pa Watson sent me over a telegram from you regarding permanence of the construction in our encampments, with relation to their possible use in the future for housing homeless civilians.[1] All of the temporary construction that we are entering into is of a type that should last for ten years if we are permitted necessary annual repairs. The exception to this is in the matter of barracks for the units of the National Guard being concentrated in the South. In these cases the men are to use framed and screened tents; but the remainder of the set-up is on the same basis of construction as above referred to, that is, roads, walks, sewers, water systems, kitchens, mess halls, latrines, recreation rooms, hospitals, etc. For National Guard organizations in the more northerly latitudes, the construction is of the cantonment type throughout; the same applies to the extensions of existing Regular Army establishments which have to be increased for the purposes of the Selective Service Act.   Faithfully yours,

GCMRL/G. C. Marshall Papers (Pentagon Office, Selected)
   1. Baruch's telegram of September 20 to the president's secretary read: "I think all of the encampments should be built with permanence in view. In case [of] another economic collapse scattered as they will be all over the country, they could be used as encampments for housing the homeless or feeding the hungry." General Watson gave Major Walter B. Smith a copy of the message and said that the president was very receptive to the idea. (Baruch's telegram and Smith's attached, undated memorandum to General Marshall are in GCMRL/G. C. Marshall Papers [Pentagon Office, Selected].)

To Lieutenant General John L. De Witt   September 25, 1940
                                                        [Washington, D.C.]

Dear De Witt: I was very much interested in your lengthy letter to General Moore, and in particular with relation to the apparent confusion regarding coordination of movements and control of matters in Alaska. I will look into this right away.[1]

   Yesterday the President approved a long list of temporary promotions in the grade of general.[2] Please explain to Peek that he was not down for a major generalcy as Corps Area commander as we were forced to limit the list at this time to what seemed the pressing of necessities.[3] I hope a few weeks later to move into the field of Corps Area commanders, along with the announcement of the new set-up involved in the separation of Corps Area from Army command and the organization of tactical corps, to make them major generals.

These makes [promotions] of course are a terrific headache to me and more so here in Washington than anywhere else for it has been necessary to jump over some of my outstanding assistants, notably George Strong, Andrews, and Miles. I hope to rectify these matters a little later, but the problem at the moment was to get this list by the President and accepted by Congress.

Also included in the list for promotion are John C. H. Lee and Groninger, one contemplated for the Army base in San Francisco and one for the Army base in Brooklyn.[4] I had assumed Lee for San Francisco because of his intimate knowledge of Alaskan matters. If you have a different idea radio me. Faithfully yours,

GCMRL/G. C. Marshall Papers (Pentagon Office, Selected)

1. The letter from the Fourth Army commander to Deputy Chief of Staff Major General Richard C. Moore is not in the Marshall papers.

2. Concerning Marshall's efforts to secure authority to make temporary promotions, see his Memorandum for the President, July 18, 1940, pp. 270–71. Six men had been given temporary promotions to major general and two to brigadier general effective September 25. On September 24, the president approved without change a new, longer list of temporary promotions (including twenty-three to major general and seventy-two to brigadier general). Secretary Stimson noted in his diary that this represented "an unusual case of exhibition of confidence on the part of the President." (September 24, 1940, Yale/H. L. Stimson Papers [Diary, 30:18].) Marshall wrote to Frank R. McCoy: "I learned indirectly from Mr. Stimson that you had done a great deal in securing his full acceptance of the list of 'makes' submitted the other day. It might interest you to know that my own people have been pressing me this morning to scratch off Terry Allen's name because of the depressing effect on other officers of such an advancement. I have left his name on the list." (Marshall to McCoy, September 25, 1940, LC/F. R. McCoy Papers.) At this time over nine hundred men stood ahead of Lieutenant Colonel Terry de la M. Allen of the Seventh Cavalry on the promotion list.)

3. Brigadier General Ernest D. Peek (U.S.M.A., 1901) was chief of staff of the Ninth Corps Area; he was scheduled to become Corps Area commander in early November, when De Witt relinquished that command. In late October, Peek and five others were promoted to major general, and another twenty brigadier generals were appointed.

4. Both Colonel John C. H. Lee (U.S.M.A., 1909) and Colonel Homer McL. Groninger (U.S.M.A., 1908) were members of De Witt's command at this time. Lee was named commanding general of the San Francisco Port of Embarkation; Groninger was named commanding general of the New York Port of Embarkation.

MEMORANDUM FOR THE ASSISTANT CHIEF OF STAFF, G-3 [ANDREWS]　　　September 27, 1940
[Washington, D.C.]

Yesterday I was before the Military Affairs Committee of the House for about two hours, being questioned regarding a number of subjects.[1] One of these was brought up in different forms by various members of the Committee, and related to the war worn subject of officers' training schools.

I told them that we were studying the proposition of conducting candidate schools in the last three months of the volunteer or trainees' service; that it would involve of course only selected men who had been conspicuous for their evident qualities of leadership[;] that it would apply only to men who were in ranks; and that for commissions with the combat branches of the Army such procedure would undoubtedly be very necessary.

I became involved in the commissioning of Elliott Roosevelt which brought up the point that for non-combatant posts men of certain specialistic qualifications might be commissioned outright in grades above that of Second Lieutenant as was done in the case of young Roosevelt.[2]

The question was asked me, what about young men who have completed three years CMTC? Would they be denied any further opportunity and would their previous three months' effort be ignored? I had not considered this at all but I hazarded the statement that we would consider that and it might be that such a young man if found evidently possessing special qualifications might be permitted to enter a candidate school of the character previously referred to.

There were a number of other slants on this particular proposition but I am passing this along to you for your consideration.

GCMRL/G. C. Marshall Papers (Pentagon Office, Selected)

1. The committee did not publish the testimony heard during this session.

2. Elliott Roosevelt, the president's second son, was inducted into the Air Corps Specialists Reserve on September 23 with the rank of captain. Charges of favoritism were immediately raised, to which Roosevelt replied on September 25. (*New York Times*, September 26, 1940, p. 25.) Orlando Ward's comment in his diary perhaps reflected the opinions of many in the War Department: "The Air Corps have put the WD in an embarrassing position by going too far with Elliott Roosevelt before taking it up with the Chief of Staffs office so on the say of the White house we commissioned him a Captain. It has been followed by a mass of similar applications as well as some hot editorial[s] particularly those by Hugh Johnson. Little does he know that the White House concurred and that they are pushing two others just as raw." (September 26, 1940, Orlando Ward Diary, photocopy in GCMRL/Research File.)

Memorandum for General Moore   September 28, 1940
[Washington, D.C.]

Subject: Work for National Youth Administration students.

Mr. Aubrey Williams and one of his assistants called on me yesterday to see what could be done towards providing more actual work for the young men the NYA is attempting to train as mechanics, carpenters, etc. He stated that they were now producing Army bunks for South Charleston arsenal in West Virginia, to replace those that had been loaned to them by the Army; that they were manufacturing some thousands of ditty-boxes, or sea chests, for the Navy, etc.

Please have this matter surveyed to see if there are any things we could give them to make to supplement our supply business. We would have to provide the material. I have thought of a simple box locker to supplement those we procure of a more elaborate nature. I understand they are making an arm rack down in San Antonio for the Army. I should think there would be a number of things that would be helpful to us to have them produce with our placing only partial dependence on them.

There is another phase to this matter which I would like considered and regarding which I talked to Mr. Williams. I am going before the Senate Committee to try to have restored to our estimates the money for 15,000 civilians. I considered yesterday the elaborate set-up for permanent post overheads. Why can't we offer the NYA jobs as helpers for all the various utility people—electricians, plumbers, carpenters, engineers, car mechanics, cooks, bakers, etc., etc. Certainly there is a possibility here of producing a tremendous amount of service without a charge against the military appropriations, at the same time offering practical instruction to a large number of young fellows.

The air people have used these boys to quite an extent on some posts, and the arsenals have used them. I believe some of the Quartermaster depots have used them. Please have some fellow with a vision talk this over with McSherry and see if we can't do something big in regard to it.[1]

GCMRL/G. C. Marshall Papers (Pentagon Office, General)

1. Aubrey Williams was the administrator of the National Youth Administration, a division of the Federal Security Agency. Lieutenant Colonel Frank J. McSherry was the General Staff's liaison with the agency, and since July 1, 1940, he had been an administrative assistant with the Labor Division of the Advisory Committee to the Council of National Defense.

To HOWARD C. BRONSON[1]   September 30, 1940
                                                [Washington, D.C.]

My dear Bronson: I have given a careful reading to your letter of September 12th and have had it gone over both by the Organization and Personnel Branches of the General Staff.

You need not have feared that I did not appreciate the value of Army bands as morale builders, and you may be sure that I will have this in mind during the coming development of our National Defense program. However, some of the points you raised, particularly with relation to musicians in the recent Second Army Maneuvers, lead me to feel that there is a misunderstanding on the part of the bandsmen themselves of one cardinal principle of this whole Army business. Everybody in the Army is a soldier, which means that he must hold himself ready, in a disciplined manner, to meet any job that the urgencies of the moment demand. Your comments I heard in the early days of the AEF where bandsmen were given a variety of duties to perform in helping out with the troops of the line. They recovered from most of these reactions as they began to get the true picture of what an Army really is.

An infantry soldier might well object to the fatigue jobs that come his way, and very frequently, as being injurious to his morale. Excess of fatigue duty is injurious to morale, but to have a soldier feel that he is justified in being resentful because he is called upon to perform such a duty, would mean that the military team no longer existed. Some commanding officers will undoubtedly mishandle their bands, just as they will mishandle other units, but I think, in general, all are well aware of the great importance of music in maintaining morale. Some may make the mistake of calling upon bandsmen to do things which injure their touch—I have known this to happen, but similar mistakes occur with relation to men of all arms and services. We cannot get perfection of direction and leadership, but we must have a team.

The War Department is aware of the problems which have arisen relative to bands and band leaders, and has devoted a great deal of time to their consideration. In the opinion of the Department, nothing has arisen thus far which would justify advocating the establishment of a separate Band Corps, and especially at this time when we are faced with the tremendous problems incident to the expansion of the Army as a whole. However, you may be assured that I personally have in mind the arguments which have been raised on both sides, and I will do my best to see in the end that the right thing is done.   Faithfully yours,

GCMRL/G. C. Marshall Papers (Pentagon Office, General)

1. Bronson was president of the United States Army and Navy Bandsmen's Association. For Marshall's previous dealings with this group, see Memorandum for the Assistant Chief of Staff, G-1, March 18, 1940, pp. 176–77.

A Heavy Task

October 1 – December 31, 1940

I must confess to an over-burdened mind and to over-crowded days— mobilization in time of peace in a democracy is a heavy task for one in my particular position.

—Marshall to Charles D. Herron
December 13, 1940

MANPOWER growth was the dominant theme for War Department leaders during the last three months of 1940; it suffused every issue and brought with it a host of problems for the chief of staff. The net gain in enlisted men and officers during this period (182,000) was nearly equal to the total in the Regular Army when George C. Marshall became acting chief of staff on July 1, 1939. Despite the passage of the nation's first peacetime conscription law, drafted men constituted only slightly more than 10 percent of this increase. The largest component came from federalizing National Guard units. Six Infantry divisions, five additional Infantry regiments, three Coast Artillery units, nine Observation squadrons, and nine other Guard units were called up during the last quarter of 1940 and added to the four divisions, eighteen Coast Artillery regiments, and four Observation squadrons that had been federalized in the last two weeks of September. (War Department, "Biennial Report of the Chief of Staff, July 1, 1941," in *Report of the Secretary of War to the President, 1941* [Washington: GPO, 1941], Chart 9, Table D, and p. 134.) The construction of cantonments and the manufacture and distribution of materiel lagged, presenting Marshall with political, social, and morale problems.

Marshall's already busy schedule became even more crowded and the pressures of his job increased. "To be perfectly honest," he wrote, "when I leave the office I find it necessary to completely detach myself from Army affairs in order to clear my mind in preparation for the next day's business. The pressures these times are terrific." (Marshall to Mrs. Elizabeth Conger Pratt, October 4, 1940, GCMRL/G. C. Marshall Papers [Pentagon Office, Selected].) To a friend in Portland, Oregon, Marshall again wrote of his strenuous days but noted: "I am blessed with a remarkably able staff. I think very few people in this country appreciate the tremendous expansion, with all its involvements, that we have been carrying out during the past six months, and particularly the past three; so much of it has been done efficiently that it has developed quite unobtrusively." (Marshall to Aaron M. Frank, October 4, 1940, GCMRL/G. C. Marshall Papers [Pentagon Office, General].)

While declining an invitation to address the Bankers Club of Chicago, Marshall wrote to his longtime friend Charles G. Dawes that "engagements made a few days ahead are usually impossible to keep. My week-ends and lulls, if any, in affairs here have been used for inspections of concentrations in the field. With Congress in session, I have necessarily had to remain close to home to be available for Committee meetings. During this time I have depended on others to make inspections, which are increasingly vital, and now I feel that to attempt engagements would further tie me to a set schedule, which I must avoid." (Marshall to Dawes, October 15, 1940, Northwestern/C. G. Dawes Papers.)

Despite the press of momentous events and the army's massive growth in size and budget, Marshall continued to concern himself seriously with the individual soldier's morale and welfare. "More than ever before," he told a national radio audience, "the efficiency of an army depends upon the quality of its soldiers." (N.B.C. Radio Address on the Progress of National Defense, November 29, 1940, p. 359.) ★

To Niles Trammell   October 1, 1940
                                                        [Washington, D.C.]

Dear Trammell: I have just received your note of September 30th, enclosing me the initial copy of "NBC Defense News."[1] I am much interested in what you are planning to do, and I think it will have a splendid effect.

I have this suggestion to offer: Your itinerary includes a number of what we might call "dead spots" in the present national defense development. For example, you have Fort Devens, Massachusetts, at which little is occurring, and have ignored the harbor defenses of Boston, where the National Guard has just been placed on duty. You have Fort Meade, again where little is occurring, and have ignored Langley Field, Virginia, which is a part of our tremendous air development. I would add Camp Jackson at Columbia, South Carolina, less than an hour's flight from Fort Bragg, where almost 20,000 troops are now concentrated. I would also add Barksdale Field in Louisiana, which is a great air base, and Fort Bliss, at El Paso, Texas, where the Cavalry Division is located, and March Field in Southern California, another great air base; and Hamilton Field near San Francisco, another air base. You have Fort Logan, Colorado on your schedule; yet the great development in the vicinity of Denver is at Lowry Field on the outskirts of the city, an Air Corps installation. There is nothing at Fort Leavenworth except the faculty of the school, working on training pamphlets; there is only the local garrison at Fort Snelling, and much the same situation at Fort Sheridan. Camp Custer is just in the process of construction, while Selfridge Field in the vicinity of Detroit, is a part of the great Air Corps expansion. Instead of Fort Thomas, Kentucky, where not much is occurring, I think your broadcast should have covered Fort Knox in the vicinity of Louisville, where the new armored force is now located.

I am just submitting this as hasty suggestions.   Faithfully yours,

GCMRL/G. C. Marshall Papers (Pentagon Office, Selected)

1. Niles Trammell, president of National Broadcasting Company, Inc., in New York City, had visited Marshall's office on September 20. Trammell's September 30 note is not in the Marshall papers.

To the Commanding General   October 4, 1940
Third Corps Area[1]   [Washington, D.C.]

Dear Parsons: I am attaching a memorandum correspondence between myself and The Adjutant General regarding Technical Sergeant Walter B. Shooter, on duty at the Fishburne Military School in Virginia, which is largely self-explanatory.[2] However, in paragraph 4 of the memorandum of The Adjutant General dated July 30th, the statement is made: "There are others with just as good records, equally deserving." I am inclined to question this. When a sergeant of the Regular Army, in addition to a highly satisfactory performance of routine duties, coaches a shooting team so that it wins a national contest two years in succession, and also the individual excellency trophy, it seems to me he has given an outstanding performance with practically no approximate competitor.

I know how difficult these matters of rank are, but I also know that the strong tendency is to fall back on a purely seniority basis without regard to exceptional cases of demonstrated merit. My rather recent experience in Chicago gave me glaring examples of a routine arrangement permitting many cases of mediocrity to go ahead of splendid efficiency.[3] I realize the difficulties of determination in these matters and the necessity for a very definite policy, but I am strongly of the opinion that exceptions, where the individual is conspicuous, are essential to the business of developing high efficiency in the Army.

I do not wish to embarrass you in this matter, so I stipulate that no acknowledgment be made of this communication, and in all probability I will not learn what happens in Sergeant Shooter's case, as I have never heard from him or of him since I saw him and inquired into his record last June.   Faithfully yours,

GCMRL/G. C. Marshall Papers (Pentagon Office, General)

1. Major General James K. Parsons commanded the Third Corps Area until his taking leave in mid-October 1940, prior to his retirement.

2. Marshall had visited Fishburne—in Waynesboro, Virginia, part of the Third Corps Area—on June 1 and had met Shooter. In a memorandum to the adjutant general, the chief of staff observed that the school's superintendent had praised the sergeant, and Marshall concluded, "It seems to me such a man should win some recognition beyond the ordinary routine regulatory method of advancement." (Marshall Memorandum for The Adjutant General, July 20, 1940, GCMRL/G. C. Marshall Papers [Pentagon Office, Selected].)

3. On this subject, see Marshall's report on the Illinois National Guard for the year July 1935 through June 1936, *Papers of GCM*, 1: 497.

October 5, 1940
[Washington, D.C.]

Subject: Assignment of Captain Leon B. Thomas,
Medical Reserve Corps (O–31420)

The above officer is at Vancouver Barracks, Washington, and has been ordered to duty for one year. I have never seen him, and until yesterday had never heard of him. However, a rather remarkable commendation of his services reached me from the wife of a Staff Sergeant at Vancouver, whom I know to be a woman of education and discernment. He seems to have saved her and her husband—an unusually fine character—by his skillful attention. As a result, in gratitude she is praying that he be considered for some hospital assignment, as at the Letterman, where adequate equipment is available.

Will you be good enough to check on this man, and if he is found to be of promise, to see that he gets an assignment suitable to his possibilities. I do not think he has the faintest idea that anyone is boosting his cause, but, frankly, I have been so irritated by heavy pressures to advance undeserving men that I would derive positive satisfaction from helping, in this manner, a really deserving man in an inconspicuous position.[1]

GCMRL/G. C. Marshall Papers (Pentagon Office, General)

1. Captain Thomas was assigned to Fort Lewis, Washington, his second station of choice, on October 15, 1940. (Mrs. Alva M. Hughes to Katherine T. Marshall, September 29, 1940, GCMRL/G. C. Marshall Papers [Pentagon Office, General]; Colonel Larry B. McAfee Memorandum for the Secretary, General Staff, October 30, 1940, ibid.)

To COLONEL MILTON G. BAKER[1] October 8, 1940
[Washington, D.C.]

My dear Colonel Baker: I have just had time to read over your note of October 4th, inviting me to make an address at the Armistice Day service at the Valley Forge Military Academy on November 10th at 2:30 in the afternoon.

In view of my inability to accept your invitation last June, I would like to accommodate you on this occasion.[2] My doubts in the matter are these: If a great deal of publicity is going to be given to what I say, then I have to make very careful preparation and I literally have not time for such, and I am unwilling to farm it out as is so often done in the political field. If I am merely talking to your young men and guests, that is something quite different, though I suppose even then I will be involved in the presence of reporters.

Will you write me quite frankly regarding this before I make a final decision.[3] I should say that I have declined practically every invitation, and have had to cancel most of my inspections recently because of the uncertainty of developments here, and the tremendous mass of important business that has to be met daily. Faithfully yours,

GCMRL/G. C. Marshall Papers (Pentagon Office, Selected)

1. Baker, a colonel in the Pennsylvania National Guard, was superintendent of Valley Forge Military Academy in Wayne, Pennsylvania.

2. Marshall had declined Colonel Baker's invitation to deliver the academy's baccalaureate address on June 2, 1940, because of prior engagements. (Marshall to Baker, March 28, 1940, GCMRL/G. C. Marshall Papers [Pentagon Office, Selected].)

3. In his October 4 invitation to Marshall, Baker had written that the address would be broadcast over a national hookup of the Mutual Broadcasting System. On October 10, however, Baker replied that Marshall's address would be unreported and unpublicized. The audience would be restricted to the Corps of Cadets and their guests and the radio broadcast would be cancelled. (Baker to Marshall, October 4 and 10, 1940, ibid.) Marshall accepted the invitation. See Marshall to Baker, November 13, 1940, pp. 349–50.

THE Tripartite Pact (also called the Berlin-Rome-Tokyo Axis), a ten-year mutual aid treaty signed on September 27, 1940, formally added Japan to the Axis coalition. This treaty, plus Britain's decision to reopen the Burma Road supply line to China on October 17, prompted Prime Minister Churchill to ask President Roosevelt to "send an American squadron, the bigger the better, to pay a friendly visit to Singapore. . . . Anything in this direction would have a marked deterrent effect upon a Japanese declaration of war upon us over the Burma Road opening." (*Churchill and Roosevelt: The Complete Correspondence,* ed. Warren F. Kimball, 3 vols. [Princeton: Princeton University Press, 1984], 1: 74.) See the editorial note on pp. 409–10.

Churchill's suggestion was the chief topic for discussion at the October 5 Standing Liaison Committee meeting. The chief of naval operations was strongly "opposed to any measures which did not fit into the general plan of operations in the event of war with Japan. He stated that the vital theater was the eastern Atlantic, and the western Pacific a secondary one." Marshall and Sumner Welles agreed with Admiral Stark. The next day President Roosevelt told Stark to cancel the orders for sending 4,000 Marines to various Pacific stations, because he wanted an army division sent to reinforce Hawaii. (Marshall Memorandum for the Secretary of War, October 8, 1940, NA/RG 165 [OCS, Categorical, Miscellaneous]. The October 5 meeting is discussed in Mark S. Watson, *Chief of Staff: Prewar Plans and Preparations,* a volume in the *United States Army in World War II* [Washington: GPO, 1950], pp. 117–18.) The General Staff was opposed to this move. Not only would it disrupt training schedules, but it would complicate the army's supply problems in Hawaii. What was really needed was anti-aircraft personnel to man the equipment already on hand in Oahu. (George V. Strong Memorandum for the Chief of Staff, October 7, 1940, NA/RG 165 [WPD, 3444–4].) ★

MEMORANDUM FOR GENERAL BRYDEN   October 9, 1940
Secret   [Washington, D.C.]

Subject: Reinforcement of Hawaii.

The following is the situation at the present time:

The President will not direct the reinforcement of Hawaii by a division, and does not specifically direct its reinforcement by any troops, but would be gratified if we could find it advisable to take some such action. The Secretary of War is in accord with this view.

Our decision is to send the 251st AA regiment of the National Guard of California, now at Ventura, whenever transportation is available.[1]

Admiral Stark notifies me that he sees no prospect of the Navy having space available in the near future, and is having difficulty in chartering additional boats to carry his own people.

I understand from the attached papers that there is no available space on Army transports until next March.

Will you have this looked into to see if we can scare up some transportation for these men?

GCMRL/G. C. Marshall Papers (Pentagon Office, Selected)

1. During the winter, the 251st Antiaircraft Artillery Regiment moved to Oahu, becoming the first National Guard unit to leave the continental United States for overseas duty. (Stetson Conn, Rose C. Engelman, and Byron Fairchild, *Guarding the United States and Its Outposts,* a volume in the *United States Army in World War II* [Washington: GPO, 1964], p. 159.)

MEMORANDUM FOR THE SECRETARY OF WAR   October 9, 1940
[Washington, D.C.]

Subject: Aviation Facilities between the United States
and Northeastern Brazil.

In order to carry out joint Army and Navy basic war plans for the defense of the Western Hemisphere it is essential that facilities for operation and the emergency movement of Army and Navy aircraft in the Caribbean area and northeastern Brazil be available at the time of the emergency. Failure to provide for such facilities will prevent the adequate air support of the expeditionary forces, as well as the full utilization of the newly acquired air bases.

Arrangements have been made on the basis of having these facilities provided by the Pan American Airways for an estimated amount of twelve million dollars. I am of the opinion that due to the urgency of the time element no other method of providing these facilities is practicable. I urge that an immediate decision be made in order to permit this work to be started.[1]

GCMRL/G. C. Marshall Papers (Pentagon Office, Selected)

1. Since May 1940 the War, Navy, and State departments had been trying to work out a program to facilitate airfield construction in Latin America that did not overtly involve the United States government. Lengthy negotiations had been under way with Pan American Airways since June. On September 7 Marshall reported to Secretary Stimson that the army, navy, and Pan American Airways had reached an agreement, and he recommended that $12,000,000 be allocated for construction from the president's emergency fund. "The immediate conclusion of the Pan American contract," he wrote, "is now more essential to our national defense than any other single matter." (Marshall Memorandum for the Secretary of War, September 7, 1940, NA/RG 407 [Classified, 580.82 (8-27-40) Bulky Package].)

The State Department, however, was not enthusiastic over the prospect that Pan American Airways might use government money to establish a monopoly over air traffic in Latin America. Assistant Secretary of State Adolf A. Berle, Jr., commented in his diary on September 30 that "this air business is getting to be almost as much of a war as the European war. . . . [Pan American Airways President Juan] Trippe's plan is monopoly or nothing; and he is quite able to play on either side of the belligerent line, or both sides at once." (*Navigating the Rapids, 1918-1971: From the Papers of Adolf A. Berle,* ed. Beatrice Bishop Berle and Travis Beal Jacobs [New York: Harcourt Brace Jovanovich, 1973], pp. 336-37, 340. See Memorandum for the Secretary of War and Under Secretary of War, March 6, 1941, pp. 438-39.) Nevertheless, the State Department gave its approval on October 24, and the contracts were signed on November 2. (Stetson Conn and Byron Fairchild, *The Framework of Hemisphere Defense,* a volume in the *United States Army in World War II* [Washington: GPO, 1960], pp. 250-53.)

To GENERAL PEDRO GÓES MONTEIRO   October 15, 1940
[Washington, D.C.]

My dear General Monteiro: I had looked forward to meeting you personally on your arrival in Washington this morning, but I have been advised by the diplomatic experts that if I did this it would be necessary for me to meet the various Chiefs of Staff as they arrive, which would be a physical impossibility. Therefore, I am sending General Crane to extend my personal welcome and to express my regrets that I cannot meet you personally.[1]

I received your message expressing your regret that you cannot have family dinner with Mrs. Marshall and myself tonight. I am very sorry but I quite understand your situation. However, at the first opportunity Mrs. Marshall and I wish to welcome you into our home.

Hoping that you have had a pleasant trip and you are in fine health, and looking forward with the keenest pleasure to renewing our friendship, believe me, with high regard   Faithfully yours,

GCMRL/G. C. Marshall Papers (Pentagon Office, General)

1. Brigadier General John A. Crane was head of the foreign liaison section of G-2. United States Army and Navy staff representatives cooperated in two series of conversations with Latin American military staff representatives, one in June, and the second between August and October 1940. In these discussions the United States sought to define a framework for military cooperation, particularly to insure that base facilities would be available to United States forces should the need arise. Staff agreements were concluded with each Latin American nation approached, except Argentina, which rebuffed the overtures. As part of these efforts to influence their military policies, Marshall invited the chiefs of staff (or equivalent) and one other officer from each of the Central and South American nations to visit the United States and to tour various military installations and defense industries. Two groups visited the United States: the first from October 1 to 14, and the second from October 16 to 30. Marshall met with the visitors several times. He was particularly friendly to Brazil's chief of staff, General Góes Monteiro, who had a special itinerary and who discussed and concluded a staff agreement with the United States on October 29. (Conn and Fairchild, *Framework of Hemisphere Defense*, pp. 178–85. See Marshall to Oswaldo Aranha, January 6, 1941, pp. 381–82.)

MEMORANDUM FOR GENERAL BRYDEN   October 16, 1940
[Washington, D.C.]

Subject: Future status of the Regular Army, National Guard, and Reserve Corps.

With reference to my hasty outline this morning of the necessity of having a "rough conception" of a future policy, prior to the meeting of the National Guard Association,[1] I am outlining below my present ideas on the subject:

That, the number of divisions to be maintained in the Regular Army will depend somewhat on the probable efficiency of the National Guard organization and that of the Reserve officer personnel—the degree of their immediate availability for active duty. Also, it will depend on the success with which at least a partial amount of preliminary training can be given in replacement centers for men to fill the ranks of the Regular Army units. For example, we might assign men to a regular unit after four months in a replacement center, giving them only eight months with a regular unit.

That, the standard of efficiency of the National Guard must be materially raised as to enlisted personnel, as to officer personnel, and as to character of training.

(a) The enlisted personnel to have served a minimum of six months in the Federal service in replacement centers. This might possibly be arranged on the basis of six months' Federal service being exempted in consideration of a three-year enlistment in the National Guard; or, making an exemption of four months' Federal service in consideration of a two-year enlistment in the National Guard. Or, if it is thought that the necessary men could be obtained, to proceed according to the present law, which frees the men enlisting in the National Guard from eight years in the Reserves. Personally, I do not think this would produce the necessary numbers.

(b) That 75% of the officer personnel with the National Guard be provided from Reserve Corps officers—products of the ROTC— who have served one year with the Regular Army after graduation; the remaining 25% to come from the ranks of the National Guard, and to be given a special schooling at our special service schools.

That, the training of the Reserve Corps be largely based on the development of the habit of recent graduates of the ROTC being given a year's active duty with the Regular establishment either in replacement centers or with regular organizations, or both.

The foregoing is merely a rough outline of how the matter appears to me at the present time.

GCMRL/G. C. Marshall Papers (Pentagon Office, Selected)

1. The editors have found no record of a Marshall conference with or memorandum to Deputy Chief of Staff William Bryden on this subject. The National Guard Association of the United States met in Washington, D.C., October 21–23, and discussion focused upon the implications for the Guard of its induction into federal service. Marshall spoke "off the record" at the October 22 banquet. (*Army and Navy Journal,* October 19 and 26, 1940, pp. 197, 203.) No copy of Marshall's speech is in the Marshall papers, but on the day of his speech Colonel Kenneth Buchanan—a National Guard officer who had been Marshall's aide between the summer of 1939 and the summer of 1940, prior to his moving to the Office of the Chief of the National Guard Bureau—called to suggest that the chief of staff assure the National Guard that its identity would not be lost and that its officers would not be eliminated for the benefit of Regular Army officers who sought commands. (Claude M. Adams Memorandum for General Marshall, October 22, 1940, GCMRL/G. C. Marshall Papers [Pentagon Office, Selected].)

To Edith Nourse Rogers[1]

October 18, 1940
[Washington, D.C.]

Dear Mrs. Rogers: Thank you for your gracious little note of October 17th, regarding Fort Devens.[2] I appreciate your thanks, but I want you to know that we merely did what seemed to be in the best interests of National

Defense. In doing this very many times we disappoint, frequently irritate, and sometimes definitely antagonize individual Members of Congress; but we have tried to make it a fixed rule to attend to the National Defense and "let the chips fly where they may."

So, it is very pleasant to have your particular note. Thank you. Faithfully yours,

GCMRL/G. C. Marshall Papers (Pentagon Office, General)

1. Congresswoman Rogers, a Republican, had been the representative from the Fifth District of Massachusetts since 1925. She was a member of the House World War Veterans' Legislation Committee and had worked since 1918 for better care of disabled soldiers.

2. Rogers had written Marshall a note of appreciation for his "co-operation and help in the building-up of Fort Devens." (Rogers to Marshall, October 17, 1940, GCMRL/G. C. Marshall Papers [Pentagon Office, General].) Although Fort Devens had been a major post during the World War, the War Department considered abandoning the post in 1930; but due in part to Congresswoman Rogers's efforts, it became a permanent authorized post in November 1931. On October 15, 1940, the War Department announced that a new Army Air Corps station would be established there. By early November plans were announced to acquire 5,700 additional acres to expand the post and to reestablish the reception center. (*Boston Herald,* October 16, p. 14, and November 5, 1940, p. 24.)

To MORSE A. CARTWRIGHT[1]   October 18, 1940
Confidential   [Washington, D.C.]

Dear Mr. Cartwright: I had your letter of September 27, together with the previous data on the general subject of Army Educational programs carefully studied by the concerned section of the General Staff. Also I gave some additional thought to it myself.[2]

In the first place, I do appreciate the fact that you refrained from pressing me in this matter, and if you had any idea of the terrific pressures that I labor under you could better understand my appreciation of your restraint.

As to the educational program itself, I am sorry to tell you that I do not think we can go into it at this time. The fact of the matter is, we have only twelve months in which to produce a seasoned trained soldier instead of the eighteen months we asked for. The majority of the men, selective trainees and prior volunteers, must be trained in the ranks of the National Guard. This organization has a tremendous task on its hands; that is, 30% strength of partially trained men must themselves give complete training to the remaining 70% now entering the ranks. All this must be accomplished in a twelve-month period, and practically all of it will require a tremendous output of physical energy and long hours. It is not believed under the circumstances we can manage another training set-up along the lines you and I discussed and you are now proposing.

We have received some very interesting data with relation to the training and fighting of the French and German Armies. General [E. J.] Requin, of the Fourth French Army,—a very distinguished officer—stated that he was required to spend 95% of his time on morale and educational programs, and had only 5% of the time for real training; the results were all but disastrous. Our observers reported to us that the French Army carried out an extensive program of educational and recreational activities for the soldiers stationed on the Maginot line to such an extent that military training was neglected. It was the observation of our officers and of the French High Command that the results were harmful and contributed to defeat. In contrast, the German Army was kept immensely busy in military and physical training; they had no educational training, as such, their time being devoted exclusively to training as soldiers. In the British training centers, the men worked eight to twelve hours a day and often engaged in night exercises. Obviously there would be little time left for academic work, even if the men's minds could dominate their physical exhaustion.

One French Division which had an outstanding record for its fighting in the recent battles in Flanders, was conspicuous for the fact that its commander devoted all of the time to military training, declining to emasculate his program in order to work up an educational-recreational program.

I am writing these things to you confidentially, that you may better understand our hesitation at the present time to inject an additional problem into the extremely difficult one that we must solve in short order.

We have given special attention to the development of a library service, and will watch very carefully to see that provision is made to render better fitted for service those men who have language deficiencies or are illiterates. Practically all of our officers are college men, which should help a great deal in these respects. The situation confronting the Army today is somewhat different from that of 1917. Our military training methods involve considerable educational value, and our standards have been considerably raised over the 1917–18 set-up.

I am sorry to tell you that as I see the situation, it will be necessary for the Army to concentrate all its efforts on military training. However, I will re-survey the field in three or four months to see if it appears advisable to alter this policy.   Faithfully yours,

GCMRL/G. C. Marshall Papers (Pentagon Office, General)

1. Cartwright was the director of the American Association for Adult Education.

2. Cartwright's letter is not in the Marshall papers. In March 1940 Marshall had written a memorandum to the Training Division stating: "I have had several communications from Mr. Cartwright and some material. They are very anxious . . . that we have some educational set-up for the men. I told him at the time of their call last fall [1939] that we were completely absorbed in reorganization and in military training at that time; that if later on a mobilization occurred, undoubtedly we would have to consider the matter of educational work for the men." (Marshall Memorandum for Assistant Chief of Staff, G-3, March 26, 1940, GCMRL/ G. C. Marshall Papers [Pentagon Office, General].)

MEMORANDUM   October 19, 1940
Secret   [Washington, D.C.]

Subject: Conference with British Purchasing Commission
regarding new British Production Program.[1]

25-Pounder: Mr. Knudsen and Mr. Vance say no.[2] Machine tool is the
bottle-neck. We understand they are adamant on this question. 1800 guns
implies a force of 1,000,000 men, therefore a difference of caliber would not
present much complication. Incidentally, deliveries on this number of guns
could not be produced on a quantity basis before the late spring of 1942,
whereas, our deliveries of 105 [mm guns], including ammunition, on a
quantity basis will commence ten months from now. It is conceivable that
we might release these deliveries to the British, the situation being as at
present. Such an arrangement would mean no serious interference with our
production and a much earlier British receipt of guns in this approximate
caliber.

2-pounder (40mm) Anti-tank and Tank guns: British are willing to take
our 37mm tank gun, but they prefer their 2-pdr. anti-tank gun. Mr. Vance
states that this would seriously interfere with our 37mm anti-tank guns; and
that the British would get into production much more quickly if they would
accept our 37mm anti-tank gun.

Anti-aircraft: The British still seem unwilling to go ahead on our production of 90mm and 37mm guns. They continue to insist on the Bofors
40mm gun. Mr. Vance states Bofors production would, (a) seriously interfere
with our production, and (b) would be a very long time in getting under
way.

303 Enfield Rifles: Mr. Vance and Mr. Knudsen are opposed to attempting production of .303 rifles, especially because the machine tool bottle-neck
would mean a very serious delay to one of our most important weapons,—
the caliber .50 anti-aircraft machine gun. Mr. Carpenter, of the Remington
plant, who was concerned with the principal production of Enfield rifles in
this country in 1918, stated that it would be 2½ years before a new plant
could be got into quantity production on these rifles.

Our proposal was that we lease for British use our complete caliber .30
rifle plant at the Rock Island Arsenal; that the Remington people set this up
in the Remington-Ilion plant in New York, where space is available and they
now have 1200 people engaged in making sporting rifles; and also where
there are machinists unemployed who are familiar with this type of work.
Mr. Carpenter was of the opinion that in ten months they would be in good
production.

The difference here is between 2½ years and 10 months, and between the
serious interference with one of our most important requirements, .50

caliber anti-aircraft machine guns (as well as caliber .30 machine guns), and a unified production program.

GCMRL/G. C. Marshall Papers (Pentagon Office, Selected)

1. Marshall probably wrote this memorandum for Secretary of War Stimson. Following the German victories on the Continent, the British government formulated a program to create fifty-five new divisions; this necessitated supplemental materiel purchases from the United States of British-design ordnance. These new orders competed with those being placed under the United States Army's Munitions Program of June 30, 1940. (See the editorial note on pp. 285–86.) To clear up the numerous problems which had developed over ordnance supply, Sir Walter Layton, director-general of programs in the British Ministry of Supply, arrived in Washington on September 22. On October 11 he submitted a memorandum detailing British requirements, the main elements of which were: 1,800 field guns; 5,250 tank guns; 3,000 antitank guns; 3,400 antiaircraft guns; and 1,000,000 rifles—all of British types. Such a program would require new factories and machine tools; but "owing largely to the demands of British industry, the machine-tool situation was likely to remain critical for at least fifteen months." (H. Duncan Hall, *North American Supply,* a volume in the *History of the Second World War* [London: HMSO and Longmans, Green and Company, 1955], pp. 184–87.)

2. William S. Knudsen, president of the General Motors Corporation, was N.D.A.C. executive in charge of the Industrial Production Division. His assistant, Harold S. Vance, chairman of the board of the Studebaker Corporation, was head of the Machine Tools and Heavy Ordnance Section.

To First Lieutenant George W. Day[1]   October 21, 1940
Confidential   [Washington, D.C.]

My dear Lieutenant Day: I have just this moment read your letter of October 15th, with your observations on anti-tank guns and mortars and on the physical condition of officers of non-combatant units.[2]

As to the weapon phase; the "current reports" you refer to are largely press twists to make news items. So far there is no evidence that the military authorities are ignoring the importance of anti-tank guns and mortars. Most of this comes from the photographic business connected with the National Guard maneuvers last summer where it was important to represent the guns in order that their integration into the general deployment would be understood. In this connection—though please consider this a confidential comment from me—I might mention the fact that the Germans used dummy tanks in their training, but this did not at all prevent them from producing tanks and using them with great effectiveness.

As to the physical condition, I was much interested in your comments regarding officers and men of non-combatant units, and am passing this on to the proper section for consideration in relation to the training this winter.

Thank you for writing,   Faithfully yours,

GCMRL/G. C. Marshall Papers (Pentagon Office, General)

1. Day, a Reserve officer, was the comptroller of the Pawling School in Pawling, New York.
2. Marshall sent Day's letter to Major General Lesley J. McNair at Army General Head-quarters with the observation, "So much of this letter as refers to physical condition of the non-combat groups, has considerable point to it." (Marshall Memorandum for General McNair, October 21, 1940, GCMRL/G. C. Marshall Papers [Pentagon Office, General].) McNair apparently did not return the letter; it is not in the Marshall papers.

B Y 1940 most black leaders shared the goal of integrating the armed services as an important step toward full participation by their race in society. Racial segregation in the military was established by law and tradition and reinforced in the army after the World War by the conviction among many white officers that black troops had not performed well in the A.E.F. By June 1940 there were only about 4,000 black enlisted men in the Regular Army—1.5 percent of the total; another 3,000 were in various National Guard units. The Selective Service Act of 1940, which would present the army with thousands of black draftees, specifically stated that in selection and training of men there was to be "no discrimination against any person on account of race or color." Separate facilities on a racial basis were not considered discriminatory if the facilities provided were equivalent. During the summer and autumn of 1940, political pressure by black spokesmen increased on the Roosevelt administration and on the army to enforce the no-discrimination policy. (Morris J. MacGregor, Jr., *Integration of the Armed Forces, 1940–1965,* a volume in the *Defense Studies Series* [Washington: GPO, 1981], pp. 5–15. See Marshall to McCormick, August 28, 1940, pp. 297–98, and Memorandum for General Shedd, September 14, 1940, p. 306.)

The official army policy regarding blacks was spelled out in a September 27, 1940, letter from Marshall to Senator Henry Cabot Lodge, Jr. The letter was drafted by Major Walter B. Smith, the General Staff officer at the time chiefly concerned with this problem. "It is the policy of the War Department not to intermingle colored and white enlisted personnel in the same regimental organization. The condition which has made this policy necessary is not the responsibility of the Department, but to ignore it would produce situations destructive of morale and therefore definitely detrimental to the preparations for national defense in this emergency.

"The War Department has been deeply concerned by unmistakable evidence of an extensive campaign being conducted at the present time to force a change in this policy. The present exceedingly difficult period of building up a respectable and dependable military force for the protection of this country is not the time for critical experiments, which would inevitably have a highly destructive effect on morale—meaning military efficiency.

"The existing policy has been proven satisfactory over a long period of years. It provides for a full percentage of colored personnel and a wide variety of military units. Our colored regiments have splendid morale, and their high percentage of reenlistments is evidence of the wisdom of the present system." (Marshall to Lodge, September 27, 1940, GCMRL/G. C. Marshall Papers [Pentagon Office, Selected].)

On the day that this letter was sent, President Roosevelt met with Walter F. White, T. Arnold Hill, and A. Philip Randolph, who insisted that the president take steps toward ending racial segregation in the armed forces. On October 9, the White House released to the press a War Department statement which briefly summarized the reasons for continuing segregation given in Marshall's letter to Senator Lodge, but which asserted that "the services of Negroes will be utilized on a fair and equitable basis." The army would accept blacks in numbers approximating their proportion to the total population (i.e., about 10 percent). Negro organizations were to be established in all branches, including the Air Corps. Blacks would be given the opportunity to attend officer candidate schools, but as officers they would be assigned to black units only. Qualified civilians were to be "accorded equal opportunity for employment" at army posts and arsenals. A week later this statement was distributed to all army commanders. (MacGregor, *Integration of the Armed Forces*, p. 15; Ulysses Lee, *The Employment of Negro Troops*, a volume in the *United States Army in World War II* [Washington: GPO, 1966], pp. 75–76; The Adjutant General to Commanding Generals of all Armies, Corps Areas and Departments, and Chiefs of Arms and Services, "War Department policy in regard to negroes," October 16, 1940, NA/RG 407 [General, 291.21 (10-9-40) M-A-M].)

Black leaders strongly objected to this implied White House approval of segregation, and President Roosevelt acted to soften the blow. On October 23 a War Department press release announced that Judge William H. Hastie, dean of the Howard University Law School, was to be appointed the secretary of war's civilian aide on Negro affairs. On October 25, Colonel Benjamin O. Davis, Sr., was nominated for promotion to brigadier general, the first time that a black had advanced to that rank in the United States Army. (Lee, *Employment of Negro Troops*, pp. 76–79.) The two following documents by Marshall reflect the president's concern over black protests. ★

MEMORANDUM FOR THE ASSISTANT   October 25, 1940
CHIEF OF STAFF, G-1 [SHEDD]   [Washington, D.C.]
Confidential

The following instructions of the President (see attached pencil slip in his hand-writing), have been received.[1]

Colored reservists must be called just as white reservists. I think our present plans contemplate a larger percentage of colored reservists, considering their total, than white reservists.

Colored reserves are to be assigned to new units. You will have to check up on our plans and see how best to do this considering the qualifications of the officers. However, this question is now [*not*] quite so pressing, as the new units have not yet been organized.

GCMRL/G. C. Marshall Papers (Pentagon Office, Selected)
1. No copy of the penciled note was retained in the Marshall papers.

MEMORANDUM FOR THE PRESIDENT   October 25, 1940
                                                 Washington, D.C.

Subject; White and Colored Quotas under Selective Service.

In accordance with your instructions of yesterday afternoon, each Corps Area Headquarters was called by telephone and ordered to confine its notification of quotas to State Governors and a total of the men required, without reference to color. These instructions reached all the Corps Areas but one prior to any action having been taken. However, in the Sixth Corps Area (States of Illinois, Wisconsin, and Michigan), it was found that the staff officer concerned, in order to permit the State Directors to make initial preparations, had informally advised them of the proper quotas on a basis of so many white and so many colored. Instructions were given this Corps Area that in making its formal requisition on the Governors, no reference to color would be made.

The instructions of the War Department to Corps Area commanders stating the terms and methods for making calls on the States, are rather lengthy and have not been treated as confidential. So far as we have been able to determine, only three copies of these instructions have gotten out of the hands of the Corps Area commanders, the War Department and the Selective Service Headquarters. These three were sent to the State Directors of Michigan, Illinois and Wisconsin. One copy was delivered to an individual in Texas, but has been withdrawn. However, the general contents of these instructions have been known to a great many people as result of frequent conferences during a long period of years.

The desires of the President in this matter might be met by issuing another directive to Corps Area commanders on the basis of altering the white and black quotas in order to increase the latter quota. The first call,—that for November 18th—provided for a lesser number of colored men than the 10% ratio. This was done because a number of colored organizations to be created will not have been activated until next January. The calls planned for January include about 15% colored quota, sufficient to make the general average that of 10%.

By making various adjustments, temporarily assigning colored recruits or trainees to reception centers rather than to organizations, we could readjust the quotas for the first call and could utilize this purpose as the reason for delaying the call on the Governors until after November 5th.[1] This would mean a corresponding delay in the date of the first reporting of trainees, which has been assumed to be November 18th.

G. C. Marshall

FDRL/F. D. Roosevelt Papers (OF, 1413)

1. General election day.

MEMORANDUM FOR GENERAL BRYDEN

October 25, 1940
[Washington, D.C.]

Subject: Secret Documents.

General Miles brought to my attention that very secret papers, such as reports of Japanese diplomatic conversations, were being circularized in this office on an ordinary buck slip. He may have spoken to you about it, but I told him to figure out just how far such circularization should go, and we would carry it out on that basis. I also told him to have prepared special leather folders conspicuously labeled "Secret documents" on the cover, and with instructions as to how they should be handled placed inside the cover. He is to work this up and utilize such means for the further distribution of secret documents.[1]

GCMRL/G. C. Marshall Papers (Pentagon Office, Selected)

1. As early as 1934 Army Signal Corps cryptanalysts were deciphering certain Japanese diplomatic codes—a process which was given the code name "Magic." On March 2, 1935, the Signal Corps began issuing to G-2 bulletins concerning these intercepted messages. In September 1939 Marshall approved the first significant increase in funding for the Signal Intelligence Service. (George V. Strong Memorandum for the Chief of Staff, September 5, 1939, NA/RG 165 [WPD, 4198].) By August 1940 the small Signal Corps group headed by Chief Cryptanalyst William F. Friedman had begun to read the extremely complex machine cipher (designated by United States cryptanalysts as "Purple") used by the Japanese for very important diplomatic messages. By mid-October a further expansion of the Signal Intelligence Service was being planned. (William F. Friedman, "Expansion of the Signal Intelligence Service from 1930–7 December 1941," NA/RG 457 [SRH–134], pp. 7, 9–10.)

To Major General Frederic H. Smith[1]   October 25, 1940
[Washington, D.C.]

Dear Smith: This is a wholly informal letter, to which no reply is to be made. I merely want to make certain that your attention has or will be called to the situation at Virginia Beach.

I understand that this is a small community, particularly in the winter period, with limited resources; that there are three regiments in the vicinity of the town, two National Guard and one Regular; that there is no common commander for the three because of their varied missions; and that the local community are not straining themselves to cooperate in providing some resources in the town to meet the heavy impact of men who show up there in the evenings. What particularly concerns me in such a situation is the fact that the Regular organization will undoubtedly shift for itself very promptly and that with no centralized direction the National Guard regiments will either be competing or complaining, or both.[2]

With every move we make being checked and double-checked by the press and by interested mothers and fathers, I want to make as much of a good impression as possible at the start rather than to be involved in a defensive situation in which we follow the old routine of stating the matter is going to be attended to or is under study. I am not even certain that you have anything directly to do with this. If you do not, please pass it on to the proper person.   Faithfully yours,

P.S.   I am enclosing a memorandum from the Morale Section of The Adjutant General's Department to an Assistant Adjutant General.[3]

GCMRL/G. C. Marshall Papers (Pentagon Office, General)
   1. Smith (U.S.M.A., 1903) was commandant of the army's Coast Artillery School at Fort Monroe, Virginia, and commanding general of the Third Coast Artillery District, which included Virginia Beach, Virginia.
   2. The three Coast Artillery regiments near Virginia Beach were the Regular Army's 71st (antiaircraft), the Pennsylvania National Guard's 213th (antiaircraft), and the New York National Guard's 244th (155-mm gun).
   3. The editors have been unable to identify this document.

Memorandum for General Pershing   October 28, 1940
Washington, D.C.

You will recall that I mentioned to you yesterday that the Under Secretary of State, Mr. Welles, had been trying to get in touch with me in the morning.

He reached me shortly after my return from the Hospital,[1] and had this request to make:

> If you could see your way clear to do so, it might be very desirable if you radioed some statement to Marshal Pétain, possibly with reference to his last message to you, to the general effect—that there exists in the United States the greatest sympathy for the French people and an understanding of the tragic situation in which they find themselves. However, if the French Government should elect to enter into an agreement with the German Government looking toward the defeat of England, especially the utilization of the French Fleet for this purpose, there would inevitably be a revulsion of feeling in this country.[2]

In the morning papers it would appear that matters have already gone well towards an agreement of some sort between the German and French Governments. I do not know how you would feel about such a proposition, and I am merely submitting it as a result of my conversation over the telephone with Mr. Welles. I am sorry I cannot get away this morning from the office to talk to you personally, but there is little I can say that is not included in the foregoing.

If you should decide to send a message to Marshal Pétain, Mr. Welles suggests that it should go through the State Department, otherwise there is little chance of its delivery, as everything that might interfere with German proposals is being kept from Marshal Pétain.[3]

G. C. Marshall

LC/J. J. Pershing Papers (General Correspondence)

1. Because of ill health, John J. Pershing lived at the Walter Reed Army Medical Center in Washington, D.C.

2. On General Pershing's eightieth birthday (September 13, 1940), French head of state Marshal Henri Philippe Pétain had sent greetings to his "old comrade in arms." (*New York Times,* September 14, 1940, p. 19.)

On October 21 British Prime Minister Churchill had requested that President Roosevelt "speak in the strongest terms" to the French about United States disapproval of any attempt to turn over the French fleet to Germany. Three days later, Adolf Hitler met with Pétain in a widely publicized conference at which the French agreed to cooperate with Germany. President Roosevelt wrote a personal message to Pétain on October 24—which was delivered to the marshal by the United States chargé at Vichy on the morning of October 26—warning against surrendering the French fleet. Pétain replied on November 1 that "the French Government has declared that the French fleet would never be given up and there is nothing which today can warrant questioning this solemn promise." (Department of State, *Foreign Relations of the United States: Diplomatic Papers, 1940,* 5 vols. [Washington: GPO, 1955-61], 2: 474–84.)

3. The following is typed at the bottom of this document in the Pershing papers: "NOTE. In reply to above suggestion, I telephoned General Marshall and asked that he communicate with Mr. Welles and say that, knowing Marshal Pétain as I do, it seemed unwise for me to cable him regarding the above subject. J.J.P."

MEMORANDUM FOR THE ASSISTANT   October 28, 1940
SECRETARY OF WAR [PATTERSON]   [Washington, D.C.]
Confidential

Dear Judge: I have arranged to move two units (one the 155mm gun regiment CAC, and one separate battalion, antiaircraft) from Fort Barrancas, and there will remain there only one Coast Artillery unit raised to war strength. It has been rather difficult to arrange this because we are already embarked on the construction program, and it is very important that no shelter be abandoned and that none be duplicated elsewhere. However, we think we have caught this in time to make such arrangements.

I feel that Commander Read's statement regarding possible interference with Naval pilot training was a sound one, that there would be interference if antiaircraft and 155mm gun firing were carried out in that vicinity. However, for your confidential information, I would like you to know that when I talked to Mr. Forrestal over the 'phone about this he remarked that one of the serious objections was the presence of the 155 gun regiment because it was a colored unit.[1] I am passing this information on to you that you may see the contrast between what the Army is taking in this matter, and how firmly the Navy is standing to protect itself. Here we have an objection by the Navy to the presence of an Army colored unit in a nearby post, at the same time that the Army is being called upon to mix white and colored troops in the same unit or companies in the same organization.

GCMRL/G. C. Marshall Papers (Pentagon Office, Selected)

1. The Pensacola Naval Air Station Auxiliary Landing Field was 2.5 miles from Barrancas, Florida. Commander Walton R. Read's statement is not in the Marshall papers. James V. Forrestal, under secretary of the navy, had written to Marshall on October 26. "Thank you very much indeed for your help to us on the situation at Fort Barrancas. We appreciate it a lot because we shall have to put a much greater strain on the facilities of Pensacola in the coming months, and the additional Army personnel, particularly with regard to the use of the ranges, would have made our problem difficult." (Forrestal to Marshall, October 26, 1940, GCMRL/ G. C. Marshall Papers [Pentagon Office, Selected].) The Fifty-fourth Coast Artillery Regiment (155-mm gun) was scheduled to be activated at Fort Barrancas, Florida, but was transferred instead to Camp Wallace near Galveston, Texas. In mid-1941 it was removed from that post at the insistence of local whites. (Lee, *Employment of Negro Troops,* pp. 99–100, 146.)

MEMORANDUM FOR THE QUARTERMASTER   October 28, 1940
GENERAL [GREGORY]   [Washington, D.C.]

Let me know just what is being done towards providing places for religious worship in the various camps and cantonments.

GCMRL/G. C. Marshall Papers (Pentagon Office, Selected)

MEMORANDUM FOR THE ASSISTANT   October 28, 1940
CHIEF OF STAFF, G-1 [SHEDD]   [Washington, D.C.]

There has been brought to my attention the question of ratings for men with the chaplains and with the recreation personnel. At the present time the chaplain, as I understand it, has to get his immediate helper from the troop complement. During this period of rapid promotion, this, as a rule, denies the individual any promotion, which means in effect that the chaplain gets either the poorer men or is unable to get the good men.

Please let me know what the status of this matter is, both as to the chaplain's immediate helper and the other men connected with the general morale program.

NA/RG 165 (OCS, 18901-100)

MEMORANDUM FOR GENERAL BRYDEN   October 28, 1940
Confidential   Washington, D.C.

Subject: Officer Candidate Schools:

In general, the attached proposal appears to be satisfactory.[1] However, I would like to be informed on one or two phases.

Is it felt advisable to have men applying for commissions rather than for us to select men for commissions? In this connection, you will probably have the entire colored personnel applying for commissions.[2]

In paragraph 2 of the attached memorandum, the data is partially based on the statement that sufficient men will apply for a second year tour of duty to avoid any difficulties in obtaining desired numbers. In the event of a continued crisis in the international situation, we would want these men; as a matter of fact, we would probably compel these men to continue on active service. But if we are looking at a continuing proposition of peace, even though a somewhat critical period in the world prevails, it would seem to me that we should avoid repeating on these reserve officers and should provide a new quota of considerable size each year. The graduates of the ROTC, particularly if money is provided to increase the advanced student numbers, and the graduates from the Candidate Schools, would provide the new units. I would be interested in knowing about what size the new quota should be under such policy.

If the Candidate Schools are well run, the product should be a very fine one because of the high degree of selectivity employed and because of the fact that these men would have had at least eight months of disciplinary training as soldiers—a much firmer foundation for future usefulness than the more casual disciplinary training of the ROTC. There is the other feature, that the larger this group, the more certain we are to face a continuation of the Selective Service law. And conversely, the smaller the group the more apt we are to have the Selective Service law revoked. If young men can feel, if they think they have the stuff, that after only eight months as enlisted men they can secure a commission, a great deal of the reluctance to such service will have been eliminated.

Coupled with the foregoing thought, it seems to me that there would be a still further adjustment having for its purpose the more rapid elimination of officers from the active list of the Reserve Corps as they approach field grades.

G. C. M.

NA/RG 407 (Classified, 352 [9-19-40] [1] Sec. 1)

1. In September 1940, after having prevented an immediate and heavy War Department commitment to expanding the Citizens' Military Training Camps concept (see Marshall to Davis, July 20, 1940, pp. 273–74), Marshall directed G-3 to study the feasibility of establishing Officer Candidate Schools. The Training and Operations Division replied that officers in the training sections of the five branches immediately concerned (Infantry, Cavalry, Field Artillery, Coast Artillery, and Signal Corps) were "unanimous in opposing the project, stating that no necessity existed therefor." Given the apparently ample supply of men in the Officers' Reserve Corps—primarily R.O.T.C. graduates—the branch chiefs did not wish to expand the O.R.C. unless the need became urgent. The G-3 memorandum conceded Marshall's point that Officer Candidate Schools might have some morale value in a democratic system, but it urged that the number of candidates selected be kept to a minimum. (Frank M. Andrews draft Memorandum for the Chief of Staff, September 7, 1940, NA/RG 407 [General, 352 (9-19-40) (1) Sec. 1].) Despite this opposition, Marshall directed that planning for O.C.S. proceed.

2. On November 19 Lieutenant Colonel Ben M. Sawbridge presented G-1's study of Officer Candidate Schools to the chief of staff. Based upon existing Mobilization Regulations, it permitted men in basic training to apply for admission to O.C.S. This would be a mistake, Marshall said. "We will have 10,000 applications; every man will get his Senator on the job. We will invite a vast amount of trouble. We want men who are preeminent in leadership. The Marines got the best group last time and we do not want to lose the next crop. We should set up a policy that the Company Commander will pick a man and final decision will be made by a conference of the officers who are acquainted with the man's ability. I will accept this because the Regulation has been drawn, but I saw the operation of the Thomason Act and think it was rotten. There was too much desk and not enough field work." (William T. Sexton Notes on Conference in the Office of the Chief of Staff, November 19, 1940, NA/RG 165 [OCS, Chief of Staff Conferences File].)

To Lieutenant General Charles D. Herron   October 29, 1940
Washington, D.C.

Dear Herron: I received a note from you this morning regarding the Governor's arrangement for the Selective Service Act, and your calling to duty the first Japanese ROTC product.[1] Also your suggestion regarding internment camps.[2] I am having the various points looked up by the sections of the Staff concerned.

As I told you when I was in Hawaii, you are a great source of comfort to me because I feel that your sound judgment and utter loyalty guarantee the full protection of our military interests in the Pacific.

Your reference to the business of the Army expansion is appreciated.[3] We are doing a great many things, and involvements are numerous and exceedingly complicated. However, we have been able so far to keep our heads above the deluge; the seed-corn planted last fall, which began to bear fruit in the early summer, has saved us in the business of this tremendous expansion. The numbers involved and the reorganizations accomplished seem very small in the light of what we have recently embarked on. However, if those preliminary moves and expansions had had to be carried out at the same time as the present program, it would have been utterly impossible to have avoided tremendous confusion—at least in the minds of the lower echelons struggling to find themselves.

I feel now that if we can go on into next March without untoward incident, the full plot will have been developed—the last phase being the establishment and gearing into full running order some 22 replacement centers of 15,000 or more men each. The worst should then be over, and even though a much greater expansion is required, so firm a foundation will have been laid that we should be able to carry on with far less difficulty than at present.

My trips about the country, and particularly those to Panama and Hawaii have been immensely profitable to me in passing on the various issues raised in the War Department. I am just going into what I hope is the last adjustment of the War Department General Staff, in the creation of an additional Deputy in whom will be centered all matters pertaining to the Air Corps, along with the divorcement of the GHQ Air Force from its temporary status under the Chief of the Air Corps. Once this set-up is in full running order, I think we can accommodate ourselves to future requirements.

McNair has taken a tremendous load off my shoulders, but is having a pretty hard time himself. He has a ten-passenger plane and he and his staff are on the go almost constantly.

We got a great deal of enjoyment from the fruit you and Louise treated us to; but I do wish I could sit down to another Hawaiian dinner like that she honored me with the night before my departure from Honolulu.

Give my ADC Jimmie my love, and tell her I hope she is keeping up professionally preparatory to serving me when the time comes. Incidentally she might be of help in coordinating some 15,000 ambitious would be Army hostesses—we only need 90.[4]   Affectionately,

GCMRL/G. C. Marshall Papers (Pentagon Office, Selected)

1. Herron wrote that he had called to active duty the first Reserve officer of Japanese ancestry, a University of Hawaii R.O.T.C. graduate, for an assignment in the quartermaster depot. But Governor Joseph B. Poindexter had "just announced the personnel of the Draft Boards and there is not one Japanese name in the lot, although 40% of the draft will be of that blood. I fear that the young Japanese will come to camp in a bad frame of mind and that my calling of the single Reserve officer will have no effect on the inevitable reaction to the Governor's action. I do not see how he could have done such a thing!" (Herron to Marshall, October 26, 1940, GCMRL/G. C. Marshall Papers [Pentagon Office, Selected].)

2. Concerning the possibility that a significant number of United States citizens being evacuated from the Far East might have to be housed in Hawaii, Herron wrote: "For your information about 3,000 evacuees from the Orient could be housed here temporarily without putting up tent camps or turning soldiers out of barracks. Should more than 3,000 evacuees be debarked here we would need immediately more cots." (Ibid.)

3. Concluding his letter to Marshall, Herron wrote: "Contemplation of the war Army that you are building makes my few remaining hairs stand on end and I am appalled by the thought of all of the decisions that must come up to you. Praise God you have a strong body as well as a good mind!" (Ibid.)

4. Marshall later wrote to Senator Joseph C. O'Mahoney: "The matter of the appointment of hostesses and librarians has caused me more time-consuming energy than the augmentation of the Army to 1,400,000. The War Department has successfully withstood terrific pressures from every direction." (Marshall to O'Mahoney, [March 10?, 1941], GCMRL/G. C. Marshall Papers [Pentagon Office, General].)

To GLENN L. MARTIN[1]
November 6, 1940
[Washington, D.C.]

Dear Mr. Martin: Arnold and I got back to town about 2:30 yesterday afternoon and I proceeded directly to the office and got in a couple of hours' work before closing time. I felt up to fast action as result of the delightful relaxation of my hours with you.

I want you to know that I appreciated very much your luxurious and gracious hospitality. I thoroughly enjoyed my day and only regret that I was not a better shot. Despite your feeling that the geese did not do just as you would have them conduct their affairs yesterday, I felt that we had a full opportunity to get the limit, that is, if we had the goods.

Thank you very much for a fine outing.[2]   Faithfully yours,

GCMRL/G. C. Marshall Papers (Pentagon Office, Selected)

1. One of the pioneers of aviation, Martin was president and chairman of the board of the Glenn L. Martin Company of Baltimore, Maryland, an aircraft manufacturer.

2. Major General Henry H. Arnold had arranged the trip in order to demonstrate to the chief of staff the effect a shortage of aluminum was having on aircraft production. At the Martin factory they found only a small part of the plant in operation. Arnold recalled that upon returning to Washington, Marshall "put in his own grim plea for more aluminum. . . . Overnight, the attitude of the men in charge of aluminum production changed." (H. H. Arnold, *Global Mission* [New York: Harper and Brothers, 1949], p. 205.) See Memorandum for the Assistant Secretary of War, December 9, 1940, pp. 365–66.

To Major General Frederic H. Smith   November 7, 1940
[Washington, D.C.]

Dear Smith: I am sending you directly the attached letter, which came to me with a tough steak. The latter had reached a point where it had to be disposed of. Do not trouble to answer this letter, but I pass it on to you as a possible hint toward a poorly run mess, for which I find few excuses.

As you will see, it is not anonymous, and I am putting this man Gardner rather out on a limb by passing it on to you. However, there may be something in it, so do not kill him until you have looked into it.[1] Faithfully yours,

GCMRL/G. C. Marshall Papers (Pentagon Office, General)

1. The "tough steak" letter from Gardner, who was probably an enlisted man in the Coast Artillery Corps, was not returned to General Marshall. For another comment by the chief of staff on army cooking, see his letter to Miss Prudence Penny, February 24, 1941, pp. 428–29. Another example of his handling of enlisted men's complaints is his letter to Private Frank W. Clay, April 7, 1941, pp. 467–68.

Memorandum for Admiral Stark   November 8, 1940
Secret   [Washington, D.C.]

Dear Betty: I sent over to you the other day—delivered to Captain Sherman, a study from the Army War Plans Division of October 31st with relation to additional funds for continuing planning and design, and initiating construction at Army Bases in British Possessions.[1] In view of our previous conversations on this subject following the President's refusal to consider the matter—after his original of $25,000,000 cash—I wanted to get your reaction before reopening the question.

I am told that the paper has been mislaid somewhere in the Navy Department, so I am approaching you direct as to the Army situation in this matter. As I understand it, the Navy has funds available which enable them to go ahead with the initial moves in the matter, meaning surveys, preparation of plans and design. $30,000 of these funds were loaned to us. Those have been exhausted, so we shall have to disband our organization or get more money within a few weeks.

War Plans is requesting that the Army make a separate request for $25,000,000 allotment out of the President's fund, $15,000,000 of which to be contract authorization. I dislike to become involved in a separate move in this matter, so I would appreciate your giving me your reaction.[2]

GCMRL/G. C. Marshall Papers (Pentagon Office, Selected)
1. Captain Forrest P. Sherman was a member of the navy's War Plans Division. The army's War Plans Division study is in NA/RG 165 (WPD, 4351–10).
2. The editors have not found a written reply from the chief of naval operations.

TO WILLARD K. SMITH[1]   November 12, 1940
[Washington, D.C.]

My dear Captain Smith: I received your note of November 18th [*8th*], and a copy of MERCURY with your article on Military History. I had not seen this, and am very glad you gave me the opportunity.[2]

I have always been puzzled, and still am puzzled, as to the most effective method of presenting various phases of our military history to the public. At present we are laying, I suppose, quite a foundation for future military history, and I am inclined to think that the mature minds of today will have been so deeply impressed by the conflicting presentations of columnists, radio commentators, etc. that they will not in their lifetime acquire an accurate appreciation of the situation, however well done the future historical presentations of the cause and effects of this period.

I would like very much to see your article on the German effort in the production of ordnance equipment.[3]   Faithfully yours,

GCMRL/G. C. Marshall Papers (Pentagon Office, General)
1. Smith, who signed his letter "former Captain, Ordnance, A.E.F.," was the editor of *News and Opinion,* a New York City publication.
2. Marshall's American Historical Association speech on December 28, 1939 (pp. 123–27), Smith wrote, had inspired him "to prepare an article setting forth the unpalatable facts of our previous military efforts." He had difficulty in getting the story published, "because editors generally admitted the same tendency to gloss over our deficiencies of which you complained." (Smith to Marshall, November 8, 1940, GCMRL/G. C. Marshall Papers [Pentagon Office, General].) Smith's "The Legend of American Invincibility" was published in *American Mercury* 51(November 1940): 295–302.
3. Smith had also written another article: "Is Germany's 'Secret Weapon' Work?" *Nation's Business* 28(November 1940): 20–22, 86–89.

MEMORANDUM FOR THE PRESIDENT   November 13, 1940
Secret   [Washington, D.C.]

Subject: Test of Flying Fortress Aircraft.[1]

Our aviation program includes the construction of a large number of long range bombers of the Flying Fortress type. These airplanes, which we consider of paramount importance to successful Hemisphere defense, have been given extensive technical tests, but thus far no airplane having comparable characteristics has been used in war.

The determination of the combat efficiency of this airplane would be of great value to us, as this would permit improvements to be incorporated in later deliveries under present contracts.

With this purpose in mind, I suggest that if a way can be found, legally and diplomatically acceptable, to secure such a test of these planes, that the necessary arrangements be made to do so.[2]

GCMRL/G. C. Marshall Papers (Pentagon Office, Selected)

1. The question of delivering to the British some of the Air Corps' most modern bombers—the B-17 "Flying Fortress"—had been under discussion since mid-June 1940. Marshall had agreed to include five of the planes in the United States portion of the destroyers-bases agreement of September 2 with Britain. (See Conference Notes, August 20, 1940, p. 292.) The B-17s were ultimately not included with the destroyers in that agreement, but by mid-September, Secretary of the Treasury Henry Morgenthau, Jr., had convinced President Roosevelt to share B-17 production equally with Great Britain. (Notes on conferences in the Office of the Chief of Staff, September 18 [meeting of September 17] and November 13 [meeting of November 7], 1940, NA/RG 165 [OCS, Chief of Staff Conferences File].) An important problem for Marshall was how the delivery of thoroughly modern materiel could be justified under the provisions of the Walsh Amendment. (See note 1, Certificate of Compliance, July 12, 1940, p. 262.) He consulted with representatives of the Attorney General's Office, and a carefully worded certificate of compliance was written, based upon arguments expressed in this memorandum, which he agreed to sign. (Claude M. Adams Notes on Conference in Office Chief of Staff, November 13, 1940, NA/RG 165 [OCS, Chief of Staff Conferences File].)

2. At a meeting on the morning of November 14 with Major General Henry H. Arnold, deputy chief of staff for air since October 1, and Major General George H. Brett (V.M.I., 1909), acting chief of the Air Corps, Marshall said: "Battle test will enable us to eliminate errors sooner. Battle tests are better than years of peace tests. . . . The earlier the test the sooner we can standardize" airplane construction with the British. Arnold and Brett agreed that twenty planes was the minimum number necessary for the test. Moreover, giving twenty of the eighty-six B-17s on hand would not seriously interfere with crew training, Arnold thought. Brett hoped that this agreement would eliminate the need to divide production evenly with the British. (Orlando Ward Notes of Conference in Office of Chief of Staff, November 14, 1940, ibid. The issue of sending B-17s to Britain is discussed in Watson, *Chief of Staff,* pp. 306–9.)

To Colonel Milton G. Baker   November 13, 1940
                                                 [Washington, D.C.]

Dear Colonel Baker: I have your letter of November 11th, enclosing the check.[1] You are very generous, and I appreciate this highly. As a matter of fact, I have never accepted any honorarium in the past, but this time I find it a very pleasant business; and it may interest you to know that I will pass it on as a wedding present to my step-daughter.[2]

My day with you at Wayne was highly interesting and very pleasant. I congratulate you on a splendid institution, and an exceptionally fine looking group of young soldiers. Their marching, discipline, and appearance were evidence of the highest military standards.[3]   Faithfully yours,

GCMRL/G. C. Marshall Papers (Pentagon Office, Selected)

1. Marshall had spoken at the Armistice Day service at Valley Forge Military Academy in Wayne, Pennsylvania, on November 10. Superintendent Baker's letter of November 11 enclosed an honorarium of $250. (See Marshall to Baker, October 8, 1940, pp. 326–27.)

2. Molly Pender Brown was engaged to Captain James J. Winn (U.S.M.A., 1929), an artilleryman stationed at Fort Davis, Panama Canal Zone. Announcements of their December wedding had been printed on November 3 in various newspapers, including the *New York Times*, sec. 2, p. 3.

3. Despite Baker's promise that Marshall's speech would go unreported, both the *Philadelphia Record* (p. 3) and the *Philadelphia Inquirer* ran stories on November 11. The chief of staff was quoted as having said: "Democracy is on trial. In order to meet the threat of total war we must combat it with total defense. Total defense is not only the building of a military machine, but the building of spirit, too. We must make every man, woman and child in this country believe we have something worth defending. We can accomplish things fast in a military way in this country because of the superiority of our reserve officers. It is due to this high type civilian body that we are doing today what many believed could not be done in so short a time." (*Philadelphia Inquirer*, November 11, 1940, p. 6.) No copy of this address is in the Marshall papers.

To Mrs. John R. Berry[1]   November 14, 1940
[Washington, D.C.]

Dear Mrs. Berry: I have just finished reading your letter telling me that two of your sons have taken their places in the Army, and pledging, as a mother, your full support to me and to them in this emergency. Nothing could be more reassuring to me than this evidence of the desire of a mother to contribute all within her power to the support of the Government in its efforts to keep this portion of a tragic world free of the horrors of war.

I appreciate most sincerely your writing as you did, and I assure you that if on my inspections I find the opportunity, it will be a pleasure for me to meet your boys.

Thank you for your invitation for me to return to Savannah. Mrs. Marshall and I have never forgotten our service there and would welcome an opportunity to return.   Faithfully yours,

GCMRL/G. C. Marshall Papers (Pentagon Office, General)

1. A Savannah, Georgia, resident who remembered Marshall from his assignment at nearby Fort Screven in 1932 and 1933, Mrs. Berry had written that two of her sons were now "a part of your great and glorious Army" and that she was "behind you and them 100%." (Berry to Marshall, October 26, 1940, GCMRL/G. C. Marshall Papers [Pentagon Office, General].)

To Sumner Welles

November 15, 1940
[Washington, D.C.]

My dear Mr. Welles: While I have thanked you personally, I wish more formally to express my appreciation of the strong support you gave me in the task of entertaining the Chiefs of Staff of the Latin-American Republics.[1]

From a purely professional point of view, I believe the visit was very much worth while in every respect, and that not only were our guests convinced of our friendly attitude; but what was much more important, I think they carried away with them the decided impression that a tremendous military power was developing in this country which could not be ignored. This latter impression, I believe, will to a considerable extent, off-set the impressive picture they get of the military power of Germany.

I would appreciate your conveying to the members of your staff who assisted us in this affair my personal thanks for the full cooperation they have given us. Faithfully yours,

GCMRL/G. C. Marshall Papers (Pentagon Office, General)

1. Concerning the October visits by two groups of military leaders from Latin America, see Marshall to Góes Monteiro, October 15, 1940, pp. 329–30.

To Major General Roy D. Keehn

November 19, 1940
[Washington, D.C.]

Dear Keehn: I have not had a moment in which to give your letter of November 11th a careful reading until this morning.[1]

I appreciate your concern over my physical condition, but I do not think you need worry about it. I blew off a little steam on you, but considering the fact that this was the first time I have allowed myself that privilege in a year and a half, I think the explosion was mild. I must confess to the necessity for tremendous restrain of feeling in the light of irritating pettiness of continued pressures on me and unjustified criticisms of the War Department, at a time when we have leaned over backward in an effort to do at least the right thing, if not, I think, more than we should. We are trying to organize an army, and we are still struggling with political aspects; given enough of the latter and we are wasting our money and gravely risking the security of the United States—to put it plainly. If everything pertaining to the Army has to be put on a town meeting basis, we might as well quit before we start.

I am writing rather frankly; however, you have written with extreme frankness and if I chose to, I could be much offended but I have ignored all that, knowing you and feeling confident of your friendship for me and your genuine desire to see me make the grade.

I think if you were to occupy my chair for thirty minutes and struggle with things of vast importance to this country, and at the same time struggle with a wide variety of superficial, irritating, and prejudicial reactions, you would marvel that we go ahead as smoothly as we do. Faithfully yours,

GCMRL/G. C. Marshall Papers (Pentagon Office, Selected)

1. Keehn had been unhappy with what he considered the pernicious influence of certain Illinois politicians on the Thirty-third Division and the Regular Army's frequent refusal to view National Guard affairs in the proper perspective. He was not reluctant to communicate his views on these issues to Marshall. His letters of October 30 and November 11, for example, are largely concerned with the army's concessionaire policies at post exchanges. Keehn recently had been elected vice-president of the National Guard Association, and on November 8 he had visited Marshall in Washington. (Keehn to Marshall, October 30, 1940, GCMRL/ G. C. Marshall Papers [Pentagon Office, Selected].)

Keehn's letter of November 11 to Marshall began: "Frankly, George Marshall, I am a little worried about your nervousness and high tension. If you will permit a very fine friend and a older head to talk with you quietly, I would like to say—Get some rest and relaxation. You know that I know you are the smartest man in the Army, but I believe some of these boys, including Keehn's insistence on getting the low-down, have gotten under your hide, which you cannot afford to let happen." (Keehn to Marshall, November 11, 1940, ibid.)

MEMORANDUM FOR GENERAL WATSON[1]   November 20, 1940
Confidential   [Washington, D.C.]

Yesterday afternoon I explained to the President the status of the delivery of heavy bombers to the British. Every day we are being probed by the press and radio commentators regarding this matter. The question is, in my opinion, do we worry along until there is a leak with additional embarrassments, or can something be said at the present time in the way of a "lead-up" to a deeply interested public—and a critical Congress.

I wish you would ascertain from the President whether I might not make the following reference to the matter if questioned on the subject today at a press conference I am due to have.

In reply to these questions regarding the release of heavy bombers to the British Government, I will say that we have arranged to give them priority on the delivery of about 26 heavy four-engine [B-24] bombers, in exchange for which the British Government have released to us enough engines to equip 41 Flying Fortresses [B-17-C] which had either been delivered to us without engines or would be delivered before the end of December. Our own engine deliveries will suffice for the future.

Furthermore, we are in the process of negotiating a satisfactory basis of exchange for the release of 20 Flying Fortresses completely equipped, except as to the Norden bombsight. If this can be arranged we feel that it will be a great advantage to us in that it will give us an actual service test of this particular type of heavy bomber prior to final commitments by us for the manufacture of more of this type.[2]

GCMRL/G. C. Marshall Papers (Pentagon Office, Selected)

1. Edwin M. Watson had been promoted to major general effective October 1, 1940.
2. Marshall's press conference statement was quoted in the *New York Times* on November 21, pp. 1, 14. The following day an editorial in that paper observed: "The American people know by now that Great Britain is fighting for their security as well as for her own. The transaction is to be justified only on the ground that the greatest possible help for Great Britain is the soundest possible defense for ourselves." (November 22, 1940, p. 22.)

To Mrs. W. H. Cathey
Confidential

November 20, 1940
[Washington, D.C.]

My dear Mrs. Cathey: I have received your letter of November 15th, regarding your son and the conditions at Camp Jackson and in Columbia, South Carolina, and have given it a careful reading. I am not only concerned over the morale of the Army we are forming, but I am deeply concerned regarding the well being of the young men in the ranks.[1]

For your confidential information, I am sending a copy of your letter, with a note from me, to the Commander of the First Army, General Drum, and to the Corps Commander, General Short, at Columbia, in which the 30th Division is serving. Also I am having my Inspector look into the matter. You may be sure that it will not be given casual treatment, and that we will do our best to have conditions such as you and every other mother would desire.[2]

In response to your request, I have avoided disclosing your name.   Faithfully yours,

GCMRL/G. C. Marshall Papers (Pentagon Office, General)

1. Mrs. Cathey explained that she was the proud mother of "one of your new soldier boys," but she felt compelled to protest to the highest authority certain conditions that she had observed during her visit to Fort Jackson, where her son was in training. "The drinking that I saw there among the soldiers is too terrible to describe." She described the problem at length, noting that her son had accepted "courageously" the army's hardships and living conditions, which to her "seemed little better than animals." Moreover, "there is no kind of recreation," and her son had been tired and ill. Nevertheless, she reported, he claimed to like the life. "I wanted to bring him home on a leave & get him well but he is so interested in his new antitank gun he didn't want to come at this time." (Cathey to Marshall, November 15, 1940, GCMRL/ G. C. Marshall Papers [Pentagon Office, General].)
2. Marshall also sent a copy of Mrs. Cathey's letter to Chief of Chaplains William R. Arnold. Major General Walter C. Short replied through Lieutenant General Hugh A. Drum. Drum and Arnold replied that the picture of life at Fort Jackson was overdrawn. (Drum to Marshall, November 22, 1940, ibid.; Arnold to Marshall, November 25, 1940, ibid.) This mother's letter and similar ones received by the War Department influenced the radio address Marshall delivered on November 29. (See pp. 355–59.)

MEMORANDUM FOR GENERAL BRYDEN November 22, 1940
[Washington, D.C.]

Give me the venereal rate for the 22d Infantry for the past three months; also give me the venereal rate for the past month in the 27th Division. Let me have the name of the Colonel and of the Lieutenant-Colonel of the 22d Infantry.

Let me know what is the reason for not giving bachelor officers commutation of quarters. The Secretary of War found a tremendous reaction regarding this.[1]

Rents and Moral conditions:

Have someone report to me what might be done to control the skyrocketing of rents near the large camps in the South, and what we can do prior to the passage of a law to improve the situation as to drinking, prostitution and matters of that sort, which are becoming very serious.

GCMRL/G. C. Marshall Papers (Pentagon Office, Selected)

1. Secretary of War Stimson had visited Fort Benning between November 16 and 20 and Fort McClellan on November 19. At Fort McClellan he had inspected the Twenty-seventh Division, New York National Guard, and the Twenty-second Infantry Regiment, a Regular Army unit of the Fourth Infantry Division. The secretary commented in his diary that he was "very much impressed" with what he saw. (Yale/H. L. Stimson Papers [Diary, 31: 150–51].) When he returned to the War Department on the morning of November 22, Stimson "had a long conference with General Marshall, lasting nearly an hour, in which I went over with him fully all the long list of recommendations which I had made concerning my observation and inspection." (Ibid., p. 153.)

To LEOPOLD STOKOWSKI November 25, 1940
[Washington, D.C.]

My dear Dr. Stokowski: I enjoyed very much your brief visit with me yesterday afternoon with Mr. Williams, and have thought over the several suggestions you made.[1]

In the first place, your most generous offer to make some appearances with your All American Youth Orchestra in the camps this winter, will be most gratefully received. It is merely a matter of finding out when and where you might coordinate such departures from your schedule. If you will give us an outline of your winter tour, I can have suggestions submitted as to the largest troop concentrations where you might conveniently appear. Such a contribution as yours should be a tremendous inspiration to Army personnel who would have the rare opportunity of seeing you and hearing your orchestra.

I am enclosing a statement of the instrumentation of Army bands, together with the recently recommended increase, and I would like very much to have your suggestions in this matter, which you offered to give me yesterday. There is also attached the locations of the various replacement centers, for which training bands are to be organized. Please look over this and let me have your suggestions as to the best point for the development of a band under your supervision, both as to type of band, and as to possible basis for the development of band leaders and principal musicians.[2] Faithfully yours,

GCMRL/G. C. Marshall Papers (Pentagon Office, Selected)

1. In 1940 Stokowski, who was best known as conductor of the Philadelphia Orchestra, had formed an All-American Youth Orchestra, composed of young musicians from each state, and had toured South America. At this time Stokowski was planning a lengthy tour in the United States and Canada for the spring and summer of 1941; he proposed to bring the youth orchestra to army camps near his tour cities. Aubrey W. Williams was administrator of the National Youth Administration.

2. In reply, Stokowski outlined his ideas for improving the army's bands, including reinstrumentation, creation of a demonstration band, schools for band leaders and principal musicians, and modernized orchestrations. "I believe a new type of band can be developed that in some ways will be more suited to open air playing, for standing still, for marching, and for men mounted on horses. With some variations and additions we could develop a kind of band that could play from armored cars while in motion or standing still. These could be very effective in motion for adding cheerfulness and morale to the troops while on long-distance, forced marches, if that is desired." (Stokowski to Marshall, November 28, 1940, GCMRL/ G. C. Marshall Papers [Pentagon Office, Selected].) For further information on Stokowski's ideas, see Marshall to Holtz, February 14, 1941, pp. 423–24.

N.B.C. RADIO ADDRESS ON THE PROGRESS   November 29, 1940
OF NATIONAL DEFENSE[1]   Washington, D.C.

The past few weeks have brought me so many queries regarding Army affairs that I feel it is desirable to outline the exact status of our military program and the progress that we have made. The majority of the questions have related to the present size of the Army and its organization; to the development of the Air Corps and the training of its pilots and mechanics; to the conditions in our camps, the progress of construction, and to the state of morale among our troops. Since we are at peace with the world, and the basic purpose of our preparations is to maintain that peace, and since this country is undertaking its present comprehensive military program because the American people demanded it, I feel that the more fully informed the American public is, the easier will be the problem for the War Department and military officials in general. Therefore, this brief review tonight of the present status of the Army.

A year ago last summer our active Army consisted of about 170,000 soldiers, 56 squadrons of combat planes, and some 2500 pilots. There were two small regiments of mechanized troops.

From a purely organizational point of view, the Regular Army had only three half-organized infantry divisions. As for larger organizations, the basic battle unit is an Army Corps, and there was not one in our Army. Furthermore, the troops on active duty in this country, meaning the Regular Army units, were scattered among one hundred or more small posts, making the training of a genuine field army a practical impossibility. As to munitions, such as guns, ammunition, equipment, and motor transportation, we seriously lacked adequate equipment for the organizations then on the rolls, and most of the materiel for which funds had but recently been provided was not due for delivery for many months to come.

Now, I wish very briefly to outline the situation of the Army at this moment, in contrast to that of a little more than a year ago:

Today there are 500,000 men in the field undergoing intensive training, and within a very few weeks this total will approach 800,000. Instead of three incomplete infantry divisions, there are today eighteen under training, with nine more soon to come. The two weak mechanized regiments have grown into an armored corps of two divisions, each of about 12,000 men.

One Cavalry division has had its missing units organized and is rapidly approaching a war strength of about 12,000 men, with a second division in process of activation. Five partially organized antiaircraft regiments on active duty in July a year ago have been increased to 22 complete regiments in the field training at the present time, with more to report in January. Similar changes have taken place in coast defense troops, Engineer regiments, communications battalions, medical organizations, and supply trains.

The Air Force of 56 squadrons has been increased to 109, and the number of pilots to 4,000. Training schools are now expanding to provide a production rate of about 1,000 pilots a month by next summer. The school for air mechanics which was graduating 1500 a year is now turning out men at a rate of 9,000 a year, and in a few months will have a yearly output of 30,000.

As to munitions, American industry is rapidly absorbing the orders for the production of vast amounts of materiel during the next eighteen months. The task is particularly difficult because we are endeavoring to fulfill tremendous orders on behalf of Great Britain, and we are trying to do all of this with a minimum of departure from our traditional democratic method of voluntary cooperation with the Government on the part of industry.

The public, I fear, has been much confused regarding this phase of the defense program by what might be called a war of statistics, incident to the charges and countercharges of an election campaign. The fact of the matter is, that through the splendid cooperation and energetic direction of the Advisory Commission for National Defense and of the groups of scientists who are working very hard to help us, the munitions phase of the program is getting well under way. We must, however, find methods for speeding up the present rate of production, and no pains are being spared to this end.

One of our most difficult problems has been the hurried erection of temporary shelter at cantonments, for the accommodation of large numbers of troops. A contract to build something within a period of a year is not to be compared in difficulty with the contract which must be completed in three months' time, involving the construction of complete utilities, and roads, hospitals, offices, and barracks for twenty to fifty thousand men. The awarding of such contracts is an exceedingly complicated business, and is only the preparatory step to the equally difficult matter of proper supervision to their completion. With time the dominant factor, this phase of the task has been a very trying one, but we are proceeding more rapidly than we at first thought would be possible. Literally, nothing has been allowed to interfere with the accomplishment of this task at the earliest possible date.

Another difficult matter has been the problem of obtaining large quantities of uniform clothing on short notice. Money for this did not become available until late last summer. Yet we have been able to meet the demands and, given a few months for the development of full quantity production, our problem will be much simplified. This has been a particularly pressing matter from the viewpoint of public opinion, because each mother looks to her son's uniform with a very critical eye, and the young soldier himself feels it is of great importance especially if his best girl happens to be in the neighborhood.

I now wish to bring to your attention two phases of the present situation which are troubling the War Department and for which the Department has no immediate remedy within its power.

There are being established in many portions of the country, particularly in the South and Southeast, tremendous concentrations of troops. In order to provide adequate space for training, it has been necessary to locate these camps where extensive plots of land could be obtained at a reasonable price. The natural result is that only small communities are normally to be found in the vicinity of the largest troop concentrations, with the further result that there is a serious lack of accommodations for the families of the officers and non-commissioned officers. The troops are in the field, it is true, but we are not at war and it is not unnatural, under the circumstances, that many men, wishing to avoid separation from their families for a year, or possibly longer, desire to move their dependents to the vicinity of the concentration areas.

As a result of this influx of families, we find that in some localities, local rents at first doubled, and now in certain areas have tripled, with indications that they will go still higher, apparently on the basis of "charge as much as the traffic will bear." This situation is unfortunate and very unfair, and I can only hope that State and municipal authorites will bring a sufficient pressure to bear to suppress this form of profiteering.

A subject of outstanding importance and one to which we have given extensive consideration is the moral and spiritual welfare of the young soldier. Our Corps of Chaplains, with one chaplain for every 1200 men, is well organized and will be adequately equipped to provide religious services and training for all denominations similar to those found in the average city parish. The Chief of Chaplains is being assisted by Dr. Paul Moody for Protestants, by Bishop John O'Hara for Catholics, and by Dr. David de Sola Pool of the Jewish Welfare Board.[2] There should be no fear that any young man will suffer spiritual loss during the period of his military service, and, on the contrary, we hope that the young soldier will return to his home with a keener understanding of the sacred ideals for which our churches stand.

However, despite the facilities which exist for the spiritual protection of the soldier, there is another serious problem arising from the establishment of these large camps, and one which troubles me more than any other. I am referring to matters that seriously affect morale, that affect the reputation of the Army, and especially that will affect the future of the young men now in the service. I am talking about the problem of handling tremendous numbers of young men who flood into the small nearby communities over the weekends, or in the evenings when their work is done.

Growing out of our experience in the World War, it had been determined many years ago that we should not have competing welfare organizations on the military reservations, and that the Army should take care of such matters and provide the recreational facilities. Congress has given us the money for the necessary construction and for the operation of such services, and these are being organized in a large way. On the reservations the Army can control matters, but when the soldier leaves the camp our troubles begin.

Human nature being what it is, establishments for the purpose of selling liquor are becoming increasingly active in the communities adjacent to the camps, and in some communities there has been an influx of persons of questionable reputation. Here we have on the one side a sordid business for the accumulation of money, and on the other the interest of every parent in the United States who has a son in the Army, not to mention the responsibility of the War Department to develop an Army of the highest quality. This situation must be brought under control before it grows serious.

It is in this field, in the communities in the vicinity of our troop concentrations, that the War Department urgently desires the assistance of every welfare organization in the country. We can manage matters on the military reservations, but, as I have said, we have little authority once the soldier goes to town. Therefore, it is of the utmost importance to the Army that the Red Cross and the YMCA, the Knights of Columbus and the Jewish Welfare Board, the Salvation Army, the various fraternal organizations, and the churches of the community, all cooperate to develop wholesome places for the soldier to go for his entertainment—places where he at least can sit down in respectable surroundings and not have to tramp the streets with the ever-present prospect of getting into trouble.

This question has received continuous thought in the War Department, and much has been done to stimulate the organization of committees of men and women familiar with local customs to cooperate with camp commanders, who have, in turn, been ordered to make contacts with the committees in communities adjacent to their camps.

Here is a field where tremendous good can be done both for the National Defense and for the future of these young men. Here is the field where, it seems to me, an obligation exists on the part of the local communities to do this work. It would appear to be but a matter of good business for communities adjacent to our camps thus to organize for the protection of the thousands of new customers that the Army has brought to their gates. But in a broader sense, there is a moral obligation on the part of both the Army and civil communities to assist these young men to lead clean, sound lives while they wear the uniform of their country.

This is not simply a matter of morals or sentiment. More than ever before, the efficiency of an army depends upon the quality of its soldiers, the men required to operate the complicated machines of this modern age. Soldiers today must be alert, active, and in condition, mentally, morally, and physically to withstand the ordeals of the enemy's onslaught from both ground and air, and still be able to carry the fight to the other fellow.

So, as we report on the progress of the past year in organizing, equipping, and developing our expanding forces, at the same time we ask your assistance in bettering the living conditions for the families of our officers and men, and in guarding the health and morale of our soldiers while they are guests in your communities. Only with your energetic assistance can we insure the integrity of our young army.

GCMRL/G. C. Marshall Papers (Pentagon Office, Speeches)

1. Marshall delivered his fifteen-minute address at 8:15 Friday evening. Entitled "Progress of National Defense" in the radio schedules, it was broadcast between a musical variety show and a popular Western drama. It originated from station WJSV in Washington, D.C.

2. Colonel William R. Arnold (Roman Catholic), an army chaplain since 1913, had been chief of Chaplains since December 1937. Reverend Paul D. Moody, A.E.F. General Headquarters chaplain, 1918–19, was director of the General Committee on Army and Navy Chaplains, 1940–41. Bishop John F. O'Hara had been auxiliary bishop of the Army and Navy Diocese since 1939. Rabbi David de Sola Pool was chairman of the Jewish Welfare Board's Committee on Religious Activities of the Army and Navy.

O F the five joint army-navy war plans proposed in 1939 (see the editorial note on pp. 100–101), only work on Rainbow 1 had been completed. Rainbow 2 and Rainbow 3 had been laid aside during the military crisis in the spring of 1940, while work was speeded on Rainbow 4 (the defense of the Western Hemisphere). In the autumn of 1940, anticipating that the United States might become involved in the war at an early date, the navy resumed serious work on Rainbow 3. Admiral Stark sent General Marshall a copy of his November 12 memorandum for the secretary of the navy (itself a revision of a November 4 memorandum) outlining the world situation and considering four possible responses by the United States. Stark favored the last—plan "D", hence the designation "Plan Dog" memorandum—which proposed conducting a vigorous offensive in the Atlantic against Germany and Italy while pursuing a limited, defensive war against Japan in the Pacific. This was "the first attempt to deal with American military strategy as a whole, comprehending the dispositions and missions of Army as well as Navy forces, on the assumption of concerted British and American operations." (Maurice Matloff and Edwin M. Snell, *Strategic Planning for Coalition Warfare, 1941–1942,* a volume in the *United States Army in World War II* [Washington: GPO, 1953], pp. 12–13, 25.)

Having read Stark's November 12 memorandum, President Roosevelt told the chief of naval operations that he wanted "War, State, and Navy to draw up a joint estimate." In the navy, Stark told Marshall, "we are much concerned with the possibility of having a war on our hands due to precipitate Japanese action, regardless of the wishes of the President or anybody else. That is why Navy has been concentrating on RAINBOW THREE." (Stark Memorandum for General Marshall, November 22, 1940, NA/RG 165 [WPD, 4175–15].)

Marshall and the army's planners, while generally agreeing with the navy's "Atlantic first" strategy, feared that the navy's version of Rainbow 3 still left the United States overextended in the Far East and its naval strength "dispersed from Singapore to the Mediterranean. . . . We stand to lose everywhere and win nowhere." (Gerow Memorandum for the Chief of Staff, November 27, 1940, ibid.) ★

MEMORANDUM FOR ADMIRAL STARK   November 29, 1940
Secret   [Washington, D.C.]

Subject: Tentative Draft, Navy Basic War Plan—Rainbow No. 3.

1. Reference your memorandum of November 22 and our telephone conversation of November 26, I have directed the War Department representatives on the Joint Planning Committee to get together with the Navy

representatives and prepare an estimate of the situation based on your memorandum of November 12. I have told our people to give this task first priority.

2. We have gone over your advance copy of Rainbow No. 3. Insofar as the Army is concerned it involves the disposition of forces approximately as follows:

Pacific Area:

Reinforcements, Alaska — 6,000 available at 10M at Seattle[1]

Reinforcements, Hawaii — 14,500 available at 10M at San Francisco

Reinforcements, Hawaii — 14,000 available between 20M and 60M at San Francisco.

Atlantic Area:

Depends upon the then existing situation. For planning purposes:

25,000 men available for embarkation at New York by 10M

25,000 additional men available for embarkation by 30M.

We can meet these requirements, but your plan does not appear to provide transportation for the overseas movement of these troops. This will probably be taken care of in the revision.

3. The War Department cannot fully subscribe to the strategical concept of the war or the operations as set forth in the plan. A serious commitment in the Pacific is just what Germany would like to see us undertake, and what the Japanese fear.

4. The directive for Rainbow No. 3 was based on a British-French domination of the Atlantic. Since then, the situation has been materially altered by the collapse of France and the status of the French fleet. Would it not, therefore, be better to approach the readjustment of Rainbow No. 3 on the basis, (1) that our national interests require that we resist proposals that do not have for their immediate goal the survival of the British Empire and the defeat of Germany; and, (2) that we avoid dispersions that might lessen our power to operate effectively, decisively if possible, in the principal theatre— the Atlantic. Such a basis might provide:

a. That our naval threat should be continued in the Pacific so long as the situation in the Atlantic permits.

b. That, so far as Malaysia is concerned, we should avoid dispersing our forces into that theatre. We should, however, assist the British to reinforce their naval set up in the Far East by relieving them of naval obligations in the Atlantic. This would provide a more homogeneous force for Malaysia and would, in effect, concentrate rather than disperse our naval establishment.[2]

NA/RG 165 (WPD, 4175–15)

1. The day mobilization was formally ordered to commence was designated "M-Day." Thus "10M" would be ten days later.

2. There are no drafter's initials on the file copy of this document, but the original was probably written by an officer of the War Plans Division. Marshall was dissatisfied with the last portion, however, and replaced it with a handwritten draft which explained the army's objections in greater detail. Marshall's draft became paragraphs 3 and 4 of this memorandum.

MEMORANDUM FOR ADMIRAL STARK[1]   December 2, 1940
Secret   [Washington, D.C.]

Subject: Joint Basic War Plans, Rainbows Nos. 3 and 5.

1. Referring to your memorandum of November 29, 1940, I will raise no further objection to the Rainbow Plan No. 3 (submitted with your memorandum to me of November 22, 1940).[2] But since the War Department does not subscribe to the concept of that plan, I would suggest that the Army and Navy also prepare an alternative plan for later presentation to the President. This alternative plan should be based on the concept outlined in paragraph 4, of my memorandum of November 29, 1940. Under such a plan the fleet would be retained initially in the Pacific and not moved at once to the Atlantic, as is contemplated in Rainbow Plan No. 5. In other words, the War Department suggestion for a Rainbow Plan No. 3 would cover only the period from the declaration of war with Japan up to the time that we initiate a major offensive in the Atlantic theatre against the Axis Powers.

2. I favor an effort to obtain the British point of view as to the help they need from us to defeat Germany and Italy. I would like to have our Military Attaché in London, Brigadier General Raymond E. Lee, participate in those conferences. If you have no objections please instruct Admiral Ghormley accordingly and advise me, so that I may issue similar instructions to General Lee.[3]

NA/RG 165 (WPD, 4175-15)

1. The file copy of this memorandum shows it to have been drafted by Colonel Joseph T. McNarney (U.S.M.A., 1915) and Lieutenant Colonel Lee S. Gerow (V.M.I., 1913) of the War Plans Division, but Marshall heavily edited the original draft.

2. Replying at once to Marshall's November 29 memorandum, Admiral Stark observed that the navy needed carefully laid plans since it had to "begin shooting the day that war eventuates. . . . Should we become engaged in the war described in Rainbow 3, it will not be through my doing but because those in higher authority have decided that it is to our best national interest to accept such a war. For this reason I regret that I can not accept the suggestion in paragraph 4 of your memorandum that we readjust Rainbow 3 and base it upon an entirely different set of assumptions which preclude war in the Far East altogether. . . .

"Basically, the suggestions in paragraph 4 of your memorandum are very similar to Rainbow No. 5. I hope that we can start active work on this plan within the next month.

However, if we are to make a useful plan for a major war in the Atlantic, I consider it essential that we know a great deal more about British ideas than we have yet been able to glean. I do not know, in fact, whether or not they have any long range plan for themselves, or whether they have realistic ideas as to what help they think they need from us to defeat Germany and Italy. Therefore, as a preparatory measure for getting their ideas on this subject, I propose that we ask them plainly what their major strategic ideas are, and how they would hope that an allied plan would prescribe the amount and nature of the assistance that our Army and Navy would give to them. If you agree with this idea, please let me know and I will tell Ghormley in London to ask them several pointed questions." (Stark Memorandum for General Marshall, November 29, 1940, NA/RG 165 [WPD, 4175-15].)

3. Rear Admiral Robert L. Ghormley (U.S.N.A., 1906) had arrived in London in August 1940 as a special naval observer. Lee—who had been military attaché in London since June—commented on his instructions, which eventuated in the American-British staff conferences in Washington of January and February 1941, in *The London Journal of General Raymond E. Lee, 1940-1941,* ed. James Leutze (Boston and Toronto: Little, Brown and Company, 1971), pp. 155-56. (For information about the American-British staff conferences, see the editorial note on pp. 409-10.)

To Major John J. Sullivan   December 2, 1940
                                                [Washington, D.C.]

Dear Sullivan: I appreciate very deeply your letter of November 30th, with its complimentary references to my recent radio effort, the more so since my younger son—who sells radio advertising, was decidedly critical of my efforts.[1]

I have avoided public statements either by radio or in the press in order to avoid the inevitable reaction of boredom on the part of the public. However, in this particular case I found it necessary to say something and to do it without delay. Later on, when we have progressed further in the business, I will probably have not only an occasion to bring the public up to date, but the necessity of soliciting their support along some particular line. I am glad to know and feel quite confident that you are ready to do your part when the time comes.   Faithfully yours,

GCMRL/G. C. Marshall Papers (Pentagon Office, General)

1. Sullivan, a Seattle, Washington, lawyer and member of the Reserve Corps, had written to Marshall that his November 29 N.B.C. radio address had been splendid. "Being accustomed as a public speaker to do a lot of radio speaking I would not hesitate as a brother officer and friend to give constructive criticism with a desire and interest for the best interests of the service to be helpful, but I can honestly and truthfully say that you are a natural. You talk slowly, your diction is splendid, and it was just as if you were speaking to all of us, and it was very effective." (Sullivan to Marshall, November 30, 1940, GCMRL/G. C. Marshall Papers [Pentagon Office, General].)

Nothing has been found in the Marshall papers regarding the criticism of Marshall's address by his stepson, Allen Tupper Brown. On Marshall's relationship with him, see Marshall to Brown, January 17, 1941, p. 394.

MEMORANDUM FOR THE SECRETARY OF WAR December 3, 1940
Secret [Washington, D.C.]

Subject: Seizure of Brazilian vessel by British Navy.[1]

With reference to Colonel Regnier's[2] statement in his memorandum to you of November 29th, outlining the British position with relation to the seizure of the "Siqueira Campos", I think that the following details of our point of view should be brought forcibly to their attention:

The Brazilian Government purchased the war materiel in question, from Germany, after seeking bids from England and the United States. England did not choose to sell the materiel, and we did not have it to sell. Therefore, the contract with Germany—the only available source. We denied the Brazilian Government their urgent request for arms and equipment, which we then had surplus. This materiel was turned over to the British Government at the time of the Dunkirk disaster. The large quantities involved have made it impossible for us to meet the requests of most of the South American countries. We have been greatly embarrassed in this situation. We are doing all in our power to build up a unified spirit in the Americas to offset the Nazi and Italian efforts to bore from within. This is a matter of great importance to us, which would seem to outweigh very decidedly the arguments of the British Government in this particular case.

We are seriously embarrassed because of our efforts to help Great Britain. The "grave breach" in the British blockade I cannot believe to be comparable to the grave embarrassment in which this Government is placed because of its present and previous policy of assistance to Great Britain.[3]

GCMRL/G. C. Marshall Papers (Pentagon Office, Selected)

1. Several shipments of German-made arms purchased by Brazil had already reached that nation, but the British government advised the Brazilian government that no further shipments would be permitted. When Foreign Minister Oswaldo Aranha's request that the *Siqueira Campos* be permitted to sail was rejected, he told the United States State Department that the Brazilian Army was determined to get the shipment and that if Britain did not relent, he would resign and permit the appointment of a new foreign minister having antidemocratic views. On November 16 the Brazilian government ordered the vessel to leave Lisbon without British permission. On November 21 the British notified Brazil that the ship had been seized and interned at Gibraltar. Brazilian authorities protested angrily. The United States chargé d'affaires in Brazil reported to Secretary of State Cordell Hull that Aranha "said that the success of all his efforts to maintain Brazilian opinion favorable to the democracies is menaced by this lamentable incident." (*Foreign Relations, 1940,* 5: 626–29, 631.)
2. Lieutenant Colonel Eugene A. Regnier was Secretary of War Stimson's aide.
3. During and after the negotiations on the *Siqueira Campos* affair, Brazilian authorities praised the United States for its attitude and Marshall for his assistance. (Ibid., 633, 638.) In response to Marshall's efforts, General Góes Monteiro said, "I consider this a most distinguished token of friendship and a valuable step for the defense of our interests, which we

Brazilians will always remember."(Lieutenant Colonel J. Bina Machado to Marshall, November 29, 1940, NA/RG 165 [WPD, 4224].) See Marshall to Aranha, January 6, 1941, pp. 381-82. The *Siqueira Campos* was released on December 15. (*Foreign Relations, 1940,* 5: 656.)

To George S. King   December 7, 1940
                                                [Washington, D.C.]

My dear Dr. King: I received your letter of December 4th, regarding the plan you have worked out for a defense system against aerial night bombing.[1]

We are very glad to get every idea on this subject, and I would suggest that you mail your plan to Dr. Vannevar Bush, Research Committee of the Council of National Defense, Carnegie Institution, 1530 P Street, Washington, D.C. We have coordinated all research matters, and this is one of them, to this Committee of scientists, of which Dr. Bush is the head. We not only have the advantage of the work of this particular group, but they have organized the research men throughout the United States so that their services and their laboratories are all available to assist us.

The particular subject you bring up is under investigation in a number of different directions, and I know Dr. Bush will be glad to have your ideas.[2] Faithfully yours,

GCMRL/G. C. Marshall Papers (Pentagon Office, General)

1. King, a physician in Bay Shore, New York, had written to Marshall for the name of someone in authority to whom he could submit his plan for serious consideration. King did not include his plan in his letter to Marshall, but noted that he had "carefully worked out a scheme with relatively small risk and relatively small financial outlay when compared to the present methods of combating night bombing, which I am sure is original and which I am positive would immediately appeal to you as an experienced Army officer."(King to Marshall, December 4, 1940, GCMRL/G. C. Marshall Papers [Pentagon Office, General].)

2. Dr. King replied that he was forwarding his ideas to Dr. Bush as well as to the Air Ministry of Great Britain. In appreciation of Marshall's personal reply to his letter, King wrote, "Your prompt reply to my personal letter regarding an idea for aerial night bombing, illustrates the fact that great men are great simply because they attend to details which smaller individuals over-look."(King to Marshall, December 9, 1940, ibid.)

Memorandum for the Assistant   December 9, 1940
Secretary of War [Patterson]   [Washington, D.C.]

Subject: Aluminum.

Dear Judge: Thursday afternoon I made a brief tour of the Glenn Martin plant, and found somewhat the same condition of affairs that had impressed me several weeks earlier.[1] A large number of jigs for B-26 medium bombers were standing idle, and presses and other heavy machinery were not carrying the full load. My queries in each case elicited the same response, a shortage of aluminum, for which orders were *placed* in June and deliveries *promised* in September.

Here we seem to have a rather complete difference of opinion—if one may use that word with regard to something where factual data should be available. On the one side we learn that there is no shortage of aluminum, and on the other I find a manufacturer who says that he cannot obtain it in sufficient quantity, and that our Army program is seriously delayed for that reason.

There was another phase of this matter that I have no data on at all, but which may have an important bearing on the situation. The Martin plant is turning out a British light bomber, and there seemed to be much more activity in that section of the plant than there was in the section devoted to the Army orders.

I am growing more and more concerned over the delivery rate for our Army planes and I am hopeful that everything possible will be done to get at the actual facts in the confusing state of affairs regarding aircraft production.

GCMRL/G. C. Marshall Papers (Pentagon Office, Selected)

1. Marshall and Major General Henry H. Arnold had toured the Martin factory near Baltimore, Maryland, during their hunting trip with Glenn L. Martin, November 4–5. See Marshall to Martin, November 6, 1940, p. 346.

MEMORANDUM FOR THE SECRETARY OF WAR December 11, 1940
[Washington, D.C.]

Attached is a proposal for the organization of a War Department Community Service Committee. Its preparation was just being completed when the announcement appeared in the press of the appointment of Mr. Paul V. McNutt as Coordinator of Health, medical, welfare, nutrition, recreation, and other related fields of activity affecting the national defense.[1]

It is very important that we bring about without further delay the coordination of the various welfare activities so that they can start their work in the communities in the vicinity of troop concentrations. At the present time each group is in a state of indecision pending a general policy as to how the matter of raising funds is to be coordinated, and just who is to do what. Meanwhile the troops lack the services of these organizations and the situation will grow serious if there is much more delay.

In a recent broadcast I referred to the necessity for active work by the various welfare organizations in the local communities adjacent to Army concentrations, explaining that we could handle matters on the reservations. They all come to me now for a definite basis of departure.[2] Would you be willing to send the attached plan to Mr. McNutt and get an informal comment by him as to whether we might not go ahead, on the War Department side, on this basis immediately, leaving to him and his committees the question of the decision as to fund raising campaigns and matters of that nature.[3]

GCMRL/G. C. Marshall Papers (Pentagon Office, Selected)

1. Paul V. McNutt was administrator of the Federal Security Agency, which had been created in April 1939 to consolidate numerous health, education, and welfare organizations. The announcement of his added duties was made by the White House on December 3. (*New York Times,* December 4, 1940, pp. 1, 20.)

2. See Marshall's radio address of November 29, 1940, pp. 358–59.

3. No copy of the plan attached to this memorandum was retained in Marshall's files. Several days later Marshall sent to the secretary a list of possible candidates for the committee. (Memorandum for the Secretary of War, December 23, 1940, GCMRL/G. C. Marshall Papers [Pentagon Office, Selected].) At his January 9, 1941, press conference, Stimson announced the formation of the War Department Committee on Education, Recreation, and Community Service. (January 9, 1941, Yale/H. L. Stimson Papers [Diary, 32: 94]; *Army and Navy Journal,* January 11, 1941, p. 504.)

MEMORANDUM FOR THE SECRETARY   December 11, 1940
OF THE TREASURY   [Washington, D.C.]
Secret

My dear Mr. Morgenthau: I have had Commodore Slessor's notes on the United States Air Production Program checked over by General Brett and his officers.[1] The following are their comments:

A careful study of these notes indicates clearly that they are based upon incomplete investigation and information; that Commodore Slessor had not at the date of these notes consulted with or conferred with the Air Corps engineers charged with development and production; that the information as furnished in his notes is contrary to much of the information furnished by other members of the British Purchasing Commission such as Mr. Fairey, Commodore Mansell and Commodore Baker;[2] that he has not personally gone into the details of any of our later models nor has he examined those models, which are available at the various factories.

Also, reading between the lines, it appears that Commodore Slessor's ultimate objectives are:

    a. Production in America of a *British design* long range bomber (the Sterling)

    b. Production in America of a new British design pursuit airplane.

    c. Increased productive capacity of the American aircraft industry (i.e. from 2500 airplanes a month, as now set up, to 4500 airplanes a month by 1943) . . .[3]

PRODUCTION.

Commodore Slessor's suggestion that the production be increased to 4500 airplanes per month is a re-statement of the request of July 24 for additional productive capacity. The means for obtaining this increased production appears to be practical. The present production capacity as now set up will reach 2500 airplanes per month, neglecting Government factories now authorized. Tentative British orders for 12,000 airplanes, now being placed, are sufficient for the first increment of increased productive capacity, suggested by Air Commodore Slessor, provided that both the Army and British place additional orders for at least 24,000 airplanes, for delivery in 1943, at an early date.

RESTUDY OF PRESENT PROGRAMS.

The suggestions made by Air Commodore Slessor for increasing production requires a *restudy* of the *delivery objectives* established *July 23 and 24* for the period June 30, 1940 to April 1, 1942. Consideration should be given at this time to the following:

(1) The release of all airplanes to the British over and above the actual requirements to equip 54 groups.

(2) The matter of finance, facilities.

(3) The matter of placing orders with proper consideration to the ability of the industry to absorb the additional load.

Personally, I am inclined to believe that there is an ulterior motive behind this statement, having in view a complete rearrangement of production and procurement procedure. I am deeply concerned over the slow rate, the dwindling rate of plane deliveries to the Army; but I am becoming even more concerned over the possible effects of the present campaign in certain portions of the press, particularly if supported by statements such as this from Commodore Slessor.

It is natural that Slessor should be dominated by the desire to help the British situation, however superficial his knowledge of conditions in this country may be at the moment. My interest must center on our situation, and I am worried over the disturbing effect this sort of thing has on the airplane manufacturer and other agencies involved.

Our problem is hard enough as it is—in time of peace with an unrestricted press, with the varied interests of Latin America, China, the British Empire, and our own vast expansion—but it is becoming increasingly difficult and confused under the various pressures, some very powerful, and each of which has a special purpose in mind. Incidentally, the recent publicity campaign directed against American types of plane in England as a reflection on the general efficiency of our program, is really an outrageous piece of business. The British Government was given what they pled for, in some cases to our serious embarrassment in training; now we are being damned in the press for that action.

Please note General Brett's statement on the subject, which is attached.[4]

GCMRL/G. C. Marshall Papers (Pentagon Office, Selected)

1. Air-Commodore John C. Slessor, until recently British Air Staff director of plans, had arrived in the United States on November 8. He was sent, he wrote in his memoirs, "to explain to the U.S. Administration the Air Staff plans for expansion and replacement of wastage." On December 3 he met with Secretary Morgenthau and presented a lengthy memorandum analyzing British needs, particularly increased bomber production, and comparing British and United States aircraft performance. (*The Central Blue: The Autobiography of Sir John Slessor, Marshal of the RAF* [New York: Frederick A. Praeger, 1957], pp. 320–30.)

2. Charles R. Fairey, past president of the Royal Aeronautical Society, was a British aircraft manufacturer. The officers were Air-Commodores L. G. T. (?) Mansell and G. B. A. Baker.

3. At this point Marshall included detailed comments by Acting Chief of the Air Corps George H. Brett defending the armament and performance characteristics of United States bombers and fighters compared with British models. He rejected Slessor's assertion that British planes then in production were superior in fighting efficiency to United States planes in production.

4. A copy of the attachment to this memorandum was not retained in the Marshall papers.

MEMORANDUM FOR MR. KNUDSEN   December 11, 1940
Confidential   [Washington, D.C.]

Confidentially, I am growing increasingly disturbed over the slow delivery rate for combat planes to the Army. The situation during November is fairly typical. The original schedule contemplated the delivery of 94 tactical planes for that month. The estimates the first week in November predicted 33 deliveries to the Army, and 406 tactical planes for export. I now find that only six tactical planes reached us in that month.[1]

Without implying criticism of the present efforts of the Aircraft industry, I must say that I am not satisfied with the status of the airplane production at present available to the Army, nor the character of the estimates for future deliveries. I am aware of a number of reasons for difference between estimated and actual deliveries, but even so this does not remove my apprehension in the matter.

Part of the responsibility for production rests with the Army, particularly that relating to design; and it is the recognized duty of the War Department to contribute in every possible way to the success of your efforts to increase production.

In view of the situation, I would like very much to have your ideas as to how our cooperation might be made more effective.[2]

GCMRL/G. C. Marshall Papers (Pentagon Office, General)

1. British Air-Commodore Slessor, who had recently been designated a British representative to the forthcoming joint staff conferences to begin in late January 1941, commented on Marshall's observation to him of the discrepancy between the number of planes delivered to the Army Air Corps and to the Royal Air Force. "General Marshall told me for instance that in November only six new aircraft were delivered to the U.S.A.F., the remainder, amounting to some three hundred, being allocated to the British—a situation of which the consequences, if they were to become publicly known, might have been extremely awkward for him and Mr. Stimson." (Slessor, *Central Blue,* p. 325.)

2. No written reply from Knudsen has been found in the Marshall papers.

To Lieutenant General Charles D. Herron   December 13, 1940
Confidential   Washington, D.C.

Dear Herron: I should have written you several weeks ago, but I must confess to an over-burdened mind and to over-crowded days—mobilization in time of peace in a democracy is a heavy task for one in my particular position.

What I wanted to tell you is this: For reasons on this side of the water, it appears desirable to send Walter Short to Hawaii instead of Krueger, and for the same reason it appears best to make the transfer at an earlier date than originally intended.[1] Therefore, Short will probably be relieved as a tactical corps commander in the early part of January and ordered to Hawaii. Whether or not he will want a leave before going I do not know, but he will be given one if he desires it and you are agreeable to that arrangement.

At the present time, Short knows nothing about this—nor does anyone else for that matter; but I intend to write to him and tell him what is brewing. I will ask him about the leave, and will radio you his desire, so that you in reply can tell me yours. If he goes direct, I imagine he will get out to Hawaii about the middle of January, though it may be later.

I am sorry to upset your plans, particularly in view of your generous willingness to go on up to the last moment, but the reasons for the transfer are important. Krueger, incidentally, I expect to hold for the command of the Third Army on Brees's retirement in the late spring—though I cannot be certain of that, so treat this as most confidential.[2]

I will not confuse this letter with any other matters. In reply be very frank with me, for you are entitled to every possible consideration.[3]   Faithfully yours,

GCMRL/G. C. Marshall Papers (Pentagon Office, Selected)

1. Major General Walter C. Short was commander of the First Army Corps at Columbia, South Carolina. Major General Walter Krueger was commander of the Eighth Army Corps at Fort Sam Houston, Texas. Marshall may have been concerned with Krueger's ability to cooperate with his navy counterpart in Hawaii. See Marshall to Krueger, April 14, 1941, pp. 473–74.

2. Lieutenant General Herbert J. Brees was commander of the Eighth Corps Area and Third Army at San Antonio, Texas.

3. In a December 20 radiogram and a December 24 letter, Herron conveyed his agreement. (GCMRL/G. C. Marshall Papers [Pentagon Office, Selected].)

To Major General Ewing E. Booth   December 21, 1940
                                                        [Washington, D.C.]

Dear Booth: I have just received your letter of December 18th, with the attached clipping, and appreciate very much your writing.[1] I am afraid the state of public confusion will continue so long as the situation in this country is critical and newspaper men make a living by filling up the news columns. As quickly as we scotch one line of approach, another one develops; and I believe this is going to continue during the present period of complete freedom for investigation and for publication.

There are many fine reporters and writers doing an excellent job these days, but there are also others who respond to the public desire for excitement, and indifference to ordinary statements of fact. Also, there are naturally some people who speak with an ulterior motive in their minds. But these are all natural reactions in a democracy, and despite the present situation I think we have gotten along pretty well.

With my affectionate Christmas greetings to Mrs. Booth and you,   Faithfully yours,

GCMRL/G. C. Marshall Papers (Pentagon Office, General)

1. Booth had retired from the army in February 1934 and was living in Los Angeles, California. He had written to praise Marshall's handling of his difficult job and had enclosed a short Associated Press newspaper story which quoted (with minor changes) the following excerpt from Marshall's December 17 remarks at the National Aeronautic Association dinner. "Today we are in many ways at the critical point in a great transition from a condition of more or less complete unpreparedness to one of tremendous military power. We are confused by statistics and by unrestrained and public debates over each difficulty or delay. Every move that we make is subjected to the closest scrutiny, and every error, real or imaginary, is pounced upon and exploited to the world. This welter of conflicting information has so confused the public mind that few realize either how much has been done, or how much remains to be done." (Speech at the National Aeronautic Association Dinner, December 17, 1940, GCMRL/G. C. Marshall Papers [Pentagon Office, Speeches].)

Marshall was "absolutely correct," Booth observed, in saying that the public was confused. Since May, Booth had given "hundreds of public talks" trying to explain "what is being done and why." Most people, he found, strongly supported preparedness and understood that delays were inevitable, "but due to pessimistic published statements and critical comments many well read people wonder if a proper start has been made in the procurement of fighting equipment." (Booth to Marshall, December 18, 1940, GCMRL/G. C. Marshall Papers [Pentagon Office, General].)

To HENRY MORGENTHAU, JR.   December 23, 1940
                                                  [Washington, D.C.]

My dear Mr. Morgenthau: Along with my holiday greetings and good wishes go my thanks for your powerful assistance in getting the Army program under way, in both men and munitions. I do not forget your determining influence on two specific occasions last May when the real beginnings of our major preparations were launched.

I wish again to express my thanks and appreciation and to wish you all good things—and far-seeing wisdom, in this coming year with its tragic possibilities.   Faithfully yours,

GCMRL/G. C. Marshall Papers (Pentagon Office, Selected)

MEMORANDUM FOR THE INSPECTOR   December 26, 1940
GENERAL [PETERSON]   [Washington, D.C.]

Please look into the business of expediting War Department administration by checking up on the possible advantage of some rearrangement being made in the conduct of offices pertaining to receiving, recording, and distribution of papers.

It seems to me that there probably is a serious delay in the transaction of business here because of the fact that the accumulative results of the day's work bank up on the recording sections, and if they close at 4:15, about the time most of this business arrives, there is an inevitable delay. I had in mind a possible arrangement whereby recording offices would have overlapping shifts so that the recording business would be carried on for several hours after the War Department formally closes. A portion of the force would come on at the normal time, and another portion two or three hours later, maybe not until one o'clock. Will you look into this and see if there is any advantage to such an arrangement.

If there are any other matters pertaining to this business, I would like to hear from you. However, do not let this delay your looking into the first matter, which should be managed expeditiously.[1]

GCMRL/G. C. Marshall Papers (Pentagon Office, Selected)

1. No reply to this memorandum has been found in the Marshall papers.

MEMORANDUM FOR THE ASSISTANT   December 26, 1940
CHIEF OF STAFF, G-1 [SHEDD]   [Washington, D.C.]

Draft a regulation covering the saluting question for *general officers* of the Army so that commanders will be spared the inconvenience and time-consuming business of the frequent salutes that would otherwise be required, considering the large number of Generals, and the fact that they are flying here and there all over the United States.

I think the matter might be handled on the basis that a general officer arriving by air will be met by an officer prepared to meet the desires of the General, but there will be no salute unless the desire for a formal reception has been indicated in advance.

I thought that this had been managed a month or more ago. Please see that it is expedited.[1]

GCMRL/G. C. Marshall Papers (Pentagon Office, Selected)

1. In mid-January the War Department announced: "During the present emergency the salutes and honors prescribed in paragraph 13a, AR 600–25, will not be rendered to officials of the Army unless the official for whom the salute and honor is prescribed has requested such honors in advance of his arrival at the post, camp, or station." (*Army and Navy Journal,* January 18, 1941, p. 512.)

DRAFT OF A POSSIBLE STATEMENT BY THE   [December 26, 1940]
SECRETARY OF WAR[1]   [Washington, D.C.]

The December 23d issue of LIFE magazine carries on page 57 the following comment:

"—if they (soldiers) want to visit Red-Light districts, the Army gives its tacit acceptance provided they patronize Army inspected houses, stop at a prophylactic station on way home."

This statement was made without the authority or knowledge of the War Department. It is calculated to create a misleading and unfortunate impression. With reference to the problems of liquor and prostitution, the Army feels that it has two obligations or duties,—first to the young soldier himself and to his parents, and secondly, to the interests of national defense.

The policy of the War Department is to proceed in every way to offset these ever present temptations, particularly in the communities adjacent to troop concentrations, by providing comfortable living conditions, wholesome recreations, and diversions for the soldiers in the camps, and through the cooperation of civilian agencies, to see that decent conditions and healthy diversions are available in the near-by towns. For the inevitable few who fail to accept their individual responsibilities for clean living and involve themselves in unfortunate contacts, the Army takes such measures as are necessary to insure that the efficiency of the Army is not impaired. There are lectures to the soldiers, instruction in personal hygiene, and insistence by the Army that the officials of the civilian communities take every possible measure for protection against the spreading of venereal diseases.

The Army recognizes two responsibilities in this matter; one to the parents for the welfare of their sons, and the other to the nation for the efficiency, meaning a healthy Army. We shall continue to spare no pains to meet these obligations.

GCMRL/G. C. Marshall Papers (Pentagon Office, Selected)

1. Marshall requested that Lieutenant Colonel Edward H. Brooks, chief of the Statistics Branch, read the proposed statement and discuss it with Secretary Stimson during the chief of staff's absence. (Maude A. Young to Brooks, December 26, 1940, GCMRL/G. C. Marshall Papers [Pentagon Office, Selected].)

To GENERAL JOHN J. PERSHING
December 29, 1940
White Sulphur Springs, West Virginia

Dear General: Katherine and I have been here since the evening of the 26th enjoying a complete rest. Except for the constant temptation to eat too much, the place is perfect for our purpose. We have luxurious quarters, take the baths and massage, walk mile every day, and sleep long hours. We have met no one and so have no war talk and no requests for this or that. Bryden telephones me at noon to get my views or desires on the important points that have come up, and he does not call each day.[1]

Both the head waiter and the german who rubs me down spoke of your being here several months one winter, working on your book. That must have been in 1929–30.

I plan to fly back to work the morning of January 2d. Katherine will drive back. We came down on the train as the weather was too bad for flying and too disagreeable for motoring. She is getting a good rest, and she needed it after ten house guests and a wedding.[2]

I am curious to hear Mr. Roosevelts radio broadcast tonight. It is likely to be of great significance.[3]

I hope your rheumatism is better and that you are feeling well. You certainly looked well when I saw you Sunday. I will be out as soon as I get back to town.

With our affectionate regards,   Faithfully,

G. C. M.

LC/J. J. Pershing Papers (General Correspondence); H

1. General and Mrs. Marshall were vacationing at the Greenbrier Hotel resort in White Sulphur Springs, West Virginia. The chief of staff had written to Deputy Chief of Staff

Brigadier General William Bryden: "I wish that you or [Orlando] Ward would telephone me of anything of importance that comes up. 12:30 would probably be the best time. I would like you to telephone me every other day in any event." (Memorandum for General Bryden, December 26, 1940, NA/RG 165 [OCS, SGS].)

2. Molly P. Brown, Mrs. Marshall's daughter, and Captain James J. Winn were married at the chief of staff's quarters at Fort Myer on December 25, 1940. The couple left to live in Panama, where Captain Winn was stationed.

3. On December 29 President Roosevelt delivered his "arsenal of democracy" fireside chat in which he called for United States arms aid to "Britain and the other free nations which are resisting aggression." (*The Public Papers and Addresses of Franklin D. Roosevelt,* 1940 volume, ed. Samuel I. Rosenman [New York: Macmillan Company, 1941], p. 641.) "I make the direct statement to the American people that there is far less chance of the United States getting into war, if we do all we can now to support the nations defending themselves against attack by the Axis than if we acquiesce in their defeat, submit tamely to an Axis victory, and wait our turn to be the object of attack in another war later on. . . . The people of Europe who are defending themselves do not ask us to do their fighting. They ask us for the implements of war, the planes, the tanks, the guns, the freighters which will enable them to fight for their liberty and for our security. . . . We must be the great arsenal of democracy. For us this is an emergency as serious as war itself. We must apply ourselves to our task with the same resolution, the same sense of urgency, the same spirit of patriotism and sacrifice as we would show were we at war." (Ibid., pp. 640, 643.)

Rich Man's Table

January 1–April 8, 1941

The visit would have an important psychological effect in that it would indicate to the Chinese that they were being considered as potential allies rather than beggars at the rich man's table. (This last phrase is mine)

—Memorandum for General Arnold
March 28, 1941

HUNGRY for aid in the early months of 1941, dozens of nations—but Great Britain especially—sought access to "the rich man's table." John J. McCloy, special assistant to the secretary of war, outlined British weaknesses in a sweeping memorandum. Their greatest needs, he noted, were in shipping, aircraft, and air crews. To maintain adequate food and munitions forty thousand tons had to be imported annually; sinkings by Germans had reduced that rate to thirty-five thousand tons. Although Britain possessed a year's supply of beef, imports of fodder and fertilizer had been reduced by the sinkings. McCloy claimed that the British needed both impounded naval vessels and new ships from the United States. Aircraft, antiaircraft guns, and .30 caliber ammunition to continue the Battle of Britain were additional priority items. (McCloy Memorandum of Talk with L. K. Thorne, February 11, 1941, NA/RG 319 [OPD, Exec. 4, Item 11].)

"As the western Allies experienced greater and greater need for airplanes, guns, ammunition, and other supplies, they sought an increased proportion of the American output. In the ultimate victory over the Axis time would show American factory production to have been an immense factor. Early foreign orders also greatly expedited the enormous development of American industry to the long-range advantage of the Army. Yet this later benefit does not alter the fact that in diverting abroad much of the flow of new equipment those early orders temporarily retarded the equipping and hence the training of the new United States Army." (Mark S. Watson, *Chief of Staff: Prewar Plans and Preparations,* a volume in the *United States Army in World War II* [Washington: GPO, 1950], p. 300.)

Marshall struggled to balance the development of the ground forces and the Air Corps with this assistance to Britain in 1941. To this end he testified twice before Congress in support of lend-lease, on March 13 and 20. He also testified in support of supplemental appropriations on February 12, March 5 and 25, to fund an army, according to mobilization plans completed at this time, of 4,100,000 men at an unspecified time in the future. ★

To Lieutenant General Daniel Van Voorhis   January 4, 1941
Confidential   Washington, D.C.

Dear Van Voorhis: I am enclosing a tentative study on the question of command in the Caribbean area, which today is being sent to G-3 for further development.[1] You will be communicated with through formal War Department channels, but meanwhile I wish to have a little informal interchange with you on the subject.

The question of a coordinated command in the Caribbean area is to me of great importance and of many complications. The Army command alone is a sufficiently complicated matter, but when we introduce the Navy into the problem, the entire affair becomes most difficult of solution. But we must arrive at a sound basis for action without delay.

The question of the coordination of the Air forces is exceedingly important, it seems to me, and will require very special treatment. It was for that reason that I sent Frank Andrews down to the Canal Zone, so that you would have a very competent man for this purpose.[2] As soon as the new Air units begin to arrive in the Caribbean region, the matter of coordination of air affairs will demand immediate treatment.

I have felt, though the Staff here does not seem to agree with me, that our present plans involve the accumulation of too many air units on permanent station in the area, considering the rapidity with which air units can be deployed providing fields and facilities are available, and also considering the heavy expense of maintaining such units on a permanent status in that region. I suggested that we should determine the minimum garrisons, and then tag units located in the Southeastern United States for reenforcements, these units to make a circuit of the Caribbean region three or four times a year, spending several weeks in the locality designated for their emergency assignment.

I hesitate to enter into a formal discussion of the complications involved in a settlement of the matter of command throughout this region between the Army and Navy, but there can be no question but what all of the Air activities must be coordinated by a single head. A possible solution might be managed on the basis of Army control during the absence of the fleet from that region, and Navy control by the Commander of the fleet when in those waters. Certainly there must not be divided control, or adjustments at the time, dependent upon personalities.[3]

I am writing you very frankly and without Staff advice, so I must ask you to treat this as a confidential discussion between the two of us.   Faithfully yours,

GCMRL/G. C. Marshall Papers (Pentagon Office, Selected)

1. In December 1940 the War Plans Division proposed the creation of a Caribbean Defense Command consisting of the Panama Canal Department (including Jamaica), the Puerto Rican Department (including the Bahamas, Antigua, and Santa Lucia), and the Trinidad Base Command (including British Guiana). The planners envisaged a theater of operations including the Caribbean and adjacent neutral areas. Peacetime preparations for such a theater of war should commence at once, according to the War Plans Division. (Watson, *Chief of Staff,* p. 462.) For Marshall's previous comments regarding the extent of Van Voorhis's command, see pp. 293–94.

2. Frank M. Andrews had been promoted to major general effective October 27 and took command of the newly formed Panama Canal Air Force in November 1940.

3. While Marshall's letter was primarily concerned with ground-air and army-navy command coordination, Van Voorhis's reply showed him to be more concerned with strategic doctrine. Cooperation with the navy should continue, he wrote, but settlement of command coordination issues should be made "when the emergency arises." More important for him

was the question of the relation of the Panama Canal Department to the new Caribbean bases. The department's mission, in his opinion, "was that of a fortress defense" against the enemy's intention of closing the canal. The Caribbean bases were outposts of that defense, not the main line, and the canal's defenses should not be weakened in order to strengthen the bases; neither did he envision "this command as constituting an expeditionary force." As for the commander of the Caribbean Defense Command, his primary responsibilities at present were training—particularly developing communications—and planning. If he was to assume new duties in a wider sphere, Van Voorhis said, he had to improve his staff, which was presently neither qualitatively nor quantitatively capable of handling the job. (Van Voorhis to Marshall, January 10, 1941, GCMRL/G. C. Marshall [Pentagon Office, Selected].)

To Oswaldo Aranha
Confidential

January 6, 1941
[Washington, D.C.]

Your Excellency: I deeply appreciate the message from you, brought to me a few days ago by the Chargé d'Affaires of the Brazilian Embassy, regarding the release by the British of the military materiel purchased by Brazil in Germany. Whatever little I had to do in the matter was gladly done, and I was happy to learn that the decision has been a favorable one.[1]

It was a great pleasure for us to welcome General Monteiro again to the United States, and I was only sorry that with so many officials I could not find the opportunity to be with him personally as much as I would have liked to have been. We did manage to have several evenings and a lunch together at my house. I trust he brought to you a favorable report of his visit.[2]

Personally, I am inclined to think that the most valuable result lay in the intimate contacts and friendships developed among the visiting officials who were together over a considerable period of time and on a most informal basis, except for stated occasions.

I wish to assure your Excellency that I have constantly in mind an effort to do everything possible to assist your Government in obtaining whatever is desired in this country. In the midst of a struggle to give Great Britain all she needs in her present crisis, along with the armament of a million and a half men in this country, it is exceedingly difficult to make all ends meet, to our great embarrassment in many directions.[3]

I have never ceased to recall your gracious courtesy and hospitality to me on my memorable visit to Brazil. I am always hoping that you will have occasion to come to Washington, that I may have the opportunity in this country to repay some of the boundless hospitality and generous treatment you personally accorded me.[4]

With great respect and high esteem, believe me   Faithfully yours,

GCMRL/G. C. Marshall Papers (Pentagon Office, Selected)

1. On the *Siqueira Campos* affair, see Memorandum for the Secretary of War, December 3, 1940, pp. 364–65.

2. On January 6 Marshall received a confidential note from Under Secretary of State Sumner Welles which included a paraphrased message from Aranha, who stated that because of the attitude of the United States, Brazilian policy would henceforth clearly favor the British cause. Furthermore, the Brazilian Army's attitude was safely pro–United States, and German influence was no longer dangerous. Aranha did observe, however, that General Go´es Monteiro's wavering attitude was a destabilizing factor. At the end of this message Welles added: "I feel that the personal regard and admiration which General Go´es Monteiro has for you is peculiarly valuable at this time and I continue to think that the closer your contact with the General is, the more stable will he become!!" (Welles to Marshall, January 4, 1941, NA/RG 165 [WPD, 4224–116].)

3. Marshall spoke with General Amaro Bittencourt, first sub-chief of the General Staff of Brazil, on January 8, 1941. He explained that little could be done to satisfy Brazil's needs for war materiel since the Allies had first claim on United States production. Bittencourt reduced his $250,000,000 request to a priority list consisting of approximately one-half of the original. The War Department then worked out a tentative schedule for the availability of items on the priority list. By mid-January 1941 Bittencourt had a clear picture of future United States armaments sales. (Stetson Conn and Byron Fairchild, *The Framework of Hemisphere Defense*, a volume in the *United States Army in World War II* [Washington: GPO, 1960], pp. 278–79.)

4. On Marshall's May–June 1939 trip to Brazil, see *Papers of GCM,* 1: 715–20.

MEMORANDUM FOR THE ASSISTANT
CHIEF OF STAFF, G-3

January 10, 1941
[Washington, D.C.]

(Attention of the Officer in Charge of ROTC Affairs)

Attached is a list of the standings of a group of 74 officers taking the Basic Field Artillery course at Sill. 12 of these officers were honor graduates of the ROTC, the remainder were recent West Point graduates.

It was anticipated by the Chief of Field Artillery that the honor graduates from the selected men, presumably the cream of the ROTC product, would be mostly in the upper half of the class. This did not prove to be the case. For example, the honor graduate from the University of Illinois, an ROTC institution of 3500 students, stands 71 in a class of 74. That is not a logical result. Florida splits the difference between one at the top and one at the bottom.

I am wondering whether or not it might be a good thing to circulate this result, confidentially, among the PMS&T's to get their comments.

NA/RG 165 (OCS, 20741-4)

Memorandum for Mr. Stettinius[1]
Confidential

January 10, 1941
[Washington, D.C.]

Dear Ed: I have had only a brief opportunity to scan Mr. Folsom's resume on the Aluminum situation, but I will take the paper home to read at my leisure tonight.[2] Meanwhile I would like to make this comment on my own observations with regard to aluminum:

I found in going into an Aviation plant myself, and in checking on other plants through some of my subordinates exactly the same situation with regard to several matters, one of which is aluminum, that I find on every inspection I personally make or members of my staff make in the field regarding construction, and more particularly clothing and items of equipment of every kind. From every trip I return to the War Department with a number of deficiencies, and without exception, after investigation by the Staff the day following my return, I am informed that the procedure is all right, the conditions are all right, but there has been a failure on the part of the people in the field to do the right thing. When I call up the Corps Area Commander or his staff, I get the same reaction from them. But the fact remains that I find the soldier without the pants or without the mess-kit or the battery without certain equipment.

We had some of the troops in the concentration of a year ago pass through the coldest weather in 22 years with but three blankets. I was assured here in the War Department that they would have the fourth almost immediately after I had called attention to it, but it took five weeks to get that blanket into the soldier's hands, and there is not much warmth in a blanket in a table of figures.

I found this in innumerable instances, and it has not always been confined to the War Department. I found it in the CCC; I found it in France, and I am quite certain I found the same condition with relation to aluminum in the manufacture of airplanes—there was only a difference of terminology.

My reaction to this thing is that there is a long-time involvement between availability and delivery, especially when there is not a large surplus of the particular materiel on hand. I suggested to Mr. Knudsen this morning the immense importance of having a field inspection service to ascertain by the most direct measures the actual conditions in the various plants so that he (Mr. Knudsen) would have a basis for running down troubles.

In our organization at the present time I have to depend in a large measure on a quadrupled Inspector General's Department, and on continuous trips by members of the staff whom I send out to look for certain things and who report to me personally. I do not normally learn these things, at least not in time, through the usual channels, and I am convinced that the only way to boil down these conflicting reports, excuses, difficulties, delays, etc., is by supplementing the routine statistical reports with a special inspection service to find out the facts at first hand.

I do not know to what extent either you or Mr. Knudsen have organized an outside inspection service. I do know that Meigs,[3] of Knudsen's office, has been going through the various plans; but as far as I can learn, there is not an extensive organization for this purpose. I am embarrassed in the matter because I am getting somewhat outside my own bailiwick, but I am finding the Army Air Service in a very serious situation regarding the steady dwindling of deliveries. Most confidentially, in July our contracts promised 94 tactical planes in November; the first of November, this prospect was reduced to 33; on the 30th of November, I found we had actually received but six planes. This is growing more and more serious for us and, within the family, I have been trying to do everything I can to help out rather than to complicate matters.

I would like very much to talk to you personally about all this.[4]

GCMRL/G. C. Marshall Papers (Pentagon Office, Selected)

1. Edward R. Stettinius, Jr., was one of seven members of the National Defense Advisory Commission (N.D.A.C.). His sphere of interest was industrial materials. Also important in this organization was William S. Knudsen, commissioner for industrial production. On January 7, 1941, President Roosevelt created the Office of Production Management, which assumed the functions of the N.D.A.C. in production, materials, and employment. Knudsen was the principal administrator of this office; Stettinius became director of the Priorities Division. (R. Elberton Smith, *The Army and Economic Mobilization,* a volume in the *United States Army in World War II* [Washington: GPO, 1959], p. 103; on the public reaction to the formation of this office, see the *Army and Navy Journal,* January 4, 1941, p. 458.)

2. Marion B. Folsom served as a member of the Industrial Materials Division of the N.D.A.C. He reported that, according to October 1940 procurement schedules, there would be a shortage in aluminum forgings for army aircraft by July 1941. Additional productive capacity was needed and Folsom had already discussed the matter with industry officials. (Folsom Memorandum for Mr. E. R. Stettinius, Jr., January 7, 1941, GCMRL/G. C. Marshall Papers [Pentagon Office, Selected].)

3. Merrill C. Meigs, a Chicago, Illinois, publisher, was an adviser on aircraft production to the N.D.A.C.

4. Stettinius reviewed Folsom's report with Marshall on January 15, 1941. He told the chief of staff that a production representative system had been established by the Aluminum Company of America (Alcoa). A representative was at each aircraft production plant to report on the use of aluminum. Alcoa would then communicate these estimates to Folsom at the new Office of Production Management. (Stettinius to W. Averell Harriman, January 17, 1941, Virginia/E. R. Stettinius, Jr., Papers.)

MEMORANDUM FOR THE QUARTERMASTER GENERAL [GREGORY]
Confidential

January 10, 1941
[Washington, D.C.]

The Secretary of War told me today that there was no objection to the

Army using as much Argentine canned beef as possible in insular bases and other places out of tariff boundaries of the United States. It would be of important assistance to our Argentine relations if considerable purchases could be made on this basis.

GCMRL/G. C. Marshall Papers (Pentagon Office, Selected)

MEMORANDUM FOR GENERAL MILES[1]   January 10, 1941
                                                  [Washington, D.C.]

What do you think of bringing our Attaché in Berlin home to talk things over?[2]

Have you heard anything at all from our people with the Army of the Nile?[3]

Has the matter of industrial plant security shaped up as it should?

Do you think combat intelligence is being pressed along the right lines with the troops? In this replacement center business, what do you think of having a small group in one of these camps devoted to combat intelligence?

Is there someone in your office who is looking for every opportunity for me to do the courteous, thoughtful thing with relation to these Latin-American officials, either in town or in their own countries?

GCMRL/G. C. Marshall Papers (Pentagon Office, Selected)

1. Brigadier General Sherman Miles had been acting assistant chief of staff, G-2, since May 1, 1940.

2. Colonel Bernard R. Peyton (U.S.N.A., 1910) had been military attaché in Germany since September 12, 1939.

3. The British Army of the Nile had launched an attack on the Italian forces in Libya in early December 1940. On January 5, 1941, the port of Bardia had fallen, and the British moved westward toward Tobruk. Major Bonner Frank Fellers (U.S.M.A., 1918) was the chief United States Army attaché with the British forces in the Middle East.

MEMORANDUM FOR THE SECRETARY OF WAR   January 10, 1941
Secret   [Washington, D.C.]

Subject: General Miles's Estimate of Colonel Ratay,
         Military Attaché in the Balkans.[1]

Miles states that Ratay is an excellent troop officer and fine leader; that he has been tremendously impressed with the organization and power of the German Army.

General Miles stated that when he was relieved as Attaché in London last April and brought home to be G-2, he had a conference on the Continent with all the European Attachés. At that time Ratay stated that Germany could over-run and subdue France whenever she was ready, but that he thought she would turn on England first and reduce England by August last. He was the only Attaché who had a full appreciation of the power of the German Army and the weakness of France.

Miles states that Ratay is rather pro-German, at least to the extent that he is on intimate terms with many German officers; that he, Miles, has not discouraged this because he felt it very important that we have someone on an intimate basis with the Germans.

General Miles thinks that Ratay errs in his judgment of the German ratio over the British in air power, that is 16 to 1. (He, Miles, thinks it is about 6 to 1), and that in some of his other estimates he is too extreme in his views. However, Ratay's estimate on the inability of England to maintain itself without our entry into the war—giving three to one as the odds in favor of Germany—is less pessimistic than that of most of the officers with General Lee in London.[2]

GCMRL/G. C. Marshall Papers (Pentagon Office, General)

1. Lieutenant Colonel John P. Ratay had been military attaché in the Balkans with offices at the United States Legation, Bucharest, Rumania, since April 20, 1939.

2. Brigadier General Raymond E. Lee was military attaché in London. He often dined with Major-General Sir John Kennedy, director of Military Operations and Plans in the British War Office, who later wrote: "Lee was a very charming and intelligent man and a good friend of ours, and he was inclined to take an optimistic and philosophical view of the prospects." (*The Business of War; The War Narrative of Major-General Sir John Kennedy*, ed. Bernard Fergusson [London: Hutchinson and Company, 1957], p. 65.) See Lee's optimistic assessment of Britain's chances to withstand a German invasion and the prospects of Germany's ultimate defeat in *The London Journal of General Raymond E. Lee, 1940–1941*, ed. James Leutze [Boston: Little, Brown, and Company, 1971], p. 44.

To Mrs. James J. Winn   January 14, 1941
                                                     [Washington, D.C.]

Dear Molly: I have wanted to write you a long-hand letter, but have never managed it, so I am dictating this note. Your mother and I have gotten a great deal of pleasure out of your first two letters from Panama, one of which arrived yesterday afternoon, telling of your club-cottage arrangements. I gathered that the trip down was delightful and that you are pleased with the lay-out in Panama.[1]

We have been terrifically busy since returning from the White [Sulphur Springs, West Virginia]. It promises to grow worse in the next two or three weeks. I am to be given some very difficult hearings before Congress, and some of the questions are going to be rather hard to handle.

I required your mother to treat herself to a mink coat today. She picked it out at Woodward & Lothrop's and will have it in time for the Inauguration ceremonies next Monday; she is very much excited. I have not seen the coat but she says it is a beauty.

This is a pretty poor excuse for a letter, but I do not want you to think "out of sight, out of mind" for I miss you constantly and particularly when the riding hour comes around. So far I have found no substitute.

With my love,   Affectionately,

GCMRL/Research File (Family)
1. These letters by Molly Brown Winn are not in the Marshall papers. Captain Winn was assigned to Fort Davis, Panama Canal Zone.

S PEAKING on January 7 over the N.B.C. radio network, Marshall described the army's development in size and responsibility during the past year. "We now have a broad and sound foundation on which to build the larger forces ordered by the American people." He acknowledged, however, that along with the gains there remained numerous deficiencies in materiel, the result of "years of public indifference to questions of national defense." These problems could not be solved overnight, but the army was preparing the manpower. Capital and labor had to provide the equipment, and "public opinion must give its wholehearted support to the enterprise. Speed and unity are imperative."

There were even certain unintended benefits for the individual and the nation from the mobilization, in the chief of staff's opinion. Training would not only benefit men's health and physique, but "a vital psychological gain should result from this service. The complete democracy of life in the ranks, the cultivation of respect for constituted authority, the acknowledgment of a responsibility for service to one's country—those influences are bound to develop a fine citizenship. The intimate contacts will promote understanding among men from every section of this great country, and from every walk of life. Personally, I believe the best medicine for the ailments of democracy flows from association in a common effort. Our self-imposed military program provides that opportunity." (Radio interview between General Marshall and Colonel J. C. O'Laughlin, January 7, 1941, GCMRL/ G. C. Marshall Papers [Pentagon Office, Speeches].)

Marshall's remarks brought an unexpected response from his Virginia Military Institute classmate Charles S. Roller, Jr., principal of the Augusta Military Academy in Virginia. Roller had happened to hear the speech from a storefront radio on a Washington, D.C., street. After the address, he commented to some young men in the crowd which had gathered that Marshall was "the kind of man we should have for the next President," a statement which "certainly was given a very warm and approving reception." Roller told Marshall that he would make a good president and wanted to "start the ball rolling" among the V.M.I. alumni toward a possible Marshall candidacy. (Roller to Marshall, January 11, 1941, GCMRL/G. C. Marshall Papers [Pentagon Office, Selected].) Marshall's response to this idea follows. ★

To Major Charles S. Roller, Jr. January 15, 1941
[Washington, D.C.]

Dear Roller: I have just read your letter of January 11th, regarding the incident concerned with my broadcast of January 7th.

I appreciate very much your flattering reactions, but I must tell you with complete sincerity that there are two phases to your comments or suggestions that would be fatal to my future. In the first place, putting such an idea into a man's head is the first step toward destroying his usefulness, and in the second place the public suggestion of such an idea, even by mere rumor or gossip, would be almost fatal to my interests.

So long as the various servants of the Government in important positions concerned with national defense devote all their time and all their thought to the straight business of the job, all will go well with America, but just as soon as an ulterior purpose or motive creeps in, then the trouble starts and will gather momentum like a snowball. So, while I appreciate very much the compliment of your letter, I ask you not to even tell your wife what you thought.   Faithfully yours,

GCMRL/G. C. Marshall Papers (Pentagon Office, Selected)

Memorandum for The Adjutant General January 15, 1941
(Morale Branch) [Washington, D.C.]

Mr. Ford Frick, President of the National League of Professional Base Ball Clubs, called on me today to tender the helpful influence of his League, and indirectly that of Judge Landis, Base Ball Commissioner to the American League—though he had not been delegated to represent the latter.[1] They had a meeting a few weeks ago in which representatives of both Leagues and Judge Landis talked over the relation of baseball to national defense. They are anxious to be of service and had in mind a number of different things.

They thought they might be able to play exhibition games, particularly during the period of the spring practice, at or in the vicinity of camps in the

Southeast; they thought they might be able to lend some assistance in the coaching business if we developed base ball in the camps; they spoke of donating the receipts from their All-Star game to the purpose of athletic equipment—but they have been led to believe that with Government appropriations, this phase of the matter is not so pressing.

He said he would appreciate it very much if they could be given early notice of what ways they might be of assistance. The early notice is necessary, as their plans have to be made long in advance.

I suggest that somebody connected with Morale affairs call on Mr. Frick, and talk over directly the various possibilities in the matter. The spring practice in the Southeast will lend itself to a very nice gesture. I believe each Club is willing to play at least one exhibition game in the vicinity of some cantonment.

GCMRL/G. C. Marshall Papers (Pentagon Office, General)

1. Since 1920 Kenesaw Mountain Landis, former judge of the federal district court of northern Illinois, had been commissioner of the American and National leagues of professional baseball clubs.

To Brigadier General Courtney H. Hodges[1]   January 15, 1941
[Washington, D.C.]

Dear Hodges: This is just a note to tell you that I have had a number of flattering comments regarding the two weeks' course you conducted for the National Guard Generals.[2] In their opinion a tremendous amount of good should flow from the instruction and also the associations and opportunities for lengthy discussions. It is evident that you and your people did a splendid job and I want you to know that I am deeply appreciative.

More and more Benning looms in our mobilization development a factor of immense importance.   Faithfully yours,

GCMRL/G. C. Marshall Papers (Pentagon Office, General)

1. Hodges had been commandant at the Infantry School, Fort Benning, Georgia, since October 1940; he had been assistant commandant during the previous two years.

2. At the end of January 1940 the normal nine-month army service school courses had been discontinued. They were replaced by short courses of twelve weeks or less: basic courses for new officers; refresher courses for selected officers; and specialized training for key officers and enlisted men. From September 1940 to December 1941, the schools focused on the hundred thousand National Guard and Reserve Corps officers being called to active duty. Inexperienced officers received basic knowledge and educational skills for training men in their units, administrative and leadership instruction for command and "a conviction of the importance of leadership in training and combat." (Robert R. Palmer, Bell I. Wiley, and William R. Keast, *The Procurement and Training of Ground Combat Troops*, a volume in the *United States Army in World War II* [Washington: GPO, 1948], pp. 260–63.)

MEMORANDUM FOR THE ASSISTANT CHIEFS OF   January 16, 1941
STAFF, G-1 [SHEDD] AND G-3 [TWADDLE]   [Washington, D.C.]

In conversation with General Lynch this morning, I was impressed with several suggestions, or comments he made:

He told me of one regiment that had had 60 company commanders in four months, and that he did not believe that was unusual.

He remarked, for example, that he was recently called upon to furnish officers for training as observers with the Air Corps, and that this meant taking them away from troops. Along with this he made the suggestion that we should have a surplus of Reserve Officers in training. In other words, at the present time we have no fat meat, and the set-up is so lean that replacements are not available for sickness, for details away, for this and that.

He felt that Benning was reaching the saturation point and yet that we had not provided sufficiently for the training of the large number of lieutenants in the National Guard who had recently been commissioned from the ranks. We discussed the proposition of having each division run a school for this purpose. My reaction to this was that it might be well done in some places, but probably would be poorly done in others, especially as each division would be busy with a special grouping for the handling of selectees.

We thought that it might be desirable to establish branch schools, with a modest outfit at the start, at places such as Meade, San Antonio, Rolla, Missouri, and Ord. Where tent camps have been vacated, the shelter problem might be met without great difficulty. This would not be the case at Rolla, Missouri, where everything has to be built.[1] It does appear to me that we will have to provide additional training facilities for the improvement of officer personnel, along with the provision of sufficient Reserve officers to prevent too serious an absenteeism from units during this special period of training.

Will you please look into this and discuss it with me informally prior to preparing any detailed report.

GCMRL/G. C. Marshall Papers (Pentagon Office, Selected)

1. Rolla was the nearest large town to the new Fort Leonard Wood, which held its groundbreaking ceremony on December 3, 1940, and was officially named a month later. The other posts and locations mentioned are: Fort George G. Meade, near Baltimore, Maryland; Fort Sam Houston, at San Antonio, Texas; and Fort Ord, near Monterey, California.

TO GENERAL JOHN J. PERSHING   January 16, 1941
Washington, D.C.

Dear General Pershing: I have had G-1 canvass every possibility under which Curtin might be commissioned with the net result of zero as far as any acceptable solution is concerned. All appointments in The Adjutant General's Department reserve are suspended except in the case of enlisted men in the Regular Army who are eligible for appointment in the grade of captain, and Curtin is too old for this grade. We have declined so many applications for Reserve commissions from persons of influence including important members of Congress that if we now make an appointment in violation of policy we will be placed in an impossible situation. I would be glad, as you know, to do anything possible for Curtin, even if you were not personally interested, but the circumstances are such that I cannot consistently approve his application.[1]   Faithfully yours,

G. C. Marshall

LC/J. J. Pershing Papers (General Correspondence)

1. Sergeant Ralph Curtin had been Pershing's orderly during the World War and continued in that service afterwards. Sergeant Crawford C. Shaeffer was also on Pershing's staff and was considered by Marshall, at Pershing's request, for an appointment as a warrant officer. Marshall could not immediately appoint Shaeffer, but he informed Pershing that the sergeant might be eligible to take the examination for warrant officer after "several months." (Marshall to Pershing, January 14, 1941, LC/J. J. Pershing Papers [General Correspondence].)

MEMORANDUM FOR GENERAL GEROW[1]   January 17, 1941
Secret   Washington, D.C.

Subject: White House Conference of Thursday, January 16, 1941.

Yesterday afternoon the President held a lengthy conference with the Secretaries of State, War and Navy, the Chief of Naval Operations and the Chief of Staff of the Army. He discussed the possibilities of sudden and simultaneous action on the part of Germany and Japan against the United States. He felt that there was one chance out of five of such an eventuality, and that it might culminate any day.

The President then brought up for opinion and discussion a number of phases of the matter:

What military and naval action we should take in that emergency; he mentioned the "Rainbow" plan and commented on the fact that we must be realistic in the matter and avoid a state of mind involving plans which could be carried out after the lapse of some months; we must be ready to act with what we had available.

He discussed the publicity we might give to our proposed courses of action,—in relation to the Philippines, fleet, the continuation of supplies to Great Britain, etc.

He devoted himself principally to a discussion of our attitude in the Far East towards Japan and to the matter of possible curtailment of American shipments of war supplies to England. He was strongly of the opinion that in the event of hostile action towards us on the part of Germany and Japan we should be able to notify Mr. Churchill immediately that this would not curtail the supply of materiel to England. He discussed this problem on the basis of the probability that England could survive six months and that, therefore, a period of at least two months would elapse before hostile action could be taken against us in the Western Hemisphere. In other words, that there would be a period of eight months in which we could gather strength.

The meeting terminated with this general directive from the President:

That we would stand on the defensive in the Pacific with the fleet based on Hawaii; that the Commander of the Asiatic Fleet would have discretionary authority as to how long he could remain based in the Philippines and as to his direction of withdrawal—to the East or to Singapore; that there would be no naval reinforcement of the Philippines; that the Navy should have under consideration the possibility of bombing attacks against Japanese cities.[2]

That the Navy should be prepared to convoy shipping in the Atlantic to England, and to maintain a patrol off-shore from Maine south to the Virginia Capes. (I am in doubt as to this southern point.)

That the Army should not be committed to any aggressive action until it was fully prepared to undertake it; that our military course must be very conservative until our strength had developed; that it was assumed we could provide forces sufficiently trained to assist to a moderate degree in backing up friendly Latin-American governments against Nazi inspired fifth column movements.

That we should make every effort to go on the basis of continuing the supply of materiel to Great Britain, primarily in order to disappoint what he thought would be Hitler's principal objective in involving us in a war at this particular time, and also to buck up England.[3]

This is a rough outline of the general understanding resulting from the discussion.

G. C. M.

NA/RG 165 (WPD, 4175-18)

1. Brigadier General Leonard T. Gerow had been acting assistant chief of staff, War Plans Division, since December 16, 1940.

2. Concerning the army's gradual buildup in the Philippine Islands, see Marshall to Grunert, February 8, 1941, pp. 414–18.

3. President Roosevelt was summarizing the United States position on these subjects in preparation for the staff meetings called the "American-British Conversations" scheduled to begin in late January. See the editorial note on pp. 409–10.

To Douglas S. Freeman   January 17, 1941
                                                        [Washington, D.C.]

My dear Dr. Freeman: Maris has just shown me your note of January 15th to him.[1]

I am a little in the dark as to your meaning when you write: "The induction is progressing by such unostentatious stages," and particularly its connection with your further reference: "We did not realize that induction would be by so many small steps." The preliminary steps have been small, but the inductions for this month will amount to about 90,000, and I believe for February about 100,000, and for March 150,000. We already have in the field, in continental United States, over 500,000 men. Some of the National Guard units have been in active training since last September and have passed into the second phase of their training program.

What we had in mind was your getting a look at some of these camps, getting a picture of the activity, and translating that from the camp over the radio to the public.

About six weeks ago I sent about 20 newspaper men on a tour. They were the fellows who work on the military news here in Washington. They came back here almost flabbergasted with the extent of the mobilization then in progress. I get the same reaction from officers of the War Department who have not been in the field recently. I send them out by air to look into this and that, and they come back profoundly impressed by what they have seen. They had the facts on paper, but it made little impression on the mind even of the trained staff officer. So far as the Congress and the general public are concerned, I have found they haven't any conception of how much is under way in the field.

This sounds very much as if I were trying to over-persuade you, and I am aware that your services are available in case I think it advisable to go ahead with this. My point is that I am much interested in the opinions expressed in your letter rather than the question of your going out in the field, and I would like very much to get your frank comments for my advice and assistance.[2]   Faithfully yours,

GCMRL/G. C. Marshall Papers (Pentagon Office, Selected)

1. Douglas S. Freeman, editor of the *Richmond News Leader*, offered his assistance as a publicist to the War Department. On January 13, 1941, Lieutenant Colonel Ward H. Maris, chief of the War Department's Public Relations Branch, proposed two plans—which had been discussed as early as October 1940—to Freeman. First, he might visit the War Department and the training camps and then publish and broadcast by radio his observations. Second, he might accompany a proposed tour by airplane of the training camps and broadcast his observations from each base. (Maris to Freeman, January 13, 1941, GCMRL/G. C. Marshall Papers [Pentagon Office, Selected].) Freeman replied that publicizing the slow rate of mobilization meant "overplaying news that has become familiar to the nation." (Freeman to Maris, January 15, 1941, ibid.)

2. Replying to Marshall, Freeman stated that he "misunderstood your original idea." He thought that a large, single induction would occur, as in 1917. Freeman told Marshall that he welcomed the opportunity to visit the camps and broadcast his observations. (Freeman to Marshall, January 18, 1941, ibid.) Maris advised Marshall to leave it up to Freeman since the chief of the Public Relations Branch did not feel that the journalist was sufficiently enthusiastic about the project. (Maris Memorandum for Chief of Staff, January 28, 1941, ibid.) There is no record in the Marshall papers of any broadcasts by Freeman.

To Allen T. Brown   January 17, 1941
Confidential   [Washington, D.C.]

Dear Allen: I have not written to you or Madge for some time, but the failure has not been because of any lack of thought of you. I have been so busy that I have barely been able to concentrate on the urgent requirements.

It was a great pleasure to see you both here, and I am sorry that my contacts were largely hurried in and out affairs. I have read your letter to your mother and also Madge's letter to her. I think Molly's letters have been sent to you two to see. Your mother is having a pretty busy time, and the Inaugural ceremonies as well as the President's Birthday Ball matters will tax her considerably for the remainder of this month.

Confidentially, this is to you alone, I would like to say this: I was somewhat concerned when I saw you during the holidays by the feeling that you were becoming more constant and uniform in the attitude of a chip on your shoulder. It seemed to me that even in casual conversation or contacts, your reaction was almost automatically along this line. I hope you will not take offense, but I wish you would have this in mind and get it under better control.[1]

GCMRL/Research File (Family)

1. A portion of this photocopied document apparently is missing; the editors have not located the original.

Memorandum for General Ulio[1] or   January 18, 1941
The Adjutant General [Adams]   [Washington, D.C.]

There is a Lieutenant Jones with Company 4480, CCC at Frogmore Hunting Island, South Carolina.[2] Will you quietly have his record of service with the CCC checked and let me know your opinion of the man.

I might say that he has asked for nothing, as a matter of fact, he is conspicuous in my mind because he does not want anything. But he came to my attention from his outstandingly efficient work in another camp, and I am always on the lookout for the real performers who are self-effacing.

GCMRL/G. C. Marshall Papers (Pentagon Office, Selected)

1. Brigadier General James A. Ulio was the assistant adjutant general.
2. Alexander L. Jones, a 1931 graduate of the Citadel and a first lieutenant in the Infantry Reserve, had served on active duty with the Civilian Conservation Corps from 1933 to 1938. In August 1939 Marshall had assisted him in returning to C.C.C. duty as a civilian.

To the Commanding General,   January 21, 1941
Camp Beauregard   [Washington, D.C.]
Radio

Senator Overton of Louisiana informs me that a criticism of Alexandria merchants has been made by soldiers on Christmas furlough in Wisconsin to the effect that two scales of prices prevail one for the soldier much higher than that for local residents. Have you any information on the subject to give me for Senator Overton before Thursday A.M.[1]

GCMRL/G. C. Marshall Papers (Pentagon Office, General)

1. Alexandria, Louisiana, five miles from Camp Beauregard, was Senator John H. Overton's hometown.

Memorandum for General Gerow   January 21, 1941
Washington, D.C.

I will probably be called before the Foreign Relations Committee on the pending Bill tomorrow or the next day.[1] I will certainly be called before the Appropriations Committee very shortly. In either case, it is likely that the following questions will be put to me:

Explain the necessity, in our situation between two oceans, for an army of 1,400,000.

In previous hearing you mentioned the possibility that a much larger force might be necessary of 3,000,000 or 4,000,000 men. Please explain the possible requirements for such a large force.

I would like you to have someone draft possible replies for me.[2]

G. C. M.

NA/RG 165 (OCS, 20822–138)

1. Following closely upon President Roosevelt's December 29, 1940, "fireside chat" on national security, in which he proclaimed that the United States had to be "the great arsenal of democracy," and upon his January 6, 1941, state-of-the-union message, in which he disclosed the concept that came to be called "lend-lease," bills to enact this idea were introduced into

Congress on January 10 as House bill 1776 and Senate bill 275. (*The Public Papers and Addresses of Franklin D. Roosevelt*, 1940 volume, ed. Samuel I. Rosenman [New York: Macmillan Company, 1941], pp. 643, 668–69.) The House Foreign Affairs Committee began hearings on January 15, and Marshall testified in executive session on January 27 and 28. (See Marshall to Bloom, January 29, 1941, pp. 400–401.)

2. The War Plans Division responded that large forces were now essential to the United States because it, unlike some European powers, had no predetermined theater of operations and no definite knowledge of the enemy forces to be opposed, and because the speed and character of modern warfare made large army and air forces necessary. The 1,400,000-man force would meet the nation's initial needs for discouraging aggression in the Western Hemisphere, but it was inadequate for war with a major power, and it would have to be doubled if Britain's fleet was lost and Japan and Germany concerted their actions. If the Axis powers were to gain freedom of action in either the Atlantic or the Pacific oceans, the United States would need army and air forces totalling 4,000,000 men or more. Even this would be small compared to present German forces. (Gerow Memorandum for the Chief of Staff, January 22, 1941, NA/RG 165 [WPD, 3674–47].) Marshall was not required to testify before either congressional appropriations committee until March; these questions were not raised at that time.

To ALLEN T. BROWN   January 22, 1941
                                                    [Washington, D.C.]

Dear Allen: Last night I found your letter of January 20th out at the house, and gave it a careful reading. It pleased me because I had feared a rather vigorous reaction to my comments, and I was most relieved and glad to find that you had undertaken to analyze my comments in rather an impersonal fashion. I hesitated in writing you as I did and after having written I decided that it was a mistake to have done so, but now that I have your reaction I feel quite differently in the matter.

The incidents I referred to were of a very casual nature and merely symptomatic in my opinion, but it was for that reason that I was concerned. They seemed to me to indicate a state of mind that I know from long experience is very unfortunate in this world and is not the way to get across in the long run. You have to save your ammunition for the big fights and avoid a constant drain of little ones.[1]

GCMRL/Research File (Family)

1. A portion of this photocopied document apparently is missing; the editors have not located the original.

To LIEUTENANT GENERAL DANIEL VAN VOORHIS   January 24, 1941
Confidential   Washington, D.C.

Dear Van Voorhis: I have been in communication with you by radio and special letters with some frequency of late, but I think it would be well for me to tell you a little of the low-down on what has been happening.

In the first place, the Secretary of War took up directly with the President the question of the air fields. I understand the President was deeply concerned and intent on an early solution being reached without further diplomatic delay. We have awaited the arrival of the new Ambassador here before seeing that this is put over in a hurry. I am in hopes that it will now reach an early conclusion and you can actually get to work.[1]

As to placing of guards on governmental ships, that grew out of the very embarrassing prospect which is approaching now, but there seemed no other solution. We cannot take any chances with the Panama Canal. If it is blocked, our whole situation in the Atlantic becomes immensely critical should there be a tragic result in England.[2]

We are having a difficult time in obtaining experienced men in certain branches of the Army, particularly quartermasters. Running one of these huge villages of fifty or sixty thousand men is a difficult matter from the viewpoint of utilities alone. General Gregory is sending some Reserve quartermasters out to Hawaii to relieve certain Regulars there for duty in this country. Nothing has come up with regard to Panama on this particular subject, but don't you think you could loosen up on some regular quartermasters if we sent you some selected reserve quartermasters or engineers?[3]

The announcement as to unified command in the Caribbean area was made by the Secretary in a press conference ahead of our reaching definite conclusions. As a matter of fact, he had not known about our intentions until that day. Someone had suggested the item as being interesting for the press, and as they lacked such on that day, the announcement was made.

Please give me your reaction on Prosser. His nomination is now in to be a Major General in view of the size of his command. If there are any men in your outfit that you think are deserving of promotion, please let me know informally and directly. Devers has gone a long way since he left your place. He is now a Division Commander, and making a fine job of it. We want to find more men of the same type, and I am willing to go down the list quite a way to get them.[4]

Your management of affairs in Panama is a source of great assurance to me. It is very comforting to feel that you are at the helm.   Faithfully yours,

GCMRL/G. C. Marshall Papers (Pentagon Office, Selected)

1. Secretary of War Stimson discussed the airfields question with the president on January 9. In his diary, Stimson characterized the Panamanian government as "unfriendly," and it was "refusing to give us, or delaying in giving us, the emergency landing fields and airdromes that we want in different parts of the Republic. All the planes which are necessary for the defenses of the Canal are crowded together in three small airdromes in a very small space and would be at the mercy of a sudden attack from the air." (January 9, 1941, Yale/ H. L. Stimson Papers [Diary, 32: 94].) On the developments in Panama, see Memorandum for the Secretary of War, March 24, 1941, p. 452. The new ambassador from Panama, Don Carlos N. Brin, presented

his letters of credence on January 17. (*Department of State Bulletin* [January 18, 1941]: 99–100.)

2. Following a meeting at the White House on January 16, Marshall directed the War Plans Division to draft instructions to Van Voorhis to place armed guards on all public vessels transiting the Panama Canal. This was done, cleared with the State Department, and sent the next day. (Gerow Memorandum for the Record, January 17, 1941, NA/RG 319 [OPD, Exec. 4, Item 5].)

3. Van Voorhis replied that although he had two new stations needing quartermasters, a survey of his staff determined that four field-grade officers could be spared for duty in the continental United States. (Van Voorhis to Marshall, February 2, 1941, GCMRL/G. C. Marshall Papers [Pentagon Office, Selected].)

4. Brigadier General Walter E. Prosser (U.S.M.A., 1905), commander of the Panama Mobile Force, would not "fit into the situation here if, by reason of seniority, he should become Department Commander," Van Voorhis wrote. Brigadier General Jacob L. Devers had served on the presidential board for the selection of air and naval bases in the Atlantic until becoming commanding general of the Ninth Division and Fort Bragg, North Carolina, on October 9, 1940. Closing out his letter to Marshall, Van Voorhis listed several officers that he considered worthy of promotion and elaborated on their qualifications. (Ibid.)

TO MRS. JOHN B. WILSON[1]   January 27, 1941
                                                             Washington, D.C.

Dear Rose: I have been on the verge of writing to you each day since my return from White Sulphur Springs the day after New Years, but events have developed too rapidly for me to turn to anything pleasant or personal.

I want particularly to thank you for the box of cookies, which were delicious and which Mrs. Marshall and I are still using for our afternoon tea when I come in from riding or from walking. Tell me where you bought them—I am assuming you did not make them.[2]

I have been hoping to receive a letter from you with some account of your settlement in New York, but as none has come I am now asking you to write. And so that you may not think I have neglected you, I will mention that I am due in ten minutes to leave here to appear before the Foreign Relations Committee on the famous "lend-lease" bill, so I am sandwiching this in between pretty important affairs of the world.

I had a fine ride in the Hall[3] yesterday morning and a rather cold one out of doors Saturday afternoon, with a great deal of mud. Since you and Molly departed I have been riding alone, and it is a lonely business.

Molly seems to be on the top of the world in Panama and thrilled over setting up her own house. Fortunately, she knows how to cook and market.

I do hope John finds his new job all that he hoped for, and that you are happy in your new environment.   Affectionately,

                                                             G. C. M.

GCMRL/R. P. Wilson Collection

1. Rose Page Wilson, Marshall's goddaughter, had recently moved to New York City; her husband had been hired as a tax expert for the Sperry Corporation on January 1, 1941. (Rose Page Wilson, *General Marshall Remembered* [Englewood Cliffs, N.J.: Prentice-Hall, 1968], p. 234.)

2. Mrs. Wilson had sent the Marshalls a box of moravian Christmas cookies as a present. (Ibid.)

3. The riding hall at Fort Myer.

To Lee L. Lowman[1]   January 27, 1941
                                                   [Washington, D.C.]

My dear Mr. Lowman: I have received your gracious note of January 25th, inviting me to be the guest of the Maryland Alumni Club on New Market Day.[2]

I appreciate your wanting me and am sorry I cannot accept. The fact of the matter is, I have already tentatively accepted the invitation of the New York Chapter, though I have slight hope of getting there. I have turned them down three successive years, and I promised to do my best this year to attend.

I cannot make dates like this because there are so many inspections that I should be making all over the United States as well as in the Caribbean area and Alaska, and I have to leave on such short notice, fitting in my desires with the various meetings of vast importance I am involved in here as well as the calls of conferences—that an evening date of this sort adds a further complication. If I fail to show up I give offense and frequently cause embarrassment. Therefore, I have had to decline.[3]

Will you please explain my situation and thank the Committee for their courtesy in inviting me.   Faithfully yours,

GCMRL/G. C. Marshall Papers (Pentagon Office, General)

1. Lowman was a Virginia Military Institute alumnus living in Baltimore, Maryland.

2. On May 15, 1864, the V.M.I. Cadet Corps was engaged as a Confederate Army unit in a pitched battle against the United States Army at New Market, Virginia. On that anniversary the corps annually commemorates this action in formal ceremonies at the institute.

3. Marshall's letter to Lowman is typical of scores of similar responses during this period.

To Allen T. Brown   January 29, 1941
                                                   [Washington, D.C.]

Dear Allen: Your telegram was so much grief to your mother until I reached home and translated its code into the grand news that the Brown family was on the way. We are both delighted and I cannot tell you how deeply we feel that this will be a tremendous factor in stablilizing your outlook and governing the development of your lives. It is great news, and I am delighted. Please give Madge my love and all of my congratulations. Whatever Hitler may do, you two are doing your full duty to make the world a better place.[1]   Affectionately,

GCMRL/Research File (Family)

1. Allen and Madge had a son, Allen Tupper, Jr., on September 1, 1941.

To Sol Bloom[1]   January 29, 1941
                                                      [Washington, D.C.]

My dear Mr. Bloom: I am much embarrassed by the press reports of an interview with me yesterday afternoon, and deeply concerned because this may cause the members of your committee to feel that I have not acted with complete good faith regarding my appearance before the committee in executive session.

The facts are these: For some time a press conference had been scheduled for Monday, but when I received the Committee's invitation to appear on Monday, the date was advanced to Tuesday, not anticipating that my testimony would cover two days. A delay of the press conference until next week was not considered advisable by my people because the newspaper men were growing very restless in their desire to interview me since I had not seen them for about two months. A later date this week was not practicable because of interference with other War Department press conferences.

It was my intention at the conference to confine myself to affairs of our Army, but the newspaper men appeared solely interested in things abroad, and as the basis of my relations with them has been one of extreme frankness, I found myself in an embarrassing situation. It was the understanding that no reference should be made to my appearance before your committee or to my views regarding the "lease-loan" bill. However, while in the main they observed this request, yet there was sufficient by way of implication to cause me deep concern.[2]

I wish you to know the facts in the case, as it is quite evident that the holding of the conference yesterday afternoon was ill advised. I hope you will accept my regrets as most sincere.   Faithfully yours,

GCMRL/G. C. Marshall Papers (Pentagon Office, General)

1. Sol Bloom, Democrat from New York, was chairman of the House Foreign Affairs Committee.

2. At a press conference on Tuesday, January 28, 1941, Marshall contended that Britain could withstand an invasion if provided with lend-lease aid. He claimed that the United States

Army Air Corps was sufficient to resist any enemy "under present conditions" but inadequate for defense if Britain surrendered. The chief of staff stated that the United States was not finished with the first phase of its expansion program and was "not planning to spare any of our existing air equipment to the British because we have not yet filled out our own program." (*New York Times*, January 29, 1941, pp. 1, 6.)

To Major General Edmund L. Daley   January 30, 1941
Confidential   Washington, D.C.

Dear Daley: This is for your eye alone, and I want you to know that I do not want a reply.

I am going to write very frankly, particularly as I have had great admiration for the way you have developed the Puerto Rican command. There have come to me from such a variety of sources rumors or hints of a phase of discontent in your command that I thought it best to make a frank report of the matter to you personally. The indications point to a very highly developed and highly trained organization; but on the other hand, all seem to indicate that little things, small requirements pertaining to the individual are having an accumulative effect which in time will possibly do harm.

I have turned this matter over in my mind to see if I could penetrate the possible causes, but I can only guess at that in writing to you because I have refrained from any questioning of people. I am inclined to think that a variety of factors are involved, the most serious one being that you, a bachelor, are unsparing of yourself and very strenuous in your demands on other people; that Bradley, your Air man, is possibly a better staff officer than a commander in his relation to handling people; that Connell, with your Air outfit, while an excellent commander is of the "driver" type who in the past has required some pressure to have him ease up from time to time before the boys exploded; and finally, that McAndrew, your Chief of Staff, is certainly not the cheery type.[1]

As I have said I have such great confidence in your ability to handle any situation in Puerto Rico, that I hesitate in any way to seem to limit your methods or activity. Therefore, I do not want you to answer this letter. I merely want you to analyze this business and see if you think maybe the pressure has been too continuously heavy and exacting, especially as to little requirements.[2] Faithfully yours,

GCMRL/G. C. Marshall Papers (Pentagon Office, Selected)

1. Brigadier General Follett Bradley (U.S.N.A., 1910) was commanding general of the Thirteenth Composite Wing of the Puerto Rican Department. Lieutenant Colonel Carl W. Connell was the commanding officer of Borinquen Field, Puerto Rico. Bradley wrote to the

chief of the Air Corps that there was personal conflict between himself and Daley and that Connell felt that Bradley had "eclipsed" him. (Bradley to Arnold, February 3, 1941, GCMRL/ G. C. Marshall Papers [Pentagon Office, Selected].) Colonel Joseph A. McAndrew (U.S.M.A., 1904) had been chief of staff of the Puerto Rican Department since April 1939.

2. On March 20, 1941, Marshall assigned Daley to command the Fifth Army Corps assembled at Camp Beauregard, Louisiana.

MEMORANDUM FOR GENERAL SHEDD   January 31, 1941
[Washington, D.C.]

Yesterday, at the request of Mr. Lowell Mellett, in charge of publicity for the President, Mr. Walter Wanger, President of the Academy of Motion Picture Arts and Sciences, and Director of the Producers Association of the Motion Picture Industry, called to see me on the general subject of the cooperation of the Motion Picture industry with the National Defense problem. Several phases of the matter were discussed.[1]

Recruiting: He stated that he had seen several of the "shorts" on recruiting and thought that the Motion Picture industry could do better by us in this respect.

Morale: He thought that a great deal could be done in the way of morale building, and mentioned a number of slants on this particular phase of the matter. He spoke of the fact that he had just learned that we would like the Industry to play down the hard-boiled sergeant— which was news to them, but which they would be glad to do. We spoke of the possibilities of the Picture Industry through its highly trained specialists, undertaking in a very serious way the business of carrying photographic publicity on the men back to home districts so that the men would feel that they were not unnoticed and that their efforts and hardships were appreciated at home. He was most complimentary to the Signal Corps for the way they were building up a group of men who would understand the Moving Picture technique phases of the business.

Training: He was less informed on this subject than any other, but ready to undertake it in the most serious fashion. The discussion was directed by me to the question of how best to have the great producing experts brought quickly to an understanding of the character of things we wish to utilize the Movie industry for. For example, I mentioned that it was possible that the Air people could be greatly helped in this matter, yet were unaware of how the Motion Picture method might be utilized to their assistance, and that if a Motion Picture expert could survey the field of what was being done, he might point out a great many things that could be covered by motion pictures. Particularly, he might suggest a better technique than our own people visualize. Incidentally, this was brought up by Stokowski in connection with his remarks about Walter Disney.[2] Stokowski thought that Disney could do some splendid work both from the morale point of view, and in the way of making people understand, along with a little amusement, exactly what the selectees' induction into the Army means in its various stages.

Recommendations:

Mr. Wanger's principal recommendation was that we coordinate our motion picture involvements all through Mr. Mellett, Recruiting, Morale, Training. He, Mellett, would pass the business on to the proper officials in the Motion Picture Industry. Mr. Mellett is the President's Coordinator of Publicity.

Mr. Wanger suggested that Carl [*Darryl*] Zanuck, a lieutenant colonel of the Reserve Corps, might be put on, at least temporary duty for a trip through some of our great training centers in order that he might quickly acquire a broad grasp of the problem, and then apply his genius to proposals for its solution. This last appeals to me as a valuable slant on the matter. It should not be difficult for us to arrange for one of the Signal Corps men who has been developed along training film lines, together with one of the recent script writers brought into the service, Mr. Zanuck, and possibly one of his assistants, to be flown by plane from Hollywood, to meet at Randolph Field, spend a day there, then look over the Artillery School at Sill, the Infantry School at Benning, possibly the Coast Artillery School at Fort Monroe, and to Washington for a brief conference. The trip from San Antonio to be by Army plane.

Will you look into this entire matter, and see what might be done to correlate the various phases.

GCMRL/G. C. Marshall Papers (Pentagon Office, Selected)

1. The motion picture industry was one of the first to volunteer its services free or on a cost basis in 1940. The production of training, recruiting, and morale films involved close cooperation between industry (including producers and actors) and government. Planning for the production of training films began in the Research Council of the Academy of Motion Picture Arts and Sciences in late 1940. Darryl F. Zanuck, who was a lieutenant colonel in the Reserve Corps, vice-president of Twentieth Century–Fox Corporation, and chairman of the Research Council, sponsored an "Affiliated Plan" for Signal Corps–industry cooperation. Major studios informed Secretary of War Stimson that they were willing to produce training films at cost. (Dulany Terrett, *The Signal Corps: The Emergency,* a volume in the *United States Army in World War II* [Washington: GPO, 1956], pp. 225–27.)

2. Leopold Stokowski and Walter E. Disney, a pioneer in producing animated sound films, had collaborated in the production of the film "Fantasia," which had been released in November 1940. Marshall had met with Stokowski shortly after the film's release; see Marshall to Stokowski, November 25, 1940, pp. 354–55.

To Lieutenant General Daniel Van Voorhis   January 31, 1941
Confidential   Washington, D.C.

Dear Van Voorhis: I have just this moment read your letter of January 29th regarding Quartermaster Construction Corps in general, and Danielson in particular. Also the comments regarding Edgerton and Stayer.[1]

To take the last mentioned first, I am not very sympathetic toward it, particularly regarding Edgerton. I think it a small-minded business, although very human, to criticize the elevation of the Governor of the Canal Zone, in these critical times, to the same rank as that held by his predecessor. Also in the face of the labor problems involved down there, and the general situation, I do not find much use for the criticisms in Stayer's case.

The reaction to the reorganization of the Construction Division up here, and your feeling regarding Danielson, is fully comprehended, and I wish to give you this confidential information. I have had a list of promotions in to the President since December 15th, most of the men urgently needed for actual commands. Some were so urgent, as in the case of Corregidor, that we have had to hold the colonel selected for that command in Manila, since his arrival six weeks ago, because several senior colonels of the Coast Artillery are on duty in Corregidor. We have had divisions here in heavy training with only one general officer in the division.

Our trouble in securing the nominations has been the President's reluctance to make so many general officers for the Army, and it has been a very difficult business to bring it to final approval two days ago, with a much reduced list. Originally, I had Danielson on to be a brigadier general to offset exactly the reaction you talk about. We have had to forego that, as well as the promotion of seven Corps Area Commanders to major generals, the customary rank for those positions, whose responsibilities have increased a dozen-fold since the days when a major general commanded the Corps Areas.

I intend, at the first possible moment, to secure the promotion for Danielson, but the latter part of your sentence recommending this puzzles me a little bit. You write ". . . at least to the temporary grade of brigadier general." The next time you write let me know what you mean by "at least." Possibly you refer to placing him at the head of the Construction Branch.

I might tell you that I have had a terrible time with this construction business. It has caused me more headaches than anything else connected with the expansion program.

There is no objection to your telling Danielson, most confidentially, that I am trying to get him promoted.

Your P.S. in regard to the confidential matter of ship guards is noted and your action appreciated.[2] A further radio on this subject went to you two days ago.   Faithfully yours,

GCMRL/G. C. Marshall Papers (Pentagon Office, Selected)

1. In early 1941, in a series of orders, the War Department reorganized the Office of the Quartermaster General, separating administrative from planning and control functions. The reorganization of the construction function began in 1940 when Congress assigned Air Corps projects to the Corps of Engineers. In late 1941, War Department and congressional concern for excessive construction costs, because of waste and duplication of effort, led to legislation granting construction functions to the Engineers. (Erna Risch, *The Quartermaster Corps: Organization, Supply, and Services*, 2 volumes in the *United States Army in World War II* [Washington: GPO, 1953–55], 1: 11–17. See Memorandum for the Secretary of War, April 1, 1941, pp. 463–64.)

In his January 29 letter, Van Voorhis complained that the reorganization of construction depressed the morale of his Quartermaster Corps personnel. He already believed that most of these men did "not measure up," but he thought there were a few capable men under his command. He considered Colonel Wilmont A. Danielson to be the most efficient and submitted his name for promotion "at least to the temporary grade of Brigadier General, if consistent with law." Both Glen E. Edgerton, governor of the Panama Canal Zone, and Morrison C. Stayer, the zone's chief health officer, had been promoted to brigadier general on October 1, 1940. Van Voorhis observed that this did not help morale among his Quartermaster Corps officers. (Van Voorhis to Marshall, January 29, 1941, GCMRL/G. C. Marshall Papers [Pentagon Office, Selected].)

2. See Marshall to Van Voorhis, January 24, 1941, pp. 396–98.

To Leonard K. Nicholson[1]   February 3, 1941
                                                            [Washington, D.C.]

Dear Nick: I have just this moment received your note of January 30th, with the original of the cartoon on me. I appreciate very much your letting me have it.[2]

These are pretty strenuous days. I can only wish that I could sit on the radiator again and cogitate on what was wrong with the administration of the Cadet Corps, and what the three of us might do and should we get something to eat.[3]

Buster Peyton is now a Corps Commander with headquarters at Columbia, South Carolina. He has under him three divisions and a number of special troops—about forty or fifty thousand men.[4]

With thanks and affectionate regards, Faithfully yours,

GCMRL/G. C. Marshall Papers (Pentagon Office, Selected)

1. Nicholson, publisher of the New Orleans *Times-Picayune*, had been Marshall's roommate all four years at the Virginia Military Institute.

2. This cartoon is on the following page.

3. Marshall comments on this use of the heating system in the V.M.I. cadets' rooms in his letter to Cadet Walter S. Grant, Jr., January 6, 1930, *Papers of GCM*, 1: 349.

4. Philip B. Peyton, also a roommate at the Virginia Military Institute, was promoted to major general on October 1, 1940, and was commanding general of the First Army Corps.

New Orleans Times-Picayune, *January 30, 1941*

MEMORANDUM FOR THE SECRETARY OF WAR   February 4, 1941
[Washington, D.C.]

Subject: Army Chaplains.

With the tremendous influx of young men into the military forces, to pass the million mark in March, the pressure on the War Department regarding the welfare of these men is steadily growing in intensity. Religious organizations, the W.C.T.U. [Woman's Christian Temperance Union] and kindred interests are increasingly urgent in their requests for reassurance and in their proposals for War Department action.

Under these conditions it is not believed that the present situation in the Corps of Chaplains is in the best interests of the service, particularly from the viewpoint of the public reaction. Under existing law, the Army is required to have one dentist in the grade of general officer. The law permits the appointment of a veterinarian in the grade of general officer. At the same time the Chief of Chaplains is a colonel. Whether or not chaplains should have military rank seems rather beside the point in the present situation. The law gives such rank, and it does not appear to be the proper moment to attempt a change in the law.

In my opinion, the Chief of Chaplains should be given rank on a parity with the chiefs of other branches and services of the Army. While the Chief of Chaplains does not head a fighting service, neither does the Judge Advocate General. Furthermore, chaplains are required, in the British Army for example, to go forward with their men in the attack formations.[1]

Under these circumstances, it is recommended that the present Chief of Chaplains, Colonel William R. Arnold, be nominated for promotion to the grade of major general.[2]

NA/RG 165 (OCS, 16379–54)

1. The issue of promoting the chief of Chaplains to brigadier general had been raised in late September 1940 when the first large group of general-officer promotions had been proposed. (See Marshall to De Witt, September 25, 1940, pp. 316–17.) At that time, Secretary of War Stimson had "reluctantly yielded" to Marshall's including Colonel Arnold on the list to be sent to the president for approval. Roosevelt, however, instructed Stimson to delete Arnold's name. (September 25 and 26, 1940, Yale/H. L. Stimson Papers [Diary, 30: 192, 197].)

2. The following is written on the bottom of the file copy of this document: "Pencil note on original: 'Sec. of War would not approve. GCM.'"

MEMORANDUM FOR THE SECRETARY OF WAR   February 6, 1941
[Washington, D.C.]

Mr. Secretary   Mr. McNutt saw the President regarding morale questions in civil communities near army camps. The President was unaware that there was such a problem![1] He directed McNutt to see me and get an agreement as to the army's role and Mr. McNutts responsibility. McNutt saw me at noon and wants me and Mr Osborn to see the President, with him, tomorrow.

I have seen Mr. Osborn and Colonel Draper, (Dillon, Read & Co.) who is working with your advisory committee.[2] They are seeing McNutt this afternoon and then will draw up a memo for me to McNutt. I will take the last up with you tomorrow A.M. before any further action is taken.[3]

G. C. Marshall

NA/RG 107 (SW Safe, Welfare and Recreational–Joint Army and Navy); H

1. For a recent example of this kind of problem, see Marshall's radio message to Commanding General, Camp Beauregard, January 21, 1941, p. 395. Secretary Stimson also reacted with surprise that the president was just discovering that there was "a real big problem." (February 7, 1941, Yale/ H. L. Stimson Papers [Diary, 33: 15].)

2. Frederick Osborn and William H. Draper, Jr., were New York businessmen acting as special assistants to Secretary Stimson. Both had served since October 1940 on the President's Advisory Committee on Selective Service, and both were now on the War Department Committee on Education, Recreation, and Community Service. On July 22, 1940, the War Department's Morale Divison was created as part of the Office of The Adjutant General. This organization was redesignated as the Morale Branch and placed under the chief of staff's direct supervision on March 14, 1941. Marshall discusses the reasons for this change in his letter to Hugh A. Drum, May 14, 1941, pp. 501–2.

3. Marshall and Osborn proposed that Charles P. Taft, younger son of the late President William Howard Taft, be appointed to coordinate the morale activities of the War Department, the Federal Security Agency, and various private organizations. (February 7, 1941, Yale/ H. L. Stimson Papers [Diary, 33: 15].)

MEMORANDUM FOR GENERAL ARNOLD

February 6, 1941
[Washington, D.C.]

Mr. Rockefeller called to see me regarding my letter to him of February 1st, of which a copy was sent to you. He was much pleased with the letter.[1]

He proposes the creation of a board of four individuals, one from the Army, with a working secretary, who will prepare the data to the propositions for the board to consider. The secretary to be, in effect, an off-shoot of the Civil Aeronautics Board in order that he might have the advantage of their office set-up. Mr. Rockefeller is very anxious that I should be on the board. I gave a tentative agreement, with the understanding that I have an alternate. Frankly he wants me on the board because of its relation to release of airplanes for use in South America. I explained exactly what our situation was in regard to this.

I do not want to involve you or Brett in this because you are very busy, but it occurred to me that the most practicable method would be for me to have as an alternate,— somebody like Griffiss, who is in close touch with you and otherwise with the Air Service.[2]

GCMRL/G. C. Marshall Papers (Pentagon Office, Selected)

1. Nelson A. Rockefeller was the president's coordinator of commercial and cultural relations with the American Republics. He supported the expansion of the Civil Aeronautics Board's authority so that it could direct an effective program to supplant Axis-controlled

airlines by United States or locally owned airlines operating in Latin America. Arnold, the author of Marshall's February 1 letter, endorsed Rockefeller's proposal. Arnold believed that German-controlled airlines provided that nation with a means for spreading propaganda, for communication with agents and fifth column movements, and for familiarizing German soldiers with Latin America. These airlines could provide bases for an invasion and, therefore, were a threat to United States security. He also agreed that the Civil Aeronautics Board was the proper institution to undertake this proposal. He supported the creation of a committee consisting of Rockefeller and representatives of that board and of the State and War departments. (Conn and Fairchild, *Framework of Hemisphere Defense,* p. 243; Marshall to Rockefeller, February 1, 1941, NA/RG 165 [OCS, 9136–61].)

2. Major General George H. Brett had been the acting chief of the Air Corps since October 1940. Major General Henry H. Arnold, who retained the title of chief of the Air Corps, assumed the duties of deputy chief of staff for air in October 1940. On this situation, see Memorandum for the Secretary of War, May 16, 1941, pp. 508–10. Major Townsend Griffiss (U.S.M.A., 1922) served in the Office of the Chief of the Air Corps as an aide to the secretary of war.

Rockefeller's proposal was not approved. Instead, the Defense Supplies Corporation of the Reconstruction Finance Corporation instituted the American Republics Aviation Division to provide funds, skilled technicians, and aircraft to United States and locally owned airlines operating in Latin America. (Conn and Fairchild, *Framework of Hemisphere Defense,* p. 244.)

ON January 29, 1941, a series of fourteen United States–British Staff Conversations began in Washington, D.C. Major General Stanley D. Embick, Brigadier Generals Leonard T. Gerow and Sherman Miles, and Colonel Joseph T. McNarney represented the United States Army. For two months the staffs discussed the respective military positions of the United States and Great Britain and the division of strategic responsibility and possible operations in the event that America entered the war. The British representatives based their strategy upon three assumptions: first, that the European theater was the decisive one; second, that Germany and Italy should be defeated before Japan; and third, that the Far East was essential to the preservation of the British Empire, and that protection of Singapore was of special importance to Far East strategy. At the sixth meeting, on February 10, the British proposed again the idea Prime Minister Winston Churchill had raised in May and October of 1940; namely, that the United States should send a naval task force to help defend the British base at Singapore. The American representatives agreed with the first two British strategic assumptions, but disagreed with the third. (Maurice Matloff and Edwin M. Snell, *Strategic Planning for Coalition Warfare, 1941–1942,* a volume in the *United States Army in World War II* [Washington: GPO, 1953], pp. 32–35.)

Miles, the assistant chief of staff for Military Intelligence, thought British assertions of an imminent Japanese attack on Malaya looked "very like concerted British pressure on us to commit ourselves in the Far East—a pressure that has been applied rather consistently during the past three months." (Miles Memorandum for the Chief of Staff, February 11, 1941, NA/RG 165 [WPD, 4175-18].) On February 12, the United States participants in the talks told Marshall that the Singapore task force proposal "would be a strategic error of incalculable magnitude." The United States Pacific Fleet "should be limited, pending the defeat of Germany, to such deterrent and containing influence" as could be rendered from Pearl Harbor operations. (Embick, Miles, Gerow, and McNarney Memorandum for the Chief of Staff, February 12, 1941, NA/RG 165 [WPD, 4402-3].)

Determined not to overextend the army in the western Pacific, Marshall declared in a February 6 conference that the United States had two active defense problems: Panama and Hawaii. Summarizing the situation at Pearl Harbor, the chief of staff said that the navy's nets for defense against submarine or plane-carried torpedoes were insufficient. Furthermore, a Japanese attack there was possible. Miles responded that the Military Intelligence Division had no evidence of a possible attack. Nevertheless, Marshall wanted the obsolete interceptors at Honolulu replaced by new planes superior in performance to any the Japanese could use from their aircraft carriers. Arnold, the deputy chief of staff for air, who was also present at the conference, recommended that thirty-one P-36s be sent immediately, followed by fifty P-40Bs. (Orlando Ward notes on the Conference in the Office of the Chief of Staff, February 6, 1941, NA/RG 165 [OCS, Chief of Staff Conferences File].)

Responding to Secretary of the Navy Frank Knox's concern about Oahu's defense, Stimson, in a letter drafted by Gerow, claimed that the "Hawaiian Department is the best equipped of all our overseas departments, and continues to hold a high priority for the completion of its projected defenses because of the importance of giving full protection to the Fleet." (For details of the projected Hawaiian defense, see Stimson Memorandum to the Secretary of the Navy, February 7, 1941, NA/RG 165 [WPD, 3583-1].)

Following the conversations, the staffs submitted a report (commonly known as ABC-1) which defined the nature of Allied cooperation in the future. They agreed on the predominant importance of the European theater in the event of global war, the maintenance of British positions in the Mediterranean, and the importance of a strategic defensive in the Far East. The United States Fleet would be employed offensively "to weaken Japanese economic power, and to support the defense of the Malay Barrier by directing Japanese strength away from Malaysia." (Quoted in Louis Morton, *Strategy and Command: The First Two Years,* a volume in the *United States Army in World War II* [Washington: GPO, 1962], p. 88.) ★

To LIEUTENANT GENERAL WALTER C. SHORT[1]   February 7, 1941
Secret   Washington, D.C.

My dear Short: I believe you take over command today, however the reason for this letter is a conversation I had yesterday with Admiral Stark.

He spoke of Admiral Kimmel, the new Fleet Commander,[2] regarding his personal characteristics. He said Kimmel was very direct, even brusque and undiplomatic in his approach to problems; that he was at heart a very kindly man, though he appeared rather rough in his methods of doing business. I gathered that he is entirely responsive to plain speaking on the part of the other fellow if there is frankness and logic in the presentation. Stark went so far as to say that he had, in the past personally objected to Kimmel's manners in dealing with officers, but that Kimmel was outstanding in his qualifications for command, and that this was the opinion of the entire Navy.

I give you this as it may be helpful in your personal dealings with Admiral Kimmel, not that I anticipate that you would be supersensitive, but rather that you would have a full understanding of the man with whom you are to deal.

Admiral Stark said that Kimmel had written him at length about the deficiencies of Army materiel for the protection of Pearl Harbor. He referred specifically to planes and to antiaircraft guns. Of course the facts are as he represents them regarding planes, and to a less serious extent regarding caliber .50 machine guns. The 3-inch antiaircraft gun is on a better basis. What Kimmel does not realize is that we are tragically lacking in this materiel throughout the Army, and that Hawaii is on a far better basis than any other command in the Army.

The fullest protection for the Fleet is *the* rather than *a* major consideration for us, there can be little question about that; but the Navy itself makes demands on us for commands other than Hawaii, which make it difficult for us to meet the requirements of Hawaii. For example, as I told Stark yesterday,—he had been pressing me heavily to get some modern antiaircraft guns in the Philippines for the protection of Cavite,[3] where they have collected a number of submarines as well as the vessels of the Asiatic Fleet—at the present time we have no antiaircraft guns for the protection of Cavite, and very little for Corregidor. By unobtrusively withdrawing 3-inch guns from regiments now in the field in active training, we had obtained 20 3-inch guns for immediate shipment to the Philippines. However before the shipment had been gotten under way the Navy requested 18 of these guns for Marine battalions to be specially equipped for the defense of islands in the Pacific. So I am left with two guns for the Philippines. This has happened time and again, and until quantity production gets well under way, we are in a most difficult situation in these matters.[4]

I have not mentioned Panama, but the Naval requirements of defense there are of immense importance, and we have not been able to provide all the guns that are necessary, nor to set up the Air units with modern equipment. However, in this instance, we can fly the latest equipment to Panama in one day, some of it in four hours.

You should make clear to Admiral Kimmel that we are doing everything that is humanly possible to build up the Army defenses of the Naval overseas installations, but we cannot perform a miracle. I arranged yesterday to ship 31 of the P36 planes to Hawaii by aircraft carrier from San Diego in about ten days. This will give you 50 of this type of plane, deficient in speed compared to the Japanese carrier based pursuit, and deficient in armament. But at least it gives you 50 of the same type. I also arranged with Admiral Stark to ship 50 P40-B pursuit planes about March 15th by Naval carrier from San Diego. These planes just came into production this week and should be on a quantity basis of about 8 a day by the first week in March.

The Japanese carrier based pursuit plane, which has recently appeared in China, according to our information has a speed of 322 miles an hour, a very rapid ability to climb and mounts two 20mm and two .30 cal. guns.[5] It has leak-proof tanks and armor. Our P40-B will have a speed of 360 miles an hour with two .50 cal. machine guns and four of .30 caliber. It will lack the rapidity to climb of the Japanese plane. It will have leak-proof tanks and armor.

We have an earlier model of this plane, the P40, delivered between August and October, but the Chief of the Air Corps opposes sending it to Hawaii because of some engine defect which makes it unsafe for training flights over water. Up to the present time we have not had available a modern medium bomber or a light bomb[er]. This month the medium bomber will go into production, if not quantity production. This plane has a range without bombs of 3,000 miles, carries 2,000 pounds and has a speed of 320 miles an hour—a tremendous improvement on the old B18 which you now have.[6] It can operate with bombs 640 miles to sea, with a safe reserve against the return trip. We plan to give you first priority on these planes. I am looking into the question of providing at least a squadron of Flying Fortress planes for Hawaii.

I am seeing what can be done to augment the .50 caliber machine gun set-up, but I have no hopes for the next few months. The Navy approached us regarding barrage balloons. We have three now under test, and 80 in process of manufacture, and 3,000 to be procured if the President will release our estimates. However, this provides nothing against the next few months. I am looking into the question of possibly obtaining some from England, but they are asking us and not giving us these days. The first test of the first forty deliveries in June will probably be made in Hawaii.

You, of course, understand the pressures on the Department for the limited materiel we have, for Alaska, for Panama, and, *most confidentially*, for the possible occupation of the Azores, not to mention the new leased bases. However, as I have already said, we are keeping clearly in mind that our first concern is to protect the Fleet.

My impression of the Hawaiian problem has been that if no serious harm is done us during the first six hours of known hostilities, thereafter the existing defenses would discourage an enemy against the hazard of an attack. The risk of sabotage and the risk involved in a surprise raid by Air and by submarine, constitute the real perils of the situation. Frankly, I do not see any landing threat in the Hawaiian Islands so long as we have air superiority.

Please keep clearly in mind in all of your negotiations that our mission is to protect the base and the Naval concentration, and that purpose should be made clearly apparent to Admiral Kimmel. I accentuate this because I found yesterday, for example, in a matter of tremendous importance, that old Army and Navy feuds, engendered from fights over appropriations, with the usual fallacious arguments on both sides, still persist in confusing issues of national defense. We must be completely impersonal in these matters, at least so far as our own nerves and irritations are concerned.[7] Fortunately, and happily I might say, Stark and I are on the most intimate personal basis, and that relationship has enabled us to avoid many serious difficulties.   Faithfully yours,

NA/RG 165 (WPD, 4449-1)

1. Short was promoted to lieutenant general and made commanding general of the Hawaiian Department on February 7, 1941.

2. Admiral Husband E. Kimmel (U.S.N.A., 1904) had been commander in chief of the United States Fleet since February 1, 1941.

3. Cavite Naval Base was located on the headland of Sangley Point in Manila Bay.

4. On August 4, 1939, the president told the War Department that Marine Corps troops were to be removed from Hawaii, Panama, and "all like places—the Army to take them over." The marines were henceforth to be used only as emergency occupation forces in places such as Bermuda, Trinidad, and Wake Island. Since they were to be the initial expeditionary force, the army was required to give them top priority in heavy artillery and certain other types of materiel. (Marshall to Strong, August 5, 1939, NA/RG 165 [OCS, 21081 (filed before 15758-42)].)

5. Marshall was probably referring to the Mitsubishi Naval Type 0, a single-seat fighter monoplane.

6. This medium bomber was probably the North American B-25 "Mitchell."

7. Short replied that he had met with both Admiral Kimmel and Rear Admiral Claude C. Bloch, commandant of the Fourteenth Naval District, Pearl Harbor. They were cooperating with Short completely in the determination of defense measures for Hawaii. Next to army-navy cooperation, Short ranked dispersion and protection of aircraft, improvement of antiaircraft defense, improvement of harbor defense artillery, and the addition of searchlights as his top priorities.

Kimmel and Short established a series of army-navy joint committees to study Hawaiian defense, especially the employment of air power. No provisions had been made for the dispersion of aircraft on existing fields, Short noted. Emergency fields on islands other than

Oahu had been designated; however, Short argued, for pursuit aircraft this was useless since Oahu would then be outside their operating radius. Bombers could use the other islands as bases, but they had to be dispersed as well. (Short to Marshall, February 19, 1941, CGMRL/ G. C. Marshall Papers [Pentagon Office, Selected (Hawaii, Navy Court, Tab 8)].)

To Major General George Grunert   February 8, 1941
Secret   Washington, D.C.

Dear Grunert: I have been working on your various recommendations and what might be done to help out despite our great deficiencies in materiel at the present time. I want you to understand that I am keenly aware of your situation and that it is purely a question of our twisting and turning to do as much of the right thing as we can at the right place.[1]

AIR — While the number of your pursuit squadrons has been increased from one to three and new planes have been made available, we realize that these are not at all up to the standard of performance that you should have though there has been a decided improvement in numbers and in quality. When compared to the performance of the present carrier based Japanese plane, the deficiencies are only too evident. Incidentally, the new Japanese plane is rated at 322 miles an hour, with a very rapid climb, with leak-proof tanks and armor, and with two 20mm machine guns and two .30 caliber guns.

Our present pursuit plane, the P40, while it has a speed of 360 miles an hour, has only four guns. All told we have received 200 of these up to the middle of October, which completed the delivery. I had under consideration equipping the Hawaiian pursuit group with these planes, but some undetermined engine uncertainty has made it inadvisable—at least in time of peace—to fly these planes in training over water. Commencing this month, we receive the improved model of this plane which will have the same speed, leak-proof tanks, armor, two .50 and four .30 machine guns. Quantity deliveries will be under way about the first week in March and the first lot of 50 will be shipped to Hawaii. I am hoping we can arrange to equip at least one squadron of yours with these planes, immediately following the shipment to Hawaii. However, I am going to leave the decision in this matter to Admiral Stark to determine which of two places he wishes, from the viewpoint of Naval defense, to be attended to first, the Philippines or the Panama Canal—I imagine it will be the Philippines.

This month production commences on a medium bomber of 3,000 miles extreme range, without bombs. It has a speed of 320 miles an hour, and carries 2,000 pounds of bombs. Quantity production should be under way by the middle of March. In all probability, the first allotment of these will go to Hawaii, and I then hope to send a few to the Philippines so that you will have one efficient bomber that can safely operate 650 miles off-shore.

The light bomber, of which we have none, should get under way in deliveries in March or April.

GUNS — We had unobtrusively withdrawn from units now in the field in strenuous training, eighteen 3-inch antiaircraft guns for shipment to you in order to provide at least some Army air defense for the Fleet anchored in Manila Bay. However, just as we were about to go through with the shipment to San Francisco, the Navy called on us for sixteen of these guns to equip special Marine battalions which are being sent to occupy islands in the Pacific, including Wake and Midway. This left us with only two guns and we have now added two more. These four will be sent to you at once, and as quickly as more can be made available, they will be sent. You will, of course, understand the difficulties of taking materiel away from units that are actually in training, with an unrestricted press watching everything we do, and a legislative battle in Congress that has reached a peak of intensity.

As to the lighter caliber antiaircraft guns, only a few of the 37mm have been delivered, but what is more important, we have not the ammunition for these guns except on a test basis. Of the caliber .50 machine guns, we must first fill out the defenses of Pearl Harbor, where there is a considerable shortage of this materiel. And naturally the anchorage of the main Fleet is our most vital consideration.

In all matters of materiel, we are in a dilemma of meeting the terrific pressure from Great Britain on the one hand—and a justified pressure, and the demands for the training of 1,400,000 men. Our numbers have increased from about 600,000 on the first of January to about 750,000 today, with the prospect of over 900,000 by the end of the month. You will see what a demand this creates, even for minimum training requirements, and yet we must have these men in shape as quickly as possible. As production gets well under way during the next three or four months, it should not be so difficult, despite all the demands, to withdraw small amounts to help you out in your situation. A very little of really modern materiel will, of course, mean a great deal to you.

PERSONNEL — I directed that you be sent more officers, and I believe 75 were to sail in January and February. I thought that this would give you some reserve of officer material. Since then I secured the President's approval to double your Philippine Scouts.[2] Just what this will require in the way of additional officers I do not know, but I suppose we are hearing from you on this subject. The construction money represents embarrassing difficulties to us though we are going over it for you, because the greatly increased costs over the original estimates have aroused Congress, and an item like yours for these Scouts merely adds fuel to the flame.

I have been setting forth the situation very frankly that you may understand the conditions here, and also that you may feel that we are doing everything we possibly can under the circumstances to assist you.

Certain portions of this letter I think had better be considered for your eye alone, but I leave this to your discretion and judgment. Faithfully yours,

GCMRL/G. C. Marshall Papers (Pentagon Office, Selected)

1. Major General George Grunert had been commanding general of the Philippine Department since May 1940. Since July he had written numerous letters requesting the reinforcement of the Philippines. (See Marshall to Grunert, September 20, 1940, pp. 314–15.) On November 2, 1940, he advised the chief of staff that the Regular Filipino Army was understrength, ill-equipped, and untrained for large-scale mobile warfare. Grunert needed five hundred United States officers for the immediate mobilization and training of Philippine units. The General Staff initially opposed Grunert's requests because of strategic and physical difficulties: the War Plans Division feared a Japanese preemptive strike and the two-ocean war that would ensue; G-1 and G-3 argued that five hundred officers could not be sent to the Philippines. By December 26, however, Marshall reversed his position. While strategic plans did not include a major commitment to defend the Philippines in the event of war, the army began a gradual reinforcement of that department as a deterrent to Japanese expansion. (Watson, *Chief of Staff,* pp. 417–24.)

2. See Memorandum, February 12, 1941, pp. 418–20.

MEMORANDUM FOR GENERAL GEROW   February 10, 1941
Secret   Washington, D.C.

Subject: Conference with the President.

This morning at eleven the Secretaries of State, War and Navy, and Admiral Stark and myself spent one and a half hours with the President. The meeting was devoted to the outcome of a conversation between the President and Lord Halifax.[1] The latter had expressed the view of the British Government that the Japanese and Germans would act offensively and simultaneously, and possibly in the very near future. Lord Halifax was hopeful that we could do something to deter Japan. The President stated that he told Lord Halifax that we had practically exhausted the "gesture" method, that we had ordered Americans out of Japan and China, we had sent the Fleet on a secret mission, and that we could not see our way clear to reinforce our Navy in the Far East. Lord Halifax was hopeful that something might be done to cause the Japanese to delay.

The President then offered this proposal, that at his meeting in about three days with the new Japanese Ambassador, the President and the Secretary of State would draw rather long faces on the situation and endeavor to give the Japanese Ambassador the impression that we were very serious in this matter of Japan's further movement toward Malaysia.[2] The President thought if this visit was preceded and followed by a series of moves on our part, the result might be deterrent of Japanese action. He suggested the following:

First, a second direction from the State Department for Americans to leave Japan and China.

Second, the long faces to be drawn by the President and Mr. Hull in receiving Nomura.

Third, two light and two heavy cruisers, six long-legged destroyers, and an airplane carrier to be dispatched on an announced "training cruise" south from Hawaii to Canton, thence via the Fiji Islands to the southern tip of Mindanao, and thence to Manila, and then to rejoin the Fleet in Hawaii.

Fourth, that we open conversations diplomatically with Japan regarding their occupation of the Spratley Islands, literally simply reefs half way between the Philippines and the Camarines, on the basis that these really pertain to the Philippines. This for the purpose of showing them our intention to safe-guard our commercial communications in between that region and Singapore.

Mr. Hull did not think any attention would be paid to the first proposal. Later on Mr. Knox suggested that the Army might make a more positive motion by following the Naval decision to move the women and children out of the Philippines. Knox favored the attitude to be followed in meeting Nomura, and eventually favored the training cruise because he had previously advocated some such move. He did not discuss the Spratley Islands.

Mr. Knox concurred with the President, except that he thought it dangerous to send an airplane carrier through the Mandate Islands, which Admiral Stark suggested as a possible route. In this connection Stark reminded us that a mistake had been made long ago in asking the Japanese if they objected to a cruise through the Mandate Islands, which we have a legal right to do, and they had so objected.

The Secretary of War did not express himself on the cruise or on the question of a second notice to Americans in Japan and China. He thought that we might gain by taking a diplomatic position immediately through Nomura as to our interests commercially that would be involved in Japanese control of Malaysia. The fact of the Dollar boats moving several times a month through this region was mentioned, etc.[3]

The meeting was suddenly broken up by the messenger's announcing new callers, and I was only able to state that we had already been considering the question of holding officers in the Philippines whose terms would expire and moving their families to the States; that we might have General Grunert become fairly active in expediting the recruiting of the additional Philippine Scouts; that we might give some publicity to the reinforcement of the Hawaiian garrison by the planes we were sending out next week and on March 15th.[4]

G. C. Marshall

NA/RG 165 (WPD, 4175-18)

1. Viscount Halifax (Edward F. L. Wood), former British secretary of state for foreign affairs, had been named ambassador to the United States on December 23, 1940. He had arrived in Washington on January 24, 1941.

2. President Roosevelt and Secretary of State Hull received Ambassador Kichisaburo Nomura on February 14, 1941.

3. The Dollar Steamship Line, which had been established in 1888 by Captain Robert Dollar to operate on Pacific Ocean routes, had been taken over by the Maritime Commission in 1938 and some of its ships operated under the name American President Lines.

4. Gerow doubted that the proposed measures would "accomplish any worthwhile result." He suggested that the president advise Ambassador Nomura of the United States's intention to help Britain defeat Germany "by all means short of war" and emphasize to the envoy "that we would view with concern any effort on the part of Japan to nullify those measures. This would be a veiled threat but it might have a useful result." In conjunction with this meeting, Gerow suggested a press release which emphasized the United States's reinforcement of the Philippines, noting increased strength in that department's ground forces, aircraft, antiaircraft, and artillery units. The assistant chief of staff wrote to Marshall that the release of this information "may worry the Japanese a bit. At least it can do no harm." (Gerow Memorandum for the Chief of Staff, February 11, 1941, NA/RG 165 [WPD, 4175-18].)

MEMORANDUM[1]   February 12, 1941
Confidential   [Washington, D.C.]

Communications with General Grunert, Commanding Philippine Department, in connection with the President's desires regarding the Japanese situation:

A radio was sent yesterday morning direct to General Grunert to give indications immediately of genuine activity in pressing for a doubling of strength of his Scout forces—from 6,000 to 12,000, and notifying him that further communication would probably follow regarding the retention of officers in the islands and the return of women and children to the United States.

Yesterday afternoon he was directed to delay the return—that is, extend the tours, of 60 of the 100 officers due to sail for home during the next two weeks. Also he was directed to return to the United States women and children, so far as accommodations would permit, of the families of officers who would normally return during the next six months. He was instructed to make no press release, but when these instructions leaked out, as they are bound to do immediately, and the press questioned him, to merely admit the facts.[2]

Shipment of munitions to England –

A report was laid on your desk yesterday to the effect that the 50,000,000 rounds of ammunition and the 250,000 rifles had all been shipped, with Halifax as their destination.[3]

Caribbean Area –

General Van Voorhis is on a tour of inspection by air, accompanied by General Andrews. He was in Puerto Rico yesterday and is in Jamaica today, and returns to Puerto Rico tomorrow. He stopped in Venezuela. The complete details to govern the administration of his increased command have not yet been determined, but he has actually been placed in command.

Most confidentially, I am considering the replacement of General Daley in command in Puerto Rico by General Collins, now in command of the Second Division at San Antonio, Texas.[4]

General Hodges, in command of the Fifth Corps at Alexandria, La. will be retired as result of his recent physical examination.[5] General Brees, the Army Commander has assumed temporary command of the Corps. I am looking over the field to locate a suitable successor to General Hodges. This is complicated by reason of the fact that the President seems determined upon the relief of General Miles—at least I was so advised last night by General Watson. He previously had intimated to me indirectly that he would be willing to promote Miles to a Major Generalcy. The problem of finding a suitable place for him is involved in the reassortment of commanders.

General Lee, now here from London, will probably be the most suitable successor to General Miles, if the latter is relieved. General Scanlon, now in London, should be returned at least for a rest, if not for completion of tour. In the interim General Malony, now in London negotiating with regard to the leases for bases on British islands, would be very suitable in the role of Attaché. All this, of course, depends on whether or not General Miles is relieved, though I think Scanlon should be brought home immediately.[6]

GCMRL/G. C. Marshall Papers (Pentagon Office, Selected)

1. This memorandum was apparently prepared for Secretary of War Stimson.
2. Marshall declared that "the recent action was taken as one of a number of means to impress Japan with the fact that we mean business—in order to discourage them against moving into Malaysia. It is also taken for the purpose of bucking up Army morale in the Philippines." The chief of staff informed G-1 that he opposed any more families of officers sailing to the Philippines. (Marshall Memorandum for the Assistant Chief of Staff, G-1, February 13, 1941, NA/RG 165 [OCS, 15036-9].)

3. On the problem concerning this materiel, see the Conference Notes, August 20, 1940, p. 292.

4. See Marshall to Daley, January 30, 1941, pp. 401–2. Major General James L. Collins, Sr., became commanding general of the Puerto Rican Department in April 1941.

5. Major General Campbell B. Hodges, who had commanded the Fifth Corps Area since June 1, 1940, retired effective June 30, 1941.

6. Brigadier General Raymond E. Lee replaced Miles as the assistant chief of staff, G-2, on February 1, 1942. Later in 1941, Brigadier General Martin F. Scanlon returned to Washington, D.C., to serve in the headquarters of the Army Air Forces. Brigadier General Harry F. Malony (U.S.M.A., 1912) was a member, from January 3 to April 7, 1941, of the President's Base Lease Commission to negotiate the acquisition of the Atlantic Ocean bases. Marshall had instructed Malony to "look into the British method of handling field forces, and Air arm in conjunction with the part played by the War Office." The chief of staff wanted to know the British methods of coordinating production, especially aircraft, and the relationship between British general headquarters, the Air Coastal Command, the navy command, and army commanders in the field. Malony also received instructions to clear up the tax issue presented by British colonies which prevented the quick and inexpensive garrisoning of those insular bases. (Malony notes on a conversation with the Chief of Staff, January 15, 1941, NA/RG 165 [OCS, Chief of Staff Conferences File].)

T HE convening of the new Seventy-seventh Congress opened another season of budgetary conferences and hearings for the chief of staff. But before the 1942 budget could be considered, Marshall had to appear before the House Appropriations Committee's Deficiency Subcommittee on February 12 to defend the War Department's request for a supplement of $680,118,000 to the fiscal year 1941 budget, which was "necessary to complete the housing and shelter of our greatly increased Army." The bulk of the appropriation covered construction projects, the expansion of the Air Corps, the Panama augmentation program of 1940, the acquisition of land for training sites, and the completion of projects authorized in fiscal 1941 but not yet completely funded. (House Appropriations Committee, *Fourth Supplemental National Defense Appropriation Bill for 1941, Hearings* [Washington: GPO, 1941], p. 3.)

"Frankly," Marshall told the committee, "we had not anticipated that the American people would ever be sufficiently aroused to authorize in time of peace such a tremendous program for the national defense, nor had we anticipated the complete collapse of the French Government in early June, along with the deadly hazard to the British of a transfer of French naval power to Germany and Italy. Furthermore, it was necessary for us to study the campaigns, the occurrences in France and Belgium, in order to benefit to the full by the lessons indicated. The last required several months to assemble the facts from our attachés and from other sources. We took every means possible to find out what had occurred and get to the heart of the matter. This brought about decisions in late summer and early fall for modifications of organizations, for different allotments of weapons, and so forth. Practically each of these decisions in some way affected requirements of a cantonment built for the purpose not only of sheltering troops but to facilitate their instruction." (Ibid., p. 12.)

As most committee members were familiar with certain aspects of the 1917 mobilization, Marshall sought to explain why the previous solutions were inadequate for the current situation. "Our purpose and problems defined by the Congress in September of 1940 are essentially different from those of 1917, and in this difference lay most of the deficiencies in the planning and estimates for troop concentrations. . . . The troops of 1917 were quartered in cantonment areas for only brief periods of training while awaiting transportation overseas. Our present Army is being quartered in its areas, we hope, for the entire period of service of most of its members. Not only that, but the recent law on the subject extends our training plan over a period of 5 years. For such a program the World War cantonment and the ideas behind its construction were not a suitable basis for estimates. What we require and what we are building is a type of cantonment adequate for the shelter, sanitation, health, and morale of the soldier." Thorough training in the United States for modern mobile warfare necessitated greater dispersal of buildings, wider roads, and improved supply and administrative organizations to use such facilities. (Ibid., p. 4.)

Assessing the War Department's lack of preparation for the mobilization, Marshall observed: "In our usual search for economy the original estimates were made dangerously low. They were a lump-sum estimate based on the cost of certain smaller camp units let to competitive bidding during 1939 and early 1940. From these cost estimates a cost-per-man factor was evolved and applied against the total number of men to be housed. The costs mentioned resulted from construction undertaken under conditions of more deliberate procedure during favorable building weather." (Ibid., pp. 4–5.)

The chief of staff noted that this budget was for an army of 1,400,000 men, a size that would be attained in June. Rejecting the notion that the War Department "let things go absolutely wild on cost," Marshall claimed that the Inspector General's Department maintained a continuous inspection of on-going army projects. Representative Clifton A. Woodrum, Democrat from Virginia, asked concerning the appropriation bill, "Is this going to do the job?" Marshall replied, "So far as we can tell at the moment, but I will not say it will do it entirely." (Ibid., pp. 4–5, 11. For a comprehensive statement on the army's construction problems, see Memorandum for the Secretary of War, March 29, 1941, pp. 459–61.) ★

MEMORANDUM FOR GENERAL ARNOLD February 12, 1941
[Washington, D.C.]

Subject: Request of Navy for loan of flying instructors.

The question has been brought up by Admiral Stark as to the possibility of our loaning them some flying instructors for a period of a few months. He had understood that we had more pilots than planes and they were in need of instructors. I do not know whether he is referring to primary instructors or basic, but if we have any men that might be spared for this purpose for two or three months, it might be a fine gesture from you to the Navy and for the War and Navy Departments in meeting certain criticisms of Congress.

GCMRL/G. C. Marshall Papers (Pentagon Office, Selected)

MEMORANDUM FOR GENERAL ARNOLD February 14, 1941
Secret [Washington, D.C.]

There was taken up with an American observer of importance in London, by the British authorities, their desire to see if they could not find several accommodations in the United States:

First: They would like to locate from 100 to 150 trained pilots, presumably Reserve Officers, who could ferry planes to England from Canada, and then do ferrying work in England from factory to fields, no combat. This would release just that many British experienced pilots and also would give some of our people a closer-up experience than we are now getting. I assume that if such an arrangement were made, it would have to be on the basis of a Reserve officer not on active duty, or that the Reserve officer would have to resign his commission, we undertaking the promise of re-commissioning him at the end of the work. The British would pay, I believe, about $150 a week.

Second: They are very anxious to know if we might not be able to drum up some experienced men to contribute to the operation of our type of 4-engined bombers. I believe this was on the basis of actual combat operations. If we found some volunteers from the Reserve Corps who would like to try this, might we not relieve them from active duty and allow them to make their own arrangements with the British. The understanding here would be, I assume, that they could expect these men would receive favorable treatment by us on being re-commissioned.

Third: They brought up again the question of the training of their pilots in this country, under the more favorable climatic conditions of the South. I think you had this up with them before, but now the matter is reaching such a state I think we ought to entertain the proposition very seriously. I assume it would have to be done by the expansion of the several schools and we would confine it, at first at least, to the preliminary flying. Then they might pass into Canada for their basic training, or it may be that a portion of the basic training might be managed in this country.

Look into all this and see what might be done, and talk with me personally before you commit yourself to a formal report.[1]

GCMRL/G. C. Marshall Papers (Pentagon Office, Selected)

1. The American observer was presidential representative Harry L. Hopkins. The British had long sought such assistance. On September 24, 1940, Arthur B. Purvis, director of the British Purchasing Commission in the United States, outlined a plan to Secretary of the Treasury Morgenthau for the training of four thousand British or Canadian pilots a year. Flight training, except for combat subjects, would be done at civilian schools. Britain had to pay the capital costs, training pay, and provide training equipment. (H. Duncan Hall, *North American Supply*, a volume in the *History of the Second World War* [London: HMSO and Longmans, Green, and Co., 1955], p. 194; on Hopkins's recommendations, see Memorandum for General Arnold, February 27, 1941, pp. 433.)

To Fred A. Holtz

February 14, 1941
[Washington, D.C.]

My dear Mr. Holtz: I have just read your letter of February 11th, requesting an interview with me, or with someone proposed by me in connection with the re-instrumentation of Army bands.[1] I will be glad to designate an officer with whom you might talk, but I do not think anything of a helpful nature would be accomplished at this particular time.

There has been a great deal of publicity regarding Mr. Stokowski's offer to help us in the present expansion of the Army, much of which is misleading. He is working on the development of two band groups for two replacement (training) centers in California. There are to be 22 of these replacement centers, and each will have a training band. Mr. Stokowski offered to undertake the training of the nucleus for these two bands, and along with it he wishes to make some experiments of ideas he has on the subject. This has led to many statements in the press of one kind or another. I am giving you the facts.[2]

Therefore I do not think there is any necessity for your discussing this particular question at this time. When definite representations are made and the matter of re-instrumentation is actually being considered, I will be very glad to have you give your views to those concerned with the decision in the matter. At the present time matters of such paramount importance are pressing us all to an extent that makes it inadvisable to anticipate discussions before the issue has actually been raised. Faithfully yours,

GCMRL/G. C. Marshall Papers (Pentagon Office, General)

1. Holtz was president of the National Association of Band Instrument Manufacturers. His letter to Marshall is not in the Marshall papers.

2. Leopold Stokowski wanted to create more "typically American music" for the bands. A nucleus of forty Regular Army bandsmen from Coast Artillery and other units in California would train fifty new musicians at replacement centers. Reinstrumentation and rescoring of music would make the bands more suited to open-air playing in a modern army. Certain woodwind and brass instruments such as the clarinet and French horn took too long for a one-year recruit to learn, were too difficult to play on the march, and could not be heard over the noise of mechanized vehicles. Stokowski wanted to replace these instruments with saxophones and the newer American-made fluegelhorns and melophones. He also proposed that popular dance music, folk music—including Negro spirituals and the works of Stephen Foster—supplement traditional march music. With the aid of the motion picture industry, Stokowski hoped to produce training films to instruct new bandsmen. (*New York Times,* January 25, p. 10, and April 6, 1941, sec. 9, p. 7.)

To R. B. Lawrence[1]   February 17, 1941
                                                    [Washington, D.C.]

My dear Mr. Lawrence: Apropos our conversation yesterday morning in the Fort Myer Riding Hall, the soldiers' group to which I had reference is called the Soldiers, Sailors and Marines Club.* The Club undertakes to provide a wholesome place in Washington for men coming into the District from the surrounding camps, where they can get a meal, bring their girl friends to a respectable spot, and to a limited extent where they can find a bed for the night on an economical basis.

The Club is now in process of enlargement to meet the new demands. It is of great importance to the morale of enlisted men, and the ladies who manage it have a hard time raising the necessary funds, which they do largely through a rummage sale which involves a tremendous effort for a limited result.

You spoke of the possibility of some sort of horse show at Myer being used to help out. I don't know about that, but I do know that the Club needs the help that publicity will give it.

Mrs. Julian Schley, the wife of the Chief of Engineers of the Army is the President of the Women's Committee that handles it and Mrs. Marshall is Vice President and I am sure these ladies would be very much interested in having you look over the Club, and know something of how much good it does. I am taking the liberty of giving them your name and address in hopes they may be able to interest you.[2] Faithfully yours,

* 1015 L St., N.W.

GCMRL/G. C. Marshall Papers (Pentagon Office, General)
1. "Larry" Lawrence was the reporter covering horses and horse shows for the Washington *Evening Star.*
2. Having visited the service club with Mrs. Schley soon after Marshall's letter, Lawrence wrote to the chief of staff that he thought he could interest his newspaper's publishers in sponsoring a horse show. (Lawrence to Marshall, February 24, 1941, GCMRL/G. C. Marshall Papers [Pentagon Office, General].)

To GENERAL JOHN J. PERSHING

February 17, 1941
Washington, D.C.

Dear General: Someone just handed me the attached clipping from a local paper regarding Eli Pershing. Recalling my questioning you about this man because of his continued pressure on me, and your replies and what you thought of him, I am sending you the clipping.[1]

I have not yet been able to have an appointment with Bishop Freeman, but I will do so as soon as practicable.[2] The last week has been a little worse than any of the preceding, and I am now starting on a series of hearings on the Hill. I was before the Foreign Relations Committee not long ago and Thursday before the Deficiency Appropriation Committee on the $700,-000,000 bill. I will be before the Senate Committee Wednesday, I think, for general questions on any subject, and I suppose most of it will relate to the Lease-loan bill. The latter part of the week I will be before the House Appropriations Committee on the big Appropriation bill. Then over to the Senate for the corresponding hearings.

We have had quite a time getting the organization going to correlate the various welfare activities in the communities adjacent to camps. This has been greatly complicated by pushes and pulls from within here in Washington, with a variety of purposes.[3]

I sometimes think that the ordinary job of Chief of Staff, even in these days, I could handle on a two-hour a day basis, but it is these other matters that are very time-consuming and exceedingly trying. If my sense of humor survives, I am all right.

I hope you are enjoying pleasant weather and are feeling better. Katherine is down with a bad case of 'flu; it started in her throat, then went to her ears, then her teeth, then the sinus and then the top of her head. It can go no higher. Affectionately,

G. C. Marshall

LC/J. J. Pershing Papers (General Correspondence)
1. Eli Pershing was a distant relative of the general's and a captain in the Signal Corps Reserve.
2. Pershing had telegraphed the chief of staff that James E. Freeman, Protestant Episcopal bishop of Washington, D.C., was "very anxious for service in some capacity. Preferably

similar to that during the World War when he was given a roving commission by Secretary [of War Newton D.] Baker to visit all commands throughout the country as a sort of co-ordinator of religious work." (Pershing to Marshall, Telegram, February 5, 1941, GCMRL/G. C. Marshall Papers [Pentagon Office, Selected].) Colonel William R. Arnold, chief of Chaplains, wanted all religious activity coordinated by corps area, army corps, and army chaplains. He thought, however, that Freeman could be used in community–army post relations. (William R. Arnold Memorandum for the Chief of Staff, February 10, 1941, GCMRL/G. C. Marshall Papers [Pentagon Office, Selected]; see Marshall to Pershing, March 10, 1941, pp. 440–41.)

3. On the difficulties of army post relations with nearby communities and of organizing facilities for soldiers, see Marshall to Stimson, February 6, 1941, NA/RG 107 (SW Safe, Welfare and Recreational–Joint Army and Navy); and Henry L. Stimson and McGeorge Bundy, *On Active Service in Peace and War* (New York: Harper and Brothers, 1947), pp. 379–80.

To James W. Wadsworth   February 21, 1941
                                        [Washington, D.C.]

Dear Senator:[1]   I have just this moment read your note of February 19th together with the copy of your letter to the "New Republic" of the same date. I have never heard of your losing your temper but if this is an indication of the result, I can only hope that you are prepared to lose it quite frequently in the coming months, to the support of the Army.[2]

Really I am very grateful to you for your vigorous resentment of this particular derogatory reference to me and my kind.

As I have often told you, and written too through the years, I hold a great admiration for your genuine patriotism and great wisdom in matters of national defense. Recently I have had added reasons for even stronger feelings on the subject due not only to your two splendid statements on the floor of the House, but more particularly to the sound advice you have given me in the present crisis.

With my thanks and warmest regards,   Faithfully yours,

GCMRL/G. C. Marshall Papers (Pentagon Office, Selected)

1. Congressman Wadsworth had formerly been a United States Senator from New York.

2. "I confess I have lost my temper," Wadsworth wrote, over a comment in "the radical minded" journal. The article, lamenting the lag in United States industrial mobilization, stated that the delays were due, in part, to the War Department's reactionary outlook, particularly blaming former Secretary Woodring and Assistant Secretary Johnson, "both of whom failed in any way to awaken sleeping and decadent army officers, whose social activities and personal well-being conditioned their entire outlook." ("We Have Repeated Britain's Mistakes," *New Republic* 104 [February 17, 1941]: 230.) This last phrase, Wadsworth told Marshall, "was more than I can stand." He wrote to the editor that the last three chiefs of staff and their staffs had "long since recognized the fact that the United States Army was not keeping pace with modern developments," but until 1939 their recommendations for increased appropriations for modernization had been rejected by the Roosevelt administration. "To call these officers decadent is atrocious, and to say that their social activities and personal well-being condition

their entire outlook is at once silly and false. No intelligent person knowing these men and knowing the facts would indulge in such a slander." (Wadsworth to the Editor, *The New Republic,* enclosed in Wadsworth to Marshall, February 19, 1941, GCMRL/G. C. Marshall Papers [Pentagon Office, Selected]. The letter and the editors' response are in *New Republic* 104[March 10, 1941]: 342–43.)

MEMORANDUM FOR GENERAL ARNOLD   February 21, 1941
Confidential   [Washington, D.C.]

Confirming my hasty conversation with you yesterday, please get underway the following, for my preliminary consideration Saturday or Monday.

Revise priority policy for distribution of planes: In view of the fact that the security of the Fleet must now be given first priority consideration in allocation of planes to units, a new breakdown or plan should be prepared as the basis of an early discussion, possibly Monday or Tuesday, by you, Emmons,[1] Brett, Gerow, and myself. I intended to give the Navy the opportunity to indicate their desires in this matter to the extent of stating where first shipments should go—Hawaii, Panama, Puerto Rico, Philippine Islands. We will probably have to get their views on the basis of partial deliveries, that is maybe single squadrons until more ships are available. We will have to consider Emmons' necessities from the view point of permitting pilots training and familiarity with new types.

Supervision of supply of materiel: What I intended to indicate to you, hastily, yesterday was that we should immediately get out a radio of instruction to air depots and to Emmons, to the general effect that, in the matter of the supply of materiel to the active units of the Air Corps, there will be a constant check by all parties concerned, forward and back, to see that the units actually have in their possession all the materiel that they need, that is available in the depot. For example, officials of a depot should visit the units which they supply to ascertain if those units have in their actual possession the equipment required. If there is a lack, and the equipment is available in the depot there should be immediate adjustment by telephone or telegraph to be confirmed later by formal requisition. And commanders of Groups, Wings, or Districts, or their staff officers should familiarize themselves with what is available at the depots and see to it that the necessary demands or requisitions are made on the depots and early deliveries secured. A sharp line of responsibility must not be drawn in this matter. While the depots are controlled by the Chief of Air Corps, and the fighting unit with their supply services are controlled by the commander of the GHQ

Air Force, the agents of both must cross the line in a cooperative effort to get prompt results as well as to develop a more harmonious relationship. No organizational set-up can succeed without the determined efforts of the principal officials concerned to develop that degree of mutual understanding and cooperation that is essential to efficiency.

The foregoing is merely a rough idea in the matter, but the point is, I find exactly the same situation here that has existed in ordinary supply between Ordnance and Quartermaster Depots, the Corps Areas, the local supply office and the troops. For example, I learned yesterday of a dearth of signal equipment in the hands of the troop of the 44th Division at Camp Dix at a time when the supply had actually been available at Camp Dix in the hands of the local Signal Officer. Instead of his checking the units to see that they had what they needed, he waited for them to come to him with requisitions. On the other side of the fence, instead of the Commanders communicating with the Signal Officer to find out where the equipment could be obtained, there was a failure on their part to display energetic leadership in the matter. I found the same thing regarding part of the engineer equipment for 155 regiments, with an unnecessary delay of several months; I found the same situation with regard to clothing, mess kits, and similar items; and you and I found a little of the same thing with regard to aluminum.

GCMRL/G. C. Marshall Papers (Pentagon Office, Selected)

1. Delos C. Emmons had commanded the General Headquarters Air Force since March 1, 1939; he had been a lieutenant general since October 25, 1940.

To Miss Prudence Penny[1]   February 24, 1941
                                                         [Washington, D.C.]

Dear Miss Penny: I have your letter of February 20th with the clipping from the EXAMINER relative to your visit to March Field.

I read your suggestions and I must agree with you that women have a touch in cooking that is seldom realized by men, particularly by Army cooks. One of our great difficulties at the present time is to see that the excellent food purchased by the Government is given fair treatment in its preparation for the table. This is always a difficult problem with a newly created army in this country where cooking is not the fine art that it is in France, for example. However, with the schools for bakers and cooks, through the valuable assistance we are getting from young men trained in cooking in the CCC, and through very rigorous inspections of the progress that is being made, I think the matter can be handled in a satisfactory fashion. I appreciated your comments and am much interested in your suggestions.   Faithfully yours,

GCMRL/G. C. Marshall Papers (Pentagon Office, General)

1. "Miss Prudence Penny," home economics editor of the *Los Angeles Examiner,* toured the Air Corps kitchens at March Field and found "good eating." In her column she advised parents of soldiers to "stop worrying" about their sons' diets. To Marshall she wrote: "You face somewhat the same problem we as Home Economists do when trying to teach the new bride, namely, untrained cooks—and we manage to surmount this difficulty. It occurred to me that the Army could do the same." She then outlined a three-part instructional plan using proven recipes and "a crew of trained women" with a mobile kitchen. (Penny to Marshall, February 20, 1941, GCMRL/G. C. Marshall Papers [Pentagon Office, General].)

TO WALTER WANGER

February 24, 1941
[Washington, D.C.]

Dear Mr. Wanger: As a result of our recent discussion regarding the expanding army motion picture activities, together with the possibility of coordinating War Department requirements with the industry through Mr. Mellett of the White House, I have caused an examination to be made of this whole subject.

I think that the enclosed copy of a letter to Mr. Mellett will give you a concise picture of how we are working with the motion picture industry, regarding which I was not fully informed at the time of our interview. In view of the present relationships, it is my opinion that we should continue to work through the Motion Picture Committee for National Defense.[1]

I am having your suggestion concerning the stimulation of newsreel publicity which will carry the activities of the soldiers back to their home communities, considered by that committee, and I count on your support in case we run into any difficulty in the matter.

Relative to your comments as to the quality of our recruiting trailer movies, they were produced as a matter of expediency to meet a particular situation at a minimum cost. In order to improve the quality of future releases, greater use will be made of the services of the committee in the production of subsequent trailers.

With regard to your suggestion that Mr. Zanuck make a trip to a number of our camps to look over our motion picture involvements, General Mauborgne is now on his way west, and will see Mr. Zanuck.[2] Also I find that an extensive survey of this field was recently made, as a result of which, arrangements are being completed to send scenario writers to selected military activities in order that they may acquire first-hand knowledge of living and training environments. When these scenario people are located, a visit by Mr. Zanuck to look over their activities probably will be desirable.[3]

Thanking you again for your genuine interest and cordial offer of cooperation, I remain Faithfully yours,

GCMRL/G. C. Marshall Papers (Pentagon Office, General)

1. Wanger, president of the Academy of Motion Picture Arts and Sciences, had suggested that all War Department activities with the motion picture industry be coordinated by presidential assistant Lowell Mellett. A letter to Mellett, drafted by Lieutenant Colonel Frank H. Partridge of the G-1 division, outlined the existing War Department–industry relationship. The previous summer, the industry had organized the Motion Picture Committee Cooperating for National Defense, a civilian board which arranged the production of training films through the Research Council of the Academy of Motion Picture Arts and Sciences. "To further interlock the industry with the War Department," the army commissioned several movie executives to act as assistants in the Signal Corps. (Memorandum for General Shedd, January 31, 1941, pp. 402–3.) Beyond training films, the War Department hoped to arrange for newsreel coverage of the army through the same procedure. Marshall considered that this organization worked "smoothly and expeditiously;" he was loath to change it in midstream. (Marshall to Mellett, February 15, 1941, GCMRL/G. C. Marshall Papers [Pentagon Office, General].)

2. Major General Joseph O. Mauborgne was the chief signal officer of the United States Army.

3. For details on Darryl F. Zanuck's trip, see Terrett, *Signal Corps: The Emergency*, p. 228.

MEMORANDUM FOR GENERAL GEROW February 26, 1941
Secret Washington, D.C.

At 10:15 this morning the President held a meeting at which were present the Secretaries of State, War and Navy (Mr. Forrestal) Admiral Stark and myself.

The President reviewed the points covered in the previous meeting with relation to our attitude in the Far East. He referred to the various moves to be made in the game, first to the direction for the withdrawal of American citizens from China and Japan, and commented on the impression that had been made on the Japanese. He referred to the excellent results which had followed from the attitude he and Mr. Hull had taken in their meeting with Nomura. He then interpolated the comment that Mr. Churchill, I believe he said, had informed him that the tension in the Far East had been somewhat removed and there appeared to be no immediate prospect of Japanese overt action in Malaysia. Also that Mr. Churchill felt we should nevertheless continue, both Great Britain and the United States, in our pressures on the situation in the Far East in order to maintain the present Japanese attitude.[1]

At this point Mr. Hull discussed a possible lack of a clear understanding between what had occurred in conversations between the British Foreign Office and the Japanese. He felt it was essential that we learn from the British just what the present understanding of their relations with the Japanese Government were, in order that we avoid a confusion in planning.[2]

The President then re-opened the question of a "Training Cruise" by several cruisers, with some destroyers, by one of three routes to Davao in the southern Philippines. He discussed the relative advantages of the several routes, and mentioned with relation to the southernmost route the advantages of making a call at Port Darwin in northern Australia. Mr. Hull thought it might be inadvisable in [*to*] make such a call because it would be, in effect, a challenge to the Japanese.

The President discussed the question of this cruise with Admiral Stark, who reiterated his belief that it was not advisable to disperse the Fleet, and also that he did not think it would have an appreciable effect on the Japanese staff.[3] The President replied that this was not a Naval or Military matter now, but a question of state policy. He remarked that he might be agreeable to the number of cruisers being reduced from four to two and the number of destroyers from six to four. Finally he directed that the Secretaries of War and Navy and Admiral Stark and myself look into the matter and propose to him just exactly what should be done.

The President next discussed the report he had received from Mr. Hopkins relative to British and German Air strength. He said the British data showed a ratio of about four to three in favor of Germany instead of the four to one rating from our G-2. He added that Mr. Hopkins had stated that the British considered there had been a loss by the Germans in the air or in accidents in landings, etc. of 6,000 planes, whereas the British had similarly lost only about 3,000. He discussed the possibility that the Germans might build up air and some land power in Tripoli, and questioned me as to the whereabouts of the Army of the Nile.

The President commented on a letter he had received from Ambassador Phillips in Italy to the effect that there was a decided change in the Italian state of mind;[4] that Mussolini was openly referred to with disapproval and that his actions had not been those of a normal man, particularly in dispersing his Cabinet officers to troop commands, even where an individual was ill and awaiting an operation. Mr. Hull confirmed this from letters he had received, adding that Mr. Phillips had reported that the Germans had skillfully sifted in to most of the control positions in the Italian Government.

After the meeting, Mr. Stimson, Admiral Stark and I met in the Secretary of War's office and discussed the question of a "Training Cruise". Mr. Stimson felt that the principal advantage, possibly the only advantage, would be the pause at Port Darwin in Australia, which was opposed by Mr. Hull. He thought it possible that the stop at Davao, which is a Japanese Colony, might stir up some excitement.[5] Incidentally, the President stated that he thought the squadron probably should not call at Manila. Mr. Stimson said he would talk to Mr. Hull over the 'phone and see if he could get a withdrawal of his opposition to an Australian stop, in case such a cruise is made.[6]

One more matter was taken up at the conference with the President, which I omitted to refer to in its proper place. During the discussion of the possible Japanese reaction to the "training cruise" I suggested the possible desirability of our following a more active course in the Philippines in the way of military preparation which would be impressive to the Japanese military authorities. I suggested as possible moves the transfer of a few antiaircraft guns from Corregidor for the protection of the Cavite anchorage, the work being started immediately on the expansion of air fields—assuming the money would be made available without waiting for Congressional action, and the immediate creation (something we were already considering) of some squadrons of planes with Filipino pilots, the planes would be those released from the squadrons due to the arrival of the Swedish and Siamese planes.[7] The President thought this would be taken merely as a gesture to protect the City, and I commented on the fact that it related purely to the protection of an anchorage. Mr. Stimson suggested that if we started work on some fields in the southern Philippines near Davao, for example, it might be more impressive. When we were leaving the President suggested the possible desirability of going ahead with the air field phase of the program.

G. C. Marshall

NA/RG 319 (OPD, Exec. 4, Item 11)

1. The president informed Ambassador Nomura that United States public opinion overwhelmingly opposed Japanese expansion in the Far East. In a dramatic warning, Roosevelt claimed that he could not restrain popular indignation much longer. Japan, he emphasized, had to realize that their actions brought civilization to the brink of war. (Adolf A. Berle recounts Roosevelt's description of the meeting in *Navigating the Rapids, 1918–1971: From the Papers of Adolf A. Berle*, ed. Beatrice Bishop Berle and Travis Beal Jacobs [New York: Harcourt Brace Jovanovich, 1973], pp. 359–60.) On February 20, 1941, Churchill had written to Roosevelt: "If Japanese attack which seemed imminent is now postponed, this is largely due to fear of United States. The more these fears can be played upon the better." (*Churchill and Roosevelt: The Complete Correspondence,* ed. Warren F. Kimball, 3 vols. [Princeton: Princeton University Press, 1984], 1: 137.)

2. British Ambassador Lord Halifax had noted the latest Japanese diplomatic initiatives in a letter to Secretary of State Hull on February 24, 1941. He wrote that after the British had expressed their concern over Japanese expansion, the Japanese quickly disavowed any military moves into Indochina. (Department of State, *Foreign Relations of the United States: Diplomatic Papers, 1941,* 7 vols. [Washington: GPO, 1956–63], 4: 48.)

3. On Stark's opposition to naval cruises as instruments of deterrence policy, see Stark to Kimmel, April 19, 1941, in *Hearings before the Joint Committee on the Investigation of the Pearl Harbor Attack,* (Washington: GPO, 1946), pt. 16, p. 2163.

4. William Phillips, a career diplomat, had been ambassador to Italy since 1936.

5. Davao was the chief port of Mindanao, second largest island in the Philippine archipelago. In 1941 two-thirds of the nearly thirty thousand Japanese nationals in the islands lived in or near Davao. (Louis Morton, *The Fall of the Philippines,* a volume in the *United States Army in World War II* [Washington: GPO, 1953], p. 6.)

6. In mid-March Roosevelt sent a naval division of four cruisers and a squadron of destroyers to Australia, New Zealand, Fiji, and Tahiti as a demonstration of United States–British Commonwealth solidarity. (*New York Times,* March 17, 1941, p. 3; see also the editorial on March 20, 1941, p. 20.)

7. In October 1940 Major General Arnold diverted aircraft scheduled for delivery to Thailand and Sweden to the Philippines. Two squadrons of P-35s arrived in the Philippines in late November, but these planes were no match for the latest Japanese models. Marshall told officials attending a February 25 meeting called to discuss aircraft reinforcements for the Pacific bases that even a single squadron of modern planes in the Philippine Department would give the Japanese some pause. Reinforcements for the Philippines were third in priority behind Hawaii and the Panama Canal, but Marshall approved the sending of a squadron each of P-40Bs and B-18s. (Notes on a conference in the Office of the Chief of Staff, February 25, 1941, NA/RG 165 [OCS, Chief of Staff Conferences File]; Arnold Memorandum for Assistant Chief of Staff, WPD, February 27, 1941, NA/RG 165 [OCS, Notes on Conferences– Decisions File]. See also Wesley Frank Craven and James Lea Cate, *Plans and Early Operations: January 1939 to August 1942,* a volume in *The Army Air Forces in World War II* [Chicago: University Press, 1948], pp. 176–77.)

MEMORANDUM FOR GENERAL ARNOLD   February 27, 1941
Confidential   [Washington, D.C.]

With reference to the re-allocation of experienced personnel, Mr. Hopkins yesterday brought to us a list of the most urgent requirements for the British, as approved by Winston Churchill. The following refer to the Air Corps:[1]

American pilots to ferry planes to England. It was stated that this would save them about 800 pilots. Mr. Hopkins reports they are very short of pilots.

Experienced crews for heavy bombers.

Set-ups, meaning I suppose personnel as well as materiel, for five training schools for pilots in this country.

All of this is but another indication of tremendous pressure which will be exerted on us regarding the allocation of experienced Air Corps personnel, both ground and air. I have been going over the distribution table you handed me yesterday, but this more recent proposal by Mr. Hopkins adds another complication to the plot. It looks as though we are going to be forced to some very radical thing or departure, and what I am concerned about is that we arrive at a solution before an unfortunate one is forced on us. Please turn this over in your mind and then see me about it personally.[2]

GCMRL/G. C. Marshall Papers (Pentagon Office, Selected)

1. For the Hopkins list of British requirements, see Robert E. Sherwood, *Roosevelt and Hopkins: An Intimate History* (New York: Harper and Brothers, 1948), pp. 257–58. For the origins of the British requests, see Memorandum for General Arnold, February 14, 1941, pp. 422–23.

2. Marshall and Hopkins discussed the British situation in early March. For details of their meeting, see Memorandum for the Secretary of War, March 10, 1941, pp. 439–40.

MEMORANDUM FOR GENERAL BRYDEN   February 28, 1941
                                            [Washington, D.C.]

Subject: Defense commands and Air Defense set-up.

I have come to the decision that the Air Defense set-up should be in time of peace under the direction and control of the Commanding General of the GHQ Air Force.[1]

Please work out the defense command with the foregoing in mind. Also I would like you to consider these factors:

The changing of the Corps Area designation to department, in order to avoid present confusion of terms.

Along with this, some consideration might be given to the possibility of reducing the number of Corps Areas by consolidation of the 1st, 2nd, and 3rd. This may be wholly impracticable, but I offer it with the thought that since Corps Area Commanders will undoubtedly have to be charged with some defense details, the more nearly the Areas coincide with the defense commands the simpler the solution.

Chaney thinks that the Air Defense Commander, who would really be the Air District Commander in time of peace, should be charged with the organization of the Air Warning Service.[2] Emmons feels that while that official is the man most interested and therefore might be charged with the organization, that the Corps Area Commander should handle the details of administration, pay, feeding, etc. I agree with Chaney that the Pursuit people are the ones vitally interested in efficient warning service and therefore would do the job much better than a less vitally interested official. There have been evidences of this already.

In setting up the defense commands I am inclined to think the two most difficult phases will be inter-relation between the Air Defense, as to the availability of antiaircraft artillery, and the relation of the defense commander to the Corps Area commander. All of this, of course, pertains to peace-time set-up. Everyone seems to be in agreement as to the theatre-of-operation set-up. However, there is still another phase of the matter. In all probability the senior commander in a defense area once the army has taken the field will be a Major General of Coast Artillery.

The foregoing is a casual statement and I would rather you treated it for your advice rather than for Staff circulation.

GCMRL/G. C. Marshall Papers (Pentagon Office, Selected)
    1. For discussions of the lengthy debates concerning air and ground defense coordination,

territorial and mobile defense of the continental United States, the respective roles to be played by Army General Headquarters and General Headquarters Air Force, and the problems of unity of command which led to the creation, on March 17, 1941, of the four Continental Defense Commands (i.e., Northeastern, Central, Southern, and Western) and of the four Air Forces (i.e., First, Second, Third, and Fourth), see Kent Roberts Greenfield, Robert R. Palmer, and Bell I. Wiley, *The Organization of Ground Combat Troops,* a volume in the *United States Army in World War II* (Washington: GPO, 1947), pp. 115–27; and Craven and Cate, *Plans and Early Operations,* pp. 152–55, 289–90. See also the notes on the conferences on air defense of February 13, 14, 18, and 19, 1941, in NA/RG 165 (OCS, Chief of Staff Conferences File).

2. Since October 1, 1940, Major General James E. Chaney had commanded the First Air District (renamed the First Air Force on March 17).

MEMORANDUM FOR GENERAL HAISLIP[1]   March 3, 1941
[Washington, D.C.]

Subject: Civilian Corps of Specialists.

Please give this matter further study. I realize that we have lists of civilian experts, but this is not at all what I have in mind. We are constantly under pressure to use the services of individuals in all categories from Anglican bishop to theatrical producer, and many of these people have talents which can be employed to advantage in some of our activities. As a rule they want some military rank or status, but it is a travesty to commission individuals who have not and who never will have any command function.[2]

The Germans have solved this problem very neatly with a uniform militarized Civil Service, and it is possible that we could adapt this to our own system. It would require legislation, which should not be difficult to obtain.

GCMRL/G. C. Marshall Papers (Pentagon Office, Selected)

1. Brigadier General Wade H. Haislip (U.S.M.A., 1912) had been assistant chief of staff, G-1, since February 19, 1941.

2. On the policy eventually followed by the Army Service Forces in the commissioning of civilian specialists, see John D. Millett, *The Organization and Role of the Army Service Forces,* a volume in the *United States Army in World War II* (Washington: GPO, 1954), pp. 100–101.

TO HENRY CABOT LODGE, JR.[1]   March 4, 1941
Secret   [Washington, D.C.]

Dear Senator: I have received your note of March 3d, requesting my advice as to the importance and value of Bill HR-1776 "insofar as upbuilding of our National Defense is concerned."[2]

In my opinion the prompt enactment of this bill into law is a matter of great importance to the proper and expeditious development of our measures for national security. The munitions program in prospect presents a colossal task which can only be accomplished under most favorable circumstances, meaning absence of confusion and simplicity of procedure. The bill has been drawn with this in mind.

Furthermore, in view of the world situation with the probable rapidity of new developments, it is my personal opinion and that of the staff, that the legal terms should be so drawn as to permit a maximum of flexibility in the allocation of the products of our production program. In a contest with an arbitrary and ruthless opponent who can take any measures he sees fit and strike where and when he wills with sudden and terrific violence, we must be prepared to act with rapidity if the British fleet is to continue to contribute to our security in the Atlantic. HR-1776 would afford this latitude as to munitions.[3]   Faithfully yours,

GCMRL/G. C. Marshall Papers (Pentagon Office, General)

1. Lodge, a Republican, was the junior senator from Massachusetts.

2. Major William T. Sexton, an assistant secretary of the General Staff, noted: "It appears that Senator Lodge called on the Chief of Staff and stated that he did not intend to further oppose the passage of the Lease Lend Bill; however, in order to justify this change before his constituents, he was addressing a letter to the Chief of Staff asking for a frank expression of opinion as to the effect of the Lease Lend Bill on the National Defense of the United States." Marshall then asked John J. McCloy, special assistant to the Secretary of War, to assist him in preparing a statement. (William T. Sexton notes on Conference in the Office of the Chief of Staff Between the Chief of Staff and Mr. McCloy, March 4, 1941, NA/RG 165 [OCS, Chief of Staff Conferences File]; Lodge's letter of March 3 is in GCMRL/G. C. Marshall Papers [Pentagon Office, General].)

Lodge initially opposed the lend-lease bill because he believed that it would grant excessive powers to the president, creating an "internal dictatorship" and weakening the nation's ability to defend itself in a period of crisis. This position received important Republican support in the hearings on the bill. (*New York Times,* February 11, 1941, pp. 1, 12.)

3. Lodge broke ranks with his Republican colleagues on March 8, as the Senate voted sixty to thirty-one in favor of lend-lease. A vote along partisan political lines, it paralleled the February 8 House of Representatives vote. Roosevelt signed the act into law on March 11, 1941. Lodge, quoting the chief of staff's letter, explained in a prepared statement that Marshall's beliefs accounted for his shift of position. (*New York Times,* March 9, 1941, p. 21.)

M ARSHALL had testified in favor of the lend-lease bill in executive sessions of the House Foreign Affairs Committee (January 27 and 28) and the Senate Military Affairs Committee (February 20). When the bill stalled in the Senate and amendments were proposed that the Roosevelt administration opposed, Secretary of War Stimson brought the chief of staff to an important March 4 meeting with key Senate leaders. Marshall described the benefits that had accrued to the United States defense effort because of aid to Britain. Stimson recorded in his diary that Marshall "gave a ripping good speech on it. . . . He made a great impression on the Senators, who evidently don't know much about the whole situation." (March 4, 1941, Yale/ H. L. Stimson Papers [Diary, 33: 56].)

On March 12, the day after he signed the lend-lease bill into law, President Roosevelt requested a $7,000,000,000 appropriation to finance the program. Marshall testified in support of the measure on March 13 (House) and March 20 (Senate). The key question Marshall was asked at these hearings was: How would lend-lease help the nation's defense? Marshall assured the committee members that the United States stood to benefit in several ways. First, "our own actual resources will not be diminished until the finished products come off the production line and are ready for shipment. Increased production will add to our strength until the time for distribution begins." Second, the lend-lease commitment would encourage the nation's friends—particularly the British and various Latin American countries—and demonstrate to potential enemies that "we mean business. . . . I think it will have a tremendously stimulating effect on the morale of the British Army. . . . Napoleon said that morale is to materiel as three is to one, and somebody remarked the other day that under many circumstances the correct ratio is more nearly 10 to 1. We have seen a nation collapse. Those who have attempted to explain the debacle have talked a great deal about lack of materiel, but it is quite evident now that the failure was primarily in morale." (House Appropriations Committee, *Defense Aid Supplemental Appropriation Bill, 1941, Hearings* [Washington: GPO, 1941], pp. 23–25.)

Finally, the lend-lease act provided that the United States would become the primary contractual party with its own manufacturers; Great Britain could no longer place its own orders directly. "At the present time we have a confusion of orders and a division of responsibility, both on the part of the manufacturer and among various interested groups which are trying to place contracts practically in competition with each other. Once this bill becomes a law the entire matter of placing contracts, the types of materiel to be manufactured, and the inspection service to be carried on during this period of production will all be coordinated. . . . If we go ahead independently with the placing of our own contracts under the recent deficiency appropriation bill approved by this committee, while at the same time the British are also placing tremendous contracts in this country, the result, lacking coordination, will be unutterable confusion and the development of new bottlenecks in addition to those we already have to contend with." (Senate Appropriations Committee, *Defense Aid Supplemental Appropriation Bill, 1941, Hearings* [Washington: GPO, 1941], pp. 19–20. Congress passed the bill, and the president signed it on March 27, 1941.) ★

MEMORANDUM FOR THE SECRETARY OF WAR   March 6, 1941
AND UNDER SECRETARY OF WAR   Washington, D.C.
Confidential

I learned yesterday from Juan Trippe, of Pan American that the first German ship to run the blockade in South America had arrived at Rio, loaded exclusively with air equipment for the Condor Lines in Brazil. There was one plane aboard and the rest of the cargo consisted of spare parts and other equipment.[1]

For some time the Condor Lines were gradually becoming ineffective, due to their inability to obtain any equipment from Germany. At the same time Pan American was endeavoring to establish subsidiary lines which would take the place of the German-controlled service. It was partly on this basis that Pan American had a foundation for its negotiations with the Brazilian Government toward the extension or building of eight airfields in Brazil for Army use.[2] There have been negotiations with the State Department, the CAA [Civil Aeronautics Administration] and the War and Navy Departments to develop the basis for financing these subsidiary lines. Trippe tells me no progress has been made because of varied interests and ideas on the subject, especially the fact that the CAA felt that the principal decision was theirs. Now at this hour Germany successfully stages a hazardous voyage to reestablish her air lines in Brazil, which also incidentally jeopardizes the contracts in which the Army is interested.

In connection with the latter I might explain that Pan American was unable to make any progress with the contracts until I radioed personally to General Monteiro. Incidentally, he seems to have been the opponent to the contracts. In compliance to my radio, he reversed himself, and the matter got under way. In the Natal district this was a serious question.

I will go into the matter in detail, but for the time being, I give you the foregoing information, which I have had no opportunity to investigate or analyze.

There is still another phase of this Pan American business which Trippe brought to my attention last night, and which I have had no opportunity to investigate. He tells me that as a development of the American Export Line's effort to parallel Pan American on the Atlantic Flight and in the Caribbean district (the TACA Lines)—there may be a public statement by Thurman Arnold against Pan American—this within a week. The House Committee definitely turned down the American Export Lines as being highly inexpeditious at this time for the Government to be involved in subsidiaries to competing lines—there is not enough business for both.[3]

The point to this matter is, a public statement at this time would do even more harm to our position in Brazil. Whatever the Department of Justice does in the way of investigation, I think it highly inadvisable at this time for a public official pronouncement to be made against Pan American. It is too important a factor in our hemisphere defense set-up to be publicly discredited—in advance of an investigation. While I have opposed giving them the right of way on new planes at this time, I have quite a contrary view on this new phase.[4]

G. C. Marshall

NA/RG 107 (SW Safe, Pan American Airways)

1. By early 1941 Axis-controlled aviation based in Brazil had expanded operations southward and westward to the Pacific Ocean. Germany's Condor line, an old, well-established firm, serviced Brazil and the southern half of the continent. The Italian LATI line provided transatlantic service from Europe to Natal and Rio de Janeiro. LATI and Air France, a Vichy firm, controlled airfield facilities from Natal southward along the Brazilian coast. The War Department believed that these Axis airlines directly threatened United States war plans for Natal and British shipping in the South Atlantic. (Conn and Fairchild, *Framework of Hemisphere Defense,* p. 247.)

2. On the Brazilian airfields, see Marshall to Van Voorhis, January 24, 1941, pp. 396–98, and Conn and Fairchild, *Framework of Hemisphere Defense,* p. 254.

3. Lieutenant General Van Voorhis strongly supported the entry of "pro-American," British-owned TACA airlines into the Panama Canal Zone in competition with other carriers. In October 1940 the American Export Airlines contracted to purchase TACA to connect the continental United States to a unified Caribbean network in competition with Pan American. At first, the War Department approved American Export's bid to take over TACA because it would lead to healthy competition in the Caribbean. (Ibid., pp. 254–56.)

In March 1941, however, the War Department enunciated a new Latin American air policy. It supported only Pan American operations south of Mexico City "until Axis-controlled lines had been eliminated in South America." The military services then refused TACA's entry into the Canal Zone. On December 4, 1941, the Civil Aeronautics Board disapproved American Export's application to acquire TACA; Pan American Airways soon secured dominance over the Latin American skies. (Ibid., pp. 246–47.)

Thurman W. Arnold was the assistant attorney general of the Justice Department's Antitrust Division.

4. Stimson noted on his copy of the memorandum: "Atty Genl will take care of this   HLS." Ward noted on the chief of staff's copy: "SW saw ATG [Attorney General] at Cabinet meeting and Arnold will make no statement".

MEMORANDUM FOR THE SECRETARY OF WAR
Confidential

March 10, 1941
Washington, D.C.

My lunch was with Mr. Hopkins alone. The conversation did not include Arnold.[1]

Mr. Hopkins was discussing a possible way of getting at the "actual necessities" on the British list. He feared that they had asked for too much, in at least some instances; and he was fearful that we might not fully understand their requirements. What he particularly wished to avoid was a delay, and yet he felt that some method of checking either in England or here might be necessary. His idea was that if the principal leaders could talk with one another, they could quickly arrive at a sound list. He cited an example of the list he brought home, which was the result of a series of cuts imposed during a conference under Mr. Churchill's supervision, and in Mr. Hopkins' presence, just before he left London.[2]

He had in mind Arnold, somebody high in rank from the Navy—possibly Stark, and myself, going over for a two or three days' conference with Portal, of the Air, Dill of the Army, and Pound of the Navy. The conversation ended with the thought that it might be Arnold and Burns—with his detailed knowledge of ordnance as well as troop requirements. The discussion was purely casual.[3]

G. C. M.

NA/RG 165 (OCS, SGS)

1. The *New York Times* reported that on this date Marshall went to the White House to discuss essential items for transfer to Great Britain under the Lend-Lease Act. (*New York Times*, March 11, 1941, p. 8.)

2. The following day, Marshall sent to Stimson a list of army equipment—mainly howitzers, ammunition, and vehicles—immediately available for shipment to Great Britain under the provisions of the Lend-Lease Act. (Marshall Memorandum for the President, March 11, 1941, NA/RG 165 [OCS, SGS].)

3. Major General James H. Burns (U.S.M.A., 1908) was the executive officer in the Office of the Assistant Secretary of War. The British chiefs of staff referred to were Air Chief Marshal Sir Charles Portal; General Sir John Dill, chief of the Imperial General Staff; and Admiral of the Fleet and First Sea Lord Sir Dudley Pound. On Deputy Chief of Staff for Air Henry H. Arnold's trip to Britain, see Memorandum for the President, April 23, 1941, pp. 483–84.

To GENERAL JOHN J. PERSHING   March 10, 1941
                                              Washington, D.C.

Dear General: I received your note of March 4th, out at the house at Fort Myer, where I was nursing an incipient cold from Friday noon to Monday morning—this morning. Mr. Osborn, Chairman of the Joint Army and Navy Morale Committee, who is an old friend and admirer of Bishop Freeman, had arranged for a conference this week when the Bishop returned to Washington. They have a definite service they would like him to help out with, in inspiring the citizens in communities adjacent to the camps to greater efforts in meeting the present serious situation. I have expected to see the Bishop on his return to the city.[1]

The fact of the matter is, the past two weeks have been terrific here, due to a number of matters, particularly the preparations for the passage of the Lease-loan Bill, as well as business in connection with its passage. My days have been spent in conferences with the State Department, at the White

House, before Committees of Congress, and with the Advisory Committee for National Defense, until I have had but an hour or two to devote to the Army, as such. Probably you can best understand my situation when I tell you that there are five Major Generals on the Staff who have been trying to see me for the better part of a week and I have not yet been able to see them,—there were just not enough hours in the day.

I will see Bishop Freeman before Friday, I hope, as I am expecting to leave here then on a rush trip of about 4,000 miles which I have to complete before Tuesday night in order to be before a Committee of Congress on Wednesday.

I have gone somewhat into detail because I do not want you to feel that I was neglecting a request of yours, but the hours have not permitted me to do what I would like to have done. I have decentralized in every direction possible, yet there is an insistence that I appear personally in this or that conference, along with the tremendous pressures for me to see this or that person individually. A threatened cold has not helped matters, but I took time by the forelock and am entirely out of the woods today and at the office. As a matter of fact, I accomplished more work at Myer than down here.

I am awfully sorry that your Hot Springs visit was disappointing and I hope that the San Antonio weather will be more considerate. You have at least escaped some very disagreeable days here in Washington.

With my love to you and Miss May, Affectionately,

G. C. Marshall

LC/J. J. Pershing Papers (General Correspondence)

1. Pershing wrote to Marshall on March 4, 1941, to inquire again if he could give Bishop James E. Freeman "some job in connection with welfare of the Army." (Pershing to Marshall, LC/J. J. Pershing Papers [General Correspondence]. See also Marshall to Pershing, February 17, 1941, pp. 425–26.) Freeman requested a blanket letter of authority to visit all army camps and speak to large gatherings of troops. The secretary of war refused this request because it would set a precedent for numerous other groups and individuals. The Morale Branch did want to arrange special speaking tours for Freeman if his health and schedule permitted. (Marshall to Pershing, March 24, 1941, LC/J. J. Pershing Papers [General Correspondence].)

MEMORANDUM FOR LIEUTENANT COLONEL GINSBURGH[1]

March 11, 1941

[Washington, D.C.]

I want to make a talk over the radio on a general hook-up, at some cantonment where ostensibly I am merely addressing, say, the officers and non-commissioned officers of the unit. I want to make a picture of the tremendous army that has been built up on a scale never before dreamed of in time of peace; I want to make both a picture and an appreciation of the wonderful morale with which all the elements, Regulars, National Guardsmen, Selectees, and Volunteers have entered into this task, their accomplishment under vile weather and uncomfortable living conditions, their cheerful endurance of long marches and strenuous training program. In accentuating or appreciating the remarkable morale which really has dominated these units up to the present time, in what amounts to the initial stages of a great experiment in democracy, I wish to mention and even elaborate on the vital importance of the solid backing of the people in public morale as well as military morale, in contrast to quibblings and bickerings, distracting arguments of statistics about production, the long debates in Congress, all of which has produced so much of confusion in the public mind that a really great and splendid achievement of the past six months has all but been overlooked, except as to columns on delays regarding the completion of this or that cantonment and no reference whatever to those that actually were completed ahead of schedule.

Will you be good enough to give me a rough outline of how I might approach this.[2]

GCMRL/G. C. Marshall Papers (Pentagon Office, Selected)

1. A. Robert Ginsburgh, a lawyer detached from the Judge Advocate General's Department, was on the staff in the Office of the Assistant Secretary of War.

2. Ginsburgh drafted speeches for the chief of staff's Army Day broadcasts to the Thirty-third Division and on N.B.C. radio, both on April 5, 1941. (For the texts of these broadcasts, see GCMRL/G. C. Marshall Papers [Pentagon Office, Speeches].)

MEMORANDUM FOR GENERAL PARKER[1]   March 12, 1941
                                                    [Washington, D.C.]

Subject: Policies and Objectives.

The Army situation today is entirely different from that on previous occasions when we have discussed Army objectives.[2] By June 30, 1941, our force will consist of 1,200,000 men in ground units, training centers and overhead, and 200,000 men in the Air Corps and its services. Ground forces in continental United States will be organized in two armies, nine corps troops, twenty-seven infantry divisions (1 motorized), four armored divisions (later to be further increased), two cavalry divisions and a cavalry brigade, and GHQ troops (including 43 antiaircraft regiments and fifteen medium tank battalions). One set of Army troops and five sets of corps troops will be complete. Other Army and corps troops will lack certain essential units.

Nine of our infantry divisions (triangular) will be at full strength (13,000), and other units will vary from 80% to 90% of full strength. The air force will include 54 combat groups containing 208 combat squadrons. Initial equipment requirements for this force will be met with the stocks now on hand and under manufacture, plus those to be procured from funds set up in current estimates. Some shortages will still exist in the requirements of this force to provide for one year of combat operation, largely in ammunition, Air Corps equipment, motor vehicles, boats, etc. Funds to meet these shortages will be authorized shortly.

With respect to the eighteen divisions of the National Guard, we are really involved in two plans. We are operating now under legislative authority which requires the return of the Guard to civil life after one year's training, and have submitted our Fiscal Year 1942 estimates on that basis. If the present critical world situation continues, it would be dangerous for us to release any seasoned divisions, and under those circumstances, it would be necessary to request funds and authority to continue the Guard in federal service for a longer period. Before making a final decision in the matter, we propose to wait and see what conditions are when the end of the training period now authorized by law approaches.

From the broad point of view, we are not concerned about funds. We do not have to fight for money—it is forthcoming as required and the machinery is in operation to provide us with manpower as needed. We are planning for a large increase in the number of our trained pilots and mechanics, but we do not anticipate difficulty in obtaining approval of this increase.[3] What we really need today is support of the program we have under way. Our organization is shaping up remarkably well toward a balanced, seasoned force in accordance with present plans. Our greatest concern is to be allowed to complete this organization without having its effectiveness destroyed by frequent changes. Unfortunately, press reports overemphasize the more spectacular phases of warfare as well as difficulties reference this or that. On this account we are under constant pressure from many directions to change, to reorganize, etc., which would result in a continuous emasculation of our program. The support of the American Legion will be particularly valuable in enabling us to continue to maintain a reasoned balance in our organization.

GCMRL/G. C. Marshall Papers (Pentagon Office, Selected)

1. Major General Frank Parker (U.S.M.A., 1894), commanding general of the Third Army before his retirement in 1936, was a member of the National Executive Committee of the American Legion and member of the American Legion mission to Great Britain in February 1941.

2. Marshall briefed Parker on the War Department's defense objectives in a letter dated September 5, 1940 (GCMRL/G. C. Marshall Papers [Pentagon Office, Selected]), and the staff updated that appraisal on January 23, 1941 (NA/RG 165 [OCS, 20316–20]).

3. On pilot training goals, see Craven and Cate, *Plans and Early Operations*, pp. 110–11.

MEMORANDUM FOR GENERAL RICHARDSON[1] March 13, 1941
[Washington, D.C.]

The attached clippings and what I read last night in TIME would indicate that the War Department's statement to the effect that we were not planning to request an extension of the tour of the National Guard had been given little publicity. This has produced a very embarrassing situation for me and for the War Department. The matter is serious. It has reopened a battle of last fall.

Please see that it is understood that there was no basis of authority for the statement that was made, which was given such publicity in the New York TIMES.

The Matter is important.[2]

GCMRL/G. C. Marshall Papers (Pentagon Office, Selected)

1. Major General Robert C. Richardson, Jr., (U.S.M.A., 1904) was director of the War Department's Bureau of Public Relations.

2. The War Department had released the following statement on March 7 to counter reports in both the *New York Times* and the *Washington Post* of an extension of National Guard service: "The War Department announces that there is no authority whatever for the statement which appeared in The Washington Post March 7, which quoted an authorized Army spokesman as stating that the War Department will request legislation to extend by six to twelve months the active duty training of the National Guard." (*New York Times,* March 8, 1941, p. 6.) *Time* magazine (March 17, 1941, p. 22) repeated the newspaper reports. Interviewed on March 20, after his inspection trip, the chief of staff told reporters that the retention of the National Guard was being considered as an option, but the decision would be made in June. "If the situation is critical then," said Marshall, "they probably will have to stay on, which will mean a simple administrative matter of getting the money for them. But if the Lord is good to us and they can be sent back home, it will involve some complex administrative problems." (*New York Times,* March 21, 1941, p. 11.)

TO WALTER WANGER March 13, 1941
[Washington, D.C.]

Dear Mr. Wanger: Your letter of March 4th was singularly appropriate as it arrived just after my preview of the sex hygiene film.[1] The forceful manner in which this difficult subject is presented leaves such a profound and lasting impression that I feel certain its effects will be far-reaching. With this picture as a criterion and the rapidly expanding Signal Corps facilities, I think my concern as to the quality or type of future training films has been greatly modified. Mr. Gordon Mitchell has conferred with the War Department and, as a result of this exchange of views, a number of minor matters have been satisfactorily adjusted.[2] The Academy of Motion Picture Arts and

Sciences has reason to be proud of its contribution to this important phase of our preparations for defense.

As to the other ways in which the motion picture industry may cooperate with the Army, apart from training, you will be interested to know that these are now heading up to the Bureau of Public Relations under Major General Robert C. Richardson, Jr. Insofar as the War Department is concerned, this Bureau will in effect constitute the clearing house—except for training—which you recommend in your letter and will, I am sure, serve to effectively coordinate all other motion picture involvements of the Army. We will keep Mr. Mellett fully informed of these activities.

I hope you will have no hesitancy in writing either to me or to General Richardson regarding any suggestions you may have in mind. We will be grateful for your assistance.

I am looking forward to meeting Mr. Zanuck on his arrival here. Incidentally, I hope on your next visit east you will have lunch with me so that we can talk things over a little more expansively.   Faithfully yours,

GCMRL/G. C. Marshall Papers (Pentagon Office, Selected)

1. In a telegram congratulating Darryl F. Zanuck, Marshall said: "Film on sex hygiene has been personally delivered by Captain Gordon Mitchell and previewed by representatives of my office and Office of Surgeon General. They are unanimous in their expressions of approval and commendation." (Marshall to Zanuck, March 6, 1941, NA/RG 407 [Unclassified, 413 (2–16–41)].) Not all the film's viewers were pleased, however, and in July Marshall wrote to Bishop John F. O'Hara of the Roman Catholic Army and Navy Diocese: "I have just approved the detailed action to amend the film on Sex Hygiene to emphasize the importance of continence in accord with certain of your suggestions." (Marshall to O'Hara, July 10, 1941, GCMRL/G. C. Marshall Papers [Pentagon Office, Selected].)

2. Wanger wrote to clarify certain points which had arisen during his February conversation with Marshall (see Marshall to Wanger, February 24, 1941, pp. 429–30) and to reiterate his opinion that "it might be worthwhile to consider some clearing-house, in Washington, representing the Government's various branches, which might serve to advise each of the Government's branches of the film work being done by the other—in order to prevent duplication and double-effort." At the top of Wanger's lengthy letter, Marshall wrote: "I want to reply. He is the most impressive type I have met in a long time." (Wanger to Marshall, March 4, 1941, NA/RG 407 [General, 413 (2–16–41)].)

DEPARTING from Washington shortly after ten o'clock on the morning of March 14, Marshall began his first extensive inspection trip since August 1940. During his five-day journey, he concentrated his attention on four ground forces and five Air Corps installations in the southeast. (Marshall described the trip in his letter of March 22 to Mrs. John B. Wilson, pp. 449–50.) He also delivered two addresses: a five-minute radio speech from Montgomery, Alabama, given as part of a program honoring the anniversary of the founding of the United States Military Academy; and a longer, informal speech before the General Association of Chambers of Commerce in Tampa, Florida. Apparently no transcript was made of Marshall's addresses.

In Washington the General Staff secretariat was enjoying a brief respite from their normally heavy load. "With General Marshall away, the office is much quieter than usual," the newest assistant secretary, Lieutenant Colonel Paul M. Robinett, recorded in his diary. (March 15, 1941, GCMRL/P. M. Robinett Collection [Diary, p. 68].) His commanding officer, Colonel Orlando Ward, also observed that "things are tranquil"; but from experience he added, "It will not last long." (Orlando Ward Diary, March 17, 1941, photocopy in GCMRL/Research File.) As usual, Marshall returned from his trip with a long list of problems, shortages, and grievances to be investigated and resolved. The following six memorandums are typical of those resulting from an inspection trip by the chief of staff. ★

MEMORANDUM FOR GENERAL ULIO[1]   March 19, 1941
[Washington, D.C.]

I learn that newly activated units are starting without any company funds. Please look into the matter of seeing whether or not some arrangements can be made to meet this situation.

[P.S.]   Could we not advance some of the Red X money and take repayment.[2]

NA/RG 165 (OCS, 16449-23)

1. Brigadier General James A. Ulio, formerly the assistant adjutant general, was in command of the new Morale Branch, which had been created on March 14, 1941. (Watson, *Chief of Staff*, pp. 232–33.)

2. The postscript concerning the Red Cross on the file copy had been added in the handwriting of Marshall's secretary.

MEMORANDUM FOR THE QUARTERMASTER   March 20, 1941
GENERAL [GREGORY]   [Washington, D.C.]

Subject: Typewriters for Fort Bragg.

General Devers at Fort Bragg[1] tells me that he requisitioned 615 machines for the Post unit and but 165 are authorized; and that he requisitioned 634 for the Replacement Center and 244 are authorized. The shortage, according to his figures, is 840. The strength of his command is 62,000.

The variance between the authorized number and the number he feels he requires is so great as to cause me to feel that some review of this is required. The strength of his command in a few months will be 62,000 and I have not detected any let-up in War Department requirements in the way of paper work.

GCMRL/G. C. Marshall Papers (Pentagon Office, General)
1. Major General Jacob L. Devers had been commanding general of Fort Bragg, North Carolina, since October 9, 1940.

MEMORANDUM FOR ASSISTANT CHIEF   March 20, 1941
OF STAFF, G-4 [REYBOLD]   [Washington, D.C.]

On a recent inspection trip I noticed at Fort McClellan, for example, that in a difficult mud situation no provision had been made for washing motor transportation. This has an unfortunate effect on the morale of a command, as the transportation presents a miserable appearance.

Another item I would like you to check on, though it is probably too late to do anything about it: In a hospital I looked at, I noted a heating system in Orlando, Florida, that looked suitable for Minnesota, also that long cor-
* ridors would have no exit doors, making the building a fire trap. Do we not have standard plans for these things that should have avoided such results?

* Doors have been cut.[1]

GCMRL/G. C. Marshall Papers (Pentagon Office, Selected)
1. This note had been added to the file copy in the handwriting of Marshall's secretary.

MEMORANDUM FOR THE ADJUTANT   March 20, 1941
GENERAL [ADAMS]   [Washington, D.C.]

Everywhere I go, out with the troops, I find complimentary references to the operation of the War Department moving picture set-up. However, I find a unanimity of feeling against the restriction on releasing pictures in less than a month, to two months in some cases, after they have been shown in the adjacent community. To me it is an absurd situation, where an army village of double and treble the size of the community has pictures one to two months older than are shown in the small theatres of that community. I think we should proceed immediately to correct this. The reasons that may have governed under the peace-time life of the Army certainly do not apply to these young men who are turned out in this emergency. They don't understand such a procedure and you can't blame them. The local theatres are overwhelmed as it is and the local communities receive the major financial benefits of the proximity of the camps.

Please let me have a comment with regard to this matter. I want the basis of taking this up directly with the moving picture people.

General Devers suggests that moving picture theatre tickets should be placed in Batteries and Companies for sale to enlisted men, as is done with Post Exchange coupons.

GCMRL/ G. C. Marshall Papers (Pentagon Office, Selected)

MEMORANDUM FOR THE QUARTERMASTER   March 20, 1941
GENERAL [GREGORY]   [Washington, D.C.]

On a recent inspection trip I noticed utility buildings at various places that had been completed but lacked equipment. For example, at Fort Bragg the cold storage plant building was ready January 16th, but the equipment will not be available until March 18—if then; the laundry building was ready February 1st, but the equipment not until March 25th; the bakery building was ready December 21st, but the equipment is not due until March 25th. I found the same situation regarding furniture. At Camp Stewart the recreation building was completed but no furniture was available; the men were in dire need of a place to go, as they are in a rather desolate location, and there stands a building empty of all equipment and furniture. I found libraries (this probably is not your business) ready for books and no books.

What is the reason for this? It would seem to me it would take less time to get the furniture, for example, than it does to build a building, particularly when ordinary standard furniture is available.

GCMRL/ G. C. Marshall Papers (Pentagon Office, Selected)

MEMORANDUM FOR GENERAL ULIO   March 20, 1941
                                                              [Washington, D.C.]

I learned from General Devers at Fort Bragg that he has no authorization for recreational facilities for the motorized and animal unit areas, involving

14,800 troops. I am referring to two theatres, service club, guest house, Post Office, telephone exchange. Also, no service club or guest house is authorized for 8,000 colored troops. Please look into this.[1]

GCMRL/G. C. Marshall Papers (Pentagon Office, General)

1. With enormous construction loads, recreational facilities received low priority; construction of both housing and facilities for black troops ranked near the bottom. Since many communities opposed the stationing of black troops on nearby army posts and creating recreational facilities for them in their towns, the War Department carefully stationed such troops to avoid controversy. (Ulysses Lee, *The Employment of Negro Troops,* a volume in the *United States Army in World War II* [Washington: GPO, 1966], pp. 97–102.)

MEMORANDUM FOR THE ASSISTANT CHIEF OF STAFF, G-1 [HAISLIP]

March 21, 1941
[Washington, D.C.]

There has been a lot of newspaper publicity, of the "jim crow" colored equality character, sent around with the allegation that this Colonel Randell is to be relieved. Will you look into this and find out if there is anything to it, and make certain that I see the papers when they come through.[1]

GCMRL/G. C. Marshall Papers (Pentagon Office, Selected)

1. On March 16, 1941, the National Lawyers Guild had charged that the armed services practiced "Jim Crow discrimination," particularly protesting the Selective Service's use of a separate quota system for drafting blacks. The guild contended that this was a "denial of the very essence of democracy." (*New York Times,* March 17, 1941, p. 19.)

The War Department had converted the Eighth Illinois Infantry to the 184th Field Artillery before its induction into federal service. The commander of this black unit failed his physical examination and the selection of a replacement was necessary. Since there were no black Regular Army officers available for command on the line at that time, the question of succession caused consternation. Congressman Raymond S. McKeough, Democrat from Chicago, informed Marshall that the black community was upset that a white officer might command the 184th. After much deliberation, Lieutenant General Ben Lear, Second Army commanding general, recommended Lieutenant Colonel Oscar Randell, a black officer from within the regiment, for promotion, thus settling the command problem. (Orlando Ward to McKeough, March 6, 1941, NA/RG 165 [OCS, 20602-132]; Lee, *Employment of Negro Troops,* pp. 198–99.)

TO MRS. JOHN B. WILSON

March 22, 1941
Washington, D.C.

My dear Rosie: I am typing this myself out at Myer. Things have been too fast or pressing at the office of late to permit of even the dictation of a hasty note. Also, I flew off on a 3,000 mile rush inspection trip the other day – saw about 200,000 troops – three divisions in one day; and when I returned the work had piled up seriously, especially in connection with the hearings on the Lease-Loan seven billons. I have had to spend a good deal of time up on the Hill.

I was much amused with your comments on The Conqueror, Hamilton, Jefferson – who, by the way, came from "a small place in the north of the south." also, your appreciation of Gertrude Atherton.[1] I was delighted to learn about Celest's raise, and especially about Tom's raise. Some time back I had Miss Thomas call up your Mother to get Tom's address and telephone number. She gave us the address – out here where we go to the nice, clean little movie theatre, Buckingham Village. But your Mother said that Tom had not put in a telephone. This last rather blocked my intention, because I am always so uncertain of my time that I cannot call up until the last moment, and I wanted to have Tom and Susie over when we were clear and they had some one at hand to look after the children; or to meet us at the movie, where we so frequently go on short notice, and sometimes get a Thursday night bite in the little restauraunt next door to the theatre.[2]

On my recent trip I touched Fort Bragg, N.C., Columbia, S.C., where we have 25,000 troops, Camp McClelland, Ala., Montgomery, Ala., Savannah and two nearby camps, Gainesville, Fla., and a camp there of 30,000, Tampa, Fla., an air base, Orlando, Fla., another air base, and Langley Field, Va – all from ten thirty Friday morning to five o'clock Tuesday evening. Wednesday a.m. at ten I was before a senate committee! Incidentally on the flight north I Flew over the water just off Myrtle Beach of your beloved Uncle. Flew two or three times around Jekyl Island to look over its exclusive colony.

I rode today and yesterday, and am riding in the morning in time to get in town and broadcast for the Red Cross at eleven fifteen. All my ridings has been alone since you and Molly left.

Write [a]nd tell me how John finds his new job and associates.

With my love to you both.

G. C. M.

GCMRL/R. P. Wilson Collection; T

1. The book to which Marshall refers is Gertrude Atherton's *The Conqueror: Being the True and Romantic Story of Alexander Hamilton* (New York: Macmillan, 1902). It was subsequently reprinted several times with the subtitle "A Dramatized Biography of Alexander Hamilton."

2. Mrs. Wilson's letter to Marshall, to which this is a response, is not in the Marshall papers; neither is it mentioned in her book. (Rose Page Wilson, *General Marshall Remembered* [Englewood Cliffs, N.J.: Prentice-Hall, 1968], pp. 240–41.) Celeste was Rose's sister, Thomas her brother, and Susan her sister-in-law. Cora Thomas had been Marshall's appointment secretary since November 1940.

To Westbrook Pegler   March 22, 1941
                                                [Washington, D.C.]

My dear Mr. Pegler: Your recent column regarding War Department officials and their civilian attire has added materially to my mail. Richardson
was forced to turn his prayer meeting suit over to the porter at his hotel.[1]
    Seriously, your reactions on Fort Bragg have proved to be very helpful,
and I hope that you visit Benning early in your tour, as I think the varied
interests there will be helpful in broadening your background.[2]
    If you can prolong your tour, I would suggest that you include these
phases of the present activities: A GHQ Air unit (the Air Base at Savannah
affords a convenient point), a new school for air pilots, bombers, etc. paralleling Randolph Field (Maxwell Field, Alabama is convenient for this),
Artillery School of Fire (the Fort Sill, Oklahoma school), one of our new
Replacement Training Centers, which once well established should meta-
morphose the development of our Army (there are a number of these
scattered about the country, and commanding officers wherever you are can
tell the most convenient for you.) They are getting under way this month—
22 of them, to be of 12,000 each.
    Your recent effort to explain the complexity of Army organization should
be helpful. Incidentally, we found that Germany has eight different types of
divisions, and a new type has just appeared in Tripoli, a fractional part of
the heavy armored divisions that operated in France and Belgium. Until we
have more experience in operating our present organizations in strength in
genuine free-handed maneuvers, it does not appear wise for us to standardize very much.
    We never have had an opportunity in our army since the Civil War, to
handle seasoned complete divisions of any type at full strength and in corps
formations. The first opportunity of this nature will come this summer. The
pressing problem now is to discipline, condition and develop in the fundamentals the National Guard divisions we have recently inducted into active
service. Changes in type later on would be a comparatively simple problem
compared to the present task.   Faithfully yours,

GCMRL/G. C. Marshall Papers (Pentagon Office, General)
    1. Pegler, who wrote the syndicated column "Fair Enough," had commented that high-
ranking army officers were more likely to "go around posing as suburban taxpayers and
leaders of the P.T.A." than to wear their uniforms. "George Marshall . . . is so bashful that he
doesn't wear his soldier suit regularly, and any officer who should dress up in the quaint
costume of his trade in Washington, except for a fancy-pants party at the White House or a
high-class scuffle at the home of some refined millionaire, would be accused of insufferable
swank and might be sent back to the soldiers for making himself conspicuous in public."
Major General Robert C. Richardson, Jr., director of the army's Bureau of Public Relations,

"wears a black suit and looks as if he were fixing to clear his throat and say, 'Brethren, let us bow our heads in two minutes of pious meditation.'" (*Washington Post,* March 1, 1941, p. 7.) Marshall later commented: "I was in favor of remaining in civilian clothes at the War Department and the big city headquarters as long as possible, though I was much opposed in every way. I know how quickly the worm turns on this, and while I was asking for large forces and asking for billions [of dollars], I didn't want a lot of uniforms plastered around Washington. I remember in the First World War we came back and we found one of the acrid comments on the army then was the number of officers around Washington . . . , and I was trying to play that down as much as possible." (George C. Marshall, interviewed by Forrest C. Pogue, February 14, 1957, GCMRL.)

2. Marshall had written to Major General Jacob L. Devers: "I note in the morning's paper that Westbrook Pegler is searching for words to properly appraise what is being done at Bragg. This reversal of form is almost revolutionary. The greater part of the reason is your capable management and leadership." (Marshall to Devers, March 19, 1941, GCMRL/G. C. Marshall Papers [Pentagon Office, Selected].)

MEMORANDUM FOR THE SECRETARY OF WAR March 24, 1941
[Washington, D.C.]

Subject: Air Fields and other Defense Set-ups in the Republic of Panama.

I have just returned from a liaison meeting at the office of Mr. Sumner Welles.

With relation to the Panama situation, the State Department is sending today a radio to our Ambassador presenting the attitude of our Government in the matter, copy enclosed. Mr. Welles states that our Ambassador will be directed to show this to General Van Voorhis immediately, and he recommends that we direct Van Voorhis to radio back his view of the matter in the light of this last communication.

Mr. Welles' attitude is that unless General Van Voorhis recommends against such action, we should direct Van Voorhis to take over all surveyed sites and start construction immediately. Meanwhile, the State Department would proceed with the further negotiations as to the terms of settlement.[1]

GCMRL/G. C. Marshall Papers (Pentagon Office, Selected)

1. At this time the army wished to acquire over seventy-five defense sites in the Republic of Panama, but negotiations for these were being delayed by questions of the extent of United States jurisdiction and tenure at the sites. Lieutenant General Daniel Van Voorhis, head of the Caribbean Defense Command, was reluctant to occupy the sites until these issues were settled. Under Secretary of State Sumner Welles told Marshall that he had "succeeded in mopping up all major difficulties concerning defense sites in Panama." During the week following this memorandum, Van Voorhis received instructions to begin occupying the positions. (Stetson Conn, Rose C. Engelman, and Byron Fairchild, *Guarding the United States and Its Outposts,* a volume in the *United States Army in World War II* [Washington: GPO, 1964], pp. 344–45. The quotation is from the Standing Liaison Committee minutes dated March 25, 1941, NA/RG 319 [WDCSA, SGS].)

MEMORANDUM FOR THE SECRETARY OF WAR　　　　March 25, 1941
[Washington, D.C.]

The attached is a letter from Assistant Secretary of State, Mr. Berle, to General Miles regarding a meeting to be held this afternoon by representatives of the Departments of State, War, Navy, and Justice (Mr. Hoover).[1] Arrangements are to be made for the coordination by a single agency (Vincent Astor as Area Controller) of intelligence and investigational activities in the New York area.[2]

Mr. Berle's memorandum indicates the concurrence of the War Department. General Miles tells me he has not heard of the matter heretofore.

I have known that Mr. Astor has been engaged in some such service in New York since 1939. As a matter of fact I was called to the White House with Admiral Stark on at least one occasion late at night to discuss with the President some item regarding which Mr. Astor had telephoned him.

Has there been any discussion of this with the President? General Miles is prepared to make his contribution to the coordination, but would like to know just what commitments have already been made.

GCMRL/G. C. Marshall Papers (Pentagon Office, Selected)

1. The editors have not found Berle's letter.

2. Regarding the coordination of domestic intelligence operations, Miles first contacted Adolf A. Berle on September 26, 1940. Berle noted in his diary: "He has been thinking over some suggestions of several weeks ago, realizing that there is more to this job of internal defense than merely intelligence and police work. He feels that J. Edgar Hoover, who is a good policeman, does not wholly take in the entire situation." (*Navigating the Rapids*, p. 337.)

In mid-February, Federal Bureau of Investigation Director Hoover charged that the Military Intelligence Division had exceeded its authority and was conducting domestic intelligence activities which were the province of the F.B.I. The G-2 staff replied that "some of the allegations and assumptions are so far from the truth as to be ridiculous. . . . The crux of the matter is that allegations have been made continually by FBI and sent to high authority without any attempt being made to verify thru or straighten them out by direct contact." Moreover, Hoover had declined to meet with G-2 to discuss the issues involved. (Hoover to Miles, February 10, 1941, NA/RG 107 [SW Safe, FBI—G-2]; staff memorandum "Charges Contained in Letter of February 10, 1941," [March 26, 1941], ibid.)

On March 19, 1941, Roosevelt appointed wealthy businessman and personal friend W. Vincent Astor as area controller of intelligence for New York. Astor, a commander in the Naval Reserve, set up a clearinghouse to establish priorities for intelligence gathering and assign responsibility to the various governmental departments for intelligence activities. (D. J. Callaghan Memorandum for the President, March 14, 1941; Roosevelt to Grace Tully, March 19, 1941; Astor to Roosevelt, April 3, 1941, FDRL/F. D. Roosevelt Papers [PSF, Astor].)

To COLONEL CHARLES L. SAMPSON　　　　March 26, 1941
Personal　　　　[Washington, D.C.]

My dear Colonel Sampson:　In reply to your letter of March 21st, I am sorry to learn that you feel the Chief of Infantry gave you an implied promise that your assignment to the Replacement Center would carry a promotion.

In the first place, promotion to a general officer passes through numerous tests and hands before final approval, and even the Chief of Staff does not have the authority to state definitely that any particular position will carry with it a promotion. Furthermore, in your case and that of the other Executives of the replacement centers, no one other than General Lynch and his immediate office had any knowledge of the selections made or that orders were being issued, except the officials handling that routine in the office of The Adjutant General. In other words, the first intimation that the Secretary of War, the Chief of Staff, the Deputy Chief of Staff, and the Assistant Chief of Staff, G-1, had in this matter was the actual issuing of the orders. Insofar as I was concerned, I knew nothing about it as to individuals until you were ushered into my office.[1]

You state that "This whole experience, under the circumstances, appears to me to have been a most ruthless and unjust humiliation and not deserved by an officer of my record and rating." You also go into details regarding personal arrangements. You introduce here detailed matters which, from the viewpoint of the administration of an army of 1,400,000 men is entirely beyond my capacity to oversee.

There are many aspects of this affair which I am not free to discuss with each individual who might be concerned, and to a certain extent, almost every colonel of infantry is concerned, and it includes some of my dearest friends. Even if I were free to go into such detail, it would be utterly impossible for me to pursue the job here on any such basis. I will say this much, which is really improper for me to divulge at this time, that I have been engaged in an effort to secure Presidential approval for a policy to take care of outstanding Infantry colonels who are above the age limit for troop commands.

Now I am going to be equally frank, and tell you that I think your letter does you a great injustice, because it inclines me to think that the state of mind you reflect may have ruined your usefulness. These are not the days for purely personal reactions, to which you have given way.[2]   Faithfully yours,

GCMRL/G. C. Marshall Papers (Pentagon Office, General)

1. Sampson, who would be sixty-two in October, was executive officer of the Infantry Replacement Center at Nacimiento, California. He wrote to Marshall that the chief of Infantry had indicated in December 1940 that his assignment would include a promotion and command of the center, but he had since learned that he was "to be superseded by a General Officer to be ordered here."

2. Retiring as a colonel at the end of June 1942, Sampson remained on active duty through January 1944.

To Major General Frank M. Andrews   March 27, 1941
Confidential   Washington, D.C.

Dear Andrews: I received your letter, and while I have only had time to give it a hasty reading, I was very glad to get your views on the correlation of Air matters in Panama & the Caribbean.[1] I have sent that portion of the letter out to be considered by the Staff. The latter part referring to Howard, of course I did not release.[2]

I was very sorry about his case, and for that reason talked to him personally and very frankly. The truth was, I found a complete unanimity of opinion everywhere in the War Department, Air office, G-1, G-3, War Plans,—all were so antagonistic, many so outraged by his high-handed methods, that it was not possible to do business with such a discordant situation existing. I was interested, and rather shocked to learn that he had no premonition of anything on his part at any time that might lead to hard feeling and lack of cooperation. For that reason especially I was completely frank in talking to him and giving him the reaction that I had obtained regarding his personality and its effect on cooperative staff action. All are agreed as to his ability and all seemed genuinely regretful that he prejudiced the usefulness of that ability by his personality.

I do not recall just where he has been sent, though I did know at the time; but I have him in mind to see if there is not some way to use his special engineering knowledge. However, unless a man can in some degree accommodate himself to the give and take of affairs it is very difficult to find a suitable place for him. You like him and he evidently is a tremendous admirer of yours, but I think you would suffer from his presence near you, and your efficiency be correspondingly affected. That is the trouble they found in each effort to place him. Arnold rather kept aloof, quite evidently because he felt that his marital relationship was a great embarrassment. My reactions came from almost every other direction.

I hope shortly that we can reach a more definite basis for the Caribbean situation, not only as relates to the Army and Navy but as to the handling of the Army aspects.[3] I am hopeful that the conference now being conducted, or about to be conducted by General Emmons under the management of Chaney at Mitchel Field will be helpful in setting everybody off on the right foot. Now that we have settled the policy concerning Air defense, it is rather a simple proposition to develop it on a common basis throughout the Army.

The staff, and legislation, and British requirements, situation present a tremendously complicated task for us here in Washington. I spend, seemingly, most of my time before committees of Congress or in meetings outside the War Department, all of rather momentous importance. I made a recent quick inspection trip of about 3,000 miles, and I hope to get off to the West

Coast in about two weeks. Heretofore it has been almost impossible for me to get out of Washington. I wish you could see the Army as it is now developing following your earlier struggles with organization. It is an inspiring spectacle. Faithfully yours,

G. C. Marshall

LC/F. M. Andrews Papers

1. Writing to Marshall, Andrews had criticized the Caribbean defense situation. In view of the threat posed by Axis-controlled airlines, he requested a defense set-up similar to London's—complete with antiaircraft guns and barrage balloons. He noted, however, that, with the help of Pan American Airways, the United States had air routes to both the west and east coasts of South America. (Andrews to Marshall, March 12, 1941, LC/F. M. Andrews Papers.)

2. Commenting on the January 20, 1941, relief from the G-3 division of Colonel Clinton W. Howard (U.S.M.A., 1915). Andrews had observed that Howard was "really a brilliant aeronautical engineer," but conceded that he was "impatient and often rude with those whose minds work slower." Andrews insisted, nevertheless, that loyalty to him and his ideas, when he was assistant chief of staff, G-3, brought trouble to many of his assistants. "I have never tried to keep out of trouble, though I believe in tact and consideration and loyalty in dealing with all those below as well as above. I have never hesitated to present things as I see them. I have never had a resentment or ill thought against the War Department on the personal side, but I have fought the War Department, often against the advice of members of my staff. . . . I fought on questions of organization, of increased mechanization, in the early days of the GHQ Air Force for an air base in Puerto Rico, and many other things, but always in the family and with my cards on the table." (Ibid.)

3. Discussing unity of command in the Canal Zone, Andrews had noted that naval activities "are primarily concerned with local defense and the Army commander who has the responsibility for that local defense should be supreme." (Ibid.)

TO BRIGADIER GENERAL JOHN P. SMITH[1]   March 27, 1941
Confidential   [Washington, D.C.]

Dear Smith: On my recent trip I gathered data on the length of time it took to get decisions or authority for this or that, as related to camp headquarters, corps area headquarters, and the War Department, and also regarding the degree of activity displayed in putting across the business of the day.

During the past three or four months I have, of course, formed tentative conclusions in the matter, but now I am rather fixed in the belief that some of the headquarters are not functioning at the speed demanded by the emergency. There is too much of the time-clock procedure. I am writing you most informally because I am going to be very frank. The last has been a frequent criticism of your headquarters from any number of directions. I am inclined to think that several of your staff are not sufficiently aggressive, energetic and far-seeing. You have a tremendous problem and I know you personally are working at it very, very hard.

Please quietly survey conditions and see if some corrective is not required.

I would prefer that this letter remain confidential between the two of us, and that it does not go into the record. In other words, treat it as a personal conversation, and in any reply you may care to make, address it to me, personal and confidential. I want to avoid at all costs harassing you or upsetting you, but on the other hand, I must be certain that this emergency is being met with the energy and whole-souled cooperation that is so necessary.[2] Faithfully yours,

GCMRL/G. C. Marshall Papers (Pentagon Office, General)

1. Smith, who was to be promoted to major general on April 4, had taken command of the Fourth Corps Area in October 1940.
2. Replying on April 1, Smith expressed surprise at hearing that there had been "widespread criticism of our operating efficiency," and he promised to take "prompt corrective measures." (Smith to Marshall, April 1, 1941, GCMRL/G. C. Marshall Papers [Pentagon Office, General].)

MEMORANDUM FOR THE SECRETARY OF WAR March 28, 1941
[Washington, D.C.]

I learned this morning that a representative of Mr. Knudsen conferred with officers of the Judge Advocate General's office yesterday to ascertain whether or not there was any legal objection to the use of Federal troops for the purpose of guarding industrial plants that we might have to take over. The OPM representative was advised that there appeared to be no legal objection, but that the proper course to pursue was to submit formally the question to the War Department.[1]

I have had no opportunity to give this particular request any consideration other than to dictate this memorandum. However, I feel that from the viewpoint of the development of our war army, aside from the matter of materiel, this is a very serious matter; that by every possible means we should seek to avoid the use of Federal troops for this purpose, in order to avoid a reaction which might be seriously damaging to the Selective Service procedure—given expert propaganda service, which would undoubtedly be the case.

I noticed that you talked about this in connection with the necessity for the early development of Home Guards, in your press conference yesterday.[2] This seems to me to be the correct line of action, and by every means we should avoid the implication that we are going to use Federal troops for this purpose, until it is evident to us that the situation demands such action and we have reached the decision to do it. In other words, when the public becomes aware of our intention to use Federal troops, the troops themselves should be enroute to the place of trouble.

GCMRL/G. C. Marshall Papers (Pentagon Office, Selected)

1. Preparing for labor-management mediation on March 27, 1941, the Office of Production Management, administered by William S. Knudsen, listed thirteen defense-related strikes—mainly in steel and automotive equipment—which involved 40,000 workers. Knudsen requested that both sides reach an agreement at the long-idled Allis-Chalmers Corporation, a major engine and machinery producer. (*New York Times,* March 28, 1941, p. 14; Yale/H. L. Stimson Papers [Diary, 33: 119].)

2. In a press conference on March 27, Stimson claimed that mobilization destabilized prices and prompted "disturbances between capital and labor." He urged the states to create Home Guards, armed by the federal government, to control these disputes. Regiments already organized in New York, Massachusetts, and Florida received his praise. (*New York Times,* March 28, 1941, p. 14; on the coal miners' strike, see Marshall to Chaffee, April 7, 1941, p. 468.)

MEMORANDUM FOR GENERAL ARNOLD   March 28, 1941
Confidential   [Washington, D.C.]

The Secretary of War had two things up yesterday:

His first question was how far you had progressed in making arrangements for your trip to England.[1]

The second matter related to General Clagett's prospective visit to China. He approved the idea of General Clagett, and I will leave it to you to prepare the directive to Clagett. Mr. Currie (the official who reported the Chinese desire to have a high ranking Air Corps official visit there) stated there were three things the Chinese thought might be accomplished by this visit:[2]

1. The officer could determine for himself the efficiency of the Chinese Air Force, from the viewpoint of its possible cooperation with us if we became involved in this war.

2. The officer could inform himself as to the adequacy of the new air fields to be constructed.

3. The officer could inform himself as to the fighting tactics and characteristics of the Japanese Air Force, from what has been learned by the Chinese Aviation Corps.

The visit would have an important psychological effect in that it would indicate to the Chinese that they were being considered as potential allies rather than beggars at the rich man's table. (This last phrase is mine)

GCMRL/G. C. Marshall Papers (Pentagon Office, Selected)

1. The chief of the Air Corps began his visit in London on April 12, 1941. His account of the trip is in *Global Mission* (New York: Harper and Brothers, 1949), pp. 215–40.

2. Stimson discussed the China situation with Lauchlin Currie, presidential administrative assistant, who had recently returned from that nation. Currie had inspected the new Soviet-built Chinese bombers and was "impressed with the efficiency of the Chinese factories for munitions." Currie presented Chiang Kai-shek's request for an air force adviser. After approv-

ing Brigadier General Henry B. Clagett (U.S.M.A., 1906), Stimson also talked to Arnold about aircraft and pilots for China. (March 27, 1941, Yale/ H. L. Stimson Papers [Diary, 33: 120–22].)

MEMORANDUM FOR THE SECRETARY OF WAR — March 29, 1941
Washington, D.C.

Subject: Causes for Under-Estimates on Construction.[1]

The following are general comments by me. The attached, however, is a carefully prepared memorandum on the subject, and the report of the House Committee on the Deficiency Appropriation which enumerates reasons, and which quotes from my testimony, to which I referred the other day:[2]

a. The World War cantonment construction formed the general basis of estimates for mobilization studies in the succeeding years. However, that construction was for temporary occupancy only, pending shipment of units to France. In succeeding years no one anticipated a world situation which would determine our people to undertake a full mobilization in time of peace. The present cantonments are for continued occupancy of at least a year by the same units. Morale, as well as other features to be mentioned later, therefore greatly affected the later construction. The decision of the people was not taken until September 1941 [*1940*].

b. Another misleading factor in the calculations resulted from the experience gained in the Air Corps augmentation, on which hearings were conducted before Congress in the spring of 1939. At that time estimates were on the basis of $400 per man for cantonment type and $285 for tent camps. This construction, however, involved little basic utility development as the temporary barracks in most instances were located alongside of permanent set-ups. Also the barracks were of a poor type compared with those erected to meet the great augmentation of the National Guard, Selective Service, etc.

c. In making estimates for construction under the full augmentation program we lacked funds for adequate engineering surveys, we lacked definite commitments by Congress until September 1940; we tried from the end of May 1940, to secure authorization for the progressive mobilization of the National Guard to begin July 1st under summer conditions. We secured this authority in September, and after securing the authority we then had to proceed to get the funds through Budgetary, House, and Senate hearings. At this time on several occasions I made clear the difficulties of getting into the winter season for this construction and pled for the immediate provision of funds. Quick action was given me then by the Committee, including a joint resolution for the Selective Service increment of construction funds. But October was on us before the money could be put to work.

d. Along with the foregoing situation under *c,* the following developments affected the construction requirements, and resulted in marked increased expense. The data gradually being collected, on a factual basis, as result of the incredible happenings in Belgium and France, made clear the necessity for certain changes in organization, notably the Armored Force and increased motorization throughout the Service. Some fully motorized units, notably the 4th Division, were decided upon. All this occurred after the preparation of the elaborate estimates. These changes involved wider roads, more extensive roads to maneuver areas, less congestion of buildings—all of which involved a greater expense. Even so, changes in plans were urged by the Chief of Field Artillery and by the Chief of Infantry, brought about by this motorized situation, which I refused to authorize because of the increased expense involved in the alterations.

e. I personally directed the painting of the buildings, the building of quarters for division, brigade, and in some instances, the equivalent of regimental commanders, and certain increases for recreational purposes. This is my definite responsibility. I failed to require sufficient recreational space for camps such as that at Hinesville, Georgia, and others in similarly isolated regions. Each company should have had a day room.

f. There were, in my opinion, two contrasting errors throughout this procedure; one was, the constructing quartermaster did not decentralize sufficiently into zone control. On the other hand, he was forced by circumstances to make his estimates with little data as to the special conditions in the various camps. Also, he had to make the best use he could under the pressures—which included a political campaign—of civilian assistance. And I am under the impression, which General Moore confirms, that a portion of his difficulties came from the misjudgment of civilian architects as to lay-out. I spoke to you specifically about [Camp] Blanding as an illustration of this matter.

G. C. Marshall

Note: Please see attached papers

I have not discussed increased labor and material cost nor increases due to necessity for overtime labor in vile weather conditions.

G. C. M.[3]

NA/RG 107 (SW Safe, Hearings [Senate Investigations])

1. This memorandum was created as part of the War Department's preparations for testimony before the special Senate committee investigating the national defense program. See

the editorial note on pp. 482–83.

2. Marshall had testified at length on February 12 concerning the army's construction problems. See the editorial note on pp. 420–21. The attachments mentioned here—"Memorandum of Statement of the Chief of Staff in re Delays in Construction" and "Statement of Increased Construction Costs for Emergency Housing"—have not been printed.

3. This note was added in Marshall's handwriting. One cause of the construction problem which Marshall did not wish to discuss publicly was raised by a member of the G-4 division; Lieutenant Colonel Stephen J. Chamberlin (U.S.M.A, 1912) argued that the army's mobilization plans had been based on the assumption that the troops raised during mobilization would move immediately into the theater of operations, which had not happened. Marshall observed that making such a statement before Congress "might be dangerous." (William T. Sexton notes on the Conference in the Office of the Chief of Staff, January 10, 1941, NA/RG 165 [OCS, Chief of Staff Conferences File].)

TO MAJOR GENERAL PHILIP B. PEYTON   March 31, 1941
                                                                [Washington, D.C.]

Dear Buster: I have your letter of March 27th, regarding the Armored Force. I agree with you completely on the question of imagination in connection with the development of that outfit—in contrast to too much concentration on carburetors and chassis. I don't think you really appreciate what they now have, because I am frequently made the recipient of what seem to be pretty wild imaginings. So it is not a cut and dried business by any means.[1]

I was very sorry the other day that I had to be so hurried in my visit with you. As a matter of fact, that particular day I had to complete my inspection at Jackson, get into conference with corps and division officers at Atlanta, inspect the 22d Division at McClellan, and have a conference with the officers of the Southeast Training Center at Montgomery, not to mention the West Point broadcast. The latter part of my day was spent flying in an open plane in a rain-storm, with one leg slowing congealing. However, I managed to keep up with the schedule.

I believe you have the President with you at Columbia today.[2] I am sorry that you could not receive him.

With affectionate regards,   Faithfully yours,

GCMRL/G. C. Marshall Papers (Pentagon Office, Selected)

1. Peyton reminded Marshall that the latter had been chosen as assistant commandant of the Infantry School in 1927 because of his imaginative leadership. "I feel that imagination is the limiting factor in the development of the Armored Force but I think that also, as in your case, imagination has to be supported by a background of study and of experience." Although reluctant to draw conclusions from previous maneuvers, Peyton argued: "I know most of the men with the Armored Force who are former tankers and I know some of the men who are reconditioned cavalrymen, who are inclined to regard mechanized equipment as steel horses. I think the tactical and strategical possibilities of the Armored Forces will more surely be

realized by men who have not the limitations of most of the people I have referred to." Peyton wanted men who "will do more than merely ape the Germans." Imaginative officers would "beat the Germans at their own game." (Peyton to Marshall, March 27, 1941, GCMRL/G. C. Marshall Papers [Pentagon Office, Selected].)

2. Roosevelt inspected troops at Fort Jackson, near Columbia, South Carolina, on the morning of March 31.

To Major General Adna R. Chaffee[1]   March 31, 1941
[Washington, D.C.]

Dear Chaffee: I sent a radio last night to the effect that the Secretary of War would not be able to make a visit to Knox this week, which probably means that I will not get there either. However, I am going to make the dash the first opportunity that presents itself.

My purpose in writing to you this morning results from a letter I have received that urges me to see some officers placed in the Armored Force who have as a dominant characteristic imagination and an aggressive mentality—if that is a proper characterization. The fear of the writer was that we would have too much of men who have been immersed in the engineering aspects rather than in the tactical possibilities. I have thought several times that there were evidences of over-doses of imagination,—however I pass this suggestion on to you. What I am coming to think is that we must be careful not to bring in men only who have merely struggled with armored vehicles. You not only will be under the necessity of introducing new blood, but I think it is highly desirable that you do this. Undoubtedly such a proposal on your part would meet an immediate resistance in most of your high ranking staff officers,—at least if my experience in the War Department is any criterion in these matters.[2]

I hope to get out to Knox some time this week, but things are getting pretty thick.   Faithfully yours,

GCMRL/G. C. Marshall Papers (Pentagon Office, Selected)

1. Major General Adna R. Chaffee was the commanding general of the Armored Force at Fort Knox, Kentucky.

2. Chaffee agreed with Marshall on the qualities necessary for leadership of the Armored Force: "Ever since the earliest experiences with the old Infantry Tank Board, when it was under General Rockenbach and I used to see them standing around arguing about the size of a bolt hole to the point where they never got any tanks and never thought about tactics, I have dreaded the same thing happening in any force that I had anything to do with; and from the earliest days I have made it a principle to go on to tactical exercises of any kind that were available, no matter what the materiel at hand has been." Chaffee informed the chief of staff that while the Armored Force had a lot of "new blood" and little experience, his regimental commanders were "all tops in their branches and have had wide experience in both staff and command other than with armored units." (Chaffee to Marshall, April 4, 1941, GCMRL/ G. C. Marshall Papers [Pentagon Office, Selected].)

MEMORANDUM FOR THE SECRETARY OF WAR   April 1, 1941
                                                      Washington, D.C.

Subject: Authority for the transfer of Construction to the Engineer Corps.

I find that the procedure to obtain this authority was so informal that there is little of positive record. So far as I can recall, and General Moore and General Reybold remember, Senator McKellar was induced to introduce an amendment to this effect on the floor of the Senate. This amendment was adopted by the Senate on August 29, 1940 as part of Section 102, Public 281, which finally became law September 9, 1940.[1]

Later when I was before the House Appropriation Committee I took up the matter, off the record, to meet an attack on the Senate amendment which was being conducted, so far as I could learn, by at least a portion of the General Contractors' Association. There was involved in it a Reserve officer who was helping out in the office of the Quartermaster General. There was also involved in the matter, as reported to me, General R. C. Marshall,—a one-time Regular who was in charge of construction during the World War, later resigned, and now holds a Reserve commission.[2] Some Members of Congress thought I was the General Marshall being referred to. To meet this situation, I made a very strong statement to the Committee that any idea of opposing this amendment would be an outrageous restriction on the War Department, particularly on me personally, in the discharge of a tremendous responsibility. I stated that every resource of the Government should be employed to meet the burdens of the day, and to deny us the right to use the highly organized and beautifully decentralized Engineer Corps to lighten the burden was unthinkable. As I recall, General Hartman was present at the time, and I told the Committee that the Quartermaster General and his Construction Chief were opposed to this amendment, which all the more convinced me of the necessity for having it included in the law, as they were being overwhelmed with the enormity of their task.[3]

                                                        G. C. Marshall

NA/RG 107 (SW Safe, Hearings [Senate Investigations])

1. For Marshall's opinion on the controversy surrounding this matter, see his April 1, 1940, Memorandum for General Watson, pp. 184–85. In August 1940, Chief of Engineers Major General Julian L. Schley, with Marshall's support, persuaded Assistant Secretary of War Robert P. Patterson to propose an amendment to the appropriation bill S. 1884. Senator Kenneth McKellar, Democrat from Tennessee, proposed the amendment that would allow the Secretary of War to "allocate to the Corps of Engineers any of the construction works required to carry out the national-defense program." (Lenore Fine and Jesse A. Remington, *The Corps of Engineers: Construction in the United States,* a volume in the *United States Army in World War II* [Washington: GPO, 1972], p. 250.)

2. Brigadier General Richard C. Marshall, Jr. (V.M.I., 1898), had been commandant at V.M.I. during Marshall's last year. During World War I, he had been chief of the army's Construction Division. He was general manager of the Association of General Contractors of America. Brigadier General Charles D. Hartman (U.S.M.A., 1908) was chief of the Construction Division.

3. On the transfer of the construction function to the Corps of Engineers, see Memorandum for Senator Truman, June 4, 1941, pp. 523–24.

To LIEUTENANT GENERAL JOHN L. DE WITT   April 2, 1941
Confidential   [Washington, D.C.]

Dear De Witt: It has come to me from several directions that Glass who, I believe, is post Commander at Lewis, has been drinking heavily, and I recall that you spoke to me about this same subject regarding him when he was Chief of Staff of the Third Division at Camp Ord.[1]
    It is rather unusual for me here in Washington to be writing to an Army commander about something that is the immediate responsibility of a Corps Area and possibly tactical Corps Commander; however we suffer very serious reactions from questionable actions on the part of senior regular officers, and I am therefore asking you please quietly to check up on this. I am not going to have a few regular officers exposing the entire regular establishment to destructive criticism.
    As I have no positive evidence in this matter, please treat what I have said as merely a suspicion.[2]   Faithfully yours,

GCMRL/G. C. Marshall Papers (Pentagon Office, Selected)
    1. Colonel Ralph R. Glass was the commanding officer at Fort Lewis, Washington.
    2. De Witt's subsequent investigation did not prove the allegations against Glass. De Witt agreed with Marshall that excessive drinking by senior officers jeopardized the army, but he believed that Glass had conducted himself properly since assuming his present position and had been warned not to allow drinking to interfere with his command. (De Witt to Marshall, April 11, 1941, GCMRL/G. C. Marshall Papers [Pentagon Office, Selected].)

MEMORANDUM FOR THE SECRETARY OF WAR   April 4, 1941
Secret   [Washington, D.C.]

Subject: Staff Conference at Singapore.

    I request authority to send the following radio to the Commanding General, Philippine Department:
    Advice has been received that the British Commander-in-Chief, Far East, will conduct a staff conference on April 18, 1941 at Singapore. The representatives of Australian and New Zealand Governments; Netherland East Indies; British Commander-in-Chief, China; British Com-

mander-in-Chief, East Indies, and the United States are invited to attend.

In this connection you are advised that there was forwarded to you on April 3, 1941, by Naval Courier, report of United States–British Commonwealth Staff Conversations recently concluded in Washington, with letter of transmittal. This report scheduled to reach you April 14. While no approval has as yet been given to the report, nevertheless you are herewith authorized to designate a well informed officer of sound judgment to represent you on the staff conversations referred to above. This authority revokes that specific part of the letter of transmittal in contradiction thereto. Agreements reached in the conference must be subject to approval by the War Department. Commander-in-Chief, Asiatic Fleet has also been authorized to send a representative and he will provide transportation for Army representative.[1]

GCMRL/G. C. Marshall Papers (Pentagon Office, Selected)

1. Under the agreement of the American-British conversations held in January and February in Washington, a further staff conference, including representatives of the Netherlands, was held in Singapore from April 21 to 27, 1941. Colonel Allan C. McBride, assistant chief of staff, G-3, of the Philippine Department, represented his commander, Major General Grunert; Captain William R. Purnell, chief of staff, Asiatic Fleet, represented his commander, Admiral Thomas C. Hart (U.S.N.A., 1897). (Matloff and Snell, *Strategic Planning for Coalition Warfare: 1941-1942*, p. 65.)

At the Singapore conversations the delegations formulated a general statement of strategy for the Far East. Emphasizing the defensive nature of operations in the Pacific, they, nevertheless, proposed the organization of air operations against Japan and Japanese-occupied territory, in the event of hostilities. The conference report stressed the importance of Luzon as a strategic base for Far Eastern operations and the importance, therefore, of the defense of the Philippine Islands. (Ibid., p. 66.)

MEMORANDUM FOR THE SECRETARY OF WAR   April 4, 1941
Confidential   [Washington, D.C.]

Subject: Supply of Munitions to American Republics.

1. For a long time the War Department has been under considerable pressure from Latin American Republics to supply certain munitions. It will be many months before we would be able to supply the particular items, in the quantities desired. These Republics have been so informed, but with few exceptions they have been given a frank statement of our reasons.

They doubt our sincerity.

2. The officers of the War Department who have been in conference with these various representatives during a long period of weeks feel that the present demands and unfavorable reactions could largely be dispelled by an authoritative statement on the subject and they propose the following:

["]The United States is making a great national effort to equip its tremendously expanding armed forces. In addition, it must supply large quantities of munitions to the British.

As long as British resistance continues, there will be no major menace to this hemisphere. If British resistance collapses, we will all be in danger.

The national safety of all countries of this hemisphere demands that the British be supplied as fully and as rapidly as possible. The United States is doing this even to the extent of delaying the equipping of its own troops, but it is doing so in the common defense of all the Americas.

Subject to agreement upon details, the American Republics can be assured that they may begin procuring their armaments in the United States as soon as our production will meet these vital prior requirements. Their armies could thus commence to receive arms only a short time after the armies of the United States have received theirs.

This frank statement is made in order that each may understand the problem facing all, and with the hope that each will continue to contribute full cooperation to the common purpose."

Whether these statements should be made, and if so, whether publicly, or confidentially to the several governments concerned, would seem to be matters for decision by the Department of State.

It is suggested this matter be formally considered by the President.[1]

GCMRL/G. C. Marshall Papers (Pentagon Office, Selected)

1. Lieutenant Colonel Matthew B. Ridgway of the War Plans Division drafted this statement because he believed that it was necessary to inform Latin American governments that substantial deliveries of munitions were impossible in the near future. In his preparation of the statement, Ridgway secured the advance approval of several officials at the Department of State before Stimson sent the draft to the secretary of state. The State Department, however, refused to issue the statement. (Conn and Fairchild, *Framework of Hemisphere Defense,* pp. 220–21.)

MEMORANDUM FOR GENERAL MOORE   April 5, 1941
                                               Washington, D.C.

Last night I had dinner with General Preston Brown. His brother-in-law, Mr. Waite, was a member of the small group. Mr. Waite, whom I have known before, is apparently the man in charge of the investigation by the Budget Bureau, under Mr. Smith, of our procedure in selecting and con-

structing cantonments.[1] I also find that he feels there were egregious blunders in the selection of cantonment areas, referring especially to Blanding, Indiantown Gap and the Antiaircraft cantonment in the vicinity of March
* Field. He feels that these selections were inexcusable, and as he is Mr. Smith's adviser and naturally determines Mr. Smith's feelings in the matter, this is a rather serious state of affairs.

Mr. Waite is a business man who gives two weeks, I believe, out of each month to this work. He has been very friendly disposed to the Army on account of his connection with Preston Brown. I think it highly advisable to go over these matters with him and see if we can alter his point of view. I suggest that you make an appointment with him to come to your office and state his views to Embick, Reybold and yourself, and give you three officers a chance to develop a better perspective for him as to the numerous influences which bore on each decision. I include Embick because of his calm and logical way of putting things, and particularly because he was in command of the Fourth Corps Area when the recommendation for Blanding was submitted to the War Department.

G. C. M.

* I am not referring to layouts.[2]

GCMRL/G. C. Marshall Papers (Pentagon Office, General)

1. Harold D. Smith was the director of the Bureau of the Budget. Henry M. Waite, a civil engineer, was a consultant for the bureau's Defense Projects Unit. Major General Preston Brown had been deputy chief of staff in 1930 and Sixth Corps Area commanding general when Marshall was senior instructor of the Illinois National Guard.

2. Moore returned the memorandum to Marshall with a note at the bottom of the page: "Held satisfactory conference at 2:30 PM April 7– RCM."

To Private Frank W. Clay   April 7, 1941
[Washington, D.C.]

My dear Clay: Since the receipt of your letter, complaining about the lack of attention you have received, your case has been investigated by the Commanding General at Fort Bragg. I am told you believe you are suffering from arthritis, but that the surgeon has been unable to make a definite diagnosis.[1] But what is more to the point, I am told that prior to December 31, 1940, your service was satisfactory, but since that date it has not been satisfactory. You married without permission; you were absent without leave on January 6th and again for three days from January 15th; you entered the hospital on January 18, and were absent without leave on January 19th.

There are more than one million young men in the Army today. If conduct such as yours was a frequent occurrence, it would be impossible to build up an efficient army and utterly impossible to administer it. The fact that the Chief of Staff of the Army has taken the time to write to you directly should indicate to you the harm done by unjustifiable complaints such as yours. It is your job now as a citizen and soldier in this great emergency to do your duty without further derelictions.

GCMRL/G. C. Marshall Papers (Pentagon Office, Selected)

1. The Office of the Chief of Staff received numerous letters from enlisted men during the mobilization period; usually their problems involved matters of discipline, morale, personal equipment, or food. Officers' problems usually involved promotion, management, or professional deportment. (For example, see Marshall to De Witt, April 2, 1941, p. 464.)

Marshall's letter to Major General Jacob L. Devers, commanding general of Fort Bragg, North Carolina, was typical of his response to enlisted men's complaints: "Entirely informally and off the record I am sending you the attached rather pathetic letter. Please do not have this fellow hazed, but have the surgeons see what the trouble is." (Marshall to Devers, April 2, 1941, GCMRL/G. C. Marshall Papers [Pentagon Office, Selected].)

To Major General Adna R. Chaffee   April 7, 1941
[Washington, D.C.]

Dear Chaffee: Our plan for dealing with disturbances, such as those which may arise in the mining area of Eastern Kentucky as outlined by you in your letter of April 3d, places on the Corps Area Commander the responsibility for observing and reporting on conditions which might require federal intervention. He is also charged with the preparation of plans to meet these emergencies.[1]

However, as you point out, your troops are practically the only ones at his disposal for such use, and I was, therefore, glad to have your report.

In the event of a decision to employ troops it would probably be necessary to release a portion of your command to the Corps Area Commander.[2] Faithfully yours,

GCMRL/G. C. Marshall Papers (Pentagon Office, Selected)

1. Chaffee had written to Marshall that 14,000 members of the United Mine Workers (U.M.W.) in Harlan and Bell counties had struck the mines after their contract expired, an action that resulted in violence and several casualties. Governor Keen Johnson of Kentucky emphasized the importance of his state's coal production to the nation's defense industries and his lack of police and National Guard troops. For these reasons, Johnson informed Chaffee that he might need federal troops. (Chaffee to Marshall, April 3, 1941, GCMRL/G. C. Marshall Papers [Pentagon Office, Selected].)

2. The bituminous coal operators accepted the U.M.W. position on the union shop and troops were not sent into Kentucky. (Byron Fairchild and Jonathan Grossman, *The Army and Industrial Manpower,* a volume in the *United States Army in World War II* [Washington: GPO, 1959], p. 67.)

To Major General George Grunert   April 8, 1941
Secret   [Washington, D.C.]

Dear General Grunert: I have issued instructions which will enable you to activate the Department Headquarters Company and an M. P. Company as requested in your letter of March 1. The matter has required a certain amount of juggling here because it interferes with established troop bases and also because all additional allotments to the Philippines must be three-year men.[1]

I can well understand your problems with regard to caliber .30 ammunition, and regret that I can do nothing for you at this time in that respect. The Army and Navy both face an acute shortage of this item, a shortage so critical that I cannot send you the 12½ million rounds previously promised until some repayment of this item is made by the British. In the event such a repayment is not made prior to June 30, 1941, further consideration will be given to an additional shipment.[2]   Faithfully yours,

GCMRL/G. C. Marshall Papers (Pentagon Office, Selected)

1. Grunert had written that he needed a headquarters company and a military police company to avoid depleting the strength of his combat troops. (Grunert to Marshall, March 1, 1941, GCMRL/G. C. Marshall Papers [Pentagon Office, Selected].)

2. "My most crying need now is ammunition," Grunert wrote. Shipments intended for the Philippines, according to him, covered only 42 percent of first priority needs for .30 caliber ammunition. President Roosevelt had authorized the transfer of fifty million rounds of .30 caliber to the British on February 5, 1941. (Grunert to Marshall, ibid.; Marshall Memorandum for General Moore, February 6, 1941, GCMRL/G. C. Marshall Papers [Pentagon Office, Selected].)

To the Commanding General,   April 8, 1941
Fort Knox, Kentucky   [Washington, D.C.]
Radio

I am planning to leave here about three P.M. today for Fort Knox and to leave Knox about eleven A.M. tomorrow. It may be that a White House meeting will prevent the trip but I will radio you later. Request no publicity no honors no ceremony no change in schedule no party. Acknowledge.

NA/RG 319 (WDCSA, SGS, Miscellaneous Correspondence)

A Great Army in the Making

April 9–June 30, 1941

I feel sometimes that we are diverted from the main issue by so much of statistics about this or that, so much of argument about this delay or that delay, this opinion or that opinion. We have a great Army in the making; it is coming into its own; it needs things, but it needs more than anything else the understanding and appreciative support from every side and on every hand in this country.

—Speech to the Chamber of Commerce
of the United States
April 29, 1941

G ERMAN successes in the Balkans and Libya were complemented by a
pro-Axis rebellion in Iraq in April 1941. Within a month Vichy France's collaborative agreements and the Nazi conquest of Crete created a new
Atlantic crisis for the United States. With military intelligence officers
expecting a German occupation of West Africa, United States political and
military leaders debated the extent and direction of the nation's involvement
in the increasingly global conflict.

In this crucible of crisis, Marshall contended with every aspect of a "great
Army in the making." Rapid mobilization had created procurement and
construction problems on a massive scale; Marshall explained these problems to a special Senate committee in April. To fund the army and the
nation's increasing support for the Allies, the chief of staff appealed to both
houses of Congress in April and June for appropriations. After he returned
on April 12 from a four-day inspection of training sites and a visit with
General Pershing in Texas, Marshall turned to the vital questions of command and promotion. ★

To Major General Walter Krueger   April 14, 1941
Secret   [Washington, D.C.]

Dear Krueger: I returned to the office this morning and found your note
of April 2d, which I much appreciate.[1]

I had hoped for an opportunity to talk to you at some length while I was
on this recent inspection trip, but circumstances prevented. Therefore, I am
forced to discuss matters with you by letter which, in the circumstances, is
rather difficult.

I do not anticipate any difficulty in securing approval for your promotion
to command of the Third Army, and I will try to settle the matter conclusively within the next few days, so that you can be certain as to your course
for the immediate future. Incidentally, we have in mind the assignment of
George Strong to replace you as Corps Commander. But more of that later.

Now, I intend to be entirely frank with you because in this great emergency my purpose is purely objective, and only personal in so far as is vital
to the maintenance of morale. I want you to accept my comments in this
light, because they are directed entirely to the purpose of the efficient development of the Third Army.

While I have known you for many years and have been well aware of
your mental ability and of your tremendous capacity and willingness for
hard work, there are several reactions of yours which have come to my
attention from a number of directions during the past year which give me
concern. In the first place, and the factor that possibly exercises the domi-

nant influence I am troubled about, is the fact that you are very sensitive to criticism, to suggestions, and to anything that you think might not reflect to the best advantage for you personally. You are a man of decided opinions, along with great ability cultivated through many years of hard work, and as a partial result of this there has grown up the impression that you have a hard time hearing other people's views and adapting them to your own use—and that you are evidently unaware of this reaction of yours. In the big picture of this emergency, you will have to follow another pattern if the best results are to be obtained.

Another phase of this same matter is your sensitiveness to possible or assumed criticism involved in any suggestions, coupled with your reaction to any course of action which you think might involve you unfavorably. There is much these days that those at the top have to take on the chin, and I must be certain that you will carry your full burden of the task in a self-effacing manner.

Finally, I have gotten the impression from a number of directions that where you do not fully agree with a policy you have a hard time working yourself up to a state of whole-hearted acceptance. I am not talking about a mere difference of views. Everybody has that about pretty much every new thing that comes up. I am referring, for example, to the desire of the War Department to have National Guard officers placed in command of Regular divisions last spring; I am also referring to the situation during the maneuvers of last May.[2] It is quite possible that you would not even be able to determine just what I am referring to. That doesn't matter, and I would not enter into any discussion of this with you in any event. I am merely trying to make my position clear to facilitate business during the coming critical period. And I want you to accept this letter as a frank statement with a sincere and a friendly purpose. I am telling you exactly what I think for the sole purpose of facilitating the development of this new army of ours, on which so much may depend.[3]   Faithfully yours,

GCMRL/G. C. Marshall Papers (Pentagon Office, Selected)

1. The editors have not found Krueger's April 2 note. Krueger commanded the Eighth Army Corps at Fort Sam Houston, Texas, from October 9, 1940, until becoming Third Army commander at San Antonio, Texas, in May 1941.

2. Marshall was probably referring to the critique of the maneuvers. On May 25, 1940, Lieutenant General Herbert J. Brees, chief control officer for the Third Army maneuvers, thoroughly criticized the leadership of the participating generals. (See Memorandum for General McNair, June 18, 1941, pp. 538–39.)

3. Krueger replied: "I offer neither explanation nor excuse, but accept your comments without reservation, in the same spirit in which they were offered, and will profit by them. I appreciate fully that, no matter in what capacity I may serve, I must obviate the impressions to which you refer. I shall do that. . . . You shall have no cause hereafter for anxiety on my account in this connection." (Krueger to Marshall, April 20, 1941, GCMRL/G. C. Marshall Papers [Pentagon Office, Selected].) On Krueger's promotion, see Memorandum for the Secretary of War, May 3, 1941, pp. 492–93.

To General Douglas MacArthur[1]   April 14, 1941
                                                [Washington, D.C.]

My dear MacArthur: You are quite correct that a bureau chief who retires prior to or on the date that he completed a four year tour would if recalled to duty be called in the grade of major general, whereas one who took terminal leave after completing a four year tour and then retired would be called to active duty in the grade of colonel.[2] However, bureau chiefs are appointed for the specific purpose of acting as chief of an arm or service, and after retirement, would probably not be recalled to active duty to again act in such a capacity. If we desired to call them for a line command they could be granted temporary promotion in the Army of the United States under the existing authority enacted last year. You are, of course, aware of the fact that any general officer called to active duty in his grade of general officer receives only retired pay and no allowances. We have legislation pending before the Congress to permit a retired general officer, if called to active duty, to draw full active duty pay and allowances. The Navy was unable to have the law so amended last year and it is possible that Congress will not amend it for us this year.[3]

I could agree with you on the desirability of having retired officers who are called to active duty serve in the highest World War grade if there had been a uniform system of temporary promotion during the World War, and if all officers on the active list who held higher grades during the World War were now serving in the higher grade. However, such is not the case. There was no uniformity in the matter of temporary promotion during the war. Some division commanders recommended promotions to fill all vacancies which occurred within their divisions, whereas other[s] requisitioned officers from outside the division to fill vacancies.

We are studying now the matter of providing temporary promotion on the basis of years of active service for retired officers who are called to active duty, granting them the same promotion which has been granted to Regular officers of the active list on completing specified years of service.

Eventually we will be back to promotion by selection, and retired officers called to active duty will have the same opportunity as officers of the active list and officers of the Officers' Reserve Corps.[4]   Faithfully yours,

GCMRL/G. C. Marshall Papers (Pentagon Office, Selected)

1. Although he reverted to his permanent rank of major general in 1935 when he assumed the post of military adviser to the Philippines, Douglas MacArthur retired in 1937 at the rank of general. He continued at his post of adviser and field marshal of the Philippine Army, a rank he had held since August 1936.

2. MacArthur wrote to Marshall that several retired officers had complained to him about the Judge Advocate General Department's ruling on the recall of officers to the active list. MacArthur noted that, through technicalities, certain officers could be recalled at lower ranks than at which they retired, while the army could recall others at ranks higher than their

retirement. "Such irregularities bring the whole hierarchy of rank into ridicule," MacArthur wrote. "They do more than that. They tend to lower markedly the morale and esprit of the entire officer corps." (MacArthur to Marshall, March 27, 1941, MML/D. MacArthur Archives [RG 1].)

3. Congress did not amend the 1919 act governing pay and allowances of general officers recalled to active duty until June 16, 1942. This amendment provided that "retired officers shall, when on active duty, receive full pay and allowances of the grade or rank in which they serve on such active duty, and when on active duty status, shall have the same pay and allowance rights while on leave of absence or sick as officers on the active list." (The Adjutant General, *Official Army Register, 1944* [Washington: GPO, 1944], p. 1619.)

4. MacArthur replied: "Your decision to place promotion on the basis of selection is in my opinion eminently sound and together with the authority to appoint officers to temporary rank in the Army of the United States completely solves in an equitable way all problems connected with rank. . . . I shall take the liberty of explaining the matter to those officers who previously protested to me." (MacArthur to Marshall, May 11, 1941, GCMRL/G. C. Marshall Papers [Pentagon Office, Selected].)

MEMORANDUM FOR GENERAL ULIO   April 14, 1941
(MORALE BRANCH)   [Washington, D.C.]

The urgent need for CCC companies in administrative capacities on all posts, camps and stations is evident. Your views as to the manner in which this can best be arranged are desired. Timely action is absolutely essential. Too many soldiers are being used on non-military activities at these places when such work could better be performed by the CCC.

The CCC can be a great factor in expediting our Army program and in assisting us to meet conditions that adversely effect morale. There is little time for studies. Can anything be done?[1]

GCMRL/G. C. Marshall Papers (Pentagon Office, Selected)
1. While dictated by the chief of staff, this memo bore Orlando Ward's signature. For Marshall's views on the administration of the Civilian Conservation Corps, see Memorandum for the Assistant Chiefs of Staff, G-1 and G-4, May 7, 1941, p. 497.

TO GENERAL JOHN J. PERSHING[1]   April 15, 1941
                                                  Washington, D.C.

Dear General: The day following my delightful evening with Miss May and you was spent in inspecting the troops of the Second Division at Leon Springs, looking over the installations at Fort Sam Houston, inspecting the Air Depot and the schools at Kelly and Randolph Fields.

I got away from Randolph about two o'clock P.M. and flew into Beauregard, Louisiana to inspect the two divisions there and Corps Headquarters.

I had intended to fly on to Shelby, but thought it advisable to attend Senator Sheppard's funeral in Texarkana; so I left Beauregard at noon the following day and arrived in Texarkana in time for the funeral.[2] I left there the same evening and flew directly east, arriving in Washington at eleven that night, and found Mrs. Marshall at Bolling Field to receive me.

Allen and his wife and Clifton were here to spend Easter week-end, so we had quite a house full, and a lovely spring day. I got in a horse-back ride and walk and a drive down to Leesburg for my first look at the house Mrs. Marshall had been negotiating for.[3]

I was so glad to have an evening with you and Miss May and delighted to see how well you are looking. I imagine this warm weather will bring you north very shortly. It is 82 in Washington today.

With affectionate regards to you both,   Faithfully yours,

G. C. Marshall

P.S.   I had my first of your Texas grapefruit Sunday morning. You were very thoughtful to think of us.   G. C. M.[4]

LC/J. J. Pershing Papers (General Correspondence)

1. Pershing was staying at the Gunter Hotel in San Antonio, Texas, with his sister May Pershing. Marshall visited them on the evening of April 10.

2. Senator Morris Sheppard, Democrat from Texas and native of Texarkana, had been chairman of the Military Affairs Committee until his death on April 9.

3. On May 5 the Marshalls paid $20,000 for Dodona Manor and its nearly four acres on the east side of Leesburg, Virginia, about thirty-five miles northwest of Washington, D.C. Mrs. Marshall described the town as "about as unreconstructed a place as you could find, alluringly replete with tradition and history." (Katherine Tupper Marshall, *Together: Annals of an Army Wife* [New York and Atlanta: Tupper and Love, 1946], p. 115.) The house was built in 1754 by George Washington Ball, a nephew of George Washington, and named by its previous owner, Northcutt Ely. For a contemporary view of the house as remodeled by Mrs. Marshall, see "The Virginia Home of General Marshall," *House and Garden,* 81(February 1942): 40–41, 80.

4. Marshall added this handwritten postscript.

Memorandum for the Secretary of War[1]   April 16, 1941
Secret   Washington, D.C.

The discussion with the President was of a general nature. Convoys were not referred to.[2]

He had us analyze the Eastern Mediterranean situation, the possible re-locations of the British ground forces from that area, and the probable field of operation for the Eastern Mediterranean fleet after withdrawal. He discussed the importance of the West Coast of Africa—Dakar in particular, at considerable length.

He directed that we re-examine the cargoes now about to be shipped for

Greece and Yugoslavia to see what portion might be withheld and what portion might be of service to General Wavell.[3]

GCMRL/G. C. Marshall Papers (Pentagon Office, Selected)

1. This memorandum was dictated but not read or signed by the chief of staff. A member of the staff carried it to Stimson's house on the afternoon of April 16.

2. Lieutenant General Stanley D. Embick accompanied Marshall to the White House on the afternoon of April 16, 1941. According to the chief of staff, Harry Hopkins had arranged the meeting in the hope that the president could grasp the fundamental strategic problems facing the nation after conversing with senior military advisers. Therefore Embick was ordered to come to Washington, D.C., by airplane that morning. Hopkins, unaware of the progress made by the American-British Conversations in defining strategic goals (see pp. 409–10), had thought a decision regarding immediate military action might have to be made soon. The meeting, which included senior naval strategists, had been prompted by the navy's desire to establish a neutrality patrol in the western Atlantic. On the morning of April 16, Secretary of War Stimson, thinking along the same lines, requested the War Plans Division to prepare detailed plans for an expeditionary force—possibly to Greenland or Dakar. (Paul M. Robinett Notes of a Conference in the Office of the Chief of Staff, 11:25 A.M., April 16, 1941, NA/RG 165 [OCS, Chief of Staff Conferences File]; Yale/H. L. Stimson Papers [Diary, 33: 162–64, 166].)

Before meeting with the president, Marshall, Embick, and several staff officers discussed a W.P.D. memorandum, drafted by Colonel Jonathan W. Anderson (U.S.N.A., 1911), recommending immediate war status for the United States. The planners believed a declaration of war would invigorate the nation's mobilization effort, support the Churchill government, and secure the Western Hemisphere. They suggested the occupation of Iceland and other Atlantic islands. Embick rejected the notion that the situation was critical; he also did not regard the Churchill government as essential to Britain's survival. (Robinett conference notes, 11:25 A.M., April 16, 1941, NA/RG 165, [OCS, Chief of Staff Conferences File]; Anderson's Memorandum for Chief of Staff, April 16, 1941, is discussed in Mark S. Watson, *Chief of Staff: Prewar Plans and Preparations,* a volume in the *United States Army in World War II* [Washington: GPO, 1950], pp. 387–91.)

3. Germany had attacked Yugoslavia and Greece on April 6, 1941. A small British expeditionary force aided the Greeks until its evacuation to the island of Crete on April 24. On March 11, the president had authorized lend-lease aid to Greece, which requested pursuit aircraft and munitions for mountain fighting. Yugoslavia had requested similar aid on April 6. With the occupation of both nations, the United States diverted this assistance to General Archibald P. Wavell, British commander in the Middle East, who faced a German encirclement of British-held Tobruk, a Libyan port city, and a German advance into Egypt. (Edward R. Stettinius, Jr., *Lend-Lease: Weapon for Victory* [New York: Macmillan Company, 1944], pp. 89–93.)

MEMORANDUM FOR GENERAL EMMONS   April 17, 1941
Secret   [Washington, D.C.]

On a recent trip which included several stations of the GHQ Air Force, I was concerned to find how little the Air Corps officers knew of the facts relating to the existing situation as to planes, prospective deliveries, and reasons for present and past difficulties. I was particularly struck with how little of this information one of your senior commanders possessed, notwithstanding the fact that he had rather recently been on duty in the office of the Chief of the Air Corps.

It appeared to me that some of the young pilots lacked in morale, evidently because of their restless impatience for modern materiel with which to work and their ignorance of the reasons which had effected the delays in the distribution of equipment. The ground troops of the Army have lacked a great deal in modern equipment and have suffered considerable hardships this past winter, but in most instances their leaders have made clear to them the difficulties of the supply situation, with the result that a high morale has been maintained.

I have had prepared a memorandum on the supply status of airplanes and I wish you would personally see to it that your general officers make such use of the information as may be necessary to bring the young officers to a better understanding of the situation.[1]

GCMRL/G. C. Marshall Papers (Pentagon Office, Selected)

1. The editors have been unable to identify the aircraft supply memorandum Marshall enclosed. Emmons replied that the chief of staff's directive was being implemented and that the explanation of "the existing situation as to planes, prospective deliveries, and reasons for present and past difficulties" would "materially add" to his officers' morale. (Emmons Memorandum for General George C. Marshall, Chief of Staff, April 21, 1941, NA/RG 165 [OCS, 19838–50].)

To Madame Jouatte[1]   April 18, 1941
                                                [Washington, D.C.]

Dear Madame Jouatte: I have just received your letter of March 10th, and was deeply touched by this notice of your whereabouts and regarding your tragic experience since last May. I was greatly relieved to learn that you were well and safe, even if banished from your home. Your good fortune in having your son and his family with you, particularly your little grandson, is one ray of sunshine for you in a gloomy world.[2]

Those days in Gondrecourt more than 23 years ago, though distant and remote, remain clearly printed in my memory—particularly your kindness to me. How little we anticipated the march of events that were to follow!

I have been very busy for more than two years, and have been Chief of Staff since July 1939. During this period I have travelled a great deal, about the United States, to Hawaii, and to Central and South America, probably some 75,000 miles—all by air except a voyage to Rio de Janeiro on a Naval cruiser.

I am sending you a small photograph, which I hope reaches you in time, though the mails are rather uncertain.

This letter carries to you my hopes and prayers for your safety and for the future of little Michel.[3]   Faithfully yours,

GCMRL/G. C. Marshall Papers (Pentagon Office, Selected)
1. Marshall had spent six months in France with the First Division of the A.E.F. at Gondrecourt and had billeted at Mme Jouatte's home.
2. Mme Jouatte wrote that she had left her house on May 13, 1940, after Gondrecourt sustained a four-hour German bombardment. With her family, she fled to Moissac in the south of France, where she remained in "exile." (Mme Jouatte to Marshall, March 10, 1941, GCMRL/G. C. Marshall Papers [Pentagon Office, Selected].)
3. Marshall's letter was given to G-2 to be sent to the United States military attaché in France for posting.

MEMORANDUM FOR GENERAL HAISLIP   April 19, 1941
Confidential   [Washington, D.C.]

I had a long talk with General O'Ryan the other day as to the best method of approaching the re-classification of high-ranking officers in the National Guard.[1] The military procedure is well understood, but the question whether in time of peace we will not become involved in very serious personal reactions is to be considered.

As a matter of snap judgment, I had in mind the possibility of creating a group of distinguished National Guard officers who would serve as an advisory committee to the Secretary of War (not to me) in the matter of classification of National Guard officers. I am not quite clear as to how they would operate, but I think if the group was composed of well known and trusted men, it might be very helpful in off-setting a reaction that the Regular Army was trying to emasculate or benzine the National Guard.

I have not studied General O'Ryan's memorandum, because first I wanted to get your reaction.[2] I had in mind some such board as this:

General O'Ryan as the Chairman

General Tyndall, who has been a division commander in the augmentation and is now retiring,

General Barrows (former President of the University of California
and Commander of the California Division, a very aggressive
Reserve officer of the old World War period) and possibly

Colonel Baker, from the Pennsylvania State staff of the National
Guard, and now the head of Valley Forge Military Academy, as
the Secretary.[3]

O'Ryan is a man of stern purpose; Barrows, I think, would operate on a very high plane; Tyndall, I am not certain about, but O'Ryan thought he would be a good man and in particular would reflect the present conditions and necessities. Baker is one of the most efficient administrators and executives I have ever seen. His school is the best run school I know of. Do not circulate this memorandum in your section.[4]

GCMRL/G. C. Marshall Papers (Pentagon Office, Selected)

1. Major General John F. O'Ryan had been the commanding general of the Twenty-seventh Division (New York National Guard) during the World War.

2. O'Ryan's memorandum is not in the Marshall papers, but his views are noted in a June 13 letter drafted by the Personnel Division (G-1). O'Ryan wanted the fitness of Reserve officers to be judged by a military board under the direction of the chief of staff rather than by an advisory board to the secretary of war. (Marshall to O'Ryan, June 13, 1941, GCMRL/G. C. Marshall Papers [Pentagon Office, Selected].)

3. The officers referred to are: Major General Robert H. Tyndall, former commanding general of the Thirty-eighth National Guard Division; Major General David P. Barrows, commanding general of the Fortieth Division (California National Guard) from 1926 to 1937; and Colonel Milton G. Baker.

4. In mid-June the War Department announced the formation of an advisory board for the reclassification of Reserve and National Guard officers unfit for active service. In the June 13 letter, Marshall advised O'Ryan that he wanted an advisory board which "would relieve the Chief of Staff and the War Department of the inevitable charge that the Regular Army was emasculating the reserve components." (Ibid.)

MEMORANDUM FOR GENERAL MALONY[1]
April 21, 1941
[Washington, D.C.]

Yesterday I had a very interesting conversation, while horse-back riding at Belvoir with the Commander of the Engineer Replacement Training Center.[2] In his opinion the instruction the Reserve officers were getting in the Training Center was much more effective than that Reserve officers were receiving in the Engineer School. The latter, of necessity, was largely theoretical, except as to some weapons, while the Training Center work was highly practical and a wonderful development in the handling of men. I gathered that it was his understanding that the head of the School at Belvoir was very much of the same opinion. If this is a correct estimate of the situation, then we are wasting effort in running schools on the basis we now do for Reserve officers, and missing a good bet in the development of officers in the Training centers.

Colonel Hoge told me that the training as he saw it was the finest development he had witnessed in his Army career, but that he had no reserve of any kind and his officers were going about 14 hours a day, either working with the men or being schooled for the next day's work. He thought that each company should have a surplus officer who would be benefiting by the training and would be available to take off the pressure. Undoubtedly we must not hold officers at training centers for prolonged periods because it would be too much strain on the individual and too discouraging to feel that he is making no progress toward a troop organization. It seems to me that there is a possibility here for a combination and an economy in our school and training effort. I do not want Hoge's opinions quoted at his expense, but I would like you to do this:

Get together an informal group, such as General Kingman, Engineers, General Hodges, Infantry, Danford, Field Artillery, Huebner from your Section, and the corresponding man from G-1, and take them down to Belvoir to see a day's work and to talk over the whole matter with the various individuals concerned. Maybe there is a good idea here, and as Belvoir is very convenient, I think you can make a preliminary check on it in an informal manner.[3]

GCMRL/G. C. Marshall Papers (Pentagon Office, Selected)

1. Brigadier General Harry J. Malony was the assistant chief of staff, G-3, from April 9 to 23, 1941.
2. Lieutenant Colonel William M. Hoge (U.S.M.A., 1916) was the executive officer of the Engineer Replacement Training Center at Fort Belvoir, Virginia.
3. The officers referred to are: Brigadier General John J. Kingman (U.S.M.A., 1904), assistant to the chief of Engineers; Major General Courtney H. Hodges of the Office of the Chief of Infantry; Major General Robert M. Danford (U.S.M.A., 1904), the chief of Field Artillery; and Lieutenant Colonel Clarence R. Huebner, chief of the G-3 division's Training Branch.

O N March 1, 1941, the Senate passed Senate Resolution 71, authorizing the establishment of a special committee to investigate the mobilization program, including the procurement of munitions and the construction of cantonments and industrial plants. On April 22 Marshall testified before the Truman Committee—named for Harry S. Truman, Democrat from Missouri, who had drafted the resolution and was chairman of the committee. In broad terms, the chief of staff sketched the military and industrial mobilization, emphasizing the time factor in production and the need to create a field army from the nation's scattered, understrength units. He noted that Congress had cut appropriations for the 1940 maneuvers. The fall of France had quickly shifted public opinion and the opinion of business leaders; the latter, Marshall said, changed from an attitude of "dividend considerations to one of purely patriotic considerations." (Special Committee Investigating the National Defense Program, *Investigation of the National Defense Program, Hearings* [Washington: GPO, 1941], pp. 160–63.)

An immediate, balanced mobilization had been impossible, the chief of staff noted, because detailed studies of the 1940 European campaigns had not been available until spring 1941. Only then could the army design its armored force, Air Corps, and support units to fight a modern war. Marshall then explained that cantonment construction and materiel procurement depended on advance knowledge of this new troop organization, which was not possible in 1940. Detailed plans made prior to 1941 were based on the experience of the World War and prompted costly, last-minute changes. (Ibid., pp. 164–70.)

Marshall acknowledged that many additional expenditures had resulted from insufficient planning. Using the example of housing costs for the Forty-fourth Division, Marshall justified his spending policy: "There was a feeling on the part of the staff that the sum ought to be pared down. I didn't think so. I didn't think we could afford at that time to jeopardize morale, to risk health and entail great many other risks that would be far more serious than a possible overestimate on the part of the authorities." (Ibid., p. 176.)

Pursuing this theme of morale, Truman asked if the mobilizing National Guard and Reserves possessed a "one-army spirit." The chief of staff answered with praise for the reserve officers that provided the bulk of the army's officer corps. "I might say in that connection . . . that the most valuable single measure of national defense we had available was the Reserve Corps built up by the R.O.T.C. That has been of more positive assistance in meeting this emergency than any other single thing that has been provided by the Congress." Marshall believed that their technical competence was superior to the hastily trained World War I officers. (Ibid., p. 178.)

Turning to the policy of selective promotion, Marshall spoke to the committee on leadership: "If leadership depends purely on seniority you are defeated before you start. You give a good leader very little and he will succeed; you give mediocrity a great deal and they will fail. That is illustrated everywhere I turn. These rapid tours I make around the country disclose that as the most impressive thing. You see the effect of leadership in handling the flu, in the construction of a cantonment, in doing anything. It depends on leadership." (Ibid., p. 180.) ★

MEMORANDUM FOR THE PRESIDENT   April 23, 1941
Confidential   [Washington, D.C.]

Subject: Training of Air Pilots for United Kingdom in the United States.[1]

Preliminary Training:

Under previous arrangements the War Department has prepared plans to establish six elementary—basic flying schools to be turned over to the British, to maintain an annual production of 3,000 pilots. To put this into effect, authority is needed for the expenditure of lease-loan funds sufficient to set up and in effect purchase the entire installation to be turned over to the British.

Later Development:

Prior to General Arnold's departure for London, a plan was developed proposing to devote one-third of our pilot training capacity for the training of British pilots. From London he cables the British acceptance of this proposition and their proposal that the arrangements be prepared by British representatives duly appointed, with our people. This involves not only the basic training but additional preliminary training and a full program of advanced training. It is to secure a production of 4,000 pilots annually.[2]

Authority is requested to proceed with this matter, amalgamating the two programs involving a total of approximately 7,000 pilots annually, except as to a deficiency in advanced training for 3,000 pilots, which at the present time we cannot see our way clear to meet.

GCMRL/G. C. Marshall Papers (Pentagon Office, Selected)

1. On Air Corps assistance to Great Britain, see Memorandum for General Arnold, February 14 and 27, 1941, pp. 422–23 and 433, and Memorandum for the Secretary of War, March 10, 1941, pp. 439–40.

2. At his April 13, 1941, meeting with the British staff in London, Arnold arranged for training British pilots in the United States, lending American pilots to assist in ferrying aircraft to the United Kingdom, and establishing a Greenland-Iceland air route across the Atlantic. (H. H. Arnold, *Global Mission* [New York: Harper and Brothers, 1949], p. 216.)

MEMORANDUM FOR GENERAL WATSON April 23, 1941
Secret Washington, D.C.

General Greely, who had been in command of the District, has been promoted to the command of the Second Division at San Antonio.[1] This leaves a vacancy for the District command.

The troops involved are those stationed at Fort Myer, the Arlington Cantonment, and the Headquarters Company located near the Munitions Building. The District Commander has a competent staff to coordinate military plans concerning the District, to arrange for ceremonies, such as parades, etc. The Commander himself has a great many obligations of a semi-official nature—social and otherwise.

Normally we would bring in a Brigadier General of the Regular Army and assign him to this post, thereby creating a vacancy somewhere in the field which would have to be filled by promotion.

Under the present circumstances, I think it advisable to order to active duty Brigadier General Albert L. Cox, of the Reserve Corps for the command of the District. He is also the Commander of the National Guard of the District, but these troops have been inducted into active service of the Federal Government. General Cox has no command in the National Guard

Divisions and, therefore, was not inducted. However, he holds a commission in the Reserve Corps as a Brigadier General.

Cox knows nothing of my idea on the subject. He has made no application for the job and brought no pressure to bear. I have been under continuous pressure from high ranking officers of the Reserve Corps to order them to active duty. In this connection the trouble is, the senior ranks of the Reserve Corps are the weakest sections of the Reserve Corps, including less of preparation and efficiency and more of mediocrity than is found among the lieutenants and captains. The detail of Cox to active duty, especially as the troops concerned are all Regulars, would do much to off-set the irritating pressures for the detail actively of other senior officers. At the same time I think Cox, who has a pronounced flair for public-spirited activities, might be very helpful in meeting the necessities for looking after soldiers on leave in Washington from Meade, Belvoir, Quantico, etc. Should a serious situation develop in the District and it appeared, after some experience, that Cox was not fully competent to handle the situation, his assignment elsewhere could be managed.

I did not care to discuss this with the Secretary, who may have objections, without some indication of whether or not such detail would be acceptable to the President.[2]

G. C. Marshall

NA/RG 165 (OCS, 18861-157)

1. Brigadier General John N. Greely had taken command of the Second Division in March.

2. Edwin M. Watson returned the memorandum to Marshall with the note "OK EMW" penned at the top of the first page. Cox was designated the commanding general of the Washington Provisional Brigade.

To Lieutenant General Hugh A. Drum   April 26, 1941
[Washington, D.C.]

My dear Drum: The attached letter from a soldier of the 44th Division, presumably a selectee, was addressed to one of the Assistant Secretaries.[1] I turned it over to McNair for his reaction, and was advised by him that possibly, or rather probably this particular man's nose was a little out of joint because of failure to be promoted, and that from General McNair's observation and that of his staff officers, there was a good bit of truth to what this man said.

I have found widely contrasting conditions in National Guard divisions, due largely to the character of young officers commissioned during the past six months. In some divisions better than 50% of these men were selected from the product of the ROTC, in others no ROTC graduate had been commissioned. The contrast in efficiency was marked, particularly as evidenced in the instruction of the selectees. The lack of the really fine background of instruction in technique given the ROTC product, was marked in the case of those commissioned directly from the ranks. The latter officers frequently do not know how to use the manuals, and we found many cases where they did not even know of the existence of the manuals. Once the elementary recruit instruction period had been completed there was a serious falling off in the standards of instruction, along with an increase of criticism and irritation on the part of alert, well educated men who had been called on to give up a year of their lives to the service of the Government.

I have used one illustration a great many times, and may have repeated it to you, but it illustrates very clearly I think the difficulties of the present situation. The ROTC graduate has fired a battery sixty times before he obtains a commission. I have gone through a National Guard division and questioned practically every 2d lieutenant in the artillery, and rarely have ever found a man who has fired a gun more than once, and usually more than 50% of them have never fired a battery at all. The same applies pretty generally to the 1st lieutenants and I found captains with much less experience in actual direction of battery firing than the ROTC's before he obtains a commission.

I think one of our most serious reactions in connection with the Selective Service Act, which may adversely affect its continuance, will be generated by the alert, well ordered minds of many selectees who have been assigned to National Guard divisions. Therefore, we must do everything in our power to remedy this situation.   Faithfully yours,

NA/RG 165 (OCS, 17529–106)
1. The editors have not found this letter.

MEMORANDUM FOR THE SECRETARY OF WAR   April 28, 1941
Confidential   Washington, D.C.

Subject: Civilian Aide to the Commander of the Field Forces.

As Commander of the Field Forces pro tem, it seems to me desirable that I have available a civilian reaction on the development of the field forces, training centers, etc.[1]

To be of real value to me, the man would have to have a reasonably good background on Army requirements, as well as a practical understanding of the influences of the human factors involved in the military mobilization of a democracy like ours. What I have in mind is, such a man traveling about the country where he could see what is going on with the troops, with no specific objective in mind other than the intense interest of a patriotic citizen. His reactions might relate to any subject that seemed of importance to bring to my attention.

There are very few people that I would be willing to risk on such a basis of contact with Army, Corps and Division Commanders, Corps Area Commanders, and lower echelons. Outstanding in my mind is Mr. Osborn.[2] I spoke to him about this and he seemed interested, but before considering the matter any further, I would like to have your approval or disapproval both as to the idea in general, and as to the individual in particular.[3]

G. C. Marshall

NA/RG 165 (OCS, SGS, Notes on Conferences File)

1. Concerning Marshall's role as the commander of the Field Forces, see the editorial note on p. 3.

2. Frederick H. Osborn was chairman of the Joint Army and Navy Committee on Welfare and Recreation, which advised the secretaries of war and navy on morale questions.

3. Stimson returned the memorandum to the chief of staff with the following handwritten note at the bottom: "Osborn is so vitally important now as head of the Morale Advisory Com that I do not like to let him go. I took this same position as to his becoming Director of Selective Service and he gave that up. Could you get someone else? HLS"

APPEARING before the subcommittee of the House Appropriations Committee on April 28 and 30, 1941, Marshall testified in support of the 1942 Military Establishment Appropriation Bill for $6,565,424,331. The bulk of this appropriation covered Air Corps purchases of aircraft, engines, and spare parts. In addition, the army proposed to complete its purchases of critical and essential materiel for its 1,418,000-man Protective Mobilization Plan force and critical items for a 2,000,000-man force. (House Appropriations Committee, *Military Establishment Appropriation Bill for 1942, Hearings* [Washington: GPO, 1941], pp. 5–20.)

Reviewing the past year's events, the chief of staff reminded the subcommittee: "Europe did blaze in the late spring and then burst into an incredible catastrophe with the fall of France. The Congress did, step by step, make available to the War Department the means for putting the military house in order. But all occurred with almost lightning rapidity, and time rather than money became the vital issue in a chaotic world." The last year had necessitated changes in mobilization plans and the new appropriation bill would pay for them, Marshall argued. (Ibid., p. 4.)

Comparing the mobilization then under way with that in 1917, Marshall noted: "There has been an opportunity to organize on a very much better basis. There has been more uniformity, more careful inspection, more education, and more logical development." (Ibid., p. 36.)

Questioned about the excessive cost of military construction, Marshall reiterated his April 22 testimony. The "political processes of the Government which require the War Department to follow certain procedure," the chief of staff declared, had contributed to the problem. Congress appropriated only a portion of his 1940 requests: "You did not give me anything for Alaska. I got only 57 planes last March, and no money for Alaska of the $12,700,000 we asked for." (Ibid., p. 37.)

Looking toward the future, Marshall advised the congressmen on preparedness: "I believe that selective service provides the only practical and economical method of maintaining the military force that we inevitably are going to be required to have in the future and I think, with all my heart, that selective service is a necessity to the maintenance of a true democracy." (Ibid., p. 39.)

Should peace return, Marshall recommended, "we should have all of the necessary available facilities to maintain the military program we think is necessary for our security. . . . We should have a very carefully defined policy of providing, through sufficient appropriation, of funds for research both as to better types of materiel and as to the means of rapidly manufacturing whatever is required. Such a policy would mean a tremendous saving, because it would cut down the reserves to be maintained." (Ibid., p. 55.)

On June 5, 1941, the House Appropriations Committee recommended a $9,800,000,000 appropriation for fiscal year 1942. This included a $25,000,000 emergency fund for the chief of staff and the provision permitting him to purchase munitions for the new armored force as needed. (Watson, *Chief of Staff*, p. 217.) ★

MEMORANDUM FOR ADMIRAL STARK   April 29, 1941
Secret   [Washington, D.C.]

Dear Betty: In our studies and efforts to develop the situation in Greenland we have a great many difficulties. We are in the process of constructing a suitable landing field on the west coast of Greenland for the staging of aircraft via Newfoundland and Iceland to England. It should make possible the ferrying of medium and light bombardment aircraft, and it is possible that this route may be in operation before the end of the summer.[1]

We are initiating a survey of the east coast of Greenland and the northeast coast of Labrador to locate possible fields for the purpose of staging pursuit aircraft on trans-Atlantic flights. The construction and supply of fields in this area presents so many difficult problems that there is little chance of completing a field on the east coast before the end of the summer of 1942. In fact it is rather probable that this route may be found impracticable.

Our Air people feel that more emphasis should be placed on the possibilities of utilizing sea-borne carriers for the purpose of ferrying pursuit planes. Such carriers might be improvised or of primary construction for this particular purpose. However, this is entirely a Naval slant to the development, and I would appreciate very much your reactions on the subject.[2]

GCMRL/G. C. Marshall Papers (Pentagon Office, Selected)

1. On April 9, 1941, the United States and Denmark signed an agreement regarding Greenland. It clarified the United States role in the defense of that island, granting rights to construct, maintain, and operate landing fields and other facilities. Army and navy surveying teams sailed from the United States on March 18 to explore the south of Greenland for possible airbase sites. (Wesley Frank Craven and James Lea Cate, *Plans and Early Operations: January 1939 to August 1942,* a volume in *The Army Air Forces in World War II* [Chicago: University of Chicago Press, 1948–58], p. 122.) Continuing on its own construction program in Greenland, the army opened its first airfield in October 1941. (Watson, *Chief of Staff,* p. 486.)

2. The chief of naval operations requested that two army transport ships, the *Manhattan* and the *Washington,* be turned over to the navy for conversion to aircraft carriers. These could be used to ferry planes across the Atlantic Ocean. The army rejected the proposal; in a May 14, 1941, memorandum to Stark—drafted by the Supply Division, G-4—Marshall noted that the army needed all its usable transports. New ships or those badly in need of repair could be converted. (This correspondence is in NA/RG 165 [G-4, 29717-65].)

SPEECH TO THE CHAMBER OF COMMERCE
OF THE UNITED STATES[1]
April 29, 1941
Washington, D.C.

The Army.

. . . I now reach the point of talking about your business as it relates to my business. Preparations today for any military effort for defense involve not only men and the proverbial rifle that is hung over the fireplace—but they involve materiel on a vast scale, of which you have heard a great deal; it is a war of smoke-stacks as well as of men. We need every possible assistance from industry; we need the most expeditious and most completely coordinated assistance that you can give us. We need a symmetrical development, and that means that every sub-contractor, as well as every general contractor or manufacturer and industrialist, must contribute in the same measure of effort and on the same ratio as to time.

You can have a very large instrument, a very impressive instrument, and have it wholly ineffective because it lacks an essential part, and that essential part is often a very small piece of the whole, but it is absolutely necessary to the operation of the main instrument. So this must be a symmetrical development.

I sometimes think that we have an unfortunate habit in the Army of talking about a balanced force. That terminology is not stimulating to thought and people do not understand exactly what we mean. However, in referring to materiel and its relation to industry, we do have great need of a balanced production—which is equivalent to a balanced force in terms of war.

We are in need of all the effort you can manage; the more you do, and the more effectively it is done, the stronger will be our position.

We are also in need, from you ladies and gentlemen, of your influence with the people back home to win their appreciation of what our soldiers are doing in the camps. There is nothing glamorous about training in the mud; there will be nothing glamorous about the long marches in the heat and dust and the difficulties and the hardships that will be involved in the tremendous maneuvers that we will conduct next summer. These young soldiers will do almost anything. I think they *will* do anything, if their efforts are appreciated, and their efforts can only be appreciated if the people at home understand the situation. I am not talking just about the man's family—I am talking about the general public. I feel sometimes that we are diverted from the main issue by so much of statistics about this or that, so much of argument about this delay or that delay, this opinion or that opinion. We have a great Army in the making; it is coming into its own; it needs things, but it needs more than anything else the understanding and appreciative support from every side and on every hand in this country.

GCMRL/G. C. Marshall Papers (Pentagon Office, Speeches)

1. Marshall addressed the twenty-ninth annual meeting of the Chamber of Commerce of the United States. In the bulk of his address, he discussed the importance of the maneuvers and the creation of corps and field armies—the essential organizations of the army team in war. The last 30 percent of the address is printed here.

MEMORANDUM FOR THE STAFF
May 2, 1941
[Washington, D.C.]

At midnight last night General Watson telephoned me that the President had received a telegram from the Governor of Arkansas to the following effect: That he had a serious situation at Arkansas City; that a negro was to be tried for rape; that he was sure they could not bring the negro to trial without troops for protection; that he requested two companies of infantry from Camp Robinson for duty probably not to exceed 36 to 48 hours. General Watson informed me that the President desired compliance with the Governor's request.[1]

General Watson was informed that under the terms of the present law, the

President had to issue a proclamation. General Watson stated the President had gone to bed and had left the arrangement of the matter with him. He was going to notify the Governor and I told him not to do that, but to leave the notification of the Governor to be made by the Commander of the corps area, General Strong, and I would telephone him.[2]

I talked to General Gullion over the 'phone, who explained the legal requirements as to the proclamation.[3] This is based on an address to people assembled for unlawful purposes. There is no assembly and action is in anticipation of an assembly. General Gullion thought the proclamation might be signed by the President but no publicity given it. He suggested that it be delivered to the U.S. Marshal. I objected to this because under the President's direction the troops would be sent to the scene and I did not wish the military commander to be exposed to the hazards of action against his command or in the face of his command with someone, possibly at a distant point, determining whether or not the President's proclamation should be publicized. He suggested sending it to the Governor. I opposed this for the same reason. If the troops were to be present at the scene of possible disturbance the commander should not be left dependent on some other party to take the determining action. General Gullion agreed. It was arranged that the proclamation and as later advised should be ready early in the morning—this morning.

I telephoned General Strong at Fort Omaha. He had already arranged for a plane to stand by with his Assistant Chief of Staff for Operations, Colonel Fred Miller, prepared to leave on short notice. He had not discussed the matter with General Truman, the Division Commander at Fort Robinson, Little Rock. General Strong had previously been advised to have no contact with the Governor, but to arrange matters so as to take prompt action if the President decided to authorize the use of the troops.[4]

I instructed General Strong to communicate with the Governor immediately, particularly to learn when the trouble was expected. The President apparently thought it was an immediate matter. General Gullion had informed me that Senator Caraway's secretary had told him during the afternoon it would not come to a head for about three days.[5]

I instructed General Strong to arrange with General Truman to send two companies to Arkansas City. I explained to him the legal technicalities with regard to the proclamation and that our intention was to have the proclamation delivered to the troop commander. General Strong requested that it be delivered to Colonel Miller, his representative, who was an officer of excellent judgment and who would be present. I told him I thought this would be the arrangement and would notify him this morning.

I had covered these details with Colonel Smith, of my staff, who was instructed to notify General Lear, the Army Commander, to release the two companies referred to and to notify General Strong accordingly. Incidentally I had told General Strong that these were my orders, even if he had not heard from Lear. General Lear had been notified earlier in the day to that effect, but General Strong did not receive notice of the release of the companies. Colonel Smith was directed by me to telephone General Lear to notify General Strong immediately of the release of the troops. Colonel Smith talked to the duty officer at General Lear's headquarters on the 'phone, and he was to notify the Chief of Staff of the Army, General Robinson.[6]

The duty officer at General Lear's headquarters telephoned Colonel Smith later on that the Governor specifically requested that Arkansas troops be not sent, and Colonel Smith directed that General Strong be notified accordingly and that the selection be left to General Truman.[7]

GCMRL/G. C. Marshall Papers (Pentagon Office, Selected)

1. Homer Adkins was the governor of Arkansas. The defendant was John Henry Riney.
2. Major General George V. Strong had been commanding general of the Seventh Corps Area since December 1940.
3. Major General Allen W. Gullion (U.S.M.A., 1905) had been the judge advocate general since December 1, 1937.
4. Strong's operations officer was Lieutenant Colonel Fred W. Miller. Major General Ralph E. Truman commanded the Thirty-fifth Division of the National Guard.
5. Hattie W. Caraway, Democrat from Arkansas, had been senator since 1931.
6. Lieutenant Colonel Walter B. Smith was an assistant secretary of the General Staff. Lieutenant General Ben Lear commanded the Second Army. Brigadier General Donald A. Robinson was chief of staff of Second Army.
7. The army sent the 140th Infantry Regiment of the Missouri National Guard to Arkansas City. Riney admitted his guilt on the witness stand. (*Washington Post*, May 18, 1941, p. 14.)

MEMORANDUM FOR THE SECRETARY OF WAR   May 3, 1941
                                            Washington, D.C.

Subject: Commander for the Third Army.

General Brees, the present commander of the Third Army, goes on leave preparatory to retirement, on May 15th. He retires June 30th, but I desired his earlier departure in order that the new Army Commander would be in charge throughout the approaching period of the Corps and Army Maneuvers. The senior army corps commander of that region is permanent Major General Walter Krueger. I wish to place him in command of that Army on May 15th.

General Krueger is a few weeks my junior in years, and was my senior in rank. He has been one of the intellectuals of the Army; is a very hard worker; is of the German type; won his commission from the ranks in the

Philippines in 1901. Krueger was head of the War Plans Division when made a brigadier general in 1936. Later on he was commander of the second triangular division at San Antonio, and of one of the improvised army corps in the maneuvers of last May in Louisiana.

General Brees considers General Krueger the proper successor for him, and as it was desirable in the development of the plans for the major maneuvers in June, July and August, I permitted Brees to tell Krueger that I had in mind proposing him for the command. If Krueger is passed over, I am inclined to think his efficiency as a corps commander would be affected.

I attach a confidential letter of mine to Krueger regarding his personal traits as a leader, and his acknowledgment.[1]

G. C. Marshall

GCMRL/G. C. Marshall Papers (Pentagon Office, Selected)

1. See Marshall to Krueger, April 14, 1941, pp. 473–74. In a handwritten postscript, Marshall noted: "The approval of the President is not necessary." Secretary Stimson returned the memorandum to Marshall with his approval.

MEMORANDUM FOR THE SECRETARY OF WAR May 5, 1941
[Washington, D.C.]

Subject: Important matters under Consideration.

1. The instructions for the commanders of bases in British possessions, withheld last week at the direction of the President—presumably on the request of Mr. Hull—leaves the commanders concerned without guidance in the event of emergency. If Mr. Hull is to secure a modification of the present instructions, I think a decision should be reached as quickly as possible.[1]

2. The President has directed that, on the request of the Governor of Arkansas, two companies of infantry be sent to Arkansas City to prevent the possible lynching at the time of the trial of a negro for rape. The date for the trial is May 15th. A Presidential proclamation is necessary, and a draft has been prepared by General Gullion and O.K'd by the Solicitor General. Signature by the President should be obtained as soon as possible in order that the Proclamation may be placed in the hands of General Strong, the Corps Area Commander, to be issued by the Commander of the troops *in the event* that a mob gathers.

3. The matter of General Miles's successor remains to be determined. The vacancy to which I wish to assign General Miles, Commander of the First Corps Area in Boston, occurs on May 15th. There should be a commander there at that time because of the tremendous activity in preparation

for the summer program. Also General Lee, if he is to be General Miles's successor, should take over here as soon after General Miles's departure as possible.[2]

4. The designation of a new commander for the Third Army.

GCMRL/G. C. Marshall Papers (Pentagon Office, Selected)

1. According to the navy's Western Hemisphere Defense Plan Number Two of April 21, 1941, the United States assumed defense for territory west of twenty-six degrees longitude and including Greenland and the Azores. Should naval vessels or aircraft from belligerent nations which did not have possessions in the hemisphere cross this line, they would be warned; if the warning was ignored, they would be attacked. The army drafted instructions to its base commanders in Bermuda, Trinidad, and Newfoundland, according to the naval plan. At this point State Department officials urged caution. Secretary Stimson then redrafted the instructions on May 10, 1941, to direct army base commanders to resist any attack by belligerents with all the force at their disposal. The army did not, however, send similar instructions to the Puerto Rican and Panama Canal departments. (Conn and Fairchild, *Framework of Hemisphere Defense*, pp. 107–9.)

2. Brigadier General Sherman Miles was the assistant chief of staff, G-2. He did not assume the corps area command until February 1, 1942. Brigadier General Raymond E. Lee, military attaché in London, replaced him on that date.

To Brigadier General Lehman W. Miller[1]   May 6, 1941
Confidential   [Washington, D.C.]

Dear Miller: It is my understanding that the Brazilian Government contemplates sending two divisions to the Natal and Recife region for maneuvers this summer—meaning their winter. It occurred to me that this presented a fine opportunity to erect a milestone in cooperative effort—especially one that would be reassuring instead of alarming to the South American people.[2]

What I have in mind is that we offer to cooperate in the maneuvers by supplying the air force—a composite group of three or four squadrons—and a sample of those units which the Brazilian Army now lacks—an antiaircraft battalion or regiment, a signal battalion and maybe a battalion of engineers and some medical troops. The Brazilian commander could be the supreme official for the purpose of the maneuvers, and we would have no combatant ground troops other than antiaircraft.

I have spoken to Mr. Welles, of the State department, regarding this and he is very favorably impressed and thought the best method of approach would be a direct one between the respective military authorities.[3] I am, therefore, outlining the affair to you in order that you may sound out the Brazilian Army officials. There is no objection to your discussing the matter with Ambassador Caffery.

Our people have been studying the possibility of carrying out such a procedure and, of course, find that the principal difficulty would be securing the necessary shipping to put the ground forces into Brazil and awaiting the time for their withdrawal. I would dislike sending our Air force without anything of ours on the ground in support. However, the first step would be to determine the possible reaction of the Brazilians to such a move. My guess, and of course it is purely a guess, is that the people would respond to this as they did to the visit of the Flying Fortresses. So long as we do not land combatant ground troops, and so long as the ground troops are the major participants and are local troops under local command, it seems to me that there is a chance of establishing a valuable precedent for cooperative action.[4]

Let me have your reactions, understanding that the entire affair is purely tentative, has not yet received Mr. Roosevelt's approval in any way, and may not be practicable of execution by us. Faithfully yours,

GCMRL/G. C. Marshall Papers (Pentagon Office, General)

1. Miller was head of the United States Military Mission to Brazil.
2. In March 1941 the Brazilian government informed Miller of its intention to garrison the northeastern states with three infantry divisions reinforced by antiaircraft units; the United States was asked to supply the units with modern equipment. When this request was rejected by the War Department in late March, Brazil opted to hold maneuvers in that region in August and September 1941. (Conn and Fairchild, *Framework of Hemisphere Defense*, p. 283.)
3. Marshall had discussed Brazil with Under Secretary of State Sumner Welles and Admiral Stark at a meeting of the Standing Liaison Committee at the State Department on the afternoon of May 5, 1941.
4. The Brazilian government was not convinced of the Axis threat to Latin America. Internal differences of opinion about a United States military presence in Brazil blocked negotiations between the two nations. (Ibid.) Concerning the stationing of troops in Northeast Brazil, see Memorandum for War Plans Division, June 21, 1941, p. 548.

To Mrs. James J. Winn   May 6, 1941
                                                  [Washington, D.C.]

Dear Molly: I have been a long time in acknowledging your letters, but there has been too much pressure and too much business, both of which are on a continuous increase.

We are so pleased that you find your surroundings and life delightful apparently in every respect. I was amused at your report to me on my series of advices, but I am glad that you did treat them seriously.

Clifton is in the hospital; Marie is here—arrived yesterday; Tris left Sunday afternoon having been here a week; Edmund Coles spent one day with us and Dr. and Mrs. Perry, of Phillips Exeter, spent 24 hours with us ten days ago. So you see the hotel still functions.[1]

The yard looks lovely now, everything is in bloom. Fleet is crazy about getting in the car when I go horse-back riding. The trouble is, he gets into anybody's car. Dumcke removed him from a stranger's car recently near the Lee mansion, where he was eating sandwiches, and yesterday the military police brought him home from Arlington cemetery. He sits down in front of all the automobiles, but as yet the Lord has been good. However, I fear the law of averages will prevail and he will have a tragedy.[2]

I sent Rosetta and Trail Runner down to Belvoir on Monday. Colonel and Mrs. Hoge will exercise them and I plan to ride there from time to time. I think Mrs. Hoge will give Rosetta fine training. Clifton had ridden her the three days before he went into the hospital. I suppose you know that she dumped Allen over her head.

I was to have left for Alaska yesterday but had to delay; again delayed today, with no prospects of leaving tomorrow. De Witt leaves Seattle on the 9th on an engineer boat to go four days by water and the remaining way by plane. I very much wish to join him, but it looks a dubious prospect at present.

With my love and affectionate regards to you both,

GCMRL/Research File (Family)

1. Tristram Tupper, a writer, was Mrs. Marshall's brother. Lewis Perry, Sr., was the principal of Phillips Exeter Academy.

2. Fleet, a dalmatian, had been given to the Marshalls by Edward R. Stettinius, Jr. Mrs. Marshall called the dog "beautiful but dumb. However, he loved his master with a devotion and adoration so complete that George's heart was touched. Fleet, in fact, was the one stupid thing in which I have ever known him to take delight." (K. T. Marshall, *Together,* p. 137.) Sergeant George Dumcke was the chief of staff's driver.

To Mrs. Allen T. Brown   May 7, 1941
[Washington, D.C.]

Dear Madge: I have not written to you and Beau for some time, but I have enjoyed your letters to Katherine.[1] My time grows more limited each day, as the pressures are constantly on the increase.

I was supposed to have left for the West Coast Monday and have been at Monterey, California to-day, to review an army corps near Tacoma to-morrow and to have sailed for Alaska tomorrow night. As it developed, I had to go to the White House yesterday; was scheduled to go today—that was postponed, and am due to go tomorrow and possibly Friday, and so my Alaska trip depends now on my joining the Army Commander out there by a direct flight to Anchorage, over Canada to the Yukon.

My sister is here now and she and Katherine have been out to see the place, where everything is in bloom. Arrangements have been made for the repapering of the hall and the living room, work to start next week.[2] At our place at Myer, they are laying a rather intermittent paved court in rear of the house under the apple-tree where we lunch in the warm weather.

I hope that nothing interferes with my trip to West Point in June, so that I may see you.

With my love   Affectionately,

GCMRL/Research File (Family)
1. "Beau" was the family name for Allen.
2. Marshall was referring to Dodona Manor, their house in Leesburg, Virginia.

MEMORANDUM FOR THE ASSISTANT CHIEFS OF   May 7, 1941
STAFF, G-1 [HAISLIP] AND G-4 [REYBOLD]   [Washington, D.C.]
Confidential

General Ulio tells me this morning that Mr. McNutt is considering a proposal to entirely remove the CCC from Army responsibility. My own reaction is that we should take it over completely or release it entirely, and in the light of the complicating factors, I think the better course is to release it.

Please look into this from the viewpoint of the changes that will be required.[1]

For the present this is confidential.

NA/RG 165 (OCS, 17622–1822)
1. On the relationship of the army to the administration of the Civilian Conservation Corps, see *Papers of GCM,* 1: 392–93. The Personnel Division of the General Staff favored release of control over the C.C.C. because the Regular officers thus made available were urgently needed for other duties. The Supply Division concurred, but noted that certain services provided by the army, such as communications and medical, would be difficult for the C.C.C. to replace. G-4 also noted that the army's assumption of total control over the C.C.C. would be complicated under existing laws. (Haislip Memorandum for Chief of Staff, May 12, 1941, NA/RG 165 [G-1, 11882–1606]; Reybold Memorandum for Chief of Staff, May 13, 1941, NA/RG 165 [G-4, 32960].) For further discussion of the army's control over the administration of the C.C.C. camps, see Marshall Memorandum for General Ulio, January 30, 1942, GCMRL/G. C. Marshall Papers [Pentagon Office, Selected].)

MEMORANDUM FOR GENERAL HENRY W. BAIRD   May 8, 1941
                                                [Washington, D.C.]

General Bryden on returning from his recent inspection trip to Pine Camp reports to me the fact that you emphasized the necessity for sending to any new camp the house-keeping elements first, namely, the Headquarters Company, the Quartermaster Battalion, and the Engineer Battalion;

also that advance parties should be stronger—not less than 25 men per regiment, including some strong backs.

I have just discussed this matter with the officer concerned with drafting orders for the movement of troops in G-3, and he tells me that the orders from the War Department allow the necessary latitude to the local commanders in control of such matters. What you emphasized to General Bryden is plain common sense, to put it mildly—what I am surprised at is the necessity for emphasizing it. Please let me have your comments on how the details of your movement were arranged.[1]

I am sending a copy of this to General Chaffee.

NA/RG 165 (OCS, 19575-34)

1. Brigadier General Baird commanded the Fourth Armored Division, which had recently moved to the Pine Plains Military Reservation (called "Pine Camp" from 1908 to 1938) in the Second Corps Area near Watertown, New York.

MEMORANDUM FOR GENERAL PHILLIPSON[1]   May 8, 1941
[Washington, D.C.]

Subject: Morale Matters.

General Bryden has just returned from an inspection trip in the First and Second Corps Areas, and brings to my attention certain matters with relation to morale.

Specifically, he reports a lack in facilities at Pine Camp. General Ulio tells me that *since* General Bryden's report he had directed that special moving picture equipment be expressed to Pine Camp and that a motion picture engineer from Washington has left for Pine Camp to install the equipment in the converted recreation building. Other measures of corrective action have also been taken. But the point is, we should not have to initiate corrective measures in Washington. Has your Morale officer been to Pine Camp and made any recommendations, or taken any action?

It seems to me all possible or practicable measures should be taken in advance of the arrival of the troops. The effect on morale is very marked in either case, favorably if there are evidences of pre-vision in their interest, and unfavorably if there is a long delay before the appropriate measures are taken.

Please check up on this, because I continue to find the same situation time after time as officers of the War Department move about in the field.

GCMRL/G. C. Marshall Papers (Pentagon Office, General)

1. Major General Irving J. Phillipson (U.S.M.A., 1904) was commanding general of the Second Corps Area.

MEMORANDUM FOR THE SECRETARY OF WAR   May 12, 1941
[Washington, D.C.]

Subject: Sale of Light Beer in Post Exchanges.

Senator Sheppard introduced a bill (S. 860, copy attached) restricting the sale of beer in cantonments and their immediate vicinity. The feeling of all the troop commanders I have seen, notably men like Haskell, is that such a restriction for cantonments would inevitably drive men away from the cantonments to dives and honky tonks, with unfortunate results.

The issue, of course, is an old one, but unfortunately it is being revived at the present time when we have the situation under excellent control. There is justification for considering beer of less than 3.2% alcoholic content (now being sold) as non-intoxicating. Although the Act of March 22, 1933, which so defined 3.2% beer was repealed with the repeal of prohibition, it was the last pronouncement of Congress on the subject, and the beer now being sold in our post exchanges complies strictly with its provisions. The automobile makes former zone limitations more or less ineffective, as it is easy for the soldier to visit places where we have no control over what is sold, or over the character and orderliness of the premises. Our troubles begin when men leave the reservation to find liquor, and the incentive to do this is stronger when they cannot get legal beer at home.

Some time back I gave an hour to the president of the WCTU and her working committee, I have written many letters explaining our point of view; and now I am receiving a deluge of letters from mothers, all of which follow a certain form, pressing for the passage of Senator Sheppard's bill.

As this is a matter of great public interest, I wanted to bring the immediate situation to your attention.[1]

GCMRL/G. C. Marshall Papers (Pentagon Office, Selected)
 1. Mrs. Ida B. Wise Smith was president of the Woman's Christian Temperance Union. On June 30 the Senate voted to drop the sections of S. 860 pertaining to alcoholic beverages.

TO BRIGADIER GENERAL HARVEY C. ALLEN[1]   May 13, 1941
[Washington, D.C.]

Dear Allen: This is an informal note to tell you that I have had various reports about the conditions in your nearby town as relates to the soldiers. I am told that the local Government is not above reproach; also that you get little cooperation from them, to the hazard of the young men of your command.

Please write me informally and directly and tell me what the situation is, and if you have any suggestions as to how I might help, include them. Faithfully yours,

P.S.   Is your Morale officer involved in other duties?[2]

GCMRL/G. C. Marshall Papers (Pentagon Office, General)

1. Allen was the commanding general of the Antiaircraft Training Center at Camp Hulen, Texas.

2. Although his morale officer was working full time at his duties, Allen noted in a lengthy response, the small town of Palacios did not have the facilities to handle his eleven thousand-man command. He suggested that the War Department support the construction of recreational facilities in the town and provide him with funds for construction on the base. (Allen to Marshall, May 19, 1941, GCMRL/G. C. Marshall Papers [Pentagon Office, General].)

MEMORANDUM FOR THE ASSISTANT CHIEF   May 14, 1941
OF STAFF, G-3 [TWADDLE]   [Washington, D.C.]

Subject: Defense Against Armored Forces.

In considering the attached G-3 paper pertaining to the defense against armored forces, I am certain that one of our urgent needs is for development, organization and immediate action on the subject of defense against armored forces, to include an *offensive weapon and organization* to combat these forces. While antitank defense normally should be a responsibility of each arm, defense against armored forces is a problem possibly beyond the capabilities of any one arm and probably requiring the organization and use of a special force of combined arms, capable of rapid movement, interception and active rather than passive defense tactics. The organization, tactical doctrine, and development of such a force seems beyond the scope of any Chief of Arm and needs thorough coordination as well as strong direction.[1]

At the risk of placing G-3 in the operating field, I believe that for the solution of this problem you should take energetic and positive steps to push this matter as fast as humanly possible. The subject should be attacked with imagination and with untiring effort. I believe that it is a function of the General Staff and should be initiated and carried through in your office. I do not want the question of another branch or arm brought up at this time.

There seems to be an element missing in the War Department General Staff, namely a group whose sole responsibility is thinking and planning on improved methods of warfare. Our organization and methods should not lag behind developments abroad. You should organize in your division a small planning and exploring branch, composed of visionary officers, with nothing else to do but think out improvements in methods of warfare, study developments abroad and tackle such unsolved problems as measures against armored force action, night bombardment, march protection and the like. Such a group should be divorced of all current matters and should work closely with the National Defense Research Committee, Inventors' Council, G-2 and the development people in G-4.[2]

GCMRL/G. C. Marshall Papers (Pentagon Office, Selected)

1. Considerable controversy attended the formulation of antitank doctrine after the fall of France. One theory held that armored forces should directly counter the advance of hostile tanks. Proponents of the opposing position, including Major General Lesley J. McNair, argued that specialized antitank units provided the most effective defense. On April 14, 1941, Marshall asked the G-3 division to study the creation of mobile antitank and antiaircraft units organized at the corps and army echelons. On April 29, he requested its opinion on their assumption of responsibility for the development, organization, and tactical doctrine of these units, which he hoped to activate for the autumn 1941 maneuvers. Marshall also proposed that G-3 coordinate all War Department studies on antitank and antiaircraft doctrine in the future. (Orlando Ward Memorandums for the Assistant Chief of Staff, G-3, April 14 and 29, 1941, NA/RG 165 [OCS, 21103–6]; Kent R. Greenfield, Robert R. Palmer, and Bell I. Wiley, *The Organization of Ground Combat Troops*, a volume in the *United States Army in World War II* [Washington: GPO, 1947], pp. 73–78.)

2. On May 15, 1941, a planning branch was established in the G-3 division to study foreign military developments and problems in modern warfare. This branch utilized information and facilities provided by the Military Intelligence and Supply divisions of the General Staff, the National Defense Research Committee, and the National Inventors' Council, as well as the chiefs of the arms and services within the War Department. (William E. Chambers Memorandum, May 15, 1941, NA/RG 165 [OCS, 21103–6].)

To Lieutenant General Hugh A. Drum   May 14, 1941
                                                  [Washington, D.C.]

Dear Drum: With reference to your letter of May 5, the purpose in establishing the Morale Branch and more particularly in making the Morale Officer in the various echelons, down to and including division, a special staff officer was intended to bring forcibly to the attention of all Army personnel and Commanders the extreme importance of the matter. Also, we had examples of serious failures or omissions in meeting this problem, and examples of outstanding performances in maintaining morale under distressingly unfavorable conditions.[1]

Training has been properly the principal consideration, but some leaders and chiefs of staff have allowed this to cloud the issue of cause and effect as to morale.

When the Morale Officer under our former organization was assistant to the Adjutant General the function of morale became fixed in the minds of some commanders as of secondary importance. Since it is rather intangible, it requires considerable initiative, authority, and imaginative thinking. It usually happened that the other more tangible duties were carried out, and little time was left for the much more important question of morale.

Under current conditions the Army and Corps officers will have less specific duties to perform than would be the case in the field, yet the effect on the lower echelons will be more pointed if even in this stage special staff officers be available to you and your Corps Commanders for whatever suggestions, assistance, and coordination they may be able to achieve. Their inspection and supervision duties will require a great deal of work and travel. Incidentally, every time your friend Jimmie Ulio goes on the road, and he travels pretty continuously, he finds deficiencies that should have been picked up locally and corrected long since.   Faithfully yours,

GCMRL/G. C. Marshall Papers (Pentagon Office, Selected)

1. The editors have not found Drum's letter. For an earlier discussion of the problem of morale, see Memorandum for the Secretary of War, February 6, 1941, pp. 407–8.

TO LIEUTENANT COLONEL CLAUDE M. ADAMS   May 14, 1941
[Washington, D.C.]

Dear Flap: I sent out to Ruth yesterday a gift from Mr. Duntz which he turned over to me as I left by small boat for my plane at Ocean Beach Monday morning. Both Duntz and Babe Morriss sent you many messages and seemed deeply concerned regarding your welfare.[1]

I had good luck on the weather this trip, but a little bad luck otherwise. We were simply pestered to death by people coming in to talk over "the situation." A perfect stranger got into the house Saturday night and stayed for 2½ hours. We went down town for dinner Saturday and I practically did not get to eat, as someone seemed always standing beside the table—being very pleasant and gracious but making it pretty difficult to get any relaxation. Fire Island has always been free of this sort of thing, so I was disappointed.

We did a lot of work about the cottage and the yard; found everything in excellent condition, and the set-up now quite luxurious with the new complete equipment in the kitchen, hot water, etc. Katherine is coming back Friday.

Business here grows still more pressing, with many outside meetings at the State Department and the White House.

I have not yet been able to get out to see Clifton, but talked to him on the phone this morning.[2] He seems to be getting along well, the only difficulty being lack of pajamas.   Affectionately,

GCMRL/G. C. Marshall Papers (Pentagon Office, Selected)

1. Adams, Marshall's aide, had a history of heart disorder and had been admitted to Walter Reed General Hospital in Washington, D.C. After his recovery, he was assigned to R.O.T.C.

duty, effective August 7, 1941, at the Staunton Military Academy, Staunton, Virginia. Marshall had recently returned from a two-day rest (May 10–12) at the Fire Island cottage.
2. Marshall's stepson Clifton was also in the hospital. See Marshall to King, August 19, 1941, p. 593.

To General John J. Pershing   May 14, 1941
                                                 Washington, D.C.

Dear General: I have not been very successful in the matter of looking up apartment accommodations immediately available. I have hopes, but as yet they have not been realized.[1]

The following will be available on the dates mentioned. They are both at The Kennedy-Warren on Connecticut Avenue. I selected that apartment house because the elevator runs directly to the garage in the basement so that you can step directly from the elevator into your car thus avoiding long walks through lobbies, steps, etc. Also the Kennedy-Warren is a quieter place than most large apartment houses, has very nice people staying there, and is air-cooled and modern.

Miss (Dr.) Julia Hahn, Assistant Superintendent of Schools, wishes to sub-let her apartment for $125 a month during July and August. It consists of one large bedroom and bath, one small bedroom with half a bath, a living room 21.6 × 14.6, a dining alcove and kitchenette. Of course it is furnished and linen and silver would be included.

Mrs. Lytle, a Navy widow, wishes to sub-let her apartment at $115 a month from June 1 to October 1. It consists of one large bedroom and bath, a living room 21.6 × 14.5, dining alcove and kitchenette, furnished, linen and silver included.

I was told that both of these apartments are furnished in good taste and are most comfortable. I forgot to mention that there is a good cafe and room service.

I have surveyed some of the other apartments and eliminated most of them in my mind because, like at Wardman Park and The Shoreham, there is a long walk from the elevators to the car through crowded lobbies and, in the case of The Shoreham, also too many steps.

My Alaskan trip was stopped at the last hour by a call from the President, which continued day after day until finally his illness delayed matters so that the whole trip had to be cancelled.[2] I got away Saturday afternoon by plane and joined Katherine at Fire Island, where she was straightening up the cottage, which has been leased for this entire summer. While it was cold, I got some relaxation in working on the grounds. I also had a couple of hours sunning on the beach. I flew back early Monday morning. Katherine does not return until Friday.

I want to invite myself to lunch as soon as you will have me again.[3]
Affectionately,

G. C. Marshall

LC/J. J. Pershing Papers (General Correspondence)

1. Pershing was staying at the Carlton Hotel in Washington, D.C.

2. For the preceding three weeks, the president's advisers had debated whether to reinforce the Atlantic Fleet. In accordance with the expanded naval duties outlined in Western Hemisphere Defense Plan Number Two, Stimson, Marshall, Stark, and Secretary of the Navy Knox advocated the reinforcement. The service chiefs argued that the United States would assume a defensive posture in the Pacific in the event of war and would need additional naval strength to protect task forces that might be deployed in the Atlantic. Secretary of State Hull initially opposed any weakening of naval strength in the Pacific that might encourage Japanese expansionism. Although Hull moderated his stance, the president approved only a small reinforcement of the Atlantic Fleet on May 13. (Yale/H. L. Stimson Papers [Diary, 34: 9–14]; Conn and Fairchild, *Framework of Hemisphere Defense,* pp. 104–10.)

3. Concerned about Pershing's health, Marshall wrote their mutual friend Charles G. Dawes: "I fear you will have a great shock when you see General Pershing. Confidentially, it is very, very sad to see the change in him in the last few weeks. We had dinner together in San Antonio about six weeks ago and he looked fine. Then I had lunch with him the day after his return to Washington, and he was in good humor, but since then he has gone down hill." (Marshall to Dawes, May 22, 1941, GCMRL/G. C. Marshall Papers [Pentagon Office, Selected].)

MEMORANDUM FOR THE SECRETARY OF WAR
May 15, 1941
[Washington, D.C.]

Subject: Weekly Staff Conference.

The National Defense Act, Section 5b, provided that the Secretary of War, The Assistant Secretary of War, The General of the Army, and the Chief of Staff should constitute the War Council of the War Department, "which council shall, from time to time, meet and consider policies affecting both the military and munitions problems of the War Department. Such questions shall be presented to the Secretary of War in the War Council, and, decision with reference to such questions of policy, after consideration of the recommendations thereon by the several members of the War Council, shall constitute the policy of the War Department with reference thereto." G.O. 48, War Department 1920, announced the formation of the War Council in conformity with the law.

Mr. Woodring usually had a meeting of a so-called War Council at 11:30 each morning—the Assistant Secretary and the Chief of Staff attending. These meetings were time-consuming, and as they usually followed no definite procedure, were ineffective.

At the present time the business of the War Department has expanded so rapidly and involves so many conflicting matters, that it is believed some such meetings should be held weekly for the purpose of orientation among the principal officials.

The following is suggested as an effective manner of procedure for this purpose:

Attendance. The Secretary, the Under Secretary, the Assistant Secretaries, and the Chief of Staff (accompanied by the three Deputies)—in the office of the Secretary of War.

Time. Monday at 9:15 A.M.

Procedure. Each in turn (normally excepting the Deputies), to be prepared briefly to outline such matters as it is believed desirable in the interest of efficient administration for all to be aware of. Discussions to be curtailed as much as possible, at the time, where they pertain only to a minority of the group.

It is suggested that the Secretary of the General Staff be present to keep an outline record of the matters discussed and of any decisions reached.[1]

GCMRL/G. C. Marshall Papers (Pentagon Office, Selected)

1. Secretary Stimson approved Marshall's agenda on May 16, 1941. (John W. Martyn Memorandum for the Under Secretary of War et al., May 16, 1941, NA/RG 165 [OCS, War Council Minutes].)

INFORMAL STATEMENT[1]   May 15, 1941
                                                          [Washington, D.C.]

Necessity for Contingent Fund

We are under a very heavy handicap because of our inability to take immediate action in many urgent cases which require the expenditure of money to correct. This is due to our rigid financial procedure, relatively unimportant under normal conditions, but now embarrassing, and at times seriously detrimental to morale and effective leadership. Some comparatively minor matter may turn the scale from reasonable comfort to serious discomfort in the living conditions of thousands of Selective Service men and strike at morale. Time, in such instances, rather than money is the vital factor.

For example, we recently found that an operating room in one of our temporary hospitals could not be used because of unusual dust conditions brought on by a drought. This might have meant the difference between life and death in an emergency, and it could have been corrected immediately by installing a small air conditioning unit.[2] Under our cumbersome fiscal procedure the responsible man on the ground would either have to wait a matter of weeks or take a chance and make an illegal purchase. Of course, if he is any good, he will make the purchase, but it is not right to force him to the choice.

Recently during the influenza epidemic some of our hospital facilities were overtaxed and as there was no way immediately to increase the number of civilian employees, we had to detail selectees to help out in emptying bed-pans, scrubbing sick rooms, and taking over similar menial work. This is not a good introduction to the military service, especially in the case of older men who have relinquished important positions in civil life, and morale suffered accordingly with severe criticisms from parents, friends, political representatives and the press.[3]

Local conditions in cantonments vary greatly and impose quite different requirements. Often these matters have a direct, a pressing relationship to the morale of the command. An immediate remedy is indicated—not next week nor next month, as usually must be the case, but immediately. It does no good to say that each of these conditions should have been foreseen. It, in my opinion, was not humanly possible to do so. But even if it were, the troops should not be denied the remedy, and immediately.[4]

The solution is a flexible contingent fund. We are asking for a change in the wording of the appropriation "Contingencies of the Army" which will permit us to cut red tape and meet unforeseen emergencies without vexatious delays. Garrisons of the new Atlantic bases, are generally isolated and present a serious morale problem. It is necessary to provide them with a great deal more in the way of welfare set-up than is allotted to troops close to civilian communities in the United States. This necessity has developed as the determination of sites in the bases progressed. A contingent fund would permit us to meet these abnormal situations promptly and without complicated administrative procedure.[5]

The matter is just as important from a tactical standpoint. It was recently discovered that administrative processes were seriously delaying the repair of boats required for mine laying. Funds were available but the routine procedure is slow, and the repairs should be made without delays. They could be made from a contingent fund and the money replaced from regularly appropriated funds when administrative difficulties had been ironed out. The importance of the change in wording and the benefit to be derived from having money immediately available is out of all proportion to the amount involved. It seems to me that in the present emergency we should be trusted to exercise the proper care and judgment in regulating its expenditure, especially as we are being trusted otherwise in the matter of billions.

GCMRL/G. C. Marshall Papers (Pentagon Office, General)

1. There is no indication in the Marshall papers for whom this document was intended.

2. During his mid-April inspection trip, Marshall visited the new Infantry training center at Camp Barkeley near Abilene, Texas. There he found that the hospital was having problems with dust in the operating rooms. He then "took special pains to check up on the operating

rooms in hospitals at four other places." (Marshall to Walter Krueger, April 24, 1941, NA/RG 165 [OCS, 21101-10].)

3. The army's problems in coordinating civilian skills with army duty classifications was a constant source of discontent among newly inducted men. Writing to a base commander about a congressman's inquiries on behalf of the mother of a chemical engineer who had been assigned routine hospital duties, Marshall observed: "The other day in Texas I found a man who had successfully run his own business at a net of from $15,000 to $20,000 and who was shuffling around bed-pans in a hospital. I think he could better have coordinated the mess-halls and a number of other things." (Memorandum for the Commanding General, Chanute Field, Illinois, May 8, 1941, GCMRL/G. C. Marshall Papers [Pentagon Office, General].)

4. Commenting on his inspection-trip observations to Major General Clement A. Trott, commanding general of the Fifth Corps Area, Marshall said that he was "concerned to find serious delays in the development of the recreational possibilities which are so important at this particular period. . . . At a number of the cantonments I have been distressed over the delays in obtaining furniture and the delays in obtaining books. Please have your Morale officer check on this closely and aggressively to see that the proper action is taken, and not merely to rest on his oars if he thinks he has done his part. My interest centers exclusively on the soldier having the clothing or equipment, or what-not, available and not merely on requisition. . . . Action in favor of the troops is what is wanted." (Marshall to Trott, April 24, 1941, ibid.)

5. When the Military Establishment Appropriation Bill for 1942 was signed by President Roosevelt on June 30, 1941, it included, under the Office of the Secretary of War, the item "Contingencies of the Army, 1942," appropriating $200,000 "for all emergencies and extraordinary expenses . . . as may be determined and approved by the Secretary of War." Under the heading General Staff Corps $25,000,000 was appropriated for a "Contingent Fund, Chief of Staff, Army, 1942," which was "for such emergent military uses as the Chief of Staff may determine to be necessary." (Treasury Department, *Digest of Appropriations . . . , 1942* [Washington: GPO, 1941], pp. 589, 591.)

TO MAJOR GENERAL GEORGE A. WHITE   May 16, 1941
Confidential   [Washington, D.C.]

Dear White: Most confidentially, I want your suggestions and your advice.[1]

The question of the return of the National Guard units to the states on the completion of twelve months' service is now a matter of urgent importance. I am told that the present uncertainty has a number of unfortunate effects, among which is a let-down in the training program, also, and more serious, a rather natural reluctance on the part of commanding officers to go ahead with the reclassification of officers in view of expected return to home communities.

I understand that a number of men of high position in civil life, who are completely willing to give their all for the national defense, are not especially agreeable to the prospect of continuing in the service if there is not urgent need for their continued contribution. Young men in the ranks, I am told, feel that after twelve months of service—unless there is a full emergency— they would be glad to take advantage of the plentiful jobs and the high pay now available in industry.

Confidentially, I think the matter, so far as an immediate announcement is concerned, will be determined more on the basis of political or public reactions than on the details which concern us in the Army, and which seriously affect morale. In other words, the question would be one of the advisability of a request on Congress at this particular time by the President to extend the period beyond twelve months. Will this provoke a reaction adverse to his present policies, and if not, should the extension be for an indefinite period, or for a year or for, say six months—the last on the assumption that certainly we will know a great more about the necessities of the situation next March.

Should, for example, the President merely announce that he contemplates asking for an extension?[2] What would be the effect of a statement at this time that the Guard is to be returned home at the completion of a year's service, in other words, that no request is to be made for an amendment to the law? The public reaction, what would that be to the present situation? The Guard reaction, what would that be with the uncertainty as to whether or not this statement could be finally carried out?

I would appreciate your writing me very frankly your views in the matter. I will treat them as confidential.[3]   Faithfully yours,

GCMRL/G. C. Marshall Papers (Pentagon Office, Selected)

1. White commanded the National Guard's Forty-first Division. Marshall sent similar letters to Major Generals Edward Martin and William S. Key.

2. See Memorandum for the President, July 16, 1941, p. 567.

3. White replied to the chief of staff: "I believe that a Presidential request on congress to extend the period of service of the civilian components will be accepted as the inevitable and only possible course." White noted that the public would expect the extension following the president's May 27, 1941, declaration of an unlimited national emergency. The Forty-first Division had listened to Roosevelt's radio address, "We Choose Human Freedom," which announced the emergency. "The opinion everywhere among the men was that the situation now was so grave that any thought of going home in September was out. It seemed to me that the transformation among them was definite, a stiffening of fiber, an acceptance of reality, the end of any doubt that this is serious business." (White to Marshall, May 29, 1941, GCMRL/ G. C. Marshall Papers [Pentagon Office, Selected].)

Key supported an extension of the Guard's service, but wanted a definite time period specified. Martin held a similar view, advising an extension until March 1942. (Key to Marshall, May 20, 1941, GCMRL/G. C. Marshall Papers [Pentagon Office, General]; Martin to Marshall, May 19, 1941, GCMRL/G. C. Marshall Papers [Pentagon Office, Selected].)

MEMORANDUM FOR THE SECRETARY OF WAR   May 16, 1941
Secret   Washington, D.C.

Subject: Nominations for Promotion.

A serious complication has developed with regard to your recent proposals of nomination for permanent promotions in the grade of major general, including the Chief of Infantry, the Chief of Chemical Warfare Service, and the Chief of the Air Corps.

The President apparently declines to accept the nominations because of his objection to Arnold. There is a bill before Congress—still in committee—which would permit the retirement of a Chief of arm after 2½ years of service.[1] This, if passed, would permit General Arnold to retire in the grade of major general. I understand, via Smith and Watson,[2] that the President now has in mind waiting until this bill is passed in order to permit Arnold to retire, or to be protected in his right to retirement as a major general, and only nominated as a brigadier general of the line.

Apparently the President will approve the remainder of the list, but even so this would not permit the appointment of General Brett as Chief of the Air Corps.[3] The present half and half arrangement between Arnold and Brett, one Acting Chief of the Air Corps, and the other by law still required to perform certain functions as Chief of the Air Corps, leaves an unfortunate uncertainty and promotes discord.

For Arnold to step down to a brigadier generalcy while Deputy would involve so much loss of prestige that he would be entirely ineffective in that positon, one grade below the Chief of the Air Corps, his former junior, and two grades below the Chief of the GHQ Air Force, also a former junior.[4]

This matter is serious and is affecting our administrative management of affairs. I think you should have a frank talk with the President. Incidentally, Smith tells me that he now thinks the President's hostility to Arnold results from the influence of Steve Early,[5] who was representative of the Associated Press in the War Department in the early 20's, when Arnold was a junior Air Corps officer at the Information Desk in the office of the Chief of the Air Corps. General Patrick then was head of the Air Corps (Chief Engineer of the AEF) and was promoting a reorganization of the Air Corps within the Army similar to the Marine adjunct to the Navy.[6] Arnold gave a press release on this and had to take it on the chin for his Chief when a great to do was made over the matter. This seems to be the background of the feeling against Arnold, which was accentuated by Mr. Morgenthau's hostility when the War Department and the Treasury Department were at cross purposes in the matter of sales of planes abroad.

Additional Nominations.

In connection with influencing the President in the foregoing matter, Smith thinks it very important that you do not raise the issue at this time of Colonel Adler's promotion. Smith gathers from Watson that the President would probably accept your recommendation in Colonel Adler's case if you urge it, but that it will increase his resistance to the Arnold matter and to future lists, which are now overdue.[7]

Please do not allow Smith's connection with these matters, particularly in relation to Early, to go further than your personal knowledge.

G. C. Marshall

NA/RG 165 (OCS, 15102–892)

1. In his memoirs, Major General Henry H. Arnold commented: "I was 'taboo' at the White House for a long time. I was not wanted there during the conferences. . . . I had a genuine worry because I had lost the President's confidence at probably the most critical period of my professional career." (Arnold, *Global Mission*, p. 186.) The bill to which Marshall refers, H.R. 3135, was never reported out of the House Military Affairs Committee.

2. Lieutenant Colonel Walter B. Smith was the administrative liaison between the chief of staff and the president's secretary and military aide, Major General Edwin M. Watson.

3. Major General George H. Brett had been appointed acting chief of the Air Corps on October 1, 1940; he was made chief of the Air Corps on May 31, 1941.

4. While he was chief of the Air Corps, Arnold was a major general ex officio. But his permanent rank was still colonel, because he had not yet notified the War Department of his acceptance of the promotion to permanent brigadier general made on December 2, 1940. On May 31, 1941, he accepted his promotion to permanent brigadier general, was promoted to the permanent rank of major general, and accepted that rank.

5. Stephen Early was the president's press secretary.

6. Major General Mason M. Patrick (U.S.M.A., 1886), chief of the Air Service from 1921 to 1927, advocated the creation of both aviation support units for the ground forces and an offensive air force with a separate command structure. The Joint Board rejected this proposal in 1923. (Craven and Cate, *Plans and Early Operations*, p. 26.)

7. Secretary Stimson had noted on March 26, 1941, that Watson claimed that the president opposed the promotion of *New York Times* general manager and Reserve officer Julius Ochs Adler. Stimson suspected that Watson was the source of the opposition. (Yale/H. L. Stimson Papers [Diary, 33: 115].)

MEMORANDUM FOR G-3: (ATTENTION COLONEL WALKER)[1]

May 16, 1941
[Washington, D.C.]

Mr. Flynn presented these papers to me personally, with oral explanation.[2] He told me that he had discussed the matter with you and that you and some other officer had actually been in the area he refers to.

This thought occurs to me: We have been mulling over the problem of the establishment of a division camp in a high altitude. There is a serious difference of opinion and a heavy cost item involved. Might not the problem be met, at least in a smaller way, in another manner. Suppose Fiske's idea of a Ski School was enlarged somewhat and there were assembled there selected officers and men from particular divisons, and organized into provisional battalions.[3] I do not now see, outside of Alaska and for a very few people in Greenland, other than a remote possibility for the employment of men at high altitudes. If such an eventuality occurred, we would at least have provisional units of selected men who could be quickly gathered together and sent to the area in question. We would at least have a beginning, and at the same time be establishing a basis for a more effective spread of the knowledge of skiing.

Naturally I have had no time to analyze the various pros and cons, so do not attach serious weight to what I propose merely because I happened to propose it.

NA/RG 165 (OCS, 21112–52)
1. Lieutenant Colonel Nelson M. Walker was in the Training Branch of G-3.
2. Thomas J. Flynn of Aspen, Colorado, had met with Marshall on the morning of May 16 and had urged that the army establish a ski academy near that mountain town. Army interest in winter and mountain troop training was stimulated by the Finnish Army's initial successes against the Soviet Army in the Russo-Finnish War. Marshall was also interested in the morale aspects of winter sports for troops stationed in cold climates. See Memorandum for Assistant Chief of Staff, G-3, September 12, 1940, pp. 303–4.
3. Lieutenant Colonel Normal E. Fiske, the United States military attaché in Italy, had recently submitted a report on the Italian Army's "disaster" in Albania, where, he said, the Italians were unprepared for either winter or mountain fighting. The lesson for the United States, he added, was that "an army which may have to fight anywhere in the world must have an important part of its major units especially organized, trained and equipped for fighting in the mountains and in winter. The army and equipment must be on hand and the troops fully conditioned, for such units cannot be improvised hurriedly from line divisions." (Quoted in Captain Thomas P. Govan, "Training for Mountain and Winter Warfare," Study No. 23, Historical Section, Army Ground Forces, pp. 3–4, NA/RG 407 [Microfilm Reel 3191, item 3813].)

D URING the summer of 1940 some 36,151 young men had completed the summer Citizens' Military Training Camps in the nine corps areas; 2,318 completed the advanced course, and 245 of these accepted appointment as second lieutenants in the Officers' Reserve Corps. An additional 2,160 older men had completed the special business and professional leaders' course; over one-third of these were from the New York–New Jersey area. (War Department, *Report of the Secretary of War to the President, 1941* [Washington: GPO, 1941], pp. 137–38.) But the preparedness advocates associated with the Military Training Camps Association, which was particularly strong around New York City, had been disappointed with General Marshall and the army's opposition to expanding the camps and to making them the chief training facilities for new officers. (See Marshall to Davis, July 20, 1940, pp. 275–76.)

The M.T.C.A.—strongly supported by Secretary Stimson, Under Secretary Patterson, and newly appointed Assistant Secretary John J. McCloy— believed that the experience of 1917–18 had demonstrated that "three months would be ample" to turn "the best brains in the country" into second lieutenants. Brigadier General Wade H. Haislip, the assistant chief of staff, G-1, argued the General Staff's position that twice as long was essential. (March 12, 1941, Yale/H. L. Stimson Papers [Diary, 33: 83–84].) Moreover, the M.T.C.A. believed that those "best brains" would not be attracted to the army if, rather than taking Reserve commissions and returning to civilian pursuits after camp, they first had to train as enlisted men and then to serve on active duty for a year; desirable men might prefer the navy, which was not imposing such restrictions. (William T. Sexton notes on Conference in the Office of the Chief of Staff, February 8, 1941, GCMRL/G. C. Marshall Papers [Pentagon Office, Selected].)

The secretary of war noted in his diary that Patterson and McCloy gave him "a long and worrisome talk" about the issue. They "felt that we ought to have training camps and think that the Army's opposition to it is simply a mark of incompetence and narrow-mindedness." (March 27, 1941, Yale/ H. L. Stimson Papers [Diary, 33: 118].) On that day Marshall had threatened to resign as chief of staff if such training camps were instituted. Marshall had discussed the possible necessity of threatening this action at a March 22 meeting with Deputy Chief of Staff Richard C. Moore and Secretary of the General Staff Orlando Ward. Five days later Ward wrote in his diary: "The Chief of Staff and the Sectary of War had it out on the matter of training camps for the sons of the rich with out their going thru the draft. He the C/S told him that aparantly the New York General Staff thought one thing and that the War Department General Staff thought another and that he could not stay as Chief of Staff if the SW took the advice of the NY out fit. It evidently was rather embarrassing to the SW but the C/S came out on top and It should be a red letter day for the army. It should seat us a little frimer in the saddle. God knows wer nearly out of it enough of the time." (Orlando Ward Diary, March 22 and 27, photocopy in GCMRL/Research File.)

Marshall later told his authorized biographer that he did not like having to take this position with Secretary Stimson. "I thought it was a very bad business for a public official to come up with a resignation proposition just because the thing didn't go his way—which is so often the case with political appointees—and I didn't think an army officer had any business doing it unless it was a matter of such great moment that he couldn't continue himself with the thing or with the affair because of a violent difference in principle. However, I was trying to save the situation and that was the only way I could think of at the time. I regretted it afterwards, though it partly accomplished its purpose." (George C. Marshall, interviewed by Forrest C. Pogue, February 20, 1957, GCMRL.)

Having stopped the movement to make Citizens' Military Training Camps the primary officer training facilities, Marshall then turned to solving the last-minute problems arising before the opening of the army's first Officer Candidate School on July 1. ★

MEMORANDUM FOR ASSISTANT CHIEF   May 17, 1941
OF STAFF, G-1 [HAISLIP]   [Washington, D.C.]

With relation to the Candidate Schools, I am getting the impression that we are going to lose some excellent material by reason of restriction of candidates to those who obligate themselves to a further year's service. If there is a full emergency, we can demand their service; if there is not a full emergency, the better the man the more apt he is to have an ambition for his progress in civil life, which would influence him strongly to return to civil life and give up the chance for a commission. On this basis, we would lose some of the best.

I am inclined to think we would get enough anyway under present conditions to meet the requirements. Also there is the feeling of G-1 with regard to the strong view that 50% of the Reserve officers should be released after a year's service commencing June 1st, and from this point of view, the fact that some of the candidates do not choose to serve a year longer would assist G-1 to proceed with the training of those Reserve officers who have not yet been called to duty.

It is true that the individual would be much more effective if he had a year's training as a commissioned officer. It may be from that point of view that the present regulation is justified. However, please consider this matter in the light of the above.

GCMRL/G. C. Marshall Papers (Pentagon Office, Selected)

To Lieutenant General Daniel Van Voorhis May 17, 1941
Confidential [Washington, D.C.]

Dear Van Voorhis: I have nothing particular on my mind to write to you about, but I do not want you to feel that "out of sight is out of mind." Things move so rapidly up here that we are inclined to lose the picture in the overseas garrisons.

The other day I held back some Flying Fortresses that were scheduled to be included in the recent flight of twenty-one to Hawaii. I did this because of the increasing seriousness of the situation in the Atlantic theater, and also because we would have had no more of this type, the most modern B-17, available in this country for crew training purposes. Yesterday I told Arnold to arrange to send a squadron of nine Flying Fortresses to Panama so that Andrews could manage the necessary crew training down there and would have available in emergency this powerful ship. We will not send down the latest model at this time, as there are only fourteen in continental United States, and further deliveries will not start until July or August. However, considering the training phase and the possible situation in the Caribbean theater, the planes being sent to you should be satisfactory.

The GHQ Air Force is getting its air defense arrangements pretty well organized. Chaney, after eight months of study and development here, including participation in an Army maneuver and following about two months in England, developed a highly effective system of air defense— meaning coordination between pursuit and anti-aircraft, communications, and warning service. The matter is now being standardized in the United States, and as early as possible we want to get the same set-up in Hawaii, Panama, and Puerto Rico and other overseas garrisons.

I had hoped to get down to Panama the latter part of April but was held here by compelling circumstances. Last week daily I was on the verge of getting off to Alaska, within an hour of departure on one day, and I am still here. De Witt is now going through the Aleutians and I was supposed to have been with him.

Most confidentially, I have disturbing reports regarding Trott's administration of the Fifth Corps Area, and I am sending General Moore out to look things over next week. Whether or not it will require an immediate change or not, I do not know, but I fear so. However, if the situation does not require immediate action, would you care to finish out your active period, after Panama, in command of that Corps Area? Please be very frank in telling me just what your reaction is. I just happened to think of this in relation to your home being in that vicinity. It would not be the policy to give you an Army command up here. In the first place, there would not be a vacancy; in the second place, your remaining period of service is too short, with the immensely complicated task that Army commanders now have.[1]

Should you be interested in this phase of the matter and want to curtail somewhat your period in Panama, I would be willing to consider such a change as early as October, but I would not want to do it before that time. Let me know what you think of it.

I know you have a very strenuous job, particularly as you get into the development of the Caribbean command and these new garrisons that are now being established. However, you are spared the daily repercussions of democracy that take up more than 25% of our time, the investigations which keep me hours and hours on the stand two or three times a week sometimes, and the conferences here and conferences there of vital moment, along with the ordinary routine of business of the Chief of Staff in the development of a war army. If I had a mine planter at my disposal and the opportunity to go fishing, I would be quite happy.   Faithfully yours,

GCMRL/G. C. Marshall Papers (Pentagon Office, Selected)

1. Van Voorhis responded: "Of course, the curtailing of my tour would start tongues to wagging. I would therefore request that, if my services are desired in October, you indicate the situation to include a statement as to why an Army assignment is not advisable and in such a way as to make it an open letter." (Van Voorhis to Marshall, May 24, 1941, GCMRL/G. C. Marshall Papers [Pentagon Office, Selected].) Van Voorhis assumed command of the Fifth Corps Area on October 1, 1941.

MEMORANDUM FOR GENERAL RICHARDSON   May 17, 1941
                                                    [Washington, D.C.]

I am wondering if it might not be a good thing to have some clever writer, whose stuff gets national circulation, prepare an article, a little of humor, and more of serious implications, as to what is now going on in relation to the work of the War Department in mobilizing and training an Army, and meeting the other requirements of planning, vital conferences, etc.

I have had as many as six letters in the same mail from a single Congressman, each one requiring some investigation, a well-prepared and courteous reply, and in view of the importance of our relations with Congress, usually a reply by me personally. Two or three days ago we had six letters from a single Senator, each requesting data, some of which required a considerable time to prepare. This, of course, was serious preparation for a speech or debate, but a little later from the same Senator comes a letter stating that an individual of the 1,300,000 reports to him that the food is neither sufficient nor palatable, and he requests me to reply on that subject.[1]

Yesterday I had five congressional calls, three visits at the request of important members of Congress which could not well be refused by me, and about twelve congressional telephone queries. Meanwhile, I have to confer with the Secretary of War, with the Secretary of State, with the President, with the members of the Staff, make some inspections and attend to the business of the Army.

A democracy makes certain requirements which have to be treated in a philosophical manner, but the matter is now progressing beyond the point of feasibility as to the functioning of the War Department in its designated field.

I am not mentioning hundreds of letters from mothers that come to me personally, because they are inevitable and natural reactions from the situation, and I can arrange to handle them and wish to sense their point of view.[2] The survey of tentative cantonment sites has provoked letters and pressures in an appalling manner. We have regarded this as somewhat inevitable, but when reflected through congressional representations from important men, it becomes an exceedingly serious matter if the War Department is to conduct its business with a fair degree of efficiency. One important member of the staff has been harassed until his efficiency is being, I think rather seriously affected.

With reference to the foregoing, this point should be made clear, that the great majority of the Members of Congress have not disturbed us at all, have never written a line, have practically never made any request on me; but the minority is sufficiently numerous to create a burden on the War Department which involves 25% of its staff to meet.

Think this over and talk to me about it. It is useless to expect that we can terminate the legislative pressures, but possibly we can moderate them; however it is to be done, we must not antagonize the group.

GCMRL/G. C. Marshall Papers (Pentagon Office, Selected)

1. Senator Harry F. Byrd, Democrat from Virginia, had written to Marshall on May 15 regarding a constituent's complaints about army food. Marshall responded immediately. "We receive complaints and suggestions ranging from criticism of the weather to plans for major joint operations, and we give all of them courteous consideration regardless of the time and effort required, but a statement that anyone in the military service lacks adequate and nourishing food is more than we can accept gracefully." He had had the complaint investigated informally, Marshall wrote, and "it developed that the complainant had gained 16 pounds in one month and that his letter was propaganda to get a cake from home." While conceding the pressures under which Congress was working, Marshall suggested that the senator "pay an unannounced visit to one of the nearby camps and inspect some of the organization messes. . . . I am confident that your impressions will be as favorable as those of other members of Congress who have made similar visits." (Marshall to Byrd, May 16, 1941, NA/RG 165 [OCS, SGS Reading File].)

2. For a typical letter from the chief of staff to a soldier's mother see Marshall to Mrs. Rose Lumetta, June 28, 1941, p. 553.

MEMORANDUM FOR GENERAL RICHARDSON   May 19, 1941
[Washington, D.C.]

Subject: Maneuvers.

I think it important that your Service begin a preparation of the public mind for the inevitable reactions from the maneuvers. I mean this:

These large maneuvers will involve long marches, lack of water, dust, heat, missed meals, and a multitude of discomforts that will require a high state of discipline, or otherwise we will have a volume of unsoldierly complaints. They will be a test not only of tactics and technique, but more particularly of the seasoned state of the Army and the character of discipline that we have developed since last fall.

If the public gets the right point of view and if the men at the same time acquire somewhat the same point of view, I think we will hear very little of unfavorable reactions. It should be easy to play this up because everyone has been told so much of the fortitude and endurance displayed by the German troops, as their most marked characteristic which determined their ability to undergo exceptional hardships and continue the campaign through Flanders into France at a high speed. "If they can do it, we can do it" is the motto to be unobtrusively hung up.

I think you ought to make a staff study of this and get under way a deliberate campaign of education.

GCMRL/G. C. Marshall Papers (Pentagon Office, Selected)

(33) General Marshall carries his battered briefcase, October 1940. He took the briefcase to France in 1917 and continued to use it after the World War.

(34) *General Marshall meets with visiting Latin American chiefs of staff at the Munitions Building, Washington, D.C., October 1, 1940.*

(35) General Marshall leads the inaugural parade up Pennsylvania Avenue on "King Story,"
January 20, 1941.

(36) President Roosevelt in the reviewing stand during the inaugural ceremonies, accompanied
by General George C. Marshall, Admiral Harold R. Stark, and Vice-President Henry A.
Wallace, January 20, 1941.

(37) Secretary of War Henry L. Stimson and General Marshall observing demonstrations of the new trackless tank, Fort Myer, Virginia, April 22, 1941.

(38) Congressman J. Buell Snyder, chairman of the House Military Subcommittee of the Appropriations Commitee, is greeted by Major General Adna R. Chaffee, chief of the Armored Force, upon arrival at Fort Knox, Kentucky, to observe the Armored Force, May 16, 1941.

(39) Demonstration of the new trackless tank at Fort Myer, Virginia, April 22, 1941.

(40) General and Mrs. George C. Marshall and their dog "Fleet," Fort Myer, Virginia, spring 1941.

(41) General Marshall enjoys a relaxing horseback ride with his dog "Fleet," Fort Myer, Virginia, 1941.

(42) General and Mrs. George C. Marshall enjoy coffee at Quarters One, Fort Myer, Virginia, spring 1941.

(43) Dodona Manor, the Marshalls' home in Leesburg, Virginia. (This photograph was taken in 1941.)

(44) James Montgomery Flagg's sketch of General George C. Marshall (May 1941), whom Flagg described as "the red-faced, sandy haired vital type—a leader."

(45) General George C. Marshall testifies before the Senate Military Affairs Committee, July 17, 1941. On the left are General Marshall and Brigadier General Wade H. Haislip. At the committee table, left to right: Senators Josh Lee, Styles Bridges, Sheridan Downey, Warren R. Austin, Robert R. Reynolds, Elbert D. Thomas, Lister Hill, Albert B. Chandler, and Chan Gurney.

(46) *President Franklin D. Roosevelt and Prime Minister Winston S. Churchill converse following divine services aboard H.M.S.* Prince of Wales, *Placentia Bay, August 10, 1941. Standing behind them at right are General Marshall and General Sir John Dill.*

(47) *President Roosevelt and Prime Minister Churchill aboard H.M.S.* Prince of Wales, *August 10, 1941. Standing behind them are General Marshall, Admiral Ernest J. King, and Admiral Harold R. Stark.*

(48) *United States and British military and naval leaders meet during the Atlantic Conference, August 1941. Left to right: Air Vice-Marshal Sir Wilfrid Freeman, Major General Henry H. Arnold, Admiral Harold R. Stark, Admiral Sir Dudley Pound, Admiral Ernest J. King, General George C. Marshall, General Sir John Dill, and Rear Admiral Richmond K. Turner.*

(49) General Marshall addresses the American Legion's national convention in Milwaukee, Wisconsin, September 15, 1941.

(50) General George C. Marshall, Secretary of War Henry L. Stimson, and Lieutenant General John L. De Witt being interviewed by the press at Fort Lewis, Washington, during the Fourth Army maneuvers, August 1941.

(51) Lieutenant General Lesley J. McNair (left) and General George C. Marshall discuss the Third Army maneuvers in Louisiana, September 26, 1941.

(52) General Marshall addresses a meeting of the Advisory Council to the Women's Interests Section of the War Department's Bureau of Public Relations, at the Munitions Building, October 13, 1941.

(53) Joint Board meeting held at the Munitions Building, Washington, D.C., November 1941. Seated around the table, left to right: Brigadier General Harold F. Loomis, Major General Henry H. Arnold, Major General William Bryden, General Marshall, Admiral Harold R. Stark, Rear Admiral Royal E. Ingersoll, Rear Admiral John H. Towers, and Rear Admiral Richmond K. Turner.

(54) *War Department General Staff, November 1941. General George C. Marshall pictured with members of his General Staff in his office at the War Department, Munitions Building. Left to right: Brigadier General Leonard T. Gerow, War Plans; Brigadier General Raymond A. Wheeler, Supply; Brigadier General Sherman Miles, Intelligence; Major General Henry H. Arnold, Air Corps; Chief of Staff Marshall (seated); Brigadier General Wade H. Haislip, Personnel; Brigadier General Harry L. Twaddle, Operations and Training; and Major General William Bryden, Deputy Chief of Staff (seated). Major General Richard C. Moore, Additional Deputy Chief of Staff, is not present.*

O N May 14, 1941, the Joint Board approved strategic plan Rainbow 5 and the Anglo-American staff agreement ABC–1. Responding to the staff agreement, the Joint Board based Rainbow 5 on several strategic assumptions: that the Associated Powers, including the United States and the British Commonwealth, would be at war with the Axis Powers, including Germany, Italy, and possibly Japan; that an offensive strategy in Europe should predominate over other theaters; and that an eventual land offensive against Germany would be conducted. (Maurice Matloff and Edwin M. Snell, *Strategic Planning for Coalition Warfare, 1941–1942,* a volume in the *United States Army in World War II* [Washington: GPO, 1953], pp. 43–46.)

In conjunction with these plans and the uncertainties in materiel procurement caused by lend-lease, the War Department recognized the need for an overall strategic estimate. Although a Defense Aid Division had been instituted under the direction of Under Secretary of War Patterson on April 10, 1941, this office could not administer a supply program without long-range plans. On April 18 both the G-4 division and the under secretary of war called for a statement of production objectives. In a May 17 conference, two days after the Vichy government's collaborative agreements with Germany, John D. Biggers, director of production for the Office of Production Management, informed Patterson and Marshall of the president's deep concern over industrial output. In the context of this new Atlantic crisis, Roosevelt wanted an intensified effort in industrial production. The chief of staff noted that procurement for future use was not a problem, but priorities had to be set. (Watson, *Chief of Staff,* pp. 331–35.) ★

MEMORANDUM FOR THE ASSISTANT CHIEF   May 21, 1941
OF STAFF, WPD [GEROW]   Washington, D.C.
Confidential

We are continually receiving suggestions as to increases and changes in armament, bombers, etc., along with suggestions of a more far-reaching nature. To provide a base of departure for meeting these proposals we should have a more clear-cut, strategic estimate of our situation from a ground, air and naval viewpoint. With such an estimate kept up to date, the various organizational, tactical and strategical questions which are constantly arising could be answered with more consistency than at present.

Such an estimate should be strategic in nature, and should include the views of the Navy and other interested governmental agencies. However, I believe it premature at the present time to make a formal approach to other departments.

Please contact other divisions of the W.D.G.S. and take the necessary steps to have an estimate prepared to be submitted to me in the rough. It should be brief. Appendices can be added at a later date to support the various statements. The initial paper could be utilized as a basis for obtaining the views of other departments. Then we could revamp the estimate.[1]

G. C. M.

NA/RG 165 (WPD, 4510)

1. The War Plans Division assigned Major Albert C. Wedemeyer (U.S.M.A., 1919) to initiate the study. On July 9 President Roosevelt gave added impetus to the project in a directive to the secretaries of war and navy; this provided Wedemeyer with the principal authority he needed to assemble information for his study from sources outside the War Department. The result was the September 10, 1941, "Victory Program," a carefully constructed, comprehensive estimate of the manpower and materiel the army would need to participate in a coalition war to defeat the Axis powers, as formulated in war plan Rainbow 5. (Watson, *Chief of Staff,* pp. 336–40.)

TO FREDERICK D. PATTERSON[1]　　　　　　　　　　　　May 24, 1941
　　　　　　　　　　　　　　　　　　　　　　　　　[Washington, D.C.]

My dear Dr. Patterson:　In reply to your confidential report on the situation in Chicago, in which you state "concerted attempts are being made to embarrass the military program in aviation which has been set up for negroes", I have referred the matter to the C.A.A.[2]

The officials of the C.A.A. state that this movement is not confined solely to the airport or the airport operators, but extends beyond that and they cannot see any steps which they might take at this time to provide a solution. I am very sorry to find that the aviation development at Tuskegee is laboring under such unfortunate disadvantages. Apparently the purpose of the movement you describe is to render ineffective the Tuskegee plan in order to get an entirely different kind of training also a different location of the school.

There seems to be little more that we can do other than to give you the best equipment and the best personnel possible, in order to provide the same standards of training at Tuskegee as at other training centers.[3]　Faithfully yours,

GCMRL/G. C. Marshall Papers (Pentagon Office, Selected)

1. Patterson had been president of the Tuskegee Institute, Tuskegee, Alabama, since 1935.
2. In December 1940 the Air Corps proposed a plan to locate a training facility for blacks at Tuskegee Institute, which already conducted a Civil Aeronautics Authority flight training program. Judge William H. Hastie, civilian aide to the secretary of war, in charge of army-black relations, disagreed with the plan. He argued that interracial cooperation in the army could not be advanced by separate training stations. The northern black press and public bitterly opposed the plan and did not want blacks trained in Alabama. Arnold rejected their

notion that racial prejudice would be less at other locations than at Tuskegee. In a May 20 memorandum to Marshall, he noted that northern blacks would risk the entire Tuskegee program on a chance of obtaining different circumstances and greater opportunity. (Ulysses Lee, *The Employment of Negro Troops,* a volume in the *United States Army in World War II* [Washington: GPO, 1966], pp. 116–19.)

3. On Marshall's continuing efforts to assist the Tuskegee Institute, see pp. 525–27.

MEMORANDUM FOR THE SECRETARY OF WAR   May 28, 1941
[Washington, D.C.]

Subject: Promotion of General McNair.

Last summer in order to decentralize the task of the War Department General Staff, and in accordance with mobilization regulations, a nucleus of General Headquarters for the direction of the field forces was created from the faculty of the Army War College. Major General Lesley J. McNair was designated as Chief of Staff and charged initially with the direction and supervision of the vast training program in contemplation.[1] He has acted for me in my temporary capacity as Commander of the Field Army. Since last September he has flown some 43,000 miles in the discharge of his duties.

The training program is approaching the peak in the large maneuvers now getting under way. The coordination of these maneuvers and the direction of the inter-army maneuvers is the task of General McNair and his staff. Also he will be intimately involved with the critical and delicate matter of relief or re-classification of high ranking officers, as a result of training inspections and of the coming maneuvers.

General McNair is personally and frequently in contact with five Lieutenant Generals and some thirty-five Major Generals. He has devised and directed the most impressive training program our Army has ever attempted. He must soon undertake the further development of his staff to take over the normal planning and operative duties of a GHQ.

General McNair has one of the best minds in the Army. He is conspicuous for loyalty, modesty and soldierly qualities. He should have greater prestige for his arduous and highly responsible duties of the coming months, especially since I am being held rather closely to Washington. Therefore I urge his immediate advancement to the temporary grade of Lieutenant General.[2]

No increase of pay or allowances is involved.

GCMRL/G. C. Marshall Papers (Pentagon Office, Selected)

1. On McNair and the activation of General Headquarters see Marshall to Van Voorhis, August 22, 1940, pp. 293–94.

2. McNair was promoted to lieutenant general on June 9, 1941.

To ROGER L. SCAIFE   May 31, 1941
                                                      [Washington, D.C.]

Dear Roger: Thank you for your note of May 29th, referring to the copy of my old World War journal, and urging that I keep the record up to date.[1] I am sorry to tell you that I have not been following your advice, and for several reasons. In the first place, I have not the time to do it, though I could have a special assistant concentrate on this business; and what I think is much more important, I am keeping my mind focused on the business of preparing an army, and ignoring so far as is humanly possible any thought of investigations, justifications, or similar matters. There is little I do today that has not possibilities of future investigation, and too frequently, the advice I receive relates to that phase of the matter. I want to keep my mind as completely free of such thoughts as possible, in other words, so long as I do not give a damn about what they say in the future, I probably will be able to do a fair job at the present time.

I probably am not making myself very clear and when I have more time I will write you at greater length. Meanwhile, thank you for your note.   Faithfully yours,

GCMRL/Research File (Verifax 1844)

1. Scaife was vice-president and director of Little, Brown and Company. Marshall had discussed publication of his memoirs, written from 1919 to 1923, when Scaife was with Houghton Mifflin in 1924. (James L. Collins, Jr., "Foreword" to George C. Marshall, *Memoirs of My Services in the World War, 1917–1918* [Boston: Houghton Mifflin Company, 1976], p. viii.) Scaife's May 29 letter is not in the Marshall papers.

To MRS. JULIAN L. SCHLEY   June 2, 1941
                                                      [Washington, D.C.]

My dear Mrs. Schley: The evening of Decoration Day I found an opportunity to visit the Soldiers, Sailors, and Marines Club. The clerk and janitor on duty showed me over the buildings.[1]

This note is to express to you and to the ladies of the Committee in charge, my congratulations on the splendid job that has been done, with my thanks for the very important contribution you have made to the morale of the Services stationed in the vicinity of Washington.

I was greatly impressed not only with the physical plant you have built up, but more especially with the evident efficiency with which it is being run. Please express to the various ladies concerned my personal thanks along with those of the War Department, for the important service they have rendered.   Faithfully yours,

GCMRL/G. C. Marshall Papers (Pentagon Office, General)
1. Denise V. Schley, wife of the chief of Engineers, was president of the Womans' Army and Navy League, the sponsor of the Soldiers, Sailors and Marines Club. On the club's earlier efforts at fundraising, see Marshall to R. B. Lawrence, February 17, 1941, pp. 424–25.

To Major General Frank R. McCoy   June 2, 1941
                                                  Washington, D.C.

Dear Frank: Thanks a lot for your letter of May 29th with the attached notes.[1] I am really very glad to have your suggestions, and in a form that I can conveniently use for reference to appropriate sections of the Staff.[2] If any further points occur to you, please write and send them in.

I have so little time for thinking things out that I am only too glad to have the advice and suggestions of someone in whom I have great confidence.

Give my love to Frances.   Faithfully yours,

                                                  G. C. Marshall

LC/F. R. McCoy Papers
1. McCoy had departed on March 5, 1941, for a three-month tour of Latin America. Sponsored in part by the State Department, he made the trip to survey United States diplomatic and military relations with the republics in the hemisphere. (*New York Times,* March 6, 1941, p. 7.) Upon his return, he wrote to Marshall and enclosed his memorandum "Casual Comments on Military Attachés and their work in South American Countries." (McCoy to Marshall, May 29, 1941, LC/F. R. McCoy Papers.)
2. The current world crisis placed greater burdens on military attachés, McCoy wrote to Marshall, and the War Department's Latin American missions were all understaffed. He also suggested that officers of Hispanic descent be assigned as attachés, that a large contingency fund be allocated to the attachés in order to "counter what the Germans are doing," and that every possible measure be taken to break up the German and Italian airlines in South America. He specifically noted the strategic importance of Iquitos, Peru, at the head of ocean-going navigation on the Amazon River and within a one thousand-mile radius of the Panama Canal. ("Casual Comments," ibid.)

Memorandum for General Arnold   June 2, 1941
                                                  [Washington, D.C.]

Please look at the attached suggestion of General Frank McCoy, following his trip around South America. I attach his map which he wishes to have returned.

How would it be to send a radio to General Van Voorhis asking that he radio us Frank Andrews' comments? If there is anything to it, we can probably bring about an important improvement of the field from here. Also, the thought occurred to me that we might take over Hugh Wells, give him a commission, find his line or something of that sort if it is of sufficient importance.[1]

GCMRL/G. C. Marshall Papers (Pentagon Office, Selected)

1. Hugh Wells was a United States citizen who owned and operated a freight airline from Iquitos, Peru. According to McCoy, the Peruvian government had recently taken over his airline and intended to appoint Wells as director of civil aviation. McCoy suggested that the War Department encourage pro–United States airlines in Brazil to extend their operations through Iquitos to Lima, Peru, to counter the possibility of German expansion into that country. ("Casual Comments on Military Attachés and their work in South American Countries," enclosed in McCoy to Marshall, May 29, 1941, LC/F. R. McCoy Papers.) In his recommendations to the War Department, Andrews agreed with McCoy that pro–United States airlines should expand into Iquitos and the Amazon Valley. Andrews also recommended supporting Wells, but had doubts about his business acumen. (Andrews to McCoy, June 16, 1941, LC/F. M. Andrews Papers.)

MEMORANDUM FOR GENERAL MILES   June 2, 1941
                                                  [Washington, D.C.]

Attached are some notes General McCoy sent me at my request following a brief conversation on the subject when he passed through Washington the other day. I am much impressed with his suggestions regarding more attachés or rather assistant attachés of Latin blood.[1] Possibly more training planes with young aviators would be helpful.

As to his reference to Steele's "American Campaigns", please purchase half a dozen sets of these books from the Infantry Journal people—who I am certain have them, and send them to Sibert, with instructions to send one set to the man to whom McCoy refers, with a card that this is being done with the compliments of General McCoy.[2]

GCMRL/G. C. Marshall Papers (Pentagon Office, Selected)

1. On the assignment of officers of Hispanic descent as attachés to Latin America, see Marshall to John F. O'Hara, July 22, 1941, pp. 573–74.
2. Colonel Edwin L. Sibert (U.S.M.A., June, 1918), military attaché in Brazil, had given a copy of the first volume of Matthew F. Steele, *American Campaigns* (Washington: GPO, 1901) to the commander at Bahia. Steele's work is a classic study of United States military history and strategy; he taught at Fort Leavenworth's service schools from 1903 to 1908. McCoy suggested that complete sets of the work should be provided to each attaché to give to senior Latin American officers.

MEMORANDUM FOR THE SECRETARY OF WAR   June 3, 1941
Secret   [Washington, D.C.]

Prince André Poniatowski, a member of the technical staff of the Headquarters of the present French Army at Vichy, has just arrived in the United

States on a confidential mission. He contacted General Miles with a statement that he had full authority to speak for the French General staff; that the French Army is not in sympathy with the Vichy Government; that he is prepared to put his own knowledge and French military experience at our disposal. Further that the French staff at Vichy are sending two officers, tank engineers, to Martinique in case we should desire to have them come to this country for consultation.

He had comments to make regarding American intervention in North Africa, predicting its success and cooperation by General Weygand if made in force.[1]

Prince Poniatowski stated that a letter would be received from our Military Attaché in Vichy vouching for him.[2] No mail having been received from Vichy in over two weeks, General Miles cabled our Military Attaché a query regarding Poniatowski. May 27th he received a reply signed "Leahy" stating that Poniatowski speaks for the French Army with full approval and authority.[3]

I have talked to him and I suggest that you give him an appointment.[4]

GCMRL/G. C. Marshall Papers (Pentagon Office, Selected)

1. General Maxime Weygand was the commanding general of Vichy French forces in North Africa. After Vichy's rapprochement with Germany, Weygand had asked the United States what help he could receive if he resisted the Germans. Poniatowski told Marshall that the French Army had relieved its older, inefficient officers and restructured its forces. He advised the chief of staff that Weygand would assist a major United States invasion of North Africa if one was mounted. (Orlando Ward notes on Conference in the Office of the Secretary of War, May 19 and June 3, 1941, NA/RG 165 [OCS, War Council Minutes].)
2. Major Robert A. Schow (U.S.M.A., November 1918) was the military attaché in Vichy.
3. Admiral William D. Leahy was the ambassador in Vichy.
4. Stimson received Poniatowski later that day. (Yale/H. L. Stimson Papers [Diary, 34:87].)

MEMORANDUM FOR SENATOR TRUMAN   June 4, 1941
[Washington, D.C.]

At your suggestion I submit herewith an informal proposal for a new set-up to handle Army construction and maintenance work. As this idea has not been submitted to the Bureau of the Budget, I am not informed as to whether or not legislation along the line indicated would be in accord with the President's program.[1]

My view is that Army construction and maintenance other than river and harbor work should be handled by an independent office separate from either the Quartermaster Corps or the Engineer Corps; that the officers should all be on a detailed status; that other employees should be civilians. It would be important to include the following provisos: That in the present emergency, in the discretion of the Secretary of War, the Corps of Engineers could remain in charge of all projects now under their control (Air Corps and outlying Atlantic bases), and also that the Secretary would have authority at any time in the future to assign work to the Corps of Engineers when, in his judgment, such a procedure is advisable in the public interest. We should never deny ourselves the utilization of trained personnel to meet an emergency.

While the problem of maintenance is not in the public or congressional eye at the present time, yet in the future it will be one of the most serious problems of the War Department, as it will consume a constantly increasing proportion of the military budget unless handled with great efficiency. This phase of the Army problem from 1920 to 1935 was an example of how not to handle this matter.

I attach an outline of a possible proposal by your Committee. This seems more advisable than to submit a draft of a proposed law.[2]

GCMRL/G. C. Marshall Papers (Pentagon Office, Selected)

1. Harry S. Truman, chairman of the Senate Special Investigating Committee examining national defense programs, charged that the army mobilization plan was an "Indian-war plan." According to Truman, insufficient planning explained many of the conditions which caused high construction costs: hasty site selection, the lack of specific programs and blueprints, and the reliance on fixed-fee contracts. As a partial solution to these problems, the Truman committee was considering a recommendation to create a separate construction division within the War Department. (Lenore Fine and Jesse A. Remington, *The Corps of Engineers: Construction in the United States,* a volume in the *United States Army in World War II* [Washington: GPO, 1972], pp. 390–91.)

2. The chief of staff's outline is in GCMRL/G. C. Marshall Papers (Pentagon Office, Selected). On August 14, 1941, the Truman committee released its report, advocating a separate construction and maintenance division, as Marshall had recommended. (Fine and Remington, *Corps of Engineers,* p. 391.) Legislation transferring the construction function to the Corps of Engineers was signed by the president on December 1, 1941. (Ibid., p. 475.)

TO MRS. JOHN B. WILSON   June 4, 1941
                                                        Washington, D.C.

Dear Rose: Thanks for your letter, though I do wish you would have your typewriter repaired.

Your comments on the streets of New York in the summer season painted an effective picture of the evils of urban concentrations. I used to see this when I lived for some months in Washington Square and took my air on a bench in the Square surrounded by countless little wops. My suggestion to you at this moment is to get a copy of "The Honorable Peter Stirling" by Paul Leicester Ford, from the library and read it. I am sure you will be much interested in the first half of the book—not in the latter half.[1]

I am sorry you did not call me up when you were in Washington, and was distressed to learn that you had the necessity for a real bout with the doctors. However, as you seem to be taking it seriously, I imagine the cause will be quickly eliminated. I was on the verge of retirement in 1911 because of a bad foot—fallen arch, I was walking with a cane. I had another serious period in 1904, when I was threatened with T.B. from exposure to winter winds at drill following two years in the Philippines. Cod liver oil knocked this out and almost took me with it. So you see, everyone has his moments.[2]

I have not had a riding companion since you and Molly left; was going it alone last night. I have the government mount Molly used, which has developed into a splendid riding animal and I find was a star polo pony at Riley.[3]

The work here grows more and more pressing. I barely have time to think.

I failed to take Tom's telephone number as the basis for getting in touch with them, but I will try to remember to do this today.

With my love,   Affectionately,

G. C. M.

GCMRL/R. P. Wilson Papers

1. Marshall probably was referring to his tour of duty as aide-de-camp to Major General J. Franklin Bell at Governors Island, New York, from April to June 1917. Ford wrote *The Honorable Peter Stirling and what people thought of him* (New York: H. Holt and Company, 1894).

2. Marshall was stationed at Fort Reno, Oklahoma, in 1904, after his Philippine tour of duty; he was inspector-instructor of the Massachusetts Volunteer Militia in 1911.

3. Concerning the horses from Fort Riley, Kansas, see Marshall to Malin Craig, footnote 2, September 19, 1939, p. 60.

MEMORANDUM FOR GENERAL RICHARDSON   June 4, 1941
Confidential   [Washington, D.C.]

Dr. Patterson, head of Tuskegee Institute, has been doing a very fine thing in assisting the Air Corps in the development of a negro aviation unit. He has been under heavy attack from the Chicago and Harlem elements, and for a time it appeared that they would succeed in emasculating the Tuskegee Air program for national defense.[1]

I have had a talk with him this morning and he mentioned the desirability of a definite program of publicity to play up what is being done for the development of negro military aviation at Chanute Field and at Tuskegee. Mechanics are being trained at Chanute Field; the other phases of the development are at Tuskegee, and the funds for a considerable amount of the construction were obtained by a loan from the Rosenthal (or Rosenwald) fund.[2] Dr. Patterson mentioned the following newspapers as being of dominant influence to negroes in this country:

Afro-American, of Baltimore
The Pittsburgh Courier, Pittsburgh, Pa.
The Journal and Guide, Norfolk, Va.
Chicago Defender. (This has been a militant newspaper, bitterly attacking the present Army policy).
Kansas City CALL, Kansas City, Missouri, and the
Scott Newspaper Syndicate in Atlanta.

It might be a good thing to have someone check up and get some photographs on this business both at Chanute Field and at Tuskegee.[3]

GCMRL/G. C. Marshall Papers (Pentagon Office, Selected)

1. The opposition to the black aviation program at Tuskegee is discussed in Marshall to Patterson, May 24, 1941, pp. 518–19.

2. The Julius Rosenwald Fund, established in 1917, provided money for programs benefiting black education and welfare.

3. For an example of press coverage of aviation training at Tuskegee Institute, see *The Pittsburgh Courier,* June 21, 1941, p. 12.

MEMORANDUM FOR COLONEL WILSON, G-4[1]   June 4, 1941
Confidential   [Washington, D.C.]

Subject: Tuskegee Institute and WPA Appropriations.

I have forgotten just what you told me as result of your last effort to obtain certain things for Tuskegee. However, this morning in a conversation with Dr. Patterson, the President of the Institute, I find that the fact that WPA decided some time back (an Alabamian made the decision) that this was a private institution, has denied them many advantages from Government activities. According to Dr. Patterson, the facts are these:[2]

The income from endowments for the institution have dwindled, as have all others, and the gifts have similarly dwindled. If the institution, which is now a non-profit organization, should be reorganized, it would make it income taxable, which would wreck them in their present work. Treat this as confidential for you alone.

He states that the decision that it was a private institution was on the hair-line order; was based solely on the fact that the continuing Board of Directors might possibly at some time in the future make such use as they saw fit of the plant. He states that some Alabama Supreme Court decisions have given the institution a public status.

Please check up unobtrusively on this matter, and then advise me. I have in mind a procedure to bring influence on the WPA to get a new decision. Such a decision would open up a number of channels for governmental assistance. They need very badly an engineering laboratory, and this is right along with their Air development for the Army Air Corps. They need more facilities—shelter and tools for vocational training, and this would assist us in the development of the negro units that we are now attempting. Look into this, please, preliminary to my taking a more definite step.[3]

GCMRL/G. C. Marshall Papers (Pentagon Office, Selected)

1. Lieutenant Colonel Arthur R. Wilson.
2. In an earlier conversation, Marshall had discussed W.P.A. funds for Tuskegee Institute with Patterson. The chief of staff recommended that the institute apply to W. G. Henderson, the W.P.A.'s state administrator in Alabama for financial support. (Marshall to Patterson, March 3, 1941, GCMRL/G. C. Marshall Papers [Pentagon Office, Selected].)
3. In a letter drafted by the G-4 division of the General Staff, Marshall informed Patterson that neither the W.P.A. nor the National Youth Administration could support civil aviation at Tuskegee Institute because it was a private institution. (Marshall to Patterson, September 2, 1941, ibid.) Patterson had also requested that a black officer serve as professor of military science and tactics at Tuskegee Institute. Lieutenant Colonel Walter B. Smith, in a letter signed by the chief of staff, noted that such duty had to be done by a Regular Army officer and no black officer was available. However, Smith wrote, the War Department could designate the officer on duty at the University of Alabama as nominal professor and assign a black Reserve officer to Tuskegee. (Marshall to Patterson, June 14, 1941, ibid.)

MEMORANDUM FOR THE SECRETARY OF WAR   June 5, 1941
Confidential   [Washington, D.C.]

The Ambassador from the Argentine called on me personally this morning to extend an invitation from his Government, in the name of the Secretary of War, for me to be present at the celebration of the anniversary of the independence of the Argentine—on July 9th. He informed me that similar invitations were being issued to the senior Army officers in Brazil, Bolivia, Chile, Paraguay, Peru and Uruguay.[1]

In an off the record discussion apropos of his appreciation of the fact that I am very closely engaged here in Washington, he commented on the rising tide of feeling as a result of the increased activity of Nazi propaganda and the recent British reverses in the Near East.[2] He thought that such a meeting at this particular moment might have great weight in influencing Army circles. When I discussed the possibility of selecting an appropriate representative other than myself—I mentioned Lieut. General Van Voorhis, he advised against any suggestion of this nature, at least from this end of the line. He thought that the inference resulting from the presence of the senior officers of the other countries and a subordinate from this country would be unfortunate, that the proposal of such substitution should come from the Argentine, but whether or not they would make it he did not know.[3]

GCMRL/G. C. Marshall Papers (Pentagon Office, Selected)

1. The ambassador from Argentina was Don Felipe A. Espil.

2. The British had been driven from the mainland of Greece in April and from the island of Crete at the end of May. In North Africa, Lieutenant General Erwin Rommel's forces continued to advance into Egypt. Meanwhile, the British had had to dispatch troops to suppress a pro-Axis revolt in Iraq.

3. After Argentina agreed to invite an officer designated by the chief of staff, Marshall instructed Major General Frank M. Andrews to attend the ceremonies in that nation. (His instructions are in Marshall to Van Voorhis, June 26, 1941, GCMRL/G. C. Marshall Papers [Pentagon Office, Selected].)

MEMORANDUM FOR GENERAL HAISLIP June 6, 1941
[Washington, D.C.]

My recent inspection trips and the letters that are coming to me now, either directly or by reference, indicate the development of a serious situation, particularly in the National Guard with relation to the older men who have been drawn under the Selective Service Act.

During the first five or six weeks of their service the problem of physical hardening occupies their minds. After that their reaction is that of an older man who finds himself feeling better than he has for years with a brain correspondingly alert. The trouble then begins because the noncoms and the junior officers in the National Guard, and some of the other junior instructors are unable to provide the necessary stimulating instruction. If they are in the Armored Force or with the few concerned in the Air Corps, the problem is not quite so difficult. But in the Infantry in particular, in the Cavalry and in the Engineers, the situation becomes serious.

We do not want second lieutenants who are, comparatively speaking, old men, but I think we have to take into account the fact that many of these Selective Service men have a mental equipment and executive and administrative experience which should enable them to do certain things much better and much more quickly than the young selectees.

What are the expedients we should take in order to meet this situation? What can we do to better the situation? It is definitely affecting morale, but what worries me is that given three or four more months, it will be a serious matter in the way of public reaction.

I hope there will be sufficient judgment in the units to promote the outstanding men to noncommissioned grades at an early date. Maybe we should advise such a course, but there must be other adjustments or we are walking into serious trouble. We must provide the cure before the disease has fully developed, and I am convinced that we are on the way to trouble.

In considering this question we must avoid the ordinary calculation of the time required to train a soldier, thinking of a boy of 18 to 22 or 23. I have found in my limited inspections men of outstanding proven business capacity standing in the ranks alongside of a kid of 21 who did not even complete high school. I understand we have a collection of certified accountants; I know there is a large number of men of proven ability. We must treat this matter in a realistic fashion and not by rule of thumb.

GCMRL/G. C. Marshall Papers (Pentagon Office, Selected)

To Major General John F. Williams   June 8, 1941
[Washington, D.C.]

Dear Williams: Recently General Key, of the 45th Division, made an inquiry relative to the assignment of a Regular Army officer as Chief of Staff for his Division. I am attaching a copy of my reply to Key, for your information.[1]

Personally, I have not been in favor of piecemeal business about the detail of Regular Army officers to the National Guard. I think a formal policy should be worked out and adopted uniformly for the entire National Guard, which must mean, of course, the acquiescence of each state—a very difficult thing to launch. My conception of the most effective manner of increasing the staff efficiency of the National Guard and promoting its training, would be to fill certain positions with Regular officers, young ones given increased rank; to have all these officers forbidden by regulations from having anything whatever to do with promotions, selection of personnel, and local relations. To have them specifically charged with problems of training and particularly with the development of team work in the staffs.

The present is no time to bring this up, therefore I am not giving you this for distribution; rather, merely to give you my idea on the subject. I think the following posts in the National Guard should be filled, as vacancies occur, by young Regular officers on a three-year detail—maybe four: Division Chief of Staff, brigade and regimental executive officers. With such an arrangement I do not think it would be necessary to detail instructors with the National Guard, because the posts I have mentioned are proper positions for officers engaged in instructional work. Incidentally, they could do their job as instructor with authority from such posts, whereas at present it is by indirection or circumlocution.[2] Faithfully yours,

NA/RG 165 (OCS, 18107–33)

1. Marshall had written to Major General William S. Key, commander of the National Guard's Forty-fifth Division, concerning the promotion of a retired Regular Army officer presently on active duty. (Marshall to Key, May 28, 1941, GCMRL/G. C. Marshall Papers [Pentagon Office, General].)

2. War Department policy was not determined until the autumn of 1941. The chief of staff wanted every vacancy in a National Guard unit filled by an officer from that unit if the man was qualified. The evolution of this policy is discussed in Watson, *Chief of Staff,* pp. 260–61.

SPEECH AT THE COLLEGE OF
WILLIAM AND MARY[1]

June 9, 1941
Williamsburg, Virginia

I am happy for the opportunity to be here this morning. There is so much of uncertainty in obligations these days that it is impossible for me to be sure of personal plans more than a few hours in advance of the scheduled moment. I am deeply gratified by the honor of the degree that has just been conferred on me. The distinction of this degree particularly appeals to me because of the implications to be drawn from the history of this institution in relation to the situation in which this country now finds itself.

If you will pardon me for being a little personal in developing my thoughts this morning, I first acquired a special interest in this college following a visit to the site of old Fort Kaskaskia in southern Illinois. To my surprise I learned that that remote locality was once conceived to be a part of the State of Virginia. The instructions which led to the dramatic capture of that picturesque little garrison led me back to Williamsburg, to the Governor of that day, Patrick Henry, and his advisers at the moment, Thomas Jefferson and George Wythe, I believe, and I found myself in the atmosphere of the early days of the College of William and Mary.

Incidentally, that famous expedition of George Rogers Clark involves some curious contrasts to similar affairs today. He received his orders from Patrick Henry here in Williamsburg on January 2nd [1778]. He started bare-handed, without troops, without equipment or munitions—all had to be organized or created. Six months later, on July 4th he had traversed nearly a thousand miles, surprised and captured his objective. The troops had been organized, armed, trained, and provided with ammunition and supplies. Each man provided his weapons, I suppose. Here is the curious phase of contrast—the necessary armed force could be created, equipped within sixty days, and carried 1,000 miles to its objective within six months; today it might cover one thousand miles in a matter of three hours, but the provision of the equipment would involve several years.

You young ladies and gentlemen have a great tradition for your guidance, a great heritage. At no previous moment in our history, I believe, has this held more of importance or significance. The founder of this institution, a determined and hard-headed cleric, went to London to secure the charter and funds. England was at war; money for educational purposes was out of the question. Yet he secured the charter and arranged for the financing of the college; he would not be denied. This college is older than the flag it flies. More than once it has been burnt and rebuilt, more than once it has been taken over by enemy forces and later reconditioned. Its history is the exemplification of the persistence of an ideal. Its graduates have performed more important duties in the development of this country than the graduates of any other institution. Whether they served their community or their country, in the state or the church, in the school or in the professions, they all demonstrated that outstanding quality of integrity. Their friends could depend on them; their country, which acknowledged their leadership, could depend on them. I wish those of our people today who are weak in spirit could be here this morning to derive inspiration from these surroundings.

It is true that we are living in a strange and unpredictable period. No idea seems too preposterous, no theory has not its defenders. At a time when civilization, according to our crude appreciation, reached a summit in achievements, we find ourselves in a great catastrophe, in which all our ideals are in dispute, the relationship between the individual and the community, between citizens and the government, between men and their God—all are questioned, all are attacked. The things of the spirit which have enabled this college to endure, which guided the great men of its early days, these seem to be trembling on the verge of the discard. The times demand courageous men with unselfish purpose and truly great ideals.

GCMRL/G. C. Marshall Papers (Pentagon Office, Speeches)
1. Following the awarding to him of a Doctor of Laws degree, Marshall delivered the commencement address at the college.

MOBILIZATION caused the War Department's Washington, D.C., work force—civilian and military—to expand rapidly to over 20,000 persons. In his annual report Secretary Stimson noted that at the end of June 1941 the army's efficiency "was impaired to a material degree by the fact that the activities of the Department were carried on in 23 separate buildings." (War Department, *Report of the Secretary of War to the President, 1941* [Washington: GPO, 1941], p. 11.) Completion of the new War Department building (which became the State Department building in 1947) reduced the scattering to seventeen buildings. Congress authorized and provided funds to construct temporary office buildings, but stipulated that they be built within the District of Columbia. (Stimson Memorandum for the President, April 10, 1941, NA/RG 107 [White House Correspondence, WD 029.21 (4-9-41)].)

By the late spring of 1941 the War Department was seeking to consolidate its offices and personnel into a few large, temporary buildings, but it considered the possible sites in the District inadequate. On June 11 Marshall testified before a subcommittee of the House Appropriations Committee to request that the construction limitations be removed so that the Virginia experimental farm site could be used. "The Arlington farms is across the Memorial Bridge. There is no stop light at all. It is property we already own. We can commence building on this site as soon as legislation authorizing construction outside of the District is enacted. It is about 4 minutes from the War Department. To be able to build our temporary office buildings on the Arlington farms site means everything to us; we can do business if our buildings are placed there." (House Appropriations Committee, *Second Deficiency Appropriation Bill for 1941, Hearings* [Washington: GPO, 1941], p. 506.) See the map on p. xviii.

In July the Appropriations Committee requested that the War Department consider consolidating its activities into a single, large building. Architects and army engineers, under the supervision of Brigadier General Brehon B. Somervell (U.S.M.A., 1914), chief of the Construction Division, Quartermaster Corps, rapidly designed a pentagonal building covering 6,500,000 square feet, to be built within a year of the appropriation of $35,000,000. (*Congressional Record,* 77th Cong., 1st sess., vol. 87, pp. 6301–2.) The bill to do this (H.R. 5412) was approved on August 25. After President Roosevelt ordered the site moved, for aesthetic reasons, a half mile further down the Potomac River, construction began in September 1941. No official name for the structure was picked until early 1942, although the shape suggested "Pentagon Building" as one of the possibilities. (Frank McCarthy Notes on Proposed War Department Building, n.d. [August 15? 1941], NA/RG 165 [OCS, SGS, Notes on Conferences and Decisions File]; Somervell Memorandum to the Secretary of War, August 20, 1941, ibid.) ★

MEMORANDUM FOR GENERAL ULIO   June 12, 1941
[Washington, D.C.]

Gertrude Ely served through the War with the 18th Infantry in the First Division. She is a wealthy woman who has given a great portion of her time to such efforts. She was a great influence for good in the First Division, particularly as she went into the advance dressing stations and labored valiantly through the heavy fighting of the Division.[1]

When she comes through Washington, I would like you or one of your principal people to talk to her.[2]

NA/RG 165 (OCS, SGS)

1. Marshall and Ely had previously discussed the duties that women could assume in the mobilization of troops. (Marshall to Ely, September 18, 1940, GCMRL/G. C. Marshall Papers [Pentagon Office, General].) In April, 1941, he gave her a letter of introduction to the commanding general of Camp Blanding, Florida, where she was to represent the Army Y.M.C.A. (Marshall to Major General John C. Persons, April 14, 1941, GCMRL/G. C. Marshall Papers [Pentagon Office, Selected].)

2. Ulio received Ely on her next visit to Washington, D.C.

To Lieutenant General Daniel Van Voorhis   June 12, 1941
Personal   [Washington, D.C.]

Dear Van Voorhis: Your endorsement of May 7th to War Department communication of April 28th regarding Air defense, was brough† to my attention by WPD.[1]

While I have not had time to go into it in detail, it is evident that you are laboring under a misapprehension as to the attitude of the War Department in the matter. There was no intention whatever to reflect on you. In studying over the arrangements in the various overseas possessions, the Department, lacking information to the contrary, assumed that the organization of your Air defense was as indicated in the basic war plans of the 1941 revision, which differed in some major respects from the organization being adopted in continental United States. The purpose of the original letter was purely to bring the differences to your attention and not at all to reflect on your procedure.

They tell me that the plan for the organization of Air defense in the Caribbean Defense Command, recently received in the War Department, indicates an organization in conformity with the general practice now being put into effect throughout the Army.

Frankly, while you have your difficulties with the Government of Panama, I do not think you have quite enough. You lack the flood of daily irritations and disturbances that we have every hour which eventually produce either prostration or a case-hardened front to the world. So far as I can, I try to deal in a very direct and semi-personal manner with the overseas commanders, but there are limits and the formal Staff productions should be received with due regard for the immense burden these people up here are carrying. Faithfully yours,

GCMRL/G. C. Marshall Papers (Pentagon Office, Selected)

1. The War Plans Division had requested that Van Voorhis review his air defenses in light of the newly organized Air Defense Command and Britain's combat experience. Van Voorhis interpreted the staff's request as a criticism of his lack of initiative. (Gerow Memorandum for the Chief of Staff, June 5, 1941, NA/RG 165 [WPD, 4270-8].) Marshall had previously mentioned reorganizing Caribbean air defense. (Marshall to Van Voorhis, May 17, 1941, pp. 513–14.)

To Lieutenant General Walter Krueger   June 13, 1941
Personal and Confidential   [Washington, D.C.]

Dear Krueger: Relative to Atkins' relief: You state in your letter, "I do not have confidence in his ability effectively to function as Chief of Staff of the

Third Army and prefer a younger man for that position. Therefore, I earnestly request that he be given a *command assignment.*"[1]

I am ordering Colonel Eisenhower to your headquarters, but meanwhile I wish a more definite recommendation from you regarding Atkins. He will be sixty-two in November, far too old for a brigade command or to propose him to the President for a major generalcy to command a division. I am, therefore, embarrassed by your recommendation of a *command assignment,* as much as I am embarrassed with the difficulty of finding an appropriate place for Atkins. General Brees expressed the same view in this matter that you have as to Atkins' qualifications for Chief of Staff of the Third Army. All of us are concerned to protect his reputation and avoid a hurt to his pride; however, the troops come first.

Please let me hear from you by air mail.[2]   Faithfully yours,

GCMRL/G. C. Marshall Papers (Pentagon Office, Selected)

1. In a letter to Marshall, Krueger had requested the relief of Colonel Joseph A. Atkins (U.S.M.A., 1904) as Third Army chief of staff. Krueger then elaborated on the qualifications of a field army's chief of staff: "In my judgment, that position demands a younger man, one possessing broad vision, progressive ideas, a thorough grasp of the magnitude of the problems involved in handling an Army, and lots of initiative and resourcefulness. Lieutenant Colonel Dwight D. Eisenhower, Infantry, is such a man, and I urgently request that he be detailed to replace Atkins as Chief of Staff of the Third Army." (Krueger to Marshall, June 11, 1941, GCMRL/G. C. Marshall Papers [Pentagon Office, Selected].) Eisenhower (U.S.M.A., 1915) had been promoted to colonel on March 6, 1941, and was chief of staff of the Ninth Army Corps at Fort Lewis, Washington.

2. In his reply to the chief of staff, Krueger recommended Atkins for an administrative command such as a port of embarkation or a reception center. (Krueger to Marshall, June 14, 1941, ibid.) Atkins retired in October 1941.

SPEECH AT TRINITY COLLEGE[1]   June 15, 1941
                                                        Hartford, Connecticut

It is a pleasure to be here this morning in surroundings that give the spiritual in us a chance to exclude the uncertainties and complexities that harass us in these unpredictable times.

These buildings represent a patriotic contribution of the Episcopal Church to the nation. They house a College whose traditions and environment have enabled her to put a distinctive stamp of her own making upon the young men who have the good fortune to matriculate here.

I can readily understand why that is so when I recall the Trinity men with whom I have come in contact.

Their period of development here not only vitalized the faculties of their minds but also aroused and intensified those latent forces of the soul that the ordinary educational process sometimes fails to reach.

I know that this association with you here this morning is good for my soul. If I were back in my office I would not have referred to my soul. Instead I should have used the word "morale" and said that this occasion increased my "morale"—in other words, was of spiritual benefit to me.

One of the most interesting and important phenomena of the last [war] was the emergence of that French word from comparative obscurity to widespread usage in all the armies of the world.

With use it took on increased significance—a significance which was not lost in the twenty years following the World War.

Today, as we strive to create a great new defensive force, we are investing the word "morale" with deeper and wider meaning.

I realize that when you read the daily press it would appear, from the headlines, that the War Department is a wholly materialistic institution whose only concern is the development and perfection of a machine—a war machine. You read of OPM, and priorities, and the production of bombers, of pursuit ships, of tanks, howitzers, rifles and shells. You come to the natural conclusion that the machine is the thing—that only steel, in one lethal form or another, absorbs the complete time and attention of the War Department.

It is true, as the daily press points out, that we are applying all of American energy, ingenuity and genius we can mobilize, to the task of equipping our new Army with the most modern and efficient weapons in the world—and in ever-increasing quantity. That is our responsibility and you expect us to meet it.

But underlying all, the effort back of this essentially material and industrial effort is the realization that the primary instrument of warfare is the fighting man. All of the weapons with which we arm him are merely tools to enable him to carry out his mission.

So we progress from the machine to the man and much of our time and thought and effort is concentrated on the disposition and the temper and the spirit of the men we have mobilized and we get back to the word "morale."

We think of food in terms of morale—of clothing, of shelter, of medical care, of amusement and recreation in terms of morale. We want all of these to be available in such quantity and quality that they will be sustaining factors when it comes to a consideration of the soldier's spirit.

The soldier's heart, the soldier's spirit, the soldier's soul, are everything. Unless the soldier's soul sustains him he cannot be relied on and will fail himself and his commander and his country in the end.

Today war, total war, is not a succession of mere episodes in a day or a week. It is a long drawn out and intricately planned business and the longer it continues the heavier are the demands on the character of the men engaged in it.

With each succeeding month, with each succeeding year, it makes always heavier and more terrible demands on the mental and spiritual qualities, capacities and powers of the men engaged in it.

War is a burden to be carried on a steep and bloody road and only strong nerves and determined spirits can endure to the end.

It is true that war is fought with physical weapons of flame and steel but it is not the mere possession of these weapons, or the use of them, that wins the struggle. They are indispensable but in the final analysis it is the human spirit that achieves the ultimate decision.

It is not enough to fight. It is the spirit which we bring to the fight that decides the issue. It is morale that wins the victory.

The French never found an adequate "dictionary" definition for the word. I don't think that any "definition," in the strict sense of the word, could encompass its meaning or comprehend its full import.

It is more than a word—more than any one word, or several words, can measure.

Morale is a state of mind. It is steadfastness and courage and hope. It is confidence and zeal and loyalty. It is elan, esprit de corps and determination.

It is staying power, the spirit which endures to the end—the will to win.

With it all things are possible, without it everything else, planning, preparation, production, count for nought.

I have just said it is the spirit which endures to the end. And so it is.

That being so I feel that it is quite appropriate and proper for me to speak a soldier's word here, on this occasion, this morning; for I am acknowledging, and gladly emphasizing, in this spiritual place, that the determining factor in war is something invisible and intangible, something wholly spiritual.

This recognition of the potency of the spiritual in war receives full consideration in the War Department. Those of us to whom you have entrusted the task of organizing, equipping and training our great new defense forces never treat it lightly when it touches our planning, preparation and calculations.

You will recall that some time ago the Press commented on instructions that went out from the War Department to all commanders in the field relative to the new type of discipline that was to be sought for our citizen armies.

I say "sought" because it is not being "imposed." It has not been found necessary to "impose" it.

The military discipline that many of us here today can look back upon, took the form, in the main, of bodily exercises.

The body reacted to it surely enough. Its appeal was physical and instinctive. It could not be said to have appealed to the spirit and the intellect. It was inculcated by playing upon the lower range of morale qualities—pride, shame, fear and, above all, habit.

"Habit" came pretty close to being everything. It was undoubtedly the objective of all that old-fashioned "squads east and west" that you still hang stories on.

This older type of discipline was the objective of all that monotonous drilling which, to be honest, achieved obedience at the expense of initiative. It excluded "thought" of any kind. As an old drill-sergeant put it one day, "Give me control of the 'instinct' and you can have the 'reason'."

The result of the method was a rigid discipline that expressed itself in a mechanical, subconscious obedience that was, to be just to it, admirable in many respects.

It was born of, and perhaps fitted to, the small professional armies of volunteers who lived under it and accomplished much through it.

But for our new armies of citizen soldiers we have achieved a type of discipline better fitted to the type of man himself as well as to the new tactics that have rendered obsolete not only the shoulder-to-shoulder formations but even the discipline based on them.

"Theirs not to reason why—theirs but to do and die" is out of the picture. Your sons and brothers and friends are being taught why orders must be obeyed; why a faulty command unhesitatingly obeyed will accomplish more than a faultless order carried out half-heartedly or with hesitation; why individuals must submerge themselves in the team if the army is to meet its obligation to the nation.

We are replacing force of habit of body with force of habit of mind.

We are basing the discipline of the individual on respect rather than on fear; on the effect of good example given by officers; on the intelligent comprehension by all ranks of why an order has to be, and why it must be carried out; on a sense of duty, on esprit de corps.

From a moral stand-point there is no question as to which of these two disciplines is the finer if you admit that respect is to be preferred to fear; the white flame of enthusiasm to the dull edge of routine; the spiritual to the instinctive.

This new discipline enables me to leave with you the assurance that the men in this Army we are building for the defense of a Christian nation and Christian values, will fight, if they have to fight, with more than their bodies and their hands and their material weapons. They will fight with their souls in the job to do, and we who are here today know that everything, ultimately, depends on the soul—for out of the heart are the issues of life.

The War Department is seeing to it that this Christian Army is not asked to live on rations alone. It has enlisted the aid of chaplains by the hundreds and is building chapels by the hundreds (555 to be exact) to give the Army the spiritual food we want it to have.

We know that in creating morale we are creating a living thing that is contagious, that spreads and fastens.

We are building that morale—not on supreme confidence in our ability to conquer and subdue other peoples; not in reliance on things of steel and the super-excellence of guns and planes and bomb-sights. We are building it on things infinitely more potent. We are building it on *belief* for it is what men *believe* that makes them invincible. We have sought for something more than enthusiasm, something finer and higher than optimism or self-confidence, something not merely of the intellect or the emotions but rather something in the spirit of man, something encompassed only by the soul.

This Army of ours already possesses a morale based on what we allude to as the noblest aspirations of mankind—on the spiritual forces which rule the world and will continue to do so.

Let me call it the morale of omnipotence. With your endorsement and support this omnipotent morale will be sustained as long as the things of the spirit are stronger than the things of earth.[2]

GCMRL/G. C. Marshall Papers (Pentagon Office, Speeches)

1. Marshall was awarded a Doctor of Laws degree by Trinity College. He then delivered this commencement address.

2. A report of Marshall's address indicates that he went beyond the text printed here in appealing for national unity. "The time has come for the people to unify completely behind this Army and Navy; to unify as quickly as we can," Marshall is quoted as having said. "The day for bickering has passed. . . . These are days for courageous men with unselfish purpose." (*New York Times,* June 16, 1941, p. 8.)

MEMORANDUM FOR GENERAL MCNAIR   June 18, 1941
                                                [Washington, D.C.]

At the conclusion of maneuvers in May 1940, a public critique was held in which General Brees discussed principally the leadership of the Commanding Generals of the opposing sides. In addition, he made rather caustic reference to the leadership of the older officers. Further, this was mimeographed and released to the press.[1]

I do not think that those portions of the critique which refer to the senior commanders should be attended by the junior officers. As a matter of fact, it might even be desirable to confine the portion of such critique to the two commanders themselves, and possibly their chiefs of staff. Certainly, such a critique should not be open to the public or released to the press.

I am inclined to think that a careful segregation of officers should be made in arranging critiques in accordance with what is to be discussed. For officers generally, the common errors should be featured—and I am inclined to think that this should be covered rapidly in a quickly prepared mimeograph, and released to the officers, possibly prior to the critique.

I do not know what your plans or directions are in this matter, but I wish you would go into it in order to avoid a repetition of the procedure of last May. Just where the press fits into the plot I do not know, but I would like you to have Richardson talk this over with you.[2]

GCMRL/G. C. Marshall Papers (Pentagon Office, Selected)

1. Lieutenant General Herbert J. Brees, the referee of the Third Army's spring maneuvers, and Major General Walter C. Short had thoroughly criticized all participating officers, including generals, in a final "public" critique on May 25, 1940. They noted the poor performance in such aspects as reconnaissance and intelligence, and criticized the emphasis on speed at the expense of tactical efficiency. The *Army and Navy Journal* published most of the critique in its June 1, 1940, edition (pp. 943, 962–64) and ran a summary of editorial comments from other newspapers on the critique in the June 15 edition (p. 998.)

2. In introducing his remarks at the critique of the first phase of the Louisiana army maneuvers of September 14–19, 1941, McNair said: "Rather extensive detailed comments are contained in the mimeographed matter just issued. It is quite possible also that the army commanders will receive later certain additional comments by letter." And in closing his observations on the second phase (September 24–28), he remarked: "Appreciation also is due the Press. All elements—news, pictures, and radio—strove only to give the true picture, and it was a very real picture. The members who covered the maneuvers accepted restrictions cheerfully, lived with the troops, and earned in many ways the respect and gratitude of us all. We hope that they will come to see us often." (Comments by Lieutenant General L. J. McNair, NA/RG 337 [Headquarters, Commanding General, AGF 354.2/2(1941)].)

O N June 18, 1941, Marshall testified on the War Department's budget before a subcommittee of the Senate Appropriations Committee. The chief of staff argued for a $10,009,655,187 appropriation for the 1942 fiscal year. Marshall noted that this appropriation bill covered the procurement of twelve thousand new aircraft for the Air Corps, a recent supplement designed to meet army and lend-lease requirements. The bulk of the appropriation covered pay, clothing, equipment and maintenance costs. When asked if the mobilization was progressing as he expected, Marshall replied that overseas demands on American industry had expanded more rapidly than estimated the previous year. Although these orders burdened United States manufacturers and forced a readjustment of army procurement, the chief of staff was satisfied with the overall state of national preparedness. (Senate Appropriations Committee, *Military Establishment Appropriation Bill for 1942, Hearings* [Washington: GPO, 1941], pp. 5–12.) ★

TO JAMES F. BYRNES[1]

June 20, 1941
[Washington, D.C.]

My dear Senator Byrnes: Knowing the deluge of congratulations you would be receiving, I have delayed a little in the hope that you might have time to read mine. I was genuinely delighted to read of your appointment, though selfishly disturbed over the loss of your powerful assistance in the Senate.

In my contacts with the Senate, particularly with the Appropriations Committee, I have felt that your backing and your guidance have been of great help and importance to me personally and to the Army program in general. A number of times you have skillfully protected me during hearings when my own inexperience was leading me into something of an impasse.

I want you to know that I was deeply appreciative of what you did for me and the Army. You have my very sincere congratulations.   Faithfully yours,

GCMRL/G. C. Marshall Papers (Pentagon Office, Selected)

1. On June 12, President Roosevelt had nominated Senator Byrnes of South Carolina to be an associate justice of the United States Supreme Court.

To GENERAL DOUGLAS MACARTHUR   June 20, 1941
Confidential   Washington, D.C.

My dear MacArthur: In your letter of May 29 you state that the Philippine Army is to be absorbed by the United States Army in the near future, and consequently, that you are closing out your Military Mission. At the present time, War Department plans are not so far reaching. Contingent upon the appropriation of sugar and excise tax funds, Grunert has recommended that about 75,000 troops of the Philippine Army engage in a period of training of from three to nine months, in order to prepare them for the defense of the Philippines. While the decision as to the termination of the Military Mission is yours, the War Department plans do not contemplate taking over all responsibilities of your Mission in the near future.[1]

Both the Secretary of War and I are much concerned about the situation in the Far East. During one of our discussions about three months ago, it was decided that your outstanding qualifications and vast experience in the Philippines make you the logical selection as the Army Commander in the Far East should the situation approach a crisis.[2] The Secretary has delayed recommending your appointment as he does not feel the time has arrived for such action. However, he has authorized me to tell you that, at the proper time, he will recommend to the President that you be so appointed. It is my impression that the President will approve his recommendation.

This letter is also an acknowledgment of your letters to the President and to the Secretary of War. Please keep its contents confidential for the present.   Faithfully yours,

G. C. Marshall

MML/D. MacArthur Archives (RG 1)

1. MacArthur's letter is not in the Marshall papers. MacArthur had recommended that the military mission be closed and that the War Department establish a Far Eastern Command with himself as commanding general. In a June 6, 1941, memorandum to Marshall, War Plans Division disagreed with MacArthur's proposal for two reasons: the British had accepted the burden of strategic defense in the region, and the United States defended only the Philippine Islands. Therefore, War Plans Division recommended that MacArthur, if activated, assume command of the Philippine Department. (Louis Morton, *The Fall of the Philippines,* a volume in the *United States Army in World War II* [Washington: GPO, 1953], pp. 15–16.)

2. Marshall had informed Stimson on May 21, 1941, that he intended to recall MacArthur and "place him in command" if a Far Eastern crisis arose. (Yale/H. L. Stimson Papers [Diary, 34: 50].)

MEMORANDUM FOR THE SECRETARY OF WAR   June 20, 1941
Confidential   Washington, D.C.

The following paragraphs summarize the problems involved in the matter of determining whether or not the National Guard is to be retained in the Federal service:[1]

MORALE   On the whole the National Guard is willing to remain in service. However, Guardsmen are pleading for an early decision in this matter, because of the effect the decision will have upon their personal activities. For example, the renting season is now under way in most communities and to arrange for their families, Guardsmen must know if they are to be released. Young men who expect to return to college are also vitally concerned because registration and other arrangements should be completed now.

EMPLOYMENT OF GUARDSMEN   There are certain laws governing the re-employment of military personnel called into service during the present emergency. Employers are insisting upon knowing now if Guardsmen will return to their jobs at the end of the year's service.

STATE INTEREST   It is imperative that the various States be informed at the earliest practicable date of the future of the National Guard. Many States are now expending funds on Home Guard units which by law must be disbanded when the National Guard is released. Other States hesitate to proceed with such organization in the present uncertainty concerning the National Guard. Some States have released rented National Guard armories when the Guard was mobilized, while other States rented State-owned armories. In any case advance notice should be furnished in order that armory facilities can be provided.

STAFF PLANNING It takes considerable time to accomplish the demobilization of the National Guard and for disposing of selectees and
large quantities of equipment involved. Instructions for demobilization should reach all concerned at least two months
before effective date. The critical date for a substantial part
of the Guard is July 15. It is imperative that this planning be
carefully worked out since it not only involves careful coordination with maneuver schedules, but also personnel, supply
and transportation problems. If not retained in the service,
some Guard units now overseas must be returned to the
United States for discharge early in August.

SELECTIVE SERVICE The decision relative to the Guard vitally affects personnel procurement rates. Requisitions for selectees must be
made six weeks prior to delivery date. This entails considerable advanced planning and coordination with the Selective
Service which cannot be done until the decision relative to
the Guard is made. This planning also involves the provision
and adequate training of cadres for units to be activated if
the Guard is released. A special training of cadres must be
initiated by July 15.

CONSTRUCTION If the Guard is to be retained, additional construction will
be necessary especially for new armored force units. This
construction should be initiated immediately to avoid winter
building and to assure the unimpeded development of the
armored force.

BASE AND TASK
FORCES Regular Army organizations are now being disrupted to
provide base and task forces. If the National Guard is retained, a part of it could be employed for these purposes. The
preparation and training of these forces for special missions
require considerable time. It is, therefore, becoming increasingly important that an early decision be made as to the
future status of the Guard.[2]

G. C. Marshall

NA/RG 107 (SW Safe, Repeal of Restrictions—Armed Forces)

1. Planning for the retention of the National Guard in federal service began in December
1940. The General Staff recognized that those units federalized first would complete their
service before the augmented Regular Army was sufficiently trained. On April 28, 1941,
Marshall told the House Appropriations Committee that a decision to retain the National
Guard would be made by June. No decision was made by then, however. President Roosevelt
advised the nation on June 17 that the government was studying the matter and that Secretary
Stimson was to make a report to him. (Watson, *Chief of Staff,* pp. 214–18.)

2. On this same day, Secretary Stimson sent President Roosevelt a lengthy memorandum
("Removal of legislative restrictions") strongly urging that a joint resolution be introduced
into Congress retaining the National Guard, the Reserve Corps officers, and the draftees in

federal service beyond the year stipulated in the 1940 legislation. The president replied on June 26 instructing Stimson to "go ahead and get something started as soon as you can." (Stimson Memorandum for the President, June 20, 1941, NA/RG 107 (SW Safe, Repeal of Restrictions—Armed Forces); Roosevelt Confidential Memorandum for the Secretary of War, June 26, 1941, ibid.) On the history of this measure and Marshall's views regarding the issue, see the editorial note on pp. 565–66.

MEMORANDUM FOR ADMIRAL STARK June 20, 1941
Confidential [Washington, D.C.]

Dear Betty: I have gone over your draft in the priority matter and had it analyzed by our procurement people, and their findings formally checked and approved by the Under Secretary of War.[1]

Mr. Lovett, Assistant Secretary of War for Air, maintains that the President intended by his directive to the Secretary of War to place the machine tools and plant equipment for the entire 4-engine land and seaplane bombing program (500 planes per month) in A-1-a priority and their production in A-1-b priority. Incidentally, the Navy 2-engine patrol plane program is also advanced from the A-1-c category to the A-1-b category to place it on a parity with the 4-engine bomber program. At the moment, I see no other way of solving the present impasse except to submit these airplane schedules to the President for his consideration and decision.

With reference to the ship program, we had hoped that the Army proposal of June 2d would be considered as a fair compromise, having in view the requirements of the British. Experience over the past nine months with Army ordnance procurement efforts has proved conclusively that Naval ordnance and Army ordnance items are of such a character that both services compete extensively for the same productive capacity in management and in plant facilities. The officers who have gone into the details of this matter, and who fully understand its implications, are unanimous in the belief that an agreement to the present Navy proposal on ordnance items will result in

(1), a serious delay in the production of Army items required for the British, and

(2), a still further delay in our immediate need for adequate quantities of equipment and ammunition for the equipment of task forces, outlying base forces, the Panama Canal defense project, and the training of the present forces. (I am very seriously embarrassed from the morale point of view by the continuation of a really seriously inadequate amount of materiel for the training of the troops, whose impatience grows with their military development. This will become glaring, I fear, as the large maneuvers develop this summer). The Ordnance procurement officers call attention to the fact that the plants producing Army equipment, which now lack only a few essential tools to achieve balanced production lines, would be required to delay still longer before getting into quantity production. They also express the opinion that an agreement to the Navy proposal will result in piling up equipment and ammunition before the ships for which they are intended are ready.

In handling this matter of priorities, I personally get into deep water regarding the technical possibilities of the various proposals, but my predicament as to the equipment of our task forces, the inability to do what you would like to have done in the Philippines, and the very serious situation in which I am becoming involved regarding the present troop development in the United States is a matter of the deepest concern to me. I cannot escape the fact that our situation as to ordnance material is tragic in the light of possible requirements of the next six months, and the present demands which I am unable to meet. I have done my best to find a way out to help you in your dilemma, and am sorry that I must stand on the proposal of June 2d.[2]

GCMRL/G. C. Marshall Papers (Pentagon Office, Selected)

1. On April 22, 1941, the navy proposed that certain programs, such as their long-range shipbuilding project, be elevated to a higher priority. On June 2 the army advanced a compromise. Army planners recognized the strategic importance of the naval programs and agreed to a higher priority for certain construction and repair projects. A second navy proposal on June 16 recommended elevation of their bomber and patrol plane programs to a higher priority level also. The War Department's procurement experts recommended to Marshall that he "take an inflexible stand" against the navy's second proposal. They argued that the navy program would produce ordnance, equipment, and aircraft before their ships were ready and that the revised priorities would hinder the army's 1941 mobilization. Their final recommendation was to maintain the June 2 army compromise and any presidential amendments. (Charles Hines Memorandum for the Chief of Staff, June 18, 1941, NA/RG 165 [OCS, 19603-20].)

2. On July 15, 1941, Secretary of the Navy Frank Knox proposed that all production priorities be set jointly by both services. In assessing this recommendation, War Plans Division suggested that priorities be established by the Joint Army and Navy Munitions Board, to be reviewed and approved by the Joint Board. (Gerow Memorandum for Deputy Chief of Staff [Major General Moore], July 21, 1941, NA/RG 165 [OCS, 19603-21-B].) To adjust priority conflicts between the military services as well as between the military and civilian sectors, President Roosevelt issued Executive Order 8875 on August 28, 1941, establishing within the Office of Production Management a Supply Priorities and Allocations Board. This policy group was composed of the chief executive officers of the principal agencies concerned with resource and production allocations.

To Harry S. Truman   June 21, 1941
                                                      [Washington, D.C.]

My dear Senator: I have just read your letter to Lieutenant Knoll at Fort Leonard Wood, and I want you to know that I highly appreciate the stand you have taken.¹ Your letter is a gem, and I shall treat it as confidential as you request. However, if all names, including yours, were omitted, would you mind our making some use of this to stop the flood of this sort of pressure?²

Your letter should certainly act as a check on the young man in question—and I hope it won't lose you a vote; but if it could be given wider application both in the field and on the Hill, our problem might be materially simplified.

Thank you very much for the stand you have taken.   Faithfully yours,

GCMRL/G. C. Marshall Papers (Pentagon Office, Selected)

1. Lieutenant Rudolph J. Knoll, stationed at Fort Leonard Wood, Missouri, had written to Senator Truman criticizing United States foreign policy. In a reply which he copied and sent to the chief of staff, Truman wrote: "While I was a Lieutenant of Field Artillery in training at Fort Sill in 1917 and later as a Captain in France, it would never have occurred to me to write a letter to Senator Jim Reed and give him my opinions of the state of the Nation. First, I was too busy with the job in hand. Second, I didn't feel qualified and, third, there was something in the Army Regulations which said that an officer in the Army should not express opinions on political subjects." Truman noted that "things may be different now" and "younger officers may be smarter." but he still would not write to a government official. (Truman to Knoll, June 14, 1941, GCMRL/G. C. Marshall Papers [Pentagon Office, Selected].)

2. With the senator's permission, the War Department issued a press release on June 29, publicizing Truman's letter and using his name. Also included in the release was the text of A.R. 600–10, Paragraph 4, which stated that political activity by soldiers to influence legislation was forbidden unless authorized by the War Department. A War Department letter to all officers, dated October 4, 1940, reinforced A.R. 600–10. (Press Release, June 29, 1941, GCMRL/G. C. Marshall Papers [Pentagon Office, Selected].)

MEMORANDUM FOR COLONEL GINSBURGH¹   June 21, 1941
                                                [Washington, D.C.]

I have been unable to focus on the problem of providing you one or two instances of my experience with non-commissioned officers indicating their importance in the military set-up. The matter is too important to be treated lightly, and lacking an appropriate example I have hesitated to produce a poor one. At the moment I can only think of these hints towards what is desired:

Throughout my service I have been opposed to the close supervision of officers over work which was appropriate to non-commissioned officers, feeling that the job would be better done if proper confidence was reposed in the NCO. For example, wherever I have been in command I have insisted that the close-order drill should be largely the problem of the 1st sergeant, and I objected to all the officers being on the drill ground in constant and intimate supervision of what the sergeant was doing. This is a little dangerous medicine to broadcast at this particular moment when we have a limited experience in the senior non-coms. and the necessity for constant supervision by everybody. Yet on the peacetime basis of the old Regular Army, I thought it was important, and always felt that we lost a great deal by having the much higher paid officers, who should have been doing planning and other advanced work of preparation, in a sense humbling the first sergeants by following at their heels.

There is a great difference of opinion in regard to this, many colonels requiring their officers to be on the drill field—by drill field I mean for close-order work—just at the time I think it should have been the first sergeant's "hour". With the diminutive companies of the peacetime Regular Army, this seemed to me all the more important because I felt the old first sergeant was a better drill master—I am not talking about extended order work or minor tactics—than the new lieutenant, and particularly, that he was better than the officer of ten or more years' service, who should mentally have progressed into wider fields of action. Our procedure, I felt, was a little like having the college professor or instructor being always present at the kindergarten or first grade work.

In my treatment of non-commissioned officers—and remember I am talking of the old Regular Army, old in the sense of prior to 1938—I always maintained a personal contact with all of the first sergeants so far as it was possible, and utilized their services at times on duties that always had been confined to commissioned officer personnel. For example, partly to relieve the strain on the small officer personnel at a post, and partly to utilize the outstanding quality of the first sergeants at that particular post, I placed the first sergeants on the "officer of the day" roster. They did this work surpassingly well, and I always felt a complete confidence in the state of the garrison when one of these men was on duty. They took it very seriously and there was little that went on in the garrison that they did not already know about. In line with this I made it a point to have them line up outside my quarters at some appropriate moment during the visit of the Corps Area Commander, and presented them personally to him.

The trouble with these examples is, they, in a sense, do not fit the present situation and they are not appropriate for me to be talking about because it amounts to praise of my system rather than of what is intended, an appreciation of the NCO.

There should be no question about the importance of the NCO; unless he is well trained, highly disciplined, loyal, and a leader you can expect very little from that organization. He must be good. The point I have been making is, we have always talked about the importance of the NCO and then seldom have trusted him twenty feet out of our sight. The trouble here is, this does not exactly suit the present day Army, so it is ticklish business.

GCMRL/G. C. Marshall Papers (Pentagon Office, Selected)
1. Lieutenant Colonel A. Robert Ginsburgh, assigned to the Office of the Chief of Staff, drafted speeches for Marshall.

VICHY'S May 15, 1941, collaborative agreement with Germany caused great concern among army planners for the security of northeastern Brazil. The Intelligence Division believed a German invasion of West Africa was probable. Marshall immediately sent Lieutenant Colonel Matthew B. Ridgway to Brazil to secure an agreement permitting the United States to station forces in the Natal region. Brazil rejected the proposal. (Conn and Fairchild, *Framework of Hemisphere Defense*, pp. 284–85.)

In response to this Atlantic crisis, President Roosevelt addressed the nation over radio on May 27. He asserted that a German occupation of any southern Atlantic islands, or Iceland or Greenland, would threaten the defense of the Western Hemisphere. Roosevelt concluded his address by proclaiming an unlimited national emergency. (*The Public Papers and Addresses of Franklin D. Roosevelt*, 1941 volume, ed. Samuel I. Rosenman [New York: Harper and Brothers, 1950], pp. 181–95.)

The United States had not yet chosen the means to counter the German threat, however. Prior to his speech, Roosevelt had ordered the army and navy to prepare a joint plan for the occupation of the Azores. The War Plans Division disagreed with this proposal and emphasized the strategic importance of Brazil. On June 6, 1941, Roosevelt temporarily resolved the question by ordering the occupation of Iceland. (Conn and Fairchild, *Framework of Hemisphere Defense*, pp. 116–23.)

Although he favored the occupation of Iceland, Marshall was intent on sending troops to Brazil. Instructed by the chief of staff to prepare a memorandum for Under Secretary of State Sumner Welles, Ridgway recommended that the army also send troops to other key Latin American nations. On June 7 the Joint Board modified his plan, proposing the immediate movement of troops to Brazil and the negotiation of transit rights for armed aircraft to cross Venezuelan and Colombian territory. Following Ridgway's plan, Marshall informed Welles on June 17 that the army wanted to send a force of 9,000 men to Natal. (Ibid., pp. 285–87.) ★

MEMORANDUM FOR WAR PLANS DIVISION: June 21, 1941
(ATTENTION COLONEL RIDGWAY) [Washington, D.C.]
Secret

In an interview with the President day before yesterday, in his bed-room, Colonel Stimson and I presented Joint Board paper regarding the establishment of some of our troops in the Natal region in Brazil. We also gave him, and he glanced through my memorandum to Mr. Welles on the same subject.

We talked over the vital importance of the matter and the necessity for speedy action. We focused on the proposition that we thought he should force the State Department to find a solution within the next two weeks. It was up to them to find a solution, but we must get action immediately.

He discussed several possibilities, but thought the most likely method, and the one he would take up with Mr. Welles, would be to get Vargas[1] to give us a limited lease—only for the period of the emergency—to establish a small air base in the Natal-Recife region. He thought that that probably would be the best, or at least the only practicable basis on which Vargas could put the thing over. He wanted the offer to come from Brazil. Behind it would be the necessity that we would back that Government. This last was not an emphatic part of the proposal, but it was involved in the conversation.[2]

GCMRL/G. C. Marshall Papers (Pentagon Office, Selected)

1. President Getúlio Vargas of Brazil.
2. Germany's June 22 offensive against the Soviet Union calmed fears of an impending Nazi occupation of West Africa and postponed any movement of United States troops to Brazil. Stimson, Marshall, and army planners still wanted to send a force to Natal, however. The army wanted to send an Infantry regiment with support troops to participate in Brazil's autumn maneuvers. Ambassador Jefferson Caffery encountered bitter opposition to this plan by Brazilians who feared that the arrival of United States ground forces would precipitate a political crisis for their government. In the autumn of 1941, Brazil settled the matter by canceling the maneuvers. (Draft of Radiogram to Lehman Miller, June 30, 1941, GCMRL/ G. C. Marshall Papers [Pentagon Office, General]; Conn and Fairchild, *Framework of Hemisphere Defense,* pp. 287–88; Caffery to Cordell Hull, June 27, 1941, Department of State, *Foreign Relations of the United States: Diplomatic Papers, 1941,* 7 vols. [Washington: GPO, 1956–63], 6: 502.)

TO THE COMMANDING GENERAL, FIRST ARMY[1] June 26, 1941
Radio. *Confidential* [Washington, D.C.]

Most confidentially we have rumblings here of a build-up in the press unfavorable to the maneuvers along the lines of criticism of lack of equipment, lack of air ground activity, lack of modernized procedure of motorized and mechanized forces. Views of enlisted men obtained from circulating press correspondents indicate that they know little of what is going on and therefore derive little instruction from the maneuvers and feel that they are losing needed basic training. The matter of equipment involves misunderstanding of why certain divisions have more than others due to logical priorities. The matter of air-ground cooperation involves misunderstanding regarding the time required to procure proper type radio installations for ground forces to communicate with air and the necessarily slow development of sufficient air units in continental United States due to advanced priorities for overseas garrisons as well as delays in production schedule. Nine groups are being brought into shape for participation in September October and November. The immediate reaction has evidently been inspired by the failures of officers and noncommissioned officers to keep their men advised of the constantly changing local maneuver situation as applied to them. Steps should be taken to correct this as quickly as possible. There is also failure on the part of civilians to appreciate the absolute necessity with or without complete equipment of training regimental and higher staffs which can only be done by actual maneuvers. Also the necessity of testing out the quality of the men that is their state of discipline and stamina when under physical and other pressures of arduous field service.

GCMRL/G. C. Marshall Papers (Pentagon Office, Selected)

1. This same message was sent to the commanding generals of the Second, Third, and Fourth armies.

MEMORANDUM FOR GENERAL PETERSON[1]   June 27, 1941
Confidential   [Washington, D.C.]

CCC: Please arrange to have your inspectors who happen to be in the various corps areas cover the management of the CCC at each corps area headquarters. I would like to have them check the apparent activity and quality of the man in charge, determine the number of changes in district commanders and the average number of changes in company commanders during the preceding six months, the character of the school for the training of CCC leaders to assist company commanders— there has been a belief these were of too short duration in some corps areas—and any other items that would give an indication as to whether or not this activity is being treated with sufficient care and supervision. I do not want to worry the corps area commander about this in the midst of his tremendous military involvements, but I want to be certain that lame ducks are not running this part of the show.

MANEUVERS: I would like your inspectors to check up on whether or not the enlisted men are kept advised of the changing situations in the maneuvers. Do they know what is going on and why? There have been reports that the men are doing the job without much knowledge of the reason why, and this is building up, from the attendant newspaper men, a tendency to criticize the conduct of the maneuvers, along with the deficiency in materiel, and the fact that some divisions have much more materiel than others (due to logical priorities). I have sent instructions to each Army Corps regarding this last matter.[2]

RELATION BETWEEN CANTONMENT COMMANDERS, UNIT COMMANDERS, AND HIGHER COMMANDERS: I would like all your inspectors to keep their eye on this subject and submit any ideas that may occur to them. The matter is exceedingly complex and doesn't seem to admit of a clear-cut solution. We have a corps area commander directly in charge of ground troop training centers, for example, responsible for the up-keep of all cantonments and military settlements within the corps area, and yet not in direct command of the people involved, and they, in turn, representing a variety of higher control, GHQ Air, Army Corps and Chief of the Air Corps. This becomes still more complicated in cases such as at Fort Bragg, where the senior officer has a huge establishment, commands a division that is part of a corps command,—General Shedd and General Drum,—has a separate artillery brigade under him that is under Army command, I believe; has a training center and a reception center that is under corps area command, etc. The army and then the corps, and the corps area, all may want certain things, which build up into a very complicated situation. No one has suggested a solution. So long as the field army is superimposed on the zone of the interior, and so long as we have major air units scattered through the United States in the zone of the interior, it will be a difficult situation. However, I think we will have to arrive at a little more definite demarcation than we have at present.

GCMRL/G. C. Marshall Papers (Pentagon Office, Selected)

1. Major General Virgil L. Peterson (U.S.M.A., 1908) had been the inspector general of the army since February 27, 1940.

2. When inspection reports showed that lack of knowledge of the maneuve. situation w..s still common among enlisted men and even among some officers (see Peterson . Memorandum for the Chief of Staff, July 16, 1941, NA/RG 165 [OCS, 14440-395]), Marsha!' again sent messages directing the commanding generals of maneuvers to concern themselves with this problem (see Marshall to Lieutenant General Walter Krueger, Telegram, Septem' er 12, 1941, NA/RG 165 [OCS, 14440-394]). After the maneuvers were completed, Mar nall praised

Lieutenant General Ben Lear, commanding general of the Second Army: "Apparently your idea of issuing simple Army news bulletins did a great deal to bring about this improvement over conditions existing in previous maneuvers." He directed that Lear's methods be brought to the attention of other commanders. (Draft by Colonel Walter B. Smith of Marshall to Lear, October 7, 1941, NA/RG 165 [OCS, 14440-403].)

To Admiral Harold R. Stark
Secret

June 27, 1941
[Washington, D.C.]

Dear Betty: I am sorry to delay so long in replying to your attached formal memorandum but it has taken our War Plans people longer than usual to make a thorough analysis, and since your letter was written many of the items noted have been accomplished or are in process of accomplishment. There are, however, certain exceptions. With regard to overseas Army forces, we have already made reductions in the war garrisons for Hawaii, Puerto Rico and Panama, and we are making efforts now to reinforce Army garrisons in the Western Hemisphere as far as practicable before M-Day, and some movements are now actually taking place. Details will be furnished to the Navy War Plans Division.[1]

With reference to other possible expeditions not specifically covered by Rainbow 5, the units and materiel to be moved should not be considered as additional, but as part of the 83,000 troops set up for transatlantic operations. This, however, does not apply to the force mentioned for West African operations. No commitment is made in Rainbow 5 nor does other agreement exist for a West African expedition. We would strongly oppose any such an operation as strategically unsound.

While the A.B.C. agreement upon which Rainbow 5 was based was studied for over two months by representatives of the Army, Navy and British, the plan should be subject to constant critical re-examination, always with a view to decisive defensive action by United States forces. As you know, we are not prepared to undertake any large scale defensive operations on land for some time to come. The question of priorities is most important and I suggest that it be studied by our respective planning committees in the light of changes which have occurred in the general situation since your letter was prepared.

We are gravely concerned over the lack of shipping necessary to transport and maintain our troops in overseas theaters. You know the difficulty of meeting such requirements for the Indigo operation and at the same time keeping on hand a reserve of shipping to meet emergency situations that might require the use of troops in South America.[2] I hope that it will be possible for you to take steps to meet this transportation problem in any of the operations mentioned in your letter. Faithfully yours,

NA/RG 165 (WPD, 4175–22)

1. Secretary Stimson approved joint war plan Rainbow 5 on June 2, 1941. Although the president did not formally approve the plan, the War Department proceeded with strategic planning on a tentative basis. According to Rainbow 5, the army would garrison Hawaii, Alaska, Panama, the Caribbean, and Iceland with forces totaling 220,900 men within the first few months of war. Air defense units and air forces, already scheduled for assignment to Britain according to the ABC staff agreements, were included in the joint war plan. The army also tentatively planned to send expeditionary forces to South America and to transatlantic destinations within six months after mobilization day. (Matloff and Snell, *Strategic Planning for Coalition Warfare*, pp. 46–47.)

Stark's May 22, 1941, letter discussed possible expeditionary forces to West Africa and Greenland, and proposed detailed planning for offensive actions against Germany. The army's War Plans Division opposed detailed planning until wartime and rejected any proposal for expeditionary forces not specified in Rainbow 5. (The W.P.D. study of Stark's letter is in NA/RG 165 [WPD, 4175–22].)

2. The Indigo operation—the occupation of Iceland—began on July 1, 1941. On July 7 United States Marines landed on Iceland. The army components of the garrison landed on August 6 and September 15.

MEMORANDUM FOR MR. McCLOY   June 28, 1941
                                                        [Washington, D.C.]

With reference to the attached draft regarding the designation of a Coordinator of Information: While I personally have not had time to inform myself as to the various aspects of the matter, in general I would be opposed to what is proposed in the draft.[1]

I am attaching a chart which presents, in a tentative manner, the character of the organization that I think should be set up, unless we have a fundamental, governmental reorganization in regard to the establishment of a higher staff with a Chief of Staff in direct contact with the President and, in effect, over and above all Cabinet officials so far as the national defense is concerned. This last seems to me wholly out of the question in our form of government. Therefore, I turn to some such organization as indicated on the chart.[2]

As I told you, at the moment I am not interested in the details of the actual organization of this debatable intelligence group or who is to be the head of it; what I am vitally interested in is where it is to be placed in the national defense scheme.

There is also attached a draft which I have not had time to analyze carefully, which might be utilized to put into effect an organization of the type indicated on the chart.

GCMRL/G. C. Marshall Papers (Pentagon Office, Selected)

1. Overlapping intelligence activities by the army, the navy, and the Federal Bureau of Investigation had caused conflict by early 1941. Several proposals to coordinate these functions

had been considered by the War Department. William J. Donovan, a World War officer and former assistant attorney general of the United States, submitted his own plan for a joint intelligence committee to Secretary Stimson. According to his plan, this committee would analyze and coordinate the exchange of intelligence information between governmental departments. President Roosevelt wanted Donovan to assume the rank of major general and report directly to him. On June 24 Marshall advised Stimson that, according to this plan, the coordinator would supplant the chief of staff's responsibility to the president. Stimson revised the proposal, making the new office a civilian position. (Preliminary proposals for a joint intelligence committee are in NA/RG 319 [G-2, MIS, 310.11 and 350.05]; on the bureaucratic conflict within the intelligence community, see Memorandum for the Secretary of War, March 25, 1941, p. 453; Marshall's opinions on the Donovan plan are in Yale/H. L. Stimson Papers [Diary, 34: 143, 146–47].)

2. Neither the draft document mentioned nor Marshall's organizational chart are in the Marshall papers. On July 3 Donovan met with Stimson and McCloy and "agreed upon the general principles. . . . The routine channels for the recommendations as to intelligence and information were to be coordinated by Donovan as they came from all the Departments which collected them—the Army, the Navy, FBI, the State Department, and all the others—information, economic and military—and then should go up through the channels, through the Joint Board and then through the Chief of Staff and the Chief of Operations of the Navy, the Secretary of War and the Secretary of the Navy, to the President." (Yale/H. L. Stimson Papers [Diary, 34: 168].)

TO MRS. ROSE LUMETTA   June 28, 1941
                                                                  [Washington, D.C.]

My dear Mrs. Lumetta: I have your letter of June 24th and am sorry that you are so disturbed and angry over the possibility of your son's remaining in the Army beyond one year.[1] The War Department does not wish to keep your boy or any of the others in the service for one day longer than is necessary for the safety of the country, but it is impossible to tell at this time what that necessity is. It depends upon world conditions which change so rapidly that no one knows what the next 24 hours will bring forth.

Unless the military situation becomes very acute the bulk of the selectees will be sent home after they complete their year of service. Some in key positions may be needed so badly that authority will be requested to retain them in service.

Millions of European mothers would be offering grateful prayers of thanksgiving if the only sacrifice they were called upon to make for their country was to be separated from their sons by a few hundred peaceful miles. To preserve that peace is our sole objective.   Faithfully yours,

GCMRL/G. C. Marshall Papers (Pentagon Office, General)

1. Lumetta questioned whether she could address Marshall as "dear sir" considering the chief of staff's intention to extend the term of service for selectees. "If you do that," she wrote, "you will have the hatred of every mother, wife and sweethearts and also the boys themselves." (Lumetta to Marshall, June 24, 1941, GCMRL/G. C. Marshall Papers [Pentagon Office, General].)

MEMORANDUM FOR ADMIRAL STARK   June 28, 1941
Confidential   [Washington, D.C.]

Dear Betty: Some time back we discussed in a Joint Board meeting the proposition of transforming the Joint Planning Committee from its present divided status—the Army members working over here, the Navy members working over in your shop—into a genuine committee of men working together all the time. The heads of the Committee apparently would have to be the respective heads of the Army and Navy War Plans Committees— Gerow and Turner—and they of course would remain in their own sections. But it seems to me the time has come to assemble the other members on a permanent basis.[1]

As the Navy interest at the present time is the dominant one from the viewpoint of possible operations, it is entirely agreeable to me for this committee to sit in the Navy Department.

Think this over during the week-end and talk to me about it Monday.

GCMRL/ G. C. Marshall Papers (Pentagon Office, Selected)

1. Created in 1919, the Joint Planning Committee studied and reported on plans under consideration by the Joint Board. The mounting volume of national defense plans formulated in 1939 and 1940 overburdened the planning committee, which consisted of the War Plans Division chiefs for both services and their senior assistants. In May 1941 the Joint Board reduced the Joint Planning Committee to only the two War Plans chiefs plus temporary working committees from their staffs. A new Joint Strategic Committee, drawn from all the officers of the army and navy War Plans divisions, assumed the duty of joint planning. (Ray S. Cline, *Washington Command Post: The Operations Division,* a volume in the *United States Army in World War II* [Washington: GPO, 1951], p. 46.) Rear Admiral Richmond K. Turner (U.S.N.A., 1908) directed the navy's War Plans Division.

MEMORANDUM FOR ASSISTANT CHIEF   June 30, 1941
OF STAFF, G-2 [MILES]   [Washington, D.C.]
Confidential

The Under Secretary of State has just informed the Soviet Ambassador that he feels our Military Attaché in Moscow should be given an opportunity to witness the operations now in progress. The Soviet Ambassador replied that he agreed with the reasonableness of the request and stated that he would transmit this proposal to his government.[1]

The President informed Mr. Welles that he wished our attaché in Moscow to check up on two things:

1. Did the Russians have any plans for destroying the cereal crops as they withdrew, particularly from the Ukraine, and if so, were they successful?

2. Had the Russians plans to destroy the oil wells in that vicinity. (Mr. Welles stated that the British had already asked him in regard to the latter in relation to some plans they were attempting to perfect to this purpose.)[2]

NA/RG 165 (OCS, SGS, Notes on Conferences File)

1. Major Ivan D. Yeaton was the United States military attaché in the Soviet Union. Constantine A. Oumansky was the Soviet Union's ambassador to the United States.

2. At a War Council meeting on June 23, Marshall had commented on the recently launched invasion of the Soviet Union. He advised the council that if the Soviets could carry out a strategic withdrawal, avoiding encirclement while sabotaging their oil refineries in southern Russia, they could deny the Germans a quick victory. Although the crops were too green to be torched, Marshall noted, a massive sabotage effort in the oil fields would prevent the Germans from swiftly exploiting their gains. (Orlando Ward Notes on Conference in the Office of the Secretary of War, June 23, 1941, NA/RG 165 [OCS, War Council Minutes].)

A Capacity for Leadership

July 1 – September 30, 1941

You are about to assume the most important duty that our officers are called upon to perform—the direct command of combat units of American soldiers. To succeed requires two fundamental qualifications—thorough professional knowledge and a capacity for leadership.

—Address for Delivery to the Graduates
of the First Officer Candidate School
September 27, 1941

M ARSHALL reported the state of the armed forces on July 1, 1941, in the biennial report of the chief of staff for July 1, 1939, to June 30, 1941. "Today the Army has been increased eightfold and consists of approximately 1,400,000 men. The ground forces in the continental United States form four armies of nine army corps and twenty-nine divisions, and an Armored Force of four divisions, soon to be increased to six. The Air Force includes 54 combat groups. . . .

"The strength of the Army is now allocated approximately as follows: 456,000 men to the 29 divisions of the field armies; 43,000 men to the Armored Force; 308,000 men to some 215 regiments or similar units of field and antiaircraft artillery, engineers, signal troops, etc., who form the corps, army, and GHQ troops to support the divisions; 167,000 men in the Air Corps; 46,000 men manning our harbor defenses; 120,000 men in oversea garrisons including Alaska and Newfoundland; and 160,000 men who provide the overhead to maintain and operate some 550 posts or stations, the supply depots, and the ports of embarkation; and finally from 100,000 to 200,000 selectees under recruit training in the replacement training centers. Our long coast lines and numerous oversea bases involve the employment of a large number of men not related to the field forces now being developed in continental United States."

A modern army must be prepared to operate in a variety of climates and terrains, the chief of staff continued. "The members of our armed forces have passed through a winter of rigorous training and are in splendid physical condition. The training and welfare agencies have produced a gratifying state of morale. Although sufficient equipment exists for training purposes, the necessary amount of critical items is still far short of requirements, and only a small portion of the field Army is at present equipped for extended active operations under conditions of modern warfare. However, quantity production has been getting under way for an increasing number of items, and the next 4 months should greatly improve the situation." ("Biennial Report of the Chief of Staff, July 1, 1941," in War Department, *Report of the Secretary of War to the President, 1941* [Washington: GPO, 1941], pp. 55–56.)

But maintaining an expanded army required more than equipment. Morale was of primary interest to the chief of staff. "The problems incident to the maintenance of a high state of morale in our expanded Army have been of primary importance during the past 2 fiscal years. The introduction of selective service, the induction of the National Guard, and the calling to active duty of a large number of Reserve officers have brought many diverse elements into the Army. This rapid expansion, coupled with the difficulties encountered in housing, clothing, feeding, and training the new Army produced many new problems in the field of morale. These special problems were recognized early in the expansion, and steps were taken immediately to solve them. As a result of these timely measures, it can be reported that a high state of morale is now clearly evident throughout our Army.

"One of the outstanding indications of improvement in morale has been the continuous diminution of court-martial rates. During the fiscal year 1940, the general court-martial rate per thousand enlisted men fell from 11 to 9; the special court-martial rate, from 23 to 21; and the summary court-martial rate, from 56 to 48." (Ibid., pp. 75–76.)

Creation of the Morale Branch in the spring of 1941 had made evident the War Department's awareness of the importance of morale activities. While the War Department assumed responsibility for morale work within military reservations, other federal agencies were responsible for morale activities outside military boundaries. Marshall then cited examples of the United States Army providing recreational, social, and entertainment services within the borders of military reservations. Athletic equipment and field houses for athletic programs were available; 185 posts had facilities for showing motion pictures; a system of mobile units to provide volunteer professional entertainment had been initiated; 113 service clubs had been constructed, most of them with a library and a cafeteria; and 297 hostesses and 96 librarians had been employed.

"While the physical comforts and recreational needs will remain in the spotlight of attention," Marshall concluded, "it is recognized that everything physical and psychological affects human conduct. The Morale Branch is constantly engaged in the study of all factors which contribute and adversely affect morale and the advance planning for morale work in the event of a movement to theaters of operation." (Ibid., pp. 76–77.) ★

To Nat Patton   July 5, 1941
[Washington, D.C.]

My dear Mr. Patton: Upon receipt of your letter of June 25th, regarding the 56th Cavalry Brigade, I had a careful investigation made from two sources.[1]

Immediately after the concentration of the Brigade at Fort Bliss the latter part of May, there was an epidemic of diarrhoea, which has been eliminated. The sick rate is now normal. The excessive rate was apparently due to a combination of factors. One was the excessive drinking of soft drinks by the men who had not become hardened to field service and therefore suffered from thirst. Another cause was failure to properly clean the mess kits, the usual difficulty with unseasoned troops. Regarding the first cause, the hospital authorities issued salt tablets for the purpose of allaying thirst during extremely hot afternoons. Also gauze masks for men on duty in the picket line, where the dust was excessive. Special screening and other measures were taken.

As to the question of morale and discontent, I find no basis for that. Approximately 50 men and 8 or 10 officers were privately questioned on the subject. But on the contrary, it was found that the morale was high, and particularly that the Brigade had taken a very effective part in a recent maneuver. The men who played the game were alert notwithstanding the heat and appeared to enjoy the experience; they were disappointed that it was terminated ahead of schedule. The officers seemed quite enthusiastic, especially over the high commendation they received on the maneuvers.

While I am giving you this data, I would prefer that you do not quote me in the press on the subject.[2]   Faithfully yours,

GCMRL/G. C. Marshall Papers (Pentagon Office, General)

1. Congressman Nat Patton, a Democrat representing the Seventh District of Texas, had requested that Marshall investigate the Fifty-sixth Cavalry Brigade stationed at Fort Bliss. "I am advised that the morale of this brigade is at a low ebb due to jealousy among the officers at the Fort and because of the fact that recently a large percentage of the men have suffered a stomach disorder that has been blamed on the mess. This is a relatively small matter, but it may become one of a number of factors that can destroy the present high morale of the army we are now so proud to have." (Patton to Marshall, June 25, 1941, GCMRL/G. C. Marshall Papers [Pentagon Office, General].)

2. Patton replied that he appreciated Marshall's prompt inquiry. "I should like to say that my good friend, the late Senator Morris Sheppard, always had the highest regard for both your ability and your endeavor, and from his own high opinion, I have gained an exalted opinion of your value." (Patton to Marshall, July 7, 1941, ibid.)

To Major General Walter S. Grant   July 7, 1941
Personal and Confidential   [Washington, D.C.]

Dear Walter: Most confidentially, I propose in August to make a sweeping change in army corps commanders in order to get younger and more experienced leadership to these mobile forces from men who have proven themselves very able in organizing and training divisions. The present corps commanders are very good men but not quite up to the jobs from the viewpoint of activity and, on the part of three Coast Artillerymen, from the standpoint of knowledge of the mobile arms.[1] I am also bringing about a change of command in Panama in September, and for this purpose will order General Van Voorhis to relieve Trott in the 5th Corps Area.

Under the circumstances and in view of your retirement date, it will help me out of a difficult situation to install your successor about the middle of August. If agreeable to you, on Embick's recommendation, I would like to have you assist him in strategical planning, in which he is now engaged.

Incidentally, he is on the Canadian Defense Board, and the Mexican Defense Board, as well as serving in a confidential capacity at the White House.[2] Also, I would like to have you serve on a general selection board which we must create. I do not imagine it would be necessary for you to change your place of residence because it probably would not be necessary for you to come to Washington every day.

Please treat everything I have said as most confidential, and please give me your frank reaction.[3]   Faithfully yours,

GCMRL/G. C. Marshall Papers (Pentagon Office, Selected)

1. The three corps commanders with Coast Artillery Corps backgrounds were Major Generals William E. Shedd (First), Frederic H. Smith (Seventh), and Walter K. Wilson (U.S.M.A., 1902) (Third). See Marshall to Wilson, October 7, 1941, pp. 631–33.

On this same day, Marshall also wrote to Lieutenant General John L. De Witt to outline the proposed changes. "I had proceeded initially on the basis that it was essential to put in older officers as corps commanders from the viewpoint of morale and more especially because it seemed much wiser to have the ultimate selection of corps commander confined to men who had had extensive divisional command experience. Also, I wanted to avoid hurting the development of these new divisions by changing commanders in the middle of the process. Now, we have gotten to the point where such change of divisional command can be carried out, I think, without too much harm." (Marshall to De Witt, July 7, 1941, GCMRL/G. C. Marshall Papers [Pentagon Office, Selected].)

2. Since the completion of the American-British staff conferences in late March, Marshall had called upon Major General Stanley D. Embick to advise not only the War Department but the president on military affairs. Secretary Stimson noted in his diary that Roosevelt considered Embick one of his trusted advisers. "He is one of our best strategists—a Retired General whom we all rely on, including the President." (April 15 and October 1, 1941, Yale/ H. L. Stimson Papers [Diary, 33: 163; 35: 103].)

3. Grant replied that while he was due to retire on January 31, 1942, he had hoped to command the Third Corps Area until December 1, 1941, but if Marshall preferred that he be relieved in August and assist Embick in strategic planning it was all right with him. "I'll conform to any plan that is for the best interests of the army and the country." (Grant to Marshall, July 9, 1941, GCMRL/G. C. Marshall Papers [Pentagon Office, Selected].)

MEMORANDUM FOR ADMIRAL STARK   July 7, 1941
Personal and Confidential   [Washington, D.C.]

Dear Betty: I have very carefully gone over Admiral Towers' memorandum and that of the Judge Advocate General of the Navy Department regarding General Arnold's rank, and I am sorry that this issue has been raised.[1]

The legal opinion of the Judge Advocate General of the Army might have been written as Admiral Towers indicates. However, this would have been with very serious consequences to the command situation in the Army. The Navy has quite a different problem, remote from our difficulties in creating a unified force out of three components, among which the professional

Regular Army group is decidedly in the minority. For example, in approximately 90,000 officers now on active duty only about 13,000 are Regulars and about half the Generals are National Guardsmen.

Arnold's case came up in connection with three others, and the decision involved will apply to a great many others.[2] As a matter of fact, Arnold while the Chief of an arm actually commanded the entire Air Corps—the GHQ Air Force being under his control—during most of his term of office. If the decision of your Naval Judge Advocate in relation to your Bureau Chiefs were to be applied to the Army, General Arnold would drop approximately 60 files among the Major Generals heretofore his juniors, and General Bryden, the senior Deputy Chief of Staff, would suffer almost as great a loss. Though in his case there is no question of a Bureau Chief status, there is the problem of a temporary commission over-lapping a permanent commission. The same issue occurs in the case of General Brett. He occupies, through definite arrangement last October, a certain seniority in the Air Corps. The decision of your Naval Judge Advocate would drop him below most of the senior officers controlling various sub-divisions of Aviation under General Brett's direct control. Similar topsy-turvy leap-frogging of rank will be the rule whenever officers of one component of the Army are appointed in another component notwithstanding the change in component occurred without hiatus and without change in powers and duties. It is this anomalous and militarily impossible condition I wish to avoid. Such a condition, moreover, would be directly contrary to the national policy of treating all components of the Army as of equal dignity and importance, and what is more important, of facilitating transfers among the components. To bolster up the National Guard I am forced at times to place temporary Major Generals of the Regular Army or Brigadier Generals in command of such units. Compared with such matters, the question of who sits senior on a board appears to me as insignificant, especially as the two individuals concerned have sat on the board for a long period in a certain order of rank.

Confidentially, I am distressed by this issue, which was raised over what seems to me to be an irritatingly small matter, because it is just such business as this that will create for us a Department of National Defense or a separate Air Corps. It comes with singularly bad taste to me at this moment when I have just deferred in the case of an Army commander who clearly ranks the Marine officer that you and I thought should be in command of an important force. Contrast this with the matter of seniority on a board, and I think it suggests an unfortunate attitude.

I am very glad you sent this to me informally so that I could reply to it informally. You and I, I think, have both done our level best to maintain a complete accord between the Army and Navy and to foster an intimate relationship. This reaction of Admiral Towers, it seems to me, is plainly contrary to that policy.

GCMRL/G. C. Marshall Papers (Pentagon Office, Selected)

1. The editors have not found Rear Admiral John H. Towers's memorandum or that of the navy judge advocate general. (For information concerning the Joint Air Advisory Committee, of which Arnold and Towers were members, see Memorandum for Admiral Stark, February 24, 1940, pp. 166–67.)

2. For information about Arnold's promotion, see Memorandum for the Secretary of War, May 16, 1941, pp. 508–10.

MEMORANDUM FOR MR. WELLES   July 10, 1941
Secret   Washington, D.C.

Reference our telephone conversation late yesterday evening:

Our Attaché in Moscow notifies us that he has been advised by the Russian officials that they are considering the matter of permitting him to go to the front. Up to the present time we have no notice of his having been accorded that privilege.[1]

With further reference to the military situation, it would appear that the German Army is on the verge of disrupting the Russian forces, that is, so separating them that they cannot act with any unity. It is believed that the German Army has reached what may be called a phase line, where there has been a pause to permit the foot divisions to get up in closer supporting distance of the armored divisions. This would be a natural pause. It is anticipated that there will be another lunge shortly, which will probably make clear the sub-dividing of the Russian forces. It is not believed their fortified lines amount to very much.[2]

In the Ukraine it is felt that the German progress has been greater than reported. However, in this particular campaign we have a minimum of armored divisions on the German side, about 2, and a considerably greater number on the Russian side. Nevertheless, the Germans appear to have advanced about 120 miles.

Measured by the map of France, the German general advance is equivalent to a movement from Germany to the Pyrenees.

While long-range estimating is a dangerous business, it looks as though about one-third of the Russian Army might be able to reorganize behind the Volga and possibly make the winter there but more probably in Western Siberia. Unconfirmed reports indicate about 10 divisions from the Eastern Siberian Army moved to the west. If this is so, the Japanese military position in Manchuria will be greatly strengthened.

I am dictating this by telephone to you.

GCMRL/G. C. Marshall Papers (Pentagon Office, Selected)

1. Efforts by the War and State departments to obtain permission for Major Ivan D. Yeaton, United States military attaché in Moscow, to visit the front were finally successful on

July 28. (Department of State, *Foreign Relations of the United States: Diplomatic Papers, 1941,* 7 vols. [Washington: GPO, 1956–63], 1: 781, 900–903.)
   2. Lieutenant Colonel Paul M. Robinett, who had begun his duties as assistant chief of staff, G-2, at Army General Headquarters the week after the June 22 German attack on the Soviet Union, observed that at the time "there was almost unanimous agreement among all military men that Russia would be quickly and decisively destroyed. The only difference of opinion seemed to be concerning how long it would take. No one that I know of had any other view." (GCMRL/P. M. Robinett Collection [Diary, pp. 176–77].)

UNITED STATES "interests are imperiled," Marshall wrote in his July 1, 1941, biennial report; "a grave national emergency exists." The army's ability to defend these interests was severely restricted by laws limiting the service of Reserve officers, National Guard troops, and draftees to twelve months and restricting the deployment of these forces to the Western Hemisphere. These restrictions should be removed, he asserted. ("Biennial Report," in *Report of the Secretary of War to the President, 1941,* pp. 56–57.)

   "The Regular Army divisions contain from 75 to 90 percent Reserve officers whose term of service is legally limited to 12 months. In other words, some 600 officers in a division under the law would soon be entitled to drop their present duties and return to their homes. The 12 months' service period of many, if not most of the officers in the first priority divisions, is now nearly completed. Must we replace most of the trained officer personnel of a division—the leaders—at the moment of departure for strategic localities? In two of the Regular divisions we have restricted the enlisted personnel to 3-year men, but in the others, of necessity, the number of selectees varies from 25 to 50 percent. The problem here is the same as for the Reserve officer personnel. The National Guard units involve three distinct limitations as to personnel—that for the National Guard unit, that for the 10 percent Reserve officers in their regiments and now being increased, and that pertaining to selectees who comprise more than 50 percent of the men in the ranks. Furthermore, a task force involves all components. While we may select regular units as the divisional components for task forces, we must utilize National Guard organizations for the special supporting units— antiaircraft, heavy artillery, engineers, etc. So we have become involved in a complete confusion of restrictive details regarding personnel." (Ibid., pp. 57–58.)

   The service-time limitation, he told the Senate Military Affairs Committee on July 9, meant that garrisoning distant posts such as Alaska and Hawaii was difficult. Units could not be sent there if a large portion of their personnel soon had to be replaced. The geographical limitation meant that units of the all-volunteer Marine Corps had to be sent instead of the United States Army to protect the nation's interests in places such as Iceland.

(Senate Military Affairs Committee, *Strengthening the National Defense, Hearing* [Washington: GPO, 1941], pp. 3–4, 10–11.)

Marshall's use of the words "task force" in his biennial report had immediate repercussions in the press and in Congress; fears were voiced that the army was preparing a 1917-style A.E.F. for action in Europe. In his testimony of July 9, the chief of staff rejected such a "confused" interpretation of the term. "As to the 'task forces' referred to in my report—I used that expression deliberately because I thought it was time that the public should become accustomed to the term. It should have no sinister significance. It means simply this: We determine for a particular, a possible mission the size and composition of the force necessary to carry it out. It may be 5,000, or 15,000, or 30,000. It is, as I have explained, a self-contained, self-supporting force. Instead of waiting until the last moment to assemble such a force as we have always done in the past—for the Santiago campaign in Cuba, the Philippines in 1898, for Siberia and Russia in 1918, and for France and Italy in 1917—we are deliberately organizing them now so far as we can foresee the possibility and are training them for their possible employment." (Ibid., p. 4.)

The political objections to removal of the geographical restrictions endangered the issue Marshall considered most important: removal of the service-time limitations. In a White House meeting on Monday, July 14, Marshall further discussed with the president and congressional leaders the timely need for lifting the legal limitations on the army. In the interest of quick passage of the service extension resolutions, the group agreed, at least for the immediate time, not to pursue abolition of the territorial restrictions. (Orlando Ward Notes on Conference in the Office of the Secretary of War, July 16, 1941, NA/RG 165 [OCS, War Council Minutes]; *New York Times,* July 15, 1941, pp. 1, 11.) ★

MEMORANDUM FOR THE PRESIDENT   July 15, 1941
                                                 Washington, D.C.

Attached is the record of my hearings before the Senate Military Committee on the question of the retention of the selectees and reserve components in the military service. I have marked certain portions which relate to the general proposition, to Hawaii and Alaska, and especially to Iceland.

In view of the discussion of yesterday, and others which may follow, you may be interested in reading those particular portions of my testimony.

G. C. Marshall

FDRL/F. D. Roosevelt Papers (OF, 1413)

MEMORANDUM FOR THE PRESIDENT   July 16, 1941
                                                     Washington, D.C.

With reference to your informal direction to me last Monday morning to ascertain the suitable time for a message by you to the Congress regarding the removal of the legal limitations now adversely affecting the Army, I have talked to the principal leaders, and have had many others queried on the subject, all, of course, confidentially. The consensus of opinion appears to be that a message from you as soon as possible would be highly desirable, in fact, they believe this will be necessary to a favorable consideration of the recommendations of the War Department.[1]

I discussed this a few minutes ago with Senator Barkley, who is strongly of the opinion that this action should be taken as soon as possible. Mr. Wadsworth and Senator Hill are of the same opinion today.[2]

There is evidently a much better understanding of the seriousness of the situation than was the case a few days ago.

                                                     G. C. Marshall

FDRL/F. D. Roosevelt Papers (OF, 1413)

1. On July 21 President Roosevelt sent a message to Capitol Hill urging Congress quickly to enact legislation which would extend the service of selectees, national guardsmen, and reservists in the army beyond one year. Roosevelt stated that the danger to United States national security was "infinitely greater" than the year before. "It is true that in modern war men without machines are of little value. It is equally true that machines without men are of no value at all. . . . Within two months disintegration, which would follow failure to take Congressional action, will commence in the armies of the United States. Time counts. The responsibility rests solely with the Congress." (*The Public Papers and Addresses of Franklin D. Roosevelt*, 1941 volume, ed. Samuel I. Rosenman [New York: Harper and Brothers, 1950], pp. 272–77.) In August the Senate, by a vote of 45–30, and the House of Representatives, by a vote of 203–202, authorized extension from twelve to eighteen months of service under the Selective Training and Service Act. President Roosevelt approved the Service Extension Act of 1941 on August 18, and three days later he issued Executive Order 8862 extending active military service to eighteen months.

2. Alben W. Barkley, a Democrat from Kentucky, had been majority leader since 1937. James W. Wadsworth was a Republican congressman from New York, and Lister Hill was a Democratic senator from Alabama.

MEMORANDUM FOR GENERAL ARNOLD   July 16, 1941
Confidential   [Washington, D.C.]

With reference to the proposition that some of our Army pursuit planes be turned over to Russia:[1]

Please make it perfectly clear that as Chief of Staff I am unalterably opposed to the release of any U.S. pursuit planes and light and medium bombers until we have first established units of these types in the Philippines for the security of the Fleet anchorage, and the defense of the Islands. We have been trying for six months to meet the Navy's demands, and that of our Army Commander in the Philippines, that the obsolescent planes be replaced at the earliest possible moment with modern types. At the present moment, with Japan's known preparations to move South, the Philippines become of great strategic importance, as they constitute both a Naval and Air Base upon the immediate flank of the Japanese southern movement.

Furthermore, up to the present time we have been unable to provide either pursuit planes or light bombers to cooperate in any way with our troops during these large maneuvers. This represents a complete deficiency in air-ground training, and we must not continue further with that state of affairs. The development of the Army demands that this be corrected, and the public reaction presents a very serious consideration.

GCMRL/G. C. Marshall Papers (Pentagon Office, Selected)

1. At his June 24 press conference, President Roosevelt had declared that the United States was prepared to extend military aid to the Soviet Union, but nothing could be done until the Soviets presented a list of needed materials. (*New York Times,* June 25, 1941, p. 1.) Ambassador Constantine A. Oumansky had presented a memorandum of general requirements to the State Department on June 30 and two detailed materiel lists on July 7. (*Foreign Relations, 1941,* 1: 779–81, 788.) The Soviet government requested nearly $2,000,000,000 worth of materiel, including three thousand bombers and an equal number of pursuit planes. (W. Averell Harriman and Elie Abel, *Special Envoy to Churchill and Stalin, 1941–1946* [New York: Random House, 1975], p. 74.)

To Lieutenant Colonel Darryl F. Zanuck   July 17, 1941
[Washington, D.C.]

Dear Colonel Zanuck: Your suggestion for educational and semi-historical courses is far from presumptuous;—as a matter of fact, I think the observations which prompted your recommendation are entirely accurate.[1]

To be perfectly frank, I believe the state of bewilderment which you have noted is the result of a very apparent lack of unity of thought throughout the country, and not a fault of training. Our difficulty lies in the fact that we are bound to avoid controversial or political subjects, or any attempt to control the views of our men on such matters. We can, and do, instruct in the obligations of citizenship and of military service, but this is about as far as we can go under present conditions.

If the situation crystallizes we can do much more, and then I think your educational courses could be pushed to the limit. Would it not be possible to do this better by motion pictures than in any other way? Give this some thought and let me have the benefit of your ideas.

The news reel did turn out well and you are to be congratulated.[2]   Faithfully yours,

GCMRL/G. C. Marshall Papers (Pentagon Office, Selected)

1. In mid-June, Zanuck had met with various arm and service chiefs and with General Marshall regarding his training film production activities. While in Washington and since returning to California, he had talked with officers recently stationed at cantonments throughout the nation. He was disturbed because the officers had reported that the majority of the draftees and newly enlisted men, were "not fully aware of the causes and the reasons for our present foreign policy." The men were "confused and bewildered by the tommyrot constantly dished out by Lindbergh and the America First Committee. I do not for a moment suggest that the United States Army delve into propaganda or exploitation, but I do recommend that educational and semi-historical courses be delivered in every camp throughout the nation, so that draftees or newly enlisted men may be told the truth and the facts about our present foreign policy." (Zanuck to Marshall, June 25, 1941, GCMRL/G. C. Marshall Papers [Pentagon Office, Selected].)

2. In his letter, Zanuck did not indicate which newsreel he had shown to Marshall. Most of the newsreel companies had begun production of films depicting various aspects of army life, and the Bureau of Public Relations hoped to use these extensively in public theaters. (Lieutenant Colonel A. D. Bruce Informal Memorandum for Lieutenant Colonel Mickelsen, March 7, 1941, NA/RG 407 [General, 413].)

MEMORANDUM FOR THE ASSISTANT   July 18, 1941
SECRETARY FOR AIR[1]   Washington, D.C.
Confidential

My dear Mr. Lovett: Last night Mr. Sumner Welles telephoned me that he had learned that the OPM and other related officials had turned down the proposition of furnishing planes to Russia. I believe he was referring to the effort made to have the British release certain planes from United States production. He stated that the President was deeply concerned over this and had "ordered" that we make a token release to Russia of P-40s and light bombers, and that we make an effort to have the British do likewise.

You are familiar with the situation regarding both of these types of planes so far as pertains to our Army. At the present time I am under four serious pressures regarding their allocation.

The great and increasing importance of several squadrons of pursuit planes and of light bombers in the Philippines to protect that Fleet base and to threaten the Japanese line of communications.

The urgent necessity of having efficient squadrons of pursuit planes and light bombers working with the ground troops in the current maneuvers. This is vitally important so far as the development of ground air team work is concerned, but it is possibly of even more pressing importance to meet the growing public pressure and criticism on this subject.

The necessity of having immediately available squadrons of pursuit and light bombers for station in Natal. Concerned with the foregoing and reflecting the State Department's urgent demands, the allocation of twelve light bombers to Brazil.

The urgings of Mr. Lauchlin Currie for us to release planes of these types to the Chinese.[2]

Now we have this directive from the Commander-in-Chief to make a token release, which means at least a squadron in each case to Russia. I feel that this should be discussed with the President personally in order that he may have a complete picture of our present dilemma in this matter. Are we to risk the Philippine situation or the Brazilian situation, or the clamor of the press in this country or the purely military requirements of training our field forces in this country?[3]

G. C. Marshall

NA/RG 107 (SW Safe, Russia)

1. Robert A. Lovett, a pilot in the Naval Air Service from 1917 to 1918, had been assistant secretary of war for air since April 1941. He had served as special assistant to the secretary of war from December 1940 to April 1941.

2. On July 23, 1941, President Roosevelt approved a Joint Board recommendation to "equip, man, and maintain" a five hundred-plane Chinese Air Force. (Charles F. Romanus and Riley Sunderland, *Stilwell's Mission to China,* a volume in the *United States Army in World War II* [Washington: GPO, 1953], p. 23.) Currie, administrative assistant to the president, had submitted the aircraft program for China in late May. In a letter to Roosevelt, Acting Secretary of War Robert P. Patterson and Secretary of the Navy Frank Knox stated: "The accomplishment of the Joint Board's proposals to furnish aircraft equipment to China in accordance with Mr. Currie's Short Term Requirements for China, requires the collaboration of Great Britain in diversions of allocations already made to them; however, it is our belief that the suggested diversions present no insurmountable difficulty nor occasion any great handicap." (Patterson and Knox to The President, July 18, 1941, NA/RG 319 [OPD, Joint Board 355, Serial 691].)

3. Lovett met with Sumner Welles on July 18 and explained that a token delivery of planes, particularly P-40s, would be "dangerous and undesirable" because the P-40s required expert service and maintenance, could not readily be flown to Russia via Alaska, and required guns and ammunition which were in an acute shortage. "It is our feeling that a 'token force' of equipment of this character might be of very doubtful benefit to the Russians since, if flight delivered, it would undoubtedly arrive in bad condition and in quantities so small as to have an effect exactly the reverse of what would be hoped for. We suggest that the Russians might reasonably wonder why the greatest industrial country in the world could only deliver a mere handful of planes." He reminded Welles that British demands accounted for over 50 percent of July aircraft production and that China had also requested aircraft. (Lovett Memorandum for the Secretary of War, July 21, 1941, NA/RG 107 [SW Safe, Russia].) See Memorandum for General Arnold, July 16, 1941, pp. 567–68.

To John Osborne   July 18, 1941
                                                 [Washington, D.C.]

Dear Osborne: I was interested in your note of the 14th, though I had already seen General Jarman's letter.[1] A number of these cases will come up, and will be corrected.

The point is, there were something over 600 vacancies, and we could not wait until the reports on the past year's work from the field had passed through the various channels and came up to the War Department. Therefore, we were compelled to make promotions at this time on the basis of ten years' efficiency records. For that reason, we only advanced 200 line officers, leaving over 400 vacancies to be filled in September, November, and January. In this way the record of the field will enable us to correct the errors in September of the first list, particularly as commanders are instructed to report specific cases where they feel an injustice has been done, with a statement of the circumstances. The November list will be three-quarters based on the work of the past year, and the final list of 150 in January will be entirely based on the work during the emergency.

It is utterly impossible for us to make a theoretically perfect performance, and largely for that reason, together with the opposition of Congress we have never been able to get started in the past—particularly because we have had no good criterion of test as the Navy has had in the Fleet, where everybody is under easy observation. Now with great field forces, we have a chance, even though they are widely scattered.

You have to break eggs to make an omelet, and I am determined to have the omelet. My only concern is that favoritism and propinquity do not do too much harm. It is very difficult to have the officer on the ground act in a cold-blooded impersonal manner regarding his immediate subordinates. He approves promotion by selection, but he is often weak in giving it a proper application to those with whom he is daily associated. Faithfully yours,

GCMRL/G. C. Marshall Papers (Pentagon Office, Selected)

1. Osborne, the associate editor of *Time* magazine, had written to Marshall that an unnamed army friend had informed him that "the recent selections for colonelcies created a very curious and disturbing situation in the Panama Coast Artillery Command," which he suggested that Marshall investigate. He noted that Major General Sanderford Jarman (U.S.M.A., 1908), commander of the Panama Coast Artillery brigade but *not* the informant, had detailed the situation in a letter to Major General Joseph A. Green, chief of Coast Artillery. Osborne emphasized, "no one in the Army acted indiscreetly or unethically in telling me about this matter. . . . I do feel that 'the good of the Army' is involved in this case. It will never be referred to in TIME, I can assure you." (Osborne to Marshall, July 14, 1941, GCMRL/G. C. Marshall Papers [Pentagon Office, Selected].) The editors have not found Jarman's letter to Green.

To Spencer L. Carter   July 19, 1941
                                                    Washington, D.C.

Dear Spencer: Thank you so much for your telegram of the 18th. It is indeed a refreshing and a heartening thing to receive such encouraging praise, and particularly from one whose good opinion I value so highly.[1] Faithfully yours,

G. C. Marshall

In contrast to your message, I am being called—a Benedict Arnold, a skunk, Hitler Marshall, a stooge, Traitor, etc, etc. GCM[2]

GCMRL/G. C. Marshall Collection (Correspondence)
  1. Carter (V.M.I., 1893), an officer of the Virginia-Carolina Chemical Corporation, told Marshall, "Your sound sensible and outspoken testimony before the Military Affairs Committee yesterday was that of a great general and a great organizer." (Carter to Marshall, Telegram, July 18, 1941, GCMRL/G. C. Marshall Papers [Pentagon Office, Selected].)
  2. Marshall added this postscript in his own handwriting.

To Colonel E. R. Warner McCabe[1]   July 21, 1941
                                                    [Washington, D.C.]

Dear McCabe: Your P.M.S. & T. Colonel Tuttle, came in to see me the other day,—he is an old friend of China and Benning days—and incidentally made a comment to the effect that he was changing station as he was being squeezed out or ousted from his present job by my Aide, Colonel Adams.[2]

I told him this was not the fact. However, I would like you to make clear to him that the selection of Adams for your job had no relation to Colonel Tuttle's relief. I try too hard to be completely impersonal in the business of being purely objective for the efficiency of the Army to have such rumors or ideas as this broadcast.[3] Hastily yours,

GCMRL/G. C. Marshall Papers (Pentagon Office, General)
  1. Assistant chief of staff, G-2, between July 1937 and February 1940, McCabe had retired from the army effective July 31, 1940. "You were always to me a breath of spring in the air, the saving grace in this bureaucracy," the chief of staff wrote following McCabe's departure from Washington. (Marshall to McCabe, March 18, 1940, GCMRL/G. C. Marshall Papers [Pentagon Office, General].) Later that year Marshall recommended McCabe for the post of superintendent of Staunton Military Academy in Staunton, Virginia, which position he assumed in early 1941. (Marshall to the Governing Board, Staunton Military Academy, November 29, 1940, ibid.)
  2. Lieutenant Colonel William B. Tuttle—who had been with Marshall in the Fifteenth Infantry in Tientsin, China, and then a student under him at the Infantry School at Fort

Benning, Georgia—had been at the Staunton Military Academy since August 1938. He had recently been reassigned to duty at Fort Sam Houston, Texas. Concerning Lieutenant Colonel Claude M. Adams's R.O.T.C. assignment, see note 1, Marshall to Adams, May 14, 1941, pp. 502–3.

3. McCabe replied that he had "made it very clear" to Tuttle that Adams's selection had not caused his relief. He assured Marshall that, as far as he knew, there had not been any rumor of favoritism regarding Adams's assignment. (McCabe to Marshall, July 22, 1941, GCMRL/ G. C. Marshall Papers [Pentagon Office, General].)

TO JOHN F. O'HARA
July 22, 1941
[Washington, D.C.]

My dear Bishop: I have just read your letter of July 20th, regarding Monsignor Vassallo and his possible detail as Military Attaché to Cuba.[1] The matter has been dropped, however I would like you to know just what brought the proposal about.

General Frank McCoy, retired, the present head of the Foreign Policy Association, was sent by Rockefeller on a tour of Latin-America. General McCoy is a man of wide experience in those countries and of very sound and conservative judgment. He represented to me the great importance of having officers from our Army in South American countries who were of Latin blood and temperament. He stated that the natural reaction of the Latin Americans to the United States and our Army was one of a Latin toward an Anglo-Saxon, without regard to the fact that we have many officers of Latin blood in the Army.[2]

General McCoy's suggestion appealed to me as a wise one, and I set about locating officers who were suited to such duties and at the same time filled his requirements. Monsignor Vassallo was the most conspicuous example of the type desired, that I had met in my Army contacts. I had been much impressed by his character and bearing and by his broad culture.

In considering the fact that he was a Chaplain it occurred to me that that might make him more effective in Latin-American countries. I did not have in mind a prolonged detail but rather a short one and more as an experiment. I also knew that he had been in Puerto Rico for a great many years, and I thought he might find it interesting to have a brief period of service elsewhere. Faithfully yours,

GCMRL/G. C. Marshall Papers (Pentagon Office, Selected)

1. As auxiliary bishop of the Roman Catholic Army and Navy Diocese, O'Hara had written to Marshall to explain why he could not approve the appointment to the attaché position of Monsignor Mariano Vassallo, who was a lieutenant colonel in the Chaplains Corps and the vicar general of the Diocese of San Juan, Puerto Rico. The shortage of chaplains and the fact that as a monsignor Vassallo's diplomatic status far exceeded that of

assistant attaché precluded his assignment, but O'Hara named four other chaplains of Hispanic descent who had the proper credentials for the job. (O'Hara to Marshall, July 20 and 23, 1941, GCMRL/G. C. Marshall Papers [Pentagon Office, Selected].)
2. See Marshall to McCoy and Memorandum for General Miles, June 2, 1941, pp. 521, 522.

TO BRIGADIER GENERAL OMAR N. BRADLEY[1]   July 22, 1941
[Washington, D.C.]

Dear Bradley: I noticed a press write-up on the Candidate School at Benning which stated that there were but eleven selectees. I wish you would write direct to me and tell me frankly what your reaction is as to the selections made for this first group.[2] Also I would like your reactions to a possible increase in the numbers within your present plant facilities, and again if we move the 4th Division away. In the latter event, quite probably a portion of the space would have to be taken up for a three months training course for National Guard and Reserve officers.

I wish you would give me your reaction to another proposition: do you think it possible to send to divisions a team which would in effect set up the faculty, demonstrate the technique and give the standards for a school for brightening up the junior officers?

I would like to have your reaction to the proposition of sending National Guard lieutenants to Training Centers as supernumeraries for a month and then passing them into the regular job of training selectees for three or four months before being returned to their regiments.[3]   Hastily yours,

GCMRL/G. C. Marshall Papers (Pentagon Office, Selected)
1. Bradley had been promoted to brigadier general in February 1941 and had become the commandant of the Infantry School in March.
2. The first men to attend the Officer Candidate School were "a fine, selected group of noncommissioned officers," Bradley replied; "a large percentage of this group will make excellent company officers." The first group had been expected to be largely from the Regular Army, "because of the limited number of selectees and National Guardsmen who have sufficient federal service." Moreover, Bradley had been informed that "many of the best qualified selectees are not interested in attending the candidate school. Apparently they want to finish their year and get back to their jobs." (Bradley to Marshall, July 26, 1941, NA/RG 407 [General, 352 (2-19-40)(1)(Sec. 1)].)
3. To Marshall's three other inquiries, Bradley responded: (1) the number of officer candidates could be expanded without difficulty; (2) he did not believe that sending such teams to divisions as the chief of staff suggested was feasible at present; (3) National Guard lieutenants should spend only one week at the replacement centers. (Ibid.) In a letter drafted in the G-1 division, Marshall replied that the number of officer candidates would be increased from two hundred per month to three hundred as soon as possible. The chief of staff agreed with Bradley's conclusions on teams to divisions and decided to drop the idea of sending National Guard lieutenants to replacement centers. (Marshall to Bradley, August 15, 1941, ibid.)

To Lieutenant General John L. De Witt   July 22, 1941
[Washington, D.C.]

Dear De Witt: I am planning for the tenth time to get out to the West Coast. Whether it will be next week or during your maneuvers between August 15 and 30, I will not be able to tell until the last moment. Today it looks as though I might possibly get away Sunday afternoon next, and in that case I would move into either Southern California or the Northwest Monday or Tuesday.

If I can manage it, I want two or three days' rest, because I need it badly. I have had only nine days in the past two years, except for that period in your house when I was offending Mrs. De Witt by avoiding entertainment. In all probability I will head into Portland, Oregon, and spend two or three days with the Hamilton Corbetts either at the seashore or trying to get some fishing. They know nothing about such an intention on my part, so please do not mention it.[1]

As soon as I have a definite idea of my plans, I will go about coordinating them with yours, but please understand that I do not want you to upset your schedule. You have too many things to manage for me to cause a complete rearrangement of your program. In other words, if you have a plan to be away in Southern California at the time I reach the Northwest, do not think of flying up there; I will meet you later on. Or if the reverse happens to be the case, you in the Northwest and I come in by the southern route, go on about your business, I will catch up with you sooner or later.[2]

I would like to go into Alaska, but I doubt if that will be arrangeable at this season or in the time at my disposal. Incidentally, you might tell Buckner most confidentially that I am trying to make him a major general and will probably succeed shortly, so I do not want him to feel that I have been unappreciative of the splendid job he has done. I am not free to go into the difficulty of my position in this matter, and I do not want Buckner to be cogitating among his friends as to just why there should be any difficulty.[3]

I have been having a very hard battle here in Washington, but I hope to complete my part of it in the next three or four days. After that it is up to the public, the Congress and the President.   Faithfully yours,

GCMRL/G. C. Marshall Papers (Pentagon Office, Selected)

1. Marshall had stayed with the De Witts March 1–3, 1940, on his way to Hawaii. During his August 1940 inspection trip, he had spent the night of August 11–12 at the Corbetts' Portland, Oregon, home.
2. Marshall and Secretary Stimson inspected Fourth Army troops one month later. The chief of staff, after a few days of fishing with Stimson at Glacier National Park, met with De Witt at Fort Lewis, Washington, on August 25. (Yale/H. L. Stimson Papers [Diary, 35: 46].)
3. The Alaska Defense Command, created in February 1941 and headed by Brigadier General Simon B. Buckner, Jr., was a part of De Witt's Western Defense Command. German Army successes in the Soviet Union increased the War Department's concern regarding that

outpost's vulnerability to Axis attack, particularly the naval bases there; consequently, the reinforcement of Alaska was granted increased priority. (Stetson Conn, Rose C. Engelman, and Byron Fairchild, *Guarding the United States and Its Outposts,* a volume in the *United States Army in World War II* [Washington: GPO, 1964], pp. 230–50.) Buckner was promoted to major general effective August 4. Marshall did not visit Alaska during his August inspection trip.

MEMORANDUM FOR GENERAL MILES
July 24, 1941
[Washington, D.C.]

I am being pressed by members of the House to give more definite information, particularly as relates to Latin-America, or the threats against our interests at the present time, which constitute the degree of imperilment of the Nation to which I have been referring, and the reasons for the declaration of a National Emergency.[1]

Will you please have someone go to work quickly on the preparation for, either release to the press, or more probably better, for the information of various legislators—who can use it in speeches—of such information as we can disclose without harm to our cause. Have in mind what has leaked out; my references to Brazil in Executive Session yesterday have partially leaked out to our great disadvantage. Whether we can make further reference to that or not, I do not know.[2]

I suggest that your people put in parentheses, for me to pass on, such things as *possibly* might be said but they or you doubt the advisability of disclosing.

You will have to work fast on this, and I put no limits as to the subject matter of hemisphere or the nations concerned.[3]

GCMRL/G. C. Marshall Papers (Pentagon Office, Selected)

1. In the House Military Affairs Committee hearings on July 22, Charles H. Elston, Republican from Ohio, asked Marshall to publicize the danger to United States security posed by Axis nation activities in Latin America. Marshall replied that the War Department had commented publicly on Axis propaganda efforts in Latin America. The chief of staff refused to discuss publicly other Axis activities. (House Military Affairs Committee, *Providing for the National Defense by Removing Restrictions on Numbers and Length of Service of Draftees, Hearings* [Washington: GPO, 1941], pp. 31–32.)

In executive session before the House Military Affairs Committee on July 23, however, Marshall informed the committee that: Brazilian President Vargas could barely contain Axis activities in his nation; Pan American Airways was upgrading airfields for United States Army use; Axis nations had efficiently and thoroughly organized propaganda agencies throughout South America; the War Department arranged to have Britain allow German munitions shipments into Brazil because the United States could not supply the Latin Americans; and the War Department refused to allow the installation of Axis-controlled governments in Venezuela or Colombia because of their proximity to the Panama Canal. (Matthew B. Ridgway Memorandum for Colonel Heard, July 24, 1941, NA/RG 165 [WPD, 4224].)

2. An Associated Press story reported that Marshall had warned the House Military Affairs Committee about possible Nazi uprisings in Brazil, Bolivia, and Colombia. (*New York Times*, July 24, 1941, p. 9.)
3. No reply from Miles has been found by the editors.

To GENERAL DOUGLAS MACARTHUR July 26, 1941
Telegram. *Secret* Washington, D.C.

Effective this date there is hereby constituted a command designated as the United States Army Forces in the Far East. This command will include the Philippine Department, forces of the government of the Commonwealth of the Philippines called and ordered into the service of the armed forces of the United States for the period of the existing emergency, and such other forces as may be assigned to it. Headquarters United States Army Forces in the Far East will be established in Manila Philippine Islands. You are hereby designated as the commanding general United States Army Forces in the Far East. You are also designated as the general officer United States Army referred to in a military order calling into the service of the armed forces of the United States the organized military forces of the government of the Commonwealth of the Philippines dated July 26, 1941. Orders calling you to active duty are being issued effective July 26, 1941. Report assumption of command by radio.[1]

NA/RG 165 (OCS, 18136–35)
1. MacArthur radioed the next day of his assumption of command. (MacArthur to TAG, July 27, 1941, NA/RG 407 [201, USAFFE].) He later sent a message to General Marshall in which he extended his thanks to the chief of staff, to Secretary Stimson, and to President Roosevelt for his return to active duty, and expressed his "appreciation for the confidence indicated by my assignment to this command. I would like to assure you that I am confident of the successful accomplishment of the assigned mission." (MacArthur to Marshall, Telegram, July 30, 1941, GCMRL/G. C. Marshall Papers [Pentagon Officer, Selected].)

To MRS. EDWARD R. STETTINIUS, JR. July 28, 1941
[Washington, D.C.]

Dear Virginia: I feel most apologetic in not having written you how much I enjoyed and appreciated the week-end you gave me, particularly as you had to combine the obligations of a hostess with the role of an invalid. I returned to town much refreshed and with a more tolerant and wholesome outlook on things in general. It was a good thing that I did because the week following was a terrific one for me.[1]

I had Brentano send you two books, which I hope you will read.[2] Both are old favorites of mine, but for different reasons. "Queed" is a Richmond story and what I would like you to notice are the discussions by Queed relating to sociology and allied matters, particularly with regard to the effect of intellectual supremacy in relation to the maintenance of a dominant race or group.

"Amos Judd" is merely, in my opinion, a little classic of romantic and dramatic fiction. It won't take you long to read it, but I want you to be frank in your impression. Katherine tells me I am too positive in my likes and dislikes, as well as too odd in my general choice of literature. As a matter of fact, I seldom read fiction.

I hope you have entirely recovered from your many stitches.   Faithfully yours,

P.S.   I expect to leave tonight for a hurried inspection in Massachusetts, flying back tomorrow night, then Thursday morning early I will probably head for the Northwest. Katherine, Fleet and I are sending you a photograph.

GCMRL/G. C. Marshall Papers (Pentagon Office, Selected)
1. Marshall had spent the weekend of July 19–20 at Horse Shoe Farm, the Stettiniuses' home near Rapidan, Virginia. Since January 1941 Edward R. Stettinius, Jr., had been director of the Division of Priorities and chairman of the Priorities Board of the Office of Production Management.
2. Marshall had the following sent to Mrs. Stettinius: Henry S. Harrison, *Queed: A Novel* (Boston: Houghton Mifflin Company, 1911); John A. Mitchell, *Amos Judd* (New York: Charles Scribner's Sons, 1901). (Marshall to Brentano's Book Stores, Inc., July 22, 1941, GCMRL/G. C. Marshall Papers [Pentagon Office, Selected].)

MEMORANDUM FOR THE ASSISTANT CHIEF   July 28, 1941
OF STAFF, G-2 [MILES]   [Washington, D.C.]

The Secretary of War would like to have an informal estimate, oral and written, on the Russian operations, in view of the data that has possibly been obtained from the recently arrived Russian Mission. The Secretary particularly wishes to have the possible effect of the guerrilla tactics evaluated. What is thought of the capacity of the Russians to carry out such a type of warfare? He would like to have a brief study of the present status of Russian industry.[1]

I wish you would make an appointment for Faymonville to see the

Secretary and tell him his impressions of what he has picked up from the Russian Mission.[2]

GCMRL/G. C. Marshall Papers (Pentagon Office, Selected)

1. On July 26 a Soviet military mission, headed by Lieutenant General Filip I. Golikov, arrived in Washington and met with the chief of staff. Marshall informed the War Council on July 28 that the Soviet Union desired war materiel and a readjustment of United States munitions aid in recognition of their assumption of the major battlefield burden. Marshall refused to make any commitments, however. He also recounted for the council the Soviets' estimate of the battlefield situation and their appraisal of the German Army. He observed that Soviet guerrilla tactics, which were "forceful and very cruel," had inflicted heavy losses on the invaders. Impressed by this evidence, Secretary Stimson criticized G-2 for not properly evaluating partisan activity. (Orlando Ward Notes on Conference in the Office of the Secretary of War, July 28, 1941, NA/RG 165 [OCS, War Council Minutes].) "I had a long talk with General Miles on the subject" after the meeting, Stimson recorded. (July 28, 1941, Yale/H. L. Stimson Papers [Diary, 34: 211].)

2. Colonel Philip R. Faymonville (U.S.M.A., 1912)—formerly a military attaché in Moscow and at this time on the staff of the Division of Defense Aid Reports—briefed the secretary of war on July 30. Faymonville asserted that, despite heavy losses of men and materiel, the Soviet defenders could hold out indefinitely; moreover, they planned to move their industries to the Ural Mountains, but they had not yet completed the task. (July 30, 1941, Yale/H. L. Stimson Papers [Diary, 34: 216–17].)

MEMORANDUM FOR GENERAL MOORE   July 28, 1941
                                        Washington, D.C.

In a telephone conversation with the President yesterday he took up the necessity for providing railroad traffic experts to assist the Russians in keeping the Siberian Railway out of Vladivostok open. Also some assistance in handling the warehouse at Vladivostok, which appears to be in a state of confusion. He spoke of the fact that the Russians did not want military officials to help them, and he suggested that civilian rail and warehouse experts might be provided.

I do not know anything about this, so I pass it to you for reference to the proper place and a follow-up in order that I may report to the President on the subject.[1]

G. C. M.

NA/RG 165 (OCS, 16446-3)

1. In reply, Deputy Chief of Staff Moore drafted a memorandum for the president which Marshall signed. The memorandum noted that the matter of United States assistance to Soviet transportation had been discussed with the Division of Defense Aid Reports and with Ralph Budd of the Office for Emergency Management. According to the chief of staff, Colonel Faymonville had stated that the Russians "would not welcome either civilian or military assistance in their administration at Vladivostok or on the Siberian Railway." (Marshall Memorandum for the President, July 30, 1941, NA/RG 165 [OCS, 16446-3].)

To General John J. Pershing   July 31, 1941
                                              Washington, D.C.

Dear General: I telephoned your apartment at the Walter Reed Sunday
[July 27] to learn if I might see you. The orderly on duty told me you were
asleep and were not feeling up to visitors that afternoon. As I left the house
shortly afterward to keep a broadcasting engagement,[1] it was not until four
o'clock that I received your telephone message that you would see me.
Unfortunately I was involved in a meeting with some British officials and,
therefore, could not get out to the Hospital that afternoon. Monday I left
for New England, and incidentally was grounded at Hartford and had to
take to the train—and did not get back to town until yesterday. I was about
to leave here at six o'clock this morning for the Northwest, and a turn
around south from California. However, last night at six the President had
me at the White House and cancelled my trip. I am leaving Saturday on
another inspection, so I cannot manage to get out to see you for another
week.[2]

I do hope you are feeling better. John Palmer told me of his visit with
you. He and Grenville Clark were very much flattered that you received
them.

I have a great deal to tell you when we get together.   Affectionately,
                                                        G. C. M.

LC/J. J. Pershing Papers (General Correspondence)

1. On July 27 Marshall had talked briefly during the 2:35–2:45 P.M. A.B.C. network
broadcast of the First Army Cantonment Chapel dedication at Arlington National Cemetery.

2. Marshall left shortly after 4:00 P.M. on July 28 for an inspection trip to Fort Devens, a
large reception center in Massachusetts, northwest of Boston. The "inspection trip" scheduled
for the weekend (he left at noon on Sunday, August 3) was actually a story invented to conceal
his participation in the Churchill-Roosevelt meetings at Placentia Bay, Newfoundland.

Memorandum for General Haislip   August 1, 1941
                                                 [Washington, D.C.]

Relative to the conversation of this morning with General Danford and
the Commanders of the Field Artillery Training Centers,[1] and the proposal
to authorize them to select members of their own commands of less than six
months' service for consideration as candidates for the Officers Candidate
Schools:

I am convinced that something of this sort must be done immediately.
I am practically of the opinion that orders should go out within a very
few days to this general effect:

A certain allotment, and not a minute one, to each Training Center which gives the commander of that center the authority to nominate for the Officers Candidate Schools men of over four months' service.

I believe this offers a really practicable means of selecting the cream of intellectual and leadership vigor that Grenville Clark and his people put forward.[2] I believe this procedure will offset the inevitable older man's reaction, which certainly would to a serious extent dominate proposals from National Guard Divisions. I believe this procedure is almost vital to the morale problem we are going to have on our hands this fall and winter.[3]

GCMRL/G. C. Marshall Papers (Pentagon Office, Selected)

1. Major General Robert M. Danford had been chief of Field Artillery since March 1938.
2. Clark was one of the founders and leaders of the Military Training Camps Association. Concerning Marshall's views on officer training, see the editorial note on pp. 511–12.
3. Assistant Chief of Staff, G-1, Brigadier General Wade H. Haislip, along with G-3 concurrence, opposed allotment quotas for replacement training centers as well as reducing the six months' service requirement. (Haislip Memorandum for the Chief of Staff, August 2, 1941, NA/RG 165 [G-1, 14679–42].) Marshall persevered and his recommendations became effective in February 1942. (Mark S. Watson, *Chief of Staff: Prewar Plans and Preparations,* a volume in the *United States Army in World War II* [Washington: GPO, 1950], pp. 271–72; Robert R. Palmer, Bell I. Wiley, and William R. Keast, *The Procurement and Training of Ground Combat Troops,* a volume in the *United States Army in World War II* [Washington: GPO, 1948], p. 95; War Department Circular 48, February 19, 1942.)

MEMORANDUM FOR THE SECRETARY OF WAR   August 1, 1941
Secret   [Washington, D.C.]

Regarding the attached report of Colonel Faymonville, with the directions of the President for the provision of planes to Russia:[1]

P-40 Pursuit Planes — Our Air people have been working with the British since last evening to let delivery on the lot of 40 of these planes in the United States that the British have expressed a willingness to release to Russia. We are planning to transport in one way or another these planes to Fairbanks, Alaska, and there to make contact with the Russians who are to fly the planes. We are requesting the Russian Government to fly their pilots and mechanics by transport planes across Siberia to Nome, Alaska. The actual training of the Russian pilots and the handling of these planes and the mechanics and maintenance of the planes will first take place at Fairbanks. It is planned to start approximately one squadron of 30 planes by the Northern Siberian Airway to see if this is a practicable proposition. If it is not, the planes will probably have to be shipped across the Pacific to an agreed on port in western Siberia. There they must be set up by our mechanics and there we must have American pilots to instruct the Russians in the flying of the planes.

The direction of the President to take 160 planes from the units of the Army Air Corps, if other American sources are not available, reduces our pursuit planes in continental United States to 6 squadrons, planes of another type. At the present moment we have only approximately 90 P-40s in active commission, the remainder are under repair, the delay being due to the shortage in spare parts because the ground-looping tendency of the plane has been productive to unusual damage to wing-tips and propellers.

4-Engine Bombers — In the B-17 and B-24 type planes, the situation in continental United States is as follows:

There are 40 B-17s in service and 30 being modernized. Of these 40, 9 are earmarked for transfer to Hawaii to replace 9 there being sent to Manila. This would leave 31 B-17s in continental United States for the training of 150 crews now in ranks or reporting by the end of next month, 170 more crews coming in during the following three months.

We may have one B-24, but I do not think it has been delivered. In the matter of preparing a competent crew to fly these heavy planes, it took the British about two months after they had gotten their men over here, and it required a much longer time for the training of the mechanical crew. We can only guess at the Russian ability, but probably at least three months would be required for the pilots.

With regard to the next class of bombers—medium, B-25 or B-26, the following is our present situation:

There are 50 B-25s in service. Of the B-26 planes, we have 50 on hand, with only 12 in commission due to shortage of propellers and defective exhaust stacks. There is no indication at the present time of propeller deliveries for the B-26 planes that would release any large number of those now on the ground.

NA/RG 165 (OCS, 20141)

1. On July 31, 1941, President Roosevelt had a forty-minute meeting with the Russian delegation made up of Soviet Ambassador Constantine A. Oumansky, Lieutenant General Filip I. Golikov, and Major General Alexander K. Repin. (Sherman Miles Memorandum for the Chief of Staff, August 1, 1941, NA/RG 165 [OCS, 20141].)

Colonel Philip R. Faymonville had met with President Roosevelt on August 1 "to confirm the report the Russian Mission had given him of their interview with the President the previous day." Faymonville reported: "The President expressed his conviction that something positive must immediately be done in the matter of sending both pursuit planes and bombers to the Soviet Union; that he did not want any telegrams sent across the water to the effect that we are people who talk much and do little. On the question of pursuit planes, he stated that two hundred planes must be sent, and that he considered it impossible to withdraw from England any of the P-40 planes already shipped there. . . . The two hundred planes should be made up of the forty which are now awaiting shipment to Great Britain, and if other American sources are not immediately available, 160 must be taken from planes in the hands of active Army Air Corps units."

"As to bombers," Faymonville continued, "the President indicated that at least token shipments of bombers of the B-17 type and the B-24 type should be made immediately and should be repeated monthly as an indication of our intent to continue supply of planes of this type." Shipment of ten bombing planes monthly should commence immediately—"five to be contributed by the United States and five by the United Kingdom. He added that this general plan had been discussed with Lord Halifax yesterday and had met with his concurrence." (Faymonville Notes on Remarks of the President at Conference Held at 12:15 P.M., August 1, 1941, attached to the above Memorandum for the Secretary of War, August 1, 1941, NA/RG 165 [OCS, 20141].) For more information concerning Colonel Faymonville, see Memorandum for Mr. Hopkins, October 10, 1941, pp. 635–36.

MEMORANDUM FOR THE PRESIDENT   August 2, 1941
Secret   [Washington, D.C.]

Subject: Transfer of Air Materiel to Russia.

The following steps have been taken toward the transfer to the Russian Government of aviation materiel:

It has been proposed to the Russian Embassy, and accepted by them—subject to the confirmation of their government—to utilize our aviation set-up at Fairbanks, Alaska, as the point of transfer of equipment, including the transition training of pilots and mechanics. The Russian Embassy has been requested to have fifty single-engine pilots, 25 mechanics and ten two-engine bomber pilots and ten mechanics flown to Fairbanks, Alaska via Nome. The Russian Embassy says that these men can be in Fairbanks by August 11.

The War Department is assembling the pilots and mechanics necessary for the ferrying of planes to Fairbanks and the training of pilots and mechanics at Fairbanks.

There are 59 modern P-forties (Tomahawks) on British order now in this country. 28 of these are at the Curtiss Plant, and the remainder have been delivered on the docks on the Atlantic seaboard. We have the Curtiss plant now uncrating the 28 at Buffalo and have directed the return from the seaboard to Buffalo of the remaining planes. As these planes all lack radio and their wiring will not permit the installation of our radio, we have cabled London to send the British radios by B-24 transport planes as quickly as possible. Meanwhile we will undertake to fly these planes into Alaska, convoying them with our planes to provide the radio control. There is some hazard in this on account of the bad weather in passing out of the North Temperate zone, but this will have to be accepted.

Our principal complication at the moment is that the British authorities in this country, with whom our Air officers have been in contact, state that they have no definite instructions to release any planes. We have committed ourselves to the extent of having their planes uncrated and others ordered to Buffalo from the seaboard. We are endeavoring to get some authorization to go ahead with the matter.

As to the bomber types, we are preparing five B-twenty-fives for flight to Fairbanks with the necessary officers to give pilot and mechanic instruction. There is a sight complication here, as the Norden and the AFCE (automatic control) has to be removed. However, we will install a substitute sight.

The only bomber, approximately medium type, that the British have under order in this country is the Lockheed-Hudson. We are discussing with them the possibility of five of these being matched with five of our B-twenty-fives. The difficulty here would be that while this British plane has its radio installed in this country, the turret is installed in England. Possibly it would be simpler for the British to fly their bomber contribution directly from Great Britain into Russia.

4,000,000 rounds of 30 caliber ammunition have been allotted, and will have to be shipped to some agreed-upon point in Eastern Siberia, possibly Vladivostok. A portion of this will be placed in the planes at Fairbanks as flight equipment during their transit flight to Siberia.

The 50 caliber ammunition required for these planes will have to be supplied by the British, who up to the present time have indicated an unwillingness to do so. Our Army reserves have been so depleted in building up to the Navy's requirements that we should not release any of this ammunition. We are arranging to provide bombs on the same basis of "missions" as the 30 caliber ammunition.

P-forties in England:

Approximately 140 P-40s of the British 200 are in England. Just what their degree of readiness for service is I do not know, but there is a probability that spare part shortage will affect the availability of a number of these planes. I understand from Colonel Burns and Colonel Faymonville[1] that you wish us to make available from our Air forces the necessary P-forties to off-set planes of this type now in England, if we could not obtain them elsewhere—presumably from British orders in this country. At the present time we have 149 P-tens [*P-forties*] in service in continental United States. The remaining 138 which have been delivered lack wing tips, or complete wings or propellers, due to the tendency to ground-loop and a shortage of spare parts.

The matter of the delivery of planes beyond the 59 first referred to can be adjusted a little bit later, as the first problem is to establish our contact at Fairbanks and get the instruction of pilots and mechanics under way.

The unadjusted difficulties of the moment in this matter are (1) the lack of authorization in this country for the British to turn over planes to us, and (2) whatever delay is involved in hearing from the Russian Government.

NA/RG 165 (OCS, 20141)
1. Major General James H. Burns, executive officer of the Division of Defense Aid Reports, and Colonel Philip R. Faymonville, of the same office, were studying the possibilities for sending military supplies to Russia. (Edward R. Stettinius, Jr., *Lend-Lease: Weapon for Victory* [New York: Macmillan Company, 1944], p. 122.)

MARSHALL was suddenly called to the White House on the evening of July 30, and directed by the president to prepare, in utmost secrecy, to leave for a meeting at sea with British Prime Minister Churchill and his military advisers. The chief of staff could take only Major General H. H. Arnold and two other assistants. The Atlantic Conference "came as a complete surprise," Marshall recalled. "The army members . . . , saving myself, had no knowledge of it until we were well up the coast on the cruiser *Augusta.*" Marshall had only instructed Arnold to take cool weather uniforms and to be prepared for an absence of about ten days. Even Secretary of War Stimson was not told where they were going. (George C. Marshall, interviewed by Forrest C. Pogue, January 15, 1957, GCMRL; H. H. Arnold, *Global Mission* [New York: Harper and Brothers, 1949], pp. 246-47; Yale/H. L. Stimson Papers [Diary, 35: 14].)

General Marshall, Admiral Harold R. Stark, and their assistants boarded ship in New York's East River on August 3. The chief of staff and the chief of naval operations traveled to the meeting site on the heavy cruiser U.S.S. *Augusta,* while Arnold and the other military men were berthed on the U.S.S. *Tuscaloosa.* Accordingly, there were no army-navy conferences until August 7, when the ships anchored in Placentia Bay, near the United States base at Argentia, Newfoundland. Major General Arnold, who had recently returned from a trip to England, was impressed with "the thoroughness with which the British prepare for such conferences. As far as I knew, we were going into this one cold." Marshall later recalled: "There was not much opportunity to plan for a specific meeting. To me the meeting was largely a get-together for the first time, an opportunity to meet the British chiefs of staff, and to come to some understanding with them as to how they worked and what their principal problems were. We were in no position at that time to lay very heavy matters before them. . . . We had so little basis for planning at the time of the meeting on the *Augusta.* So only the things that were almost self-evident could be discussed by us." (Arnold, *Global Mission,* pp. 247-48; Marshall interview, January 15, 1957.)

In his memoirs Arnold wrote that he had advocated—and had gained acceptance from President Roosevelt, General Marshall, and Admiral Stark for—a three-point program of general principles: "(1) Development of our Army, Navy, and Air Force to meet the present international situation;

(2) As a policy, give to the British, the Chinese, and other foreign governments only such items as they could use effectively, after first meeting our own requirements under our adopted plan; (3) No commitments to be made until our experts had an opportunity to study the proposals and requests, with all their ramifications, made by the British." (Arnold, *Global Mission,* p. 248.)

Saturday morning, August 9, the battleship H.M.S. *Prince of Wales* entered Placentia Bay carrying Churchill and his party, including a thirteen-man military mission headed by Admiral of the Fleet Sir Dudley Pound; General Sir John Dill, chief of the Imperial General Staff; and Air Chief Marshal Sir Wilfrid R. Freeman, vice-chief of the Air Staff. A continuous round of business meetings and social gatherings ensued which lasted until the conference ended three days later.

The British service chiefs had prepared a "General Strategy Review" with which they hoped the American leaders would agree. Marshall, Stark, and Arnold received copies of the review on August 10 in preparation for the next day's meeting. The British Army, the document stated, was "immeasurably stronger than it was last September," but still deficient in armor. Moreover, there had been "considerable improvement" in the British position in the battle for the North Atlantic sea lanes, "though this may be only temporary." In West Africa the British possessed no forces with which to contain German and Vichy French threats to Allied communications and shipping. The Middle East had to be held; the loss of the British position in that region "would have disastrous effects." In the Far East, it was essential that Singapore be held in order to maintain communications and supply lines "vital to the successful continuance of our war effort," and the British were "making constant efforts to provide the requisite forces." The review then made a strong plea for immediate United States intervention in the war, which "would revolutionize the whole situation." But the intervention had to come soon; "the longer it is delayed the greater will be the leeway to be made up in every direction."

The British chiefs of staff foresaw four important areas in which United States intervention would help to win the war. First, control of the seas and their adjacent lands by the Allies would be assured, "even if Japan intervened." Second, the British assumed that the German Army could not be defeated, "even if the Russians are able to maintain an Eastern Front," until the Allies destroyed "the foundations upon which the war machine rests— the economy which feeds it, the morale which sustains it, the supplies which nourish it and the hopes of victory which inspire it." This could not be accomplished by massive armies attacking along definite fronts, as in 1914–18, but by a bombing offensive "on the heaviest possible scale," supplemented by blockade, partisan activities, and a propaganda campaign. United States bombers would "swell the air offensive against Germany." Third, when Germany was driven to its knees, United States armored forces would join the British in suppressing remaining resistance and in occupation duties. Fourth, American entry into the conflict would bolster Allied and undermine Axis morale; it "would not only make victory certain, but might also make it swift." (General Strategy Review by the British Chiefs of Staff, July 31, 1941, attached to L. C. Hollis to Marshall, August 10, 1941, NA/ RG 165 [WPD, 4402–62].)

At a lengthy meeting on August 11, Admiral Pound began to discuss the review point by point. Admiral Stark emphasized that while the United States military was willing to cooperate as much as possible with the British, under current national policies, there were definite limits to this cooperation. Careful planning and coordination were essential, and he told the British chiefs that they would receive a formal reply after United States military leaders had studied the document on return to the United States. Marshall commented briefly on the commitment of army forces to Iceland and perhaps also to the Azores and the bulge of Brazil, but he noted that these forces had to be taken from the limited supply of trained forces at his disposal. He also emphasized the serious drain on United States supplies and shipping that the British efforts in the Middle East were causing and noted that each new commitment of forces worsened matters. Marshall cautioned the British to improve their internal coordination before making supply requests of the United States, so as not to exacerbate further the production priorities battle.

Marshall and Stark informed the British chiefs of staff that the United States was determined to reinforce its defenses in the Philippine Islands, which would serve to strengthen Britain's position in the Indian Ocean and at Singapore. Could the British, they inquired, assist this project by modifying their aid requests? The supply question was the chief subject of discussion at the August 12 meeting. (Charles W. Bundy Memorandum for the Chief of Staff, August 20, 1941, NA/RG 165 [WPD, 4402–62].)

Upon their return to Washington, Marshall and Arnold briefed Secretary Stimson on the meetings, particularly on the supply discussions. The secretary noted: "I found that what the practical British were after was action and that they had no idea at all of how the cupboard was bare so far as the United States was concerned. In that respect we are going to have a hard time. All they want now is great big 4-engine bombers, regardless of the fact that we are behind in those bombers mainly because they knocked them so hard in the beginning." (August 14, 1941, Yale/H. L. Stimson Papers [Diary, 35: 31].)

While the British were disappointed with the outcome of the Atlantic Conference, it did produce certain significant political results. The leaders agreed upon greater coordination in supply, a warning to Japan against further expansion into Southeast Asia and the Pacific, and a declaration of peace aims called the "Atlantic Charter." Released to the press on August 14, the eight-point charter declared that the two nations sought: no new territories or any territorial changes without the consent of the people affected; world political and economic freedom; and the disarmament of aggressor nations, "pending the establishment of a wider and permanent system of general security." (*Foreign Relations, 1941,* 1: 368–69.) Churchill later wrote: "The profound and far-reaching importance of this Joint Declaration was apparent. The fact alone of the United States, still technically neutral, joining with a belligerent Power in making such a declaration was astonishing." (Winston S. Churchill, *The Grand Alliance* [Boston: Houghton Mifflin Company, 1950], p. 444.)

An important result of the conference was the personal relationships established or strengthened between British and American leaders. Of all the British representatives at the conference, Sir John Dill most impressed General Marshall, and the two chiefs of staff formed a friendship, lasting until Dill's death in 1944, that was of great importance in Anglo-American relations. (Katherine Tupper Marshall, *Together: Annals of an Army Wife* [New York and Atlanta: Tupper and Love, 1946], p. 96.) ★

To Brigadier General John McA. Palmer   August 15, 1941
                                                    Washington, D.C.

Dear John: I returned last night to find your note of the 4th.[1] Thank you for your support of me. I need it these days because I am getting knocks from every side.[2]

This would be a longer letter, but I find my desk piled to the ceiling with matters to be attended to, due to an absence of ten days.

With my love to you and Maude,   Affectionately,

                                                    G. C. M.

LC/J. McA. Palmer Papers

1. Palmer had written to Marshall: "A few days ago I took up the cudgels for you in a modest way. One of my disciples, a man of some influence, wrote me that you were apparently against what he called the 'Washington-Palmer idea' and that you were really building up an 'Uptonian' regular army.

"My reply was as follows: 'I am highly flattered that you should refer to our traditional military policy as the "Washington-Palmer idea", but you are clear off as to what General Marshall is doing. Marshall *is* increasing the regular army but not in the vicious way that was adopted in 1861 and 1917. He is increasing it by bringing citizen officers and soldiers into it for the period of the emergency (essentially as Washington and Knox proposed in 1790) and not by making it a scheme for the permanent promotion of *all* regular army officers without reference to their individual merits. In this way he is fitting an expanding regular army into the original Washingtonian pattern. I opposed the Uptonian idea because it was predicated upon the absurd theory that *all* professionals are superior, *per se,* to *all* non-professionals. Marshall has no sympathy with that absurdity. He is seeking and advancing able men whether professional or non-professional and he is getting rid of incompetents and back numbers, whether professional or non-professional. In fact he has been following the Washingtonian policy as closely as was possible in a great emergency where there was almost nothing to build on.'" (Palmer to Marshall, August 4, 1941, GCMRL/G. C. Marshall Papers [Pentagon Office, Selected].) For more information on Palmer's ideas about military policy, along with Marshall's comments, see *Papers of GCM*, 1: 329, 333–34, 348.

2. Testifying before the House Military Affairs Committee on July 22, 1941, Marshall commented that he had received unfavorable mail since issuing his biennial report. Of the 241 unfavorable letters, most of them showed evidence of collusion and duplication of phraseology, and a large number had come from a small German group in Brooklyn and from another group in Passaic, New Jersey. He noted that 23 percent were "marked by extreme personal abuse or threats of violence against the President or the Chief of Staff." (House Military Affairs Committee, *Providing for the National Defense by Removing Restrictions on Numbers and Length of Service of Draftees, Hearing* [Washington: GPO, 1941], pp. 8–9.) See Marshall to Baruch, August 19, 1941, pp. 591–92.

TO MRS. J. FRANKLIN BELL[1]   August 16, 1941
                                              [Washington, D.C.]

My dear Mrs. Bell: I have just learned from Sally Chamberlin[2] that you have been exercising on a stepladder with disastrous results. I am immensely relieved to learn that no bones were broken, but Sally tells me you suffered a strained back. I hope this is not proving a serious discomfort and that you will get back into normal condition very quickly.

I suppose you have received a great deal of advice on the matter of the stepladder so I won't add mine to your irritations. But please do look before you leap the next time.

Your performance reminds me of a reference in Lord Frederick Hamilton's book "The Days Before Yesterday" where he tells of his mother at eighty-five being found out in the garden giving a demonstration on stilts for the benefit of a great grandchild. Later on the same lady at ninety, was found with a club in her hand and a stable-boy as a companion, watching a rat-hole down which they had put a ferret.[3] I am not offering this as suggestions for you, but merely as a defense for you against criticisms of your tip-toeing on a stepladder.

With my love,   Affectionately,

GCMRL/G. C. Marshall Papers (Pentagon Office, General)

1. Marshall had been an aide to Major General J. Franklin Bell for a year beginning in July 1916. Concerning his relations then with General and Mrs. Bell, see *Papers of GCM*, 1: 98–99.

2. Sally G. Chamberlin was Marshall's social and personal secretary.

3. Frederick S. Hamilton, *The Days Before Yesterday* (London: Hodder and Stoughton, 1920).

MEMORANDUM FOR GENERAL HAISLIP   August 18, 1941
                                                  [Washington, D.C.]

I will probably be leaving tomorrow for a week's absence with the Secretary.[1] In view of this, I think it is important that a press release be made tomorrow morning on the question of extension of service. The manner of stating our intentions will be of critical importance. We must not appear to be taking action because of unfavorable reactions, but rather because the period of completion of twelve months' service is approaching for a considerable increment of the Army. I have not time to draft such a document, but I am dictating a few notes, which appear below:

In view of the approaching termination of twelve months' service for the first increment of the National Guard (some 150,000 men) inducted in September and October, and Reserve officers, and the selectees who were inducted in November, the War Department today announces that the following instructions were being issued concerning the matter.

Assuming our present situation continues without more serious developments, enlisted men of the National Guard and selectees will be released from active duty under the following priorities: 1st, hardship cases, 2d, men of 28 years of age or older not holding non-commissioned rank, and such men holding non-commissioned rank who so desire. 3d, married men who so desire. Men whose three-year term of service has been completed will be discharged unless they desire to reenlist. War Department directions provide that the release from active duty of men of 28 years and over will be completed by December 31st, provided the men will have had at least six months' training.

Under the assumption that we do not become more seriously involved, it is anticipated that other selectees as well as enlisted men in the ranks of the National Guard will be released from active duty after an average of about 17 months' total active service, the periods varying from 14 to 20 months depending on the location of the unit and its schedule of preparation.

Instructions were issued by the War Department in March (?)[2] directing that 50% of the Reserve officers would be released from active duty at the completion of twelve months' service. This policy will be carried out in order to provide places for some 30,000 Reserve officers who have not yet been called into service and should be trained, and also to permit the employment of a monthly output of approximately 1200 officers commissioned from the ranks of the Army.

The details have not been completed for covering a similar procedure of relief from service regarding officers of the National Guard.[3]

GCMRL/G. C. Marshall Papers (Pentagon Office, Selected)

1. Marshall left Washington on August 20 with Secretary of War Henry L. Stimson for an inspection tour of the Northwest. They returned to Washington on August 28. (Yale/H. L. Stimson Papers [Diary, 35: 42–49].)

2. February. (*New York Times*, August 20, 1941, p. 10.)

3. The War Department issued a statement similar in wording on August 19, 1941. The plan would release about 200,000 from active duty: 150,000 National Guardsmen, 10,000 Reserve officers, 20,000 selectees who were inducted in November and December, and 20,000 National Guard officers. (Ibid., pp. 1, 10.)

To Bernard M. Baruch

August 19, 1941
[Washington, D.C.]

My dear Mr. Baruch: Smith has just shown me your note with the very pleasant and complimentary reference to me.[1] I appreciate your good opinion, particularly at the present time when hard knocks are rather numerous.

Quite evidently, with the debates in the background and the magazine articles playing up the situation, and especially with a group now insisting on demoralizing the Air Corps with investigations, I am in for a hard winter. It has been intensely interesting and quite tragic to watch the violent change in morale commencing with the recent debates on the prolongation of service. Up to June we really had a remarkable state of morale, but seemingly in a moment with these violent discussions, parents became stirred up and individual soldiers were taught to feel sorry for themselves.[2]

I have always felt surprised that in our democracy we were able to achieve a Selective Service system late last summer, but I guess it was hoping too much to think that we could continue the strenuous preparation to meet this emergency without great difficulties. There is no more delicate problem than troop morale, and with such a slender margin of public approval to back us, it is no easy matter to build up the highly trained and seasoned fighting force that we must have available as quickly as possible. However, we are going to do it if too many of us do not lose our tempers.

I am off in the morning on another inspection trip, this time to the Northwest and I will not be back until about the 28th. As soon as I am in town again I hope you will have lunch with me under my apple-tree at Myer. Maybe your griefs about materiel will serve to assuage my troubles about personnel.[3]   Faithfully yours,

GCMRL/G. C. Marshall Papers (Pentagon Office, Selected)

1. Lieutenant Colonel Walter B. Smith, assistant secretary of the General Staff, had sent Baruch two copies of Marshall's biennial report. (Smith to Baruch, August 4, 1941, GCMRL/ G. C. Marshall Papers [Pentagon Office, Selected].) Baruch replied to Smith, "Thank you for

what you did and tell General Marshall that he is hitting on all cylinders and gaining a wider respect and confidence, to which I think he is justly entitled." (Baruch to Smith, August 4, 1941, Princeton/B. M. Baruch Papers.)

2. Both *Time* and *Life* magazines had published articles on August 18, 1941, about the low state of morale in the army. A *Life* staff member had spent a week with a National Guard division in the South and had interviewed four hundred privates. According to the reporter: "The most important single reason for the bad morale in this division appears to be national uncertainty. . . . Not more than 5% of the men in this division believe that the emergency is as serious as President Roosevelt insists." ("This is What the Soldiers Complain About," *Life* 11[August 18, 1941]: 17–18.) The *Time* article claimed that a low state of morale affected two-thirds of the 1,531,800 men under arms. In a Mississippi camp the previous week uniformed men had booed newsreel pictures of President Roosevelt and General Marshall. "Said an old army sergeant: 'Give us a shooting war and there won't be a morale problem.' . . . Last week the civilian soldier's real complaint was that he had no worthwhile job to do." ("Problem of Morale," *Time* 38[August 18, 1941]: 35–36.) Threatening desertion at the end of the initial twelve months' period of service, soldiers had scrawled the letters "OHIO" (Over the Hill in October) on latrine walls and artillery pieces. Marshall later recalled, "People have forgotten entirely the hostility of that time. *Life* magazine played it up at great length—this OHIO movement. . . . Certain phases of democracy make it quite a struggle to raise any army—probably should, I guess. But in the great tragedy the world was in at that time, it made it doubly hard." (Marshall interview, January 22, 1957.)

3. Baruch, chairman of the War Industries Board during the World War, was an unofficial presidential adviser and had been meeting weekly with Roosevelt. The New York banker also had given lectures on industrial mobilization at the Army War College. (*New York Times,* July 28, 1941, p. 1; July 29, 1941, p. 7; September 5, 1941, p. 11.) In the spring Baruch had published an article about the War Industries Board and the importance of the Priorities Division: "industrial mobilization must have as a center of everything a priorities division which synchronizes the whole war effort, at the same time providing for the maximum possible satisfaction of civilian needs." (Bernard M. Baruch, "Priorities: The Synchronizing Force," *Harvard Business Review* 19[Spring 1941]: 261–70.)

To Major General Campbell King   August 19, 1941
                                                    [Washington, D.C.]

Dear King: I have just received your note regarding the problem of morale and the understanding of enlisted men of the world situation. We have been working on some such method as you suggest and I am particularly glad to have your slant on the matter.[1] It has been very difficult for us to do much of this sort of thing without being charged with conducting a propaganda service under the power of military control and in opposition to the minority group in Congress. So long as we are on a peacetime basis, this situation will be very trying, and I expect to have a difficult time in the coming months. However, there have been no easy times since I became Chief of Staff, so I am rather hardened to the ordeal.

Katherine and I were talking about Harriott and you the other day and wondering what sort of a summer you had. I have been away a good bit recently and am leaving tomorrow morning on an inspection trip to the West Coast. K. is down at Leesburg spending our substance on the plumber, the painter, the carpenter and the like. She is having a great time over our new home. Incidentally I recall at this moment that I have a clipping in a drawer giving a picture of the house and something of its history.[2] I enclose it with this note.

Allen married last June a year ago and lives in Poughkeepsie, where he has a job in a newspaper and radio chain. His wife is expecting a baby in a few days. Molly, in Panama, has similar expectations in November. Clifton has to give up his New York job and go in the hospital for an operation on his feet; he has been having trouble with them for almost five years. They had exhausted the radium treatment, as a matter of fact they had done too much of it, and finally he had to have an operation, which Keller[3] performed and which apparently has been successful, though it put him out of action for two and a half months. He had a similar experience with his job in Chicago and was either in the hospital or at home under treatment here for nearly six months. Now he has a good job in a local bank and is delighted with it, as he has a natural facility for figures and likes the people with whom he is associated. He and I ride every morning at six o'clock. Katherine and I usually walk in the late evening or go swimming in the Post pool. I practically never go out at night, and try to get to bed at nine or nine-thirty.

I am sending you a copy of my Report, which stirred up such a hubbub, so that you can read the entire discussion, which few people have taken the trouble to do, though they had a hell of a lot to say about it.

With my affectionate regards to you both,   Faithfully yours,

GCMRL/G. C. Marshall Papers (Pentagon Office, Selected)

1. King had written favorably of Secretary of War Stimson's August 15 radio address to the army in which he explained why it was vital to the national defense to have the authority to extend the service times of selectees, National Guardsmen, and Reserve officers by eighteen months. (*New York Times,* August 16, 1941, pp. 1, 6.) King then proposed: "In view of the rumors of criticism by the enlisted men (not of the regular army) as to the necessity for this country to be prepared for emergencies, and the implication that they do not see the necessity for their being required to go thru a prolonged period of training, I suggest that it might be advisable to condense the facts set forth by Mr. Stimson in some simple form (preferably illustrated by a map) suitable to a soldier's mentality and have it presented *orally* to each company or similar organization by suitable officers specially qualified to make an impression when speaking to soldiers." (King to Marshall, August 16, 1941, GCMRL/G. C. Marshall Papers [Pentagon Office, Selected].)

2. For more information on Marshall's Leesburg, Virginia, house, see Marshall to Pershing, April 15, 1941, p. 477.

3. Colonel William L. Keller was a surgeon at Walter Reed General Hospital. See *Papers of GCM,* 1: 310, 312.

MEMORANDUM FOR THE INSPECTOR   August 19, 1941
GENERAL [PETERSON]   [Washington, D.C.]

Subject: The selection of Individuals for the Officer Candidate Schools.

There have been some disappointments in the type of the men selected for these candidate schools. While leadership was specifically prescribed as the dominant factor in the selection and education in effect made of secondary importance, it appears that some boards seriously ignored general background and education in the selections. It would appear that some of the preferred individuals were more suitable material for noncommissioned grades than for commissioned.

As there has been a continuous and heavy pressure to authorize the commissioning of individuals after very brief service, practically selecting them before their induction into the Army, it is of importance that the procedure for the recruitment of the officer candidate schools be above criticism and that any errors that may have been made be corrected as quickly as possible. Therefore, the following instructions:

Please have a rapid inspection made of the procedure of the boards in the various corps areas and of the candidates in the several schools. As it is important to learn the results of this inspection as quickly as possible, it will be necessary to have at least three inspectors on the job.

I suggest that all the inspectors designated for this duty should collectively interview the boards of the Second, Third and Fourth Corps Areas. It might tend to produce a more uniform appreciation of conditions throughout the country.[1]

GCMRL/G. C. Marshall Papers (Pentagon Office, Selected)

1. The editors have not found Inspector General Virgil L. Peterson's investigative report, but for Marshall's comments on the investigation, see Marshall to Devers, September 24, 1941, pp. 617–18. In September Assistant Chief of Staff, G-1, Wade H. Haislip wrote that all commanders were anxious to cooperate to improve O.C.S. selection. "It is believed that the action by the Chief of Staff in causing The Inspector General to investigate the method and procedure of selecting candidates has, in large part, already corrected many of the evils that were found to exist in the selection for the first course." (Haislip Memorandum for the Chief of Staff, September 26, 1941, NA/RG 165 [OCS, 21167–54].)

TO WALTER G. ANDREWS   August 19, 1941
[Washington, D.C.]

Dear Ham: I am just leaving on an inspection trip, and before I go I want you to know how much I appreciate your unselfish stand in assisting the passage of the recent legislation concerning our citizen-soldiers.

You have been a great source of strength to me on numerous occasions, but never more so than during this recent Congressional struggle. My sincere thanks go to you.[1] Faithfully yours,

GCMRL/G. C. Marshall Papers (Pentagon Office, General)

1. Andrews was a Republican congressman from New York and a member of the House Military Affairs Committee. He replied, "The narrowness of our margin made it a very trying ordeal, but when I recall the original conference in [Speaker of the House Sam] Rayburns office, I am not disheartened and I have a feeling that sentiment will improve as we would have it." (Andrews to Marshall, August 27, 1941, GCMRL/G. C. Marshall Papers [Pentagon Office, General].) See Marshall to Leland M. Ford, September 19, 1941, pp. 612–13.

MEMORANDUM FOR THE SECRETARY OF WAR   August 29, 1941
Secret   [Washington, D.C.]

With reference to Mr. Roosevelt's letter to you regarding the difficulty experienced in providing spare engines, spare parts, tools, and operating supplies, such as anti-freeze compounds for the planes being turned over to Russia,[1] I suggest that the President be given the following information at the Cabinet meeting:

In the first place our entire Air Corps is suffering from a severe shortage in spare parts of *all* kinds. We have planes on the ground because we cannot repair them. As a matter of fact, we have been forced for the time being to take about one-fifth of the new planes to provide parts for the older planes that we are keeping in the air.

Mr. Oumansky and his Russian associates were informed of this situation. He stated that airplane spare parts were not a problem and that he would be satisfied if the Russians were given spare engines and engine spare parts. It appears that 20% spare engines are ample, and twelve spare engines have been forwarded to Amtorg Corporation to be included with the shipment of planes. Furthermore, a complement of engine spare parts, with the exception of generators and starters have been furnished.

With regard to tools, in addition to the spares which are normally furnished with planes and engines, a complement of miscellaneous tools went forward for shipment with the planes.

With regard to fuels, lubricants, etc., the Amtorg Corporation was advised as to the situation, and is making direct procurement of these supplies. All of the facilities of the War Department were placed at their disposal to assist them in every way possible.

As to the airplane spares, although Mr. Oumansky stated that airplane spares were not a matter of immediate concern, necessary action has been taken to insure that a full complement of airplane spares will be shipped within thirty days.

If any criticism is to be made in this matter, in my opinion it is that we have been too generous, to our own disadvantage, and I seriously question the advisability of our action in releasing the P-forties at this particular time; I question this even more when it only results in criticism, and I think the President should have it clearly pointed out to him that Mr. Oumansky will take everything we own if we submit to his criticisms. Please read their attitude toward our Attaché, which I sent you this morning.

GCMRL/G. C. Marshall Papers (Pentagon Office, Selected)

1. President Roosevelt had written to Secretary Stimson: "I have been following the initial efforts of the War Department to effect early deliveries of a limited number of pursuit planes to the Soviet Government. In connection with this shipment, it has been brought to my attention that some difficulty is being experienced in providing spare engines, spare parts, tools, and operating supplies, such as anti-freeze compounds. In my opinion failure to make this shipment complete, in such a way as to be immediately serviceable and effective for combat operations abroad would entirely defeat the purpose for which this shipment is being made. In view of this situation, it is my desire that every consideration be given to sending with the airplanes the requisite supplies and equipment from existing stocks in amounts approaching as nearly as possible those which would be required for our own forces operating under similar conditions." (Roosevelt to the Secretary of War, August 27, 1941, FDRL/ F. D. Roosevelt Papers [PSF, 16].)

MEMORANDUM TO THE PRESIDENT[1]   August 29, 1941
[Washington, D.C.]

Colonel Frank P. Lahm retires from active service on November 30th at 64 years of age. He is our oldest Army pilot and he was the first military aviator in the world. He gained air prominence by winning the first Gordon Bennett International Balloon Race in a flight from Paris to Dale, England. He designed the admirably arranged Air Corps Pilot School at Randolph Field and, I understand, has never seen the place since he laid out the plot.

I submit his name to you for appointment as a temporary Major General, as a temporary recognition of his past services. It would only be effective until November 30th. I have in mind ordering him to Randolph Field for the day of his retirement in order that appropriate ceremonies may mark this occasion.

May I have your approval for his nomination?[2]

GCMRL/G. C. Marshall Papers (Pentagon Office, General)

1. This document was written by Marshall for the secretary of war's signature.
2. On September 9, 1908, Lahm (U.S.M.A., 1901) became the first army officer to fly as a passenger in a Wright Brothers aircraft. On October 26, 1909, he and Fredric E. Humphreys (U.S.M.A., 1906) became the first certified military pilots. Lahm received temporary promo-

tion to major general from September 15 to November 29, 1941, and he commanded the Gulf Coast Air Corps Training Center with headquarters at Randolph Field, Texas, from October 1941 until he retired with the rank of brigadier general on November 30, 1941.

To Admiral Harold R. Stark
Secret

August 29, 1941
[Washington, D.C.]

Dear Betty: I am of the opinion that the United States forces in Iceland should be under one commander, who should be given, to the extent legally possible, full authority and responsibility. The Commander's authority should not be restricted to that contemplated in "Joint Action of the Army and the Navy" for the exercise of "unity of command."[1]

In order to give the Commander of United States Forces in Iceland the authority legally possible over the combined forces, I propose that Marine forces in Iceland be detached for service with the Army. There is attached hereto a joint letter transmitting to the President a draft of an Executive Order which will accomplish the proposed detachment.[2]

Since the Army contingent will sail on or about September 5, it is very desirable that this matter be expedited. Faithfully yours,

GCMRL/G. C. Marshall Papers (Pentagon Office, Selected)

1. Joint Board Serial 514, *Joint Action of the Army and Navy* (Washington: GPO, 1935), was a lengthy, frequently revised, loose-leaf book which served to "assemble in one volume all joint policies, agreements, or instructions which have been approved by the War and Navy Departments, with a view to securing effective coordination." (Ibid., p. iii.) The president could appoint either an army or a navy officer to command a joint operation. This commander was empowered "to coordinate the operations of the forces of both services" by organizing task forces, assigning missions, designating objectives, and providing logistical support. But he could not issue "instructions as to dispositions for, or methods of, operation in the accomplishment of missions assigned solely to forces of the service to which the commander does not belong, nor control of the administration, discipline, or technique of the operations of such forces." (Ibid., p. 7.)

2. President Roosevelt did not issue the proposed executive order. A revision was sent to him, which he issued as a presidential directive to the secretaries of war and navy on September 22. (NA/RG 319 [OPD, Joint Board, Serial 697]; Watson, *Chief of Staff*, pp. 488-89.) See Memorandum for the Secretary of War, September 5, 1941, p. 600.

To Mrs. James J. Winn

September 4, 1941
[Washington, D.C.]

Dear Molly: I have not written you for some time for I have been almost constantly on the move. First I was away about twelve days on the Churchill rendezvous, and then after two days in town left again for Illinois, Denver, Glacier National Park, the Northwest, San Francisco, Cheyenne, Omaha, and home. I spent two days in Glacier Park on horseback and fishing, the latter without much success because of heavy showers. The scenery was magnificent and the outing much appreciated.

For the first time since July 4th I got down to Leesburg and spent last Saturday afternoon and Sunday there, most of the time on a ladder or in trees doing pruning your mother wanted attended to. Fortunately I was in easy telephone reach because I had to talk to Hyde Park and to Washington five or six times on pretty important matters.

I see a recent War Department policy will make Jim a major.[1] You are getting a promotion entirely too quickly; a long period of incubation as the wife of a lieutenant is excellent training. However, I am glad you are to have the advantage of a major's choice for quarters.

Your mother received a letter from Kay, who was very enthusiastic about you, your hospitality and your apartment. Your mother is at Leesburg now wrestling with the painters, carpenters and plumbers. The garage is about completed and the tool-house in place of the stable was finished two weeks ago; the smaller details around the house are being attended to now. I think she has spent about $1000 to date, but all of it is in a good cause I believe against the future.

With my love,   Affectionately,

GCMRL/ Research File (Family)

1. Two weeks previously the War Department had announced a promotion policy whereby temporary promotion by selection was extended to all grades. According to the War Department's statement, the policy combined "permanent and temporary promotion of Reserve officers with temporary promotion of Regular Army officers to remove inequalities" between the two components of the army. "Last June the War Department instituted a procedure of temporary promotion by selection to the grade of colonel for Regular Army officers. This departure from the rule of seniority is giving the Army more vigorous leadership." (*Army and Navy Journal,* August 23, 1941, p. 1449.) Captain James J. Winn was promoted to major on October 10, 1941.

ARMY planners began, during the summer and autumn of 1941, to revise their views of the defensibility of the Philippine Archipelago in the face of growing Japanese military power. Formerly, they had assumed that the islands could offer only a temporary citadel defense of the naval facilities around Manila. (Louis Morton, *The Fall of the Philippines,* a volume in the *United States Army in World War II* [Washington: GPO, 1953], p. 65.) By mid-summer of 1941, however, "as a result of the alignment of Japan with the Axis,—followed by the outbreak of war between Germany and Russia, the strategic importance of the Philippines was enhanced." (Marshall [draft by W.P.D.] to MacArthur, October 18, 1941, NA/RG 165 [WPD, 4175-18]. See Memorandum for General Arnold, July 16, 1941, pp. 567–68.) Accordingly, revisions to the Far East portion of basic war plan Rainbow 5 were initiated and further steps were taken to reinforce the Philippines. ★

To LIEUTENANT GENERAL DOUGLAS MACARTHUR[1]   September 5, 1941
Telegram No. 121. *Secret*   [Washington, D.C.]

Consideration being given by army navy to possibility of dispatching one first class National Guard division to Philippines approximately eighteen thousand men. This involves heavy demand on shipping in view of tremendous obligations in Atlantic. It also involves serious convoy problem with jeopardy to naval craft passing mandate bases. It further involves future heavy tonnage requirements for supply to Philippines with probability of this being rendered impracticable. Your views are desired. In this connection you are informed that we are planning in any event to send you nine additional Flying Fortresses in early October and a similar number in November together with additional though uncertain numbers of pursuit planes and we hope some modern light bombers and additional tanks. Additional personnel, not necessarily organizational, to man this equipment can be sent as you desire. Also we can supply trained replacements for any of your present Regular personnel being utilized in organization of Philippine Army or for minor increases of your command.[2]

GCMRL/G. C. Marshall Papers (Pentagon Office, Selected)
   1. MacArthur, having returned to active duty on July 26, 1941, received the rank of lieutenant general on July 29, 1941.
   2. "I do not consider it necessary for defense purposes to dispatch a US Army Infantry division at this time," MacArthur replied. "Equipment and supply of existing forces are the prime essential instead of reinforcements except comparatively minimum required to meet special needs." He then outlined several special needs, including more aircraft and antiaircraft supplies, concluding: "I am confident if these steps are taken with sufficient speed that no further major reinforcement will be necessary for accomplishment of defense mission." (MacArthur to Marshall, Telegram No. 277, September 7, 1941, NA/RG 407 [Classified, 320.2 (7-28-41)(3)].) See Memorandum for Admiral Stark, September 12, 1941, pp. 605–6.

MEMORANDUM FOR THE SECRETARY OF WAR   September 5, 1941
Secret   [Washington, D.C.]

The Indigo expedition under General Bonesteel sailed yesterday afternoon.[1]

Mr. Forrestal signed the joint letter from the two of you requesting the issuance of an Executive Order by the President to place the Marines in Iceland under command of the Army. General Holcomb, Commandant of the Marine Corps, submitted a very urgent remonstrance in this matter, which Admiral Stark disapproved, at my request.[2]

Mr. Hopkins brought to Admiral Stark yesterday the proposition of a "former Naval personage" to turn over to U.K. October 1st twelve passenger liners and twenty freighters to facilitate the movement into the Persian Gulf.[3] Stark talked to me and went over with General Reybold the question of how many Army transports could be diverted alone for this purpose, as we are already short-handed and are chartering commercial boats for both Alaska and the Philippines, we could not release transports.

GCMRL/G. C. Marshall Papers (Pentagon Office, Selected)

1. "Indigo-3" was the army's short title for the August 16, 1941, "Joint Army and Navy Directive for Augmenting the Existing British Defenses in Iceland with Troops of the U.S. Army and the U.S. Marine Corps." (NA/RG 319 [OPD, Joint Board, Serial 697-3].) Major General Charles H. Bonesteel (U.S.M.A., 1908) was head of the Iceland Base Command.

2. Citing the "administrative difficulties" that would ensue, Major General Thomas Holcomb opposed assigning the marine contingent to the army command. (Holcomb Memorandum for Admiral Stark, September 4, 1941, NA/RG 319 [OPD, Joint Board, Serial 697].) He preferred that the command relations follow precisely the prescriptions in paragraph 7 of *Joint Action of the Army and Navy,* thereby limiting Bonesteel's authority to operational orders and precluding instructions regarding Marine Corps administration and discipline. Marshall thought Holcomb was "unduly concerned over the command set-up proposed." Maintaining discipline and morale would be difficult enough for Bonesteel, particularly during the winter, and Marshall insisted that Bonesteel be able to exercise authority over the marines in Iceland in disciplinary and administrative matters. Admiral Stark agreed. (Marshall Memorandum for Admiral Stark, September 5, 1941, ibid.; Marshall to Stark, September 9, 1941, NA/RG 165 [OCS, 21224-45-B].)

3. President Roosevelt had received British Prime Minister Winston S. Churchill's request on September 1. (*Churchill and Roosevelt: The Complete Correspondence,* ed. Warren F. Kimball, 3 vols. [Princeton: Princeton University Press, 1984], 1: 235-36.)

MEMORANDUM FOR THE PRESIDENT   September 6, 1941
Secret   [Washington, D.C.]

Subject: Organization of the first Army contingent for Iceland.

You may be interested in the following details incident to the removal and replacement of selectees and Reserve officers who were legally debarred from serving in the first contingent being sent to Iceland. For the entire force, eighty-two per cent of the Reserve officers volunteered, while only twenty-two per cent of the selectees did so.[1]

The 10th Infantry regiment, less one of its three battalions, (93 officers and 2200 men) required the replacement of one-fourth of its officers and over one-third of its enlisted men, this in addition to volunteers obtained from the battalion left behind. The Field Artillery Battalion (30 officers and 520 men) required the replacement of only three of its thirty officers, but the turnover of enlisted men was in the same proportion as in the Infantry. To obtain replacements for those who would not volunteer it was necessary to comb another Infantry regiment, the Medical Battalion and remaining Artillery organizations of the Division, and a near-by General Hospital.

The specialized Services offered an even more difficult problem. One company of three officers and one hundred and fifty men necessitated transfers from nineteen different organizations. Even key instructors from special schools had to be drafted into the ranks.

As the units in the first contingent are in general parts of larger organizations of the 5th Division, the portions of the larger organizations which were left behind were drained of experienced three-year men; also they have had to absorb those men who declined to volunteer.

The organization of additional forces of this nature will require the disruption of approximately three regiments for every one sent and, even so, with small probability of securing volunteers of certain specialists essential to forces of this type. I am instructing the Staff to see that a special effort is made between now and next spring to bring units destined for Iceland to full strength with three-year men. The difficulty in this matter is that we are only able to secure a limited number of volunteer enlistments and the high priority for these as well as the desire of the volunteers themselves is for the Air Corps, and to a lesser extent, the armored force—neither of which are involved in the problem of providing the additional garrison for Iceland.

NA/RG 165 (OCS, 21224–39)

1. Draftees and members of the Officers' Reserve Corps and the National Guard could not be required to serve outside the Western Hemisphere, except in United States possessions. See the editorial note on pp. 565–66.

MEMORANDUM FOR THE PRESIDENT September 6, 1941
[Washington, D.C.]

The present morale situation in the troops of the Army, resulting from the debates in Congress, as well as press and radio activities, presents a very difficult problem. While the troops in 90% of the organizations have weathered the storm in excellent shape—as a matter of fact in every instance where we have had good leadership in the higher command—nevertheless the home influence presents a continuing difficulty. Parents have been so confused as to the facts or logic of the situation and so influenced by what they read of a critical nature that something must be done to bring them to an understanding of the national emergency and of the necessity for a highly trained Army.[1]

Within the War Department organization we are doing our best to counteract this weakness on the home-front, but as it relates to the civil population, I recommend that this phase of the matter be taken in hand by the Civilian Defense organization, to which it was assigned. In my opinion, Mr. President, prompt action is necessary.[2]

GCMRL/G. C. Marshall Papers (Pentagon Office, Selected)

1. Marshall had emphasized the importance of the home in bolstering army morale in a message published in the August 1941 *Ladies' Home Journal.* "Morale and physical fitness are attributes of a good soldier. In this new Army of ours we are paying a great deal of attention to both, as each supplements the other. . . . Our men are not being called upon to endure rigors for which they are unprepared—they have been trained and conditioned during the past months like athletes. No detail affecting their health and well-being has been overlooked. Their religious welfare has been most carefully provided for and is the subject of continuous inspection. Morale matters in general are under constant supervision. The hardships the men in training will be called upon to bear will probably not require as much of courage as this period of separation from their families. The training they are receiving is vital to our security, and encouragement from home is vital to their morale." (George C. Marshall, "A Message to the Women of America," *Ladies' Home Journal* 58[August 1941]: 6.)

2. In an effort to counter the problem of impaired army morale, on August 19, 1941, the War Department had named a civilian, Frederick H. Osborn, as chief of the Morale Branch with the temporary rank of brigadier general. (*New York Times,* August 20, 1941, p. 1.)

The Office of Civilian Defense had been established by executive order on May 20, 1941, to coordinate national, state, and local civilian defense activities. It was directed "to facilitate constructive civilian participation in the defense program, and to sustain national morale." (Executive Order No. 8757.) New York City Mayor Fiorello H. LaGuardia had been appointed director of the office. For President Roosevelt's reply, see the note to Memorandum for the President, September 25, 1941, pp. 618–19.

To GENERAL SIR JOHN DILL
September 9, 1941
[Washington, D.C.]

My dear Sir John: This morning I received your note of August 20th, together with General Spears's book, which I am taking home to read at the completion of the day's chores. I appreciate your remembering our conversations about Spears and this book; but I much more appreciate the generous phrasing of your note.[1]

There has been some discussion of my going to London for the meeting preparatory to the Joint Mission to Moscow. However, it was not arrangeable at this particular time. Most of my decisions could be taken here, as they related to the decision regarding the maximum limit of materiel we could spare during the next few months.[2] I am in the midst of a maneuver of some 500,000 troops, a legislative battle over a separate Air Corps,[3] the instructions from the White House to make a strong presentation before the Congressional Committees on the new Lease-loan appropriation about to be launched, and several other almost as important matters. A little later I hope things will clear up so I will have more liberty of action.

I felt greatly reassured by my conversations with you, and I propose writing to you personally and very frankly whenever any matters arise which I think merit such attention. I am depending on you to treat me with similar frankness, and I am quite sure you will do so.

Since my return from Newfoundland I have been inspecting in the Middle West, in Colorado, during the maneuvers of the Fourth Army in the Northwest, many of our air installations in California, and some of our large training centers at Cheyenne, Wyoming, and Nebraska. I returned last night from another air trip, intensive as to mileage but very brief as to time.[4] Meanwhile, between and during these activities I have been involved in reaching a decision regarding allocations of materiel. However when I think of your responsibilities, my obligations and troubles seem quite trivial.

With very warm regards,   Faithfully yours,

GCMRL/G. C. Marshall Papers (Pentagon Office, Selected)

1. In a handwritten note to Marshall, Dill had said: "This is just a line with the book I promised to send you to let you know how greatly I appreciated the opportunity of meeting you. I had heard so much about you before and now that I know you I feel immensely pleased. I wish you every possible success in the great task upon which you are engaged & I sincerely hope that we shall meet again before long. In the meantime we must keep each other in touch in the frank manner upon which we agreed." (Dill to Marshall, August 20, 1941, GCMRL/G. C. Marshall Papers [Pentagon Office, Selected].)

Dill had most likely sent to Marshall a copy of Brigadier-General Edward L. Spears's *Prelude to Victory* (London: Jonathan Cape, 1939). Spears described and analyzed the great offensive of 1917, a period in which "the relations between the British and French Armies were put to their greatest strain." Spears concluded the Preface with a hope that the volume would "contribute to a better understanding of days when it seemed as if the only constant factor, the one thing that could be relied upon absolutely, was the unfailing endurance and courage of both French and British soldiers." (*Prelude to Victory,* p. 15.)

2. At their Placentia Bay conference, Churchill and Roosevelt had decided to send a joint mission to the Soviet Union to ascertain what Russian materiel needs the United States and Great Britain could supply. To head the mission Churchill appointed Lord Beaverbrook, minister of supply, and Roosevelt named W. Averell Harriman, who had been in London as the president's lend-lease expediter since March 1941. At the time Marshall wrote this letter, Harriman was in Washington, D.C., assembling the personnel for his mission and working out the details of the United States position. Discussions in London were scheduled to begin on September 15 to prepare a combined British-American aid list for the mission. (*Foreign Relations, 1941,* 1: 825, 829–30.) On September 12 Churchill was notified that Lieutenant

General Stanley D. Embick was "being sent to London to represent the Chief of Staff in the discussion." (*Churchill and Roosevelt: The Complete Correspondence,* 1: 241.)

3. For Marshall's views on a separate Air Force, see Speech to the American Legion, September 15, 1941, p. 610.

4. During August 20–28, Marshall and Secretary of War Henry L. Stimson had made a combination relaxation-inspection tour of the Northwest. Marshall inspected the bombsight school at Lowry Field, Colorado (August 22); and the Boeing plant at Seattle, Washington (August 25); witnessed the take-off of the Twentieth Pursuit Group at Hamilton Field, California (August 27); and inspected the Quartermaster Replacement Center at Fort Francis E. Warren, Wyoming (August 27). He arrived in Washington, D.C., on August 28. (Yale/ H. L. Stimson Papers [Diary, 35: 42–49].)

On September 8 Marshall had flown to New York City and back. He attended a conference at First Army Headquarters at Governors Island that was attended by the army corps and division commanders, corps area commanders, and the Coast Artillery district commanders for the purpose of discussing the upcoming maneuvers. Lieutenant General Hugh A. Drum thanked Marshall for attending. "The officers appreciated the time you took to journey here and back, and especially your fine explanation of the problems that you have to solve. You cleared the atmosphere greatly in connection with the ammunition and it will help them in their problems of esprit de corps, etc." (Drum to Marshall, September 9, 1941, GCMRL/ G. C. Marshall Papers [Pentagon Office, Selected].)

MEMORANDUM FOR THE PRESIDENT
Secret

September 9, 1941
[Washington, D.C.]

The following extract from a personal letter from General MacArthur to me may be of interest to you:

"The Philippine Army units that have been called are now (August 30) mobilizing in a most satisfactory manner and the whole program is progressing by leaps and bounds. President Roosevelt's proclamation had a most momentous effect throughout the Far East.[1] Locally it changed a feeling of defeatism to the highest state of morale I have ever seen. It was hailed with the utmost enthusiasm by all classes. You, Secretary Stimson, and the President may congratulate yourselves on the excellent timing of the action.

"I wish to express my personal appreciation for the splendid support that you and the entire War Department have given me along every line since the formation of this command. With such backing the development of a completely adequate defense force will be rapid."

By commercial vessels from San Francisco on August 26th and September 8th, the following personnel and materiel have been shipped to Manila:

One antiaircraft regiment
One tank battalion (less one company) with 50 tanks
Fifty latest model P-forty pursuit planes, along
    with ammunition, and some other items of materiel.

The departure of the Flying Fortress squadron from Hawaii was delayed because of the run-way at Wake Island. It is now en route and arrived at New Britain this morning. It should be in Manila tomorrow, or the next day.

GCMRL/G. C. Marshall Papers (Pentagon Office, Selected)

1. Roosevelt's military order of July 26, 1941, called the military of the Commonwealth of the Philippines into federal service. (*Code of Federal Regulations, 1941 Supplement* [Washington: GPO, 1942], p. 350.)

MEMORANDUM FOR ADMIRAL STARK   September 12, 1941
Secret   [Washington, D.C.]

Dear Betty: You asked me about what we are doing for the Philippines:[1]

August 26: There sailed from San Francisco part of a regiment of antiaircraft troops and some reserve supplies.

September 8: There sailed from San Francisco the remainder of the antiaircraft regiment, a tank battalion of 50 tanks, 50 of the latest pursuit planes, and the personnel to man them, which brings the modern pursuit planes in the Philippines up to 80.

September 18: 50 self-propelled mounts for 75 cannon to be shipped from San Francisco, and 50 more tanks.

Today The squadron of nine Flying Fortresses landed in Manila after successfully flying the route Midway, Wake, New Britain, Dutch East Indies.

September 30: Two squadrons (26 planes) of Flying Fortresses will leave San Francisco for Hawaii en route to the Philippines.

October: A reserve of pursuit planes will have been in process of shipment, about 32 in October, rising to a total of 130 by December.

November: Probably a reserve of six to nine of the super Flying Fortresses, B-24 type planes will be transferred to Manila. These planes will have an operating radius of 1500 miles, with a load of 14,000 bombs, which means that they can reach Osaka with a full load and Tokyo with a partial load. They have pressure cabins and can operate continuously 35,000 feet for bombing.

December: Another group of Flying Fortresses, some 35 planes, goes to Manila.

A group of dive bombers, some 54 planes, also goes.

A group of pursuit, some 130 planes, along with two additional squadrons to build up the previous pursuit group, will be dispatched.

A 50% reserve is being established for all these planes.

GCMRL/G. C. Marshall Papers (Pentagon Office, Selected)
1. Stark's query may have been oral, since the editors have found no document on the issue from the chief of naval operations.

SPEECH TO THE AMERICAN LEGION[1]   September 15, 1941
Milwaukee, Wisconsin

This National Convention of the Legion finds our country in the midst of a tremendous defense effort. It finds the Army at a momentary climax of the most extensive and strenuous peacetime training program in the history of this or, possibly, any other country.

A great deal of water has gone over the dam since your first convention in 1919. Unfortunately it carried with it, by way of erosion, most of the military power created by your youthful vigor and your willingness to serve the country in those other critical days. Obsolescence had a similar effect on materiel.

Since the transition of you men from the ranks of the Army to the ranks of the Legion, your organization has fathered and has urged, year after year, military policies and appropriations which if they had been accepted by the people and the Congress, would have found us in 1938 so strong in being and so powerful in immediate prospect, that the influence of this country might have given a different turn to the tragic history of the past two years.

No other group of men and women in this country can render such powerful support to the War Department as yours, and at no other time has this support been so necessary as it is today. In the past you have urged adequate appropriations for defense. Today, money is not the acute problem—the Congress has been ready to provide the desired appropriations. What we lack and what we must have is an understanding by every family in America of the gravity of our situation. They should understand what it takes in discipline, in training, and in time to make a dependable army, and they must realize what infinite harm can be done through ignorance of military requirements and unwitting cooperation with agencies working in the interest of potential enemies.

The problems of preparing our present military forces are quite different from those with which you men were familiar in 1917. In those days the matter of equipment was solved by the tremendous productive capacity which had been developed in England and France after three years' concentrated military effort. Our troops were sent overseas barehanded, versed only in the basic training of the soldier. Divisions were equipped in the field, trained within sound of the guns along the lines held by our Allies. Corps and armies were actually organized on the battle-field. Units were placed in the line at our convenience. Tactical errors, the results of faulty leadership, were not fatal, although unnecessary losses resulted, since they were localized by the very nature of the sector warfare of that period.

The technique of 1917 is outmoded today. The specialized training for a particular type of operation gives way to the necessity for perfect teamwork in fast-moving operations over any type of terrain. A high degree of technical and tactical knowledge is necessary, from the individual soldier to the commanders of the highest units. Skilled initiative is a mandatory requirement. The complicated coordination of fire power, ground and air, must be managed at top speed, and for a surprising variety of weapons, with little or no opportunity to rehearse the procedure or to gain familiarity with the ground.

The training of this modern Army has been steadily progressive in nature. The soldier is given thirteen weeks of basic military education, including specialized training for his branch of the service. He is then assigned to a tactical unit where he passes through a period of unit training. The man who entered the Army last fall is now engaged in a final phase of training—that is, field service as a member of large military units. These maneuvers have been in progress all summer, with constantly increasing forces, until they are now culminating in the operations of three field armies, involving three-quarters of a million men.

It is difficult to overemphasize the importance of the maneuvers. You veterans who served in France will recall the fog of battle and the utter confusion which often prevails when large military forces come to grips; you probably remember the tremendous difficulties of ammunition and food supply; the great strain placed on field communications and the difficulty of their maintenance; I know you realize the stern necessity of willing obedience and firm discipline. In actual battle these matters are of decisive importance and they cannot be simulated on the parade ground. The present maneuvers are the closest peacetime approximation to actual fighting conditions that has ever been undertaken in this country. But what is of the greatest importance, the mistakes and failures will not imperil the nation or cost the lives of men. In the past we have jeopardized our future, penalized our leaders and sacrificed our men by training untrained troops on the battlefield.

The maneuvers also constitute a field laboratory to accept or discard new methods of applying fundamental tactical principles. They enable us to perfect close liaison between combat aviation and ground units. They permit of test of a possible solution to the secret of defense against tanks. By actual field operations we are determining the proper tactics for the employment of armored units. The development of our mechanized reconnaissance units is being accelerated by experience with the difficulties and uncertainties created by masses of troops operating over wide distances. Opposing divisions are kept in the dark as to the size, equipment, and other capabilities of their immediate opponents. The results at times have been startling. In some cases divisions would have been annihilated; in others they would have been captured. On the field of battle such events would be tragic. Today they are merely mistakes. We can correct them, replace the ineffective leaders, and go ahead. As an insurance policy against whatever operations our troops might be called upon to perform, the cost of these maneuvers represents a trifling premium to pay. Tremendous sums of money have been spent on our national defense effort, but I know of no single investment which will give this country a greater return in security and in the saving of lives than the present maneuvers.

Although we have streamlined the Army, blistered feet and aching bones are still the lot of the recruit, and heavy burdens and long marches the role of the majority of the soldiers. Tank and truck travel may be fast but it is far from luxurious, really a severe hardship, which the men must be trained to endure.

Strenuous as the past year has been on the troops, we find that all but a few have gained weight and that despite the tremendous increase in the size of the Army during the past year, the death rate has actually decreased from 3 per thousand to 2 per thousand. Although we moved hundreds of thousands of men from all parts of the United States into tent camps in the middle of winter, the sickness rate in our Army camps was, and is, generally below that of the average civilian community. Our soldiers probably constitute the healthiest group of individuals in the world today.

Along with the progress of the past year, we have encountered problems that have taxed our ingenuity to the extreme and there is one in particular which I wish to discuss tonight. It is a very serious matter for it strikes at the taproot of military efficiency.

Although the President has proclaimed a state of emergency, the Army for all practical purposes is still operating under peacetime conditions. Perhaps it is this unusual, unprecedented situation which has resulted in a lack of understanding by the public as well as parents of soldiers and the soldiers themselves, regarding fundamental military requirements. The power of an army cannot be measured in mere numbers. It is based on a high state of discipline and training; on a readiness to carry out its mission wherever and whenever the Commander-in-Chief and Congress decide. Any compromise with *those* requirements and *that* purpose not only minimizes our efforts but largely vitiates our development of military power.

This Army belongs to the American people—it is their Army, your Army. What it does, what it is, are naturally matters of personal interest to all of our people; not only to those who have relatives in uniform, but to every citizen depending on the army for security. Despite the pros and cons which have attended every issue debated during the past year, whether on the floors of Congress, in the press, or over the radio, I am certain that everyone is in agreement on one point—that is, this country must have the best army in the world.

Now, as veteran soldiers, I submit to you men of the Legion the impossibility of developing an efficient army if decisions which are purely military in nature are continuously subjected to investigation, cross-examination, debate, ridicule, and public discussion by pressure groups, or by individuals with only a superficial knowledge of military matters, or of the actual facts in the particular case. I submit that there is a clear line of demarcation between the democratic freedom of discussion which we are determined to preserve and a destructive procedure which promotes discontent and destroys confidence in the Army.

As Chief of Staff I am largely responsible for the military program and for the decisions of subordinates. Mistakes have been made and it is to be expected that more will be made. However, I am certain that we in the Army are the most severe critics and also that we can best detect deficiencies and we are better prepared to determine the method for their correction.

Please have these considerations in mind. A sane, a wonderful step has been taken by this country in adopting a policy of preparing its military forces in time of peace, as the wisest of precautionary measures in the face of a world crisis. The very fact that the nation has shown such unprecedented [foresight] in a military way presents the most serious difficulty for those responsible for the development of the army. With a clear-cut task before us well-known to the troops, the development of the army would be comparatively a simple matter. But *must* we *declare war* in order to facilitate training and morale? *Must* you *burn down* the building in order to justify the Fire Department?

The local posts of the Legion can do much to bring the people at home to a better understanding of the requirements of the situation. Even you veterans probably do not realize the result of appeals of the young man angling for a home-made cake or bragging to his parents or his girl of the hardships he endures, or grousing over the failure of his leaders to recognize his particular ability by immediate promotion. The War Department at times receives a veritable avalanche of criticisms or pressures resulting from such ordinary soldier reactions as these. The incidents in themselves are often amusing, as in the case of the mother who complained that her son wasn't getting enough to eat, and we found her boy had gained sixteen pounds in twenty days. But the total effect is really serious. As I read confidential reports from abroad there is a startling similarity between our present situation in this respect and that which affected the late lamented Army of France. Criticism, justified or otherwise, is to be expected. In fact, it is as inevitable as a Congressional investigation, but when its *nature* or *purpose* is to cause disunity within the Army, I say, direct such criticisms at me personally, but leave the Army alone. Don't tear down what you are striving so hard to build up.

Let me cite an example of what I mean. Take the matter of a separate Air Force. Because we are convinced that the establishment of a separate Air Force would not only be a grave error but would completely disrupt the splendid organization now in process of building, we are accused of being unprogressive, jealous of prerogatives and incredibly short-sighted.

On the basis of a cold-blooded analysis of facts, the matter has been studied in great detail by the War Department during the operations in which foreign nations are now involved. I can assure you that nothing has developed as a result of the present war which indicates that a change should be made in the present setup in the United States. Comparisons are drawn that two nations whose air forces have attained the greatest success have so-called separate air forces. Here again we encounter a confusion of facts. Consider, for instance, the case of our friends, the British. Except for the gallant and truly remarkable defense of the British Isles which is a special problem having little application to our problem of hemisphere defense, the lack of unity of command between the air and ground forces has courted disaster in virtually every operation they have undertaken. In the operations in Belgium, and France, in Norway, in Greece, in Crete and in the Middle East this lack of unity of command has remained a continuous, unsolved problem. In fact, the British have found it necessary to modify the separate air arm idea with respect to naval aviation. More recently they have been improvising special groups to operate more closely with ground troops.

The ex-democracy of France had a separate air force which operated on a basis similar to that which some individuals are now proposing that we adopt. France was defeated and reduced to a state of vassalage in a five-week's campaign. The Italian air force which nurtures the theory of total war from the air and which has so-called independent control has yet to be effective in the present war. Contrary to popular belief, the German air force is not independent of the ground arms in the generally conceived sense, but is closely coordinated by means of a system of command and staff over and above all civil departments, which would not be acceptable to a democracy such as the United States. The German government is geared throughout for the primary purpose of making war through a superlatively centralized form of control. Hitler is Commander-in-Chief, but he operates through a Chief of Staff of a Supreme Staff which plans, directs, and controls the operations of the Army, Navy, and Air Force, and is responsible only to the head of the Government. Through this machinery a campaign is planned, the organizations—air, ground and naval—are allotted, and a Commander is designated. He organizes and trains this task force and at the appointed time carries out the campaign, with every available resource of Germany in support. He may be a ground officer, an air or a naval officer. But he is in sole charge of every phase of the operation.

It is needless to say that the American people are not likely to establish a military oligarchy for this country, and lacking such an organization the German system would be ineffective. As a matter of fact, we have adapted to our own use a setup that approximates that of Germany as closely as is possible under our system of government.

Just a year ago the President gave final approval to the Selective Training and Service Act and to legislation authorizing reserve components to be called into federal service. The importance of these two measures for the national defense was tremendous. They constituted a reversal of the historic and almost tragic policy that the United States would prepare for war only after becoming involved in war. Our peacetime military force was maintained for minor transactions, not to meet a first-class foe; a perilous policy, and one of extreme extravagance in men and money when the emergency arose. The greatest security which this nation can possess is a powerful navy, backed by a well-trained army, together so strong that no foreign nation will dare to provoke a war. The Army is now in the making, but it must go through another winter of training under field conditions before it is fully prepared; and it must have the understanding and support of the people at home.

You gentlemen are practical soldiers. You can understand the difficulty of handling large masses of men under conditions of warfare. You recognize the meaning and importance of discipline. You realize how easy it is to tear down, and how difficult it is to build it up. During this emergency the sound policies of the Legion have been a tower of strength to the War Department and to commanders in the field, and it is to you that I look for the support necessary to the accomplishment of our objective.

The spirit and determination that were yours twenty-three years ago, in the Meuse-Argonne, at San Mihiel, or in a training camp at home, must be instilled in the men of this new Army. You can understand this and I know you will help. There is a further responsibility which I place upon you. I look to you to educate the people at home as to the necessities of the times. Without a united country it will be impossible to build the type of Army we must have. We cannot build the best army in the world unless the people of this country are behind it.

I am a soldier and I have spoken to you as one soldier to another. I have but one purpose, one mission, and that is to produce the most efficient Army in the world. Given the American type of soldier and our war industries operating at top speed; given your aggressive support on the home front, and it can be done, and it will be done in time.

GCMRL/G. C. Marshall Papers (Pentagon Office, Speeches)

1. Marshall sent the ribbons and medals that he received at the Legion convention to Edward R. Stettinius, Jr.'s, youngsters. In a letter to Mrs. Stettinius, Marshall wrote: "I am sending you some loot from the Legion Convention, to be bestowed upon Joseph and Wallace. Tell them that the advantage is all on their side. They can wear the ribbons and the medals and still not have to listen to me make a speech." (Marshall to Mrs. Edward R. Stettinius, Jr., September 19, 1941, GCMRL/G. C. Marshall Papers [Pentagon Office, Selected].)

MEMORANDUM FOR THE COMMANDING GENERAL, September 18, 1941
FIRST ARMY[1] [Washington, D.C.]

It has come to my attention that a number of general officers have relatives as members of their staffs. This practice has serious objections. The presence of such individuals on the personal or official staff of a commander has an unavoidably adverse reaction in the minds of both superiors and subordinates in their dealings with the commander concerned. I am convinced that under present conditions such a practice does not serve the best interests of the Army.

It is desired, therefore, that in your command you take steps informally and quietly to have relatives of general officers who are members of the personal and official staffs of those officers assigned to other duties prior to December 31, 1941.[2]

NA/RG 165 (OCS, 21320–1)

1. Identical letters were sent to the commanding generals of all corps areas, armies, departments, Armored Force, and Air Force Combat Command.

2. Concerning the use of relatives as aides, see note 1, Marshall to Herron, April 1, 1940, p. 184.

TO LELAND M. FORD[1] September 19, 1941
[Washington, D.C.]

My dear Mr. Ford: I have been concerned to learn of the unfavorable political reaction of some of your constituents to your vote upon the matter of the extension of service of selectees and officers and men of the Guard and Reserve Corps. I suppose this was inevitable but it is rather depressing to find that when a man acts against his own personal interests and courageously takes a stand purely in the interest of the nation at large, he should not be judged accordingly.[2]

You voted for the national defense and I assume that your action was to some extent influenced by my statements to a number of congressmen of the Republican party. I do hope that this proof of your courage and patriotism will not be used to your political disadvantage. It should mark you as a representative your constituents could trust to do his full duty to the country.[3]   Faithfully yours,

GCMRL/G. C. Marshall Papers (Pentagon Office, General)

   1. Congressman Ford, a Republican, had represented California's Sixteenth District since 1939.
   2. Ford had sent to Marshall a copy of a letter which he had written to E. O. Blackman, chairman of California's Sixteenth District Republican Central Committee, in reply to a letter from Blackman with reference to Ford's having voted in favor of retaining the selectees. Ford told Blackman that he realized that his vote was unpopular, but that it was "the necessary thing to do," and that "the safety of our country hinged on our decision." Ford had been among an audience of Republican congressmen to which Marshall had spoken at the Army and Navy Club. "At this meeting he was interrogated by every one of the Congressmen including myself, and so far as I could see it, there was nothing else for us to do but vote to keep these selectees in." At the meeting Marshall "went into the matter of distribution of troops, percentage of selectees in each division, their status, etc. I believe if our people were wholly aware of what this situation is that there would be no question in their mind as to the course to be taken." Ford concluded that Chief of Staff Marshall was better able to determine the needs of the army than was the average layman. "A good department head will tell you things you ought to know and not the things you like to hear. I think that General Marshall comes under this qualification, and I would stake my life that he is sound. He is a fighting man and an able man, and if the politicians would leave him alone I think we would be much better off." (Ford to Marshall, September 11, 1941, and attached Ford to Blackman, September 3, 1941, GCMRL/G. C. Marshall Papers [Pentagon Office, General].)
   3. Ford replied that he had talked with many of his constituents in Los Angeles County and had received their approval when he explained to them that he had absolute confidence in the War and Navy departments and that "this was no time for any partisanship." (Ford to Marshall, September 23, 1941, ibid.)

MEMORANDUM FOR GENERAL MOORE   September 22, 1941
Secret   [Washington, D.C.]

The President at the conference today brought up the question of tanks.[1] In brief these were his directions:

For you to proceed with an effort to find a way to double tank production.

For you to proceed in every way possible to increase the present tank production between now and July 1, 1942, by 25% so that the expedited deliveries could go to export.

For us to release 50 tanks, light or heavy or both, over and above our present promised releases, out of the production of the next three months.

In this last connection I commented on the fact that the matter of penalizing ourselves in addition to 50 tanks was not really the serious phase of the matter. What we would be troubled about was that this was merely a lead-up to still heavier diversion from us to the British and Russians. He accepted this last comment in good part but gave me no assurances, however I at least made the point.[2]

GCMRL/G. C. Marshall Papers (Pentagon Office, Selected)

1. Marshall and Secretary of War Stimson had met with President Roosevelt at noon at the White House. The minutes of a conference two days previous in the chief of staff's office with representatives from G-1, G-3, G-4, and W.P.D. called to discuss preparation of information for the meeting with the president reveal that Marshall anticipated discussing "a proposal to reduce the strength of the Army in order to make available more materiel for other purposes. . . . The proposals which have been made are as follows: (1) to reduce the size of the Army; (2) to reduce the amount of materiel being used by our Army; (3) to reduce the strength of our forces in the bases. The Chief of Staff pointed out that whatever data is presented to the President must be in concise form and not contain technical language of any kind. Each particular subject should be covered in not more than one paragraph. The Chief of Staff also pointed out that steps are being taken to reduce the garrisons in Hawaii and Panama; that the situation in the Philippines might be decisive within the next two months, and that our present augmentations there, particularly of air, are of outstanding importance. The question of reducing the forces in the bases is tied in with the continued maintenance of the British Navy." (William T. Sexton Notes on Conference in Office Chief of Staff, September 20, 1941, NA/RG 165 [OCS, Chief of Staff Conferences File].)

2. That same day Marshall wrote to Colonel Robert W. Crawford (U.S.M.A., 1914) of War Plans Division about his meeting with Roosevelt, where the president had reviewed a memorandum entitled "Ground Forces" prepared by War Plans Division. "I do not believe he is of the opinion that there should be any reduction in the military forces," Marshall wrote. "I think he is looking everywhere to find ways and means to secure materiel for Russia." (Marshall Memorandum for Colonel Crawford, September 22, 1941, GCMRL/G. C. Marshall Papers [Pentagon Office, Selected].)

TO MAJOR GENERAL CHARLES H. BONESTEEL   September 23, 1941
Secret   [Washington, D.C.]

Dear Bonesteel: During an interview with the President yesterday he talked quite a bit about the situation in Iceland. He was concerned over the divided command status—between the British and ourselves. He was desirous of continuing to send troops to Iceland during the winter—in small groups—in order to permit a continued return to England of small groups and the return to the United States of the misfits. He was concerned by someone's comment to him that there was too much of a concentration of troops around Reykjavik, presenting a vulnerable target to heavy bombing.

With regard to the command status he asked me how many U.S. troops we should have in Iceland before we could press for the command of the ground and air forces to be turned over to you. I told him 20,000 but he seemed to feel 15,000 would be sufficient to justify our requesting the transfer of command. I told him that the British might concede the point in order to oblige him personally, but that they would be very loathe to do so; that in any event they must continue to exercise command over the naval base, which is an integral part of their Northwest Passage convoy service. I believe the present agreement is that the transfer should be made when we have two-thirds of the force. Let me have your comments on this.[1]

Regarding his desire to continue the movement of our troops to Iceland during the winter, the understanding was that I would look into the question of the Navy's reactions as to the matter of tonnage and convoy service; that if we found it possible to send small increments we would do so. But I told him that the limiting factor at the moment would be the reorganization necessary legally to qualify troops to go to Iceland, that we had almost destroyed the 5th Division, and were engaged in diverting 3-year enlistments to the division to prepare the reinforcements for next Spring. Also I told him that to bring back groups of one or two hundred misfits might well induce men who were not charmed with the prospects of an Iceland winter to compete for the misfit class. Give me your reactions to this.[2]

As to over-concentration in the vicinity of Reykjavik, you will have to advise me on the subject. I imagine the principal difficulty is the development of adequate shelter in other localities and the lack of road communications and diversional facilities.[3]

Please treat all of the foregoing as confidential to yourself and to General Homer.[4]

If there is anything we can do to help you meet winter conditions, don't hesitate to advise us officially, and if you think the matter is very urgent send a copy of your official request direct to me by name. Faithfully yours,

GCMRL/G. C. Marshall Papers (Pentagon Office, Selected)

1. Bonesteel replied that the command situation was not a problem between his forces and the British. "To date we have had the finest relations with them, due in a great measure to the personality and common sense of Major General H. O. Curtis, the G.O.C. [general officer commanding]. I mention this at length, because you know that under present conditions, i.e., the United States not at war, we operate with the British under the principle of mutual cooperation and the question of 'command' does not apply. . . . He commands his forces and I command mine, but with very close cooperation not only in purely military matters but also in the many complex problems of relations with the Icelanders, etc., that the occupation engenders. . . . The number of troops of either army present does not in my opinion, affect the situation." (Bonesteel to Marshall, October 10, 1941, NA/RG 165 [WPD, 4493-165].)

2. Reykjavik harbor was seriously congested, and Bonesteel warned against increasing the number of shipments to Iceland. "If the schedule of United States ships is maintained during the next three months and also that of the British, there will be more cargo arriving than can be unloaded." He also emphasized the need to cull the "misfits" prior to sending units to Iceland and agreed with Marshall's assessment of the probable effects on his troops' morale of a "misfit convoy." (Ibid.)

3. The majority of the troops in and around Reykjavik were British, Bonesteel replied. "I have made every effort to keep our combat troop installations out of the city and will continue to do so, however this will become an acute problem when the relief of the British is effected."

There was a decided shortage of available land suitable for camps in the Reykjavik area, according to Bonesteel, and the Icelanders resented encroachment on their cultivated lands. (Ibid.)
  4. Brigadier General John L. Homer was chief of staff of the Iceland Base Command.

To CHARLES J. GRAHAM[1]   September 23, 1941
                                                [Washington, D.C.]

Dear Charlie: I wish it were possible for me to accept your tempting invitation to the Woodmont Rod and Gun Club's first shoot of the season on the 15th of November. There is nothing I would like better than to be a member of your party but unfortunately for me, I expect to be in Panama at that time.
  Am sure that I would enjoy meeting Wendell Willkie, particularly under such informal and agreeable circumstances, and as to my political faith—I have never voted, my father was a democrat, my mother a republican, and I am an Episcopalian.[2]
  Thank you many times for asking me to join you on this alluring outing, I am indeed sorry that I cannot be with you.   Faithfully yours,

GCMRL/G. C. Marshall Papers (Pentagon Office, Selected)
  1. Graham, president of the Pittsburgh and West Virginia Railway Company, had invited Marshall to attend the opening dinner and shoot scheduled for mid-November at the Woodmont Rod and Gun Club in nearby Maryland. (Graham to Marshall, September 22, 1941, GCMRL/G. C. Marshall Papers [Pentagon Office, Selected].)
  2. Graham had written to Marshall: "Am inviting Wendell Willkie, and while he may not be of your political faith, he is certainly 100% for the Administration in connection with its foreign policy and am sure you would enjoy knowing him." (Ibid.)

MEMORANDUM FOR THE SURGEON GENERAL[1]   September 23, 1941
                                                [Washington, D.C.]

I have just been talking to Colonel Truman Smith whose retirement becomes effective today. I am interested in the red tape involved in his retirement and I would like you to look into his particular case as possibly symptomatic of the condition which might be corrected.
  He is afflicted with diabetes. This was determined by the Walter Reed authorities in August 1939, or thereabouts. The annual physical examination in January 1940 and again in January 1941 recommended that he be sent before a retirement board.

The problem was on what status we should continue to use his services in the War Department, and I suspended action on the retirement proceedings until the middle of last July and then directed that the recommendations from the annual physical examinations be carried out.

Here is a case of a Regular Army officer who has a clear case of diabetes, who was not fighting for retirement nor was he fighting against retirement, there would seem to be no financial hazard to the Government involved.

Since my direction in the matter, of July, to go ahead with Colonel Smith's retirement, well over two months have elapsed during which he has had three more physical examinations which have involved your doctors and your record people and have accumulated quite a mass of papers.

Please look into this and see if there are not circumstances under which your people could handle cases like this expeditiously and help all of us. I fully understand how careful you must be in the case of a citizen-soldier who is looking to retirement status for financial reasons and in the case of a regular officer who is fighting retirement, and I recognize that there must be a certain routine manner of handling such cases, but can't you evolve some more simplified procedure for cases regarding which there is no debate.[2]

GCMRL/G. C. Marshall Papers (Pentagon Office, General)
1. Major General James C. Magee had been the surgeon general since June 1, 1939.
2. The editors have not found the surgeon general's reply.

To Major General Jacob L. Devers   September 24, 1941
[Washington, D.C.]

My dear Devers: I had a special investigation made of the selection of men for the Officer Candidate Schools, and while I have not had time to gain more than a superficial reaction in the matter, it is evident to me that some very inefficient administration occurred which gave us far below the average quality we should have obtained. The most adverse report is against the selection of candidates for the Armored Force school, therefore I would like you to look into this personally as soon as you get back to Knox.

I do not know to what extent the following comments apply to your school, as they were submitted in regard to the general proposition, but I recite them for your information:

Selections were not always impartial, especially in the case of local boards; too many clerks and old non-commissioned officers were selected as well as men whose past records showed trial and conviction for such offenses as desertion, assault and battery, and disrespect to their superior officers. Some men were sent to school who had previously failed to complete non-commissioned officer courses in the same school.[1]

Faithfully yours,

GCMRL/G. C. Marshall Papers (Pentagon Office, Selected)

1. Devers had commanded the Armored Force headquarters at Fort Knox, Kentucky, since August 1. He replied that the recent graduates were "the cleanest finest group of second lieutenants that I have seen anywhere. If the quality of this group is the lowest of all the schools, then, indeed, the army has nothing to worry about." Devers's only reservation about the group was that 50 percent of them were older than he preferred. He reported that there was no indication of any partiality shown by the local or final boards. Of the 250 candidates who had been authorized, only 231 had been selected. Of the 178 who were graduated, 56 were clerks, 9 were supply sergeants, and 13 were selectees; 38 were over twenty-nine years of age. One had been convicted of desertion in 1934, but he had since completed six years of "continuous excellent service." Devers concluded that they would not be able to fill their quota of 250 for the class entering in October, and that "instructions have been given to improve the quality of candidates." (Devers to Marshall, October 1, 1941, GCMRL/G. C. Marshall Papers [Pentagon Office, Selected].) See Memorandum for the Inspector General, August 19, 1941, p. 594.

MEMORANDUM FOR THE PRESIDENT

September 25, 1941
[Washington, D.C.]

Dear Mr. President: In answer to your note of September 23rd regarding my ideas on the subject of bolstering up civilian morale, I make this suggestion:[1]

General Osborn tells me there is a civilian morale division in the Office of Civil Defense under the provisional name of Division of National Unity. Osborn has had some contact with this group and understands that they have spent several months working up plans which seem to have real merit. My suggestion, and I referred to it in my memorandum to you of September 6th, is that these people be told to start aggressively to carry out their plans. I assume that a message or suggestion from you would be all that is necessary to set the machine in motion.

I am embarrassed in the matter because this business would seem to be the responsibility of Mr. LaGuardia's organization, and I imagine he would be resentful of my instigating pressure on him to allow his people to get under way with their ideas. However, the results of a lack of action in the purely civilian field react to the great complication of my task.

GCMRL/G. C. Marshall Papers (Pentagon Office, Selected)

1. On September 23 President Roosevelt had replied to Marshall's September 6 memorandum concerning civilian morale (see pp. 601-2). "I have not had a chance to send you a line in reply to your memorandum of September sixth," wrote the president. "In effect you say: (a)

The boys in camp are O.K. (b) The parental influence hurts the morale of many of them. (c) Please, Mr. President, do something about this weakness on the part of the civilian population. Got any ideas?" (Roosevelt to Marshall, September 23, 1941, GCMRL/G. C. Marshall Papers [Pentagon Office, Selected].)

MEMORANDUM FOR ADMIRAL STARK September 25, 1941
[Washington, D.C.]

Dear Betty: In relation to your navy story, the following are the facts:[1]

During maneuvers we prescribe the menus for each day and the rations necessary to these menus are then shipped up from the depots to the daily railheads accordingly. In other words, 500,000 men have the same bill of fare. So, if it happens to provide for french toast and your navy man wants soft-boiled eggs, he will have to go back to the navy for his breakfast. For .8 of an egg per man is sufficient for french toast or a scramble. The limiting factor is 50¢ per ration but the distribution of these fifty cents is determined in advance over the period of the entire maneuvers. There is still another complication which you probably will not advertise—you get 60¢ a day in the Navy. We get 50¢.

GCMRL/G. C. Marshall Papers (Pentagon Office, Selected)

1. The chief of naval operations had sent to Marshall a copy of a "yarn" from navy pilots complaining about the insufficiency of the food at the Beaumont, Texas, army mess where they had been eating while participating in the maneuvers in Louisiana. (Stark to Marshall, September 23, 1941, GCMRL/G. C. Marshall [Pentagon Office, Selected].) Deputy Chief of Staff for Air Arnold had likewise been "declaiming" about the parsimonious egg ration. "Maybe they need for [*more*] egg in the air than on the ground," Marshall wrote at the bottom of the letter from Stark. Arnold commented that his investigation of the egg situation had elicited the following teletyped response: "There is no trouble with the food at Beaumont. Everybody is satisfied. The Mess Officer says so." (Arnold Memorandum for General Moore, September 24, 1941, ibid.)

ADDRESS FOR DELIVERY TO THE GRADUATES OF [September 27, 1941]
THE FIRST OFFICER CANDIDATE SCHOOL[1] [Washington, D.C.]

You are about to assume the most important duty that our officers are called upon to perform—the direct command of combat units of American soldiers. To succeed requires two fundamental qualifications—thorough professional knowledge and a capacity for leadership. The schools have done all that can be done in the limited time available to equip you professionally, and your technique of weapons and tactics should rapidly improve with further study and actual practice. However, they cannot provide you with qualities of leadership—that courage and evident high purpose which command the respect and loyalty of American soldiers.

You were selected as officer candidates because you give evidence of possessing these qualifications. Whether or not you develop into truly capable leaders depends almost entirely upon you personally.

Your school work has been under ideal conditions from an instructional standpoint; but when you join your organizations, you will find many difficulties and deficiencies complicating your task. There will be shortages in equipment, for example. These are being made good as rapidly as possible, but so long as they exist they are a challenge to your ingenuity and not an invitation to fall back on an overdose of close order drill and the other necessary but stultifying minutia which so irked the Army of 1917 that we still suffer from the repercussions.

Warfare today is a thing of swift movement—of rapid concentrations. It requires the building up of enormous fire power against successive objectives with breathtaking speed. It is not a game for the unimaginative plodder. Modern battles are fought by platoon leaders. The carefully prepared plans of higher commanders can do no more than project you to the line of departure at the proper time and place, in proper formation, and start you off in the right direction. Thereafter, the responsibility for results is almost entirely yours. If you know your business of weapons and tactics, if you have inspired the complete confidence and loyalty of your men, things will go well on that section of the front.

There is a gulf between the drill ground or cantonment type of leadership and that necessary for the successful command of men when it may involve the question of sacrificing one's life. Our Army differs from all other armies. The very characteristics which make our men potentially the best soldiers in the world can be in some respects a possible source of weakness. Racially we are not a homogeneous people, like the British for example, who can glorify a defeat by their stubborn tenacity and dogged discipline. We have no common racial group, and we have deliberately cultivated individual initiative and independence of thought and action. Our men are intelligent and resourceful to an unusual degree. These characteristics, these qualities may be, in effect, explosive or positively destructive in a military organization, especially under adverse conditions, unless the leadership is wise and determined, and unless the leader commands the complete respect of his men.

Never for an instant can you divest yourselves of the fact that you are officers. On the athletic field, at the club, in civilian clothes, or even at home on leave, the fact that you are a commissioned officer in the Army imposes a constant obligation to higher standards than might ordinarily seem normal or necessary for your personal guidance. A small dereliction becomes conspicuous, at times notorious, purely by reason of the fact that the individual concerned is a commissioned officer.

But the evil result goes much further than a mere matter of unfortunate publicity. When you are commanding, leading men under conditions where physical exhaustion and privations must be ignored; where the lives of men may be sacrificed, then, the efficiency of your leadership will depend only to a minor degree on your tactical or technical ability. It will primarily be determined by your character, your reputation, not so much for courage— which will be accepted as a matter of course—but by the previous reputation you have established for fairness, for that high-minded patriotic purpose, that quality of unswerving determination to carry through any military task assigned you.

The feeling which the men must hold for you is not to be compared to the popularity of a football coach or a leader of civic activities. Professional competence is essential to leadership and your knowledge of arms, equipment, and tactical operations must be clearly superior to that possessed by your subordinates; at the same time, you must command their respect above and beyond those qualities.

It is difficult to make a clear picture of the obligations and requirements for an officer. Conditions of campaign and the demands of the battlefield are seldom appreciated except by veterans of such experiences. The necessity for discipline is never fully comprehended by the soldier until he has undergone the ordeal of battle, and even then he lacks a basis of comparison—the contrast between the action of a disciplined regiment and the failure and probable disintegration of one which lacks that intangible quality. The quality of officers is tested to the limit during the long and trying periods of waiting or marching here and there without evident purpose, and during those weeks or months of service under conditions of extreme discomfort or of possible privations or isolations. The true leader surmounts all of these difficulties, maintaining the discipline of his unit and further developing its training. Where there is a deficiency of such leadership, serious results inevitably follow, and too often the criticism is directed to the conditions under which the unit labored rather than toward the individual who failed in his duty because he was found wanting in inherent ability to accept his responsibilities.

Remember that we are a people prone to be critical of everything except that for which we are personally responsible. Remember also that to a soldier a certain amount of grousing appears to be necessary. However, there is a vast difference between these usually amusing reactions and the destructive and disloyal criticism of the undisciplined soldier.

Mental alertness, initiative, vision are qualities which you must cultivate. Passive inactivity because you have not been given specific instructions to do this or to do that is a serious deficiency. Always encourage initiative on the part of your men, but initiative must of course, be accompanied by intelligence.

Much of what I have said has been by way of repetition of one thought which I wish you gentlemen to carry with you to your new duties. You will be responsible for a unit in the Army of the United States in this great emergency. Its quality, its discipline, its training will depend upon your leadership. Whatever deficiencies there are must be charged to your failure or incapacity. Remember this: the truly great leader overcomes all difficulties, and campaigns and battles are nothing but a long series of difficulties to be overcome. The lack of equipment, the lack of food, the lack of this or that are only excuses; the real leader displays his quality in his triumphs over adversity, however great it may be.

Good luck to you. We expect great things of you. Your class is the first of which I believe will be the finest group of troop leaders in the world.

GCMRL/G. C. Marshall Papers (Pentagon Office, Speeches)

1. Marshall was unable to attend the graduation exercises at Fort Benning, Georgia. Brigadier General Omar N. Bradley, commandant of the Infantry School, sent his regrets. "We are very sorry that you were unable to come to Benning today for our officer candidate graduating exercises. All three groups of candidates will be assembled and your address will be read to them. Each candidate will also receive a copy." (Bradley to Marshall, September 27, 1941, GCMRL/G. C. Marshall Papers [Pentagon Office, Selected].)

To Major General Ernest D. Peek   September 29, 1941
                                         [Washington, D.C.]

Dear Peek: I flew in from Louisiana last night and this morning found your note of September 26th. When I was at the maneuvers last week General De Witt had told me of your misfortune and since my return I have had not only your letter but also a letter from him.[1] I am terribly sorry you had such hard luck, and I feel badly because it has been induced by the strenuous program I have called on you to meet in the 9th Corps Area. I might tell you that this has happened a number of times in the last six months and on each occasion it has been the direct result of the terrific demands on the individual concerned. Now I do hope that you will follow the safe course and not wreck your health permanently by attempting to rush back to a heavy military burden, or otherwise call heavily on your reserves.

I am arranging to have Lane take over temporary command of the Corps Area, and I think that General Benedict will probably be given the permanent assignment. He now commands a Corps in the Third Army.[2]

My sympathy goes as much to Anne as to you because I know how deeply she will grieve over your being laid up at this time. With affectionate regards to you both,   Faithfully yours,

GCMRL/G. C. Marshall Papers (Pentagon Office, Selected)

1. Marshall had left Washington on September 25 to inspect the Louisiana maneuvers and had returned on September 28.

Peek, commander of the Ninth Corps Area, had written expressing his appreciation for Marshall's "kind consideration and message of thoughtfulness" relayed by Lieutenant General John L. De Witt. Peek had been in the hospital since September 9, recovering from a heart attack, and had written to Marshall concerning command during his absence while on sick leave. (Peek to Marshall, September 26, 1941, GCMRL/G. C. Marshall Papers [Pentagon Office, Selected].) Meanwhile, De Witt had written to Marshall recommending Brigadier General Arthur W. Lane (U.S.M.A., 1905) to command temporarily the Ninth Corps Area pending disposition of Peek's case. "He hesitated at first to agree that he should give up command of the Corps Area out of loyalty to you," wrote De Witt. "He felt that he should retain the command if it is possible for him to do so. I told him that was foolish; that in your conversation with me you clearly indicated that you felt he should retire if he had a heart condition." (De Witt to Marshall, September 25, 1941, ibid.)

2. Major General Jay L. Benedict, superintendent of the United States Military Academy from February 1938 to November 1940, was commander of the Fourth Army Corps at Jacksonville, Florida. He assumed command of the Ninth Corps Area on November 3, 1941.

To George A. Beecher   September 30, 1941
                                              [Washington, D.C.]

Dear Bishop Beecher: I returned from the Louisiana maneuvers last night[1] to find your letter of September 27th. It is a very pleasant thing to hear from you again, and exceedingly gratifying to read your generous comments regarding me personally, and to find that you are so stalwart in your attitude toward the practical business of our national security.[2]

I have been very happy in my relations with the religious organizations in connection with the development of this emergency army, largely, I think, because of the splendid character and capacity for leadership of the current Chief of Chaplains, Colonel William R. Arnold. He is a Catholic, but his attitude has been completely non-sectarian and his judgment in choosing advisors has been admirable. Through his advice and guidance, and with his leadership among the chaplains, I have been able to make tremendous strides in this phase of our responsibilities.

I have been criticized for the building of too many chapels and too few buildings for purely military purposes, but I feel that we are generally involved in a great experiment to see if much more cannot be done than has ever been practical in the past. In effect we are treating the Chaplains Corps in exactly the same manner we treat the other officers regarding training, tactics, or supply. We have tried to exert the same care in the selection of chaplains that we endeavor to exert in the selection of troop leaders. This is probably the most important phase of the whole matter, because without the capacity for leadership a chaplain almost does more harm than good. I was really pleased several months ago to receive a letter from Bishop O'Hara, who had been on our advisory council, stating that he thought we were working the catholic chaplains too hard.[3] This meant to me that our efforts in the religious field were as strenuous as we try to make them in the purely military field.

I often look back on our pleasant days at Fort Benning, particularly our rides. I hope you have suffered no continuing ill effects from your automobile accident and that Mrs. Beecher is in good health.

With my warm regards to both of you,   Faithfully yours,

GCMRL/G. C. Marshall Papers (Pentagon Office, General)

1. Marshall returned from the Louisiana maneuvers on September 28. He most likely dictated this letter on September 29, although it was typed on September 30.

2. Beecher, Episcopal bishop of the Missionary District of Western Nebraska, had been Marshall's horseback riding companion at Fort Benning. "I have related to my various congregations on Sunday mornings the deeply anchored confidence I have in you and your powerful leadership of our troops in this tragical world situation," Beecher had written to Marshall. "I know that it does no harm to tell our people who you are and what you are doing. It helps to stimulate their confidence and warm them up to a more rational and helpful patriotism. I have been hammering at the disloyal groups who have been plying their schemes to disrupt this country by creating factions and sectionalism against the Administration and his associates who are trying to crush Nazism and all it stands for at the earliest possible date. . . . I have told our people how much I thought of you and referred to several incidents in which you demonstrated that type of Christian character which makes us all proud of you as a national leader in a time of distress. I recall in this connection the order you issued for all troops not on specific duty to be granted the privilege of attending the Good Friday services last Lent." (Beecher to Marshall, September 27, 1941, GCMRL/G. C. Marshall Papers [Pentagon Office, General].)

3. The letter to which Marshall refers is not in the Marshall papers.

MEMORANDUM FOR THE HONORABLE ROBERT P.   September 30, 1941
PATTERSON, UNDERSECRETARY OF WAR   [Washington, D.C.]
Confidential

Subject: Morale of the Army.

1. Your memorandum of August 14, together with accompanying papers, relative to the morale of the Army, particularly in National Guard divisions, and suggestions for remedying unsatisfactory conditions, has been noted by me and circulated through the Staff.[1]

2. The conditions to which you refer have been matters of great concern. As a general comment, I would say that morale is a function of command. Therefore, as far as the efforts of the Army itself are concerned, the initial corrective measure to be undertaken is improvement of officer personnel. We are attempting to accomplish this not only by elimination of the incompetent, but, of greater importance, by gradually sending all of our officers to the service schools. This is a tremendous task, and is taxing our facilities to the utmost. I feel that morale problems will disappear as the professional knowledge of officers is increased. Soldiers will tolerate almost anything in an officer except unfairness or ignorance. They are quick to detect either.

The Regular Army is not bothered by poor morale because its officers have attained professional knowledge either at schools or through practical experience. National Guard officers have not had these opportunities, and the morale of their units reflects the deficiency. Of approximately 25,000 officers of the National Guard or on duty with the National Guard, only 6800 have completed a course of instruction at a service school; many of these were graduated long before the present emergency. We must educate the remaining officers of the National Guard before we can expect a rise in the esprit of their units. We are attempting to do this. At the Infantry school, for example, there are now 2,450 officers undergoing instruction. Of this number, 1400 are National Guard officers and 600 are Reserve officers commissioned from civil life. The school is also training 600 officer candidates, as well as offering specialist courses which train enlisted men as motor mechanics and radio operators. It is contemplated moving the 4th Division from Fort Benning about January 1 in order to permit an expansion of the student capacity of the Infantry school. At that time, it is planned to increase the number of officer candidates in the school to 900 in order to train the Infantry's share of those to be trained annually.

3. You suggest in your memorandum that the officer candidates be increased to 25,000 per year in order to create more incentive for selectees. We are now training 14,280 officer candidates each year and of these, 60% will be selectees. Adding the number of R.O.T.C. graduates commissioned each year, we are producing 24,000 second lieutenants annually, a figure far in excess of any needs which can be foreseen at this time. Considering the limited training facilities and equipment available, and also a scarcity of qualifying instructors, I do not feel that we can both increase the number of officer candidates and pursue a policy of educating officers now on our rolls. As a measure for increasing efficiency and morale, I consider the latter project to be far the more important.

GCMRL/G. C. Marshall Papers (Pentagon Office, Selected)

1. Patterson had written to Secretary of War Henry L. Stimson: "I am concerned over the morale of the troops, particularly the troops serving in National Guard Divisions. From

sources that are too reliable to be treated lightly, I am informed that large numbers of the men are discontented and dislike the service. They will remain in it after the year is up but without enthusiasm." He noted four main causes: no sense of urgency; dissatisfaction with officers; lack of work; and lack of initiative. To remedy the situation Patterson suggested that the critical situation regarding national safety be clearly explained; incompetent officers be removed; the training program be stiffened; and the number of men attending Officer Candidate School be increased to 25,000 a year as soon as possible.

At the bottom of the memorandum Stimson had replied: "I approve this. I will talk with you as soon as I return from the West.   H.L.S." (Patterson Memorandum for the Secretary of War, August 14, 1941, LC/R. P. Patterson Papers.)

Peak of Difficulties

October 1 – December 6, 1941

Each day I think I have reached the peak of difficulties and pressures, but last week was the worst of all, a combination of Russian affairs, the Japanese situation, supplies to England, the political pressures, developments in relation to National Guard and some Regular officers over relief from command, the development of the next period of training for the Army, the approaching hearings on the Lease-Loan, etc., etc. do not give me many peaceful hours.

—Marshall to Mrs. James J. Winn
October 20, 1941

GCMRL/Research File (Family)

MILITARY affairs abroad presented both opportunities and dangers for Marshall. Britain had not been invaded; the Soviet Union had not yet collapsed. But both respites meant that pressures increased on the War Department to divert materiel from the United States Army. The danger of war grew rapidly in the Far East, but the situation seemed far from hopeless—if the final break could be delayed through the winter of 1941–42. Properly positioned, the Air Force's new heavy bombers might yet be used as a threat to deter Japanese expansion. It was "now apparent," two of the Air Force's leading officials wrote during the period, "that air forces may completely disrupt nations; that air forces can dictate terms at peace tables; that the threat of air forces can accomplish without dropping a bomb the breakdown of opposing diplomatic morale." (H. H. Arnold and Ira C. Eaker, *Winged Warfare* [New York and London: Harper and Brothers, 1941], p. 260.) In this light, reinforcing the Philippine Islands assumed increased importance.

At home Marshall faced another combination of danger and opportunity. The intensity of the army's morale problem among draftees and National Guard troops began to abate after mid-August, when Congress passed the bill permitting the extension of the period of service. During the September maneuvers in Louisiana, Marshall found much that pleased him during his inspections. While he discovered a remarkable improvement in large-unit management, problems of command and coordination remained at the highest echelons—the corps and field army levels. "Basic training" for the army was over and Marshall concentrated his efforts on improving the quality of the general officers.

Marshall's vigorous efforts to cull the improperly assigned, the inefficient, the unimaginative, and those lacking physical and mental vigor from the ranks of field-grade and general officers, particularly in National Guard units, produced a "flood of political pressure." Although convinced that he had the backing of the public and of most members of Congress, the chief of staff worked to prevent complaints against the War Department from causing congressional obstacles to the mobilization effort. (Marshall to Krueger, October 30, 1941, pp. 655–57.) ★

To ALLEN T. BROWN
October 4, 1941
[Washington, D.C.]

Dear Allen: In my letter the other day I purposely made no reference to your flattering proposal to me, to be the Godfather of young Tupper.[1] I intended to make this the subject of a separate letter. I must confess now that the business of Mr. Hitler diverted me from my purpose. I have only just recalled that I have made no comment.

I am flattered and pleased at being chosen for this responsible position, however you will realize, knowing how reluctant I am about giving advice, that I am not very well qualified for being a Godfather. However, I will do my best as soon as the young man can listen and there is some prospect of analysing what is said.

I have been going home towards noon the last two days, to nurse a flu germ and apparently I have gotten by the worst. Your mother is all right and resting from her travels. She still makes dashes down to Leesburg, taking three men with her to do a rush job on this or that. However, Mrs. Johnson has arrived now and I imagine the last tasks have been completed and there only remains to pay the bills.[2]   Affectionately,

GCMRL/Research File (Family)

1. Allen Tupper Brown, Jr., had been born on September 1.
2. Mrs. Marshall had been remodeling Dodona Manor in Leesburg, Virginia. She had leased the house to her friends Mr. and Mrs. Aymar Johnson of Islip, Long Island.

To Colonel Hjalmar Erickson[1]   October 6, 1941
                                                                [Washington, D.C.]

Dear Erick: I received your note of October 2d with your comments and questions regarding the Army maneuvers.

The development in division and corps management was remarkable; the supply procedure from corps areas through the depots and rail-heads to the troops was about as good as we are ever going to get it. You were right in your question regarding the training of the small units, though we did manage to accomplish this in the so-called Regular divisions on a remarkably satisfactory basis.[2] We have to go at it again with the National Guard units, along with considerable change in officer personnel.

Of course in all of this you will have to remember that the Army had no previous time standard as a basis, because we never had the opportunity to go through the entire cycle up to Army maneuvers. The improvement between the first small maneuvers of a couple of divisions through the inter-corps maneuvers of five to six divisions, the army maneuvers of eight to twelve divisions, and finally the inter-army maneuvers of about 450,000 troops, was amazing. The show started last June. The First Army maneuvers, which will involve five additional divisions are now getting under way in the corps phase and will culminate the end of November.

Throughout the Louisiana affair the men bore the hardships in great shape. It was very impressive to find a maneuver covering practically an entire State.

With warm regards,   Faithfully yours,

GCMRL/G. C. Marshall Papers (Pentagon Office, Selected)

1. Erickson, who had served with Marshall in the First Division in 1918, was living in Reno, Nevada. He had retired in 1923 because of disability in line of duty, but he had been retained on active duty until 1932. (With the president's consent, the army could retain or recall to duty retired officers, although those above the rank of major served with reduced pay and allowances.)

2. After complimenting Marshall on the favorable newspaper reports of the fall maneuvers, Erickson observed that while the higher commanders and services had been tested, he "wondered how the lesser commanders and *their* men (who make victories possible) stood up to the test after such a short period of training behind them." (Erickson to Marshall, October 2, 1941, GCMRL/G. C. Marshall Papers [Pentagon Office, Selected].)

TO BRIGADIER GENERAL CHARLES H. CORLETT[1]   October 6, 1941
[Washington, D.C.]

Dear Corlett: I received your note of thanks regarding your appointment. There were no thanks due me; you owe your promotion entirely to your record. I knew nothing of you other than the fact that you were on the list of five submitted by the Office of the Chief of Infantry, and what was far more important to my mind, four different officials endeavored to get your services for important posts. The last determined me on your selection at this particular time.[2]   Faithfully yours,

GCMRL/G. C. Marshall Papers (Pentagon Office, General)

1. Corlett (U.S.M.A., 1913), former chief of staff of the Ninth Army Corps, had been promoted to brigadier general effective September 30, 1941, and given command of the army base at Kodiak, Alaska.

2. This letter is typical of numerous responses by the chief of staff to letters thanking him for promotions or assignments. See Marshall to Patton, July 19, 1940, p. 272.

TO MAJOR GENERAL WALTER K. WILSON[1]   October 7, 1941
Confidential   [Washington, D.C.]

Dear Wilson: I received your letter of September 18th, and am glad to know that you have recovered from your injuries. By this time you should be back to normal.

In reply to your comments regarding your services with the Third Army

Corps, it is apparent that you do not understand the planning that lay behind the original assignments. In France in 1918, I saw the unfortunate results of corps command by individuals who had never commanded divisions in actual operations. This same lack of divisional knowledge adversely affected the GHQ decisions. So I was determined in this present emergency that corps commanders should have a sound basic knowledge of divisional requirements and operations. In order to do this it became necessary to make assignments which in effect were temporary, of older officers to army corps during the period of basic training, while other officers were organizing divisions and learning the divisional business. It was my desire that the latter officers should have at least one maneuver experience before being chosen for corps commander. The initial corps commanders were to be assigned to positions for which they were especially qualified. Under this policy the changes were made which carried you to the command of the West Coast Defenses.[2]

There is another angle to this business regarding which I think I should speak very frankly. It must be apparent to everyone with an understanding of the vast military problem on our hands, that I have to go ahead on the basis which seems most likely to produce effective results for the army as a whole, meaning the men in the ranks and the general problem of national defense. My most difficult task is concerned with the higher commands and it is made the more difficult by the benign practices of the old army, where time was of little moment and high command was privileged to the nth degree. I might tell you, and most confidentially, that General McNair's greatest concern and that of all of his officers is the problem of corps command. That was the greatest lesson of the Louisiana maneuvers, though we have carefully avoided any publicity on the subject. The difficulty flows, of course, from our inexperience in this field; there is a vast difference between theoretical concepts and practical operations, particularly when cast in an unlimited field of activity such as that in Louisiana.

I have written you very frankly, and to a certain extent as indicated, most confidentially. Regarding your own service, there has been no question. General De Witt highly approved of you as a corps commander.[3]   Faithfully yours,

GCMRL/G. C. Marshall Papers (Pentagon Office, General)

1. Wilson had commanded the Third Army Corps between December 1940 and July 1941, when he was relieved and given command of the Ninth Coast Artillery District. He wrote to Marshall on September 18—shortly after completing seven weeks of hospital treatment for accident injuries—to express his disappointment with losing the corps command and to assure the chief of staff: "I shall enter upon my new assignment with as much energy and enthusiasm as I have always shown in my work." (Wilson to Marshall, September 18, 1941, GCMRL/ G. C. Marshall Papers [Pentagon Office, General].)

2. Since July 1941 the following corps commanders had been relieved and given new commands: William E. Shedd (First); Henry C. Pratt (Second); Walter K. Wilson (Third); Jay L.

Benedict (Fourth); Frederic H. Smith (Seventh). See Marshall to Grant, July 7, 1941, pp. 561–62.

3. The Third Army Corps was a part of Lieutenant General John L. De Witt's Fourth Army. Marshall wrote on Wilson's September 18 letter: "The facts were: Gen. McNair was strongly of opinion that the Army Corps was not being developed as a tactical unit; that De Witt had been so busy with Alaska that he had somewhat overlooked training necessities. GCM"

To HARRY H. WOODRING
October 8, 1941
[Washington, D.C.]

My dear Mr. Woodring: I have just received your note of October 6th, and appreciate what you have to say, and particularly learning something of what you are doing. I will show Mrs. Marshall your paragraph of advice regarding some restraint in my activities.[1] Unfortunately, the shoe is really on the other foot, she is the one who is over-doing, and I am constantly worried about my inability to restrain her from doing what she feels she must do, but what is beyond her strength. However she is in reasonably good health at the present time.

I follow a very rigid schedule, and so far have been able to get along without developing a nervous tendency to lose my temper, though I am frequently on the verge of doing so.

I ride at six, for about eight miles; get to the office about 7:45, and go home for lunch—a seven-minute trip; get away from work between five and five-thirty; and we practically never go out in the evening. I think we have been to two dinners in the last two months.

I do not let the telephone reach me unless it is a call from the White House or the Secretary, and I do not allow anyone else to intrude on our evenings, because inevitably they talk shop. Mrs. Marshall and I frequently go canoeing on the Potomac, where I get in about an hour of good paddling up-stream, then we drift back, eat our supper and get home about 9:30. Or we go to a pleasant movie theatre in one of the small communities beyond Fort Myer where we are unknown and there are always vacant seats and a place to park your car. Or we stay home and read. This phase of our existence is rather hard and restrictive on Mrs. Marshall, but I find it essential to my own activities and unless I get to bed early, generally about nine o'clock, I am mentally too slow on the following day to focus on the wide variety of problems that reach me every hour. Even with your long experience here I do not believe you can visualize the complexities of affairs at the present time.

I got to the maneuvers in Louisiana twice and each time was called back to Washington. They were really a great success and to me very impressive.

Covering almost an entire State with practically no areas barred to the troops, and involving some 450,000 men and 600 planes, the war picture was very realistic. Apparently we have mastered the technique of supply, of providing replacements in the field, of evacuating the sick, prisoners, etc., and of handling large organizations with facility. The deficiencies were in the basic training of small units in the National Guard and in weaknesses in leadership. Both of these are in process of being corrected and present no unsurmountable difficulties.

I am happy to know that Mrs. Woodring is now fully herself again. We were all very much worried about her condition.[2]

With warm regards to you both,   Faithfully yours,

GCMRL/G. C. Marshall Papers (Pentagon Office, Selected)

1. The former secretary of war had written that work on his farm near Topeka, Kansas, was keeping him "busy as a Chief of Staff." He warned Marshall not to "permit even the unexcelled services of an almost providential selected Chief of Staff to go beyond a point where no strong, healthy patriot can afford to give. Remember there will be another war in a decade or so and you want to leave this one after your supreme command so that you may enjoy a peaceful, happy retirement on a little country estate on the Potomac or down in the old Dominion State. I saw one Chief of Staff let the mental strain of work and worry almost wreck him physically." (Woodring to Marshall, October 6, 1941, GCMRL/G. C. Marshall Papers [Pentagon Office, Selected].)

2. General and Mrs. Marshall had sent a telegram to Helen Woodring during her recent stay in the hospital.

To MAJOR GENERAL EDWARD MARTIN   October 9, 1941
[Washington, D.C.]

Dear Martin: I have about made up my mind that General Garesché Ord will probably be the best choice to succeed you in command of the 28th Division. He has had a valuable experience and has made a fine record with the 1st Division and, as I recall, you esteem him highly and he knows your people.[1] I have the following to suggest for your consideration:

How would it be for you to initiate the proposal that Ord should succeed you, and that he be attached to the Division about November 1st to accompany you through the maneuvers pending your transfer to other duties the latter part of the month. Possibly this procedure may not appeal to you, but I thought it might save you embarrassment if the proposal and publicity start with you at your headquarters.[2]

If this course appeals to you, I will confidentially arrange that your proposal meets the proper response from General Fredendall and General Drum.[3]

Will you please write to me directly and frankly.   Faithfully yours,

GCMRL/G. C. Marshall Papers (Pentagon Office, Selected)

1. At this time Brigadier General J. Garesché Ord (U.S.M.A., 1909) was assistant division commander of the First Division. Between July and September 1940 he had served as senior instructor of the Pennsylvania National Guard (Twenty-eighth Division).

2. Martin's division had been called into federal service on February 17, 1941. In his reply to Marshall, he wrote: "I had hoped that I might complete my year in the Army as Commander of the 28th Division. . . . From the standpoint of defense, if a member of this Division could be placed in command it would have a most favorable reaction as far as the National Guard is concerned." (Martin to Marshall, October 15, 1941, GCMRL/G. C. Marshall Papers [Pentagon Office, Selected].) Ord took command of the division on February 17, 1942.

3. The Twenty-eighth, Twenty-ninth, and Forty-fourth divisions constituted Major General Lloyd R. Fredendall's Second Army Corps, which was itself a part of Lieutenant General Hugh A. Drum's First Army.

MEMORANDUM FOR MR. HOPKINS[1]   October 10, 1941
Confidential   [Washington, D.C.]

Dear Harry: As I recall, you spoke to me the other day about the detail of Colonel Faymonville as Attaché in Moscow. A specific request has not yet come in, but I suppose we will hear from Harriman in due time.[2] Meanwhile for your eye only, I send you the following resumé which confirms other reports that I had received from several quarters more than a year ago. I am giving you this because I think it might be well for you casually to bring the matter up with Mr. Bullitt, who is referred to in the following comment:

"I don't know him well, but I do know that competent men who have served with him, such as ex-Ambassador Bullitt and Mr. Henderson of the Russian Division of the State Department, have serious doubts as to his judgment and his impartiality wherever the Soviets are concerned."[3]

Personally, we had a great deal of difficulty in controlling him recently while he was serving as a guide to the Russian group.[4] He was quite oblivious to instructions and almost defiant of regulations. Of course, the big problem in Moscow is to have the confidence of the Russians, and I imagine he will probably manage that better than anyone else we can send over. There is this further consideration, however. I assume that we will eventually have a mission with the Russians on a parity with the one in London and the one in China, and in that case the man in Faymonville's position over there should be made a general officer.[5]

GCMRL/G. C. Marshall Papers (Pentagon Office, Selected)

1. President Roosevelt had designated Harry L. Hopkins to "advise and assist" him on lend-lease matters. (Robert E. Sherwood, *Roosevelt and Hopkins: An Intimate History* [New York: Harper and Brothers, 1948], p. 267.)

2. Philip R. Faymonville had been military attaché in the Soviet Union between July 1934 and February 1939. Following the German invasion of the Soviet Union in June 1941, Faymonville had been recalled to Washington from his post as Fourth Army ordnance officer and had been assigned to work in the Division of Defense Aid Reports, which handled lend-lease matters. In early September he was selected to be a member of the Harriman aid mission to the Soviet Union. When that mission left Moscow on October 4, 1941, Faymonville, at Harry Hopkins's request, remained to act as lend-lease representative. The reports he sent to Washington regarding the likelihood of the Soviet Union's survival in the face of the German onslaught were markedly more optimistic than those of the United States military attaché. (Sherwood, *Roosevelt and Hopkins*, p. 395; Department of State, *Foreign Relations of the United States: Diplomatic Papers, 1941,* 7 vols. [Washington: GPO, 1956–63], 1: 846.)

3. The quotation is from Sherman Miles Memorandum for the Chief of Staff, September 30, 1941, NA/RG 165 [OCS, 20241].) William C. Bullitt had been ambassador to the Soviet Union from December 1933 to May 1936. Loy W. Henderson had been assigned to the Moscow embassy between 1934 and 1938; since October 1938 he had served as assistant chief of the Division of European Affairs.

4. Various members of the Soviet military mission, who had arrived in Washington on July 26, were still in the United States in October. In a memorandum for Major General Arnold, Marshall commented: "I will have to talk to Hopkins this morning about the question of bombers for the Russians. His desire is to get the forty-odd Russian aviators out of town, and I understand from him that one of the complications has been the lack of deicing equipment for the B-25s and B-26s. What may I tell him?" (Marshall Memorandum for General Arnold, October 8, 1941, GCMRL/G. C. Marshall Papers [Pentagon Office, Selected].)

5. In mid-January 1942, Hopkins raised the question of Faymonville's rank. As former Ambassador Laurence A. Steinhardt had left his post on November 12, 1941, and no new ambassador had been named yet, Hopkins wrote: "Faymonville is not only our Lend-Lease representative but he is the only real contact the United States Government has with the Soviets. That is a realistic fact which must be taken into consideration when we are dealing at such long range with Stalin. Faymonville knows the Russians and understands them. The Russians like him. He needs prestige. The Russians must believe that we have confidence in him. It seems to me that the way to do that is to give him temporary rank. Could he be made a Major-General? I know something of the War Department's misgivings about Faymonville but I think the circumstances warrant your endorsement of him in the light of the political and military situation in Russia. While I don't want to overestimate this, I really believe that if you would put your hand on Faymonville's shoulder it would not only give him confidence but aid him immeasurably in dealing with the Russian situation." (Hopkins to Marshall, January 15, 1942, ibid.) Faymonville was promoted to brigadier general effective January 22, 1942.

To LIEUTENANT GENERAL WALTER KRUEGER   October 11, 1941
Confidential   [Washington, D.C.]

Dear Krueger: I have just received a communication initiated by General Gerhardt after a consultation with me, regarding the possible promotion of Colonel Harry H. Johnson, 112th Cavalry, to the grade of Brigadier General.[1] I have noted your comments and those of McNair which support your recommendations.

There are two phases to this matter. One is that it was not the intention to remove General Gerhardt from the command of this brigade for some time to come, probably three or four months. I had in mind if it was found advisable to promote Colonel Johnson, to attach him to the First Cavalry Division where his tutelage in the job would be carried on during the period General Gerhardt was getting the Texas brigade in good shape.

General McNair makes the point that "it is believed that all troop units, including the National Guard in federal service, are entitled to the best leadership obtainable."

This is certainly correct in principle, but its practical application is a very difficult matter, both in the National Guard and the Regular Army. It is of great importance that we be supported in our present procedure to improve leadership. Therefore, wherever an opportunity presents itself to take action that will disprove accusations that we, the Regular Army authorities, are prejudiced and unfair to the citizen-soldier, it is most helpful to do so.

A heavy pressure has developed against me and the Secretary of War from the Chairman of the Foreign Relations Committee (now handling neutrality legislation) and from the Texas Representatives regarding the relief of General Birkhead, the manner of notifying Birkhead and the specific rumors that other drastic reliefs are being applied to Texas officials.[2] The same reaction is developing from other parts of the country. This was to be expected, but it is very helpful if it happens to lie within our power to do something of the nature I have described. The possible promoting of Colonel Johnson seemed to be such an opportunity.

I assume that he cannot be a Gerhardt or a Harry Chamberlin.[3] As a matter of fact, I know that there are Regular Cavalry Generals who do not approach that standard, but I thought that if he had the qualifications Gerhardt described, it offered a very favorable occasion to nullify the present reactions against the War Department.

I want you to treat this letter as for your eye alone, and I would like you to write me very frankly on the subject.[4]   Faithfully yours,

GCMRL/G. C. Marshall Papers (Pentagon Office, Selected)

1. Brigadier General Charles H. Gerhardt (U.S.M.A., April 1917) had been appointed commanding general, Second Brigade, First Cavalry Division, in mid-July 1941. Johnson had risen through the ranks of the Texas National Guard to command the Dallas-based 112th Cavalry Regiment in September 1941.

2. Major General Claude V. Birkhead, a lawyer who had commanded the Texas National Guard's Thirty-sixth Division since 1936, was relieved of his command in mid-September and replaced by Brigadier General Fred L. Walker of the Regular Army. At the same time, Brigadier General Walter B. Pyron, commanding general of the Fifty-sixth Cavalry Brigade—of which Johnson's 112th Cavalry was a part—was relieved of command. Secretary of War Stimson recorded in his diary that on the morning of September 15, "Senator Tom Connally of Texas, the Chairman of the Committee on Foreign Relations, bounded in with his hair standing up on end, full of anger and resentment because two Texas Generals of the National Guard had been retired and sent back from active duty. This was the first brick from the working of the purge and it came very quickly. Connally is an old friend of mine and I made him sit down and cool off and then we talked to him about it but he professes to be perfectly

implacable on it and has got to have satisfaction." The secretary called the chief of staff, who convinced Stimson that the reliefs were unavoidable. (September 15, 1941, Yale/H. L. Stimson Papers [Diary, 35: 66–67].)

3. Brigadier General Harry D. Chamberlin (U.S.M.A., 1910) had preceded Gerhardt as commanding general of the Second Cavalry Regiment. At this time he was commanding the Cavalry Replacement Training Center at Fort Riley, Kansas, but within the month he was to be given the Fourth Brigade of the Second Cavalry Division.

4. Krueger replied that he was impressed with Johnson's abilities and accomplishments. "I shall keep my eye on his performance and if he proves his capacity, and I am reasonably sure that he will, I shall be glad to recommend him for promotion, say on or about December 1st." (Krueger to Marshall, October 20, 1941, GCMRL/G. C. Marshall Papers [Pentagon Office, Selected].) See Marshall to Krueger, October 30, 1941, pp. 655–57.

TO COLONEL FAY W. BRABSON[1] October 11, 1941
Confidential [Washington, D.C.]

Dear Brabson: Yesterday I received an envelope in your handwriting enclosing clippings regarding the return of the 45th Division.[2] This reminded me of my intention of some time past to write you a note.

This must be confidential, but I want you to know that it had been my hope to find it possible to give Camp Commanders, of the larger installations, the rank of Brigadier General. I approved your transfer to that line of duty, and Beebe's assignment to Camp Jackson,[3] with that end in view. However, I was unable to put this across, which is a matter of deep regret to me.

While I have been allowed great freedom in the selection of officers for promotion, there have been two presidential limitations or restrictions which have steadily increased in severity. One refers to staff appointments which are constantly opposed, in contrast to a willingness to permit promotions for troop commanders, and the other refers to the age of officers recommended for advancement. The combination of these two factors has had marked effect on what has occurred. By staff appointments, I mean any position other than a tactical command. The exceptions have been largely in the Ordnance Department and for important foreign countries, or where the officer was being penalized by the job he was held on because of his marked qualifications for high troop command.

It would have given me a great deal of pleasure and satisfaction to have seen you approach your retirement period in the grade of general officer. I am sincerely sorry that I have not been able to accomplish this.   Faithfully yours,

GCMRL/G. C. Marshall Papers (Pentagon Office, Selected)

1. A friend of Marshall since they were students together at the Infantry and Cavalry

School at Fort Leavenworth in 1906–7, Brabson commanded Camp Barkeley, near Abilene, Texas.

2. The Forty-fifth Division (composed of National Guard units from Oklahoma, Arizona, Colorado, and New Mexico) had recently returned to Camp Barkeley from the September maneuvers between the Second and Third armies on the Texas-Louisiana border.

3. Colonel Royden E. Beebe had been a student with Marshall and Brabson at the Infantry and Cavalry School. He was scheduled to take command of the post at Fort Jackson, South Carolina.

MEMORANDUM FOR ADMIRAL STARK October 13, 1941
[Washington, D.C.]

Dear Betty: Having noticed the care-worn brief case you carry, I told our Air Corps to have one made for you like mine. It is not an exact duplicate and may not be quite so convenient, but it is a little larger—which I think better fits your case. Please accept it with the compliments of the Air Corps and the Army.

I have two pleasant things to communicate. General Bonesteel, our Commander in Iceland, sent me in a personal letter a most complimentary reference to the Navy. He stated that the handling and management of the convoy for his command to Iceland was carried out with superb efficiency, to the admiration of all the Army contingent; also that on arrival in Iceland, the Marines had made every possible preparation and turned to with a lively hand to assist with the unloading.[1]

In the Maneuvers in Louisiana, the contribution of the Navy and Marine Corps bombers was not only of great importance to the success of the maneuvers, due to our shortage in such aircraft at this time, but was carried out with a perfectly splendid spirit of cooperation and with outstanding efficiency. A little later when all the returns are in, I will send you an official letter of appreciation.[2] However, I want you to know without further delay how much we appreciate their cooperation and their work, and how wise I think it was to include these services with the Army, in marked contrast to what apparently has been happening abroad.[3]

GCMRL/G. C. Marshall Papers (Pentagon Office, Selected)

1. The editors have not found this letter.

2. Eight squadrons of aircraft from the United States Navy and Marine Corps participated in the September maneuvers. The marines were part of the Second Air Task Force with Lieutenant General Ben Lear's "defenders." The navy squadrons were with Lieutenant General Walter Krueger's "aggressor" forces as part of the Third Air Task Force. (*Army and Navy Journal,* September 6, 1941, p. 2. For a brief account by a navy participant, see Harry D. Felt, "VB-2 Partaking in Army Field Maneuvers—1941," Naval Aviation Museum *Foundation* 5[Spring 1984]: 10–13, 67.)

3. For Marshall's comments on the problems the British were having in this regard, see p. 610.

To Major General Lloyd R. Fredendall   October 13, 1941
Confidential   [Washington, D.C.]

Dear Fredendall: Most confidentially, I am sending you the attached letter with these comments:[1]

In the first place I am disturbed by this recital of General Muir's approach to the proposition. This business of declaring purges is quite a different matter than the actual business of cleaning house. It seems to me if the procedure described was followed by Muir it bids fair to set up a sort of reign of terror under which the cure is even worse than the bite. Certainly it completely ignores the effect on the public and inevitable political pressures, and will quickly build up a barrier of bitterness between the Regular Army components and the National Guard which will destroy the unity of the Army. We now have public approval for action towards improving leadership, but we will lose it or have the issue seriously confused as a result of tactless methods.

In this particular case, I have known Ritchel intimately and on duty with the National Guard. He is a tremendous worker, relentless in the pursuit of what he does and very able. He is not prepossessing in appearance. My reaction to him—and he was my Executive officer at one time, was that he responded so quickly to my directives that he rather harassed me with immediate proposals for the solution. Certainly he gave no impression of slowness or lack of vigor.

Apropos of what he says, I am concerned over what seems to be Muir's intention to have only his own people, that is his own selections. This is a desirable state of affairs, from Muir's viewpoint, but if it is brought about by ruining the careers of other people, then it is most unfortunate.

I am writing to you in this direct, informal and most confidential manner because I am disturbed over the repercussions that are now rapidly building up and will soon present a difficult problem for me to meet. I am disturbed because I feel that much of this could have been avoided by better judgment on the part of commanders as to what they state to their officers. In other words, the reliefs could have been accomplished just as expeditiously with less of threats of purges.[2]

I do not want you to mention to Muir that Ritchel has written to me. I want you to treat this case as symptomatic of a condition. I will probably give Ritchel another assignment, another regiment in another place, but what I do not want is a continuation of the oral methods related by Ritchel, which I assume was a fairly accurate report.[3]   Faithfully yours,

GCMRL/G. C. Marshall Papers (Pentagon Office, Selected)

1. Marshall had received a lengthy letter dated October 12 from Lieutenant Colonel Charles S. Ritchel (U.S.M.A., 1915), who had known Marshall since 1929. He had been a student under Marshall during the 1930–31 academic year at the Infantry School and had served

under him in Chicago between 1933 and 1935 as an instructor with the Illinois National Guard. The chief of staff had helped to get Ritchel assigned to command the 174th Infantry Regiment, a part of Brigadier General James I. Muir's (U.S.M.A., 1910) Eighty-ninth Brigade of the Forty-fourth Division, which was then engaged in maneuvers in North Carolina.

"I am in a terrible jam," Ritchel wrote, "and I can conscientiously and truthfully state it is through no fault of my own. My case is so serious that I feel that I must present it to you for your consideration." When he reported on October 3, Ritchel stated, Muir received him coldly, told him that the 174th Infantry was the worst regiment he had ever seen, and expressed doubts about Ritchel's capacity to lead because he had not had a troop command since 1930. Ritchel thought that his command had performed creditably in the maneuvers given their two days of preparation under him. Five days after Ritchel arrived, Muir became commanding general of the division. "He immediately called all the Field Officers together and informed them that the Division was in a very sad state of affairs from every standpoint and that he was going to get rid of a lot of officers, especially in the higher grades. I ran into him during the next day and he informed me that he had or was going to put in a requisition for officers for key positions that he personally knew." Muir told Ritchel that he lacked force, that he was incapable of command, and that his relief would be requested. The general rejected Ritchel's request for an inspector general to consider his case. (Ritchel to Marshall, October 12, 1941, GCMRL/ G. C. Marshall Papers [Pentagon Office, Selected].)

2. On October 18 Marshall sent Fredendall a report of further officer disaffection in Muir's division. "I have had other rumors regarding the 44th Division under Muir's administration which are not at all reassuring to my mind. I very much fear his method of procedure is one where the cure may be worse than the bite, because of ramifications of the reactions spreading throughout the country." (Marshall Memorandum for General Fredendall, October 18, 1941, ibid.) The Forty-fourth was a National Guard division from New York and New Jersey.

3. Fredendall had the division's administration investigated. He reported that "Muir's talk had a very good effect," that Ritchel's relief was justified, and that he had disapproved of an inspector general's investigation to avoid placing "another blot on Ritchel's good record." But there was a reason which could not be brought out officially, Fredendall wrote, that made Ritchel's reassignment desirable. "One of the complaints of the enlisted men of the 174th Infantry as developed by an investigation conducted by the II Army Corps Inspector General was that there were too many Jewish officers assigned to that regiment and, correctly or incorrectly, Lieut. Col. Ritchel was assumed to be a Jew." (Fredendall to Marshall, October 20, 1941, ibid.) Marshall assigned Ritchel to the Fourth Division, but Ritchel soon requested to be returned to the Inspector General's Department, where he had previously served.

WOMEN as individuals and as organized groups made known to the War Department their desire to participate in the military mobilization. Their services had been found necessary during 1917–18 both at home and abroad, although the context within which they had to operate was poorly organized and coordinated. The General Staff did not undertake to study this problem seriously until early 1941, by which time the tone of official statements had become more accepting of the possibility of extensive use of women.

Congresswoman Edith Nourse Rogers of Massachusetts visited Marshall during the early spring of 1941 and told him that she was going to introduce a bill to establish a corps of 25,000 women to fill professional, technical, and service positions in the army. The chief of staff asked for time to study the issue and set his G-1 staff to work drafting a bill that the army could support. To emphasize that the women were to serve *with* but not *in* the army, the Personnel Division endeavored to write a bill that made the distinctions of duty, rank, and privilege between the army and the proposed women's auxiliary as great as possible. Rogers introduced H.R. 4906 ("A Bill to Establish a Women's Army Auxiliary Corps for Service with the Army of the United States") on May 28, 1941, but it remained for months in the Military Affairs Committee without hearings. (Mattie E. Treadwell, *The Women's Army Corps,* a volume in the *United States Army in World War II* [Washington: GPO, 1954], pp. 16–20.)

Reporting on the W.A.A.C. bill, the War Department's Budget and Legislative Planning Branch observed that "this Branch understands that the Chief of Staff has informally approved the proposed legislation, and therefore makes no comment." (Memorandum for the Deputy Chief of Staff, June 18, 1941, NA/RG 407 [General, 291.9 (6-2-41) sec. 1, pt. 1].) Lieutenant Colonel John H. Hilldring, at this time assigned to G-1, later recalled that by the summer of 1941 Marshall was worried about the possibility of future manpower shortages; he also thought it inefficient for the army to attempt to train men for specialties like typist or telephone operator that women had taken over in civil life. Finally, he was impressed by women's desire to serve. While there was no immediate need to incorporate large numbers of women into the army, Marshall wanted to be prepared for immediate action should the need arise. (Treadwell, *Women's Army Corps,* p. 20.) The Bureau of the Budget was not impressed with the need for the bill, however, and in a letter dated October 7 it notified the War Department that enactment of the bill would not be "considered as being in accord with the program of the President." (John B. Blandford, Jr., to the Secretary of War, October 7, 1941, NA/RG 407 [General, 291.9 (6-2-41) sec. 1, pt. 1].)

Marshall may have received this letter shortly before delivering the following informal address to a group of twenty or thirty presidents of national women's organizations. The meeting had been arranged by Oveta Culp Hobby, co-publisher of the *Houston Post,* who had taken what she presumed to be the short-term position as chief of the War Department's Women's Interests Section in the Planning and Liaison Branch of the Bureau of Public Relations. She suggested that the chief of staff talk to the women as the mothers of soldiers, fearful of what was happening to their sons and lacking accurate information on military life, and assure them that their boys were being adequately fed, clothed, and sheltered. (Hobby Memorandum for Major W. T. Sexton, October 7, 1941, GCMRL/G. C. Marshall Papers [Pentagon Office, General].) Instead, Marshall chose to talk about discipline, a term and concept that he had learned confused and disturbed civilians. ★

October 13, 1941
[Washington, D.C.]

It may seem to some of you that of all the possible topics which an Army officer might choose to discuss before a group of ladies, discipline would be the least likely. The word, in familiar usage, suggests the enforcement of rules, a system of control, by means which are essentially masculine, and most of all military. The feminine method, which is widely known to be more effective for the purpose it serves, is one of persuasion and a subtle, if persistent, reiteration.

Thus it is that although the feminine and masculine methods of accomplishment differ as to technique, both have a common purpose—that of insuring the cooperation of those for whose conduct and safety the directing agent may be responsible.

The methods followed by the two governing forces to which I refer have been developed through the years by a process of trial and error. Each has its advantages and disadvantages, yet each has been found sufficient and effective for the purpose it seeks to serve. One follows the route of gentle but firm guidance. The other presupposes a foundation of guidance in the right direction and seeks to pick up where the first leaves off.

This may account for the general impression that the Army fosters a particularly stern quality of discipline. I can assure you that such is not the case.

It may be helpful to consider first the origin of the term "discipline," and the development of the methods of instruction and standards of performance which have come to be associated with military procedure, in all parts of the world. Discipline itself comes from the same stem as the word "disciple." It implies above all else a relationship between human beings, a basis for effective and concerted action or thought. Such a relationship affects the senior as well as the junior. Perhaps the most general misapprehension of military discipline is the thought that it has to do only with punishment, and that it is something which affects the subordinate only, in any given situation.

Military discipline is in effect a method of education. The most useful result of a disciplinary system is to familiarize the individual with a particular way of doing something, so that when a new problem confronts him, he will act in a pre-determined way. Ideally, the action should be so familiar, so nearly instinctive, that he thinks of it as his own idea. I am sure that the thought is familiar to you ladies, for it is essentially the method by which the average husband decides, independently, to do exactly what his wife thinks best.

Discipline is not an end in itself, but a means to an end. Some civilian critics of military organization and method have said, in times past, that discipline is a sort of fetish of the military mind, that it serves no useful purpose, that it bears no real relationship to the functioning of a modern army. But military discipline, intelligently administered, can be a great creative and positive force. It has evolved in very much the same way that civil law, and the discipline, or discipleship, of the school, the family, and other social groups, have evolved. It is a means, and an essential means, to the effective functioning of military organizations, of whatever size; whether the squad of eight to twelve men, the company of two hundred, the division of fifteen thousand, or our whole armed force of now somewhat more than a million and a half. In fact, it is equally essential to the functioning of the smallest military unit of all, the single private soldier, who in modern war far more often than in the past may have to carry responsibilities and make independent judgments of great importance.

For the purpose of discipline is merely to make a better soldier, and thereby a better army. Discipline cannot be expected to make brave soldiers; there are many moral and spiritual factors in war which depend far more upon the early training of the individual in the home than upon anything which the Army can superimpose upon such training. But discipline can make a soldier more confident of himself and of the military team of which he is a member; and such confidence is certainly an important factor in determining his behavior in a critical situation.

It seems unlikely that there can be many among you who have sons old enough for military service. But no doubt you have older brothers who are in the Army, and some of you have young sons who, after a lapse of years, will join the colors. I am glad to assure you that the matter of discipline, as it is practiced in our American Army, is principally one of continuing and intensifying the intelligent discipline of the home, and the school. If the ground work had not been done long before the individual soldier reached the age of induction, or if there were things which he had to unlearn upon entering the military service, our task would be hopeless. The Army, and the nation, are therefore heavily in the debt of American mothers, whose gentle but unyielding discipline has shaped the national character. And if allowance be made, as I am sure it should be made, for the influence of the feminine virtues upon the masculine mind, then yours is a continuing responsibility, and, to the Army, the final and inescapable authority.

GCMRL/G. C. Marshall Papers (Pentagon Office, Speeches)

1. Marshall made his remarks shortly after 10:00 A.M. in the Munitions Building's General Council Room.

MEMORANDUM FOR THE SECRETARY OF WAR   October 14, 1941
Secret   Washington, D.C.

Subject: Ordnance and Air Corps Mechanics for Russia.

We have been directed from the White House, through the Lease-Loan organization, to send officers and soldiers to Russia in the event that we cannot obtain civilians for the purpose of insuring proper maintenance and use of our materiel.[1] For the past week we have been endeavoring to obtain the necessary civilian personnel. General Moore now informs me that neither the Air Corps nor the Ordnance Department have been able to persuade any American company to agree with Amtorg to send mechanics to service airplanes, tanks, and other equipment being shipped between now and October 31st. Negotiations with Curtiss-Wright, American Car and Foundry, Chrysler Company, and Sperry Company, have been unsuccessful. Prospects for successful recruitment of civilian mechanics appear to be dim. Therefore, the question of sending officers and enlisted men will be acute before the end of the week.

There are two important considerations involved in the sending of officers and soldiers to Russia.

In the first place, do we order them or do we endeavor to have them volunteer, and if we order them do we send them in organized units capable of looking out for themselves—at least to a certain extent—in the way of administration, food and other arrangements, or do we turn them loose, as it were, on their own individual initiative in Russia?

In the second place, if we send officers and soldiers as individuals or ship them as organized units, what is the political repercussion at the present time and what would it be if they are lost to us, as very easily can be the case? And what will the repercussion be if we order them, and they themselves wish to avoid such detail.[2]

There is attached the directive from the White House on this subject.

G. C. Marshall

NA/RG 165 (OCS, 21302-19A)

1. The directive read: "It is the desire of the President that the material agreed on to be released for procurement by the Union of Soviet Socialist Republics and for delivery in October be delivered in the most expeditious way possible. The delivery of this material will take precedence over defense aid transfers to other countries. In case it is impracticable to obtain civilians to accompany this material by contract with Amtorg, it is desired that officers and enlisted men of the U.S. Army be furnished as observers to make certain that the material is properly employed and maintained." (Sidney P. Spalding Memorandum for the Secretary

of War, October 8, 1941, NA/RG 165 [OCS, 21302-19A].) The New York City-based Amtorg Trading Corporation was the official purchasing and sales agency for the Soviet Union in the United States.

2. At the top of this memorandum Marshall added: *"Note:* The Secretary of War directs that we endeavor to obtain volunteers from the Army and place them in Russia in the same status as the specialists and mechanics we have sent to England and Cairo. If volunteers are not obtainable, then he will discuss the problem with the President.   G. C. M." By the end of the month fifteen civilian and fifty-one military technicians had volunteered, but the Soviet government was unwilling to permit them to enter the country. Harry L. Hopkins, who had visited the Soviet Union in late July 1941 to offer aid, tried to reverse this decision. "Both Harriman and I understood from our talks in Moscow that technicians would be welcomed. We believe that it is essential that these technicians precede the equipment." But the Soviets refused to change their minds. (*Foreign Relations, 1941,* 1: 848, 859–60.)

To LIEUTENANT GENERAL FRANK M. ANDREWS[1]   October 14, 1941
[Washington, D.C.]

Dear Andrews: I have been intending for some days to get off a letter to you regarding your new responsibilities. However, I have been so pushed and pulled with Congressional hearings and trips back and forth to maneuvers, that I had to leave the details to the various sections of the War Department.

Your new job involves, first of all under present circumstances, the security of the Canal against sabotage, which involves our relationship with the Government and people of Panama. Tactically, the defense of the Canal itself is largely one of guarding against a surprise or trick attack from the air, and this involves what it seems to me is one of your most difficult problems—the maintenance of a more or less continuous alert by a considerable portion of the anti-aircraft artillery. Just how you will maintain their morale against the monotony of service in isolated stations is going to be a difficult proposition. Apropos of this, I proposed on my last visit to Panama that we ought to look into the question of hiring San Blas indians, for attachment to the anti-aircraft artillery, to do the heavy and the dirty work at gun positions; which would also permit a reduction in personnel at these isolated stations.[2]

Your shelter and racial problems in the Canal Zone are exacting in their requirements. I think you can lean heavily on the advice of Stayer in connection with the racial phase of the matter.[3]

Outside the Canal Zone you have so many problems it is difficult for me to pick out a particular one for comment.

Confidentially, I have been led to feel that possibly Talbot, at Trinidad, has been so deep in the matter of morale and ordinary living conditions that he has not been sufficiently realistic in his defense planning against the possibility of some sudden raid development.[4]

The problem in British and Dutch Guiana is evident. I think we should do everything possible to help those commanders with facilities to make life bearable. I have a special fund to use at my discretion and if there are things you need to have procured, out of the ordinary or without delays, don't hesitate to call on me for immediate action.

I have already talked to you about the problem of communications, particularly when it comes to coordinating ours with those of the Navy. I am now in the midst of talks with WPD over unified command in the Caribbean theatre.

We are to send you, I believe, a National Guard regiment to replace the Regular regiment being transferred to Trinidad. I wish you would make a special effort to get these fellows into the harness, and to help them in every way possible to improve their efficiency, especially that of the young lieutenants who, in many instances, lack the basic technical training.

We are in the midst of a development of far-reaching effects in our air reinforcements to the Philippines. This, of course, interferes to a certain extent with the promptness of delivery of new equipment to you.

This is a hasty note but I did not want to delay longer before writing to you. Faithfully yours,

GCMRL/G. C. Marshall Papers (Pentagon Office, Selected)

1. Andrews had been made commanding general of the Caribbean Defense Command and promoted to lieutenant general effective September 19, 1941.

2. Marshall later told members of the Caribbean Defense Command staff that his idea of using the San Blas Indians had not been favorably received. (William T. Sexton Notes of Conference in the Office of the Chief of Staff, October 29, 1941, NA/RG 165 [OCS, Chief of Staff Conferences File].)

3. Two major construction projects begun in 1940 (a road and a set of canal locks) created a labor shortage in Panama, causing the United States to import foreign laborers, including blacks from Jamaica. They were but a small portion of the thousands of imported workers, however. (Stetson Conn, Rose C. Engelman, and Byron Fairchild, *Guarding the United States and Its Outposts,* a volume in the *United States Army in World War II* [Washington: GPO, 1964], pp. 319–22.) Brigadier General Morrison C. Stayer had been charged with handling the racial aspects of the labor problem. (See Memorandum for Mr. Martyn, September 14, 1940, pp. 306–7.)

4. Brigadier General Ralph Talbot, Jr. (U.S.M.A., 1905), was commanding general of the Trinidad Sector of the Caribbean Defense Command. His sector included the bases in Trinidad, St. Lucia, and British Guiana. A force had already been assembled in Trinidad awaiting orders to move into Dutch Guiana (Surinam).

MEMORANDUM FOR THE QUARTERMASTER GENERAL [GREGORY]

October 15, 1941
[Washington, D.C.]

Mr. McCloy[1] brought to my attention the fact that families of officers and senior enlisted men of some of the organizations recently sent to the

Philippines have been denied commissary privileges although they are living in close proximity to Army posts.

I realize there is a strain on our commissary system but believe that everything possible should be done to make it easier for the families of officers, particularly junior officers, who are on foreign service. I wish you would look into this personally and go as far as possible in extending commissary privileges to these families.

GCMRL/G. C. Marshall Papers (Pentagon Office, Selected)

1. John J. McCloy had been assistant secretary of war since April 1941. In his memoirs, Secretary Stimson praised McCloy at length. "So varied were his labors and so catholic his interests that they defy summary. For five years McCloy was the man who handled everything that no one else happened to be handling." (Henry L. Stimson and McGeorge Bundy, *On Active Service in Peace and War* [New York: Harper and Brothers, 1948], p. 342.)

To GENERAL JOHN J. PERSHING   October 18, 1941
                                                              Washington, D.C.

Dear General: I have just this moment read your very gracious note of October 16th, which I appreciate tremendously. I always get a great deal of satisfaction out of my talks with you and am only sorry that they are so infrequent.[1]

The last three or four days have been pretty much the worst of all, with the pressing problems of the Japanese, the Russian situation, the British Near East problems, further developments of our own army augmentation and reorganization of the personnel element, and now straight political pressure that is occurring steadily regarding release from command.

You comment on Senator Clark's attack.[2] This one was in the paper, but there are many others somewhat similar directed at me or at the War Department generally. The most difficult phases of my problem are the unnecessary or rather the avoidable rumpuses. I mean the tactless or unfortunate methods of accomplishing reliefs. I am already deep in the matter of controlling those individuals who are so fearful of their own command that they are inclined to terrorize everybody else below them. It doesn't matter much how great the deficiencies are in leadership, I find myself very impatient with the man in the field who orates too much, and tactlessly, to his subordinates. The job is hard enough at best, and it is awfully hard for these
* higher commanders in the field, but under present conditions in the development of the Army some finesse is required.

I have just signed a letter to an old friend of mine whose relief from command of the Second Division is recommended, General Greely.[3]

I gave your message to Katherine and she is really anxious to join with me in the next luncheon date I have with you.   Affectionately,

G. C. Marshall

* This does not refer to Lear[4]

LC/ J. J. Pershing Papers (General Correspondence)

1. Pershing had written: "You can scarcely realize how much pleasure it gives me to have you come out [to Walter Reed General Hospital] for luncheon with me. Aside from your personal presence, it gives me an opportunity to keep more or less in touch with what is going on in the Army. I am happy to know that everything seems to be doing quite well, although I do hear once in a while considerable criticism as to the discipline in some of the divisions. And in this morning's paper I notice that Bennett Clark has criticized General Lear for relieving General Truman. These things are to be expected and to some extent are unavoidable. Thank heaven I was free from all that sort of thing in the A.E.F." (Pershing to Marshall, October 16, 1941, GCMRL/ G. C. Marshall Papers [Pentagon Office, Selected].)

2. In a letter to the chief of staff dated September 11, Lieutenant General Ben Lear had requested that Major General Ralph E. Truman, commanding general of the Thirty-fifth Division (National Guards of Missouri, Kansas, and Nebraska) be relieved from command. This was done at the end of the month. (Haislip Memorandum to The Adjutant General, September 29, 1941, NA/ RG 165 [OCS, 8136–25].) Truman decided to resign rather than accept another assignment. When Lear sent senior senator from Missouri Bennett Champ Clark a telegram informing him of Truman's decision, Clark released his reply to the press. "It is, of course, the old Army game which does not intend to leave a National Guard officer, no matter how efficient, in command of a National Guard division. You are trying to blame the tactical defeat which your Army suffered on Truman and various other National Guard officers, which is exceedingly unfair. You should retire yourself rather than make General Truman the goat." (*New York Times,* October 16, 1941, p. 11.) Major General Truman was Senator Harry S. Truman's cousin.

3. No copy of the chief of staff's letter to Major General John N. Greely was retained in the Marshall papers. Greely was assigned to the Army Group, Washington, D.C., and directed to organize a military mission to the Soviet Union.

4. Marshall added the asterisks and postscript in his own hand.

To Major General Herbert A. Dargue[1]   October 13 [*18*], 1941
[Washington, D.C.]

Dear Dargue: I have received your note of October 17, together with the pamphlet on your recent Air Defense test. I have looked through the pamphlet, and previously had talked over the recent maneuver with some of the Air officers.[2]

It was a matter of very genuine disappointment to me that I was not able to get up to New York last Wednesday. A combination of uncertain weather and terrific pressure that developed that morning in connection with Japanese matters and shipments to Russia made it extremely difficult for me to leave town, and a White House interview definitely terminated my previous plans for that day.[3]

It is an increasing source of assurance to me to follow the constant development in Air defense started with such slender resources by General Chaney. During the maneuvers the other day I felt for the first time that we were really getting somewhere so far as the field forces were concerned, but unfortunately I did not see your set-up though I did go over the Alexandria Warning service center. Again Washington interfered with my plans, as I was called back here on both of my visits to Louisiana.[4]

I think it is especially fortunate that you should have been involved in the same month with the mobile army Air program and the fixed defense Air set-up. I have been fearful that we would find ourselves too heavily developed along fixed defense as a result of the impressive demonstrations in the British Isles, and would lack a full and practical development for the coordination of air and ground troops. While we will always have to be prepared in an organizational way against sporadic air raids on coastal cities or manufacturing areas, the odds are that our principal military activity will be outside the United States, with ground troops heavily dependent upon air support. The distant bombing problem appears in many respects much more easy of organizational arrangement because only one force, and a very special one, is involved.

When you come to Washington, I would like to talk over your recent experiences.   Faithfully yours,

GCMRL/G. C. Marshall Papers (Pentagon Office, General)

1. Dargue had commanded the Nineteenth Wing in the Panama Canal Zone until called to Washington to become the assistant chief of the Air Corps in October 1940. In July 1941 he had been promoted to major general and given command of the First Air Force, which had its headquarters at Mitchel Field, New York.

2. In response to Dargue's invitation, Marshall had decided to visit the First Air Force's "'Interceptor Maneuver' . . . designed for the training of the organization which has been developed as a defense against aerial attack." (Dargue to Marshall, October 7, 1941, GCMRL/ G. C. Marshall Papers [Pentagon Office, General].) When the chief of staff was unable to attend, Dargue sent him a "restricted pamphlet we got up on the Air Defense Test." (Dargue to Marshall, October 17, 1941, ibid.)

3. Marshall was perhaps referring to the events of Thursday, October 16, when, as Secretary Stimson recorded in his diary: "I, at the last moment, received a message from the President that he had cancelled the Cabinet Meeting at 2:00 and instead had called a meeting of Hull, Knox, myself assisted by General Marshall, and Stark. Hopkins was also there. . . . It was a very important meeting on the subject of the crisis in Japan, which has grown very acute. The Japanese Cabinet has fallen and a new Cabinet will probably be chosen which will be much more anti-American." (October 16, 1941, Yale/H. L. Stimson Papers [Diary, 35: 136].) The following day the emperor designated Lieutenant General Hideki Tojo as premier.

4. Dargue had replaced Major General James E. Chaney as commanding general of the First Air Force after Chaney was sent on a special mission to Great Britain in May 1941. During the September maneuvers, Dargue had commanded the Third Air Task Force.

To Generals Drum, De Witt,   October 21, 1941
Lear, and Krueger   [Washington, D.C.]
Memorandum for The Adjutant General
Radio. *Confidential*

Please have the following radiogram sent in code to General Drum, General De Witt, General Lear and General Krueger:

"I hear rumor that a syndicated article is about to issue to the effect that three of four Army Commanders are to be relieved.[1] This is merely to notify you that the foregoing is news to me. MARSHALL"

GCMRL/G. C. Marshall Papers (Pentagon Office, General)

1. Marshall's messages were transmitted between 9:13 and 10:03 P.M. The column—Drew Pearson and Robert S. Allen's "Washington Merry-Go-Round"—appeared on the morning of October 22. It said that Drum, De Witt, and Lear would be "replaced chiefly on the basis of their showing in the field maneuvers . . . by younger men with greater tactical ability." (Washington *Times-Herald,* p. 8.)

To Lieutenant General Ben Lear   October 25, 1941
                                              [Washington, D.C.]

Dear Lear: I received your letter regarding the "Merry-Go-Round" article yesterday, and this morning your P.S. note of the 24th stating that you hoped I "didn't mind my suggestion as to possible action concerning the 'Merry-Go-Round' article."[1]

In the first place I was very glad to have your view. I had seen Drum personally and his view was identical with yours. In the same mail with your letter came one from De Witt along the same line as yours.

Our problem here is to avoid having columnists, radio men and the press generally involve us, with deliberate intention, in denials or assertions regarding leading, and frequently baseless statements. It is news to them to keep the pot boiling, and it is very difficult for us to determine just when to intervene and how to go about it. Anything that suggests a limitation on the freedom of the press produces an instant and general reaction with a variety of counter accusations, not necessarily relevant to the particular issue.

In this particular instance, I had a tip that something of this sort was to be published, but just when and just what I did not know. For the peace of mind of the Army Commanders I endeavored to reach them that afternoon with my message. It was thought advisable to code it because we had no assurance that such an article was going to be published. It develops that the coding process and other transmission procedure delayed the arrival of the message until late that evening at the various Army Headquarters, and the decoded message was not delivered until the next morning, which happened to be the morning of the publication of the article.

General Surles[2] and I have discussed at length the proper procedure, and as a result he is endeavoring to arrange at the White House to have the President use this incident as an example of destructive press procedure, an article without foundation of fact and calculated to weaken command in the Army at a very critical moment in its development. Whether or not we succeed in doing this I cannot tell you positively at this writing, but if we do not we will take another tack either through the Secretary of War or me personally in whatever manner seems advisable.[3]

Incidentally, my message to the Army Commanders was released to the Service papers for publication today and at the same time turned over to the press.   Faithfully yours,

GCMRL/G. C. Marshall Papers (Pentagon Office, Selected)

1. Lear had written to Marshall on October 23 to thank him for his prompt response to the newspaper column and to "suggest that a matter of this sort should be quickly and certainly acted upon by the War Department. A statement from you or from the Secretary of War would go far to re-establish the confidence that such a column undermines. And since your Army Commanders cannot answer it themselves, they must look to Washington for the answer." (Lear to Marshall, October 23, 1941, GCMRL/G. C. Marshall Papers [Pentagon Office, Selected].)

2. Brigadier General Alexander D. Surles (U.S.M.A., 1911) had been director of the War Department Bureau of Public Relations since August 1941.

3. Marshall asked Secretary Stimson to comment on the issue at his October 30 press conference. (Marshall Memorandum for the Secretary of War, October 30, 1941, ibid.)

To Brigadier General John McA. Palmer   October 25, 1941
[Washington, D.C.]

Dear John: I just received your note of October 24th.[1] I told the National Guard group yesterday afternoon that I not only had no objection to their consulting with you but I would appreciate it very much if they did. You probably have already heard from them in the matter.

They started off, I fear, in a state of confusion and probably suspicion, aggravated by the fact that the War Department did not want to scatter these studies around the country with the inevitable release to the press, as the matter is still in too formative a stage. We did want them to be thinking it over, but from what I hear in a very hasty inquiry, they are considerably stirred up and got the impression we were trying to rush legislation through.

This is not the case at all. We have been mulling this plan over forward and back for the past five months with the National Guard officers here in the War Department. I have talked over its details formally with the National Guard Association, and particularly with Reckord and Martin, of Pennsylvania, and others. We have to go ahead for planning purposes only at this time, because the law prescribes a certain period for the National Guard. We must have a plan to meet that possibility.[2]   Hastily yours,

P.S.   Tell Maude confidentially that Katherine had a fall in the house due to the slippery floors, while I was off in South Carolina Thursday. She fell, striking a chair and breaking four ribs and banging her head pretty badly. She has been in Walter Reed since Thursday. They have not yet been able to take an X-ray. I have only seen her once and she cannot see visitors.

GCMRL/G. C. Marshall Papers (Pentagon Office, Selected)

1. Palmer had written that Major General John F. Williams, chief of the National Guard Bureau, "telephoned me and asked me to meet a group of National Guard Officers who were studying a plan of permanent military organization recently proposed in the War Department. They asked me if I would study the plan with them and advise them especially in its relation to our national military policy. I told them that I could not consider such a proposal except with your knowledge and consent. As they were to have an appointment with you later in the afternoon I told them to speak to you about it." (Palmer to Marshall, October 24, 1941, GCMRL/G. C. Marshall Papers [Pentagon Office, Selected].)

2. By mid-October 1941 certain National Guard units had been in federal service for a year or more. The problem, as Marshall posed it to his staff at an October 15 meeting, was to establish some device "for preserving the Guard as a Reserve in so far as possible. For the purposes of this discussion, let us suppose that in February or March our status is as it is today; that we are in the war only informally as at present, and yet fully on guard. Then suppose that under these circumstances public sentiment would require us, or we would think it desirable, to release the National Guard. What would be the requirements and the procedure to keep it from dissolving so far as to be of no value to us?" The following day Marshall and his advisers tentatively decided to initiate planning on the assumption that certain units should be released beginning in February 1942. Two months prior to this action the new policy would be announced, but it would be emphasized that the nation's total combat forces were being expanded by the creation of a trained reserve and that the army's total strength was not being reduced. (Frank McCarthy Notes on Conference in General Marshall's Office, October 15 and 16, 1941, NA/RG 165 [OCS, Notes on Conferences File].)

To Mrs. James J. Winn   October 29, 1941
[Washington, D.C.]

Dear Molly: Thursday morning at 6:30 (October 23d) your mother slipped on the floor near the door of the pool-room and fell backwards striking her back against the corner of a chair, which being against the wall did not give to the impact. She broke four ribs, the 8th to the 11th, and bruised a nerve in her back badly. Fortunately Clifton heard her fall and had the good sense to leave her on the floor with a pillow under her head. [The doctor came?] over at once, but he kept her on the floor for about two hours. Then they got her on a stretcher, took an X-ray in the house, and later that afternoon moved her to Walter Reed.

She has had a very painful time up to yesterday, but the possible complication of pneumonia did not develop. Yesterday morning they bound her up in tape and she was even able to sit up in a chair for a brief period. Up to that time, however, she could not move even a few inches without agonizing pain.

I have delayed writing to you until she was well out of the woods. I see her at noon each day, and Clifton goes out at night. She has had a day and night nurse, [but?] now only has a day nurse. Since yesterday's taping she has made rapid improvement and is very cheerful, because of the relief from so much acute pain. I imagine there will be a great change in the next twenty-four hours. She had a good night last night and has cut down on codeine and things like that. I think that from now on it will be a matter of impatience to get away from the hospital, though I doubt if she leaves there for another ten days or two weeks. She has been deluged with flowers, but we have protected her from all visitors. [Malin] Craig got in to see her last night, with a very dainty negligee he had shopped for, and she is very proud of. I understand he is taking some satisfaction in informing kindly women who telephone him on various rumors, that he knows nothing about it.

I will keep you advised, but there is nothing now to worry about except the fact that she has had such hard luck.

For your own [sake?]—which you will ignore—the moral of this tale is, get rid of those damned high-heeled bed-room slippers with leather soles. I talked to you and your mother about this [week?] in and week out for years, and all I get are broken ribs. She gave me the devil on the subject just a week before the accident when I made them take up an Oriental rug in the living room where you step off to the porch from the dining room. She told me I was very difficult to live with. (Miss Young is defending the women now with a cynical smile.) However, you were worse than she was along these lines and you have ribs like she has—also expectations. This is a very hasty note.

With my love,   Affectionately,

GCMRL/Research File (Family)

To Lieutenant General Walter Krueger   October 30, 1941
Personal and Confidential   Washington, D.C.

My dear Krueger: A list of proposed nominations was submitted to the President yesterday. Whether or not it will be approved I do not know. On the list was the name of Colonel Johnson for promotion to the grade of brigadier general.

I had your note expressing the possibility that you might be able to recommend him for promotion about December 1st.[1] When I first submitted this list, his name was not on it nor the name of any other National Guard officer. The Secretary of War made the point that if it were possible to include the name of a single National Guard officer in this list, it would be very helpful at this time.[2] We canvassed the Army through GHQ, and but two names were suggested, Johnson and a colonel of coast artillery in Alaska. The latter has been quite outstanding, so the two were included.[3]

The situation is approximately this: We have public backing for the improvement of leadership by the relief of officers from command who in our opinion are not up to the desired standard. However, as I will refer to later, there have been, as was to be expected, so many allegations of a relentless attitude on the part of the Regular Army with favoritism to their own people, and more particularly charges that our methods have been unnecessarily brusque or brutal, that the reaction has been building up in many quarters a feeling of opposition that might easily be capitalized in an unfortunate investigation. The Merry-Go-Round article regarding the relief of Army Commanders added greatly to the embarrassment in this matter.

I have been able to maintain our position in these matters, but it grows more and more difficult because a flood of political pressure would break loose the minute a line of attack can be found. The relief of General Birkhead and General Pyron produced a very serious reaction in important circles. Jesse Jones, the Reconstruction Finance Corporation Director and Secretary of Commerce, was deeply concerned in this matter; also Senator Connally, the Chairman of the Foreign Relations Committee.

What I am leading up to is this: Everyone had been educated to the point of accepting the necessity for drastic changes in command, but what has weakened my hand has been the method of its application. In the minor details it would seem that there could have been better handling. The two Texas reliefs have given rise to serious criticisms, however incorrect, that little courtesy was shown these officers; that they received their notice, in one instance in the middle of the night, and in the other instance, General Pyron, while on a march, and in such a way that he thought he was being put in arrest, and there was some doubt as to whether he would even have time to change his clothes. I do not know just what happened, but I do know that I have had to defend our procedure to the Secretary of War, to the Under Secretary of War, and to others who have heard these reports.

I might discount them on the basis that there was sure to be a super-critical attitude on the part of the men being relieved. However, General Bryden and I have been much disturbed in the cases of General Greely and of General Collins. Both of these men assert that they had no intimation that they were judged so unsatisfactory as to be considered for relief, until they were notified from the War Department.[4] If this is so, the procedure is entirely wrong. It should not be left to me to notify these people that they are unsatisfactory.

I do not know George Strong's side of the case, nor yours, but I feel very definitely that in both instances these officers should have been told directly what the trouble was, both before the final decision was made, and certainly when the final decision was taken.

Whenever it is possible to handle matters for the individual so as to spare him humiliation by delay of a week or two in announcement, even if he steps out of command, or by ordering him to some other point ostensibly for some other purpose, such action should be taken. A tactless or brutal procedure that might be excused on the battlefield, if pursued in times of peace like these, will wreck us in our vital purpose of improving the leader-ship of the Army.

I am sending General Haislip down to talk to you and General Lear about the situation.   Hastily yours,

G. C. Marshall

GCMRL/G. C. Marshall Papers (Pentagon Office, Selected)

1. See Marshall to Krueger, October 11, 1941, pp. 636–38.

2. Concerning this episode, Secretary Stimson noted in his diary: "When Marshall submit-ted to me the other day a new list of General Officers in the shape of promotions, I found there were no National Guard Officers among them and I sent it back with the message that I thought that it had better wait until we had some National Guard Officers to include in it. This morning he came in with General McNair to discuss the matter and tell me the reason. McNair told me his views. He is the man who has had charge of the training of the forces and of the recent maneuvers. The demands of the war of movement which we have got to face are such that it takes a man who is so trained that the right decision and the right movement come to him as a matter of habit—he is necessary to meet the situation. This is McNair and Marshall's argument. The National Guard Officers have not yet got that and as a result, although they have tried and have considered several of them, there were none that they could recommend as being as good as the competing Regular Officer who could be had in their place. The situation, as they pointed out, has completely changed from the last war in that now the Generals of Divisions, the Generals of Corps, and the Generals of Armies have got to have a much more active post and position than they had in the last war. When the Division Commanders went into the line in the last war they were hedged on both sides by veterans and they didn't have much to do but to sit in their chateaux in the rear of the lines and pass on very small matters. Then, furthermore, Marshall told me something that I had not known—that whereas the progress of the Army Schools had not gone very far at the time of the last war,

now they for twenty years have been putting in very intensive training at Leavenworth and the Army War College and the other schools which has produced a far higher grade of proficiency in the part of the Regular Officers. Apparently the strain of these schools has been terrific. Marshall told me that at one time it was such that it produced a series of suicides at Leavenworth which was so serious that they had to close the school; in other words, the men were under such strain, and competitive feeling that they were killing themselves. The result is now that both these men, Marshall and McNair, think that we would not be doing our duty to the soldiers if we did not put them under the very best Division Commanders and from Divisions up, now. Later perhaps there will be some National Guard Officers now in the position of Regimental or Brigade Commanders who will then be fit for the higher posts but at present they are not as adequate as competing Regulars. Well, we went over the list and I again pressed my point. Perhaps they may be able to find one National Guardsman who they think will be fit to go up from a Brigade to a Division Commander." (October 27, 1941, Yale/H. L. Stimson Papers [Diary, 35: 165–66].)

3. Lieutenant General McNair had reluctantly recommended Colonel Harry H. Johnson (112th Cavalry) and Colonel David P. Hardy (250th Coast Artillery) for promotion. "I fail to see the wisdom of promotions such as these," he added, "when one ponders the welfare of the Country and of the troops commanded. I believe that a citizen officer in general should be content to reach the highly responsible grade of colonel, and that the high command should be by selected professional soldiers." (McNair Memorandum for General Marshall, October 24, 1941, NA/RG 165 [OCS, 15102-893].)

4. Krueger had ordered Major General John N. Greely replaced as commanding general of the Second Divison; Major General George V. Strong, who had commanded the Eighth Army Corps since May 1941, had ordered Brigadier General Leroy P. Collins replaced as commanding general of the Eighteenth Field Artillery. (Greely to Marshall, October 21, 1941, GCMRL/G. C. Marshall Papers [Pentagon Office, Selected]; Statement of Brigadier General Leroy P. Collins Regarding Relief from Command of 18th Field Artillery Brigade, October 18, 1941, GCMRL/G. C. Marshall Papers [Pentagon Office, General].)

AID to China in its struggle against Japan had begun in late 1939, and in May 1941 that nation had been added to the list of recipients of United States lend-lease materials. To improve China's handling of lend-lease, the United States established an "American Military Mission to China," headed by Brigadier General John Magruder, who had served in China as a military attaché between 1920 and 1930. A graduate of the Virginia Military Institute (1909) and formerly the commandant there (1932-35), he had known Marshall since 1915. (See *Papers of GCM,* 1: 95–96.) Magruder arrived in Chungking in mid-October 1941 and met with Generalissimo Chiang Kai-shek on October 27 and 31. (Charles F. Romanus and Riley Sunderland, *Stilwell's Mission to China,* a volume in the *United States Army in World War II* [Washington: GPO, 1953], pp. 7, 16, 27–28, 31, 38.)

The Chinese leader stressed his fear that the Japanese Army was poised to launch a major drive against the southern city of Kunming, aimed at cutting the Burma Road, China's last important supply link with friendly powers. Magruder agreed with Chiang's assertion that "the key city to the Pacific was Kunming and no doubt if that city was destroyed, China would fall," an attack on Malaya would follow, and "nothing in the world would then stop a war in the Pacific." Thus the only way to preserve peace in the Pacific was for the United States to issue a warning to Japan strong enough to deter their Kunming adventure and for the United States and Great Britain to give China significant air reinforcements. "Lend-lease quotas of material for aviation as now scheduled will be insufficient and arrive too late. The only hope is if Singapore forces or units, properly organized, from Manila could arrive in time to give real aid to defending Chinese troops." (Magruder to War Department, Radio, October 28–29, 1941, NA/RG 165 [WPD, 4389–27]. The Chinese expressed these views to President Roosevelt, Secretary Morgenthau, Lauchlin Currie, who was in charge of lend-lease to China, and the State Department. See *Foreign Relations, 1941,* 5: 740–46.)

Colonel Charles W. Bundy, chief of the War Plans Division's plans group, and Colonel Thomas T. Handy (V.M.I., 1914) studied Magruder's lengthy dispatch, and Bundy presented their reply to the chief of staff. The G-2 division had serious doubts about the imminence of a Japanese drive on Kunming. If it was launched, the only aid the United States could give China would result in the significant weakening of the Philippine Islands defenses, there was little likelihood that the aid would be effective, and "such action would almost certainly bring on war with Japan, a condition desired above all others by the principal enemy—Germany. A primary objective of our strategy should be to avoid a two-front war. . . . No involvement should be risked which would lessen the main effort against Germany. With Germany defeated, the Far Eastern situation can be readily retrieved." (Gerow Memorandum for the Chief of Staff, November 1, 1941, NA/RG 165 [WPD, 4389–27].) ★

MEMORANDUM FOR THE RECORD BY   November 1, 1941
COLONEL CHARLES W. BUNDY   Washington, D.C.
Secret

Subject: Immediate Aid to China.

1. I took the War Plans memorandum on the above subject, dated November 1, 1941, to General Marshall about 9:30 a.m. on this date.

2. General Marshall read it very carefully, went over the situation on the map, and entered into quite a discussion concerning General Magruder after I had pointed out General Magruder's suggestions at the end of the radiogram.

3. He stated he knew Magruder very well and that he blamed himself

somewhat for not calling in Magruder before he left and cautioning Magruder against his weaknesses. He stated that he knew Magruder when he was in China before, and General Marshall was himself in China. When the Japanese were about to advance on Nanking, Magruder, from his sympathy with the Chinese and from his viewpoint as gathered by his experience in China, became quite stampeded. General Marshall also said that he was so busy and had so many other responsibilities at the time that he did not call General Magruder in just before he left and that his stand now would be that he knew Magruder so well that he, General Marshall, could properly interpret Magruder's messages.

4. General Marshall went into quite a discussion of the Philippine reinforcements and the remarkable secrecy under which movements had so far taken place. He set the date as to our really effective reinforcement to be December 10, 1941, and said that after that date, but not before, he thought it would be advantageous for the Japanese to learn of our really effective reinforcements.

5. He then said, "But what shall we do with the immediate question concerning Mr. Currie and what should be our answer to him?" I replied that I thought it was of first importance that Mr. Currie should be impressed with the fact that the War Department did not have an unsympathetic attitude towards Chinese aid; that he should be informed of the actual G-2 estimate of the possibilities of the advance on Kunming and be given as full a picture as possible of the over-all world-wide situation. General Marshall agreed and went on to say that he thought Mr. Currie should be informed of not only of what I had spoken of but should be given a full explanation of our reinforcements to the Philippines and their effect on the real situation in the Far East, especially with reference to the Chinese situation. He authorized me to tell Mr. Currie of the current and prospective reinforcements to the Philippines, on the condition that Mr. Currie would not pass this information along to anyone.

6. General Marshall concurred in War Plans view of the great undesirability of becoming involved in war in the Far East, but pointed out that a strong stand meant nothing unless an actual action followed in case of necessity, and that while it was undesirable to engage in a Far Eastern war, our policy could not expressly guarantee non-involvement should the Japanese advance to the southward. I understood him to agree fully in the undesirability of any United States forces participating in a purely Chinese war.[1]

7. He instructed me to get in touch with Mr. Currie at the first opportunity and to go over with Mr. Currie the general and special situations as indicated above. I have secured an appointment with Mr. Currie at 12:45 p.m. today.[2]

C. W. Bundy

NA/RG 165 (WPD, 4389-27)

1. Admiral Stark and the navy's planners were similarly fearful that the United States would do something that would precipitate a war with Japan before the navy was prepared. As senior member of the Joint Board, Stark called a special meeting for November 3 to coordinate policies and to caution the president. (Colonel William P. Scobey Memorandum for Record, November 2, 1941, NA/RG 319 [OPD, Exec. 8, Book A]. The minutes of the meeting are in NA/RG 319 [OPD, Joint Board Minutes].) On November 4 Marshall and Stark met with Secretary Cordell Hull and other officials at the State Department to impress upon them the military view of the Far Eastern crisis. (November 4, 1941, Yale/H. L. Stimson Papers [Diary, 36: 2].) Two days later the chief of staff and the chief of naval operations signed a memorandum for the president (dated November 5) setting forth their views and warning that the best deterrent to Japan was a strong position in the Philippines. "By about the middle of December, 1941, United States air and submarine strength in the Philippines will have become a positive threat to any Japanese operations south of Formosa. The U.S. Army air forces in the Philippines will have reached its projected strength by February or March, 1942." Until that time, war in the Far East had to be avoided. (Marshall and Stark Memorandum for the President, November 5, 1941, NA/RG 165 [WPD, 4389-29].)

2. Bundy's November 2 Notes on Conference with Mr. Currie at the State Department are in NA/RG 165 (WPD, 4389-27).

To Lieutenant General Ben Lear   November 1, 1941
Personal and Confidential   [Washington, D.C.]

Dear Lear: I received your letter regarding a commander for the 27th Division. Orders are issuing today placing General Pendleton [*Pennell*] in command of the Division.[1]

Your proposal regarding the assignment of General Robinson to the command of the 33d Division was brought to my attention with the recommendation that it would be unwise to do this.[2] I concur, but I think it important to give you my specific reasons. Before doing so, I would like you to get a picture of what is going on here. I can probably save time in doing this by enclosing a copy of a letter I wrote to Krueger the other day. I ask you to look over this letter before reading any further.

The reaction here after release from command grows more and more intense. I had assumed from the start that we would have a most difficult time, and that probably no one relieved from command would agree to the justice of the procedure. However, the weight of the objections and criticisms has largely hung on the procedure of relief. General Truman sent me a long letter on this subject, with which I do not think it worth while to worry you, and I have covered this subject in the attached letter to Krueger.[3]

Now as to Robinson and the 33d Division: My first objection is his age. To relieve a National Guard commander and replace him with a man over sixty at a time when we are resisting heavy pressures to make exceptions to our age limits recently announced, in my opinion would be most unfortunate. Added to this would be the inevitable criticism that you were seeking to place your own Chief of Staff when he as a matter of fact was practically over-age in grade at the time of the assignment.

I go into details in this matter because I feel a reluctance in restraining the action of an Army Commander, who is in a position of tremendous responsibility and a difficult position, to put it mildly. I mean by this that I feel greatly embarrassed whenever I cannot see my way clear to give you complete support. However, I do feel that while we lack intimate touch with the actual situation in the field, we have a broader perspective from this office.

Haislip was to see you yesterday and no doubt made our situation clear. The problem now is to get over the next six weeks without serious repercussions which might be built up into embarrassing Congressional attacks or investigations. We have public opinion strongly behind us on the general issue and I have the backing of most of the Congress; but it is very easy to upset this balance of power by tactless or crude procedure, whatever the basic merits of the case.

This is a hastily dictated letter, so please accept it as such. Faithfully yours,

GCMRL/G. C. Marshall Papers (Pentagon Office, Selected)

1. Marshall had written to Lear requesting his views on the possibility of designating Brigadier General Alexander E. Anderson, who commanded a brigade of the New York National Guard, to head the division when Major General William N. Haskell retired. Haskell had suggested Anderson. (Marshall to Lear, October 27, 1941, NA/RG 165 [OCS, 20241–239B].) Lear replied that Anderson had "done fairly well," but he did not have the "technical, tactical or command experience qualifying him for command of a unit of the importance of an infantry division." Lear noted that Haskell had recently recommended for promotion Brigadier General Ralph McT. Pennell (U.S.M.A., 1906), who commanded the Fifty-second Field Artillery Brigade. (Lear to Marshall, October 28, 1941, GCMRL/G. C. Marshall Papers [Pentagon Office, Selected].)

2. Brigadier General Donald A. Robinson had been chief of staff of the First Cavalry Division (July 1939–October 1940), the Ninth Corps (November 1940–February 1941), and the Second Army (March–October 1941). At the end of October he was made the commanding general of the Cavalry Replacement Training Center at Fort Riley, Kansas.

3. Lear replied that he would "be very happy in completely carrying out your desires, especially with reference to relief of National Guard officers." He then discussed the circumstances surrounding his relief of Major General Ralph E. Truman. (Lear to Marshall, November 3, 1941, ibid.)

To Lieutenant General Hugh A. Drum   November 3, 1941
Personal and Confidential   [Washington, D.C.]

Dear Drum: I have just this moment read your letter of October 31st regarding the 28th and 29th Divisions. I believe I sent you with my letter of

October 27th copy of a letter I wrote to General Martin and his reply.[1] I did this merely to give you one method I had attempted to devise for lessening the embarrassment of these reliefs. I thought if it proved acceptable to Martin we could probably have somewhat a similar procedure with Reckord. I had two purposes, the one just mentioned, and the one mentioned by you—that is to give the new Commanders experience in seeing the divisions operate in large maneuvers.

Your reply puzzles me in regard to Ord.[2] He was the principal choice of General Martin for the Pennsylvania job of Instructor just as I became Chief of Staff, and I think we brought him back from the Philippines for that purpose. They liked him and I believe he liked them; so I thought other things being equal, he was a good choice. Personally, I have never served with Ord and know him only by reputation.

I have no doubt at all regarding Gerow, either as to his temperament or as to ability as a leader, tactician, etc.

Gullion is going to see me today to talk over a proposal I made to him that he select Reckord to be Provost Marshal General of the Third Corps Area. Those posts will be very important in the future as Gullion develops his job, which has many ramifications including relations with the LaGuardia organization, responsibility in these strike matters, etc.[3]

Whom would you have in mind to replace Russell in case his relief is indicated?[4] I have several men on a tentative list that I think have special qualifications. Omar Bradley, now Commandant of the Infantry School, who is outstanding for any job in the Army. Terry Allen, of the Second Cavalry Division, who is now attached to the 4th Division to learn more of the Infantry game. He took the Infantry School course, was weapons instructor at Riley, in fact wrote their pamphlet on this subject, and is outstanding as a leader. And his work in this regard during the recent maneuvers was so notable as to excite comment. He can do anything with men and officers, though unprepossessing in appearance and apparently casual in manner. Christian, of the Field Artillery, has done a particularly fine job at a Training Center, but I do not know how well suited he would be at the present time for a division commander.[5] I feel that the men selected to command these National Guard divisions should be of such outstanding character that no one could possibly question their efficiency, and what is even more important, they should be of a type to win the devoted loyalty of the entire command.

In this respect, I have been disturbed by the frequent rumors I hear regarding Muir, particularly relating to his statements regarding reliefs and purges. They come to me from many different directions and I am filled with considerable concern regarding his development of the 44th Division. He has a hard job, it is but he has been given three Regular subordinate commanders which should help him to put his house in order without so many indications of arbitrary and vocal methods. I trust I am being misled by the exaggerations of those adversely affected.

I will give your message to the Secretary,[6]   Faithfully yours,

GCMRL/G. C. Marshall Papers (Pentagon Office, Selected)

1. Marshall had written to Drum to ask the First Army commander's informal and confidential advice as to the best method of relieving National Guard Major Generals Edward Martin and Milton A. Reckord and placing them in acceptable posts after they had been retired for reaching the age limit of sixty-two. Marshall wrote that he feared that they would "hold on like grim death to their divisions, but we cannot make exceptions on this age business." (Marshall to Drum, October 27, 1941, GCMRL/G. C. Marshall Papers [Pentagon Office, Selected]. Marshall enclosed a copy of his letter to Martin of October 9, 1941, pp. 634–35.) Drum replied that he thought the two men should be permitted to take their divisions to their home stations after the maneuvers, as immediate relief "would be quite unfortunate," but he did not offer any suggestions as to future jobs for Martin and Reckord. (Drum to Marshall, October 31, 1941, GCMRL/G. C. Marshall Papers [Pentagon Office, Selected].)

2. Marshall had told Drum that he had Brigadier General J. Garesché Ord in mind for command of the Twenty-eighth Division. Drum replied, "In addition to Ord, General John A. Crane is worthy of consideration. Crane has developed a good deal during these maneuvers, and in many ways I think he has more force and character than Ord. [Leonard T.] Gerow should make a good commander. In the long run Ord may develop adequately, although there are some doubts in my mind. I am not sure of his ability to handle officers without irritating them unduly." (Drum to Marshall, October 31, 1941, ibid.)

3. Fiorello H. LaGuardia was director of the Office of Civilian Defense. Strikes affecting defense industries had risen markedly during 1941, particularly during the third quarter. In October, the peak month of the year, sixty-nine new strikes began that interfered with war material production. Army troops had briefly been used in June to maintain production at the North American Aviation Corporation, and on October 31 troops took over the facilities of Air Associates, Incorporated. (Byron Fairchild and Jonathan Grossman, *The Army and Industrial Manpower,* a volume in the *United States Army in World War II* [Washington: GPO, 1959], pp. 57–68, 204–5.)

4. Major General Henry D. Russell, a Georgia lawyer, was commanding general of the Thirtieth Division (National Guards of Georgia, North Carolina, South Carolina, and Tennessee). Drum wrote: "Russell is a fine man and does his best, but has two weaknesses— one, he is not a tactical commander; the other is that he will not clean house. Consequently, I fear he will have to go." (Drum to Marshall, October 31, 1941, GCMRL/G. C. Marshall Papers [Pentagon Office, Selected].)

5. Brigadier General Thomas J. J. Christian (U.S.M.A., 1911) had been commanding general of the Field Artillery Replacement Center at Camp Roberts, California, since November 1940.

6. Drum had ended his letter with a request that Marshall "extend my thanks to the Secretary for his statement" relative to the Washington Merry-Go-Round article. (See Marshall to Lear, October 25, 1941, pp. 651–52.)

To Allen T. Brown   November 3, 1941
                                                [Washington, D.C.]

Dear Allen: Your mother came home yesterday at two o'clock with her nurse in attendance. She made the trip comfortably, though Fleet almost knocked her down as they helped her out of the car. At first she was a little tired and then seemed to make a marked improvement the same evening. She insisted on coming down in the elevator for dinner in the dining room, and spent all her time on the porch.

Last night I went into her room four or five times and she was sleeping each time but once. I found out this morning she got up once herself and then went on the porch at six o'clock and was able to fix herself comfortably in a chair. The nurse is still in attendance from 7:30 in the morning until 6:30 at night.

I think she will probably make rapid strides during the next two or three days. Colonel Kirk tells me that ribs heal very quickly, due to the free circulation of the blood.[1]

This is just a hasty note,   Affectionately,

GCMRL/Research File (Family)

1. Colonel Norman T. Kirk, whom Marshall had once called "a splendid surgeon and a dandy fellow," was stationed at the Walter Reed General Hospital in Washington, D.C. (*Papers of GCM,* 1: 538.)

MEMORANDUM FOR GENERAL GEROW   November 5, 1941
[Washington, D.C.]

Last night shortly after my return to the Department, Stanley Hornbeck telephoned me.[1]

He expressed appreciation of my "lucid picture" of the situation; he shared my estimate of the recent messages from Magruder; he felt that the picture these messages conveyed had caused the State Department more worry than there was actual need for.

He then got down to the real purpose of his telephone message, stating that the State Department had only received copies of Magruder's messages because of their contacts with Lauchlin Currie; that the Department received copies of the messages from the Naval Attaché; that he did not know whether we intended to cut them off from any knowledge of what our Mission developed or not; that he hopes that copies of the messages might be sent direct to the State Department.

The embarrassing point here quite evidently is that the Naval Attaché messages do go to the Department and the Mission messages do not.[2]

GCMRL/G. C. Marshall Papers (Pentagon Office, Selected)

1. Stanley K. Hornbeck, an expert on the Far East and the State Department's adviser on political relations for that area since 1937, had been present at the November 4 meeting between Marshall, Stark, and Hull concerning the Pacific crisis. (See note 1, Memorandum for the Record by Colonel Charles W. Bundy, November 1, 1941, p. 660.)

2. G-2 was instructed to send to the State Department those portions of the military mission's dispatches the army thought might interest them. (Marshall to Hornbeck, November 13, 1941, GCMRL/G. C. Marshall Papers [Pentagon Office, Selected].)

MEMORANDUM FOR THE SECRETARY OF WAR   November 5, 1941
Washington, D. C.

The Navy is very anxious to father a prize fight in New York on January 9th between Joe Louis and Max [*Buddy*] Baer. Mike Jacobs has guaranteed them $25,000 for such a fight, to be used for welfare activities in the isolated bases. Joe Louis and Max Baer are agreeable to the arrangement.[1]

The difficulty in the matter is that Joe Louis may be inducted between now and that date. This is a matter over which we have no control, and the Selective Service people are unwilling to arrange a deferment. Admiral Stark is very anxious to have the fight in order to get the money, and he wants to know if we would be willing to allow Louis to fight, and more particularly to train for the fight, if he happens to be inducted before that date.

An exception to be made in this case in the nature of permitting Louis a portion of each day for training and giving him probably ten days' furlough just prior to the fight, might be made on the basis that it was being done specifically at the request of the Navy. Whether or not Louis would undertake such a fight with limitations on his training activities, I do not know, but in making the preliminary answer to Admiral Stark I would like your view as to whether or not you would frown on the arrangement just described.[2]

G. C. Marshall

GCMRL/G. C. Marshall Papers (Pentagon Office, Selected)

1. Max Baer, Buddy's older brother, had been heavyweight boxing champion between June 14, 1934, and June 13, 1935. Joe Louis had been champion since June 22, 1937. Louis had defeated Buddy Baer on May 23, 1941. Mike Jacobs was the boxing promoter of the Twentieth Century Sporting Club.

2. At the bottom of this memorandum, Marshall wrote: "Secretary states 'use your own judgement. The idea does not appeal to me'. GCM"

MEMORANDUM FOR ADMIRAL STARK   November 6, 1941
[Washington, D.C.]

Subject: Joe Louis.

As I told you over the phone, we have no power with relation to the

Selective Service induction procedure, and the Selective Service people expressed unwillingness to grant Louis a further deferment—one already having been granted him. In this connection, there has been a feeling that his manager or lawyer was endeavoring to secure delays until his 28th birthday in March, which would eliminate him from draft consideration.

As to his availability for the fight on January 9th in the event that he is inducted into the Army prior to that date, we will be willing to grant him reasonable training opportunities, as well as a furlough from Christmas to include the day of the fight. It would be necessary in doing this for us to state, if pressed by critics or newspaper men, that this exception was made at the request of the Navy.[1]

GCMRL/G. C. Marshall Papers (Pentagon Office, Selected)

1. Louis knocked out Buddy Baer in the first round. The champion passed his physical examination on January 12 and was inducted into the army on January 14. (*New York Times,* January 13 [p. 20] and 15 [p. 11], 1942.)

MEMORANDUM FOR COLONEL SMITH[1]   November 6, 1941
[Washington, D.C.]

One of my orderlies, Private Charles R. Thompson, 5th Class Specialist, A.S.N. R-6062214, has been with me almost two years. I have delayed in making him a sergeant because of the unfortunate effects these promotions seem to have when given to orderlies. However, Thompson has had twenty-three years' service, he has been very faithful, and is quite important to the smooth running of my establishment. Added to this, I find that his predecessor, or rather the man who was his senior in the house, and who was fired by me for neglecting his duties and was reduced from sergeant to private, was transferred to Fort Meade and almost immediately made a staff sergeant, then a technical sergeant, and is now a first sergeant.

Under these circumstances I wish to have Thompson promoted to the grade of staff sergeant.

I also wish to have my horse orderly, whose name can be obtained from the Detachment, made a sergeant. He is now a corporal. Mickelsen handled this direct with the Detachment commander,[2] and we hesitated to promote this man. But the fact remains that under existing circumstances anyone who stays with me loses heavily in rank if he belongs to the negro personnel. It is, therefore, difficult to hold a good man in contentment.

GCMRL/G. C. Marshall Papers (Pentagon Office, General)

1. Walter B. Smith was secretary of the General Staff.

2. Lieutenant Colonel Stanley R. Mickelsen, formerly an assistant secretary of the General Staff, was stationed at Camp Pendleton, Virginia, at this time.

N.B.C. RADIO BROADCAST ON THE CITIZENS'   November 11, 1941
DEFENSE CORPS   [Washington, D.C.]

The anniversary of the Armistice of 1918 is a day of renewed tributes to the memory of those who made the great sacrifices of the last war. It also has been the occasion for rejoicing over the victorious conclusion of that war.

Today's anniversary finds us with little reason for rejoicing. Instead we have reached a moment in our history, I believe, when the civilian should definitely take his place in the general preparation of the country to meet the tragic circumstances of these fateful days. The Navy on the seas and the Army in our distant outposts are prepared to do their duty. Behind them a powerful military force is rapidly being developed. Industry is now moving into high speed production of munitions. Finally, today, on the 23d anniversary of that futile armistice, the President inaugurates a week to prepare for the organized cooperation of civilians in our defense effort.

To organize the home front for the protection of the civilian communities, a new arm—the Citizens' Defense Corps—is in process of formation. Somewhat like the army with its various arms and branches, this Corps has its air-raid wardens, its auxiliary police and fire fighters, its First Aid and hospital service, its Signal Corps and Motor Corps, its engineers and other special units. Men and women to form these ranks will do so voluntarily along with their normal daily tasks. The details of organization have been or will be explained to you by local committees, by speakers on the radio, and through the medium of the press.

Mayor LaGuardia has been charged by the President with the tremendous task of organizing this Corps of citizens. At the outset he is faced with the problem of convincing 130 million people whose shores have seen no invader for a century-and-a-quarter, of the need for this step. He must convince them of the necessity for organizing against any eventuality.

Mr. LaGuardia has asked me to give you my opinion as to the importance of this task he has undertaken. From the standpoint of the soldier, the urgency of this project is difficult to overemphasize. An army is no stronger than the people behind it. Soldiers require the whole-hearted support of their home fold. They are entitled to it. They must have it. Furthermore, soldiers need to be reassured that measures have been taken to care for their families, to protect them in an emergency.

We pride ourselves on being an energetic and determined people, not easily duped and far from gullible, but we live in a free land and with such kindly relations to one another that we fail to appreciate the dangerous possibilities of the present situation. We should realize that the more we, as a nation, influence the course of this war, the more important it becomes for us to protect every phase of our national life against the efforts of the Axis

Powers to deter or to weaken us. The difficulty of arousing our people to a clear understanding of what must be done varies, somewhat directly, with the distance of their homes from the Atlantic and Pacific seaboards. And yet that apparent security of distance presents a great weakness to the German mode of procedure.

We must be prepared on the home front against both the direct methods of sabotage, and against the indirect and subtle methods of propaganda. It is not difficult for the inhabitants of coastal communities to recognize the necessity for organizing an Air-raid Warning Service. It is more difficult to convince people in the interior of the country that some of the most serious schemes for destructive action against our interests are possibilities in their midst.

It seems best to speak very frankly on this particular subject. The Government today is constantly on guard against damage to our industries or their products, but we must be prepared for a sudden and wide-spread attempt at sabotage directed against the entire munitions industry, including the critical utilities and transportation facilities. Nothing should be taken for granted. We should assume that at a given moment wholesale sabotage may be attempted by the far-reaching organization which has secretly and ceaselessly been planning for just such an occasion. We must be prepared against the confusion that so easily can be created in large centers of population, and we must be organized to look after our people at home in any emergency, whatever the nature.

However, while not minimizing the seriousness of the possibilities just mentioned, I personally am more concerned over the effects of the clever methods of Axis propaganda which for a long time have been directed against the development of our entire defense program. A portion of my daily mail is more or less a direct repercussion of such German scheming. The letters come from families who are worrying about their boys in the Army, who have been led to believe, for instance, that the soldiers lack food, lack proper shelter or medical attention. They come from members of Congress who have been similarly misled. This process of misrepresentation and distortion has been carried on with persistence and skill. Sometimes the results are seriously disturbing.

Let me give you an example. Last summer, incident to the democratic process of congressional debate on the question of the extention of service, public interest centered on the Army; everything concerned with the troops—their training, the conditions under which they were living, and the state of their equipment—were the subject of wide-spread discussion and publicity. In this connection I wish to read an extract from the instructions issued by the German Ministry of Propaganda last April: "It is more effective," these instructions state, "when the American press provides propaganda for our mill than if we do it ourselves." Now what happened last summer? The debate was on, the criticisms of our good faith and judgment were naturally frequent, and the more unfavorable reactions of individual soldiers were broadcast. Mass desertions were reported to threaten the Army in October.

Throughout the press of Latin America we found comments and conclusions seriously prejudicial to our interests, being given wide publicity, along with clever distortions of the facts. I read similar articles in the Italian papers, assuring their people that a breakdown of military preparation in this country was in progress. But the cleverest move to capitalize on this golden opportunity for sabotage was a rumor skillfully planted among the men in National Guard units that a large number of soldiers, more than a thousand, had deserted en masse from a certain Regular Army division. The men had been fed this particular rumor because such an occurrence in the Regular Army was indicative of a general breakdown in discipline. The actual fact in this matter was that the division in question had one lone desertion in the period referred to. And yet there had been spread throughout a large part of the Army this carefully planted attack on the soundness of our military organization. Back at home mothers were confused and prejudiced to an extent that was both pathetic and alarming. In certain districts known to have a number of people opposed to the strengthening of our means of defense, the reactions to this propaganda were increasingly evident.

There have been many examples of this same general nature, examples of skillful borings from within to weaken the power of the Government. We no longer live in a "snug, over-safe corner of the world." We cannot continue to be naive and credulous. On the contrary, we should set ourselves with determination to see this thing through as a united people. For these reasons, I believe that the Citizens' Defense Corps will serve a vital purpose in completing our general organization for the security of America, and I am sure that it will exert a strong influence in combating secret and destructive efforts to divide and confuse our people. I urge the whole-hearted cooperation of the leaders in every community to complete the organization of the Corps.

GCMRL/G. C. Marshall Papers (Pentagon Office, Speeches)

To Lieutenant General Hugh A. Drum   November 12, 1941
Personal and Confidential   [Washington, D.C.]

Dear Drum: I have just read your letter of November 8th regarding the 28th and 29th Divisions.[1] In your previous letter you emphasized the importance of having the prospective commanders of these two divisions present with them for at least the last phase of the maneuvers. As the time for this is rapidly approaching, a decision will have to be made. Therefore, I am placing the matter in your hands as to the attachment of Ord to the 28th, and will send Gerow to report to you for temporary duty at the end of this week.

You can handle the matter with Martin and Reckord and as to the press release. I imagine the best way to meet the latter problem, from the viewpoint of the two National Guard officers, will be to state that at an announced later date after the return of the divisions from the maneuvers the two Regular officers mentioned will be assigned to those commands due to the relief of Martin and Reckord under the age limitation provision; the present attachment was merely to give the Regular officers an opportunity to see the divisions operating under full field conditions—or something of that sort. Knowing how sensitive both these men are, it might be well to let them see the proposed press release before it is issued, in order that they might have an opportunity to offer any suggestions.

The matter of the Corps Area Provost Marshal General has not materialized as I hoped, so do not mention that.

I am planning to look in on the maneuvers next week, earlier if practicable. The trouble now is I am—most confidentially—deeply involved in the possible employment of almost 100,000 troops in the coal mine regions,[2] along with a number of serious matters connected with the Japanese crisis, and the presentation of a new six billion dollar deficiency appropriation. Faithfully yours,

GCMRL/G. C. Marshall Papers (Pentagon Office, Selected)

1. Replying to Marshall's November 3 letter, Drum wrote that in regard to Gareschè Ord, "I am willing to try him out and believe that my personal influence will carry him through." In addition, he had informally discussed their future status with both Martin and Reckord; Drum reiterated his October 31 opinion that they should be relieved after their divisions returned to their home stations following the maneuvers. (Drum to Marshall, November 8, 1941, GCMRL/G. C. Marshall Papers [Pentagon Office, Selected].)

2. Strikes by the United Mine Workers of America in the "captive" mines (i.e., those owned by the steel companies) threatened to curtail steel production during the autumn of 1941. The principal issue in the strike was the miners' demand for a union shop (i.e., all nonunion workers would be required to join the union in order to continue working). The strike began on September 15 and was twice interrupted by mediation attempts. On November 10 the National Defense Mediation Board voted against the United Mine Workers and the strike immediately resumed. The War Department debated a plan for sending troops into the coal fields to take control of mine production, but by November 22 President Roosevelt had persuaded the union and the owners to submit to arbitration and the strike was ended. The arbitration board's decision in the miners' favor was handed down on December 7. (Fairchild and Grossman, *Army and Industrial Manpower*, pp. 66–67; *New York Times*, November 23 [pp. 1, 39] and December 8 [pp. 1, 43], 1941.)

November 13, 1941
Washington, D.C.

Statement By General George C. Marshall,
Chief of Staff, U.S. Army

This morning's papers carry reports that the War Department is conducting a recruiting campaign for three-year enlistments for overseas service. Several of these articles are calculated to give the impression that we are engaged in building up an expeditionary force, and one paper I understand has already taken us to Africa.[1]

During the past year the War Department has been working to increase the number of volunteers, or three-year men to meet the increased requirements for the present overseas garrisons, such as Panama, Hawaii, and the new Atlantic Bases; also to supply the large numbers required for Air Corps units, together with a sufficient percentage of long service men to give stability to the Regular organizations in the United States, particularly the technical armored corps.

In addition, the Army has been endeavoring to provide the necessary numbers of volunteers to carry out the President's announced policy of relieving the Marines in Iceland and the elements of the British Army stationed there. The recruiting campaign to secure men for the Iceland command was initiated last August at Camp Custer among the units of the Fifth Division. We still have to meet the necessity for 10,000 men for this purpose.

The War Department has also felt that it was highly desirable to have at least one division out of the thirty-four divisions of the Army, the First Division, 100% volunteers, in order that it could be placed on an equal footing with the Marine division with which it has been training for some months in a provisional corps.

To summarize, these requirements amount to 36,000 volunteers a month, of which 25,000 are required for the Air Corps alone. The recruiting necessary for these normal and well known purposes evidently gave rise to the articles which appeared in the papers this morning. In this connection approximately 25,000 men volunteered in October, which is 9,000 short of the monthly number required.

There is no foundation whatsoever for the allegation or rumor that we are preparing troops for a possible expedition to Africa or other critical area outside this hemisphere.

GCMRL/G. C. Marshall Papers (Pentagon Office, Speeches)

1. The *New York Times* (November 13, 1941, p. 15) printed without comment the two

stories that had caused what the War Department regarded as an alarming reaction elsewhere: a United Press item stating that the army was "asking National Guardsmen and selectees to re-enlist for three-year terms in the Regular Army and to serve overseas if necessary"; and a brief Associated Press article stating that the army was "asking members of the armored force whether they would be willing to serve overseas." The comments by certain newspapers, Stimson noted in his diary, was "evidently a movement by the Isolationists to try to affect the vote" on the revisions of the Neutrality Act of 1939 which would permit the arming of United States merchant ships and the sending of them into belligerents' ports. (November 13, 1941, Yale/ H. L. Stimson Papers [Diary, 36: 22].) President Roosevelt had requested the revisions on October 9, 1941; the legislation had passed the Senate but was stalled in the House. On November 12 House Speaker Sam Rayburn, Democrat from Texas, and Majority Leader John W. McCormack, Democrat from Massachusetts, had written to the president asking for a letter supporting the revisions. The president's message was sent on November 13. (*The Public Papers and Addresses of Franklin D. Roosevelt,* 1941 volume, ed. Samuel I. Rosenman [New York: Harper and Brothers, 1950], pp. 487–90.)

Secretary Stimson wrote that he had decided to "put out a statement on the floor of the House during the debate and put it in the hands of McCormack, so that the real facts could be given fully. I called up the President and he told me to go ahead. I called up McCormack and he said that was fine and he and I decided that the best man to do it was Marshall who, of course, represented the head of the Army which had been doing this thing. So Marshall and I hurried along with our work and together with the aid of the officers who knew the facts, we drafted a statement which he signed and sent up to McCormack and it got there in time for the debate and I think had some influence. Late in the afternoon we got word that the Bill repealing Section II, III and VI of the Neutrality Law had successfully passed the House, although by the close vote of 212 to 194. It was a tremendous relief to me, because the atmosphere has been steadily setting against the movement lately." (November 13, 1941, Yale/ H. L. Stimson Papers [Diary, 36: 22–23].)

To Brigadier General John McA. Palmer   November 13, 1941
Confidential   [Washington, D.C.]

Dear John: Orders were supposed to have issued today placing you on active duty. The understanding is, pursuant to our telephone conversation, that you have no obligations of office or office hours, that you are merely available to me for consultation in the matter of Army organization as pertaining to the citizen forces, and that you are immediately available as a consultant to the Executive Committee of the National Guard people, who have already requested your advice. I attach a copy of a letter I have addressed to the three National Guard officers of this committee who called on me the other day, which is self-explanatory.[1]

Now, most confidentially, I am sending you, in the form of a possible press release, an outline of future action by the War Department which intimately concerns the National Guard. Whether or not we follow this plan must be maintained for the present as a close secret, because if we announced something and then later the international situation prevented us from going through with it, we would be immediately charged with another breach of promise. I send you this in order that you can turn over in your mind the ideas presented so that at some later date I can call you up and arrange a conference on the subject. Meanwhile, if you feel disposed you can discuss the matter with Colonel Leitch in G-3 or General Twaddle of that section.[2] Understand, I am not pressing you in any way for an immediate reply. Also please understand that this press release might not be used until after the New Year. Faithfully yours,

GCMRL/G. C. Marshall Papers (Pentagon Office, Selected)

1. Marshall wrote to Brigadier General Charles H. Grahl and Major Generals George E. Leach and Ellard A. Walsh: "It occurred to me that in justice to General Palmer and as a valuable assistance to you gentlemen that it would be appropriate to place him on active duty. Accordingly I have taken this action today and I am notifying you as a member of the National Guard Executive Committee that he is at the disposal of that committee in an advisory capacity." (Marshall to Grahl, November 13, 1941, GCMRL/G. C. Marshall Papers [Pentagon Office, Selected].) For previous correspondence on the National Guard reorganization issue, see Marshall to Palmer, October 25, 1941, pp. 652–53.

2. Lieutenant Colonel William B. Leitch was a member of the Mobilization Branch of G-3

MEMORANDUM FOR GENERAL MOORE   November 14, 1941
                                                Washington, D.C.

Mr. Harriman has just talked to me prior to his departure tomorrow morning for London. He and General Chaney apparently are in agreement as to a certain method of procedure whereby Harriman releases to Chaney all technical details concerning the lease-loan munitions, and reserves to himself the more or less political and similar matters of that nature.[1] However, he wishes to feel free to obtain from General Chaney such data regarding details as may be necessary to his, Harriman's, general understanding of what is happening.

He said Chaney told him that I had so ordered matters, but I have no recollection of this. Will you please put me straight on what I have done, if anything, and what I should do in the way of directions to Chaney to carry out Harriman's desire.[2]

G. C. M.

NA/RG 407 (Classified, 400.3295 [8-9-41] Sec. II)

1. Major General James E. Chaney, the special army observer in London, had been a member of the United States military aid mission to the Soviet Union headed by W. Averell Harriman. He had returned with the mission to Washington in mid-October for a month of consultations on various aspects of Soviet aid. (*The London Journal of General Raymond E. Lee, 1940–1941,* ed. James Leutze [Boston: Little, Brown and Company, 1971], pp. 280, 419–22; W. Averell Harriman and Elie Abel, *Special Envoy to Churchill and Stalin, 1941–1946* [New York: Random House, 1975], pp. 108–9.)

2. The War Plans Division drafted a letter for Deputy Chief of Staff Richard C. Moore's

signature which reiterated Chaney's responsibilities as the War Department's lend-lease representative and the necessity for his avoiding diplomatic and political issues "except when military necessity dictates otherwise. . . . It is General Marshall's desire that you continue to cooperate fully in every practicable way with Mr. Harriman. Toward this end it would be well to create an early opportunity to assure Mr. Harriman that any information he may desire will be gladly furnished." (Moore to Chaney, November 19, 1941, NA/RG 407 [Classified, 400.3295 (8–9–41) Sec. II].)

TO MRS. JAMES J. WINN

November 15, 1941
[Washington, D.C.]

Dear Molly: This is just a note to tell you about your mother, in case you do not trust her statements about herself. She was getting along very well about a week ago, but the day before the nurse left they went for a brief ride and then for a short walk. The result was she took a very definite backward step and was utterly miserable for the succeeding three or four days. However, after re-strapping Monday morning and commencing with some vitamin pills, she has made quick improvement and today seems well along the way to a comfortable recovery. I took her to The Buckingham[1] last night, and she told me this morning that she had slept very well, better than since her accident, and felt much stronger.

As a matter of fact, she is planning possibly a flight with me to Pompano in Florida, where the Stettiniuses have a luxurious dune cottage, far removed from any other establishment and within actual sight of the Gulf Stream. The plan is for me to leave her there and return to the maneuvers in North Carolina and then to spend Thanksgiving with the Stettiniuses and possibly bring your mother back Saturday or Sunday.

However, the crisis in the coal strike, Japanese negotiations, and the probability that I will have to appear before Congress on a six or seven billion dollar deficiency appropriation Monday, Tuesday or Wednesday threatens to cancel all my pleasurable plans. In addition, I am under the necessity of getting down to the maneuvers.

I hope to get to Panama before Christmas, just when depends on too many things to attempt to give a date. The trouble is, if I go I wish to include the Caribbean Bases, and such a trip would require about ten days. During this period of critical issues arising every twenty-four hours, it is very difficult for me to delegate responsibility and leave town. I am perfectly willing to delegate, and have already done so; the trouble is the White

House, the Committees of Congress, and the Secretary insist on seeing me personally.

With my love and an urgent desire to see the baby,[2]   affectionately,

P.S.   Your mother greatly appreciated your writing the day after your ordeal. Whatever effort you gave to the letter was much repaid by calming down her various fears.

GCMRL/Research File (Family)
1. A motion-picture theater near Fort Myer.
2. James J. Winn, Jr., had been born November 7 at Colón, Panama.

WITH the mid-October formation of the Tojo government in Japan, President Roosevelt and his principal military advisers recognized the deterioration of the Far Eastern situation. Roosevelt did nothing, however, to accomodate Japanese expansion in either China or Southeast Asia. (Conn and Fairchild, *Framework of Hemisphere Defense*, p. 154.) United States military planners came increasingly to believe that reinforcement of the Philippines could deter Japanese expansion southward.

By mid-autumn W.P.D. planners were arguing that "unexpected Russian opposition to Germany, continuance of Chinese resistance, economic pressure exerted by the United States, Great Britain and the Dutch, and the uncertainty of the outcome of war with the Associated Powers have caused Japan to hesitate." The Philippines were a major roadblock to Japan's continued southward expansion, and removal of this obstacle "would be a hazardous military operation, if opposed by strong aviation forces (United States and Associated Powers). For air support of such an attack on the Philippines, Japan must rely on carrier-based aviation and intermittent support from long-range aircraft based on Taiwan. The cost of this operation would be so great that Japan will hesitate to make the effort except as a last resort." W.P.D. recommended immediate shipments of modern combat planes to the islands. "Starting with 1942, the aviation strength will be raised to a total of 170 heavy bombers, 86 light bombers, and 195 pursuit." ("Strategic Concept of the Philippine Islands," October 8, 1941, attachment [Tab 1] to Marshall to MacArthur, October 18, 1941, NA/RG 165 [WPD, 4175-18]. Concerning air reinforcements see Wesley Frank Craven and James Lea Cate, *Plans and Early Operations: January 1939 to August 1942,* a volume in *The Army Air Forces in World War II* [Chicago: University of Chicago Press, 1948], pp. 175–93.) ★

MEMORANDUM FROM ROBERT L. SHERROD   November 15, 1941
TO DAVID W. HULBURD, JR.[1]   Washington, D.C.

Subject: General Marshall's conference today[2]
Restricted

Seven Washington correspondents, representing the three press associations, the New York Times, the Herald Tribune, TIME and Newsweek, were
called by the War Department early this morning, asked if they could
appear at 10:15 for a secret conference with General Marshall.[3] Because
General Marshall's comments are of a highly confidential nature, only one
copy of this report is being sent to New York and one copy being kept here.

General Marshall explained his embarrassment in calling the conference
and said anyone who did not care to share secrets was at liberty to leave
before he started talking. But there were some things he had to tell to key
press correspondents in order that their interpretations of current and
forthcoming events did not upset key military strategy of the United States.

The U.S. is on the brink of war with the Japanese, said the General. Our
position is highly favorable in this respect: We have access to a leak in all the
information they are receiving concerning our military preparations, especially in the Phillipines. In other words, we know what they know about us
and they dont know that we know it.[4]

Under great secrecy the U.S. is building up its strength in the Phillipines
to a level far higher than the Japanese imagine. General MacArthur is
unloading ships at night, is building air fields in the carefully guarded
interior, is allowing no one within miles of military reservations.

Most important point to remember is this: We are preparing for an
offensive war against Japan, whereas the Japs believe we are preparing only
to defend the Phillipines. All their information indicates that. For instance,
the Japanese reports show that we have 18 old B-18 bombers in the
Phillipines. As a matter of fact, we have 35 Flying Fortresses already
there—the largest concentration anywhere in the world. Twenty more will
be added next month, and 60 more in January. We are piling a large
proportion of our new materiel into the Phillipines, several shiploads a week
of it. Our new 75 mm. guns are being sent there. So are our 105's. There are
already 100 tanks in the Phillipines and another shipload in arriving next
week. New equipment for making beachhead landings is already there. On
Sept. 30 the dive bombing outfits which were participating in the Louisiana
maneuvers departed for an unknown destination. They are arriving in the
Phillipines Tuesday.[5]

This information will be allowed to leak to the Japanese (it is miraculous
that they haven't learned about the Flying Fortresses, but the two attempts
that have been made to publish the fact have been thwarted). But it must be

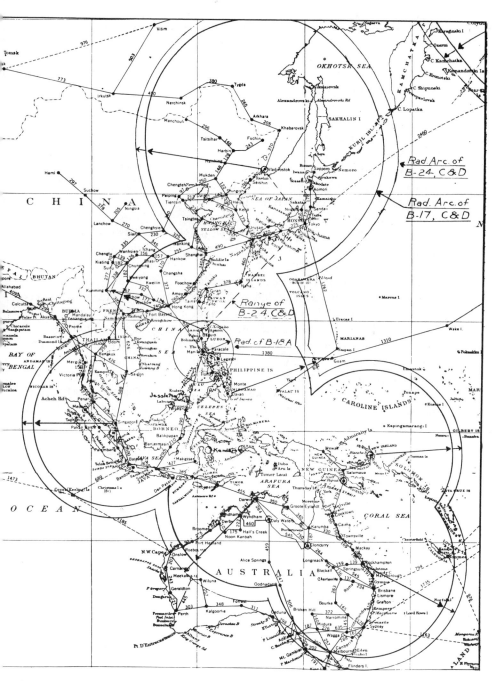

One version of the map General Marshall used at his secret press briefing to describe the coverage afforded by United States B-17s and B-24s operating out of bases at Vladivostok, the Philippines, Singapore, and Australia. Not shown here are the arcs from bases in Alaska, Hawaii, and American Samoa.

allowed to leak privately, from the White House or the State Department directly to Japanese officials—presumably Kurusu.[6] If it got out publicly, the Army fanatics in Japan would be in a position to demand war immediately, before we were better fortified. But if the leak is confined to Japanese officials, these officials can say to the cabinet: "Look here. These people really mean to bomb our cities, and they have the equipment with which to do it. We'd better go slow." In that way, no public face-saving would be necessary, and war might be averted. The last thing the U.S. wants is a war with Japanese which would divide our strength. The Germans are pushing the Japanese from 19 directions to get them into war with the U.S., as everyone knows.

If war with the Japanese does come, we'll fight mercilessly. Flying fortresses will be dispatched immediately to set the paper cities of Japan on fire. There wont be any hesitation about bombing civilians—it will be all-out. Arrangements are being made to provide landing fields for flying fortresses in Vladivostok, and it's likely that landing fields can be provided with safety in China. The B-17 Flying Fortresses cannot make the round trip to Japan from the Phillipines—not quite. But they can fly over the Phillipines to Vladivostok.[7] And the new B-24's, which will be dispatched to the Phillipines as soon as they start coming off the line, can make the round trip.

The U.S. is preparing to fight throughout the Pacific. Gasoline and bombs are already at landing fields in Australia, New Zealand, Borneo, and half a dozen other spots, and they are being sent to India, where the British are not prepared to protect shipping in the Indian Ocean. General Marshall has a map which is a series of connected semi-circles and quarter-circles forming a loop around the entire Western Pacific. The semi-circles extend from Australia to Alaska, though the Alaskan portion is thus far drawn in dotted lines. The Japanese-mandated-island naval bases are highly vulnerable in this map showing the ranges of our bombers from various bases.

Flying weather over Japan is propitious now. The rainy season is ended, and high-flying big bombers could wreak havoc. The Japanese have no pursuit planes that can reach the B-24's, which could bomb the islands at will.

The Grand Strategy does not include the use of much naval force. Marshall indicates that he believes U.S. bombers can do the trick against Japanese Naval strength and against Japanese cities "without the use of our shipping." Evidently, the U.S. Naval strength has been drained into the Atlantic until there is not enough left to pit against the Japanese Navy.[8]

But the important point is, Marshall re-stated, that none of this preparing for an offensive war be allowed to leak to the Japanese public. "Nothing that I am telling you today is publishable, even in hinted form," he said.

Marshall's second point relates to the first. The National Guard is to be sent home. It will be replaced gradually by new divisions of selectees—four new triangular divisions of Regular Army are being formed now. The selectees who are being discharged will become the new National Guard, in that they will be formed into reserve divisions. It is expected that about half the selectees will go into this new National Guard. Old National Guard camps will be transformed into new Replacement Training Centers. It is impossible to build new $30,000,000 cantonments, which require six or eight months, so the old ones will be used—and there's no point in building new ones.

Marshall wants to keep the period of service under Selective Service down to 13 or 14 months—rush them through as fast as possible, then stick them in the reserves. As a matter of fact, eventually he expects to have about 18 Regular Divisions and 14 Reserve (new National Guard) divisions. He expects to get the pay of these new reserves raised from a dollar to two dollars per day of training. Chief aim is to let each man who has had a year of training know where he is supposed to go—to what outfit he belongs—in case it is necessary to call him up again. A discharged selectee will leave the Army saying to hell with everything, but within six weeks or so he'll be edging toward the Armory to join the boys. He must re-join within six months to be of much service. Old-style drill in the Armory is out.

What Marshall fears most is that this news, when it is broken, will come out in headlines: "National Guard Sent Home," indicating that the strength of the Army is being depleted. The effect of that might be disastrous in the delicate Japanese situation. We want to put up a big front to the Japanese, without forcing them into face-saving war measures.

As a matter of fact, the strength of the Army is not being depleted with this virtual dissolution of the National Guard. The strength of the Army is over 1,800,000 now, and it wont be allowed to go down. It will soon reach 2,000,000. There will be a small depletion in Infantry divisions, of which there are 34 now, most of them old, large square divisions. And there will be only 32, more of which will be smaller and triangularized (Marshall wants to keep an adequate complement of the old square divisions, but the trend is the other way). But the added strength will come in the Air Corps and the Armored Force, of course.

Marshall is having trouble with enlistments. They are far too slow. And the Navy is having trouble with the same thing.

———

Again: NONE OF THIS IS FOR PUBLICATION. Neither is the fact that those 54 planes pulled out of maneuvers yesterday are going to Iceland. ###

GCMRL/H. W. Baldwin Papers; T

1. Sherrod, a Washington correspondent for *Time* magazine since 1935, had covered military affairs since June 1941. An associate editor of *Time,* Hulburd supervised the magazine's news bureaus from New York City.

2. Using the memorandum printed here as a basis, Sherrod published a description of Marshall's press conference in Overseas Press Club, *I Can Tell It Now*, ed. David Brown and W. Richard Bruner [New York: E. P. Dutton and Company, 1964], pp. 39–45. Brief notes on the conference are also available by Ernest K. Lindley ("Excerpts from a highly confidential interview with General Marshall," GCMRL/H. W. Baldwin Papers) and Edward E. Bomar (Oklahoma State/Paul Miller Papers).

3. In addition to Sherrod, the six correspondents present were: Edward E. Bomar (Associated Press); Harold Slater (International News Service); Lyle C. Wilson (United Press Associations); Charles W. B. Hurd (*New York Times*); Bert Andrews (*New York Herald Tribune*); and Ernest K. Lindley (*Newsweek* magazine). Brigadier General Alexander D. Surles (U.S.M.A., 1911), director of the War Department's Bureau of Public Relations, was also present.

4. Certain Japanese coded messages regarding the reinforcement of the Philippines, which were intercepted and translated by United States Army and Navy cryptanalysts, are printed in Department of Defense, *The "Magic" Background of Pearl Harbor*, 8 pts. (Washington: GPO, 1977), vol. IV appendix, A155–61. A report by the Office of the Chief of Naval Operations, dated November 27, 1941, showed that the Japanese underestimated the number of heavy bombers stationed in the Philippines but grossly overestimated the number of other aircraft. (Ibid., vol. IV, 118; vol. IV appendix, A168–69.) On November 15 Japanese commanders engaged in planning the seizure of the Philippine Islands held their final meeting. "The Japanese plan was based on a detailed knowledge of the Philippine Islands and a fairly accurate estimate of American and Philippine forces." Lieutenant General Masaharu Homma was alloted approximately fifty days to complete the seizure of Luzon. (Morton, *Fall of the Philippines*, p. 57.)

5. The personnel of the dive-bomber unit arrived in the Philippines on November 20, but their aircraft were delayed and consequently never reached their destination. (See Marshall to Commanding General, Port of Embarkation, San Francisco, November 29, 1941, pp. 687–88.) Bomber reinforcements were likewise delayed unexpectedly. (Craven and Cate, *Plans and Early Operations*, p. 183.)

6. Saburo Kurusu, formerly Japanese ambassador to Belgium and later to Germany, was scheduled to arrive in Washington, D.C., on November 15 to assist Ambassador Nomura in his discussions with Secretary of State Cordell Hull.

7. Ernest K. Lindley's notes on Marshall's comments on this point read: "At present we have no arrangement with the Russians, but if we get into war out there, we would expect to have an arrangement." (Lindley, "Excerpts," GCMRL/H. W. Baldwin Papers.)

8. Beside this paragraph Sherrod added a handwritten comment dated August 29, 1945: "The danger period is the first ten days of December, Marshall said. If we get by that, we're OK until February. By then MacArthur will have plenty in the Philippines." Lindley's notes read: "Japanese cities are very vulnerable—and so are their naval bases. When we get the B-24s out there they will be able to fly higher than any pursuit plane the Japanese have, and if the weather were suitable for precision bombing, would be able to play havoc with Japanese naval bases. We expect the Japanese navy to appreciate this factor, when they learn about it. . . . Our aim is to blanket the whole area with air power. Our own fleet, meanwhile, will remain out of range of Japanese air power, at Hawaii. . . . We believe we have in the Philippines sufficient troops to make an attack by the Japanese extremely hazardous, and by December 15, we will feel secure there." (Ibid.) On November 3, Marshall had told the members of the Joint Board that the main involvement in the Far East would be naval, but he believed that by mid-December the army's forces in the Philippines would be of such strength as to "have a deterrent effect on Japanese operations." (William P. Scobey Minutes of Meeting, NA/RG 319 [OPD, Joint Board Minutes].)

Hanson W. Baldwin obtained a copy of Sherrod's memorandum for use in his *Great Mistakes of the War* (New York: Harper and Brothers, 1950). He wrote to ask Marshall if he had been correctly quoted; Marshall replied that "the gist of the interview . . . is apparently correct." The prospects he had indicated on that occasion were defeated, however, by the failure of the air reinforcements to arrive on schedule, the inadequacies of the Philippine air fields, the Air Force's overestimation of the big bombers' effective combat range, and their underestimate of the difficulty of bombing moving ships. (Marshall to Baldwin, September 21, 1949, GCMRL/ H. W. Baldwin Papers.)

To MAJOR GENERAL ROY D. KEEHN November 19, 1941
[Washington, D.C.]

Dear Keehn: Your letter of November 13th came just as I was leaving for the maneuvers in the Carolinas. Since my return I haven't had a moment for anything personal, spending most of my time before committees of Congress.[1]

With regard to Kent, I agree with Homer that it is very important that he take additional work before committing himself to West Point.[2] What you tell me of his record would seem to indicate that he has no difficulties with books, and I hope he is sufficiently mathematically inclined not to be troubled in that field. It is important that he have a solid grounding in mathematics. Also I think it is a good thing for a boy to have at least a year in college before going to West Point. He might point his work towards entering the Academy in the summer of 1942, though he would have a broader outlook a year later despite the loss in rank due to the delay.

I am sorry to hear that Roy is not getting along with his commanding officer.[3]

I note your quotation from Dawes.[4] His point of view is quite understandable; however, what few seem to realize is that we have to operate this machine as an army, and such reassignments are exceedingly hard if not impossible to avoid in an army. For the first I prohibited any transfers from the National Guard, with the result that the much smaller Regular army was torn to pieces in order to find men and officers to do what had to be done. For example, a Regular army office starting with 200 men in August a year ago had not only to build itself up but was called upon to provide over 9,000 men, many of them picked men, for other units of special installations. There were a number of cases where Regular divisions lost 50% of their field officers in two months' time, usually the picked men—to provide the faculties for the new schools or enlarged schools, instructors for the great training centers, and the nuclei for new units. We have very few antiaircraft regiments in the Regular Army, and a great many National Guard units. The consequence has been, we had to rip the regular regiments to pieces time after time. This could not continue beyond a certain point where we must have certain units ready for immediate service.

Under these circumstances, the National Guard was brought into the picture to share its portion of these necessities. You see Dawes is talking about after the emergency, while I am involved in the emergency and its requirements. So far as possible we have endeavored to preserve the unity of the National Guard as such, but it is very difficult as the Army develops.

Mrs. Marshall is better now and in Florida, but she had a very painful time. Faithfully yours,

GCMRL/G. C. Marshall Papers (Pentagon Office, Selected)

1. On November 16 General and Mrs. Marshall flew to Fort Lauderdale, Florida. The next morning the chief of staff flew to Charlotte, North Carolina, to visit various maneuver sites before leaving by train for Washington, D.C., that evening. He arrived in his office on the morning of November 18; a few hours later he went to the Capitol to testify before the House Appropriations Committee in support of the War Department's request for $6,687,369,046 under the Third Supplemental Appropriation Bill. This money was chiefly to fund the maintenance of the National Guard in federal service; to increase ground force strength by 150,000 enlisted men; to mobilize, train, and maintain the Philippine Commonwealth Army; to activate the Aircraft Warning Service; to expand the Army Air Forces from fifty-four to eighty-four groups; and to provide ordnance items, especially tanks and special radio equipment. (House Appropriations Committee, *Third Supplemental National Defense Appropriation Bill for 1942, Hearings* [Washington: GPO, 1941], p. 54.)

2. Keehn's younger son, Kent, wished to apply for admission to the United States Military Academy, and Keehn wrote to Marshall asking advice on the boy's preparation. He had previously talked with Brigadier General John L. Homer on the subject.

3. Major Roy D. Keehn, Jr., was serving with the 106th Cavalry, which was commanded by Lieutenant Colonel Charles R. Johnson, Jr. (U.S.M.A., April 1917).

4. Colonel Charles C. Dawes was the commander of the 202d Coast Artillery Regiment, a Chicago component of the Illinois National Guard that had been called into federal service on September 16, 1940, and stationed at Fort Bliss, Texas. As a member of the National Guard Association Executive Council, Keehn had written to Dawes requesting his views on the army's treatment of the Guard. Keehn quoted at length Dawes's comments. The colonel was displeased with the number of men his unit had lost through transfer. Moreover, "so many of our Selectees are not coming from Illinois that we are rapidly losing our character as Illinois troops. I think this is a mistake and should be corrected." Regarding training, he observed: "We have pushed the Guard to just about the limit. I always had the feeling that my regiment reached its peak in 1939." (Keehn to Marshall, November 13, 1941, GCMRL/G. C. Marshall Papers [Pentagon Office, Selected].)

T HE long drive by the army's air component toward either autonomy within the army (at least) or independence from the army (at best) gathered renewed momentum with the heavy bomber's advent and with the General Staff's increasing organizational problems as mobilization progressed. (H. H. Arnold, *Global Mission* [New York: Harper and Brothers, 1949], pp. 161–65; Otto L. Nelson, Jr., *National Security and the General Staff* [Washington: Infantry Journal Press, 1946], pp. 314–34.) The author of the official army history of the Office of the Chief of Staff noted that "the

turning point in the movement for autonomy and unity of the air forces came in March of 1941" when Marshall held a series of meetings with his air staff on the relation of the Air Corps to the General Staff. (Mark S. Watson, *Chief of Staff: Prewar Plans and Preparations,* a volume in the *United States Army in World War II* [Washington: GPO, 1950], p. 291.) What resulted on June 20 was a revision of the basic regulation defining the status, functions, and organization of the air component (Army Regulation 95–5) creating the Army Air Forces. Leonard T. Gerow, the infantryman who was head of the W.P.D., noted in his office diary that the airmen had gained "a complete autonomy similar in character to that exercised by the Marine Corps of the Navy." (June 13, 1941, Gerow Diary, NA/RG 319 [OPD, Exec. 10, Item 1].)

While supporting increased autonomy for the air forces, Marshall had long opposed independence, in part because he believed that the airmen had not developed an adequately trained and experienced staff. (Marshall, interviewed by Forrest C. Pogue, February 14, 1957, GCMRL.) In addition, he told Assistant Secretary for Air Lovett and Generals Arnold and Brett, "the big problem in establishing a separate Air Corps would be the necessity for setting up administrative personnel—Quartermaster, Engineer, Medical. I saw what the Air Corps ran into in Chicago when they undertook to fly the air mail" in early 1934. (William T. Sexton Notes on Conference in the Office of the Chief of Staff, April 4, 1941, NA/RG 165 [WPD, Chief of Staff Conferences File].) The new version of A.R. 95–5 represented a notable gain for the airmen, but "in actual practice a number of defects soon appeared," and the Air Force continued to press for a more fundamental reorganization of the War Department. (Craven and Cate, *Plans and Early Operations,* pp. 114–16; Nelson, *National Security and the General Staff,* pp. 337–42.) ★

MEMORANDUM FOR THE SECRETARY OF WAR   November 26, 1941
Confidential   [Washington, D.C.]

A proposed revision of AR 95–5, Army Air Force, General Provisions, (attached) was handed me by Mr. McCloy as a statement of what certain members of the Air Corps felt was desirable.[1] It represents their interpretation of what a separate Air Staff involves.

The suggested regulation can be summarized quite briefly. (1) It contemplates complete separation of the Air Force from the rest of the Army;—

control by the War Department of the Air Force being exercised only by the Secretary of War and the Chief of Staff. (2) It establishes a separate Air General Staff described as "a component but autonomous part of the War Department General Staff." This Staff operates subject to the direction of the Chief of Staff under a Commanding General, Army Air Force, who is given command of all air operations whether conducted independently or in conjunction with other forces.

A serious weakness in this organization is the establishment of two General Staffs, one for ground and one for air. This results in no staff at all in the sense of a General Staff to coordinate the operations of the Army as a whole, since only the Secretary of War or the Chief of Staff could exercise that authority personally. It is inevitable that much duplication of effort and great confusion would result from the absence of staff control in matters which affect both ground and air, such as war plans, combined operations and training, budgetary and legislative matters and particularly supply.

Another serious defect of the proposed organization is the centralization of military command of the air force exclusively in the Chief of Staff. Actually the Chief of Staff is only commander *pro tem* of the field forces.[2] In the event of any major effort, a field commander must be designated, since effective command cannot be exercised from the War Department. Under the proposed regulation, the Commanding General, Field Forces, would be denied direct control of a powerful element, air support, necessary in the successful prosecution of combat operations unless he transmitted his requests to the Chief of Staff in Washington who, alone, would have authority to order air operations in support of a plan of action. This complicated system you will recognize as similar to the one that greatly embarrassed the British efforts in France in June of 1940, and is still embarrassing them in Egypt.

The reorganization of the Air Force contemplated in this regulation may be desirable if it is accompanied by a reorganization of the remainder of the War Department to permit an adjustment to the changed setup. Such a reorganization would provide for a real General Staff, functioning under the Secretary of War and the Chief of Staff, to coordinate the operations of the air and ground staffs. Moreover, a system for command of combined operations in the field would be required if the mistakes of the present war are to be avoided.

The whole thing resolves itself into a question of timing. We have under consideration a proposal for the reorganization of the Army command system as illustrated by the attached diagram,[3] and you will note that the important change is the grouping of air, ground and supply activities under their own commanders who are provided with *operating* general staffs. Coordination is provided by an over all general staff which it is contemplated will be much smaller and more compact than at present. My personal reaction to this plan is favorable, but I feel that its development on a practicable basis will be difficult. We have been working on it for some time. It would be a mistake, I think, to make further changes in our present setup unless they fit in with the general idea, just outlined for a major reorganization. The ink is hardly dry on the original draft of 95–5 and General Spaatz (Arnold's Chief of Staff) says that the Air Staff has not yet had time actually to work itself into the original set-up.[4] Also, as a matter of practice many of the things proposed are actually being applied to daily business. I recommend that no further change be made at present.

GCMRL/G. C. Marshall Papers (Pentagon Office, Selected)

1. The June 20, 1941, revision of Army Regulation 95–5, which created the Army Air Forces is discussed in the note to Marshall to Baruch, August 19, 1941, pp. 591–92. Despite the gains they had made as a result of the regulation revision, airmen still disliked both the degree of control exercised over the Air Force by Army General Headquarters or the influence on air planning of the War Plans Division. (See Spaatz Memorandum for the Assistant Chief of Staff, War Plans Division, October 24, 1941, NA/RG 18 [Classified, 321.9].)

2. Concerning the official definition of Marshall's job as chief of staff, see the editorial note on p. 3.

3. The diagram and attendant documents are in NA/RA 165 (WPD, 4558).

4. Brigadier General Carl Spaatz (U.S.M.A., 1914) had been the chief of the Air Force staff since October 1940.

AT a November 5 Imperial Conference, Japanese leaders opted for war if the United States and Great Britain did not meet their demands by November 25. To break the stalemate, Ambassador Kurusu proposed a truce on November 20 that would return diplomatic relations to the status quo ante July 26, 1941: Japan would withdraw from southern Indochina pending the restoration of peace with China or a general peace settlement in the Pacific; the United States would lift trade restrictions while pledging not to interfere with any China settlement. To establish a modus vivendi for the Far East, Roosevelt was ready to release frozen assets if Japan withdrew troops from southern Indochina. The president refused, however, to accomodate Japanese expansion in China, even within the framework of the Kurusu proposal. After it received only half-hearted support from Britain and opposition from China, Roosevelt dropped his proposal. (*Churchill and Roosevelt: The Complete Correspondence,* ed. Warren F. Kimball, 3 vols. [Princeton: Princeton University Press, 1984], 1: 275–78.) A formidable Japanese task force sailed on November 26 to attack the United States fleet at Pearl Harbor. ★

November 26, 1941
Secret [Washington, D.C.]

Subject: Japanese Convoy Movement towards Indo-China.[1]

About a month and a half ago we learned through Magic that the Japanese Government informed the Vichy Government that they proposed to move approximately 50,000 troops into Indo-China in addition to the 40,000 already there by previous agreement.

Today information has accumulated to the effect that a convoy of from ten to thirty ships, some of 10,000 tons displacement, has been assembled near the mouth of the Yangtse River below Shanghai. This could mean a force as great as 50,000, but more probably a smaller number. Included in this ship concentration was at least one landing-boat carrier. The deck-load of one vessel contained heavy bridge equipment. Later reports indicate that this movement is already under way and ships have been seen south of Formosa.

The officers concerned, in the Military Intelligence Division, feel that unless we receive other information, this is more or less a normal movement, that is, a logical follow-up of their previous notification to the Vichy Government.

I will keep you informed of any other information in this particular field.[2]

GCMRL/G. C. Marshall Papers (Pentagon Office, Selected)

1. This document—drafted by Marshall for Secretary Stimson's signature—apparently followed a G-2 report on the subject that Stimson had sent to the president that morning. When informed of the military convoy, the secretary recorded, President Roosevelt "fairly blew up," because "it was an evidence of bad faith on the part of the Japanese that while they were negotiating for an entire truce—an entire withdrawal—they should be sending this expedition down there to Indo-China." (November 26, 1941, Yale/H. L. Stimson Papers [Diary, 36: 50–51].)

2. Marshall returned to the Carolina maneuvers shortly after dictating this memorandum and did not return to Washington until the evening of November 27. Meanwhile, the talks with Japan had broken down and President Roosevelt directed that the military send warning messages to the commanders most likely to be immediately affected by hostilities. Drafted in the War Plans Division and sent, bearing Marshall's name, to the commanding generals in the Philippines, Panama, Hawaii, and San Francisco, the War Department's message began: "Negotiations with Japan appear to be terminated to all practical purposes with only the barest possibilities that the Japanese government might come back and offer to continue. Japanese future action unpredictable but hostile action possible at any moment." The navy's more pointed message began: "This dispatch is to be considered a war warning." (Gerow Memorandum for the Chief of Staff, November 27, 1941, NA/RG 165 [WPD, 4544-13]; November 27, 1941, Yale/H. L. Stimson Papers [Diary, 36: 53–54]; Watson, *Chief of Staff*, pp. 505–9; both messages are quoted on p. 508.)

To the Commanding General, Port of
Embarkation, San Francisco[1]
Personal and Confidential

November 29, 1941
[Washington, D.C.]

My dear General: I learned two days ago that the shipment of a group of dive bombers, personnel, planes and other materiel had been made on a ten-knot boat. This involved a further delay of, I think, thirteen days in Hawaii until the convoy of slow-moving boats could be made up. The result of this is the delay in the arrival of this vital defensive unit until December 25th in the Philippines.[2] General Gerow, in the War Plans Division, takes to himself the failure to follow through in this matter to make certain that a unit of such great importance did not go on the slowest of boats and did not suffer an unusual delay in Hawaii.

I am writing to you, for direct reply, to have you tell me just what happened in relation to the placing of this unit on a slow boat. Off-hand, it seems to me that any high ranking officer concerned with the embarkation of troops to the Philippines during the present emergency would have realized the vital importance of this particular group, and would have at least raised the question as to the advisability of its being placed on such a boat.

The harm has been done, but I am now concerned with the avoidance of repetitions of such incidents. I have never been satisfied with the War Department relationship with the Ports of Embarkation, because the Department can never be an efficient command post agency, considering direct operation of affairs.[3]

Please let me have a very frank statement in this matter, not only of what occurred, but as to the future.[4]   Faithfully yours,

GCMRL/G. C. Marshall Papers (Pentagon Office, General)

1. Colonel Frederick Gilbreath (U.S.M.A., 1911) had commanded the Port of Embarkation since November 14, 1941; he would be promoted to brigadier general on December 15.

2. The fifty-two unassembled A-24 dive bombers of the Twenty-seventh Bombardment Group (L) were aboard the transport *Meigs,* which was delayed in leaving Hawaii until November 24 when a convoy of seven vessels was formed to be escorted by the U.S.S. *Pensacola.* When word of the Japanese attack of December 7 reached the convoy, it was diverted to Australia. The group's air and ground personnel had reached the Philippines on November 20; when the war began, the men became, for all practical purposes, a part of MacArthur's infantry. (Craven and Cate, *Plans and Early Operations,* pp. 183, 192, 225–26.)

3. Similar command failures concerning supply handling had concerned the chief of staff recently. At a November 3 meeting Marshall said that a shipment of bombs sent in late September would not reach Singapore until December 18. But what particularly bothered him was that the War Department did not understand why such delays occurred. "We can have no more of this. This is the poorest command post in the Army and we must do

something about it, although I do not yet know what we will do." (Frank McCarthy Notes on Conference in General Marshall's Office, November 3, 1941, NA/RG 165 [OCS, Chief of Staff Conferences File].)
4. Gilbreath's reply is not in the Marshall papers.

To Colonel Ralph H. Goldthwaite[1]   December 1, 1941
Personal and Confidential   [Washington, D.C.]

My dear Colonel Goldthwaite: It is barely possible that I will get out to your establishment a day or two before Christmas, to stay there ten days or two weeks and give myself an opportunity to rest up. In all probability Mrs. Marshall will be with me, as she too is much in need of a restful period for recuperation, having, in addition to her normal burdens, broken four ribs a month ago.

I am writing you this note in order that you may make tentative reservations for us, but at the same time I do not wish anyone, I repeat, anyone, to know that there is any possibility of my visiting Hot Springs. Such publicity would defeat the entire purpose of my visit and would force me to abandon that plan. I have never been in the Hospital, but Mrs. Marshall has and I am inclined to think, judging from her description, that if you could give me a double room or two small adjoining rooms, it would be the best arrangement for our convenience.

Of course, all my plans are entirely dependent upon the international situation and the President's desires at the time. At best, I could not give you more than a week's notice.   Faithfully yours,

GCMRL/G. C. Marshall Papers (Pentagon Office, General)
1. Goldthwaite was commanding officer of the Army and Navy General Hospital at Hot Springs National Park, Arkansas.

To Admiral Harold R. Stark   December 2, 1941
                                          [Washington, D.C.]

Dear Betty: I have just had handed to me your letter with respect to the proposed letter from the Secretary of the Navy to the Secretary of War on the subject of enlisting 30,000 men in the Navy from the present Army.

Unfortunately, this proposal is not acceptable. The Army is barely able at the present time to maintain three-year enlistments for the rapidly expanding Air Corps, and for the task forces, which must be free of territorial limitations. Any additional load placed on our present program would make it impossible of accomplishment. Even with the great demand for volunteers, our own Air Corps is prohibited from recruiting in units of other arms. Present Army training facilities are even now insufficient for our own requirements. A further consideration is the fact that in replacing 30,000 white selectees, the Army would have to take 3,000 additional negro selectees. We are already heavily over-burdened with an excess of colored troops, and I could not agree to a still greater proportion.[1]

I am sorry that I cannot see my way to help you in this matter. Faithfully yours,

GCMRL/G. C. Marshall Papers (Pentagon Office, Selected)

1. Army policy established in October 1940 declared that blacks would be inducted in accordance with their proportion in the general population (i.e., 10.6 percent); furthermore, black units would be established in all branches. Low levels of education among blacks, however, presented the army with a major problem. At reception centers, all newly inducted men took the Army General Classification Test, which measured general educational achievement. After basic training, those with high scores usually were sent to Officer Candidate School or to the more technical branches; those scoring lowest became semiskilled soldiers, laborers, or were discharged. Between half and two-thirds of all blacks taking the test scored in the lowest category. A large percentage of the highest-scoring blacks were assigned to the units requiring a significant degree of education and skill; other black units were thus left with a high proportion of what the army considered poor soldier material. (Ulysses Lee, *The Employment of Negro Troops,* a volume in the *United States Army in World War II* [Washington: GPO, 1966], pp. 76, 242–44.)

To FIELD MARSHAL SIR JOHN DILL   December 2, 1941
MEMORANDUM FOR THE ADJUTANT GENERAL   [Washington, D.C.]
Radio. *Secret*

Please send the following radio in secret code to General Lee, Military Attaché, American Embassy, London, for Field Marshal Sir John Dill:

"I hope you will proceed to your new assignment by way of the United States and I would be honored and delighted if you would be my guest during your transit of this country.[1] Mrs. Marshall joins me in a similar invitation to Lady Dill. We can travel very comfortably by air following the warmer southern route. You can see what you choose of our military effort and enjoy something of the scenic beauty enroute Indian antiquities of the Southwest Grand Canyon and West Coast. Marshall."

NA/RG 165 (OCS, 18565-45)

1. Dill's resignation as chief of the Imperial General Staff, announced on November 18, was to become effective December 25, 1941, his sixtieth birthday. He was raised in rank to field marshal and designated the governor of Bombay. (*New York Times,* November 19, 1941, pp. 1, 6.)

MEMORANDUM FOR COLONEL BUNDY   December 2, 1941
Secret   [Washington, D.C.]

With reference to our ineffective efforts to secure at least some insight on the air fields in eastern Siberia, Mr. Bullitt suggested to me today that our Consul General, Mr. Ward, would probably be able to get something for us on this.[1] It would at least be worth the effort to get an inquiry to him direct, but it will be necessary that he does not confuse the issue.

Ambassador Steinhardt felt that some of our people, by implying to the Russians that we wanted this data for possible use in operations against Japan, had defeated our previous efforts, which were about to be successful.[2]

GCMRL/G. C. Marshall Papers (Pentagon Office, Selected)

1. President Roosevelt had announced on November 25 that former ambassador William C. Bullitt would soon leave on a mission to the Near East as the president's special representative; he was to study the political, military, and lend-lease aid situations. Angus I. Ward was the United States consul general in Vladivostok.

2. The question of United States air bases in eastern Siberia was a major issue when the new Soviet ambassador, Maxim M. Litvinov, arrived in Washington on December 7. Litvinov told Secretary of State Hull that such a concession would prompt a Japanese attack with disastrous results for the anti-Axis cause. (*New York Times,* December 9, 1941; Memorandum of Conversation, by the Secretary of State, December 11, 1941, *Foreign Relations, 1941,* 4: 742–44.)

MEMORANDUM FOR GENERAL MOORE   December 3, 1941
Secret   Washington, D.C.

The President has decided against the use of a Naval aircraft carrier for the transportation of planes to Basra for delivery to the Russians. He directed that the movement be expedited by other ships and used the expression "Hurry, Hurry, Hurry!"

General Arnold has been following this matter. I wish to be certain that the President's directive is carried out because now the responsibility rests, in a large measure, with us.[1]

G. C. M.

GCMRL/G. C. Marshall Papers (Pentagon Office, Selected)

1. The first members of the United States Military Iranian Mission reached Basra, Iraq, in November 1941. A shipment of four light bombers (A-20s) left New York on November 28 and reached Basra on January 23, 1942. The first plane was delivered to the Soviet Union in February. (T. H. Vail Motter, *The Persian Corridor and Aid to Russia,* a volume in the *United States Army in World War II* [Washington: GPO, 1952], pp. 28, 127.)

To Andrew J. May   December 3, 1941
                                                    [Washington, D.C.]

Dear Mr. May: The writer of the editorial you sent me has very decided opinions on the subject of military sanitation. Actually we have been under tremendous pressure from the advocates of both sides of the prophylaxis question and the forces seem to be about equally divided although the opponents of venereal prophylaxis are normally less drastic in their demands than Dr. Howard. We have encountered a great deal of opposition on religious grounds to some of our preventive measures, but few critics have objected to the establishment of medical prophylaxis stations.[1]

On the other hand the American Medical Association and the various nation-wide organizations engaged in fighting venereal infection would submerge us in a storm of protest if we were to accede to demands to abandon our medical preventive measures. We make every effort by means of moral, educational and recreational measures to keep our men away from the possibilities of infection. Local commanders frequently place establishments and areas off limits for soldiers. Moreover, the War Department stands ready to invoke the provisions of your Act the moment it is apparent that local authorities cannot satisfactorily handle conditions in their communities that are harmful to the health of our soldiers. We have not, however, neglected the sound advice of our own surgeons and of the American Medical Association to provide all possible medical means of prevention for those men who expose themselves to infection in spite of our efforts.

Notwithstanding statements to the contrary the Army venereal rate is lower than that of any other armed service, and considerably lower than that of civilian communities corresponding in size to our large camps. We propose to keep it that way. I must ask you to accept my assurance that we are giving careful consideration to the proposals of both parties to the controversy.[2]   Faithfully yours,

GCMRL/G. C. Marshall Papers (Pentagon Office, General)

1. Congressman Ulysses S. Guyer, Republican from Kansas, had inserted into the *Congressional Record* (vol. 87, pt. 14, pp. A5090–91) an editorial by Dr. Clinton N. Howard in the November 1941 issue of *Progress*—the official organ of the International Reform Federation—which included "a shocking revelation" of the "incentive to sin" resulting from the army's handling of prostitution near bases and from its policies on prophylactic measures.

2. Congressman May replied: "My whole purpose in writing you was to keep you posted as to the situation in Congress and the possibility of a storm of criticism from a few fellows who want to demagogue." (May to Marshall, December 5, 1941, GCMRL/G. C. Marshall Papers [Pentagon Office, General].)

To James Grafton Rogers[1]   December 3, 1941
                                              [Washington, D.C.]

My dear Dr. Rogers: I think you told me during our drive last fall to the
Rocky Mountain National Park[2] that you were working on an article or a
book on Stonewall Jackson. I think I told you at the time that there was a
very interesting collection of notes on service in his command by a Lexing-
tonian whom I had known during my VMI days. It was my intention to
send you the book last September, but it was not until yesterday that I
located it. It goes to you by today's mail.[3]

I found more of the real color of these campaigns in this book than in
anything else I ever read. Possibly this was due to the fact that I knew a
great many of the people. The battery commander, Captain Poague, was the
military store-keeper at the VMI when I was a cadet.[4] He was a very silent
little man and it never dawned on me that he was a great warrior in his
youth. As a matter of fact, there is a special monument marking the spot
where Poague's battery turned back the break-through at the "bloody
angle" at Spotsylvania Court House.   Faithfully yours,

GCMRL/G. C. Marshall Papers (Pentagon Office, Selected)

1. Rogers was master of Timothy Dwight College and professor of law at Yale University.
2. General Marshall and Secretary Stimson were in Colorado between August 20 and 22
on their trip to the Pacific Northwest. Rogers, Stimson's friend and assistant secretary of state
under him (1931–33), accompanied them on a trip to the park on August 21. (Yale/H. L.
Stimson Papers [Diary, 35: 43].)
3. The book Marshall sent was Edward A. Moore, *The Story of a Cannoneer Under
Stonewall Jackson, in Which is Told the Part Taken by the Rockbridge Artillery in the Army
of Northern Virginia* (New York and Washington: Neale Publishing Company, 1907).
4. William T. Poague was military storekeeper at the Virginia Military Institute between
1884 and 1912.

To Lieutenant General Ben Lear   December 3, 1941
Personal   [Washington, D.C.]

Dear Lear: I have gradually gotten the reactions from the various Armistice
Day parades of the Second Army, and today came your note on Ridley's
letter transmitting the clippings covering the parade of the Sixth Division in
St. Louis. It is evident that you did a grand job in this business of carrying
the Army back to the people, and I anticipate that it will have both
beneficial and lasting effects.[1] Here in the East, the First Army was closely
occupied, and therefore, made no appearance, but there will be considerable
military movement of units from south to north, which will partially accomplish the same purpose.

I am sorry I was not able to join up with you during the maneuvers. As usual I was under heavy pressure, though this time more imperative than during the Louisiana affair. I had so little time at my disposal that I could make no appointments which might prevent my seeing the troops in operation, so I confined myself to moving rapidly all day long and seldom saw other than corps command posts, though I did see a great deal of first line action.

I have been considering a get-together of higher commanders, but whether this will be in two echelons, one here and one later at some point in the field, such as Benning, I do not know. In any event, however, I shall certainly see you then.

My attention now is closely focused on the Philippines and the possibilities of that situation.   Faithfully yours,

GCMRL/G. C. Marshall Papers (Pentagon Office, Selected)
   1. In mid-October Marshall had directed that when the Carolina maneuvers ended, army, army corps, corps area, Armored Force, and division commanders make an effort to stimulate athletic, educational, and entertainment activities in their commands and to see that soldiers presented "a more military appearance" when on pass. "It is now highly desirable to bring the public to an appreciation of the present army and an understanding of its requirements. This can best be accomplished by taking advantage of favorable opportunities, not involving serious interference with training, by authorizing the appearance of troops in parades or exhibitions in the large centers of population. The coming Armistice Day presents an opportunity of this character." (Marshall Memorandum of General Instructions, October 17, 1941, NA/RG 165 [OCS, 19246–67].)

To LIEUTENANT GENERAL HUGH A. DRUM   December 4, 1941
Personal and Confidential   [Washington, D.C.]

Dear Drum: I was sorry not to see you during the Maneuvers. Both of my visits were of such short duration that I could not reach back to Army Headquarters without depriving myself of at least a brief opportunity to see troop actions. On my second trip of about thirty-six hours I did manage to see your Corps Commanders and had quite a talk with Fredendall, but only a brief stop with the others. Incidentally, Grunert flew east from San Francisco and proceeded directly to the maneuver area in order that he might have the benefit of seeing his Corps in action. I imagine the experience will be very helpful to him.[1]

I only got one good look at your improvised anti-tank units, but it appeared to me that splendid progress had been made along these lines.

Altogether the Maneuvers seemed to indicate a definite advance in tactics and technique in the higher echelons over what appeared to be the case in

Louisiana. I am told that leadership in subordinate units showed some improvement, but there is still a long way to go in raising the minor tactical standards. However, all will better recognize the necessities in these matters in subsequent training. Also I think the increased ammunition allowance now possible will tend to improve the handling of weapons.

We are discussing a get-together, somewhat on a round table basis, for higher commanders, probably in January and possibly at Benning. This will be for the purpose of evolving a better understanding of the air-ground technique, the handling of armored units, coordination of artillery firing, as well as a resumé of the lessons of the Maneuvers. It will also afford an opportunity to inform everyone on the intimate details of the international situation and the development of our various foreign garrisons, and similar matters.

For the past few weeks we have been in a very critical situation, which has required my more or less constant presence in Washington.

With my congratulations on your conduct of the Maneuvers, Faithfully yours,

GCMRL/G. C. Marshall Papers (Pentagon Office, Selected)

1. Orders issued on October 23, 1941, relieved Major General George Grunert from command of the Philippine Department and assigned him temporarily to Fourth Army Headquarters in San Francisco. He was scheduled to become commanding general of the Sixth Army Corps, a component of Drum's First Army, upon the relief of Major General Karl Truesdell.

To MRS. ALLEN T. BROWN   December 5, 1941
[Washington, D.C.]

Dear Madge: I appreciated your letter and was glad to find you enjoyed the game, however depressing the final score.[1] I was not present, being unable to leave Washington because of critical matters pending at the time. Neither you nor Allen made any mention of the other people in the box. I wonder if you met them. General Arnold, the Chief of the Air Corps, and his wife were there, and I am pretty certain Allen had met him; Glenn Martin, the Aircraft manufacturer from Baltimore, was there with a friend; the other couple was supposed to be the Secretary of Commerce and RFC Chairman, Jesse Jones and his wife but he telephoned me a request to have a niece use the tickets. Whether the niece was an old maid or a ravishing blond, I do not know.

Katherine is improving constantly and now manages a walk as far as the cemetery, which has an unpleasant implication but is our frequent daily objective in search of peace of mind. As a matter of fact, after some of the stormy days and weeks here, I think a cemetery would be pretty nice.

I get in a ride almost every day, and Fleet is now an accomplished coach dog when it comes to following and obeying.

General Stayer was here from Panama yesterday and told us all about Molly and her baby.

With my love to you both,   Affectionately,

GCMRL/Research File (Family)

1. Margaret Brown's letter is not in the Marshall papers. The Browns had attended the army-navy football game in Philadelphia on November 29. The Naval Academy won 14–6.

TO MRS. JAMES J. WINN   December 6, 1941
                                                            [Washington, D.C.]

Dear Molly: Stayer was here the other day for lunch with us and, of course gave your mother the last word regarding you, much to her reassurance.

She is progressing rapidly towards complete recovery though two of the fractures are still in the gristle stage, at least they were when she was X-rayed a week ago. She went to a hurriedly arranged and purely informal dinner at Alice Longworth's the other night and seemed to enjoy it thoroughly. The previous Saturday evening she went to a very formal dinner, mostly Supreme Court, and apparently enjoyed that very much. The following day we had lunch alone with Lord and Lady Halifax; that was a very pleasant affair.[1]

My Panama dates are still uncertain. I had thought I might be able to make the trip between the 12th and Christmas, but conditions here will prevent that. Now it appears that I will get down some time in January. It is probable that I will go to the West Coast before Christmas, though that will depend on the international situation. Everything is so unsettled that it is out of the question for me to make additional plans. In addition, I am taking a rather heavy political beating these days, as a result of the large appropriation bills, regarding which I must testify, and the acute battle between the Isolationists and the Administration supporters. Added to this are a few bouquets that come from those who have been relieved from command. Most of this last has been quietly carried out, but the repercussions are severe and numerous nevertheless, and I am the target.

Your mother talks constantly about going to Panama, inquiring into rates, schedules, etc. I have grave doubts about the advisability of such a trip. She is going too strong now, and is a poor combatter with hot weather.

Besides, from a purely personal standpoint, I have just about enough steam to do this job and if I am involved in her being down with an illness in addition to the job, it quickly goes beyond my resources.

I have written to the Commanding Officer of the Hot Springs General Hospital to make tentative reservations for us for the Christmas holiday period. I doubt if we can make any use of it but it does no harm to make the preliminary arrangements.

With my love,   affectionately

GCMRL/Research File (Family)

1. Alice Roosevelt Longworth, the late President Theodore Roosevelt's daughter, had been one of the most influential hostesses in Washington social life for many years.

Appendix 1

The War Department: Principal Officials and Organization Chart 1939–41

The men listed below served in the designated capacities during the period covered by this volume. Many of their tours of duty began prior to or ended subsequent to this period; the dates given here are from the official beginning to the official end of their service in the position. It was not uncommon for an official to take several weeks of accumulated leave prior to the official termination of his duties or for his designated successor to begin work at this time.

The offices listed have been given their official designations as of January 1, 1941. Occasionally there would be changes; for example, the Army Air Corps became the Army Air Forces on June 20, 1941.

Secretary of War
Harry H. Woodring....................September 25, 1936–June 20, 1940
Henry L. Stimson ....July 10, 1940–September 21, 1945

Under Secretary of War
Robert P. Patterson....................December 16, 1940–September 26, 1945

Assistant Secretary of War
Louis A. Johnson ....June 28, 1937–July 25, 1940
Robert P. Patterson....................July 31, 1940–December 15, 1940
John J. McCloy.........................April 24, 1941–November 29, 1945
Robert A. Lovett (Asst. for Air).....April 26, 1941–December 15, 1945

WAR DEPARTMENT GENERAL STAFF
Chief of Staff
George C. Marshall....................July 1–August 31, 1939 (Acting)
                                     September 1, 1939–November 18, 1945

Chief of Staff, General Headquarters
Lesley J. McNair ....July 9, 1940–July 13, 1944

Deputy Chief of Staff
Lorenzo D. Gasser (acting).........July 1, 1939–May 30, 1940
William Bryden ....June 1, 1940–March 16, 1942
Richard C. Moore (add'l DCS) ....July 22, 1940–March 8, 1942
Henry H. Arnold (DCS for air)....November 11, 1940–March 8, 1942

Assistant Chief of Staff, G-1 (Personnel)
William E. Shedd......................October 1, 1939–February 18, 1941
Wade H. Haislip ....February 19, 1941–January 19, 1942

Assistant Chief of Staff, G-2 (Intelligence)
E. R. Warner McCabe ....July 1, 1937–February 29, 1940
Sherman Miles ....April 30, 1940–January 31, 1942

Assistant Chief of Staff, G-3 (Operations and Training)
Robert McC. Beck ....March 7, 1938–August 3, 1939
Frank M. Andrews....................August 4, 1939–November 22, 1940
Harry L. Twaddle ....November 23, 1940–April 8, 1941
Harry J. Malony.......................April 9–23, 1941
Harry L. Twaddle ....April 24, 1941–March 8, 1942

Assistant Chief of Staff, G-4 (Supply)
George P. Tyner.......................April 16, 1937–January 20, 1940
Richard C. Moore......................January 21, 1940–July 20, 1940
Eugene Reybold (acting)...............August 4, 1940–September 8, 1941
Raymond A. Wheeler ....September 9, 1941–November 25, 1941
Brehon B. Somervell...................November 25, 1941–March 8, 1942

Assistant Chief of Staff, War Plans Division
George V. Strong ....October 16, 1938–December 14, 1940
Leonard T. Gerow.....................December 16, 1940–February 15, 1942

Secretary of the General Staff
Orlando Ward...........................July 3, 1939–August 30, 1941
Walter B. Smith........................August 31, 1941–February 3, 1942

ARMS AND SERVICES

Chief of the Air Corps
Henry H. Arnold ....September 28, 1938–March 8, 1942

Chief of Cavalry
John K. Herr ....March 26, 1938–March 9, 1942

Chief of Coast Artillery
Archibald H. Sunderland ....April 1, 1936–March 31, 1940
Joseph A. Green ....April 1, 1940–March 9, 1942

Chief of Engineers
Julian L. Schley........................October 18, 1937–September 30, 1941
Eugene Reybold ....October 1, 1941–September 30, 1945

Chief of Field Artillery
Robert M. Danford....................March 26, 1938–March 9, 1942

Chief of Infantry
George A. Lynch ....May 24, 1937–April 30, 1941
Courtney H. Hodges ....May 31, 1941–March 9, 1942

Chief Signal Officer
Joseph O. Mauborgne ....October 1, 1937–September 30, 1941
Dawson Olmstead.....................October 1, 1941–June 30, 1943

The Adjutant General
Emory S. Adams ....May 1, 1938–March 2, 1942
The Inspector General
Walter L. Reed.........................December 1, 1935–December 23, 1939
Virgil L. Peterson.....................December 24, 1939–June 5, 1945
The Judge Advocate General
Allen W. Gullion ....December 1, 1937–November 30, 1941
Myron C. Cramer ....December 1, 1941–November 30, 1945
The Quartermaster General
Henry Gibbins.........................April 1, 1936–March 31, 1940
Edmund B. Gregory ....April 1, 1940–January 31, 1946
Chief of Ordnance
Charles M. Wesson ....June 3, 1938–May 31, 1942
Chief of the Chemical Warfare Service
Walter C. Baker.......................May 24, 1937–April 30, 1941
William N. Porter ....May 31, 1941–November 28, 1945
The Provost Marshal General
Allen W. Gullion.....................July 1, 1941–April 27, 1944
The Surgeon General
James C. Magee ....June 1, 1939–May 31, 1943
Chief of Finance and Budget Officer
Frederick W. Boschen...............April 23, 1936–April 22, 1940
Howard K. Loughry.................April 23, 1940–June 1, 1945
Chief of Chaplains
William R. Arnold ....December 23, 1937–February 14, 1945
Chief of the National Guard Bureau
Albert H. Blanding....................January 31, 1936–January 30, 1940
John F. Williams ....January 31, 1940–January 31, 1946
Executive for Reserve Affairs
Charles F. Thompson ....September 16, 1938–June 9, 1940
John H. Hester........................June 21, 1940–March 23, 1941
Frank E. Lowe ....June 5, 1941–August 10, 1942

Note: The above information is derived from the comprehensive list in James E. Hewes, Jr., *From Root to McNamara: Army Organization and Administration, 1900–1963* (Washington: GPO, 1975), pp. 379–409.

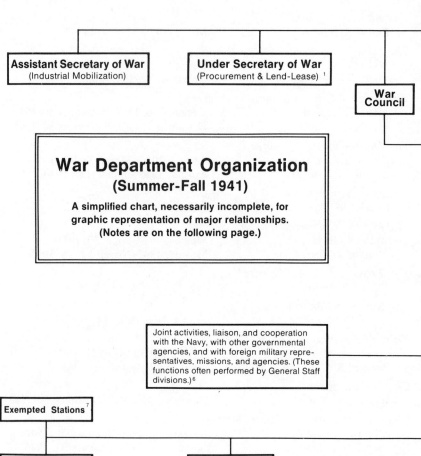

| **Assistant Secretary of War**
(Industrial Mobilization) | **Under Secretary of War**
(Procurement & Lend-Lease) [1] |

**War
Council**

War Department Organization
(Summer-Fall 1941)

**A simplified chart, necessarily incomplete, for
graphic representation of major relationships.
(Notes are on the following page.)**

Joint activities, liaison, and cooperation
with the Navy, with other governmental
agencies, and with foreign military representatives, missions, and agencies. (These
functions often performed by General Staff
divisions.) [6]

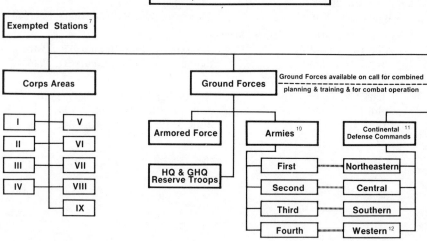

Exempted Stations [7]

| **Corps Areas** | | **Ground Forces** | Ground Forces available on call for combined
planning & training & for combat operation |

I	V
II	VI
III	VII
IV	VIII
	IX

| **Armored Force** | **Armies** [10] | **Continental** [11]
Defense Commands |

HQ & GHQ **Reserve Troops**	First	Northeastern
	Second	Central
	Third	Southern
	Fourth	Western [12]

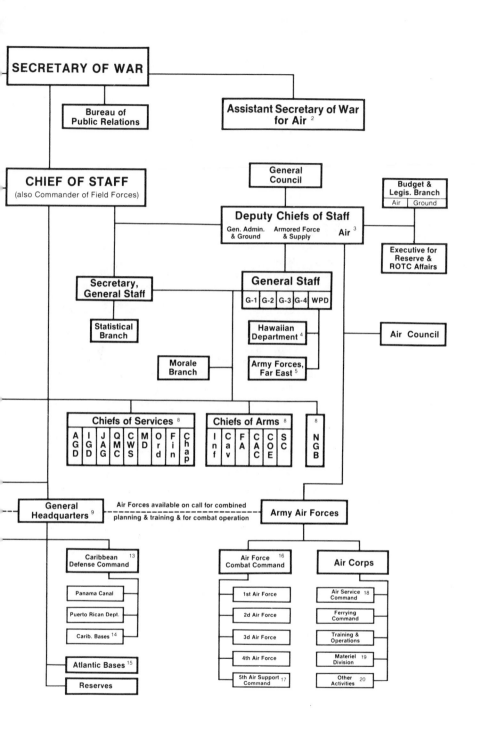

SECRETARY OF WAR

Bureau of
Public Relations

**Assistant Secretary of War
for Air** [2]

CHIEF OF STAFF
(also Commander of Field Forces)

General
Council

Budget &
Legis. Branch

Air	Ground

Deputy Chiefs of Staff

| Gen. Admin.
& Ground | Armored Force
& Supply | **Air** [3] |

Executive for
Reserve &
ROTC Affairs

**Secretary,
General Staff**

General Staff

G-1	G-2	G-3	G-4	WPD

Statistical
Branch

Hawaiian
Department [4]

Air Council

Morale
Branch

Army Forces,
Far East [5]

Chiefs of Services [8]

| A
G
D | I
G
D | J
A
G | Q
M
C | C
W
S | M
D | O
r
d | F
i
n | C
h
a
p |
|---|---|---|---|---|---|---|---|---|

Chiefs of Arms [8]

| I
n
f | C
a
v | F
A | C
A
C | C
O
E | S
C |
|---|---|---|---|---|---|

[8]

| N
G
B |
|---|

**General
Headquarters** [9]

Air Forces available on call for combined
planning & training & for combat operation

Army Air Forces

Caribbean [13]
Defense Command

Air Force [16]
Combat Command

Air Corps

| Panama Canal | | 1st Air Force | | Air Service [18]
Command |
| Puerto Rican Dept. | | 2d Air Force | | Ferrying
Command |
| Carib. Bases [14] | | 3d Air Force | | Training &
Operations |
| | | 4th Air Force | | Materiel [19]
Division |

Atlantic Bases [15]

| 5th Air Support [17]
Command | | Other [20]
Activities |

Reserves

Notes to the War Department Organization Chart

1. All procurement except aircraft (less armament).
2. All air functions with civilian officials.
3. The deputy chief of staff for Air (Major General Henry H. Arnold) was also the chief of the Army Air Forces. He exercised his command of the Air Forces through his own Air Staff.
4. In the case of the Hawaiian and Philippine departments, the chief of staff exercised command directly through the department commander, via the War Department General Staff. The War Plans Division was primarily concerned with overseas departments. For other overseas establishments, command was exercised through General Headquarters.
5. At this time the Philippine Department was part of a larger command—the United States Army Forces in the Far East. Lieutenant General Douglas MacArthur commanded both.
6. Included participation on the Joint Board, the United States–Canadian Joint Board for Defense, cooperation with the British Mission, with Lend-Lease, and with other agencies.
7. Exempted stations were those posts exempted from the administrative control of the corps area commander. These included arsenals, ordnance depots, quartermaster depots, and army schools.
8. Service and arm abbreviations: AGD = Adjutant General's Department; IGD = Inspector General's Department; JAG = Judge Advocate General's Department; QMC = Quartermaster Corps; CWS = Chemical Warfare Service; MD = Medical Department; Ord = Ordnance; Fin = Finance Department; Chap = Chaplains; Inf = Infantry; Cav = Cavalry; FA = Field Artillery; CAC = Coast Artillery Corps; COE = Corps of Engineers; SC = Signal Corps; NGB = National Guard Bureau.
9. G.H.Q. superseded the War Plans Division in the organization and control of task forces and operations. It also directed the training of the Ground Forces and combined air-ground training.
10. Each army included its assigned corps (with component divisions and corps troops) and army troops.
11. Each defense command in the continental United States included (as applicable) its component sectors, its harbor defense, its mobile ground troops (as assigned by army and corps), and its air force (when so directed by the War Department). The army commanders also served as commanding generals of the defense commands. Mobile troops for the defense commands were assigned from the armies, corps, and G.H.Q. reserve. As applicable, defense commands were coordinated with naval coastal frontiers for cooperative action and joint defense operations.
12. Included Alaska.
13. Activated in February 1941 to place the Panama Canal and Puerto Rican departments and all bases protecting the approaches to the Panama Canal under a unified command. The command was placed under G.H.Q. on December 1, 1941. The Caribbean Defense Command and its component organizations were coordinated with the naval sea frontiers for cooperative action and joint defense operations.
14. These bases included army establishments in the Bahamas, Trinidad, St. Lucia, Jamaica, Antigua, British Guiana, Surinam, Curaçao, and Aruba.
15. These bases included army establishments in Iceland, Greenland, Bermuda, and Newfoundland.
16. Commanded the tactical air forces in the continental United States. Air units sent to overseas establishments came under the command of the commander of the area to which they were assigned.
17. Specially organized for the support of armored forces.
18. Included air service areas and air depots.
19. Included procurement and development.
20. Included inspection, personnel, legal, medical, and fiscal affairs, buildings and grounds.

Appendix 2

Published Congressional Testimony
of George C. Marshall, 1939–46

Marshall's facility in informing and persuading Congress was an important aspect of his job, particularly during his first two years as chief of staff. Proceedings have been published for fifty hearings at which Marshall testified before various congressional committees during the 1939–46 period. The Marshall portions of these publications have not been reproduced in the Marshall papers volumes because they are widely available, the quantity is large, and the transcripts contain significant amounts of non-Marshall material.

The list below gives the date Marshall testified, the committee before which he appeared, the title of the publication, and certain locating information. The latter includes (in parentheses) the size of the publication, the pages on which Marshall's testimony appears (e.g., GCM = pp. 16–47), the Congressional Information Service, Inc., accession number to *U.S. Congressional Committee Hearings on Microfiche* (e.g., CIS = [76]H1190–1), and the Superintendent of Documents number (e.g., Y4.M59/1:D36/17). A list of published testimony for the period after 1946 will appear in the volume covering Marshall's years as secretary of state.

Information concerning Marshall's appearances before Congress for which testimony was not published appears in the Marshall Chronology in the front of this volume. The editors are aware of thirteen such appearances: July 6, 11, and 18, 1939; January 16, March 27, May 20, 21, and 28, June 4, September 3 and 26, 1940; January 27 and February 20, 1941. Transcriptions of Marshall's remarks of July 11, 1939, and June 4, 1940, are in GCMRL/ G. C. Marshall Papers (Pentagon Office, Testimonies).

1939   *76th Congress, 1st Session*

Jan. 19   HOUSE MILITARY AFFAIRS: *An Adequate National Defense as Outlined by the Message of the President of the United States, Hearings . . . [on H.R. 3791].* (iii+139 pp.; GCM = pp. 29–44; CIS = [76]H842–7; Y4.M59/1:D36/17)

Feb. 21   SENATE MILITARY AFFAIRS: *National Defense, Hearings . . . on H.R. 3791, an Act to Provide More Effectively for the National Defense by Carrying Out the Recommendation of the President in His Message of January 12, 1939, to the Congress.* (iii+324pp.; GCM = pp. 285–90; CIS = [76]S580–10; Y4.M59/2:D36/9)

Mar. 22   SENATE FOREIGN RELATIONS: *Providing Government Facilities to the Governments of American Republics for Certain Purposes, Hearing . . . on S. J. Res. 89 . . . to Authorize the Secretaries of War and of the Navy to Assist the Governments of American Republics to Increase Their Military and Naval Establishments.* (ii+24pp.; GCM = pp. 5–6, 22; CIS = [76]S581–5; Y4.F76/2:Am3)

1939   76th Congress, 3d Session

Nov. 27   HOUSE APPROPRIATIONS: *Emergency Supplemental Appropriation Bill for 1940,*
& 30   *Hearings . . . [on H.R. 7805].*
(ii+331pp.; GCM = 1–22, 133–41; CIS = [76]H867–1; Y4.Ap6/1:Em3/7)

1940   76th Congress, 3d Session

Feb. 23   HOUSE APPROPRIATIONS: *Military Establishment Appropriation Bill for 1941, Hear-*
& 26   *ings . . . [on H.R. 9209].*
(ii+924pp.; GCM = pp. 1–48; CIS = [76]H879–1; Y4.Ap6/1:W19/3/941)

Mar. 28   SENATE MILITARY AFFAIRS: *Purchases of Implements of War by Foreign Govern-ments, Hearing . . . on S. Res. 244, a Resolution to Investigate the Effect of Armament Sales to Foreign Governments Upon Prices and Delivery of Armament to the Government of the United States.*
(iii+18pp.; GCM = pp. 12–16; CIS = [76]S622–9; Y4.M59/2:W19/7)

Apr. 8   SENATE MILITARY AFFAIRS: *Promotion of Promotion-list Officers of the Army, Hearing . . . on S. 3712, a Bill to Provide for the Promotion of Promotion-list Officers of the Army After Specified Years of Service in Grade.*
(vi+26pp.; GCM = pp. 11–15; CIS = [76]S626–14; Y4.M59/2:P94/9/pt.1)

Apr. 9   HOUSE MILITARY AFFAIRS: *Promotion of Promotion-list Officers of the Army, Hearings . . . on H.R. 9243, a Bill to Provide for the Promotion of Promotion-list Officers of the Army After Specified Years of Service in Grade.*
(iii+25pp.; GCM = pp. 17–23; CIS = [76]H878–11; Y4.M59/1:P94/4)

Apr. 30   SENATE APPROPRIATIONS: *Military Establishment Appropriation Bill for 1941, Hear-*
May 1   *ings . . . on H.R. 9209.*
& 17   (ii+445pp.; GCM = pp. 14–71, 403–33; CIS = [76]S623–3; Y4.Ap6/2: W19/941)

May 29   HOUSE APPROPRIATIONS: *Senate Amendments to the Military Establishment Ap-propriations Bill for 1941, Hearings . . . .*
(ii+72pp.; GCM = pp. 1–31; CIS = [76]H890–4; Y4.Ap6/1:W19/3/941/supp.)

May 31   SENATE APPROPRIATIONS: *Emergency Relief Appropriation Act Fiscal Year 1941, Hearings . . . on H. J. Res. 544.* [Marshall testified in favor of using the CCC to help the army train certain service personnel.]
(ii+285pp.; GCM = pp. 191–97; CIS = [76]S630–1; Y4.Ap6/2:R27/2/941)

June 4   HOUSE APPROPRIATIONS: *Supplemental National Defense Appropriation Bill for 1941, Hearings . . . [on H.R. 10055].*
(ii+195pp.; GCM = pp. 64–73; CIS = [76]H890–5; Y4.Ap6/1:D36/2/941)

June 15   SENATE APPROPRIATIONS: *First Supplemental National Defense Appropriation Bill for 1941, Hearings . . . on H.R. 10055.*
(ii+53pp.; GCM = pp. 1–11; CIS = [76]S630–4; Y4.Ap6/2:D36/2/941)

July 12   SENATE MILITARY AFFAIRS: *Compulsory Military Training and Service, Hear-ings . . . on S. 4164.*
(iv+400pp.; GCM = pp. 327–49; CIS = [76]S629–15; Y4.M59/2:M59/8/rev.)

July 24 HOUSE MILITARY AFFAIRS: *Selective Compulsory Military Training and Service, Hearings . . . on H.R. 10132.*
(iii+64pp.; GCM = pp. 100–111; CIS = [76]H887–1; Y4.M59/1:M59/20 pt.1)

July 24 HOUSE APPROPRIATIONS: *Second Supplemental National Defense Appropriation*
& 26 *Bill for 1941, Hearings . . . [on H.R. 10263].*
(ii+257pp.; GCM = pp. 121–35, 251; CIS = [76]H890–6; Y4.Ap6/1: D36/2/941-2)

July 30 SENATE MILITARY AFFAIRS: *Ordering Reserve Components and Retired Personnel into Active Military Service, Hearing . . . on S. J. Res. 286.*
(iii+33pp.; GCM = pp. 3–20; CIS = [76]S629–13; Y4.M59/2: R30/3)

Aug. 5 SENATE APPROPRIATIONS: *Second Supplemental National Defense Appropriation*
–6 *Bill for 1941, Hearings . . . on H.R. 10263.*
& 15 (ii+257pp.; GCM = pp. 1–33, 229–44; CIS = [76]S630–5; Y4.Ap6/2:D36/2/941/2)

Aug. 20 SENATE MILITARY AFFAIRS: *Uniformity in Temporary Promotions in the Army, Hearings . . . on S. 4207.*
(iii+14pp.; GCM = pp. 3–14; CIS = [76]S649–4; Y4.M59/2:P94/10)

Sept. 19 HOUSE APPROPRIATIONS: *Third Supplemental National Defense Appropriation Bill for 1941, Hearings . . . [on H.R. 10572].*
(ii+138pp.; GCM = pp. 31–42; CIS = [76]H890–7; Y4.Ap6/1:D36/2/941-3)

Sept. 30 SENATE APPROPRIATIONS: *Third Supplemental National Defense Appropriation*
& Oct. 1 *Bill for 1941, Hearings . . . on H.R. 10572.*
(ii+56pp.; GCM = pp. 1–30; CIS = [76]S647–1; Y4.Ap6/2:D36/2/941-3)

1941   77th Congress, 1st Session

Feb. 12 HOUSE APPROPRIATIONS: *Fourth Supplemental National Defense Appropriation Bill for 1941, Hearings . . . [on H.R. 3617].*
(ii+383pp.; GCM = pp. 1–13; CIS = [77]H909–2; Y4.Ap6/1:D36/2/941-4)

Mar. 5 HOUSE APPROPRIATIONS: *Fifth Supplemental National Defense Appropriation Bill for 1941, Hearings . . . [on H.R. 4124].*
(ii+315pp.; GCM = pp. 3–17; CIS = [77]H923–5; Y4.Ap6/1:D36/2/941-5)

Mar. 13 HOUSE APPROPRIATIONS: *Defense Aid Supplemental Appropriation Bill, 1941, Hearings . . . [on H.R. 4050].*
(ii+76pp.; GCM = pp. 22–25; CIS = [77]H909–3; Y4.Ap6/1:D36/3/941)

Mar. 20 SENATE APPROPRIATIONS: *Defense Aid Supplemental Appropriation Bill, 1941, Hearings . . . on H.R. 4050.*
(ii+88pp.; GCM = pp. 19–24; CIS = [77]S658–1; Y4.Ap4/2:D36/3/941)

Mar. 25 SENATE APPROPRIATIONS: *Fifth Supplemental National Defense Appropriation Bill for 1941, Hearings . . . on H.R. 4124.*
(ii+176pp.; GCM = pp. 15–28; CIS = [77]S658–2; Y4.Ap6/2:D36/2/941-5)

Apr. 22 SENATE SPECIAL INVESTIGATING [TRUMAN] COMMITTEE: *Investigation of the National Defense Program, Hearings . . . pursuant to S. Res. 71.*
(viii+396pp.; GCM = pp. 159–84; CIS = [77]S665–0–A; Y4.N21/6:D36/pt.1)

Apr. 28 HOUSE APPROPRIATIONS: *Military Establishment Appropriation Bill for 1942,*
& 29 *Hearings . . . [on H.R. 4965].*
(ii+783pp.; GCM = pp. 1–60; CIS = [77]H921–2; Y4.Ap6/1:W19/3/942)

June 11 HOUSE APPROPRIATIONS: *Second Deficiency Appropriation Bill for 1941, Hearings . . . [on H.R. 5166].*
(ii+974pp.; GCM = pp. 505–7 ;CIS = [77]H916–3; Y4.Ap6/1:D36/941-4)

June 18   SENATE APPROPRIATIONS: *Military Establishment Appropriation Bill for 1942, Hearings . . . [on H.R. 4965].*
(ii+118pp.; GCM = pp. 1–12; CIS = [77]S666–5; Y4.Ap6/2:W19/942)

July 9   SENATE MILITARY AFFAIRS: *Vitalization of the Active List of the Army, Hearing . . . on S. J. Res. 88* [making it easier to remove army officers from active duty].
(ii+14pp.; GCM = pp. 3–14; CIS = [77]S693–4; Y4.M59/2:Ar5/15)

Strengthening the National Defense, Hearing . . . Statement of General George C. Marshall in Connection with Retention of Selectees and Reserve Components in the Military Service Beyond One Year.
(ii+14pp.; GCM = pp. 1–14; CIS = [77]S693–5; Y4.M59/2:D36/12)

July 15   HOUSE MILITARY AFFAIRS: *Temporary Appointment of Officers, Hearings . . . on H. J. Res. 199.*
(iii+10pp.; GCM = pp. 1–9; CIS = [77]H925–5; Y4.M59/1:Of2/11)

Vitalizing the Active List of the Army, Hearings . . . on H. J. Res. 203 [making it easier to remove army officers from active duty].
(ii+14pp.; GCM = pp. 2–14; CIS = [77]H925–6; Y4.M59/1:Ar5/15)

July 17   SENATE MILITARY AFFAIRS: *Retention of Reserve Components and Selectees in Military Service Beyond Twelve Months, Hearings . . . on S. J. Res. 92 . . . and S. J. Res. 93.*
(iii+254pp.; GCM = pp. 2–40; CIS = [77]S668–3; Y4.M59/2:R30/4)

July 22   HOUSE MILITARY AFFAIRS: *Providing for the National Defense by Removing Restrictions on Numbers and Length of Service of Draftees, Hearings . . . on H. J. Res. 217, H. J. Res. 218, H. J. Res. 220, and H. J. Res. 222, Joint Resolutions Declaring a National Emergency, Extending the Terms of Enlistments, Appointments, and Commissions in the Army of the United States, Suspending Certain Restrictions Upon the Employment of Retired Personnel of the Army, Making Further Provisions for Restoration of Civil Positions to Members of the Army on Relief from Military Service, and for Other Purposes.*
(iii+165pp.; GCM = pp. 1–41; CIS = [77]H925–10; Y4.M59/1:P36/18)

Sept. 22   SENATE MILITARY AFFAIRS: *Construction Activities of the Army, Hearings . . . on S. 1884* [transferring all army construction activities to the Corps of Engineers].
(iii+49pp.; GCM = pp. 17–26; CIS = [77]S675–10; Y4.M59/2:C76/7)

Sept. 29   HOUSE APPROPRIATIONS: *Second Supplemental National Defense Appropriation Bill for 1942, Hearings . . . [on H.R. 5783].*
(ii+461pp.; GCM = pp. 330–45; CIS = [77]H932–1–A; Y4.Ap6/1:D36/2/942–2/pt.1)

Sept. 30   HOUSE MILITARY AFFAIRS: *To Make Provision for the Construction Activities of the Army, Hearings . . . on H.R. 5630* [transferring all army construction activities to the Corps of Engineers].
(iii+84pp.; GCM = pp. 11–23; CIS = [77]H933–6; Y4.M59/1:C76/5)

Oct. 14   SENATE APPROPRIATIONS: *Second Supplemental National Defense Appropriation Bill for 1942, Hearings . . . on H.R. 5788.*
(ii+166pp.; GCM = pp. 48–59; CIS = [77]S673–3–A; Y4.Ap6/2:D36/2/942–2/pt.1)

Nov. 18   HOUSE APPROPRIATIONS: *Third Supplemental National Defense Appropriation Bill for 1942, Hearings . . . [on H.R. 6159].*
(ii+265pp.; GCM = pp. 44–78; CIS = [77]H932–2–B; Y4.Ap6/1:D36/2/942–3/pt.2)

1942   77th Congress, 2d Session

Oct. 14   HOUSE MILITARY AFFAIRS: *Lowering the Draft Age to 18 Years, Hearings . . . on H.R. 7528.*
(iii+165pp.; GCM = pp. 41–53; CIS = [77]H966–6; Y4.M59/1:D78/2)

Oct. 14   SENATE MILITARY AFFAIRS: *Lowering the Draft Age to 18 Years, Hearings . . . on S. 2748.*
(iii+108pp.; GCM = pp. 3–20; CIS = [77]S695–3; Y4.M59/2:D78/3)

1943   *78th Congress, 1st Session*

Sept. 20   SENATE MILITARY AFFAIRS: *Married Men Exemption (Drafting of Fathers), Hearings . . . on S. 763, a Bill Exempting Certain Married Men Who Have Children from Liability Under the Selective Training and Service Act of 1940, as Amended.*
(vii+312pp.; GCM = pp. 241–92; CIS = [78]S721–1; Y4.M59/2:M34/3/rev.)

1945   *79th Congress, 1st Session*

May 25   HOUSE APPROPRIATIONS: *Military Establishment Appropriation Bill for 1946, Hearings.*
(ii+860pp.; GCM = pp. 1–18; CIS = [79]H1052–3; Y4.Ap6/1:W19/3/946)

June 16   HOUSE SELECT COMMITTEE ON POSTWAR MILITARY POLICY: *Universal Military Training, Hearings . . . Pursuant to H. Res. 465.*
(vii+614pp.; GCM = pp. 567–78; CIS = [79]H1091–1–A; Y4.P84/8:M59/pt.1)

Sept. 25   HOUSE APPROPRIATIONS: *First Supplemental Surplus Appropriation Rescission Bill, 1946, Hearings . . . Part 2.*
(ii+836pp.; GCM = pp. 499–545; CIS = [79]H1065–0–B; Y4.Ap6/1:Su7/3/946/pt.2)

Oct. 18   SENATE MILITARY AFFAIRS: *Department of Armed Forces, Department of Military Security, Hearings . . . on S. 84, Bill to Provide for a Department of Armed Forces, Secretary of the Armed Forces, Under Secretaries of Army, Navy, and Air, and for Other Purposes; S. 1482, Bill to Establish a Department of Military Security, To Consolidate Therein the Military Security Activities of the United States, and for Other Purposes.*
(ii+707pp.; GCM = pp. 49–65; CIS = [79]S779–7; Y4.M59/2:Ar5/18)

Dec. 6   JOINT COMMITTEE ON THE INVESTIGATION OF THE PEARL HARBOR ATTACK: *Pearl*
–13   *Harbor Attack, Hearings . . . Pursuant to S. Con. Res. 27 . . . Part 3.*
(xvi+pp. 983–1583; GCM = pp. 1049–1439, 1499–1541; CIS = [79]S811–pt.1–C; Y4.P31:P31/pt.3)

1946   *79th Congress, 2d Session*

April 9   JOINT COMMITTEE ON THE INVESTIGATION OF THE PEARL HARBOR ATTACK: *Pearl Harbor Attack, Hearings . . . on S. Con. Res. 27 . . . Part 11.*
(xvi+pp. 5153–6650; GCM = pp. 5175–5200; CIS = [79]S811–pt.4–B; Y4.P31:P31/pt.11)

Index

Anglo-French Purchasing Board, 224
Antiaircraft guns: funds for, 229; shortages of, 415; testing of, 277–78, 288
Antiaircraft Training Center, 500
Antiaircraft units, volunteer, 201–3
Aranha, Oswaldo, 23, 364; document to, 381–82
Architects, 460, 532
Argentia, Newfoundland, 585
Argentina: Axis influence in, 527; beef purchases by U.S. Army, 385; independence celebration, M. invited to, 527–28; military cooperation agreement with U.S. rejected by, 330
Arkansas, 490–92
Arkansas City, Ark., 490–92
Arlington Cantonment, Va., 312, 484
Arlington Experimental Farm, 312–13, 531–32
Arlington Memorial Bridge, 20, 531
Arlington National Cemetery, 580, 694–95
Arlington Park Race Track, 15, 245, 266–67
Armies, U.S.: commanders of, 12, 305, 473–74, 651–52, 655; First, 281, 604, 692; Second, 281, 492, 661, 692; Third, 78, 133, 280–81, 370–71, 492–93, 534, 539; Fourth, 49–50, 102, 155, 281, 603, 694
Armored divisions, U.S.: 4th, 497–98
Armored forces, U.S.: civilian schools, use of, 276–77; congressional enthusiasm for, 99; construction necessary for, 542; D.C.S.'s role in, 289; defense against, 500–501; Infantry Tank Board, 462; influence of European fighting on, 460; leadership characteristics needed for, 461–62; maneuvers (1940), involvement in, 281; Officer Candidate School for, 617–18; public relations advantages of, 84; Seventh Cavalry Brigade (Mechanized), 141, 276; strength (1940), 356; technical details, danger of excessive concern with, 462; volunteers favor over other ground units, 601
Arms and equipment: bombs, shortage of, 239; foreign purchases of, 73, 151–52, 221–22, 198, 334–35; legality of sale to belligerents, 221; obsolete ordnance, sale of, 221, 237–38; quality of U.S., 91; time needed to produce, 163, 249. *See also* Small arms; United States Army: equipment and supplies
Army Air Forces: Aircraft Warning Service, 682; Air Defense Command, 202; airpower, importance of, 629; appropriations for, 189, 229–30, 308, 420, 539; construction for, 157, 215; expansion and development of, 52, 99, 101–2; Joint Air Advisory Committee, 166–67; National Guard, relations with, 19; praised by M., 7–8; public relations advantages over ground forces of, 84; Thomason Act, 54. *See also* Arnold, Henry H.

—aircraft: exchange of, 239; Japanese and U.S. planes compared, 412, 414; president's ideas re production, 212–13, 224, 228; production and delivery of, 286, 366, 368–70, 384, 478–79, 568, 582–84; purchases by Allies, 17, 212, 222–24, 368–70, 401; squadrons, increase in, 356. *See also* individual aircraft by number
—autonomy or independence for, 509–10, 563, 682–85; M.'s opposition to, 610–11, 683–85
—bombing: night attacks, defense against, 261, 365; pictures of, public reaction to, 84; importance of, British views on, 586; Japan, use against planned, 678; organization for, 650
—equipment and supplies: bombs, shortage of, 239; bombsights, 247, 352, 584; delivery to active units, priority of, 427; lack of, influence on morale, 478–79; oxygen bomb, political pressures re, 254; parts and supplies, shortages of, 595–96
—G.H.Q. Air Force, 117, 212, 237, 345, 478; defense, role in, 434, 513–14; maneuvers, participation in, 80, 93–94; supplies, cooperation re, 427–28
—ground forces: air support for, 650; competition with, 84, 198, 601; familiarity with needed, 144–45; recruiting from prohibited, 689
—Latin America: Brazil, B-17 flight to, 74–75; Brazil, maneuvers in, 494–95; Caribbean, coordination in, 379–80; facilities desired in, 328–29
—maneuvers, 237, 281; air-ground training, 177, 568–70; joint army-navy, 80, 93–94, 101–2, 154
—organization: Caribbean defense, importance of, 379–80; D.C.S. for supply and construction, 289; independence, unprepared for, 683; mobile and fixed defense strategies, influence on, 650; president's promotion policy, effects of, 509; reorganization (1940), 345; U.S. air defenses, reorganization of, 434–35
—overseas bases and fields: Alaska, 189, 215, 488; Hawaii, 246, 410, 412–14, 513; Panama Canal, 158–59, 380, 397, 513; Philippines, 414–15, 432–33, 676, 678
—pilots: appropriations for training of, 213; blacks, flight training for, 518–19, 525–27; British, U.S. training for, 484; civilian training schools for, 224–26; ferrying aircraft to U.K., agreement for, 484; military pilots, first certified, 596; training and production of, 33, 212, 223–24, 356
—regulations: basic air component regulation (A.R. 95-5), 683; recruiting from other branches prohibited, 689; spouses on army aircraft, 268
—schools: Advanced Flying, 144–45, 177; Tactical, 144–45, 290

staff, 16, 390–91; preparedness, support for, 60–61; public statements requested by M., not made, 63, 641; statement on neutrality law revision urged by M., 63; supports age-in-grade promotion bill, 236–37; visits by M. to, 43, 175, 476–77

Pershing, May, 161, 172, 476–77

Pétain, Henri Philippe, 341

Peterson, Virgil L., documents to, 372, 549–51, 594

Peyton, Bernard R., 385

Peyton, Philip B., 405; document from, quoted, 461–62; document to, 461–62

Philadelphia, Pa., 102–3, 202

Philippine Department: aircraft reinforcements for, 568, 675–76, 680, 687; commander of, 36, 315; defenselessness, press emphasis on, 315; Japanese estimates of U.S. strength in, 676, 680; naval reinforcements not sent to, 392; officers' families, evacuation of, 418–19; reinforcements and supplies for, 292, 414–16, 432–33, 587, 659–60, 687; strength, increases in, 415, 418–19; strengthening of, requests for, 314–15, 469; U.S. Navy requires equipment intended for, 411. *See also* United States Army Forces in the Far East

Philippine Islands: army of, 540, 604; attention of M. focused on, 693; Davao, Japanese influence in, 431–32; defensibility, changing War Department attitudes re, 100, 598–99; governors of, 26, 115; M.'s duty in, 40–41, 142–43; morale, improved by army mobilization, 604; naval training cruise to, considered, 430–32; strategic importance of, 465, 568–69, 605, 675

Philippine Scouts, 89, 315, 415, 418

Phillips, Thomas R., 261

Phillips, William, 431–32

Phillips Exeter Academy, 495–96

Phillipson, Irving J., 498; document to, 498

Photography: aerial, use of, 69; public relations value of, 84

Physical fitness, 193, 335–36, 602

Pine Camp, N.Y., 497–98

Pine Plains Military Reservation, N.Y., 498

Pitcher, William L., 41

Pittman Resolution (1939), 33

Pittsburgh, Pa., 169, 171

Pittsburgh and West Virginia Railway Co., 616

Placentia Bay, Newfoundland, 585–86

Plan Dog (1940), 360

Plattsburg, N.Y., 281

Poague, William T., 692

Pocono Manor Inn, 11

Poindexter, Joseph B., 346

Poland, 47–48, 83, 99, 111, 120

Poniatowski, André, 522–23

Pool, David de Sola, 358–59

Poore, Benjamin A., 207; document to, 207

Port Darwin, Australia, 431

Portal, Sir Charles, 440

Portland, Oreg., 25, 289, 323, 575

Ports of Embarkation: New York, 179–80, 317; procedures of, studied by G-3, 180; San Francisco, 138, 179–80, 317, 687

Potomac River, 275–76, 532, 633

Poughkeepsie, N.Y., 269–70

Pound, Sir Dudley, 440, 586–87; photo of, 516(#48)

Powder, James W., 127, 242

Powers, D. Lane, 168–69

Pratt, Elizabeth Conger, document to, quoted, 323

Pratt, Henry C., 632

Pratt, John L., photo of, 260(#1)

Press: antimobilization propaganda, used for, 668–69; army commanders, M. denies imminent removal of, 651–52; black newspapers, 518–19, 525–26; criticism of army by, 298, 340, 371, 442; defenselessness of Philippines, stories re, 315; effectiveness of, 123–24, 348; leaks to, 186–87, 313, 352, 576–77; maneuvers, reporting on, 315, 335, 539, 548–50; M.'s use of, 22–23, 60; press conference statements, M.'s concern re congressional reaction to, 400–401; reaction to M.'s American Historical Association speech, 139–41; reporting emphasizes spectacular, 443; secret press briefing by M., 676–81; timing of announcements, influence on, 397; tours of army posts, M.'s encouragement for, 393; War Department, relations with, 38. *See also* Associated Press; *Army and Navy Journal*

Prince of Wales, H.M.S., 586

Prosser, Walter E., 397–98

Prostitution, 373–74, 691

Protective Mobilization Plan, 167, 221, 231; appropriations for, 204, 216–17, 487; defined, 20; draft needed to implement, 264; size of forces for, 163

Public Buildings Administration, 301

Public opinion: ahead of president re intervention, 203, 215, 217; army attempts to affect re maneuvers, 136–37; favors army efforts at leadership changes, 640, 655, 661; history textbooks, influence on, 123–25; impatience of, 274; military budget cuts, pressure for, 173; mobilization, shifting opinion re, 123–24, 248,